THE AMERICAN SCENE

THE AMERICAN SCENE

THE AMERICAN SCENE

Edited by

Barrett H. Clark

and

Kenyon Nicholson

ILLUSTRATED BY

Arvia MacKaye

D. APPLETON AND COMPANY

NEW YORK : LONDON : MCMXXX

PREFACE

The American scene—from New England to California, from Canada to the Gulf of Mexico: our country in its characteristic external aspects, its people and their daily affairs, speech and thought; a bird's-eye view and a cross-section, an impressionistic picture of imposing dimensions; America made articulate, her people on farms and in city flats, in mines and factories, stores and offices, at one time and between the covers of a single book, living their respective half-hours in the theater of the mind—this ambitious scheme has been slowly worked out by the editors. For a couple of years we have been trying to select our material and arrange it in such form as to stand complete within the narrow bounds of a single mosaic that would express and exhibit a sufficient number of groups and persons within those groups, all living their lives against their proper backgrounds, and affording the reader some notion of what these United States are; the fields and cities and mountains, the homes and working places; not a statistical survey, not a study, but a composite to appeal to the senses and the imagination.

It is for this reason that we have chosen plays to tell our story, for the dramatist is a painter and a singer rather than a commentator.

v

Although it has not always been possible to find exactly the play that presents a typical locality and group of people, although certain parts of the country have not yet found their interpreters, and although the purpose of the book demanded that it be kept within reasonable space limits, we believe that what we have chosen is characteristically American and essentially true.

It is not possible at this time to determine precisely how far any artist must go in reproducing the atmosphere of any particular place before he can be regarded as "native" and in a country like America, where a thousand localities offer a thousand different atmospheres, it is impossible to take any one play and call it characteristically American. It is for this reason that we have tried to let our authors express the differences between one place and another, to exhibit as many divergences from national standardization as possible; we consider every local province chosen by our authors as important and as interesting as every other.

This book is no anthology in the usual sense; it is not just a collection of plays; we have consciously and deliberately tried to weld into a unified whole elements that seemed diverse just as the makers of epics used to knit together, and elaborate, the legends and traditions of their people, but with the difference that we have not, naturally, tried to rewrite the plays of our authors. Had these plays, however, been the products of some age-old civilization, inherited by us in oral form, it is not inconceivable that some writer might have linked them together as a kind of dramatic epic forming, as it does, a composite and running narrative. Although we know who the authors are and when each play was written, we look up the impulse that brought them into being as part of an immense enthusiasm by which all of us are now driven to do our share toward realizing our national destiny. Though we cannot be sure what is to be, we are at least conscious that it is up to us to know our country and express, by whatever means, whatever stirs our imagination.

PREFACE

None the less, we ask the reader to supply for himself some such narrative, to make an effort of the imagination and fancy us opening this American pageant with some such preamble as—

> *America we sing—the rocks and rills*
> *The hills and valleys,*
> *Farms and coal mines*
> *Black factories and blue lakes*
> *White mountains rimmed with fog, and the*
> *Dark-green woods of the North, and the*
> *Bright green forests of the Far West—*

Here, in short, is an honest statement of our intention, a hint of our ultimate aim. This composite epic with all its faults, has grown out of our love of the land and its people, and our strong faith in the work of its dramatists.

B. H. C.
K. N.

CONTENTS

CONTENTS

GREASY LUCK
BY RACHEL FIELD

PERSONS IN THE PLAY

EUNICE STARBUCK
DAVID FOLGER
ABBIE GARDNER
COUSIN CHASE

GREASY LUCK *

THE parlor of a Nantucket house in the heyday of the whaling period. It is furnished plainly but with great dignity, old-fashioned mahogany chairs and tables, family portraits and prints of ships and whaling about. A door right leads into hall. EUNICE STARBUCK is seated on an old sofa, sewing some squares of patchwork together. She is pretty and appealing, about twenty-seven, with a rather serious, sensitive face. Her hair is parted smoothly in a quaint fashion and her flowered muslin dress is voluminous and billowing.

ABBIE: [Calling from street outside the window.] Eunice, can I come in? Are you all alone?

EUNICE: [Going to the window and leaning out.] Why, Abbie, come right in. I looked for you to be at the shearin' too. [She goes to the door and opens it to admit another

---

* A native American phrase, coined in Nantucket, New Bedford and New England coast towns, which meant: "A good voyage to you and come back with plenty of whale-oil aboard." To wish a whaleman "Greasy Luck" was the equivalent of our "Bon Voyage."

girl about her own age, but gayer and more lively of manner. This is ABBIE GARDNER, who wears a bonnet and shawl. EUNICE and she kiss one another affectionately.] I had a little slatch in my work and come in here to cool off from the kitchen-fire.

ABBIE: [Seating herself and taking off shawl.] There, I knew they'd go off an' leave you with the preservin' on your hands! It wouldn't of hurt your Cousin Anna or Molly or Sophie to stay behind for once an' let you an' David enjoy yourself at the shearin' same's everybody else.

EUNICE: What about you an' John bein' there, Abbie?

ABBIE: Oh, it ain't the same thing for John'n me. We're gettin' to be old married folks now. Don't need to go off cruisin' to sociables an' shearin's. Anyhow I couldn't leave the baby all day. She's commencin' to cut her teeth. [Leaning forward the other girl and speaking more seriously.] It's you I'm thinkin' of, Eunice Starbuck; it's a shame the way you let 'em all put things on you.

EUNICE: The raspberries would of spoiled if we'd kept 'em over till to-morrow an' I always was a better hand at preservin' than Cousin Anna or the girls. Just did up twenty-seven jars o' jam an' the raspberry shrub's strainin' in the pantry now.

ABBIE: An' there you sit lookin' as if you'd never been near a stove all day! I declare I hope David's sensible to the kind of wife you're goin' to make him.

EUNICE: [Laughing.] Well, David does like my raspberry jam. [Changing subject politely to her guest.] John'll be leavin' soon, I hear. They say the *Hesper's* most fitted out.

ABBIE: John thinks she'll be shipshape by the end o' next week.

EUNICE: How long they signin' for?

ABBIE: [With the cheerful acceptance of a whaler's wife.] Only a year this time an' of course if they strike greasy luck might not be more'n nine or ten months.

EUNICE: [Holding out her patchwork.] What do you think o' this for the centre o' my quilt? I got it out to show David. He'll be stoppin' by most any time now. [She points out the fine bits of her work while ABBIE bends nearer to admire.] It's my own designin'. I mean to call it "The Blowin' Whale" pattern. I cut it after that picture [pointing to one on the wall] from an old gray flannel shirt o' Cousin Enoch's.

ABBIE: It's just as natural as life, Eunice; I don't see how you ever did it.

EUNICE: I guess David won't think so much of the whale's looks. The tail's kind of queer, but then I couldn't be expected to know whales same's he does.

ABBIE: It's a lovely pattern and David's got no call to pass remarks on it. He ain't struck so many whales himself he can afford to.

EUNICE: That's not David's fault, Abbie, an' you know it, no matter what anybody says. He's been first in the long boats time an' time again.

ABBIE: I never said he wasn't, Eunice. But how many whales has he got to his credit?

EUNICE: Folks can't always *get* the whales they sight. David says if he had a dollar for every one he's give chase to the last seven years we'd have enough to get married an' set up housekeepin' to-morrow.

ABBIE: Well, I wish he had then! I want to see you two married and settled. I declare I felt like cryin' myself when I heard the *Huntress* was back with salt water in her casks for ballust stead o' good sperm-oil. David didn't make a cent over'n above his costs, I 'spose?

EUNICE: No, not much of a lay * this time. [With a little

---

* A share or percentage. All whaling voyages were conducted on the profit-sharing basis. Each man received his proportionate part of the proceeds of the voyage.

sigh.] Does seem's if there was a spell set against him every trip.

ABBIE: I know. Honest, Eunice, I'd rather John's ship had come back without a barrel of oil this trip an' David had had his turn of luck.

EUNICE: Wishin's no use, Abbie, but I'd be real ungrateful not to thank you just the same.

ABBIE: [Speaking with an effort.] I had to come over to-day; there's something I thought you'd ought to know. I'd want you to do the same by me if 'twas John, 'stead o' David. You'n I've always been closer'n most an'—

EUNICE: If it's somethin' 'bout David—

ABBIE: 'Tis, but it's not his fault. There's been lots o' talk—oh, nothin' you'd be likely to hear, down to the wharves mostly. No one blames him for it, only it's natural they don't want to take chances.

EUNICE: I can't get the drift o' this, Abbie, you've got to tell me out plain.

ABBIE: John says David's tried to get a berth on every ship that's in, but no one's willin' to sign him up for another trip 'count o' his bein' such a Jonah.

EUNICE: Oh, they—they call him that, do they?

ABBIE: 'Tisn't because they don't like David, it's just his luck. They daren't risk havin' him aboard.

EUNICE: There's not another man from Nantucket better at harpoonin'.

ABBIE: But the rest o' the crew's likely to grumble. You know the notions they get on a long trip, an' no one wants trouble among the men.

EUNICE: [Low, to herself.] I thought he acted kind of down lately.

ABBIE: Eunice, you'd better watch out or he'll go an' sign articles on the *Maypole*. You heard 'em callin' for men for her just now an' John says they're so hard put to get a crew they'll take any one with a pair o' hands and feet.

6

EUNICE: The *Maypole!* Not that leaky old tub! Why she wasn't even built for whalin'! I've heard say she's hardly seaworthy an' they aim to make a three-year voyage. [She breaks off aghast.]

ABBIE: John's tried to reason him out of it, but he says David's terrible set. His pride's hurt an' he won't listen. I guess he will if you talk to him; he's bound to. It's same's in quiltin'—if you want things to hold, you've got to hook 'em real firm.

EUNICE: Don't seem's if I could put through another spell o' the waitin', Abbie. Maybe if I was married same's you, with children an' a house o' my own 'twouldn't be so hard, but the way things are now an' the way they've been the last six years— [She makes a little discouraged gesture.]

ABBIE: I know, you've had it harder'n most, livin' here on your cousins. David shouldn't expect you to go on forever like this. That's why I come around now without waitin' a minute. I had to tell you how 'twas, an' about Cousin Chase—

EUNICE: About Cousin Chase?

ABBIE: Yes, he's comin' round here later to see you'n David. It's 'bout David's goin' in to the store with him. He's been pesterin' John for months back an' it sort o' come to me this afternoon 'twould be the very thing for David. Good pay an' a steady job an' likely as not a share in the business after a year or two.

EUNICE: An' those rooms over the store that no one uses now. They'd be real good to set up housekeepin' in. They've got a nice view of the harbor an' we could have 'em all to ourselves— [She breaks off and goes on doubtfully.] But David doesn't have any opinion o' landlubbers an' he may not—want—

ABBIE: You've got to *make* him want to, Eunice. Dear knows I'd be the last one to keep a man from followin' the sea, but 'tisn't as if he hadn't for seven years now. It's time

7

he, thought o' your part an' how you'll be throwin' away the best years of your lives this way.

EUNICE: Oh, I know—I know.

ABBIE: I got scared hearin' the talk 'bout the *Maypole* sailin' with the tide to-morrow mornin' if they could get enough men. That's why I come right along ahead o' Cousin Chase. He said he'd stop by in half or three-quarters of an hour. I thought there'd be time for you to sound David first.

EUNICE: It was good of you, Abbie, real good. You've always stood by me an' I don't know what I'd of done without you. [She starts at a sound from outside.] There's David now. I can tell his step.

ABBIE: I'll be goin' then; don't let on I said anything to you, Eunice, but I thought you'd ought to know.

EUNICE: [Moving toward door with her.] I expect David couldn't bring himself to tell me before. He hates to let on when things touch him real hard. [In her old manner.] Drop in again when you can an' I hope the baby's teeth'll stop botherin' soon.

[As they open the door DAVID FOLGER appears on the threshold, a pleasant-faced, powerfully built six-footer of twenty-eight or nine, dressed in the heavy, seafaring clothes of the time, rather long, full trousers, clumsy boots, home-made shirt and short jacket. He is naturally kindly and cheerful, though he can be proud and stubborn as well. Although it is evident that he is in love with EUNICE, he is first and foremost a whaleman, bred to the sea.]

ABBIE: Afternoon, David.

DAVID: Afternoon, Abbie. Why ain't you over to the shearin'?

ABBIE: I got plenty to keep me busy right here. Just ran in to see Eunice's new quilt pattern. [Half out of the door she turns and speaks significantly to EUNICE.] You remember what I told you, Eunice, 'bout that hookin' part. Looks

8

GREASY LUCK

to me as if you'd better get started soon. [Abbie goes out.]

DAVID: [Looking after her.]   What she mean by that?

EUNICE: Oh, she was just givin' me some advice. That's quiltin' talk. [She runs over to him and catches eagerly at his coat sleeve.] What kept you so long down to the wharves, David? I thought you'd never come. [He bends down to kiss her, then straightens up and looks a little guiltily toward the door.] It's all right. The folks are all off to the shearin'.

DAVID: [Kissing her with hearty and rather awkward affection.] Well, that's a comfort. Don't know what 'tis 'bout your Cousin Anna, but I'd rather face a fightin' whale or an ugly crew'n take one o' those sideways looks of her's. I can't ever do or say a thing right when she's by.

EUNICE: [With a little sigh.] I know. S'posin' you'd had her over you for fifteen years same's I have?

DAVID: [Dropping down on the sofa and drawing her beside him.] I'd of taken to sea earlier'n I did, that's all! [He pulls out his pipe, then hesitates.] She'd know if I was to smoke my pipe in here, I expect?

EUNICE: [Taking up her sewing.] You know how she feels 'bout tobacco smoke, 'specially in here with the new curtains.

DAVID: [Putting the pipe away reluctantly.] Well, I wouldn't want to do nothin' to make trouble for you.

EUNICE: [Slipping her hand in his.] You can smoke anywhere you've a mind to when we have a house of our own. I'll be so glad to have the curtains smell of tobacco, for that'll mean you're home, not off whalin'. [There is a second's pause. It is plain that she is trying to begin all the things that are uppermost in her mind to say to him.] David, I—I haven't said anythin' 'bout it till now. You an' I haven't had a proper chance alone together before. I knew you were worryin' an' things hadn't gone so's you could put by a cent

9

an' I didn't want to bother you, only I've got to ask you now. It means everythin' to me an'—

DAVID: [Stooping to pick up the work which has slipped from her lap to the floor, he fingers it curiously, only half listening to her words.] What's this? Somethin' fancy you're up to? [He twists and turns the square in his hands.] Well, if it ain't a whale as true's I live! A blowin' whale.

EUNICE: I'm glad you like it. Nothin' left to do now but sew it on to the middle square o' the quilt. There's not another such pattern anywhere on the Island. I commenced it the day you left on the last voyage. This white's from my old poplin, remember?

DAVID: I wouldn't be likely to forget. You wore it to meetin' time we were first cried.

EUNICE: [Leaning closer to him.] There's bits of most all my dresses sewed into it. [She rubs her cheek softly against his sleeve.] I was so lonesome for you all the time I was makin' it seems as if that's all in it, too, even if it don't show.

DAVID: [Stroking her hair.] Missed me like that, did you? Honest?

EUNICE: Oh, David, do you have to ask? [Clinging closer to him and speaking with soft earnestness.] It's goin' to be our marriageable quilt.

DAVID: [Repeating her words slowly.] Our marriageable quilt— [He breaks off and goes on in sudden bitterness.] It's goin' on seven years since we first commenced to talk o' that.

EUNICE: Seems as if I couldn't put through another spell o' the waitin', David. Seven years is long for anybody, but it's longest for a girl like me, livin' on other folks' charity an' not getting younger or prettier or—

DAVID: Don't you talk like that. You know I've never had eyes for no other woman. I never see any sort of a she-rig could stand alongside you!

EUNICE: My, but it's good to hear you say that, [with a

10

sudden burst of honesty] even if I know my color ain't what 'twas when you first asked me. My cheeks were pink all the time then, not just when I've been over the fire or walkin' in the wind. An' that line didn't use to be there— see? [She touches her forehead lightly and breaks off.] A girl can't help gettin' fearful sometimes.

DAVID: Thought I might fetch back a Chinese lady or one of those black ones with a ring in her nose, did you? [He draws her closer to him.] Why, there ain't any sort o' foreign jadehopper I'd look at twice.

EUNICE: [Slowly, her face upturned to his.] 'Tisn't only that, dear, sometimes it's folks themselves changing—in their feelin's, I mean, an'—an' gettin' used to doin' without each other. [She turns to him in a sort of pent-up desperation.] Oh, David, if I ever thought you—

DAVID: Now there's no call for you to go an' get yourself all wadgetty. You'd ought to know me well enough after all these years.

EUNICE: How much have I seen of you in the last seven?

DAVID: Why as much as most folks in these parts, I guess. I don't know exactly.

EUNICE: Well, I know. I've figured it all out on paper an' in my head. It comes to three month an' nineteen days all told.

DAVID: 'Twould of been longer if I'd had greasy luck an' could of stopped ashore between whiles, but you know how it's been?

EUNICE: [With a little sigh.] Oh, I know. [Very tensely.] David, you do want to get married? You'd do anything so's we could, wouldn't you?

DAVID: Why, yes, that is, anythin' in reason.

EUNICE: Then you'll listen to Cousin Chase when he comes.

DAVID: Cousin Chase?

EUNICE: Yes, he's comin' here. He wants to talk to you 'bout a proposition an'—

DAVID: If it's got anythin' to do with that store o' his—

EUNICE: Oh, David, if he gives you a chance, don't throw it away.

DAVID: I got plans of my own.

EUNICE: You wouldn't go an' sign articles for any voyage without you told me first?

DAVID: Why what would you know 'bout a vessel or ship's articles, Eunice?

EUNICE: I know a vessel's not much good when they have to cry her up an' down streets for weeks 'fore they can sign up a crew, same's they're doin' with the *Maypole*.

DAVID: Don't you go believin' all the things you hear.

EUNICE: [Unable to keep back her anxiety any longer.] David, you haven't signed articles to ship on her next trip, have you?

DAVID: No, not yet, I haven't.

EUNICE: You—you're sure you're tellin' me the truth, dear?

DAVID: You never doubted my word before.

EUNICE: [Flinging her arms about him.] An' I'm not doubtin' you now; I'm not really. It's only I'm all put about in my mind so's I don't hardly know what I'm sayin'. [There is a sound of a door-knocker outside. They spring apart and EUNICE hurries out to open the front door, speaking as she goes.] That'll be Cousin Chase at the door now. You'll listen to him for both our sakes? [She runs back to DAVID once more and they kiss. DAVID's eyes follow her and he shifts a little uneasily on his feet. It should be evident to the audience that he is moved more by her personality than by her arguments.]

[Presently EUNICE reappears at the door, followed by a small elderly man. He wears a home-made quaintly cut suit, and walks as if he were a little rheumatic.]

12

EUNICE: [At the door.] David, here's Cousin Chase to see you. [She pulls forward a chair and takes his hat.]

COUSIN CHASE: [Good-naturedly.] Long's they said you weren't down to the wharves I presumed likely I could find you up here with Eunice.

DAVID: [Smiling at EUNICE.] Well, it's a pretty good place to be. I don't mind who hears me say so.

COUSIN CHASE: [Seating himself and mopping his face.] That's right. That's the way I like to hear young folks talk.

EUNICE: [With a little deprecating laugh.] We're not such dreadful young folks any more, David'n me.

COUSIN CHASE: [Patting her hand affectionately.] You'll always seem so to me even if 'tis—let's see, how many years now since you an' David commenced keepin' company?

EUNICE: Goin' on seven. David's been twice round the Horn in 'em an' dear knows where else besides.

COUSIN CHASE: [Wagging his head.] Time he stayed put a spell. This roamin' the globe for whale-blubber's all right for awhile, but where's it all come to in the long run?

DAVID: It comes to a pile o' money if you strike it greasy like the *Isabella* did last voyage. Eight hundred and thirty barrel o' sperm. I guess Ira Swain and Will Coffin can have 'bout anything they fancy from now on.

COUSIN CHASE: There's other ways of makin' a pile besides goin' to sea for it. It's that I come round to talk over with you.

EUNICE: [Moving toward door tactfully.] Well, I guess you don't need me round. I'll go see to those raspberries. [From the doorway.] Maybe you'd try a glass of my shrub if I was to bring it to you, Cousin Chase?

COUSIN CHASE: Don't you trouble yourself, Eunice. What I got to say to David won't take me long. [She goes and there is a pause as the two men settle back into their places again.] No, won't take me long to say or you to hear me out—an' I want you should understand me right

13

from the start. I'm not aimin' to turn you from the sea. I've lived too long round these parts to try that. But I come here to make you a proposition, fair an' square, an' you can take it or not as you've a mind to. [He sits back studying the other.] How old have you got to be, David?

DAVID: Twenty-eight last January.

COUSIN CHASE: I see. Things don't appear to be so good's they might be with you?

DAVID: Well, can't say's they are right now. I've been runnin' pretty close to the wind lately.

COUSIN CHASE: 'Twas the same last voyage, an' the one 'fore that. Can't see's you've made much headway.

DAVID: Most every one gets caught in the doldrums one time or another. There's bound to be better weather ahead if you can just keep holdin' on. I'm willin' to take my chances along with the rest.

COUSIN CHASE: You've got Eunice to think of, too, remember. But I didn't come here to talk o' that. From all I hear it looks as if they ain't exactly pesterin' you to ship with 'em this trip, so I thought a good steady job ashore might not seem so bad to you for a change.

DAVID: You mean you're offerin' me a berth in the store with you?

COUSIN CHASE: Yes, it's been gettin' too much for me to carry alone lately. Oh, I've had one an' another take a hand busy spells, but you know well's I do it's easier growin' peas at sea than 'tis to get a smart man to help you out on land. Course, I *could* send to Boston, but I don't hanker to take an Off-Islander in with me, for I mean it should be a share in the business after a six months' trial.

DAVID: That's a generous proposition.

COUSIN CHASE: I've got no family of my own an' I want to feel easy in my mind 'bout the business bein' in good hands after I'm gone. Eunice is my Cousin Ruth's girl an' that's another reason. I'm fond o' Eunice—like to see her mar-

14

ried an' raisin' a family, 'stead of goin' on here where she's at every one's beck an' call.

DAVID: She ain't always goin' to be.

COUSIN CHASE: Those rooms over the store have been empty ever since Sister Mary died an' I went to live up street. You an' Eunice could have 'em an' welcome. Move your things right in next week if you want to.

DAVID: Eunice would like that, but I'm fearful I wouldn't. I—

COUSIN CHASE: Give yourself plenty of time. Talk it over together. Whalin's no kind of a life after a man's thirty, unless he's master or mate with a share in the vessel.

DAVID: I'm a long ways from that yet. Still, I can't see myself anchored to a counter the rest of my days; not anyways till I've showed 'em I can have greasy luck same's the rest.

COUSIN CHASE: [Rising.] That's it—that's the trouble with whalin'. It's hard work an' dirty work, but just because there's always that chance o' luck—

DAVID: That's how 'tis!

COUSIN CHASE: Don't be too hasty decidin' this, an' remember, David, I've come to you in good faith. I didn't like that talk I've been hearin' 'bout you shippin' on the *Maypole*.

DAVID: I thought somebody must of put you up to comin' here to-day.

COUSIN CHASE: I'd made up my mind to offer it to you anyways, but I wanted to be sure you knew, 'fore you had a chance to do somethin' you might be sorry for later on. I'd certainly hate to see any man throwin' himself away on that leaky old blubber-hunter.

DAVID: 'Sposin' a man can't get a berth on any better vessel?

COUSIN CHASE: [At the door.] Then I'd say better try

his hand at some different line. [Opening the door.] Stop in the store to-morrow if you're down that way. I can show you the books an' if it's "yes" we can put things down in black an' white. I'm prepared to pay you good wages.

DAVID: Thank you for askin' me. I'll stop in—if I'm anyway's round to-morrow.

[COUSIN CHASE does not pay attention to these last words for he has spied EUNICE in the hall outside and beckons her in.]

COUSIN CHASE: Well, Eunice, we've had our little talk an' now I'm goin' down to the back garden to take a look at your Uncle Enoch's early cucumbers. He maintains his are three inches ahead o' mine, so I told him I meant to measure 'em myself first chance I got. [He takes out a piece of string from his pocket, smiling over it.]

EUNICE: [Rejoining him at the door.] Now's a good time to do it. Uncle Enoch won't be back till late from the shearin'. Want I should show you where they are?

COUSIN CHASE: [Moving off.] Oh, I can find 'em. Don't you trouble.

EUNICE: Better come back this way; that paint's not dry on the back gate yet. [Instantly she turns to DAVID, all eager hopefulness. She goes over to him quickly, catching at his arm.] David, tell me—quick!

DAVID: [Patting her shoulder, absently.] Well, what you want me to tell you, dear?

EUNICE: Why if he made you the offer—'bout goin' in the store with him, an' if you said you would?

DAVID: Oh, he made me the offer right enough.

EUNICE: An' you took it? David, you told him you would.

DAVID: He said I was to think it over, but I guess I know my answer without much thinkin'.

EUNICE: Oh, David, you will take it, won't you? It's a chance in a hundred.

16

DAVID: For those that want it, maybe, not for me.

EUNICE: You said you'd do anythin' so's we could get married.

DAVID: I said I'd do anythin' in reason, but when it comes to workin' behind a counter, helpin' to fit out ships an' crews, can't you see I couldn't do it, dear?

EUNICE: You'd get used to it.

DAVID: Think o' what they'd be sayin' 'bout me an' the laughs they'd be havin' over me behind my back. "There's David Folger," they'd say, "quit whalin' 'fore he'd even got to be third mate. He's a credit to Nantucket, ladlin' out soft soap from a bucket 'stead of oil from the try-pots an' measurin' off calico when he used to be first in the long boats!"

EUNICE: 'Sposin' they do talk an' laugh now'n then. What's that to you an' me? There wouldn't be one of 'em that wouldn't envy you comin' home from work every night o' the year 'stead of a week here an' a month there in two, maybe three years. [Clinging to him closer.] David, if you really loved me, same's you used to, you wouldn't—

DAVID: [Drawing her to him almost fiercely.] Don't you talk foolishness like that when you know there's no one else but you means anythin' to me. Why sometimes if I let myself get thinkin' how much I want you—all to myself—

EUNICE: An' all you've got to do is say "yes" to Cousin Chase an' we'd be comfortable an' settled the rest of our lives. That's all you've got to do, but you won't.

DAVID: [Smoothing her hair as he tries to make himself clear.] You don't rightly understand. Maybe it's somethin' no woman can, but it's like this: I've got to show 'em I can do as well's anybody. Just because they're callin' me a Jonah and not wantin' to take me's the very reason I've got to go.

EUNICE: Let 'em say what they want to, long's we know it's not true.

DAVID: If I turn landlubber now it certainly would look as if I thought they were right; as if I allowed I was beaten—an' I ain't beaten. I'll show 'em I can have greasy luck, too, even if I do have to ship on the *Maypole*.

EUNICE: [With a little frightened cry at the name.] Oh, David, not that! You said you wouldn't!

DAVID: I said I *hadn't*. Oh, I know she's not much of a vessel, but she's the only one that'll take me an' after all she's got as good a chance to get whales as the best of 'em.

EUNICE: David, you can't go on her. You can't. It was bad enough before when you shipped on the *Huntress* an' the *Tropic Bird* an' the rest. They were all fitted proper an' built for whalin' an' 'twas never for more'n two years. Now you're askin' me to go through three years of it. Think what that means for us both!

DAVID: Do you 'spose I've been thinkin' of anythin' else the last week? I tried every other way I could think of, but it's no use. Get a name for anythin' an' it'll follow you round the globe.

EUNICE: Folks forget, though, dear. They forget dreadful easy.

DAVID: Not always, an' anyways I wouldn't. I'd know I'd given up too soon. I wouldn't have no respect for myself the rest o' my days.

EUNICE: But three years, David. That would mean ten years waitin' all told an' maybe even then—[She breaks off, trying to force back the tears that are beginning to come.] In three years I'll be past thirty. [Holding more tightly to him as if he were already leaving her.] Oh, if you want me you'd ought to take me now 'fore the best o' me's gone waitin' and workin' for other folks.

DAVID: [Moved by her words and tears.] Eunice, I'd give my right hand to be able to.

18

EUNICE: I could have had Ira Swain in the old days. He pestered me to marry him hard enough, but I put him off to wait for you. [In a last desperate effort.] Not that I'm holdin' it up against you, dear. I'd do the same all over again, only we've each of us got just one life apiece an' folks get old so soon, an'—an' such a lot can happen.

DAVID: There now, you mustn't get thinkin' such thoughts.

EUNICE: How can I help it when I see life goin' on all round me? Other folks lovin' an' weddin' and raisin' children same's you'n I planned to do.

DAVID: An' we will yet.

EUNICE: 'Sposin' you never come back! 'Sposin' the *Maypole* goes to the bottom.

DAVID: Hush, dear, don't say such things.

EUNICE: You know the danger as well as I do. You know Martin Macy an' Hiram Mitchell went down an' lots beside. [Her tears gathering headway.] An' 'sposin' I was to take sick an' die. Why, I could be under a tombstone months an' years 'fore you'd even know—

DAVID: Eunice, you mustn't carry on so. It chills me all up to hear you.

EUNICE: David, if you love me same's you say, you won't do it. You won't ship on the *Maypole*. I've never asked anythin' of you before an' I won't ever again.

DAVID: Eunice, I—I didn't know 'twas like this with you.

EUNICE: You know now, an' 'tisn't too late to stay on with Cousin Chase.

DAVID: I'm all at sea—don't know what I'd ought to do.

EUNICE: [More tense.] Anythin' could happen in three years, David. I might get like Hester Swain. You know how 'twas with her after Jim was drowned. She got seein' an' hearin' things—things that weren't real at all. She wasn't always queer like that, not till after she'd had more'n she could stand.

DAVID: [Frightened and holding her closer.] But you're

not like her—you— [He breaks off and it is plain a struggle is going on in him.] Eunice, if I thought I'd driven you to anythin' like that I'd—

EUNICE: Oh, David dear, you're not goin' to put your pride before our love.

DAVID: Maybe I could hold out against you if I—if I didn't love you an' want you so!

[He holds her closer in another kiss. As they stand so there comes distantly from the street the sound of a bell and a voice raised in a sort of monotonous chant. It is the Town Crier coming steadily nearer so that little by little his words grow in distinctness as he cries the same news over and over.]

EUNICE: Thank God you're goin' to stay, David, I can see it in your eyes.

DAVID: I expect maybe it is my turn to give in—turn about's fair play.

[Crier's voice and bell outside, very distinct now.] Oh, yez—oh, yez—oh, yez—wanted—able-bodied young men to sign articles for three-year whalin' voyage—ship *Maypole,* Nantucket built, Andrew Coffin, Master; Ethan Gardner, mate. Sails with the tide to-morrow mornin'—all clothin' an' necessities furnished on credit of the voyage. Oh, yez— oh, yez—oh, yez.

[DAVID and EUNICE stand perfectly still, listening in spite of themselves. As he listens DAVID stiffens visibly. He becomes the whaleman again rather than the lover. EUNICE feels him slipping from her hold and tries to distract him.]

EUNICE: There's that furniture o' mother's stored in the barn. You could get John to help you fetch it down to the store to-morrow— [He does not answer. His head is lifted as he listens to the Crier, repeating the cry, but growing more distant now.] You hear me, dear?

DAVID: [Rousing himself suddenly.] I didn't hear nothin' but that. An' I won't hear nothin' else all the rest o' my days unless I go. I'll hate myself an' you an' our love an' everythin'. I was a fool to think I could stay behind.

EUNICE: But, David, you'd forget.

DAVID: Forget! Hearin' that every day! Why every time one sailed I'd be cursin' myself to think I wasn't aboard her an' 'twould be worse when one came in loaded to the decks.

EUNICE: I want my chance at happiness, too.

DAVID: 'Twouldn't bring you no happiness bein' anchored to a man that knew himself for a coward an' a fool, an' I'd know I was one. Eunice, you've got to let me go.

EUNICE: Oh, David, it's a terrible thing you're askin' of me. I can't do it—I can't.

DAVID: [Holding her close, but looking on beyond her.] I'll make it up to you yet. We're goin' to strike it greasy this trip. I can feel it in my bones. [A curious note of elation comes into his voice.] When I take my turn at the watch I'm goin' to see farther'n any one yet. "There she blows!" I'll cry, fit to burst my lungs! [Unconsciously his voice rises. He is all animation and excitement as he has not been before. EUNICE stares at him in fascinated helplessness.] It's got to be, I tell you.

EUNICE: [Feeling him slipping from her and knowing she is going to yield eventually.] Oh, David, there must be some other way. There's upward o' three thousand Nantucket men off whalin' now. Have you got to go too?

DAVID: [Simply, but with absolute sureness.] That's it—I've got to go too. You see how 'tis, dear, you do see?

EUNICE: Yes, I see—everythin's dreadful plain to me.

DAVID: [Relieved.] I knew you would. You're Island born an' raised— The *Maypole's* old an' we'll be short-handed, but that don't matter, I'll get a better chance at the harpoonin' an' maybe we'll stop off the Indies or China an' I'll be fetching you the finest silk that's made—

EUNICE: An' she sails with the tide to-morrow mornin'.

DAVID: Kind of short warnin', but I've got my chest ready. [He loosens his hold gently and turns to go.] Leave me go now to sign for the voyage. I'll be back by the time you're through with the supper things. We can have two or three hours together 'fore I have to go aboard. [EUNICE stares at him fixedly as he moves toward door.]

EUNICE: [Brokenly.] David! [He turns at her cry and goes back to her again. EUNICE clings to him and he kisses her again.]

DAVID: Nobody like you, Eunice, nobody in the world.

EUNICE: [Keeping back her tears with difficulty.] Or you, David, I—I guess you were born for somethin' bigger'n a countin'-house. Guess I'd rather have you same's you are—[she breaks off and shivers a little, then hurries on] no matter what happens—

DAVID: [Who has put her down gently and reached the door.] Maybe if you was to wish me greasy luck I'd stand more chance o' havin' it, dear.

EUNICE: [Turning toward him and struggling against her tears.] Greasy luck to you!

[He goes quickly out of the door without a backward glance. EUNICE stands staring after him, and only when she hears the front door bang, does she give way to her feelings. Then she sinks down on the sofa, crying with low, strangling sobs. After a moment COUSIN CHASE appears in the doorway, where he stands silently watching her, his hat in one hand and his handkerchief evidently filled with one of the garden cucumber plants carefully balanced in the other. At sight of her tears, he tiptoes in, his old face full of concern.]

COUSIN CHASE: Why, Eunice, whatever's come over you, child? [She looks up but cannot answer.] There ain't anything wrong? Where's David?

EUNICE: [Brokenly.] David's—gone.

COUSIN CHASE: Well, not very far I guess—

GREASY LUCK

EUNICE: Far's any man can. [Sitting up and trying to compose herself.] He's gone to sign articles—for the *Maypole*—they're sailin' with the tide to-morrow mornin'—

COUSIN CHASE: The *Maypole!* [Full of concern and sympathy.] Three years out. An' I thought he'd come round to my proposition. I thought between us we'd reasoned some sense into him. [Patting her shoulder.] I did my best, Eunice, an' I'm sorry, real sorry for you.

EUNICE: [Pulling herself together with sudden spirit.] Never mind 'bout that! I'm glad—

COUSIN CHASE: But I thought your heart was set on gettin' married?

EUNICE: An' so 'tis. 'Course I tried to make him stay —any girl would, but I'm proud he didn't just the same. [With a triumphant upward tilt of her head.] Whatever anybody says 'bout David Folger 'twon't be to call him one o' your stand-behind-the-counter, stay-ashore men!

COUSIN CHASE: [Turning to go out again.] Well, it does beat all how women are made!

[He makes a little clicking sound under his breath and goes out shaking his head as if the whole species were beyond him. EUNICE sits till after he has gone. Her breath still comes short from her spasm of crying, but she has herself in hand now. She wipes her eyes determinedly and reaches for her work-basket. Mechanically she puts on her thimble and picks up the centre square of the Blowing Whale Quilt, smoothing it out on her knee before she begins to work on it. Outside the Crier's bell and call sound faintly, a word or two distinguishable now and again. EUNICE is sewing quietly.]

BOUND EAST FOR CARDIFF
By Eugene O'Neill

PERSONS IN THE PLAY

YANK
DRISCOLL
COCKY
DAVIS
SCOTTY
OLSON
PAUL
SMITTY
IVAN
THE CAPTAIN
THE SECOND MATE

BOUND EAST FOR CARDIFF

THE seamen's forecastle of the British tramp steamer *Glencairn* on a foggy night midway on the voyage between New York and Cardiff. An irregular shaped compartment, the sides of which almost meet at the far end to form a triangle. Sleeping bunks about six feet long, ranged three deep with a space of three feet separating the upper from the lower, are built against the sides. On the right above the bunks three or four port holes can be seen. In front of the bunks, rough wooden benches. Over the bunks on the left, a lamp in a bracket. In the left foreground, a doorway. On the floor near it, a pail with a tin dipper. Oilskins are hanging from a hook near the doorway. The far side of the forecastle is so narrow that it contains only one series of bunks. In under the bunks a glimpse can be had of seachests, suit cases, seaboots, etc., jammed in indiscriminately.

At regular intervals of a minute or so the blast of the steamer's whistle can be heard above all the other sounds.

Five men are sitting on the benches talking. They are

dressed in dirty patched suits of dungaree, flannel shirts, and all are in their stocking feet. Four of the men are pulling on pipes and the air is heavy with rancid tobacco smoke. Sitting on the top bunk in the left foreground, a Norwegian, PAUL, is softly playing some folk song on a battered accordion. He stops from time to time to listen to the conversation.

In the lower bunk in the rear a dark-haired, hard-featured man is lying apparently asleep. One of his arms is stretched limply over the side of the bunk. His face is very pale, and drops of clammy perspiration glisten on his forehead.

It is nearing the end of the dog watch—about ten minutes to eight in the evening.

COCKY: [A wizened runt of a man. He is telling a story. The others are listening with amused, incredulous faces, interrupting him at the end of each sentence with loud derisive guffaws.] Makin' love to me, she was! It's Gawd's truth! A bloomin' nigger! Greased all over with cocoanut oil, she was. Gawd blimey, I couldn't stand 'er. Bloody old cow, I says; and with that I fetched 'er a biff on the ear wot knocked 'er silly, an'— [He is interrupted by a roar of laughter from the others.]

DAVIS: [A middle-aged man with black hair and mustache.] You're a liar, Cocky.

SCOTTY: [A dark young fellow.] Ho-ho! Ye werr neverr in New Guinea in yourr life, I'm thinkin'.

OLSON: [A Swede with a drooping blond mustache—with ponderous sarcasm.] Yust tink of it! You say she wass a cannibal, Cocky?

DRISCOLL: [A brawny Irishman with the battered features of a prizefighter.] How cud ye doubt ut, Ollie? A quane av the naygurs she musta been surely. Who else wud think herself aqual to fallin' in love wid a beauthiful, divil-may-care rake av a man the loike av Cocky? [A burst of laughter from the crowd.]

28

COCKY: [Indignantly.] Gawd strike me dead if it ain't true, every bleedin' word of it. 'Appened ten year ago come Christmas.

SCOTTY: 'Twas a Christmas dinner she had her eyes on.

DAVIS: He'd 'a' been a tough old bird.

DRISCOLL: 'Tis lucky for both av ye ye escaped; for the quane av the cannibal isles wad 'a' died uv the belly ache the day afther Christmas, divil a doubt av ut. [The laughter at this is long and loud.]

COCKY: [Sullenly.] Blarsted fat 'eads! [The sick man in the lower bunk in the rear groans and moves restlessly. There is a hushed silence. All the men turn and stare at him.]

DRISCOLL: Ssshh! [In a hushed whisper.] We'd best not be talkin' so loud and him tryin' to have a bit av a sleep. [He tiptoes softly to the side of the bunk.] Yank! You'd be wantin' a drink av wather, maybe? [YANK does not reply. DRISCOLL bends over and looks at him.] It's asleep he is, sure enough. His breath is chokin' in his throat loike wather gurglin' in a poipe. [He comes back quietly and sits down. All are silent, avoiding each other's eyes.]

COCKY: [After a pause.] Pore devil! It's over the side for 'im, Gawd 'elp 'im.

DRISCOLL: Stop your croakin'! He's not dead yet and, praise God, he'll have many a long day yet before him.

SCOTTY: [Shaking his head doubtfully.] He's bod, mon, he's verry bod.

DAVIS: Lucky he's alive. Many a man's light woulda gone out after a fall like that.

OLSON: You saw him fall?

DAVIS: Right next to him. He and me was goin' down in number two hold to do some chippin'. He puts his leg over careless-like and misses the ladder and plumps straight down to the bottom. I was scared to look over for a minute, and then I heard him groan and I scuttled down after him.

29

He was hurt bad inside for the blood was drippin' from the side of his mouth. He was groanin' hard, but he never let a word out of him.

COCKY: An' you blokes remember when we 'auled 'im in 'ere? Oh, 'ell, 'e says, oh, 'ell—like that, and nothink else.

OLSON: Did the captain know where he iss hurted?

COCKY: That silly ol' josser! Wot the 'ell would 'e know abaht anythink?

SCOTTY: [Scornfully.] He fiddles in his mouth wi' a bit of glass.

DRISCOLL: [Angrily.] The divil's own life ut is to be out on the lonely sea wid nothin' betune you and a grave in the ocean but a spindle-shanked, gray-whiskered auld fool the loike av him. 'Twas enough to make a saint shwear to see him wid his gold watch in his hand, tryin' to look as wise as an owl on a tree, and all the toime he not knowin' whether 'twas cholery or the barber's itch was the matther wid Yank.

SCOTTY: [Sardonically.] He gave him a dose of salts, na doot?

DRISCOLL: Divil a thing he gave him at all, but looked in the book he had wid him, and shook his head, and walked out widout sayin' a word, the second mate afther him no wiser than himself, God's curse on the two av thim!

COCKY: [After a pause.] Yank was a good shipmate, pore beggar. Lend me four bob in Noo Yark, 'e did.

DRISCOLL: [Warmly.] A good shipmate he was and is, none betther. Ye said no more than the truth, Cocky. Five years and more ut is since first I shipped wid him, and we've stuck together iver since through good luck and bad. Fights we've had, God help us, but 'twas only when we'd a bit av drink taken, and we always shook hands the nixt mornin'. Whativer was his was mine, and many's the toime I'd 'a' been on the beach or worse, but for him. And now—

[His voice trembles as he fights to control his emotion.]
Divil take me if I'm not startin' to blubber loike an auld
woman, and he not dead at all, but goin' to live many a
long year yet, maybe.

DAVIS: The sleep'll do him good. He seems better now.

OLSON: If he wude eat someting—

DRISCOLL: Wud ye have him be eatin' in his condishun?
Sure it's hard enough on the rest av us wid nothin' the
matther wid our insides to be stomachin' the skoff on this
rusty lime-juicer.

SCOTTY: [Indignantly.] It's a starvation ship.

DAVIS: Plenty o' work and no food—and the owners ridin'
around in carriages!

OLSON: Hash, hash! Stew, stew! Marmalade, py damn!
[He spits disgustedly.]

COCKY: Bloody swill! Fit only for swine is wot I say.

DRISCOLL: And the dishwather they disguise wid the name
av tea! And the putty they call bread! My belly feels loike
I'd swalleyed a dozen rivets at the thought av ut! And sea-
biscuit that'd break the teeth av a lion if he had the misfortune to take a bite at one! [Unconsciously they have all
raised their voices, forgetting the sick man in their sailor's
delight at finding something to grumble about.]

PAUL: [Swings his feet over the side of his bunk, stops
playing his accordion, and says slowly]: And rot-ten po-tay-
toes! [He starts in playing again. The sick man gives a
groan of pain.]

DRISCOLL: [Holding up his hand.] Shut your mouths, all
av you. 'Tis a hell av a thing for us to be complainin' about
our guts, and a sick man maybe dyin' listenin' to us. [Gets
up and shakes his fist at the Norwegian.] God stiffen you,
ye squarehead scut! Put down that organ av yours or I'll
break your ugly face for you. Is that banshee schreechin'
fit music for a sick man? [The Norwegian puts his accordion in the bunk and lies back and closes his eyes. DRIS-

COLL goes over and stands beside YANK. The steamer's whistle sounds particularly loud in the silence.]

DAVIS: Damn this fog! [Reaches in under a bunk and yanks out a pair of seaboots, which he pulls on.] My look-out next, too. Must be nearly eight bells, boys. [With the exception of OLSON, all the men sitting up have on oilskins, sou'westers, seaboots, etc., in preparation for the watch on deck. OLSON crawls into a lower bunk on the right.]

SCOTTY: My wheel.

OLSON: [Disgustedly.] Nothin' but yust dirty weather all dis voyage. I yust can't sleep when weestle blow. [He turns his back to the light and is soon fast asleep and snoring.]

SCOTTY: If this fog keeps up, I'm tellin' ye, we'll no be in Carrdiff for a week or more.

DRISCOLL: 'Twas just such a night as this the auld *Dover* wint down. Just about this toime ut was, too, and we all sittin' round in the fo'castle, Yank beside me, whin all av a suddint we hear da great slitherin' crash, and the ship heeled over till we was all in a heap on wan side. What came afther I disremimber exactly, except 'twas a hard shift to get the boats over the side before the auld teakittle sank. Yank was in the same boat wid me, and sivin morthal days we drifted wid scarcely a drop of wather or a bite to chew on. 'Twas Yank here that held me down whin I wanted to jump into the ocean, roarin' mad wid the thirst. Picked up we were on the same day wid only Yank in his senses, and him steerin' the boat.

COCKY: [Protestingly.] Blimey but you're a cheerful blighter, Driscoll! Talkin' abaht shipwrecks in this 'ere blushin' fog. [YANK groans and stirs uneasily, opening his eyes. DRISCOLL hurries to his side.]

DRISCOLL: Are ye feelin' any betther, Yank?

YANK: [In a weak voice.] No.

32

DRISCOLL: Sure, you must be. You look as sthrong as an ox. [Appealing to the others.] Am I tellin' him a lie?

DAVIS: The sleep's done you good.

COCKY: You'll be 'avin your pint of beer in Cardiff this day week.

SCOTTY: And fish and chips, mon!

YANK: [Peevishly.] What're yuh all lyin' for? D'yuh think I'm scared to— [He hesitates as if frightened by the word he is about to say.]

DRISCOLL: Don't be thinkin' such things! [The ship's bell is heard heavily tolling eight times. From the forecastle head above the voice of the lookout rises in a long wail: Aaall's well. The men look uncertainly at YANK as if undecided whether to say good-bye or not.]

YANK: [In an agony of fear.] Don't leave me, Drisc! I'm dyin', I tell yuh. I won't stay here alone with every one snorin'. I'll go out on deck. [He makes a feeble attempt to rise, but sinks back with a sharp groan. His breath comes in wheezy gasps.] Don't leave me, Drisc! [His face grows white and his head falls back with a jerk.]

DRISCOLL: Don't be worryin', Yank. I'll not move a step out av here—and let that divil av a bosun curse his black head off. You speak a word to the bosun, Cocky. Tell him that Yank is bad took and I'll be stayin' wid him a while yet.

COCKY: Right-o. [COCKY, DAVIS, and SCOTTY go out quietly.]

COCKY: [From the alleyway.] Gawd blimey, the fog's thick as soup.

DRISCOLL: Are ye satisfied now, Yank? [Receiving no answer, he bends over the still form.] He's fainted, God help him! [He gets a tin dipper from the bucket and bathes YANK's forehead with the water. YANK shudders and opens his eyes.]

YANK: I thought I was goin' then. Wha' did yuh wanta wake me up fur?

33

DRISCOLL: [With forced gayety.] Is it wishful for heaven ye are?

YANK: [Gloomily.] Hell, I guess.

DRISCOLL: [Crossing himself involuntarily.] For the love av the saints don't be talkin' loike that! You'd give a man the creeps. It's chippin' rust on deck you'll be in a day or two wid the best av us.

[YANK does not answer, but closes his eyes wearily. The seaman who has been on lookout, SMITTY, a young Englishman, comes in and takes off his dripping oilskins. While he is doing this the man whose turn at the wheel has been relieved enters. He is a dark burly fellow with a round stupid face. The Englishman steps softly over to DRISCOLL. The other crawls into a lower bunk.]

SMITTY: [Whispering.] How's Yank?

DRISCOLL: Betther. Ask him yourself. He's awake.

YANK: I'm all right, Smitty.

SMITTY: Glad to hear it, Yank. [He crawls to an upper bunk and is soon asleep.]

IVAN: [The stupid-faced seaman who came in after SMITTY twists his head in the direction of the sick man.] You feel gude, Jank?

YANK: Yes, Ivan.

IVAN: Dot's gude. [He rolls over on his side and falls asleep immediately.]

YANK: [After a pause broken only by snores—with a bitter laugh.] Good-bye and good luck to the lot of you!

DRISCOLL: Is ut painin' you again?

YANK: It hurts like hell—here. [He points to the lower part of his chest on the left side.] I guess my old pump's busted. Ooohh! [A spasm of pain contracts his pale features. He presses his hand to his side and writhes on the thin mattress of his bunk. The perspiration stands out in beads on his forehead.]

DRISCOLL: [Terrified.] Yank! Yank! What is ut?

34

[Jumping to his feet.] I'll run for the captain. [He starts for the doorway.]

YANK: [Sitting up in his bunk, frantic with fear.] Don't leave me, Drisc! For God's sake don't leave me alone! [He leans over the side of his bunk and spits. DRISCOLL comes back to him.] Blood! Ugh!

DRISCOLL: Blood again! I'd best be gettin' the captain.

YANK: No, no, don't leave me! If yuh do I'll git up and follow you. I ain't no coward, but I'm scared to stay here with all of them asleep and snorin'. [DRISCOLL, not knowing what to do, sits down on the bench beside him. He grows calmer and sinks back on the mattress.] The captain can't do me no good, yuh know it yourself. The pain ain't so bad now, but I thought it had me then. It was like a buzz-saw cuttin' into me.

DRISCOLL: [Fiercely.] God blarst ut!

[The captain and the second mate of the steamer enter the forecastle. The captain is an old man with gray mustache and whiskers. The mate is clean-shaven and middle-aged. Both are dressed in simple blue uniforms.]

THE CAPTAIN: [Taking out his watch and feeling YANK'S pulse.] And how is the sick man?

YANK: [Feebly.] All right, sir.

THE CAPTAIN: And the pain in the chest?

YANK: It still hurts, sir, worse than ever.

THE CAPTAIN: [Taking a thermometer from his pocket and putting it into YANK'S mouth.] Here. Be sure and keep this in under your tongue, not over it.

THE MATE: [After a pause.] Isn't this your watch on deck, Driscoll?

DRISCOLL: Yes, sorr, but Yank was fearin' to be alone, and—

THE CAPTAIN: That's all right, Driscoll.

DRISCOLL: Thank ye, sorr.

THE CAPTAIN: [Stares at his watch for a moment or so;

35

then takes the thermometer from YANK's mouth and goes to the lamp to read it. His expression grows very grave. He beckons the MATE and DRISCOLL to the corner near the doorway. YANK watches them furtively. The CAPTAIN speaks in a low voice to the MATE.] Way up, both of them. [To DRISCOLL]: Has he been spitting blood again?

DRISCOLL: Not much for the hour just past, sorr, but before that—

THE CAPTAIN: A great deal?

DRISCOLL: Yes, sorr.

THE CAPTAIN: He hasn't eaten anything?

DRISCOLL: No, sorr.

THE CAPTAIN: Did he drink that medicine I sent him?

DRISCOLL: Yes, sorr, but it didn't stay down.

THE CAPTAIN: [Shaking his head.] I'm afraid—he's very weak. I can't do anything else for him. It's too serious for me. If this had only happened a week later we'd be in Cardiff in time to—

DRISCOLL: Plaze help him some way, sorr!

THE CAPTAIN: But, my good man, I'm not a doctor. [More kindly as he sees DRISCOLL's grief.] You and he have been shipmates a long time?

DRISCOLL: Five years and more, sorr.

THE CAPTAIN: I see. Well, don't let him move. Keep him quiet and we'll hope for the best. I'll read the matter up and send him some medicine, something to ease the pain, anyway. [Goes over to YANK.] Keep up your courage! You'll be better to-morrow. [He breaks down lamely before YANK's steady gaze.] We'll pull you through all right—and—hm—well—coming, Robinson? Dammit! [He goes out hurriedly, followed by the MATE.]

DRISCOLL: [Trying to conceal his anxiety.] Didn't I tell you you wasn't half as sick as you thought you was? The Captain'll have you out on deck cursin' and swearin' loike a trooper before the week is out.

YANK: Don't lie, Drisc. I heard what he said, and if I didn't I c'd tell by the way I feel. I know what's goin' to happen. I'm goin' to— [He hesitates for a second—then resolutely.] I'm goin' to die, that's what, and the sooner the better!

DRISCOLL: [Wildly.] No, and be damned to you, you're not. I'll not let you.

YANK: It ain't no use, Drisc. I ain't got a chance, but I ain't scared. Gimme a drink of water, will yuh, Drisc? My throat's burnin' up. [DRISCOLL brings the dipper full of water and supports his head while he drinks in great gulps.]

DRISCOLL: [Seeking vainly for some word of comfort.] Are ye feelin' more aisy loike now?

YANK: Yes—now—when I know it's all up. [A pause.] You mustn't take it so hard, Drisc. I was just thinkin' it ain't as bad as people think—dyin'. I ain't never took much stock in the truck them sky-pilots preach. I ain't never had religion; but I know whatever it is what comes after it can't be no worser'n this. I don't like to leave you, Drisc, but—that's all.

DRISCOLL: [With a groan.] Lad, lad, don't be talkin'.

YANK: This sailor life ain't much to cry about leavin'— just one ship after another, hard work, small pay, and bum grub; and when we git into port, just a drunk endin' up in a fight, and all your money gone, and then ship away again. Never meetin' no nice people; never gittin outa sailor town, hardly, in any port; travellin' all over the world and never seein' none of it; without no one to care whether you're alive or dead. [With a bitter smile.] There ain't much in all that that'd make yuh sorry to lose it, Drisc.

DRISCOLL: It's a hell av a life, the sea.

YANK: [Musingly.] It must be great to stay on dry land all your life and have a farm with a house of your own with cows and pigs and chickens, 'way in the middle of the land where yuh'd never smell the sea or see a ship. It must be great to have a wife, and kids to play with at night after supper when your work was done. It must be great to have a home of your own, Drisc.

DRISCOLL: [With a great sigh.] It must, surely; but what's the use av thinkin' av ut? Such things are not for the loikes av us.

YANK: Sea-farin' is all right when you're young and don't care, but we ain't chickens no more, and somehow, I dunno, this last year has seemed rotten, and I've had a hunch I'd quit—with you, of course—and we'd save our coin, and go to Canada or Argentine or some place and git a farm, just a small one, just enough to live on. I never told yuh this cause I thought you'd laugh at me.

DRISCOLL: [Enthusiastically.] Laugh at you, is ut? When I'm havin' the same thoughts myself, toime afther toime. It's a grand idea and we'll be doin' ut sure if you'll stop your crazy notions—about—about bein' so sick.

YANK: [Sadly.] Too late. We shouldn'ta made this trip, and then— How'd all the fog git in here?

DRISCOLL: Fog?

YANK: Everything looks misty. Must be my eyes gittin' weak, I guess. What was we talkin' of a minute ago? Oh, yes, a farm. It's too late. [His mind wandering.] Argentine, did I say? D'yuh remember the times we've had in Buenos Aires? The moving pictures in Barracas? Some class to them, d'yuh remember?

DRISCOLL: [With satisfaction.] I do that; and so does the piany player. He'll not be forgettin' the black eye I gave him in a hurry.

YANK: Remember the time we was there on the beach and had to go to Tommy Moore's boarding house to git shipped? And he sold us rotten oilskins and seaboots full of holes, and shipped us on a skysail yarder round the Horn, and took two months' pay for it. And the days we used to sit on the park benches along the Paseo Colon with the vigilantes lookin' hard at us? And the songs at the Sailor's Opera where the guy played ragtime—d'yuh remember them?

DRISCOLL: I do, surely.

YANK: And La Plata—phew, the stink of the hides! I always liked Argentine—all except that booze, caña. How drunk we used to git on that, remember?

DRISCOLL: Cud I forget ut? My head pains me at the menshun av that divil's brew.

YANK: Remember the night I went crazy with the heat in Singapore? And the time you was pinched by the cops in Port Said? And the time we was both locked up in Sydney for fightin'?

DRISCOLL: I do so.

YANK: And that fight on the dock at Cape Town— [His voice betrays great inward perturbation.]

DRISCOLL: [Hastily.] Don't be thinkin' av that now. 'Tis past and gone.

YANK: D'yuh think He'll hold it up against me?

DRISCOLL: [Mystified.] Who's that?

YANK: God. They say He sees everything. He must know it was done in fair fight, in self-defense, don't yuh think?

DRISCOLL: Av course. Ye stabbed him, and be damned to him, for the skulkin' swine he was, afther him tryin' to stick you in the back, and you not suspectin'. Let your conscience be aisy. I wisht I had nothin' blacker than that on my sowl. I'd not be afraid av the angel Gabriel himself.

YANK: [With a shudder.] I c'd see him a minute ago with the blood spurtin' out of his neck. Ugh!

DRISCOLL: The fever, ut is, that makes you see such things. Give no heed to ut.

YANK: You don't think He'll hold it up agin me—God, I mean.

DRISCOLL: If there's justice in hiven, no! [YANK seems comforted by this assurance.]

YANK: [After a pause.] We won't reach Cardiff for a week at least. I'll be buried at sea.

DRISCOLL: [Putting his hands over his ears.] Ssshh! I won't listen to you.

YANK: [As if he had not heard him.] It's as good a place as any other, I s'pose—only I always wanted to be buried on dry land. But what the hell'll I care—then? [Fretfully.] Why should it be a rotten night like this with that damned whistle blowin' and people snorin' all round? I wish the stars was out, and the moon, too; I c'd lie out on deck and look at them, and it'd made it easier to go—somehow.

DRISCOLL: For the love av God don't be talkin' loike that!

YANK: Whatever pay's comin' to me yuh can divvy up with the rest of the boys; and you take my watch. It ain't worth much, but it's all I've got.

DRISCOLL: But have ye no relations at all to call your own?

YANK: No, not as I know of. One thing I forgot: You know Fanny the barmaid at the Red Stork in Cardiff?

DRISCOLL: Sure, and who doesn't?

YANK: She's been good to me. She tried to lend me half a crown when I was broke there last trip. Buy her the biggest box of candy yuh c'n find in Cardiff. [Breaking down—in a choking voice.] It's hard to ship on this voyage I'm goin' on—alone! [DRISCOLL reaches out and grasps his hand. There is a pause, during which both fight to control themselves.] My throat's like a furnace. [He gasps for air.] Gimme a drink of water, will yuh, Drisc? [DRISCOLL gets him a dipper of water.] I wish this was a pint of beer. Oooohh! [He chokes, his face convulsed with agony,

40

his hands tearing at his shirt front. The dipper falls from his nerveless fingers.]

DRISCOLL: For the love av God, what is ut, Yank?

YANK: [Speaking with tremendous difficulty.] S'long, Drisc! [He stares straight in front of him with eyes starting from their sockets.] Who's that?

DRISCOLL: Who? What?

YANK: [Faintly.] A pretty lady dressed in black. [His face twitches and his body writhes in a final spasm, then straightens out rigidly.]

DRISCOLL: [Pale with horror.] Yank! Yank! Say a word to me for the love av hiven! [He shrinks away from the bunk, making the sign of the cross. Then comes back and puts a trembling hand on YANK's chest and bends closely over the body.]

COCKY: [From the alleyway.] Oh, Driscoll! Can you leave Yank for arf a mo' and give me a 'and?

DRISCOLL: [With a great sob.] Yank! [He sinks down on his knees beside the bunk, his head on his hands. His lips move in some half-remembered prayer.]

COCKY: [Enters, his oilskins and sou'wester glistening with drops of water.] The fog's lifted. [COCKY sees DRISCOLL and stands staring at him with open mouth. DRISCOLL makes the sign of the cross again.]

COCKY: [Mockingly.] Sayin' 'is prayers! [He catches sight of the still figure in the bunk and an expression of awed understanding comes over his face. He takes off his dripping sou'wester and stands, scratching his head.]

COCKY: [In a hushed whisper.] Gawd blimey!

CHUCK
AN ORCHARD FANTASY
By Percy MacKaye

PERSONS IN THE PLAY

DEACON DOYLE
ELIJAH
ABEL
LETTY

CHUCK

THE scene is laid in an old township of New Hampshire, early in the twentieth century. An orchard hillside, on an afternoon in late August.

The foreground is shadowed by apple-tree boughs, beneath which a footpath winds between piles of ripe, sweet apples, climbs the slope toward the background, and disappears behind bushes of elder and witch-hazel, the latter in golden bloom. Below these bushes, and partly screened by others in the left foreground, the edge of an eddying pool is visible, flecked with sunbeams and leaf-shadows and blotched with the luminous red of cardinal flowers.

The pool is evidently the shallow curve of a brook, for the plash of a waterfall tinkles behind the bushes, and occasional spray glistens through the greenery. Near the further bank of the pool is a low, flat boulder, behind which a less trodden path leads from the main footway into the hazel cover.

In the center middleground rises a grassy knoll, the top of which is scarred yellow by the gravel of a woodchuck's

45

burrow, partly excavated, it would seem, by a spade, which stands, thrust upright now, in the débris nearby. Fringing the knoll are low bushes of huckleberry, lamb-kill and sweet-fern; behind it, the orchard slopes down steeply toward the right; beyond it, through the apple trees, are glimpses of rolling, summer hills.

An oriole is singing somewhere in the leafy sunshine.

On the ruined doorsill of his burrow a WOODCHUCK, squat on comfortable haunches, sits nibbling an ear of corn.

Deaf to the one and blind to the other, enters—along the footpath—DEACON DOLE, a spare, black figure in Sabbath-day garb. His shrewd, shaven face, home-cut gray hair and stiff-kneed gait are those of a Yankee farmer about seventy. He walks slowly, clutching a black book in one hand, twice pausing to look back along the path.

From away on the left, a deep-toned bell resounds with regular cadence.

With the bell tones, intermittently from beyond the bushes, are mingled the shrilly notes of a tin flute, piped merrily.

Of a sudden, conscious of the flute, the DEACON stops and listens; stoops and peers among the bushes; then gazes reflectively at the WOODCHUCK's hole, whose occupant, at his approach, has retired within, all but his furry noddle. As the old man turns aside curiously to examine this, a low, giggling laughter is distinctly audible. The DEACON's face darkens. Again the flute notes trill, in the intervals of the bell.

THE DEACON: [Stands stiffly erect, and calls in a loud, harsh voice.] Chuck!—Chuck!

A VOICE: [Deep like the DEACON's, but faint, as if far away.] Chuck!—Chuck!

[With troubled look, DEACON DOLE turns again to the footpath and is resuming his measured walk, when the sharp report of a gun causes him to exclaim and start back. The WOODCHUCK's head vanishes.]

46

CHUCK

The Deacon: [Screwing his face.] Damn him! [Then hugging tighter his book, he mutters.] Lord, on Thy day— into temptation!

A Voice: [From behind the bushes, musical and vibrant with laughter.] Chucky! Chucky! Whoa, thar! [Through the hazels behind the boulder, Abel enters and bounds, with a hop, skip and jump, to the top of the knoll. There he stands reloading his gun, and clucking his cheek like a chipmunk.] So, old Bunker! Shot into your breastworks, did ye? Godfrey, you've got book larnin' for field sarvice!

[Abel is a young fellow, about twenty: a half-wild figure, clothed in tattered yellow undershirt and blue overalls, frayed half to the knees—his bare arms and legs sun-browned and splotched with wood-stains. His expression just now is sly and twinkling, as his small squirrel eyes squint through his tousled tow hair. On his head are laid great green lily-pads, tied by long, rubbery stems under his chin. From his belt hang the pelts of small animals, grayish brown. From one hip-pocket sticks a tin flute, from the other a cartridge box.]

The Deacon: [Glowering.] Mornin', Chuck! [Abel drops his gun and starts up, scared by the voice.] Dressed for meetin', I see, and keepin' the Sabbath 's usual. [Pointing to the lily-pads on Abel's head.] What ye call it— bonnet, or hat?

Abel: [With the gleam of a grin.] Them's cure for sun-stroke!

The Deacon: Oh!—What have ye—hired out to a new trade, sence ye broke jail?

Abel: [His look growing subtle and sullen.] What trade?

The Deacon: [With the ghost of a thin smile.] Murder.

Abel: What ye goin' to run me in for now?

The Deacon: Killin' your kin, be ye?

Abel: [Amazed, then amused.] Now, thar! So ye thought I took that shot—

47

THE DEACON: Oh, not at me. I ain't no kin o' yourn now, nor you ain't none o' mine. [Points to the burrow.] I was makin' reference to them thievin' field-rat folks o' yourn, the lusty varmin that farrowed ye, and swapped ye off, in my first-born's cradle, for a son o' mine; them thar, that namesaked ye, your huckleberry brethren—the woodchucks. [Smiling, acidly.] Thou shalt not commit Murder, saith the commandment!

ABEL: [Who has listened with growing good humor, shows the skins at his belt and laughs.] If ye mean old Bunker in thar—look a-here! I've skun the hull family, 'ceptin' the old man.

THE DEACON: So ye have; so ye have.

ABEL: I tried to dig him out with the spade; but while I was bangin' down his front door, he put on his sneakers and slipped out the back ell. [Laughs reminiscently.] I tell ye: he ain't forgot his calc'latin' tables—the old un!

THE DEACON: [Ruminating, with relish.] So he ain't; so he ain't!

ABEL: I pretty nigh cotched him last week, though. I hadn't no gun, so he jest sot thar and winked. Then I fetched a grab—but Jehu! he can bite, when ye try to pull his leg.

THE DEACON: So he can! And speakin' o' calc'latin', how many times, do you calc'late, I've told you to clear out? [ABEL grins.] Eh? Answer me: how many?

ABEL: [Taking out his flute.]

So I answered him, as I thought good:
"As many red herrin's as grow in the wood."

[He plays a snatch on the flute, hopping to his tune.]
THE DEACON: [Shaking his book at him.] Quit it! Quit, I tell ye! [ABEL puts up his flute, but continues to twiddle dumbly on his left middle finger thrust in his mouth.] I'm a square man. I wa'n't chose to be deacon for nothin'. I'm

48

fair and square at catechisin', and I'm givin' you one more chanct to answer me back fair and square.

ABEL: [Saluting.]   Fair and square, sir.

THE DEACON: Answer me: How much chores have ye arned your victuals with, Chuck—well, say, in the last six months?

ABEL: [Grinning, sits on the burrow and lilts.]

> How much wood would a woodchuck chuck,
> If a woodchuck would chuck wood?

THE DEACON: [Shaken with anger.]   Damn ye! Clear out, or I'll have ye haled back to jail. Git offn the place! [He moves toward ABEL.]

ABEL: [Springing up, turns sullen again.]   Guess it's my place, too!

THE DEACON: Ye guess so!

ABEL: And my folks, too.

THE DEACON: Yourn? Ha!

ABEL: One o' ye, anyhow.

THE DEACON: Which?

ABEL: The gal—Litty.

THE DEACON: Stop: ye *daresn't* name her! The gal ye've brought to shame in your father's house; her as I 'dopted when her own folks died, and raised her to be the woman in my own house, with my own sons—good Lord!—and to share in the victuals and the chores.

ABEL: [Lilting.]   And the chores, good Lord, and the chores!

THE DEACON: Yes, the chores: She never shirked 'em till you brought her to shame, and made her grow slack, a-hankerin' for you and the vanities and lusts of the varmin you 'sort with.—And the likes of you my flesh and blood—a Dole!

ABEL:

> Dole! Dole! Dole!
> Says the De'il to the dead man's soul!

THE DEACON: And look at your brother 'Lijah—town clerk a'ready, and redeemed in the Lord's grace: and him a year younger.

ABEL: Pity I wa'n't born o' legal age, like 'Lijah!

THE DEACON: True 'nough: you make me a pretty son and heir, don't ye?

ABEL: Sun and air's pretty much all you've give' me to grow on.

THE DEACON: Yes, thank God for 'Lijah! But you—you've lied and you've drunk; you've lazed and you've lusted and you've stole: you've stole from your own home folks, and you've ravished in the house of your father. But 'Lijah, your brother, he's redeemed ye. He's put ye in jail.

ABEL: [Grinning.] Has he *kep'* me thar?

THE DEACON: And he's takin' poor Letty to meetin', to marry her himself, lawful—this day and mornin'.

ABEL: [Taking out his flute.] If they *git* thar!—*If* they git thar! [He trills a repetition of the lilt.]

THE DEACON: [Seizing up the gun from the ground.] What ye mean by that, ye whistlin' do-no-good?

ABEL: *If,* says I; *if!*—What's the dif?

THE DEACON: [Examining the cartridge in the gun, trembles with rage.] So! You was layin' for your own brother with this gun, was ye? Now, then, I'm done with ye, for al'ays and all. Git out, you lustin' rat, you rollin' stone o' Satan, ye! You filanderin', murderin' pest, git outn here! Git outn my life, git outn my home and my fields. I'll fodder the likes of ye no more. [He raises and aims the gun at ABEL, who dodges involuntarily.] Git off! [Staring at the gun's nozzle, ABEL backs slowly away, rounding toward the bushes.] And I warn ye, Chuck, the last time: keep in hidin'— [Points to the woodchuck's hole.] —like him. For if ever I set eyes on ye ag'in, trespassin' on my acres, I'll shoot ye, for the ground-hog that ye be, and bury ye thar in your own burrer. Git!

CHUCK

[Reaching the boulder, ABEL pauses, looking down at it, and smiling a quiet, absent-minded smile, seems to forget the gun and the glowering DEACON. Loosing from his head the water-lily pads, he drops them in the ferns by the rock. Above him, a locust rasps its drowsy midsummer whirr. Listening, he stoops, pulls a broad grass-blade, splits it leisurely, lays it between his two thumbs, and blows on it—through his lips—a buzzing, locust-like noise. THE DEACON, setting his jaw, lets the gun-barrel sink slowly to the ground. Buzzing his grass-blade, ABEL idles along the hazel path, and disappears. The church bell, which has rung at regular intervals, now ceases to sound.]

THE DEACON: [Climbing the footpath—gun and book in hand—mutters, as he goes from sight.] Son and heir! Son and heir!

[From the left now are heard the reverberating tones of a church organ, and soon after—the voices of a small congregation, singing. In the still summer air, the words of their hymn are half distinguishable.]

THE VOICES:

> Praise God, from whom all blessings flow;
> Praise Him, all creatures here below;
> Praise Him above, ye heavenly host;
> Praise Father, Son and Holy Ghost!
>   Amen!

[While the voices are singing, ABEL reappears from the bushes and, lying on his back upon the shady slope, plays an answering improvisation on his flute. As he does so, he keeps his eyes fixed on the burrow, out of which ere long the head of the WOODCHUCK emerges. Catching sight of it, ABEL turns over on his stomach, and—still fluting with the fingers of one hand—elbows himself, with hitches, through the huckleberry shrubs, nearer and nearer to the burrow. Reaching it, he raises his head suddenly, and grabs with one hand. The WOODCHUCK dodges in and dis-

51

appears. ABEL scrambles headlong after him into the burrow—his heels kicking the air.]

ABEL: [Coaxingly.]   Chuck! Chuck!

[Voices are heard in conversation. ABEL wriggles outward, replaces his heels by his head, rubs the fresh earth from his eyes and hair, and peers blinking above the embankment, where only his brown head is visible.]

A WOMAN'S VOICE: [As in pain.]   I can't, 'Lijah: I just can't go on 't.

A MAN'S VOICE: 'Tain't only a few rods to the meetin' house.

[Enter LETTY and ELIJAH. The former is a slight girl, in her teens, calm-browed, with large, soft eyes. She is still in the faint bloom of an early beauty fragile as an hepatica. Signs of drudgery and scant fare, however, are beginning to show in the just perceptible stoop of her figure and the shape of her hardened hands. She is dressed with plain simplicity, except for the white folds of a bride's veil, pinned to her hair. ELIJAH, clean-cut of features, resembles somewhat his father, but lacks the DEACON's dignity of years and power. He wears a styleless black suit, and speaks with a querulous sharpness, tempered at times by a conscious effort to seem kinder than he feels. LETTY, limping, reaches one hand toward ELIJAH for support, but he either does not notice, or ignores, the gesture.]

LETTY: [Pausing, speaks faintly.]   I'm so sorry: I can't stand no longer.   [Swaying, she sinks upon the ground.]

ELIJAH: [Uneasily, looking away.]   We're late. Father's gone ahead long ago. *He* got acrosst safe. Where's it hurt ye?

LETTY: [Painfully.]   My ankle. When I fell in the brook, it got twisted, I guess.

ELIJAH: I'd like to catch the mean-livin' rascal that sawed the footbridge. I'll run him in for't.

52

LETTY: I'm glad 'twas me, anyhow; and you was behind.

ELIJAH: Yes, I was just 'bout to set my foot on 't, when 't went down with ye. Lucky you didn't wet your shoes.

LETTY: 'Twas 'most dried up—the brook.

ELIJAH: Wonder who did it! [With sudden suspicion.] Letty!—Was it *him?*

LETTY: [Timidly.] Who?

ELIJAH: Oh, you know, I guess: you'd oughter. Well, if it's him, I'll jail him for that over again.

LETTY: Please, but—

ELIJAH: [With deliberate politeness.] Come, Letitia: I'll help ye 'long the path.

LETTY: I can't.

ELIJAH: *Can't?* What will ye—set *here* and get married? [Smiling an anemic smile, he extends one hand for her to rise.] Guess you ain't calc'latin' on a weddin' by a woodchuck's hole!

LETTY: [Trying hard to smile.] No; I don't scarcely know what—

ELIJAH: Come: the minister's spoke and paid for. It's fixed we're to jine him in the vestry, after meetin' 's out.

LETTY: It's such a pity—

ELIJAH: [Stiffening.] *How!*

LETTY: I mean—me bein' laid up.

ELIJAH: Well, you don't reckon I'm to carry ye, do ye?—Smart looks we'd make at meetin'—me heftin' ye like a bale o' hay! No, thank ye: I'd never hear the last on 't. Come; git up; do!

LETTY: [In an agony of embarrassment, tries to stand, but sinks down again.] 'Tain't no use, 'Lijah; I'm 'bliged to ask ye to go back to the four corners and ask old Miss Dikewell to lend me her crutches: she'll help me out—just to get to meetin' and back.

ELIJAH: Crutches, ah? [Taking out his watch.] Quarter past 'leven. You al'ays did make mountains outn mole-hills.

LETTY: I'm so sorry.

ELIJAH: [Morosely.] Married on crutches! and next mornin'—the doctor, I presume!

LETTY: No, 'Lijah—

ELIJAH: *No,* I guess too! A bad start, I call it. Well, seein' ye can't come respectable, I s'pose I've got to get ye the crutches: but mind—no doctor! [He goes off along the path, right.]

[Letty crouches over her foot in pain. From the wood-chuck's burrow, ABEL whistles low. LETTY sits back, pale, and listens. Still hidden, ABEL sings a snatch.]

ABEL:

> Come 'cross lots, come 'cross lots,
> Says I to Molly, to Molly my gal!

LETTY: [Starting half to her feet.] Abel!

ABEL: [In a loud whisper.] Litty!

LETTY: [Staring about.] O Chuck, where be you?

[Wriggling from the burrow, ABEL scrambles down the slope—ardent, and covered with brown earth—and embraces her suddenly.]

ABEL: It's me! [He kisses her.]

LETTY: [Struggling feebly.] No, no! [She sinks back helpless, and moans.]

ABEL: Gal, what's hurtin'? Which foot is it?

LETTY: [Faintly.] Go 'way, quick.

ABEL: [Feeling her ankle.] Why, it's all swole up. [Whipping out a jackknife from his pocket, he cuts the shoe-laces, deftly slips off the shoe, flings it away, and draws off the stocking, while LETTY murmurs faintly: "Don't, please."] It's cold water 't wants. Wait a bit. [Taking the stocking, he dips it in the pool, hurries back with it dripping, and wraps it carefully round the ankle.] Smart, doos it? [He looks anxiously in her face. She nods.

54

Looking quickly round, he sees a tin-can cover, fills it from the brook, brings and holds it to her mouth.] Swig—jest a mite! [She drinks.] That's nice. Onet more. Sun's hot. [She drinks again.]

LETTY: [Reviving.] Thanks.

ABEL: Durn thanks. You won't never forgive me.

LETTY: What for?

ABEL: 'Twas me: *I* sawed it.

LETTY: Sawed what?

ABEL: The foot-bridge. I never reckoned on it bustin' through with *you*. I calc'lated on *them*.

LETTY: Them?

ABEL: The old man, and 'Lijah. With a good ten-foot tumble, I calc'lated on a wooden leg apiece.

LETTY: [Painfully.] Oh, Chuck!

ABEL: Born fool, me! Might a-knowed Old Nick would leave *them* in luck, and *you* in the lurch. [At her expression, he grows tenderly anxious.] Doos it hurt hard, Litty, my gal?

LETTY: I ain't yourn no more, Abel.

ABEL: [Quickly.] Why not?

LETTY: [Touching her veil.] Ain't you noticed—this?

ABEL: [Starts up, flushing.] Yare: I noticed it. [He pulls it suddenly from her head. With the action, her bright hair falls about her shoulders, and she reaches toward him, with a startled cry.]

LETTY: Chuck! Chuck! Chuck! What ye doin'?

ABEL: [Rolling the veil into a ball, with both hands.] Now ye see it— [He springs to the woodchuck's hole and stuffs the veil in.] —and now ye don't! [He stands staring at her, as she starts to her knees, with outreached arms.] Goda'mighty! You're some pretty!

LETTY: What'll I do? 'Lijah's comin' back.

ABEL: [Coming to her.] What of it! You're my gal, ain't ye?

LETTY: You've broke jail: he'll put ye back again.

ABEL: [Scornfully.] *Him* put me back—I guess! Watch him tryin'!

LETTY: He'll tell your father at meetin'. Go 'way, quick!

ABEL: [Striding down the path.] The meetin' 's goin' to be right here.

LETTY: Come back! The Deacon said he'd shoot ye, if he catched ye again on the place.

ABEL: That's the Deacon's long suit—talk!

LETTY: And what'll I do without my shoe and my veil! [She starts to limp toward the woodchuck's hole.]

ABEL: [Hurrying to her.] Stop your goin' on that ankle, Litty.

LETTY: [In despair.] I can see him now. He's runnin'. Oh, hide! Hide, quick!

ABEL: If I hide us both, will you be my gal, and not hisn?

LETTY: [Throwing her arms about his shoulders, as he lifts her.] Oh, dear! O Chuck! Hide, quick!

ABEL: [With a proud smile, bearing her toward the brook.] My, your hair! It smells like hazel blooms.

[Lightly he springs with her into the bed of the brook, and disappears behind the bushes. They have hardly disappeared, when ELIJAH comes hurrying up the path, tucking the ends of a handkerchief into his sweating collar. He carries a pair of crutches. Pausing, dumbfounded, he searches about with his eyes.]

ELIJAH: [Calling.] Letty! Letitia! Where be ye? Letty!

[Suddenly he darts forward and picks up LETTY's shoe from the grass. He examines it carefully, pulling out some of the cut laces. Then his eyes narrow, his face hardens, and he flings the crutches on the ground, with an ugly muttering. Pocketing the shoe, he hurries off toward the church. For an instant, ABEL's head appears through the bushes, looking after him. Then the faint thunder of the organ rolls once more through the orchard, and the sound of the congregation, singing]:

THE CHURCH VOICES:

> All hail the power of Jesus' name,
>> Let angels prostrate fall;
> Bring forth the royal diadem,
>> And crown him Lord of all;
>> And—crown—him
>> Lor—or—ord of all!

[Through these more distant voices, the voice of ABEL, close by, sings from behind the bushes, mingling with the organ tones.]

THE VOICE OF ABEL:

> Come 'cross lots, come 'cross lots,
>> Says I to Molly, to Molly my gal!
> Joe Pie weed is tall and yeller,
> Cider-pears hang low and meller,
> Stoop down, and scoot t' meet your feller
>> Where th' ain't no tattletal'.

> O Joe Pie, Joe Pie,
>> If galin' and gospel don't 'gree,
> We'll give the good folks the go-by—
>> Molly my gal, and me!

THE CHURCH VOICES:

>> And—crown—him
>> Lor—or—ord of all!

[The organ still rolls. Behind the bushes, the tin flute trills a few notes. Then ABEL reënters, through the hazels, carrying LETTY, in whose loosened hair he has stuck white water-lilies and cardinal flowers. In her hand she holds a bunch of half-opened lily buds. ABEL sits on the low boulder—placing LETTY, a clinging wisp of a girl, beside him. Both her feet are now bare.]

ABEL: [Starting to sing again.]

> Come 'cross lots—

57

LETTY: [Putting her hand over his mouth.] Shh!

ABEL: He's clean out o' hearin'. [Wetting his forefinger in his mouth, he holds it in the air.] The wind 's from the meetin' house.—Mind where you're settin'?

LETTY: [With a happy cry.] Why, the boulder—it's ourn!

ABEL: Rec'lect, do ye?

LETTY: The first time I come 'cross lots, and you met me here: Oh, Chuck!

ABEL: The moon come out; and afterwards we waded for lilies.

LETTY: Lily-time—a year ago!

ABEL: And you made head-gear on 'em: the pads for me, and the blooms for youself. Do it ag'in, gal, won't ye? [Picking up the pads, which he dropped by the boulder.] Look, here's mine, made a'ready. You've got the star-buds thar. Make youself a genu*ine* bride-veil, will ye?

LETTY: If you want me.

ABEL: *Do* I? [He caresses her. She begins to weave the water lilies together.] How's the off hoof now, little heifer? No more hurt feelin'?

LETTY: Seems I ain't no feelin' nowheres, 'ceptin' here. [She feels of her throat, and swallows.]

ABEL: And here? [He kisses her on the mouth. She clings to him impetuously.]

LETTY: O Chuck! When he don't find me at meetin', he'll fetch your father.

ABEL: Not s' long 's the praisin' lasts. Hark: they're off ag'in. [He halloos, to the organ tones]:

> Come 'cross lots, come 'cross lots,
>   Says I to Molly, and let down the bars!

[The Voices of the congregation resume their singing, while ABEL—swaying LETTY on his knee—carols his counter-song.]

58

THE CHURCH VOICES:

> Oh, would like yonder sacred **throng**
> We at His feet might fall,
> And join the everlasting song,
> And crown Him Lord of all!

ABEL:

> Bull and heifer drink in the meader,
> Boy and gal are tired o' the treader;
> Skin out—when the sky is growin' redder—
> And steal your fun from the stars.

> O Joe Pie, Joe Pie,
> If pairin' and preachin' don't gee,
> We'll give the good Lord the go-by—
> Molly my gal, and me!

THE CHURCH VOICES:

> —Lor—or—ord of all!—A-men!

[The organ ceases. There is silence, except for the burring of a locust.]

LETTY: [In an awed whisper.] They've stopped. He'll be tellin' your father.

ABEL: Not yit; the preachin' 's goin' on. We've got the hull sarmon to lie snug in—snug 's a bug in a rug.

LETTY: You guess we're safe and sure here?

ABEL: Safe as salvation, and sure as sinnin'. [He fondles her hair, looking happily in her eyes. She returns his gaze, yearningly.]

LETTY: Boy—and you love me—after all?

ABEL: Guess ag'in. [He kisses her.]

LETTY: I thought 'twas all over. That's why I took 'Lijah. They couldn't a-made me done it nohow, if it hadn't a-been—hadn't a-been—for Nan.

ABEL: Now don't you fuss 'bout Nan. Nan 's no sort. She's jest a cider gal.

LETTY: What's a cider gal?

ABEL: Oh, when Jack takes his drop, he wants his Jill. But that ain't lovin'.

LETTY: I don't make out.

ABEL: No; you wa'n't never drunk: that's why. I was drunk: that's all.

LETTY: [Gently.] Wa'n't that 'nough?

ABEL: 'Nough for the preachers, I reckon. Ye ain't jined them yit, have ye?

LETTY: No, Chuck, no. But 'Lijah said how you loved her, and your father said how—seein' he'd 'dopted me— my child would have to be born reg'lar into the church and the family, and bear the name o' Dole; and so 'Lijah wanted me for himself; and they was both afeard—

ABEL: You better bet they was! They was both afeard they wouldn't have nobody to do the chores for nothin': no gal to cook and scrub and clean and do the milkin'. Skeered o' the chores; it's a family failin'! Born-brother 'Lijah and me, we're twins thar! But for gittin' rid o' chores, I'd ruther steal a heifer than a gal.

LETTY: Oh, that heifer! When your father missed it from the barn, and you was arrested—

ABEL: [Gleefully.] Born-brother 'Lijah, *he* signed the warrant!

LETTY: [Grave, and wide-eyed.] No!—him?

ABEL: [His grin splitting into laughter.] But he bought the heifer! O Lordy! He bought back his own heifer for five dollars more 'n I sold it to Sam Williams for; and Sam he set up the drinks for me, with the balance! [Wiping the tears of his laughter.] O Lordy! That was w'uth the price of admittance to jail.

LETTY: But now you've broke loose before trial, what'll happen to ye?

ABEL: Never fret. Sam he's constable, and he won't run me in twice, if the homefolks don't pinch me. Meanwhiles, with the price of 'Lijah's heifer, I've bought me— [He feels in his back pocket.] —look! [He takes out two bits of cardboard, and holds them merrily before her eyes.]

LETTY: What's them?

ABEL: Two tickets to the White Mountains—for a weddin' spree.

LETTY: A weddin' spree? Ourn?

ABEL: Wouldn't be 'Lijah's, would it?

LETTY: [Gazing on the tickets with bewildered happiness.] Us two: the White Mountains: O Chuck!

ABEL: That's my signature, and it's goin' to be yourn hencefor'ards, world without end, et cet'ry. Jest *Chuck*— that's our new callin'-card:

ABEL CHUCK and LITTY CHUCK

The doorplate of old Dole is *chucked!* It's our call to arms, Litty: Damnation without remuneration—if that ain't misery, make the most on 't! Chuck the home tea-party overboard: Chuck the hull shootin' match—chores, church and fam'ly! Them's our stars and stripes, and we'll hist 'em on that thar Bunker's Hill. [He points to the WOOD-CHUCK'S mound.]

LETTY: [Examining more closely the pieces of cardboard.] But they ain't return-tickets!

ABEL: What's the good o' returnin'?

LETTY: But where'll we put up, when the little 'un comes?

ABEL: In the deacon's cow-barn?—I guess *not!* No, s'ree! The old man called me a varmin critter: told me to pack and jine the other chucks. Wall, so I will, and take my mate along. I reckon we can nose for our livin' as good as them other gipsies. I've watched 'em sence I was so high —the chuckfolks. Durn if I don't think they're happier 'n housefolks. They ain't domestic, nor they ain't wild; but they live on the fat o' both stock. [Pointing to the burrow.] Thar's that sly old parson o' the pastur'—old Chuck-the-

dirt: Lordy, ain't I seen him mornin's, with his fur bib
tucked under his chin, breakfastin' on 'Lijah's celery and
parsnips, when 'Lijah himself was goin' empty-bellied,
drivin' his garden stuff t' market. Chucks cute? Now I
guess! That's why they're cussed by the durn-fool housefolks.

Housefolks hoe and harrer; chuckfolks feed and farrer.
Housefolks borrer trouble; chuckfolks lend it out at interest. Housefolks help the devil; chuckfolks help 'emselves.
'Course, every beggar must bide his chanct, but I guess,
Litty, you and me are cute 'nough to dig a snug burrer
somewhars, and raise up a litter on somebody *else's* lot, whar
we can share the crops and dodge the taxes. Anyhow,
you're 'cute 'nough *lookin'!* [He caresses her. Suddenly,
she seizes his arm, startled.]

LETTY: Listen: what's that?

ABEL: [Listening.] What like?

LETTY: Like a great bird, screamin' far off, and callin'—
callin' to its young uns.

ABEL: Like what it *is*, Litty—callin' to you and me. It's
Love-each-other, gal. It's the great mountain bird a-swoopin'
down on us. It's the White Mountain train, whistlin' crosst
the valley.—It'll be at the Junction in ten minutes.

LETTY: Are we goin', true 'nough?

ABEL: Tuck up your hair. How's the foot?

LETTY: [Joyously.] Oh, I ain't got none: I'm flyin'.

ABEL: Put on your veil, lily-bride. [He helps her fasten
the woven lilies on her head, he himself putting on his
former head-gear of lily-pads.]

LETTY: But where'll be the weddin'? There ain't time.

ABEL: The' ain't nothin' but time: ten minutes.

LETTY: But where—

ABEL: Didn't I say the meetin' would be right here?

LETTY: But where's the proper minister? [With a bright

thought.] They say, gipsy gals jump over a broom to get married.

ABEL: [Warningly.] Shh! Don't embarrass his worship. He's a shy sort. [Mysteriously he points to the top of the mound, where the WOODCHUCK, partly visible, sits sunning himself on his haunches. ABEL speaks low.] Ain't *he* proper 'nough?

LETTY: Him? What for?

ABEL: Why, for the ceremony. He's the most expensive prophet in the county: when he jest stirs out and looks at his shadder, the market-folks tremble in their boots. But we ain't sparin' expense to-day, Litty. I've spoke our license from *him*. So now for the ceremony!

LETTY: [Laughing for the first time—a happy, hysterical, young laugh.] Ain't you funny, Chuck!

ABEL: Ssh! Not so loud. He'll stay and jine us, if we behave. He 'preciates my comin' without no gun.—Now, do as I do. [He tiptoes forward; she follows, holding his hand.]

LETTY: Chuck, ain't you funny!

ABEL: [With a profound bow and boy-like flourish, addresses the WOODCHUCK.] Reverend Mr. Wood—of the renowned family of Chucks—we, male and female, of your honor's own kin and communion, bein' nat'ral born sinners (and glad of it), poachin' in your honor's parish (off and on), for some twenty seasons (more or less), and havin' published our banns (from time to time), in the presence of chipmunks, woodcocks and water-wagtails, duly assembled therefor, do now respectfully petition your experienced worship to unite us, one t' other, in the blessin's of wedlock, accordin' to the ancient rites and ceremonies of orchard communities.

Yours truly—Amen! [ABEL now turns about, and assumes a low, guttural tone.] Do you, boy, kiss this gal because ye love her? [In his own voice.] I do. [He

63

kisses LETTY. Then speaks again, guttural.] Do you, gal, kiss this boy, because ye love him? [He nudges LETTY.]

LETTY: [Shyly.] I do. [She kisses ABEL. Through the orchard the church organ begins again to roll.]

ABEL: [Guttural.] Will you, boy, stick to this gal, so long 's ye love her? [In his own voice.] I will. [He hugs LETTY; then speaks again, guttural.] Will you, gal, stick to this boy, so long 's ye love him? [He nudges LETTY again.]

LETTY: [In a low voice.] I will. [She draws closer to him.]

ABEL: [Guttural.] Then do I now pronounce you, man-chuck and woman-chuck, *mates!* Kiss, and be kind to your little chucks.—Amen!

ABEL and LETTY: [Together.] Amen! [They kiss each other on the mouth. The WOODCHUCK vanishes into his burrow. From nearby, the Voices of the congregation sing to the organ. As they become aware of this, ABEL and LETTY look at each other, listening.]

THE CHURCH VOICES:

> Lord, dismiss us with Thy blessing;
> Fill our hearts with joy and peace;
> Let us each, thy love possessing,
> Triumph in redeeming grace:
> O refresh us,
> O refresh us,
> Traveling through this wilderness.
> A—men!

LETTY: [Tugging at ABEL's arms.] Run! Meetin' 's out. Run, Chuck! [Hand in hand, they run up the mound, at the top of which LETTY's ankle gives way, and she sinks down.]

ABEL: What—the hoof ag'in, little heifer? [He lifts her in his arms. Holding her a moment, they stand gazing off toward the valley, where a long, deep whistle sounds.]

64

CHUCK

LETTY: It 's callin' us, Chuck: the great bird—*Love-each-other!*

ABEL: It 's callin' us to the hills, gal—the hills! [The report of a gun resounds. ABEL starts back, and stumbles. LETTY screams and hides her face. Holding her on his left arm, ABEL raises his right defiantly, and shouts:] Never skun me! [Waving toward the church.] So long, Brother 'Lijah! The minister 's waitin'!

[Putting his thumb to his nose, he twiddles his fingers mockingly; then springing with LETTY down the further slope, he disappears. The shadows in the orchard are lengthening. A locust rasps in an elm. Faint crickets cheep in the grass. An oriole flutes from an apple tree. From his hole, the WOODCHUCK crawls cautiously out, nosing, as he does so, a crumpled and earth-soiled veil, which clings to his bristly hair, half clothing him. Pulling from his burrow an ear of corn, he sits up on his haunches, silently nibbling it—his small eyes half shut in the sunshine. Faintly from below, sounds the voice of ABEL, singing:]

> Come 'cross lots, come 'cross lots,
> Says I to Litty, to Litty, my gal!

[The WOODCHUCK nibbles on.]

THE QUARRY
By J. Audrey Clark

PERSONS IN THE PLAY

Lige Burke
Reporter
Charles Higgins
Gus Hawkins
Em Cady
Zeke Tasker

THE QUARRY

THE basement of SHERIFF HIGGINS' home which has been transformed into the cell room of the County Jail, Middlebury, Vermont. In the center of the back wall is a door. One makes an elbow-turn and ascends the stairs to the street level. It is a special entrance at the side of the house so that legal "visitors" won't rub shoulders with social callers—thus obviating any mutual embarrassment which might arise from such encounters. The right side of the room and part of the back, as far as the door, is taken up with the iron "coops." To the left of the entrance, half-hidden by posters and wanted-notices pertaining to the duties of the sheriff's office, is a sort of secret panel.

In the corner is a gun rack with a couple of rifles. Against the left wall is an old-fashioned desk, used by the sheriff to store his records and other papers. On it are an oil lamp, some newspapers and a checkerboard. There are no windows. Ventilation is obtained by small gratings in each cell, and illumination comes from a couple of unshaded electric light bulbs suspended from the ceiling. There are two or three plain kitchen chairs in the room. LIGE BURKE, a tall, easy-going Vermonter is discovered sitting with his feet planted on the desk, reading a newspaper. He has a scraggly mustache—the color is nondescript, being prejudiced in favor of a "terbaccy jooce" hue. He wears an old felt hat, which one feels he never removes, even when he goes to bed, high boots which are very muddy, and besides his keys he has a huge revolver strapped to his side. Near his chair is a cuspidor to which he has had recourse now and again, as evidenced by the little splashes around it. Without taking his eyes off the paper, LIGE turns his head and ejects a stream of "jooce" in the general direction of the proper receptacle.

An iron door clangs at the top of the stairs and a REPORTER comes hesitatingly down. He wears a turned-in felt hat, a brown raincoat, goloshes and carries a crooked umbrella on his arm. With his horn-rimmed glasses and the newspaper crammed in his pocket, he presents a rather pedantic air. He seems timid—either on account of his surroundings or because this may be his first important assignment. The REPORTER looks around the room, shakes his rain-soaked umbrella, then knocks on the door jamb.

LIGE: [Without looking around.] Come in.

REPORTER: I am a reporter from the United Press Service.

[LIGE lowers his paper and gets ready to receive him. He turns around and catching sight of the insignificant looking little man, he registers disgust and goes right back to his original position, and resumes his reading of the newspaper.]

REPORTER: Are you Mr. Burke?

LIGE: Thet's me.

REPORTER: I understand that kidnapper's been captured. I wonder if you would let me have an interview with him?

LIGE: He's in custidy all right enuff. But he ain't arrived yit.

REPORTER: May I interview him when he comes?

LIGE: I daon' knaow abaout thet. Yeh'll hev teh wait an' ast the sheriff.

REPORTER: May I wait here?

LIGE: Suit yehself, young felleh. [He makes another try at the cuspidor and returns to his newspaper. The REPORTER glances around the cell room and then takes a chair at the table.]

REPORTER: Say, Mr. Burke—would you mind giving me some dope on how they caught this Hawkins? [LIGE starts to fold up his paper and gets set to review the case.]

LIGE: Wal—abaout—

REPORTER: Of course, I know the story up to the capture.

LIGE: The' catched him five o'clock this mawnin' in a ba'n. [Picks up paper and goes back.]

REPORTER: Was the girl with him?

LIGE: She wuz with him.

REPORTER: Was she—hurt any?

LIGE: Nao. He hadn't teched heh. Slep' in Joe Taggett's ba'n las' night feh teh git in aout the rain. But the' musta ovehslep' 'cause Joe spied 'em when he got up this mawnin'.

REPORTER: Taggett caught them, eh?

LIGE: Nao. Joe called the Sheriff an' *he* tuck Hawkins inteh custidy.

REPORTER: Where's the Sheriff now?

LIGE: Drivin' in with the prisoneh—his "quarry," he calls him! I reckon they're held up at cawt. Yeh didn' stop in *theh,* did yeh?

REPORTER: Why no, I thought they'd bring him to jail first.

LIGE: Wud awdinar'ly. But the Sheriff thought best teh

git it oveh with 'fore any trouble sta'ted. Naobody knaows the prisoneh's a-comin'—an' the' wun't knaow 'til he's safe in the coop! [With a knowing wink he aims for the cuspidor, smugly satisfied with this brilliant piece of strategy on the part of the local constabulary.] The's afeared a mob might git him oveh teh Granville. Yew newspapeh fellehs hez everyone all riled up agin thet hired man.

REPORTER: Well, one can't fail one's public. They must have the lurid details!

LIGE: Thet's why the' didn' dast leave him in the lock-up oveh teh Granville. They'da lynched him—sure as shootin'.

REPORTER: Why drive way down here to Middlebury?

LIGE: Wal, young felleh—*this* is the Caounty Seat!

REPORTER: Oh, is it?

LIGE: Yesseh! I shud say as much. All the jewdicial mattehs feh Addison Caounty is transacted right here. Why, we got the finest Cawthaouse in the State of Vehmont.

REPORTER: Is that so?

LIGE: Yesseh! An' the Soopreme Cawt jidges comes twicet a year teh dispense with justice!

REPORTER: Oh. Were you with the posse, Mr. Burke?

LIGE: Was I with the posse? [He glares at REPORTER with disgust; sticks out boot, points to mud; and spits.] Was I with the posse!! [He shakes his paper out disdainfully; starts reading.]

REPORTER: Excuse me. I didn't know. . . . [Glances at his watch.] Well, maybe I'd better come back later. Tell the Sheriff— [He is interrupted by the sound of voices and shuffling feet, denoting the arrival of the sheriff and "quarry." HIGGINS calls to his posse:]

HIGGINS: [Outside]. Much 'bliged, boys. Guess I'll be able teh handle him fum here 'thaout any fuss.

[Pompously in courtroom chant.] I hereby o-ficially, an' a-cordin' teh law, dismiss an' excuse fum futheh dooty, the posse and special deputties in the case of Peeple *vee-ess*

HAWKINS. [In his natural drawl.] Yeh kin go haome naow, boys.

LIGE: [Draws his gun.] Betteh stand well back, young felleh. Gus's a desput figgeh. The "quarry's" got a bad recud!

HIGGINS: [Outside.] Git daown theh, Gus.

[The REPORTER moves back out of range of gunplay. The iron door clangs shut. SHERIFF HIGGINS, a short pudgy man, full of self-importance, marches his quarry down stairs at the point of his revolver. The SHERIFF is dressed in riding breeches, high-laced boots, a sheepskin coat and a corduroy hunting cap. GUS HAWKINS, the "desperate kidnapper" of newspaper fame, is a medium sized, much bedraggled individual, wearing a rain-soaked brown cap, a heavy army shirt without a tie, an old sweater under his suit coat, and the bottoms of his trousers are stuffed into typical farmhand footgear—a pair of rubber shoes with high felt tops. His hands are shackled in front of him. He has a five-day growth of stubble on his face, and he is extremely in need of soap and water. His face bears a wide-eyed, bewildered stare.]

LIGE: Haowdy, Gus.

GUS: H'lo.

HIGGIN: Wal, Lige—got my quarry. In competition with and in spite of the hull dang State Militia. [He pulls up a chair.] Set down, Gus. Take the cuffs off him, Jaileh. Guess he'll behave hisself all right. [HIGGINS shakes the rain off his coat and hat, and hangs them up. GUS sits down. LIGE removes the shackles.]

LIGE: Gled teh see yeh with us, Gus.

GUS: [He evinces no interest in his welcome, nor in the room.] Air yeh?

LIGE: Yesseh! But not ez gled ez Cha'lie is, eh, Cha'lie?

HIGGINS: [Complacently.] Wall—b' doin' my dooty I guess I ain't lost nuthin'.

LIGE: [Goes over to the hook to hang the shackles up.] I reckon y'ain't. Next teh Gus here, yewr name's ben right prominent feh th' past five days!

HIGGINS: Lige, yew gao up theh an' see thet them deputies daon' hang araound!

LIGE: [Starts out; then as an afterthought.] Oh, say— [Spits.] Here's a felleh thet says he's fum the newspapehs.

HIGGINS: Thet sao?

REPORTER: Yes, sir.

LIGE: [Glances contemptuously at REPORTER.] I reckon he must be one of them "sob-sistehs"—heh-heh! [He goes out, cackling at his own wit.]

REPORTER: I'm from the United Press Service. I wondered if you'd let me have an interview—

HIGGINS: [Breaks right in.] Gled to hev yeh. Yeh may say thet afteh a ha'd an' long chase, I finally got m' man. 'Thaout sleep er rest I hunted the fugitive an'—

REPORTER: Excuse me, Sheriff. I wanted to interview *Hawkins*. . . .

HIGGINS: Oh— *Him.* Wal, I guess yeh kin. Haow abaout it, Gus?

GUS: Huh?

HIGGINS: Want teh tell yewr story teh the repawteh?

GUS: Mebbe.

HIGGINS: Yeh daon' hev teh 'f yeh daon' want teh.

GUS: Daon' I?

HIGGIN: Nao, yeh daon'. But 'twun't do yeh nao ha'm.

GUS: Wun' it?

HIGGINS: Gao ahead an' tell him whut yeh telled me comin' in the cah. He'll print jist whut yeh tell him. [Turns on the REPORTER sharply.] Wun't yeh?

REPORTER: [Startled.] Yes—yes.

SHERIFF: [Clapping him kindly on his shoulder.] Gao ahead, Gus. [HIGGINS goes to his desk where he starts to make out his reports.]

GUS: Awright. [The REPORTER turns to draw up a stool. His umbrella slides off his arm to the floor. GUS politely picks it up and holds it out to him. As the REPORTER turns around, he is startled until he realizes GUS' intention.]

REPORTER: Oh—thank you. [GUS takes his seat. The REPORTER draws up his stool, and taking out his pad, prepares to begin his interview.]

REPORTER: What was the first thing that happened after you left Trumbull's cabin?

GUS: [After a moment.] It rained.

REPORTER: I don't mean the weather! What did you do? [Draws out cigarettes.] Here, have a smoke? [GUS pulls out a pipe, and REPORTER starts to withdraw the cigarettes; GUS reaches and takes one, which he crumbles up and puts into his pipe.]

GUS: Match?

HIGGINS: [Swinging around from his desk.] Here y'are, Gus, naow daon' be afeared. Tell him jist whut yeh telled me as we druv up.

GUS: Ain't much teh tell.

HIGGINS: Wal, sta't off abaout th' raow yeh hed.

GUS: Wal—her old man sta'ts teh raow 'th me jis' atteh suppeh.

REPORTER: Wait— Who's "her old man"?

GUS: Old Trumbull. . . . Tessie's paw.

REPORTER: [Making a note.] A—ah. Go on.

GUS: 'Nen he sta'ts teh raow 'th *heh!*

REPORTER: Well, what was this row about?

GUS: Well—he—she—

[Stutters; then says defiantly.] 'Twan't true!

REPORTER: *What* wasn't true?

HIGGINS: [Sees his chance and assumes command of the situation.] He 'cused Gus'n heh of misdoin's. Didn't he, Gus?

GUS: Uh-huh.

75

REPORTER: And you told him. . . ?

GUS: He's a gol-damn liar. I ain' done nuthin'—she ain' nutheh.

HIGGINS: Then makes a sta't at heh an' chases heh raound the room. Ain' thet right, Gus?

GUS: Yep.

HIGGINS: He threatened teh kill heh.

REPORTER: Oh— What did he say?

GUS: Called heh names.

HIGGINS: He says: "I'll larn yeh teh sta't disgracin' us Trumbulls. I'll kill yeh, yeh little harlot!" Ain' thet sao, Gus?

GUS: Uh-huh. [His attention is absorbed by the way his pipe is drawing.]

REPORTER: Well, what happened then?

HIGGINS: Then he fired Gus, 'n telled him teh be off his place by mo'nin'. An' Gus telled him he'd best not tech Tessie. Didn' yeh, Gus?

GUS: [Finds something interesting in the smoke curling up.] 'Sright.

REPORTER: Then what did you do?

GUS: Went aout teh th' ba'n.

REPORTER: What did you go out there for?

GUS: Tend stock. Theh 'uz a sick hoss I uz' lookin' atteh. [To HIGGINS.] Poor hoss—[sighs]—'feared she ain' gonna live.

HIGGINS: Epizoodi, Gus?

GUS: Nao— [Lifts his leg to show him.] She had a spavin—right here.

REPORTER: Never mind the *horse*—tell us about the girl!

HIGGINS: Oh—yes—uh . . . she asts Gus teh take heh with him. Didn't she, Gus?

GUS: Yep.

REPORTER: And you said you would. Where did you intend taking her?

76

GUS: Jis' enywhehs—so's heh old man cudn' git at heh.

REPORTER: Oh. . . . Why did you take blankets?

GUS: I dunno. Tessie. She tuck 'em.

REPORTER: When did you first know you were wanted?

GUS: When I 'uz shot at. [Pulls off his cap.] Come mighty nigh gittin' hit, too. See wheh th' bullet went thoo m' cap. Made me run, I tell yeh!

REPORTER: When was that?

GUS: [Putting on his cap.] Day afore yestidy— Guess it wuz day afore yestidy. [He looks inquiringly at HIG-GINS.]

HIGGINS: Thet's right, Gus. A felleh 'phoned in, he'd seen yeh an' tuck a crack at yeh.

REPORTER: They had the militia—the soldiers out for you. Didn't you see any?

GUS: Yep.

REPORTER: How many did you see?

GUS: I dunno. Raows 'n raows. . . .

REPORTER: Didn't you know they were looking for *you?*

GUS: Nope.

REPORTER: Well, what on earth did you think they were doing?

GUS: P'radin'.

HIGGINS: These sojers ain't wuth a damn anyhaow. It takes the p'lice teh git theh man! Eh, Gus?

GUS: [Grins affably.] 'Sright.

REPORTER: [Leans forward.] Come now, Hawkins— you're accused of kidnapping Tessie Trumbull. We know that—have known that for five days. But why did you *abduct* Tessie?

GUS: Why I whut? Say, Misteh. . . . [He starts to rise threateningly.]

HIGGINS: [Putting a restraining hand on his shoulder.] Naow, Gus— He jis' wants teh knaow why you tuck the gehl with yeh.

77

GUS: [Sits back.] Oh. 'Cause I wanted feh teh help heh.

REPORTER: Sure about that? Trumbull says you and the girl were in love.

HIGGINS: Whut abaout thet, Gus?

GUS: I like heh.

REPORTER: But you're not in love with her?

GUS: 'Uz I gonna marry heh, yeh mean?

REPORTER: Well—yes.

GUS: Nope. Nuthin' like that.

REPORTER: But, that dark night—alone—with the blankets—

HIGGINS: [Jumps up.] Naow he hezn't ha'med the gehl none, young felleh! Even the deestrict 'torney's convinced o' thet.

REPORTER: All right, Sheriff. We'll let it go at that. [He glances at HAWKINS, his attention is caught by his hands.] Say, Hawkins—how did you ever expect to get away with your hands tattooed like that? [GUS looks at his hands; the others regard them too. The backs are covered with sailor devices.]

GUS: [Grins.] Neveh thot of 'em. Putty good drawin's ain' the'?

REPORTER: I should think so. Been in the navy?

GUS: Two months.

REPORTER: That's not a very long enlistment. Get discharged?

GUS: Nope. Left afore then.

REPORTER: A deserter!

GUS: Nope. Jis' got tired of it an' went haome.

REPORTER: Part of that bad record of yours, eh?

GUS: Yep.

REPORTER: You're a pretty desperate character, aren't you?

GUS: Uh-huh.

REPORTER: Were you ever arrested before that?

GUS: Yep.

REPORTER: What for?

GUS: Happen' teh go inteh a shack when the' wan't no one theh.

REPORTER: You happened to go in—was the door open?

GUS: Oh, nao. Hedda bust a winda fust.

HIGGINS: [Laughing sympathetically.] Jist one o' them annoying details, hey Gus?

GUS: [Grins.] 'Sright.

REPORTER: So you've been pinched for burglary, eh?

GUS: "Unlawful entreh"—thet's whut the' called it.

REPORTER: Now see here, Hawkins, you shouldn't have gone into that shack and you shouldn't have left the navy the way you did!

GUS: Yeh. Thet's whut *he* said.

REPORTER: *Who* said?

GUS: Th' jidge. Kin I have some more o' thet city terbaccy? It smokes right sma't.

REPORTER: Sure thing. [Tosses the package and matches.] Keep the pack.

GUS: Thanks. [Hurriedly lights one; then grins.] Betteh here'n in them woods, ain't it?

HIGGINS: But I'm afeard yeh can't stay long. Yeh didn't ha'm the gehl an' I can't hold yeh.

REPORTER: But the district attorney's sore as—*hell!*

HIGGINS: Humph! He's up feh re-election an' he ain't convicted no one yit.

LIGE: [Calls from the outside.] Cha'lie! Cha'lie! Hell's abustin' aout front.

HIGGINS: [Rising.] Whut's thet?

LIGE: Tom just spotted a craowd comin' daown here hotfoot teh lynch Gus. The're agaoin' teh take jistice inteh theh aown hands!

HIGGINS: Not 'f I git up theh afore *they* do! Lige, put Gus in a cell. [LIGE opens the cell door.] Naow, Gus

79

—yeh betteh hop in theh. The' may be trouble. I'd like teh knaow haow in hell they faound aout Gus wuz here!

LIGE: Tom says as haow they're comin' teh avenge the' wrongin' of the gehl.

HIGGINS: But the' ain't ben nao wrongin' to be avenged!

LIGE: The' wun't be-lieve thet.

HIGGINS: Lige, yew stay daown here an' guard aour quarry. I'll gao upstairs an' pussuade them fellehs theh wun't be nao neckin'. [Dashes up: the door clangs.]

REPORTER: How am I going to get out?

LIGE: [Calmly expectorates.] Y' ain't. Leastwise not feh a while. An' I reckon yeh mightn't git aout alive 'f yeh tried jist naow.

REPORTER: Well, I hope there won't be any shooting. [Upstairs a couple of shots are fired.] Wh—what's that?

LIGE: Thet's Cha'lie bein' pussuasive.

REPORTER: Has anything like this ever happened before up here?

LIGE: Nao. Can't 'membeh thet theh has. Yew neveh heard of enything like this did yeh, Gus?

GUS: Once.

REPORTER: When?

GUS: The time my grandad borrowed a hoss. [REPORTER turns impatiently away and into a gun held by LIGE. He is scared.]

GUS: Say, misteh—will you do somethin' for me?

REPORTER: Ye—yes—of course.

GUS: I wish yew'd find out haow Vi'let is.

REPORTER: Violet who?

GUS: Th' hoss up at Trumbull's place. She 'uz purty sick when I left. She had a— [He starts to show spavin on his leg.]

REPORTER: Say—you'd better be thinking a little about yourself, Hawkins.

GUS: Awright, gimme a match. [REPORTER takes a box

80

of matches and tries in vain to scratch one. GUS takes it and lights it calmly. REPORTER is shaking as he tries to return box to his pocket.] Whut's the matteh, misteh? Daon' yeh feel good?

REPORTER: Of course, I'm perfectly all right. [Several shots are fired upstairs. The REPORTER nearly collapses.] W—what are they doing now?

LIGE: I guess Cha'lie's havin' a ha'd time, makin' them come raound teh his way of thinkin'.

REPORTER: I don't feel safe down here!

LIGE: Wal—we kin go up an' see whut's doin' enyhaow. We may be needed. Here. [He presses gun into REPORTER's hand.]

REPORTER: Oh—no—not that!! I'll stay down here and guard the quarry.

LIGE: [Lifting his two rifles menacingly.] I said—we may be needed! [REPORTER resigns himself to his fate and starts out. LIGE follows.]

GUS: Whut time's it?

LIGE: [Glancing at his watch.] It's abaout three minutes afteh twelve. Why? Yew ain' gaoin' naowhehs, air yeh, Gus?

GUS: Wheh's m' dinneh?

LIGE: We'll see abaout it lateh!

[GUS makes a tour of inspection in his cell. He sits and rocks on the stool. The door under the stairs bursts open with a crash, and two determined looking men enter with guns. They stand cautiously surveying the room.]

GUS: Haowdy. [The men pay no attention to him. EM CADY advances stealthily and goes part way up the stairs looking around.]

GUS: Lookin' feh Lige? He's upstairs somewhehs.

EM: Nao. We've found who we're lookin' feh.

GUS: Have yeh?

EM: Yesseh!

GUS: Who is it?

EM: Try and guess.

GUS: Can't.

ZEKE: Cut thet stuff aout, Em. We ain't got nao time feh foolin'. Git him aout.

EM: Wheh's th' keys?

GUS: Lige's got 'em.

EM: We'll have to wait 'till he comes down.

ZEKE: Hope he daon' bring Higgins along. [Upstairs LIGE's voice is heard: *"All right, Cha'lie. I'll go right daown. But the' ain't nuthin' doin' daown theh!"*]

EM: Sh—sh! [To GUS.] Not a word, now.

GUS: [Gets up and comes to the bars; grins.] Nope. Wun't say nuthin'. It's a s'prise, ain't it? [The iron door clangs. LIGE and REPORTER come down the stairs. The two men crouch in the corner.]

LIGE: 'F I was sheriff I'd lock 'em all up—thet's whut I'd do!

EM: Yeh can put up yewr hands, Lige Burke—*thet's* whut yeh kin do, right quick!

GUS: Look who's here, Lige.

LIGE: [Hands going up.] Wal—Em Cady and Zeke Tasker! Wheh did yew come fum?

REPORTER: [Turns for stairs.] Oh, my God!

ZEKE: Come back here, young telleh. [REPORTER stops short.]

EM: Reckon yew'n Cha'lie fehgot the entrance from the old Cawthaouse. Wal—I didn't. So me an' Zeke here thought we'd kinda drop in an' *visit* Gus.

LIGE: Right kind o' yeh. I knaow he 'ppreciates it.

EM: I reckon he'll 'ppreciate it a dang sight more afore we gits thoo!

ZEKE: Yesseh! We 'laow as haow we'll sorta "speed th' wheels o' jistice" feh him.

82

Em: Zeke, keep 'em covehed. [He takes gun and keys from Lige and goes over to the cells.] Oh—I see yeh've got a cell open a-ready. Thet's right nice of yeh teh save us the trouble! Naow—step right in theh—an' be quick abaout it!

Lige: [As he goes in a cell followed by Reporter.] Yew ain' gainin' nuthin' by this high-handed at-ti-tude, Em Cady. Jidge Wylie's on his way daown fum Montpelier teh 'tend teh this case!

Em: Nao need o' waitin' feh Jidge Wylie teh try him. We got a jidge waitin' aout theh right naow—a well-knaown an' powehful figgeh. Maybe yeh've heerd tell o' him afore—*Jidge Lynch!*

Gus: I used teh work feh him.

Em: Shut up—yew! Yew ain't so sma't as yew think. [Walks over to Gus.] Wal—the' got yeh—didn't the'!

Gus: Yep. Betteh here'n in them woods, too.

Zeke: [Tensely.] Do yeh knaow whut yeh're goin' teh git naow, Hawkins?

Gus: M' dinneh?

Em: [Trying to fit keys in lock.] Dinneh—hell! Yeh varmint, yewr goin' teh git a few feet o' hemp araound yewr *neck*.

Gus: [Watching his attempt to open door.] Betteh try a smalleh one, misteh.

Zeke: Smalleh *whut?*

Gus: Key.

Zeke: Hurry up, Em. We ain' got much time.

Em: Dang it—I daon' knaow which key it is!

Zeke: Which key is it, Lige?

Lige: [Lounging against bars.] The one thet fits.

Em: Bring him aout an' make him open the cell, Zeke.

Zeke: [Walks over and examines Lige's cell.] Say— yew'll hev teh bring them keys. This door's locked.

Em: Hell! [He joins Zeke and both men work at lock.

83

HIGGINS appears at the top of the stairs, draws his revolver and starts down.]

HIGGINS: Haowdy, boys! I'd be much 'bliged 'f yeh'd raise 'em up high. [Both men wheel around, their hands go up.]

HIGGINS: Take his gun, Lige. Jist step oveh here, Em. Lucky thing Tom spied yeh leavin' the craowd, or yewr scheme mighta worked. Tell 'em which key'll let yeh aout, Lige.

LIGE: The brass one.

HIGGINS: All right. Zeke, s'posin' yew jist turn araound an' let them aout. [ZEKE does so; LIGE and REPORTER come out; the jailer gets his gun and removes other men's weapons.]

LIGE: Naow we'll see who'll be occipyin' a cell!

GUS: They c'n have this one.

HIGGINS: I gotta betteh plan. Boys, I could 'rest yeh feh this. But I ain' agoin' teh 'f yeh'll do as I say.

EM: Whut do yeh want?

HIGGINS: Lissen: Gus here ain't done nuthin' wrong—leastwise nuthin' teh make sech a fuss oveh. I want yeh teh go aout an' break up thet craowd. 'F yeh do thet—I wun' hold yeh.

GUS: C'n I have a match? [But no one pays any attention.]

EM: So Hawkins's got yew standin' up feh him, hez he? A lot of jistice we gits araound these pa'ts. The o-ficials in cahoots with th' creeminals!

HIGGINS: An' a lot o' jistice we'd git 'f we 'laowed a craowd o' scatteh-brains teh git theh way!

ZEKE: [The doubting Thomas.] Haow d'yeh knaow he ain' done nuthin' wrong?

HIGGINS: Got a statement fum the doctor. An' the deestrict 'torney's con-vinced he's inn-o-cent too!

GUS: Say—c'n I have anotheh match?

HIGGINS: Keep still, Gus. We got suthin' teh settle fust.

EM: [He glances at ZEKE, ZEKE nods.] Wal—'f the dees-trict 'torney's not willin' teh press the case—

HIGGINS: An, I'm not willin' teh press yewrn—?

EM: You win, Sheriff. We'll break up the meetin' feh yeh.

HIGGINS: Thet's right, boys [smiles], I knaowed yeh'd lissen teh reason!

[GUS is slightly impatient to have a light so he starts to shake the door to attract their attention. To the surprise of the men, the door opens. GUS goes calmly to table, picks up a box of matches to light his pipe again, returns to his cell. Solemnly shutting the door behind him, he sits down and starts scratching matches. EM and ZEKE look at each other. Their thoughts are unprintable. LIGE starts to chuckle.]

EM: Well—I'll be a—

LIGE: Heh—heh! Nex' time try the door fust, boys. I wuz afeard that yeh might do it any minute. The door wan't locked. Ain' been since Jed Tompkins lost the key 'baout a year agao. Heh—heh!

HIGGINS: Show our visitors teh the door, Lige. And Em —the meetin's oveh.

EM: Okay, Sheriff. [LIGE takes the men out.]

HIGGINS: Guess I got there just in the nick o' time, Gus. Yesseh, 'f it hadn't been feh me—they'd a jerked yeh inteh E-ternity 'thaout much "haowdy-do!"

REPORTER: He's right, Gus. You want to thank the sheriff that you're still breathing.

GUS: [Comes to bars.] Say, sheriff. . . .

HIGGINS: Daon' thank me . . . I on'y done m' duty!

GUS: I wuzn't gonna thank yeh. Theh's suthin' wrong with these gol—damn matches.

BLOOD O' KINGS
A PLAY OF THE HUDSON VALLEY
By Jane Dransfield

PERSONS IN THE PLAY

JIM
SAM
GUY
TONY
MIKE
GEORGE
KEP
FOS DUANE

BLOOD O' KINGS

THE scene of the play is Jim O'Brien's "Place" in the brickyard region of the Hudson Valley on Verplanck's Point, a wooded peninsula which, with Stony Point opposite, forms the northern boundary of Haverstraw Bay at the beginning of the Highlands. The time is the early 1900's. The "Place" is in an isolated spot near the river front, with no houses near. The room is clean, neat, well lighted from a large, shining center oil lamp hanging from the ceiling. To the left is the bar, with a cash register, a plate of hard-boiled eggs, and the usual appurtenances. To the right is the outer door. Chairs and tables are at either side. To the right is a Victrola, with records on a shelf above it. In the rear, curtains of cheap, bright-patterned velour hang drawn together. To the right of these curtains, on a stand, is a box with a slit in the top like a ballot box. Above this box, tacked to the wall, is a placard on which is printed in large capitals by hand the word "CÆSAR." On the left is another similar box, above which the placard is marked "ALEXANDER." In the rear right corner hangs a fykes fish net. An overcoat hangs on a peg near the door. When the curtains are opened later in the action, there is disclosed a pit sunk fully three feet beneath the level of the floor, and also lighted by a center hanging oil lamp. This is the cockpit. In a cage, not visible except as one looks down into the pit, to the right, is a pure white fighting-cock. To the left a similar cage with a black cock.

It is evening. JIM stands behind the bar, washing glasses. Blue-eyed, clean-shaven, immaculately neat, a muscular man of middle age, he has completely the air of being master on his premises. SAM and GUY sit at a table, right, playing cards. SAM is a strapping woodsman, GUY is undersized, white-faced, already in the grip of "consumption," the prevailing disease of the region. SAM is about to deal.

GUY: Say, we ain't settled on yit what we ur playin' fer, nickels or dimes.

SAM: Make it nickels. Save up fer "Cæsar" an' "Alexander," when the rest of the fellus cums in. [Turns to JIM.] Jim, what's the reason yo' allas give yer cocks them two names?

JIM: They was good fighters, them two men.

SAM: Friends of yourn?

JIM: You poor fish! They're dead, hundreds of years, but they was fighters like them gentlemen up the River at West Point nowadays. Only they was kings—always out for big stakes. Liked to read about 'em when I went to school.

SAM: Guess I never got thet fer in readin', over in Buchanan. [Turns back to the game.]

JIM: Alexander was a kind of Greek, Cæsar an Italian.

GUY: A wop, like Tony? Gee!

JIM: All wops ain't wops, Guy. Don't you know that? [The deal finished, SAM waits for GUY to play, and turns again to JIM.]

SAM: What breed ur the cocks, this time, Jim?

JIM: Best southern stock, Warhorses, way back, and Claibornes. Same as Shrove Tuesday fight, last year. Full as fiery as the Birchins and Mealy Greys of the Shrove Tuesday fights I used to go to when I was a boy in North England. Gee! them was some mains, boys, hundreds of cocks up, and bets! Never saw nothing like 'em over here. This one cock show ain't in it.

SAM: Thought you war Irish, Jim.

JIM: Born in Ireland, raised in North England country—much like this about here, rocks, and land not good for much. That's one reason I guess I settled here for good. Kind of like it hereabouts. Skiddaw ain't got it beat over Bear Mountain for bein' pretty at sunset, an' Derwent Water itself don't shine no more like silver than Haverstraw Bay does this minute out there in the moonlight.

SAM: Shrove Tuesday; what kind of a day is thet?

JIM: Day before Ash Wednesday, kind of a church day.

SAM: Gosh! Jim, cockfights ain't got nottin' ter do with religion.

JIM: Sure, they ain't. But when Shrove Tuesday comes around, the March two years old is in best trim. Still, Sam, you know what they say, when the cock stops crowing, the day of judgment comes.

GUY: Do yo' spur yer cocks, Jim, fer fightin'?

SAM: Yo're a sweet babe, Guy. Spur 'em! Yo' mus' think this is goin' ter be a barnyard affair.

GUY: Wull, I ain't never been at but one cockfight afore. Then I war too fur off ter see much. Over at Halloran's. [The door opens. TONY, a swarthy Italian of about forty, half enters, and pauses. MIKE, a younger Italian, lithe and handsome, stands behind him.]

JIM: Evening, Tony.

TONY: Evenin', boss. Mike, coma in?

JIM: Friend of yours?

TONY: Cousin.

JIM: All right. Come in. [TONY signals MIKE to follow

him in. SAM and GUY continue their game.] Shut the door, Tony. [TONY shuts the door, then advances to the bar with MIKE.]

TONY: Hees name Mike Caluori. He from Chicago. Work there year. Lives in Croton. He not married. Got lotsa money, boss.

JIM: Evening, Mike. Glad to know you.

MIKE: [His voice is soft and melodious.] Evenin', boss.

TONY: How much teeket, Jim?

JIM: Same price, always same price for cockfights. Two dollars.

TONY: [Places two dollars on the counter.] Alla right. Mike, you pay two dollar, too. [MIKE takes out a roll of bills, hands JIM a five. JIM makes the change from the cash register.]

JIM: Price of tickets, Mike, goes to house, same as drinks.

MIKE: Yeh. [JIM puts the money for the tickets into the cash register. MIKE puts fifty cents on the counter.]

TONY: Mike wanta good drink, boss. He no speak much, yet.

[JIM prepares a drink for MIKE, then deposits the coin in the register. MIKE stands at the bar, TONY goes to the boxes, examines them, and the signs, and then looks into the pit.]

GUY: Halloran don't charge no admission fer cockfights. [The door opens slightly, unnoticed by anyone.]

JIM: All right. Them as wants to get malaria sittin' round Halloran's pigsty is welcome.

GUY: Oh, I ain't findin' no fault, Jim.

TONY: Jim, you tella Mike how he put up hees money.

JIM: Pari mutuel, Mike. Five dollars unit.

SAM: Up at Halloran's we bets among ourselves.

JIM: I run my place, Sam, to suit myself. If you don't like it, get out.

SAM: No harm meant, Jim.

TONY: [Joining MIKE.] Mike no understan', boss.

JIM: [Leans over the counter toward MIKE, and takes some slips of cardboard from his pocket.] It's like this, Mike. There's two cocks fighting. One is white. His name is "Cæsar." The other is black. His name is "Alexander." You choose your bird. For each five dollars you put into the box that has the name of your cock above it, you get one of these slips to put in with it. Write your name on the slip, see? I put it down here, too, on this slate. [Shows MIKE a slate.] So there's can't be no cheating. Five dollars, one slip, ten dollars, two, and so on. Understand?

MIKE: Yeh.

JIM: Them as bets on the winning cock gets the pile to divide among 'em, according to the number of slips you put in. Cash register cuts in for ten per cent. See?

MIKE: Yeh. Alla right, boss.

TONY: [Leads MIKE toward the pit.] You bet on Cæsar, Mike, whita cock. He got very red comb, big.

JIM: Tony, you let Mike choose his own cock. Both birds is equal, hustlers from the start and always good for one last kick.

SAM: Thet's right, Jim. No tips on the races. [TONY and MIKE look into the pit. TONY turns to JIM.]

TONY: Say, when you gona start theesa fight?

[The door is thrust open, and GEORGE, KEP, and RED enter. GEORGE and KEP are grown men, RED a youth with a shock of red hair.]

JIM: Here's the rest of the boys, now. Evening, George. Evening, Kep. Evening, Red. [The men respond, GEORGE standing at the door.]

GEORGE: Fos Duane is outside, wants to cum in.

JIM: Nothing doing. Shut the door. [GEORGE shuts the door, then joins KEP and RED at the bar. All purchase tickets and drinks. JIM is busy serving them.]

SAM: [Over the game.] Thet's played, Guy. No takin' back.

[The door opens again, and Fos DUANE enters. He is a powerful negro, proud, quick, bold, with the grace of his race.]

JIM: [He stops his work, as he sees Fos.] No admission, Fos.

Fos: [He closes the door and leans against it.] I'se got the price of a ticket. [His voice is deep and vibrant.]

JIM: No go. [MIKE and TONY at the pit, SAM and GUY from the card table, the others from the bar, turn toward Fos, scenting a contest.]

Fos: Been workin' a month, steady. Can put up good an' strong. [Shows a roll of money.]

JIM: Makes no difference. Get out of here.

Fos: [Indicates TONY and MIKE.] Sell them ginks tickets?

JIM: Sure.

Fos: But not me?

JIM: [Comes from behind the counter and faces Fos.] Sorry, Fos. Can't be done.

Fos: That new fella thar, he's as black as me.

JIM: Mebbe, but he's not nigger.

Fos: No tickets to niggers, eh?

JIM: Same as no booze.

[MIKE and TONY sit at a table, and play "crap." SAM rises and throws a quarter down on the counter.]

SAM: Oh, cum on, Jim. Give me a quarter whisky, ef we've got ter stay here jawin'.

[JIM goes behind the counter again and serves SAM. GEORGE, KEP and RED saunter toward the pit, part the curtains, look in. GUY joins them. Fos advances toward the bar. JIM holds up his hand warningly.]

JIM: No, Fos. I've got my rules, an' I stick to 'em. [SAM takes a hard-boiled egg, breaks the shell away and

stands eating the egg.] Same as the government sticks to
its rules of the fykes fishing. [Indicates the nets in the
corner.] When the spring comes, and I want to let down
them nets in the River, I can't let 'em down, only when and
where the government says.

Fos: [Scornfully as he sits down at a table.] My word!
Jim O'Brien, is you as big as de government? [Guy saunters down and looks over the Victrola records.]

Jim: No. But I'm the keeper of this place. Fifteen
years I've been here, an' never a sheriff inside my door, nor
no complaints. Always ran a decent place. I don't take no
risks. Niggers is risks. [Setting away the glasses.]

Fos: W'en did de Lor' Gawd make yo' de jedge o' niggers? Mebbe some niggers is risks. Not me, not Fos
Duane.

Jim: All niggers is risks.

Fos: Yo' got some pertic'lar hunch agin me.

Sam: He's thinkin' of Mamie, Jim. His Mamie Rose.

Fos: Mamie ain't in on dis. Dere's some things as women
don' hev nothin' tuh do wid.

Sam: Mebbe, some things, but mighty few. I tell yo' Jim,
Fos is thinkin' of thet day las' summer when Mamie cum
here all dressed up like a queen in a yaller dress, wid a
red rose in the top of her hair. You wouldn't let her
come in, 'member? [Jim nods, putting away the last glasses
and tidying the counter, preparatory to what he intends to
do.] She sat on the doorstep, an' sung to yo'. Fos cum
along, an' made her go up ter hum wid him. He's sore
'bout Mamie, Fos is.

Fos: [Starts up.] Dat's a lie, Sam Brown. Mamie don'
trouble me, no moh. She wen' down souf las' fall when
de brickyards shet down, same as de robins fly down to de
rice fields. I won' see Mamie no moh. Dis is deeper 'an
women 'tween Jim an' me.

[Guy starts the Caruso record, "O Sole Mio." Fos sits

95

down again. MIKE looks up from his game and sways to the music.]

MIKE: Tony—nica music.

TONY: [Rises impatiently.] Say, boss, when theesa fight gona begin?

JIM: [Comes from behind the bar, a set look on his face.] Just a minute, my friend. Don't get impatient. [Goes toward Fos threateningly.] Fos, you're holdin' up the game. All the boys is here. Get out.

Fos: Jes' cas I'se a nigger, eh? Ain't a nigger got a right to a leetle 'citin' pleasure, aftuh workin' hard, same as anybody? An' who made me a nigger anyhow?

JIM: Guy, stop that jazz. [GUY stops the Victrola. MIKE continues humming the tune. TONY sits down again.]

JIM: I told you I was sorry, Fos, an' I mean it. But rules is rules. If you've got to spend the evening somewheres, go up to Halloran's in the Hollow.

Fos: I heared what yo' said. I war outside de dohr. I ain't got no hankerin' tuh git de chills an' feber. I like it betta heah.

JIM: There's the door, Fos.

Fos: [Rises.] Listen tuh me, Jim O'Brien, an' all of yo'. [All turn toward Fos, listening, except TONY and MIKE, who continue at "crap."] In de brickyard de boss don' objec' tuh me workin' 'longside Sam an' dis pale-faced Guy, here, who's goin' tuh quit dis worl' pretty soon. An' neider do Sam an' Guy objec', 'cept as how I stacks up more brick in one hour 'an they does in two. An' de boss on de railroad, he don' kick 'gainst my workin' 'longside Tony, an' new guineas, lak his frien' here. An' dey don' kick, neider, far as I see.

JIM: That's different. Working is different. It ain't the same. [He takes hold of Fos's arm to lead him toward the door. Fos shakes him off and saunters toward the

96

pit. The men part, and let him look in. He becomes excited.]

Fos: Hi! Dar's a black cock up. I bet twenty on de nigger cock. He's my color. [Takes out his money, goes to deposit it in the box at the left, but JIM intervenes.]

JIM: No, Fos. Rules is rules. Come, I've been patient with you. Now be a gentleman, and get out.

Fos: [After an instant's hesitation.] All right. I'se gwine. [Puts his money back into his pocket and crosses to the door, where he turns.] But yo', Jim O'Brien, as keeps dis place, an' yo', Same Brown, as hev rudder go trampin' through de woods any day wid a gun 'an work, an' yo' pale face, as is soon tuh die—an' yo', Tony, rich as a bank president, de hull o' yo' as thinks yo' is better 'an me—listen to Fos Duane. Dar's kings in me, blood o' kings! [The men start to laugh, but JIM, who stands at the counter sorting the betting slips, his back partly turned toward Fos, signals them to silence.] Nobody tol' me I war born o' kings—nobody need tuh. I knows. I knows. I can feel 'em inside o' me. An' de kings I war born from, dey went free—black kings, whose skin shone lak de sun, an' who hed women slenda as de new moon—kings as dug gol' out o' de groun', who nebber took no guf, who nebber stacked no bricks, who hunted game bigger 'an Sam ebber dreamed o'—kings who nebber died o' no white disease, nor kep' no bar, nor worked on no railroad, nor no Albany boat. [Obedient to JIM's wishes, the men still keep silence.] An' now yo' drive me out, cas I'm nigger, an' niggers is risks. An' I'se gwine tuh go. I'se gwine—tuh oblige yo' all. [Opens the door.]

JIM: That's a good fellow, Fos. Good-night. [Fos passes through the doorway. Before the door is shut, the men break into loud guffaws. Fos instantly stops, his hand on the knob, listening. The door conceals him from them.]

GUY: Gee! whet do yer think of thet?

SAM: Born of kings, is he? Ha! ha! Sure, niggers is got some imagination.

JIM: Yes, that's why they're risks. [JIM draws his slips together. SAM slaps George on the back, still laughing.]

SAM: Say, George, next time we go to Peekskill we'll buy a crown at the five an' ten, an' we'll tie it on Fos's head wid a red ribbon. See! King Fos of the Verplanck brick-yards! King Fos Duane! Ha—ha—ha! Hell! Blood of kings in him!

[As SAM speaks, Fos lifts himself up to his full height proudly, his face growing dark and ominous. The men join in SAM's laughter. Slowly Fos draws a pistol from his pocket. JIM comes from behind the bar.]

JIM: All ready, now, boys, for the fun. [Crosses to the rear and draws the curtains aside, disclosing the lighted pit. Fos closes the door. The men gather together at the pit.] Allow me to introduce "Cæsar," the white cock. And "Alexander," black. Now, boys, get out your cash, before I put on the steels. Remember, both birds is equal, full-breasted, proud and lofty. Boney, too, notice! Just four pounds apiece, March two-year-olds. In fine feather, fed up on butter, eggs and rosemary. Look at their fiery eyes. Even if they didn't want to, they've got to fight. Something inside of 'em makes 'em. Both is bloody heelers, an' close hitters. It's just a matter of choice.

[The men have been getting their money ready as JIM speaks. As they make their bets, JIM hands them the proper number of slips, a pencil, if necessary and then records the bet on the slate on the counter. The men write their names on the slips, then deposit them with their money in the right or left boxes, according to their choice of cock. JIM watches the money as it goes into the boxes to be sure the amount tallies with the slips.]

KEP: Fifteen on white cock.

JIM: Three slips. There you are, Kep.

TONY: Feefty dollar, whita cock, too.

JIM: Good, Tony. Ten slips for you. Right box.

GUY: Two units on "Alexander." He's as black as hell.

JIM: One's your limit, Guy. You need your money for medicine.

GUY: Bin insured sence I war ten. There 'ull be plenty to bury me, an' buy Maud a good black suit, too. Thet's ull I care. I got the ten, Jim. Ain't no fun 'less yo' risk somethin'.

JIM: One's your limit; get me? Break the law, if you have to, but break it decent, I say. Then there's no trouble coming. Here you are—one.

GEORGE: Thirty on "Cæsar."

RED: I wisht I hed some money. Kep, lend me some.

KEP: Nottin' doin'.

JIM: Six for you, George.

SAM: Ten on "Cæsar."

JIM: One slip's your limit, too, Sam, same as Guy.

SAM: Oh, guf, Jim.

JIM: You've got kids, an' a sick wife. You're out of work.

SAM: Thet's why I'm bettin', ain't it?

JIM: One slip, or get out. [SAM accepts the slip, but unwillingly.] Well, Mike, what do you say? You're the last.

MIKE: Yeh. Forty-five dollar.

JIM: Two twentys and a five. All right. Nine for you. Good! What's it on?

MIKE: Blacka cock.

JIM: Left box. "Alexander." [He finishes recording the bets and puts the slate on the counter.] All ready, boys. [He crosses and leaps down into the pit. The men gather around, excited. JIM releases and spurs one cock, then the other. He is seen moving rapidly about the pit.]

Tony: Mike, look, Jim spur cocks. [Instantly the second bird is released and the fight begins. The excitement grows tense, the men leaning forward over the pit.]

Guy: Atta boy! atta boy!

George: Keep yer head up, Cæsar. Don't peck.

Tony: Hi! hi!

[The door slowly opens, and Fos enters, pistol in hand. He is unnoticed. He stands, waiting.]

Sam: Go it, Cæsar! Give him hell.

Kep: Tear his eyes out—thet's the bird.

Mike: Santa Maria!

[The men are so absorbed in what is taking place in the pit that still they do not notice Fos. He advances slowly, comes to the center, and turns out the hanging lamp. The lamp in the pit, however, sheds its glare into the faces of the men, so they do not notice even this. He creeps forward, and because of his height can see into the pit over the leaning forms of the men. The cockfight is now in full swing, the birds attacking furiously, but nothing is heard except an occasional whirr of angry wings, between the exclamations of the men. These exclamations are almost simultaneous.]

Guy: Go it, Alec! Go it! Rip him up the guts.

George: Atta boy! Cæsar! Cæsar!

Mike: Santa Maria! Hi!

Sam: Ram his brains out, yo' son of a gun you. Cæsar!

Red: Stop yer pushin', can't yer? Lemme see.

Kep: Shet up! Yo' didn't put up nottin'. [Fos, as he watches, becomes wildly excited.]

Fos: Hey! hey! Alexander! Fifty dollar on Alexander. I bet fifty on de black cock. [Raises his pistol and shoots into the ceiling.] Eberybody heah me. Fifty dollar on Alexander is the bet o' Fos Duane.

Jim: [From the pit.] Hell! What's that?

Sam: It's Fos, Jim. [Jim springs to the side of the pit.

The men draw back from Fos, so that he faces JIM, with SAM beside him.]

JIM: Get out of here.

FOS: When I gets good an' ready. [SAM seizes Fos's hand, which holds the gun.]

SAM: I've got him, Jim. [Fos shakes SAM off easily.]

FOS: Take yo'r dirty han's off me, yo' damned crown buyer, yo'. [JIM draws his gun.]

JIM: Get out of here, or I'll shoot you dead.

FOS: Shoot ef yo' wants tuh. I'se made up my mind tuh see dis fight, an' I'se gwine tuh see it, ef I does it wid dead eyes.

JIM: Who put out that lamp?

FOS: Me!

JIM: Thought you'd escape notice, did you?

FOS: Didn't wan' tuh spoil de fight too soon. But when I gets 'cited, my gun jes' goes off, natural. Betta let me stay, Jim.

JIM: No.

FOS: Den I stays, anyhow. [He drops his gun into his pocket, pulls out a roll of money and stuffs it into the box on the left.] I put up fifty dollars, see? On "Alexander," de black cock. He's my color. [As he does this JIM leaps from the pit, gun in hand.]

KEP: Aw, let him stay, Jim. What's the difference?

JIM: No.

FOS: Yo' ain't gwine tuh shoot me, Jim O'Brien. Youse too 'fraid o' de sheriff, yo' is. Yo' run a decent place, yo' does. [He finishes putting his money into the box, then turns toward the crowd.] Boys, we'se missin' de fight, we is. [He moves toward the pit. JIM drops his gun into his pocket and gets in Fos's way.]

JIM: Sam! George! Boys! Let's put him out. [Fos puts his hand into the pocket into which he had dropped his pistol.]

Fos: De firs' guy as lays a finger on me, gets a ball in de guts. See? I ain't 'fraid o' no po' white sheriff. [He swings a chair to the edge of the pit, sets it down backwards, and straddles it.] I'se gwine tuh view dis fight from a box seat.

Jim: Fight's off. Cocks go back to their cages.

George: Jim, thet ain't fair. Our money's up.

Jim: You get your money back, all of you. I said Fos ain't comin' to this fight, an' he ain't. [He leaps back into the pit.] This is my place, an' I run it to suit myself. Get me? [He stoops to catch one of the cocks. Fos springs down into the pit.]

Fos: Yo' let them birds alone, Jim O'Brien. [Jim rises and faces Fos.]

Jim: You black devil, you! [He reaches his hand for his pistol, but Fos is too quick for him, pinions his arms behind his back, and holds them in a viselike grip, from which Jim struggles to free himself.] Damn you! Let me go! [Sam leaps down into the pit to Jim's assistance. Others start to follow.]

Fos: Get back! All o' yo'. Dis is 'tween Jim an' me. I can hol' him in one han', I can. What I said 'bout de gun I means. [Sam stops where he is. He looks at the birds, then shouts out.]

Sam: Boys! The black cock's down! He's dead. Cæsar's won! [All rush to look into the pit.]

Fos: Wait! Mebbe the black cock *is* down. But he ain't dead. He roll hees eyes. Give him time.

Jim: [Struggling in Fos's grip.] Let me go, damn you!

Fos: Yo' jes stays where yo' are, honey!

Jim: If the black cock don't get up in twenty counts, Cæsar's won. One, two, three—

Fos: [As Jim continues to count, "three, four, five, six, seven."] He raise hees head!

Jim: Eight, nine, ten, eleven—

Fos: [Jim is counting, "twelve, thirteen, fourteen."] Get up! Go it, comrade! Yo' ain't done fer yit.

Jim: Fifteen, sixteen, seventeen—

Fos: He's up! Go it—go it—give him hell— [The men forget Jim and Fos, lean in tense excitement over the pit.]

Sam: Cæsar, don't let him beat yer—ram him!

Mike: Santa Maria! Black cocka—hi!

George: Cæsar! Cæsar!

Fos: Hey, Cæsar's down! He's dead. [Releases Jim, leaps back into the room, the men parting to let him pass.] De black cock's won! Ha, ha, ha! Black's de lucky color dis time, sure.

Sam: What do yer say, Jim?

Jim: Black's won! [The black cock in the pit crows a shrill pæan of victory.]

Fos: Sure black's won! Hear him sing hees song o' victory lak a brass bugle. [Jim cages the black cock, leaps back into the room, and then turns on Fos.]

Jim: I'll get even with you for this.

Fos: I ain't got no ebil eye, tuh make de white cock lose.

Jim: I mean for coming back, where you weren't wanted. [Takes a key from his pocket, unlocks the padlocks on the betting boxes and takes out the money.]

Fos: 'Twarn't me did it—it war de crown on my head, tied on by a red ribbon, by Sam. It war somethin' stronger in me 'an me, Jim O'Brien.

Jim: S'pose you're waiting now for your money. [He takes the money to the counter, where he counts it. To make the best of his defeat in his contest with Fos, he assumes his usual business manner.]

Fos: Sure I is.

Tony: Mike, you win. Blacka cock win. You standa drinks all around.

Mike: Yeh. Sure.

Jim: Two hundred all told. Ten percent to the house.

[He figures on the slate. Fos sits on the edge of a table, waiting.]

SAM: [Sarcastically.] S'pose yo'll take a trip, Fos, on yer winnin's. Mebbe yo'll go down south ter see Mamie.

FOS: Mamie don' int'rest me no more. I done tol' yo' dat.

GEORGE: Better ship ter China.

FOS: I ain't gwine tuh China, neidder. I'se gwine tuh stay right whar I is, right heah, in de Verplanck brickyards.

JIM: [He has finished figuring on the slate, and counts out the money.] Nine for you, Guy. Eighty-one for Mike. Ninety for Fos. [GUY and MIKE take their money.]

FOS: [He speaks from his position on the table across the room.] Somebody han' me my money, please. [SAM, GUY, TONY, and MIKE are at the bar. KEP, RED, and GEORGE are looking in the pit. No one stirs.] Nobody willin', eh? Den I gets it mysel'. [Saunters to the bar, takes the money.] S'pose yo'-all is wonderin' what I'se gwine do wid dis heap o' money. [The men at the pit come forward. All turn toward Fos.] Stan' treat, mebbe yo' think. Or mebbe you think I buys a gold crown for my head. [He goes toward the door, where he turns, his back against it. He holds the money in his hand.] What I wan' wid dis dirty money? All I want war to see dis fight. To win. [He flings the money high into the room toward the men.] Didn't I warn yo'? Dar's blood o' kings in me. [He opens the door, and goes out. The men scramble for the bills.]

THE LAST STRAW
BY BOSWORTH CROCKER

PERSONS IN THE PLAY

FRIEDRICH BAUER
MIENE
KARL
FRITZI
JIM LANE

THE LAST STRAW

THE kitchen of the BAUER flat in the basement of the Bryn Mawr, a large apartment house in New York City. A window at the side gives on an area and shows the walk above and the houses across the street. Opposite the window is a door to an inner room. Through the outer door, in the center of the back wall, a dumb-waiter and whistles to tenants can be seen. A broken milk-bottle lies in a puddle of milk on the cement floor in front of the dumb-waiter. To the right of the outer door, a telephone; a gas-range on which there are flatirons heating and vegetables cooking. To the left of the outer door is an old sideboard; over it hangs a picture of Bismarck. Near the center of the room, a little to the right, stands a kitchen table with four chairs around it. An ironing board is placed between the kitchen table and the sink, a basket of dampened clothes under it. A large calendar on the wall. An alarm-clock on the window-sill. The time is a little before noon. The telephone rings, MRS. BAUER leaves her ironing and goes to answer it.

MRS. BAUER: No, Mr. Bauer's out yet. [She listens through the transmitter.] Thank you, Mrs. Mohler. I'll tell him just so soon he comes in—yes, ma'am. [MRS. BAUER goes back to her ironing. A grocer boy rushes into the basement, whistling; he puts down his basket, goes up to MRS. BAUER's door and looks in.]

LANE: Say—where's the boss?

MRS. BAUER: He'll be home soon, I—hope—Jim. What you want? [He stands looking at her with growing sympathy.]

LANE: Nothin'. Got a rag 'round here? Dumb-waiter's all wet. . . . Lot of groceries for Sawyers.

MRS. BAUER: [Without lifting her eyes, mechanically hands him a mop which hangs beside the door.] Here.

LANE: What's the matter?

MRS. BAUER: [Dully.] Huh?

LANE: Oh, I know.

MRS. BAUER: What you know?

LANE: About the boss. [MRS. BAUER looks distressed.] Heard your friends across the street talkin'.

MRS. BAUER: [Bitterly.] Friends!

LANE: Rotten trick to play on the boss, all right, puttin' that old maid up to get him pinched.

MRS. BAUER: Was she an old maid?

LANE: The cruelty to animals woman over there [he waves his hand]—regular old crank. Nies put her up to it all right.

MRS. BAUER: I guess it was his old woman. Nies ain't so bad. She's the one. Because my two boys dress up a little on Sunday, she don't like it.

LANE: Yes, she's sore because the boys told her the boss kicks their dog.

MRS. BAUER: He don't do nothin' of the sort—jus' drives it 'way from the garbage pails—that's all. We coulda had that dog took up long ago—they ain't got no license. But

Fritz—he's so easy—he jus' takes it out chasin' the dog and hollerin'.

LANE: That ain't no way. He ought to make the dog holler—good and hard—once; then it'd keep out of here.

MRS. BAUER: Don't you go to talkin' like that 'round my man. Look at all this trouble we're in on account of a stray cat.

LANE: I better get busy. They'll be callin' up the store in a minute. That woman's the limit. . . . Send up the groceries in that slop, she'd send them down again. High-toned people like her ought to keep maids. [He mops out the lower shelf of the dumb-waiter, then looks at the broken bottle and the puddle of milk inquiringly.]

MRS. BAUER: [Taking the mop away from him.] I'll clean that up. I forgot—in all this trouble.

LANE: Whose milk?

MRS. BAUER: The Mohlers'.—That's how it all happened. Somebody upset their milk on the dumb-waiter and the cat was on the shelf lickin' it up; my man, not noticin', starts the waiter up and the cat tries to jump out; the bottle rolls off and breaks. The cat was hurt awful—caught in the shaft. I don't see how it coulda run after that, but it did—right into the street, right into that woman—Fritz after it. Then it fell over. "You did that?" she says to Fritz. "Yes," he says, "I did that." He didn't say no more, jus' went off and then after a while they came for him and— [She begins to cry softly.]

LANE: Brace up; they ain't goin' to do anything to him. [He comes into kitchen hesitatingly.] Say! . . . He didn't kick the cat—did he?

MRS. BAUER: Who said so?

LANE: Mrs. Nies—says she saw him from her window.

MRS. BAUER: [As though to herself.] I dunno. [Excitedly.] Of course he didn't kick the cat. Fritz is so quick-tempered he mighta kicked it 'fore he knew what he was about. No one'd ever know how good Fritz is unless they lived with him. He never hurt no one and nothing except himself.

LANE: Oh, I'm on to the boss. I never mind his hollerin'.

MRS. BAUER: If you get a chance, bring me some butter for dinner—a pound.

LANE: All right. I'll run over with it in ten or fifteen minutes, soon as I get rid of these orders out here in the wagon.

MRS. BAUER: That'll do.

[She moves about apathetically, lays the cloth on the kitchen table and begins to set it. LANE goes to the dumbwaiter, whistles up the tube, puts the basket of groceries on the shelf of the dumb-waiter, pulls the rope and sends the waiter up. MRS. BAUER continues to set the table. Boys from the street suddenly swoop into the basement and yell.]

CHORUS OF BOYS' VOICES: Who killed the cat! Who killed the cat!

LANE: [Letting the rope go and making a dive for the boys.] I'll show you, you— [They rush out. MRS. BAUER stands despairingly in the doorway shaking her clasped hands.]

MRS. BAUER: Those are Nies's boys.

LANE: Regular toughs! Call the cop and have 'em pinched if they don't stop it.

MRS. BAUER: If my man hears them—you know—there'll be more trouble.

LANE: The boss ought to make it hot for them.

MRS. BAUER: Such trouble!

LANE: [Starts to go.] Well—luck to the boss.

MRS. BAUER: There ain't no such thing as luck for us.

LANE: Aw, come on. . .

MRS. BAUER: Everything's against us. First Fritz's mother dies. We named the baby after her—Trude. . . .

Then we lost Trude. That finished Fritz. After that he began this hollerin' business. And now this here trouble— just when things was goin' half ways decent for the first time. [She pushes past him and goes to her ironing.]

LANE: [Shakes his head sympathetically and takes up his basket.] A pound you said?

MRS. BAUER: Yes.

LANE: All right. [He starts off and then rushes back.] Here's the boss comin', Mrs. Bauer. [He rushes off again.]

LANE's VOICE: [Cheerfully.] Hello, there!

BAUER's VOICE: [Dull and strained.] Hello!

[BAUER comes in. His naturally bright blue eyes are tired and lustreless; his strong frame seems to have lost all vigor and alertness; there is a look of utter despondency on his face.]

MRS. BAUER: [Closing the door after him.] They let you off?

BAUER: Yes, they let me off—they let me off with a fine all right.

MRS. BAUER: [With a hard little laugh.] They think you did it then!

BAUER: The judge fined me, I tell you.

MRS. BAUER: Fined you! . . . O Fritz! [She lays her hand on his shoulder.]

BAUER: [Roughly, to keep himself from going to pieces.] That slop out there ain't cleaned up yet.

MRS. BAUER: I've been so worried.

BAUER: I can't stand it, I tell you.

MRS. BAUER: Well, it's all over now, Fritz.

BAUER: Yes, it's all over . . . it's all up with me.

MRS. BAUER: Fritz!

BAUER: That's one sure thing.

MRS. BAUER: You oughtn't to give up like this.

BAUER: [Pounding on the table.] I tell you I can't hold up my head again.

III

Mrs. Bauer: Why, Fritz?

Bauer: They've made me out guilty. The judge fined me. Fined me, Miene! How is that? Can a man stand for that? The woman said I told her myself—right out—that I did it.

Mrs. Bauer: The woman that had you—[he winces as she hesitates] took?

Bauer: Damned—

Mrs. Bauer: [Putting her hand over his mouth.] Hush, Fritz.

Bauer: Why will I hush, Miene? She said I was proud of the job. [Passionately raising his voice.] The damned interferin'—

Mrs. Bauer: Don't holler, Fritz. It's your hollerin' that's made all this trouble.

Bauer: My hollerin'! . . . [The telephone rings; she answers it.]

Mrs. Bauer: Yes, Mrs. Mohler, he's come in now.—Yes.—Won't after dinner do?—All right.—Thank you, Mrs. Mohler. [She hangs up the receiver.] Mrs. Mohler wants you to fix her sink right after dinner.

Bauer: I'm not goin' to do any more fixin' around here.

Mrs. Bauer: You hold on to yourself, Fritz; that's no way to talk; Mrs. Mohler's a nice woman.

Bauer: I don't want to see no more nice women. Hollerin'!—that's what's the matter with me—hollerin', eh? Well, I've took it all out in hollerin'.

Mrs. Bauer: They hear you and they think you've got no feelings.

Bauer: And I was goin' after the damned cat to take care of it.

Mrs. Bauer: Why didn't you tell the judge all about it?

Bauer: They got me rattled among them. The lady was so soft and pleasant—"He must be made to understand, your Honor," she said to the judge, "that dumb animals has feelin's, too, just as well as human beings"—*Me,* Miene,—made to understand that! I couldn't say nothin'. My voice just stuck in my throat.

MRS. BAUER: What's the matter with you? You oughta spoke up and told the judge just how it all happened.

BAUER: I said to myself: I'll go home and put a bullet through my head—that's the best thing for me now.

MRS. BAUER: *Ach,* Fritz, Fritz! [The clatter of feet is heard.]

CHORUS OF VOICES: [At the outer door.] Who killed the cat! Who killed the cat!

[BAUER jumps up, pale and shaken with strange rage; she pushes him gently back into his chair, opens the door, steps out for a moment, then comes in and leaves the door open behind her.]

BAUER: You see? . . . Even the kids . . . I'm disgraced all over the place.

MRS. BAUER: So long as you didn't hurt the cat—

BAUER: What's the difference? Everybody believes it.

MRS. BAUER: No, they don't, Fritz.

BAUER: You can't fool me, Miene. I see it in their eyes. They looked away from me when I was comin' 'round the corner. Some of them kinder smiled like—[He passes his hand over his head.] Even the cop says to me on the way over, yesterday: "Don't you put your foot in it any more'n you have to." You see? He thought I did it all right. Everybody believes it.

MRS. BAUER: [Putting towels away.] Well, then *let* them believe it. . . . The agent don't believe it.

BAUER: I dunno. He'da paid my fine anyhow.

MRS. BAUER: He gave you a good name.

BAUER: [With indignant derision.] He gave me a good name! . . . Haven't I always kept this place all right since we been here? Afterwards he said to me: "I'm surprised at this business, Bauer, very much surprised." That shows what he thinks. I told him it ain't true, I didn't mean to hurt it. I saw by his eyes he didn't believe me.

MRS. BAUER: Well, don't you worry any more now.

BAUER: [To himself.] Hollerin'!

MRS. BAUER: [Shuts the door.] Well now holler a little if it does you good.

BAUER: Nothin's goin' to do me good.

MRS. BAUER: You just put it out of your mind. [The telephone rings. She answers it.] Yes, but he can't come now, Mrs. McAllister. He'll be up this afternoon. [She hangs up the receiver.]

BAUER: And I ain't goin' this afternoon—nowhere.

MRS. BAUER: It's Mrs. McAllister. Somethin's wrong with her refrigerator—the water won't run off, she says.

BAUER: They can clean out their own drain pipes.

MRS. BAUER: You go to work and get your mind off this here business.

BAUER: [Staring straight ahead of him.] I ain't goin' 'round among the people in this house . . . to have them lookin' at me . . . disgraced like this.

MRS. BAUER: You want to hold up your head and act as if nothin's happened.

BAUER: Nobody spoke to me at the dumb-waiter when I took off the garbage and paper this morning. Mrs. Mohler always says something pleasant.

MRS. BAUER: You just think that because you're all upset. [The telephone rings; she goes to it and listens.] Yes, ma'am, I'll see. Fritz, have you any fine wire? Mrs. Mc-Allister thinks she might try and fix the drain with it—till you come up.

BAUER: I got no wire.

MRS. BAUER: Mr. Bauer'll fix it—right after dinner, Mrs. McAllister. He can't find the wire this minute—soon's he eats his dinner.

BAUER: You'll see. . . .

114

Mrs. Bauer: Come now, Fritz, give me your hat. [She takes his hat from him.]

Voices in the Street: [Receding from the front area.] Who killed the cat! Who killed the cat! [Bauer rushes toward the window in a fury of excitement.]

Bauer: [Shouting at the top of his voice.] *Verdammte* loafers! *Schweine!*

Mrs. Bauer: [Goes up to him.] Fritz! Fritz!

Bauer: [Collapses and drops into chair.] You hear 'em.

Mrs. Bauer: Don't pay no attention, then they'll get tired.

Bauer: Miene, we must go away. I can't stand it here no longer.

Mrs. Bauer: But there's not such another good place, Fritz—And the movin' . . .

Bauer: I say I can't stand it.

Mrs. Bauer: [Desperately.] It . . . it would be just the same any other place.

Bauer: Just the same?

Mrs. Bauer: Yes, something'd go wrong anyhow.

Bauer: You think I'm a regular Jonah. [He shakes his head repeatedly in the affirmative.]

Mrs. Bauer: Folks don't get to know you. They hear you hollerin' 'round and they think you beat the children and kick the dogs and cats.

Bauer: Do I ever lick the children when they don't need it?

Mrs. Bauer: Not Fritzi.

Bauer: You want to spoil Karl. I just touch him with the strap once, a little—like this [he illustrates with a gesture] to scare him and he howls like hell.

Mrs. Bauer: Yes, and then he don't mind you no more because he knows you don't mean it.

Bauer: [To himself.] That's the way it goes . . . a man's own wife and children. . . .

Mrs. Bauer: [Attending to the dinner. Irritably.] Fritz,

if you would clean that up out there—and Mrs. Carroll wants her waste-basket. You musta forgot to send it up again.

BAUER: All right.

[He goes out and leaves the door open. She stands her flatiron on the ledge of the range to cool and puts her ironing board away, watching him at the dumb-waiter while he picks up the glass and cleans up the milk on the cement floor. He disappears for a moment, then he comes in again, goes to the drawer and takes out rags and a bottle of polish.]

MRS. BAUER: [Pushing the clothes-basket out of the way.] This ain't cleanin' day, Fritz.

BAUER: [Dully, putting the polish back into the drawer.] That's so.

MRS. BAUER: You've got to eat a good dinner and then go upstairs and fix that sink for Mrs. Mohler and the drain for Mrs. McAllister.

BAUER: I tell you I can't stand it. . . . I tell you, Miene. . . .

MRS. BAUER: What now, Fritz?

BAUER: People laugh in my face. [He nods in the direction of the street.] Frazer's boy standin' on the stoop calls his dog away when it runs up to me like it always does.

MRS. BAUER: Dogs know better'n men who's good to them.

BAUER: He acted like he thought I'd kick it.

MRS. BAUER: You've got all kinds of foolishness in your head now . . . You sent up Carroll's basket?

BAUER: No.

MRS. BAUER: Well— [She checks herself.]

BAUER: All right. [He gets up.]

MRS. BAUER: It's settin' right beside the other dumb-waiter. [He goes out.] O Gott!—O Gott!—O Gott! [KARL and FRITZI come in. FRITZI is crying.]

MRS. BAUER: [Running to them.] What's the matter? [She hushes them and carefully closes the door.]

KARL: The boys make fun of us; they mock us.

FRITZI: They mock us—"Miau! Miau!" they cry, and then they go like this— [FRITZI imitates kicking and breaks out crying afresh.]

MRS. BAUER: Hush, Fritzi, you mustn't let your father hear.

FRITZI: He'd make them shut up.

KARL: I don't want to go to school this afternoon. [He doubles his fists.]

MRS. BAUER: [Turning on him fiercely.] Why not? [In an undertone.] You talk that way before your little brother. —Have you no sense?

FRITZI: I d-d-d-on't want to go to school this afternoon.

MRS. BAUER: You just go 'long to school and mind your own business.

KARL AND FRITZI: [Together.] But the boys. . . .

MRS. BAUER: They ain't goin' to keep it up forever. Don't you answer them. Just go 'long together and pay no attention.

KARL: Then they get fresher and fresher.

FRITZI: Yes, then they get fresher and fresher. [MRS. BAUER begins to take up the dinner. The sound of footfalls just outside the door is heard.]

MRS. BAUER: Go on now, hang up your caps and get ready for your dinners.

FRITZI: I'm going to tell my papa. [He goes to the inner door.]

MRS. BAUER: For God's sake, Fritzi, shut up. You mustn't tell no one. Papa'd be disgraced all over.

KARL: [Coming up to her.] Disgraced?

MRS. BAUER: Hush!

KARL: Why disgraced?

MRS. BAUER: Because there's liars, low-down snoopin' liars in the world.

KARL: Who's lied, Mama?

MRS. BAUER: The janitress across the street.

KARL: Mrs. Nies?

FRITZI: [Calling out.] Henny Nies is a tough.

MRS. BAUER: [Looking toward the outer door anxiously and shaking her head threateningly at FRITZI.] I give you somethin', if you don't stop hollerin' out like that.

KARL: Who'd she lie to?

MRS. BAUER: Never mind. Go 'long now. It's time you begin to eat.

KARL: What'd she lie about?

MRS. BAUER: S-s-sh! Papa'll be comin' in now in a minute.

KARL: It was Henny Nies set the gang on to us. I coulda licked them all if I hadn't had to take care of Fritzi.

MRS. BAUER: You'll get a lickin' all right if you don't keep away from Henny Nies.

KARL: Well—if they call me names—and say *my* father's been to the station-house for killing a cat . . . ?

FRITZI: Miau! Miau! Miau!

MRS. BAUER: Hold your mouth.

FRITZI: My father never was in jail—was he, Mama?

KARL: Course not.

MRS. BAUER: [To FRITZI.] Go wash your hands, Fritzi. [She steers him to the door of the inner room and he makes his exit.]

MRS. BAUER: Karl!

KARL: [Turning to his mother.] Was he, Mama?

MRS. BAUER: Papa don't act like he used to. Sometimes I wonder what's come over him. Of course, it's enough to ruin any man's temper, all the trouble we've had.

CHORUS OF VOICES: [From the area by the window.] Who killed the cat! Who killed the cat! [There is the sound of feet clattering up the area steps. FRITZI rushes in, flourishing a revolver.]

FRITZI: I shoot them, Mama.

THE LAST STRAW

Mrs. Bauer: [Grabbing the revolver.] *Mein Gott!* Fritzi! Papa's pistol! [She examines it carefully.] You ever touch that again and I'll . . .

Fritzi: I'll save up my money and buy me one.

Mrs. Bauer: [Smiling a little to herself.] I see you buyin' one. [She carries the revolver into the inner room.]

Fritzi: [In a loud voice and as though shooting at Karl.] Bang! Bang! Bang! [Karl strikes at Fritzi; Fritzi dodges.]

Mrs. Bauer: [Coming out.] You wash your dirty hands and face this minute—d'you hear me?

Fritzi: That's ink stains. I got the highest mark in spelling today. Capital H-e-n-n-y, capital N-i-e-s—Henny Nies, a bum. [Mrs. Bauer makes a rush at him and he runs back into the inner room.]

Karl: [Sitting down beside the table.] Do we have to go to school this afternoon?

Mrs. Bauer: You have to do what you always do.

Karl: Can't we stay home?

Mrs. Bauer: Why? Why?

Karl: I ain't feelin' well.

Mrs. Bauer: Karlchen! . . . *shäm' dich!*

Karl: Till the boys forget. . . .

Mrs. Bauer: Papa'd know somethin' was wrong right away. That'd be the end. You mustn't act as if anything was different from always.

Karl: Sayin' *my* father's been to jail!

Mrs. Bauer: Karl . . .

Karl: Papa'd make them stop.

Mrs. Bauer: Karl, don't you tell Papa nothing.

Karl: Not tell Papa?

Mrs. Bauer: No.

Karl: Why not tell Papa?

Mrs. Bauer: Because—

Karl: Yes, Mama?

119

Mrs. Bauer: Because he *was* arrested yesterday.

Karl: [Shocked.] What for, Mama? Why was he—

Mrs. Bauer: For nothing. . . . It was all a lie.

Karl: Well—what was it, Mama?

Mrs. Bauer: The cat got hurt in the dumb-waiter—Papa didn't mean to—then they saw Papa chasin' it—then it died.

Karl: Why did Papa chase it?

Mrs. Bauer: To see how it hurt itself.

Karl: Whose cat?

Mrs. Bauer: The stray cat.

Karl: The little black cat? Is Blacky dead?

Mrs. Bauer: Yes, he died on the sidewalk.

Karl: Where was we?

Mrs. Bauer: You was at school.

Karl: Papa didn't want us to keep Blacky.

Mrs. Bauer: So many cats and dogs around. . . .

Fritzi: [Wailing at the door.] Blacky was my cat.

Mrs. Bauer: S-s-h! What do you know about Blacky?

Fritzi: I was listening. Why did Papa kill Blacky?

Mrs. Bauer: Hush!

Fritzi: Why was Papa took to jail?

Mrs. Bauer: Fritzi! If Papa was to hear. . . . [She goes out.]

Fritzi: [Sidling up to Karl.] Miau! Miau!

Karl: You shut up that. Didn't Mama tell you?

Fritzi: When I'm a man I'm going to get arrested. I'll shoot Henny Nies.

Karl: Yes, you'll do a lot of shooting. [Fritzi punches Karl in the back.]

Karl: [Striking at Fritzi.] You're as big a tough as Henny Nies.

Fritzi: I'm going to be a man just like my father; I'll holler and make them stand around.

Karl: What you need is a good licking. [The telephone rings, Karl goes to it.]

120

KARL: No, ma'am, we're just going to eat now.

FRITZI: [Sits down beside the table.] Blacky was a nice cat; she purred just like a steam engine.

KARL: Mama told you not to bring her in.

FRITZI: Papa said I could. [There is the sound of footfalls. BAUER and his wife come in and close the door behind them.]

MRS. BAUER: [Putting the dinner on the table.] Come, children. [To BAUER.] Sit down, Fritz. [She serves the dinner. KARL pulls FRITZI out of his father's chair and pushes him into his own; then he takes his place next to his mother.]

MRS. BAUER: [To BAUER, who sits looking at his food.] Eat somethin', Friedrich. [She sits down.]

BAUER: I can't eat nothin'. I'm full up to here.

MRS. BAUER: If you haven't done nothin' wrong, why do you let it worry you so? [The children are absorbed in eating.]

FRITZI: Gee, didn't Blacky like liver! [MRS. BAUER and KARL look at him warningly.]

MRS. BAUER: You eat your dinner.

BAUER: [Affectionately, laying his hand on FRITZI's arm.] Fritzi.

FRITZI: [Points toward the inner room.] I'm going to have a gun, too, when I'm a man.

[BAUER follows FRITZI's gesture and falls to musing. There is a look of brooding misery on his face. KARL nudges FRITZI warningly and watches his father furtively. BAUER sits motionless, staring straight ahead of him.]

MRS. BAUER: [To BAUER.] Now drink your coffee.

BAUER: Don't you see, Miene, don't you see? . . . Nothing makes it right now; no one believes—no one.

MRS. BAUER: What do you care if you didn't do it.

BAUER: I care like hell.

MRS. BAUER: [With a searching look at her husband.] Fritz, when you go on like this, people won't believe you didn't do it. You ought to act like you don't care . . . [she fixes him with a beseeching glance] if you *didn't* do it. [BAUER looks at his wife as though a hidden meaning to her words had suddenly bitten into his mind.]

BAUER: [Aloud to himself.] A man can't stand that. I've gone hungry . . . I've been in the hospital . . . I've worked when I couldn't stand up hardly. . . .

MRS. BAUER: [Coaxingly.] Drink your coffee, drink it now, Fritz, while it's hot. [He tries to swallow a little coffee and then puts down the cup.]

BAUER: I've never asked favors of no man.

MRS. BAUER: Well, an' if you did . . .

BAUER: I've always kept my good name. . . .

MRS. BAUER: If a man hasn't done nothin' wrong, it don't matter. Just go ahead like always—if—

BAUER: If—if—

MRS. BAUER: [To the boys.] Get your caps now, it's time to go to school. [KARL gets up, passes behind his father and beckons to FRITZI to follow him.]

FRITZI: [Keeping his seat.] Do we have to go to school?

BAUER: [Suddenly alert.] Why, what's the matter?

FRITZI: The boys—

MRS. BAUER: [Breaking in.] Fritzi!

[The boys go into the inner room. BAUER collapses again.]

MRS. BAUER: [Looking at him strangely.] Fritz—if you didn't . . .

BAUER: I can't prove nothing—and no one believes me. [She is silent under his gaze.] No one! [He waits for her to speak. She sits with averted face. He sinks into a dull misery. The expression in his eyes changes from beseeching to despair as her silence continues, and he cries out hoarsely.] No one! Even if you kill a cat—what's a cat against a man's life!

122

MRS. BAUER: [Tensely, her eyes fastened on his.]   But you *didn't* kill it? [A pause.]

MRS. BAUER: Did you, Fritz? *Did* you? [BAUER gets up slowly. He stands very still and stares at his wife.]

KARL'S VOICE: Mama, Fritzi's fooling with Papa's gun. [Both children rush into the room.]

KARL: You oughta lock it up.

MRS. BAUER: [To FRITZI.]   Bad boy! [To KARL.] Fritzi wants to kill himself—that's what. Go on to school. [Boys run past the area.]

VOICES: Who killed the cat! Who killed the cat!

[At the sound of the voices the boys start back.   Instinctively MRS. BAUER lays a protecting hand on each. She looks around at her husband with a sudden anxiety which she tries to conceal from the children who whisper together. BAUER rises heavily to his feet and walks staggeringly toward the inner room.]

MRS. BAUER: [In a worried tone as she pushes the children out.]   Go on to school.

[At the threshold of the inner room, BAUER stops, half-turns back with distorted features, and then hurries in. The door slams behind him. MRS. BAUER closes the outer door, turns, takes a step as though to follow BAUER, hesitates, then crosses to the kitchen table and starts to clear up the dishes. The report of a revolver sounds from the inner room. Terror-stricken, MRS. BAUER rushes off into the room.]

MRS. BAUER'S VOICE: Fritz! Fritz! Speak to me! Look at me, Fritz! You didn't do it, Fritz! I know you didn't do it! [A sound of low sobbing . . .]

After a few seconds the telephone bell. It rings continuously.

MONEY
By Michael Gold

PERSONS IN THE PLAY

MOISHA
YONKEL
ABRAM
HYMAN
MENDEL
POLICEMAN

MONEY

A GLOOMY East Side cellar in New York City, a cobbler's shop by day, now in the deep of night the sleeping place of five weary men. In the darkness their forms are seen vaguely, like queer distorted sacks flung on these old mattresses. No sheets cover them, and they are dressed in undershirts and pants. Some wear socks, others are barefooted. Three or four wooden steps, seen through a glass window, lead up to the East Side street of tenements and night. A faint shaft of light from an arc-light breaks through the glass window of the door, and illuminates the cellar with a goblin glow.

Four of the men are sleeping; one of them snores. But the fifth, REB MOISHA, the cobbler himself, is sitting up on his mattress and uttering mournful sighs. He is a thin, pale man, with a reddish beard, feverish eyes, and shoulders hunched by long years at the bench.

MOISHA: [In a low voice, so as not to disturb the others.] Gottenu, Gottenu, Gottenu! [He sighs again, then slowly lifting himself, and stepping softly as a thief, he lights a

127

candle and looks about the shop, sighing all the while. One of the sleepers stirs restlessly, and MOISHA stands stock still. A moment later he is searching again.] Where is it? Where can it be? [He feels about the walls, under and above his cobbler's last, everywhere. He wrings his hands.] Is it really gone? Gottenu, gone?

[The restless sleeper stirs again, and then sits up and looks at MOISHA. He is a very thin little Jew, a shoelace peddler, with anemic body and a black wiry beard that stands out sharply on his pallid face.]

YONKEL: Again you wake me, Moisha. I am a weak man; I must sleep; the doctor of the big hospital said I need rest.

MOISHA: I know—forgive me, Yonkel. You know what I am looking for.

YONKEL: But why should you wake me? Is it right? And for a whole week it has been—for a whole week. Every night I must lie here and listen to you looking—looking—looking.

MOISHA: [Humbly.] It comes on me, Yonkel. All day I work and put it out of my head. I say, "Well, it is past, the money is gone, now I will begin another struggle." But in the night, when there are no shoes to be mended, when I am alone, then it comes. I must look. I cannot help it.

YONKEL: But the money is gone, Moisha. You are looking for a shadow. You lost it somewhere, in the street, or somewhere. Be a man. Go to sleep, and stop worrying.

MOISHA: No, it is here. It *must* be here. How *could* it be any other place? See how I came to lose it, Yonkel, and tell me whether the money could have been lost any place else but in the cellar. Listen. This is how it was: It was seven o'clock that night, and I sat here alone counting the money, $100 in bills, $5 and $10 bills, $12 in silver, $112 in all. As I was counting I heard a customer coming

128

down the steps, so I quickly tied up the money in my handkerchief and put it—

YONKEL: I have heard all this before, Moisha. What do
you want of my life? Sleep, in God's name, sleep! [He
lies down himself.]

MOISHA: [Mournfully, sitting down on his mattress.]
Yes, I will do as you say. I will try to sleep, Yonkel. I
will shut my eyes and maybe peace will come. [Shuts his
eyes for a moment.] But it is no use, Yonkel!

YONKEL: Ai, let me alone.

MOISHA: [Mumbling, then rising to wail.] No use. One
cannot shut out the world and its troubles by shutting one's
eyes. It is here, Yonkel, in my blood, in my brain, in my
heart. It is a disease only death can cure. Yes, O God, let
me die. Be kind. When a cat or dog is very sick, men
kill it. Be as kind, O God. My heart is broken, and you
let me live on and suffer. Why is this, O God? Why—

ABRAM: [A stout, outright sort of Jew, a carpenter with
sparse black beard and big voice, wearing a red flannel undershirt. He turns on his mattress and looks at MOISHA sleep-
ily.] Why is what, Moisha? Did you speak to me?

YONKEL: Ai, he is looking for his money again, Abram!

ABRAM: Can't you sleep, Moisha?

MOISHA: How can I? You understand.

YONKEL: How can we? We have our troubles, many as
great as yours. No man is happy. See, I have been sleeping, and I know that in a few years I may die. The doctor
said so, but what can I do?

MOISHA: The money *must* be here somewhere. Anyone
can see that.

YONKEL: Moisha, I swear it, I swear it on my mother's
grave, that if you keep me awake another night, I will take
my mattress and move. I pay you a dollar a month rent,
and I have my rights. I will stand no more.

ABRAM: Shah, Yonkala, shah, not so loud. You seem

to take Moisha's wandering at night more bitterly than all of us. It is not necessary.

YONKEL: I am sorry for him, Abram, but he must not be a fool. And I am a sick man, God knows, and I must have fresh air and good food and rest, the doctor said.

ABRAM: All right, just let him alone and he will go to bed. Won't you, Moisha?

MOISHA: [Taking up candle and looking at them pitifully.] Just once more I will look for the money and then I will not bother you again. Just once. It must be here. Money is not like water, to run away into the cracks or be dried up into the air. It *must* be here. Gottenu, it must be— [His voice goes off into a pitiful mumbling, as he taps and feels about the cellar in its corners with the candle in his hand.]

ABRAM: [Calling after him.] Moisha, what is the use, there is nothing to do. The money is gone, so take up your burden again and be brave. This will not help.

MOISHA: Yes, Abram. Yes, Abram. [But he continues looking.]

ABRAM: [Whispering to the peddler YONKEL.] Did you see the look in his eyes? Like a fire, Yonkel, that burns him up. He will go crazy.

YONKEL: No, he will get over it, with God's help.

ABRAM: I am afraid for our poor Moisha, Yonkel. I fear for him.

YONKEL: Men have lost money before.

ABRAM: Yes, but it is a terrible thing to work a whole year for the devil. And see what the money meant to Moisha. We would weep, too, if we had lost it.

YONKEL: Yes, it meant everything to him.

ABRAM: We all know you love money, Yonkel, but not for the same reasons as Moisha. You would not need to suffer so much if you had lost— How much was it he lost, Yonkel?

130

YONKEL: About $112, he said.

ABRAM: $112! To Rothschild it would mean nothing. And for Moisha it means life and death. Everything is so different for the rich and the poor. I think God made two worlds for us to live in. [The carpenter sighs in his beard.]

YONKEL: Better call him again, Abram.

ABRAM: Yes, we must get him to bed; Moisha!

MOISHA: Just a minute. I will look in this other corner, and then come.

ABRAM: Ai, let him look. Let him hope. It is better than nothing.

YONKEL: But hope won't find his money. And there isn't a hole or corner or spider's web of this old cellar he hasn't searched.

ABRAM: If we could only help him! If we only knew where the money is! How do you think it was lost, Yonkel?

YONKEL: How should I know? Am I a fortune teller?

ABRAM: Well, what do you think anyway?

YONKEL: I don't know. He lost it in the street maybe; or maybe it was stolen from him. Who can tell?

ABRAM: Stolen? How do you know? I never thought of that. Yes, it might have been stolen. But how? Who would have done such a thing?

YONKEL: Why do you ask me? I didn't say I knew it was stolen. I only said I *thought* so. It is—

[They hear a loud crash. MOISHA has stood up suddenly, and has thrown over two empty packing cases in the back of the room. He is coming toward them excitedly, the candle fluttering. The two other sleeping Jews have been roused by the sound and are looking around them dazedly.]

MENDEL: [One of the two, a young, sickly man with a slight mustache; a sweatshop worker.] What was that?

ABRAM: [To MOISHA, who stands over him.] Have you found it, Moisha?

131

MOISHA: No, no, but I heard what Yonkel just said! Is it true, Yonkel?

HYMAN: [The other of the two sleepers, a white-haired old man, with a feeble, high voice.] God in heaven, the money again? You are like an owl, Moisha, crying as soon as it is dark.

MOISHA: [Almost hysterical with excitement.] Yes, but listen, Hyman, Yonkel has just told me something new. He says the money was stolen. Perhaps we will find it now. Oh, who stole my money, Yonkel, who was it stole my money?

MENDEL: God in heaven, no sleep again.

YONKEL: What is the matter with you two? Are you both crazy? Or are you trying to drive me crazy? I drop a word and you make a mountain of it. Have I said I knew the money was stolen, Abram? I said it might have been stolen. That was all. Now let me alone.

MOISHA: But it is true, it is plain, it is clear. Yonkel just said—

ABRAM: No, he only said he *thought* the money was stolen. That is true, Moisha.

HYMAN: Why did you put such a thought in his head, Yonkel?

MOISHA: [Obsessed now by the idea.] Abram, it is plain as day to me now. Why have I not seen it before? Have my brains been stolen, too? It does not matter what Yonkel said, but I know now the money was not lost. It was stolen.

ABRAM: Ai, now you have a new worry. Forget this idea.

MOISHA: Listen, Abram. I see how it all happened. I was sitting that night, all alone here by the candlelight, counting my money, $112, in bills $100, in silver $12. It was about seven o'clock, and none of you were yet home. Then as I am counting—

HYMAN: You have told us this many times, Moisha.

MONEY

MOISHA: Listen! Listen! Now it is clear! I am counting the money, and as I am counting I hear a step on the stair. I put the money quickly away, here in a hole in the mattress where I always kept it. The door opens and a customer enters. It is a boy with a pair of shoes to be heeled, and he sits down, takes them off, and waits, while I work on them. As I work Mendel comes in, then Hyman and Abram. You eat your suppers. Hyman had herring and bread, I remember, and Mendel corned beef sandwiches. I finish the shoes and the boy leaves. Then we sit and talk a little, Yonkel and I. Abram and Mendel play cards, Hyman reads a newspaper. Then I blow out the candle and we go to bed. I remember it all like yesterday. In the morning, at about six, I awake. Abram has already gone to work, as always. The others are still sleeping. I go to open the door to let in the fresh morning air. I come back and look in the mattress for my money. I do not find it. It is gone. It has vanished like a cloud. Now, how could I have lost it? It must have been stolen; there was no other way! Abram, am I right?

ABRAM: You know what you are saying, Moisha?

MOISHA: Yes.

ABRAM: You mean, then, Moisha, that one of us stole it?

MOISHA: What else can I believe? There was no one else in the cellar all that night. Tell me, is there anything else to believe? [The other men look at each other blankly.]

HYMAN: You see what you have done, Yonkel.

ABRAM: Can there really be a thief among us?

MENDEL: But didn't you go out for rolls, Moisha? You might have taken your money with you then.

MOISHA: I hadn't gone for the rolls yet. No.

HYMAN: No one here would have taken your money, Moisha.

ABRAM: Yes, it is impossible. You didn't think of it till now; don't believe it any more.

133

MOISHA: But where is my money?

HYMAN: It *must* have been lost, Moisha.

MOISHA: Where could I have lost it? I went nowhere.

ABRAM: Moisha, we are all of us poor men. And we are weak men, and bad men, bad as the rest. For a little money we have to work and pay with our blood and sweat. It would be easy to tempt us. But, look at us, Moisha Can you really believe one of us would have robbed you of what meant so much to you?

MOISHA: [Weeping.] No, I do not believe it. I did not even dream of it before, until Yonkel spoke of it. But was there any other way the money could have disappeared that night, unless someone stole it? Tell me, Abram.

ABRAM: I don't know what to think, Moisha.

HYMAN: I can't believe it! It would have been like stealing a man's child, to steal that money from you.

MOISHA: [Wailing mournfully, in the orthodox Hebrew singsong.] Yes, it was my child, you all knew that. It was the wife and children in Poland I have not seen for five years. I have starved and struggled to save enough to send for them, and now the money is gone. Oh, you are Jews, you have suffered and been lonely, in this strange land! Who of you could have done this?

ABRAM: I swear it, Moisha, no one.

MOISHA: [Throwing his arms about him and weeping.] Good, kind, beloved Abram, who has always been true as gold to me, was not the door locked all that night? Were not only we five here? What have they done to me? Why have they taken my life, my hope away?

MENDEL: He can search us, Abram. I know I have not touched his money.

ABRAM: Do you want to do that, Moisha?

MOISHA: Oh, what will it help? It is a week now the money is gone, and searching will not find it. No, give it back to me. Have pity, pity, pity! [Weeps with face in hands.]

ABRAM: I don't know what to do. What can we do for him, Hyman?

HYMAN: Moisha—

MOISHA: [Looking at them wildly, his voice high and despairing.] No, I will not search you! No, I will ask you each, in the name of the God of Israel, in the name of your own brothers and sisters, your own wives and children in Poland, did you take it? I weep before you, I throw my tired old body on the ground before you, I ask again and again: Did you take my money? What does a man live for, I ask you? Does he live only to work, to make shoes in a dark hole away from the sun? No, he lives for his children, to see them grow up strong and happy, and to reach greater things than he himself has reached. That is what a man lives for. But you have taken my children away from me. Oh, who has taken my life away from me? Did you take it, Hyman? Hyman, dear, I beg you, have you taken my children from me? Tell me, I will forgive you if you did. Did you?

HYMAN: How can you ask that, Moisha? Strip me to the skin; search everything I have.

MOISHA: What can I believe, Hyman? Was it you, Mendel? Did you do it? Have you my money? Give it back; only give it back; I will not reproach you; I will be glad to forget. Mendel, did you?

MENDEL: What are you saying to me, Moisha?

MOISHA: Did you?

MENDEL: No, no. How could I?

MOISHA: Abram, did you? I must know, I must find my money. Would you have done such a thing to me, Abram? Or you, Yonkel? Tell me, in God's name. Tell me.

ABRAM: Moisha, I sooner would have cut off my right hand. You know that.

YONKEL: [Lifting his face from his hands.] I did not take it, Moisha.

MOISHA: You have never known wife or children, Yonkel. But you saw your brother killed by the Cossacks, and you know what it is to lose loved ones. Don't you know where my money is, Yonkel?

YONKEL: [Tears running down his pale face, his voice broken.] Why do you ask me again? I have told you I don't know.

MOISHA: So what can I do? Where can I turn now? You say none of you took my money. But it was stolen from me, I know that.

HYMAN: Before you were sure you forgot or lost the money somewhere; now you are sure it was stolen. Don't you see how mad this all is, Moisha?

MOISHA: It is not mad. Don't try to put me off, Hyman. One of you *must* have it. Or all of you took it and are keeping it from me. That is the way you stole it; you did it together. You must give it up now, do you hear?

ABRAM: [To YONKEL.] Now he is really mad. I told you it would drive him mad.

YONKEL: [His face in his hands.] Oh, don't speak to me, Abram.

MOISHA: [Pacing the floor, while the others watch him in awe.] Yes, you have all been plotting against me. I can see that now! It is clear. But you will not succeed, do you hear? I will not be killed so easily. I will fight. I will make you give it up. I will—

ABRAM: Moisha!

MOISHA: [Screaming as he breaks away from ABRAM's hand.] Let me be! I know what I am doing. And I know how to make you give it up. I will lock the door on all of you, and go for a policeman. That is what I will do. He will make you tell the truth, he will make you give up my money! You will listen to his club, you hard-hearted men who wouldn't listen to my tears. And how I trusted you all, how I believed you were my friends! Now you have stabbed me in the heart; you have taken what is only a little money to you, but to me is life! Murderers, give me back my money! For the last time, give me back what I have suffered for, give me back my wife and children!

ABRAM: [Going to the door and standing by him.] Don't shout, Moisha. Moisha, be reasonable, listen to us!

MOISHA: No, I have listened long enough! I have asked for the truth from thieves long enough. I am going to call a policeman now. I will show you. I will make you all confess. I— [He starts to go out.]

ABRAM: [Holding him.] Moisha, for God's sake, what would you do?

MOISHA: Ah, is it you, Abram? You whom I trusted most of all?

ABRAM: What do you mean?

MOISHA: See, he trembles already! He is afraid of the policeman; it was he that took the money! Now we know— now we know—Abram— [He turns white and half faints into ABRAM's arms.] Ah, my heart! [ABRAM takes him to the cobbler's bench and seats him there.]

ABRAM: Bring some water, Mendel! Quick! [They press the water on Moisha. He sips it, and opens his eyes slowly.] Quiet, Moisha, quiet!

MOISHA: [Sobbing.] I cannot do it over again, I tell you! You see how my heart has failed me. I have not the strength to starve, to wait another five years in this cellar. No.

HYMAN: Moisha—

MOISHA: Yes, it is all over for me. Ai, ai! It is over— My sun and moon have gone out; I wish I could die.

ABRAM: Shah, Moisha dear! [He takes MOISHA's hand. There is a little space of quiet. Then MOISHA looks up with big staring eyes.]

MOISHA: Listen. I have solved it all. I do not need the money. Some night when I am alone I will take my cobbler's knife and cut my throat. That will be best.

ABRAM: What are you saying? Moisha, do not—

MOISHA: [In a fresh burst of tears.] But what else can I do? Am I not dead now? I have no strength, no hope, to begin again. It is over for me. I will cut my throat. I will kill myself. I will not wait for God to be kind. I will end it all.

HYMAN: Moisha, dear! [MOISHA becomes weak again. They give him more water. He shuts his eyes and gasps, while the tears flow down his cheeks.]

MOISHA: Dear, kind, good friends, Jews who know what it is to be a Jew and suffer, why have you done this to me? Why have you killed me? Have I ever injured one of you? Have I ever taken from you one thing that was yours? Have I not lain here with you night after night, and been one of you? I am no stranger. And you saw—

YONKEL: [Suddenly springing up from the mattress where he has been moodily sitting all through this. He looks wildly at Abram, and clutches at his shirt.] My God, Moisha! [The rest look at him, startled. His long pale face is white as a madman's. His eyes burn with fever.]

HYMAN: What is wrong, Yonkel?

YONKEL: I can't stand this, I can't stand this! [He sits down on his mattress again.]

MOISHA: Yes, what shall I do, Yonkel? You see, how terrible life has become for me. It is hopeless. Yonkel, you remember when you were sick, and lay a month here night and day. I charged you no rent, and tended you, and now see what has become of me. What shall I do? Shall I—

YONKEL: [Springing up.] Stop! Stop, Moisha! Here is your money!

138

[He pulls out a small canvas bag from where it was tied by a string around his neck, next to the skin. As he hands the bag to MOISHA, he is seized by a violent fit of coughing. MOISHA seizes the money eagerly, uttering gurgling sounds of joy, and counts the contents of the bag. Meanwhile ABRAM comes over to the coughing YONKEL and hits him a hard blow on the jaw. YONKEL falls, coughing in an uncontrollable spasm that shakes his whole frame.]

ABRAM: You louse!

MENDEL: [Shaking his head.] And this is God's world!

HYMAN: [Mildly, as he strokes his white beard.] Better leave him alone, now, Abram. His coughing is on him again.

ABRAM: [Fiercely, as he pushes YONKEL's body aside with his foot.] The thief! The louse! It is no Jew, no man here, it is a mean little blood-sucking louse!

HYMAN: He is very sick. We had better put him on the mattress.

ABRAM: I won't help a louse! I would rather kill it!

HYMAN: Here, Mendel, help me. [They lift YONKEL, who is still coughing, on to his mattress. They give him MOISHA's water.]

MOISHA: [Coming over to Abram.] The money is all here, thank God! $112, all here!

ABRAM: And now you are happy again, yes, Moisha?

MOISHA: No, when was I happy before? And I will not see them yet—my family. I need $60 more, and it will take many months to save it. But I will eat less, I will work more, I will save, save, save!

ABRAM: Shah, Moisha, you will strain your heart again. Lie down on the mattress and rest!

MOISHA: Yes, yes, I must rest. [ABRAM helps him to lie down.] Abram, you will forgive what I said to you before? I did not mean it; I was half crazy.

ABRAM: I understand, Moisha.

MOISHA: It has all been like a bad dream to me. [YON-
KEL begins coughing again.]

ABRAM: Yes, a bad dream, but not yet ended for some.
A policeman will be here yet, and we will see what a louse
gets for stealing.

HYMAN: I think, Abram, we should let him alone now!
He is very sick.

YONKEL: No, he is right; Abram is right, Hyman.

ABRAM: I am right, am I?

YONKEL: Yes, Abram. I deserve everything.

ABRAM: So why did you do it? You know it was wrong
now, so how could you have done it? You knew why
Moisha was saving, was starving himself to a shadow.

YONKEL: [Coughing.] I—I—saw how—

ABRAM: Don't explain. I will tell you why you did it.
I have met your kind before. It is because you are one of
those Jews who have a lust for money. It is the food of
your soul, like blood is the food of the louse. Don't tell me,
I know. Suck—suck—suck, suck till you've sucked all your
brothers dry. What a man. Hah! [He spits in disgust.]

YONKEL: Yes, Abram.

ABRAM: Yes, Yonkel! Yes, you whine, it is true, Abram!
You admit you are one of those whose religion is to steal and
lie and kill and betray—all for money!

HYMAN: There are many like that in the world, Abram.
They are very wealthy.

ABRAM: But I am not like that. I have always worked,
you know that, Hyman. I have always paid my full price
of blood and sweat for my bread. I have been honest. I
have tried to hurt no man.

HYMAN: That is why you are poor.

ABRAM: There are many other poor and honest men.
There are many.

HYMAN: Yes, there are too many of us, Abram.

ABRAM: What do you mean? You speak in riddles. What I know is: let the world be good or bad, a man should be a man. That is what I believe. One ought not make others suffer—as Yonkel made you suffer, Moisha.

YONKEL: I suffered, too. [He has another spell of coughing.]

ABRAM: You suffered!

YONKEL: Yes.

ABRAM: Bah! You *will* suffer. You have still to know what Moisha here felt. I am going to have you arrested.

MOISHA: [Slowly opening his eyes.] No. I think it isn't necessary, Abram.

ABRAM: What? Is there to be no honesty in the world? I say thieves must be punished!

YONKEL: I suffered, yes, I did. You don't believe it, Abram! Let me—

ABRAM: But I won't listen to you, I tell you! I will hear you in the court. I will hear you tell the judge how you suffered.

MOISHA: Let him be. He should not have stolen my money. But I have it back.

ABRAM: What do you think, Hyman? Do you think we ought to let such a thief go?

HYMAN: It is hard to tell, Abram. You are so sure, but I am not. What can one do in this world where there is more evil than good? Let him go, maybe.

MENDEL: I heard a speaker on the street say once that the rich are all thieves. But no one punishes them.

ABRAM: [Pounding one fist into the other.] Do not try to confuse me. The thing is simple—it happened in this cellar. I have eyes, I have ears, I have seen and heard how this happened. Yonkel stole the money. It was like sucking the heart's-blood from Moisha. It was unnecessary, too. Yonkel was not starving. He took it because of his black lust for money. He is a louse. As soon as he stops coughing I will take him to the station house! [He gets up and stamps about fiercely.]

YONKEL: [Breaking into sobs.] Don't have me arrested, Abram! Don't have me put into one of those cold, dark prisons where I would die soon. There is no one with a kind heart in a prison—I would go mad there. Don't let him do it, Moisha dear! I am a Jew, we are all Jews together. I came from the same town in Poland you did, Moisha. . . .

ABRAM: You didn't remember you were Moisha's kinsman before!

YONKEL: I didn't want to take your money, Moisha, no, no, I didn't. I cried as I took it from the hole in your mattress that night. I knew what it meant to you, and how you worked for it. Believe me, Moisha, I cried for you, Moisha!

ABRAM: You make my head go round. You cried, and yet you took it.

HYMAN: Let us hear him out, Abram. Let him tell why he did it.

ABRAM: But I don't understand. Why should he do it if he cried?

HYMAN: Let him explain. People are like that, Abram. You are made of one piece, like a big tree. You don't understand how people can be both good and bad. Let him explain.

YONKEL: Yes, that's how it is, Hyman. Don't let him have me arrested. Let him arrest the thing in me that got up in the night and went to the money. Oh, how it seized on the money, so glad and hot, while I stood by and wept for you, Moisha! . . . And Moisha, when I saw you suffering all this week, I could bear it the least of all of us. . . . I lay here listening to you—I groaned with you—I tore my flesh— but what could I do? [Another fit of coughing.] One night, and then another, I got up—I—and tried to give the money back to you somehow. I stood over you in the darkness, and my tears fell on your white face, and I could have kissed you for pity. I heard you groan, and I knew what was making your whole body shake, and burning it like a fever. It was terrible. I took out the money and started to place it where it belonged, but I could not. I could do nothing. It was like watching a friend drown, and having a life preserver in one's hand, and being unable to throw it. What could I do? Does a man always conquer the beast he meets in a forest? And can a man always conquer the beasts inside himself? What could I do? [He coughs, and HYMAN hands him the water.]

HYMAN: Drink, Yonkel.

YONKEL: Thanks. Yes, so it happened for three nights. You will not believe it, but I could not return the money. And I would go back to my mattress and lie there, and shiver all night with fear. I was afraid—afraid of Money! What was it—this Beast that God has put into the world? It was in many men, eating and eating their happiness, making them cruel to each other. I was afraid of it. I would feel it move around the room, filling the corners and coming toward me, to spring at my throat. I would be afraid to open my eyes, for fear I would see it standing above me with its hot breath. I was afraid I might see its yellow eyes, that change to green, and look upon men. Do you understand, Moisha? Do you understand, Abram?

ABRAM: I don't know. But talk on, Yonkel. You were always a good talker.

MOISHA: In the old country, I remember, you did not care for money, Yonkel. But here you seem to have become a miser. It is the old Yonkel that is talking now.

YONKEL: No, in Poland I did not care for money—Moisha remembers that. I was a poor young Talmud student there, but happy. I lived on a radish a day, I slept on the hard benches of the synagogue, I cared for nothing but to live with my soul and to study the sacred books. In the quiet of the room where I sat, I would hear angels' wings moving like music. A joy was in me, for I was alone in a place where there was only God. The world never touched me. Poland is a terrible land for the Jews, but they helped each other, they were friends. I never starved, I was taken care of, they understood my passion. And I would not have cared if I starved—I lived above Life and Death then. It is hard for me to believe it now. I am different now. See how thin and unhappy I am now. But I have money. I have learned to care for money. How did it happen? I remember how it began. I remember when I came here, how friendless I was. It was all different here from Poland. What good did my Talmud study do me, what good was it that I heard angels' wings? I went into a shop where they paid me a few dollars a week. I bent over a machine and fed it my strength and my thoughts, my blood and my desires. And it turned out pants. And it turned out cloaks. I slaved and I slaved—and nothing came of it. There were slack times, and strikes, and days when I was sick. I went to work in a grocery store after that. And I slaved and was sick there, too. Nothing came of it all. I was always poor. And no one cared for me when I had no money. The boss laid us off, or let us walk out on strike, and no one cared. I was sick, and no one cared if I died or lived. I had no money! Something said to me, something in this land—Get money! It is not enough to study the Talmud, to work, to be a man. You must have money! And a great fear seized on me, the Beast entered me, and I suddenly grew afraid of being poor. I gave up God, for the Beast was jealous. And I tried to make money, for it is stronger than God. With it I could despise and stand above the world, as I stood above it without money in Poland, with only my soul. Yes, I felt the fear! Men are shot down for want of money. Men are crucified for want of money. Men who have no money live in cellars like this, and are lonely for their children. Don't you awake in the night, sweating cold, Abram, and wonder how long your job will last, what your old age will be like, who would care for your children if you should die? Thoughts such as these? Don't the fear of poverty ever come to you, Moisha, and you, Hyman, and you, Abram?

HYMAN: Yes, it does.

MENDEL: Yes.

MOISHA: Yes, often.

ABRAM: Yes, and on me, too. . . . I understand what you are saying, Yonkel. It is true. Money is a terrible thing. But may I ask you something?

YONKEL: Yes.

ABRAM: I can understand how a poor man would get to fear poverty so much he would do anything to escape it. I have felt that myself. But I have beat it down, because I have felt—well, if there are so many poor in the world, I can be poor with them, too. But I can understand your feelings, too, Yonkel. What I cannot understand is this— how could you have stolen money from Moisha? If you took it from a rich man or a worthless man, or if you cheated someone, as these millionaires do, it might not have been so bad. But to take it from Moisha!

YONKEL: I know, I know, Abram. Don't you see that is what has made me suffer? I knew what a terrible thing it was to take Moisha's money from him. I knew it more than all of you. I never knew it more than at that moment in the night when I took it. It was like a madness on me, but I could not stop it. And yet in that moment, I was sanest, too. Like a flash of lightning I saw myself for the first time in many years, and I saw what the desire for money had made of the old Yonkel. I started by thinking I would make money my slave, and I saw in that moment I had become its slave. There is a story in one of the old Hebrew books that explains. It is about a little village to

145

which there came every night a great, terrible snake and ate one of the children. This went on for many years and the people prayed to God but got no help. Then a very learned Rabbi there, taking pity on the people said, "Since God does not help us, we will use other ways." And he went out into the forest to fight the snake, and he stayed there seven years, battling the snake, night and day. He used every means, but they seemed to fail. At last he thought, "There is only one way left." So he chose that way, and changed himself into a snake, too, with flat head, and poison dripping from his mouth. And for another year he fought the snake that had eaten the children, and finally he conquered it. But when he returned to the village to tell them of his victory the people fled before him. And he wept when he remembered that he was no longer a man, but was a snake, whose delight is to poison and to kill all that it sees. Do you understand? . . . And now I will ask you something, Abram.

ABRAM: Yes, Yonkel.

YONKEL: You were angry before, and called me a louse. I do not blame you. [With a fierce cry of passion.] But I ask you, Abram, who made the louse? Who put it into the world to live on the blood of men? Who gave it that appetite and body?

ABRAM: It must have been God.

YONKEL: Then who but God is to blame for its ways? Is the louse to blame? . . . No. And then am I to blame for what I have become? Is not the thing that made me so to blame? Is not Money to blame, Money the real God of the world? Oh, my fellow Jews, you who are so meek and suffering, you who understand, I tell you I am my own worst enemy. Money has made me so. I am sick, but I live in this cellar, because I wish more money. I want a quiet mind, with the thoughts that move through all the universe and are free and joyful. But I have let this mind

146

be killed by the one hungry thought—the thought of money. I loved Moisha—here, I pitied him and wished him good fortune and a way out of his misery. But you saw what I did to him—for a little money. Oh, I am sick, I am sick with the disease of money! If I could find where it is in my breast, if I could find this cancer in my soul, I would take a terrible knife and stab it out! But would that cure it? No, for the whole world is sick with it, the whole world is its own worst enemy! I could sell or give away the little goods I peddle, I could throw my money in the river, and tomorrow I would feel free. But the next day I would be seeing men strain and sweat and hurt each other for money. And the fever would come on me again, too, and I would say: It is necessary to have money to live. It is necessary to have much money to stand above the world. And it is true—it is necessary! But it is also necessary to be a man, and to think thoughts that fly to God and are beautiful. It is necessary to be kind, and it is also necessary to make money! What does it all mean? Do you see how sick I am with it all? I am a thief, an enemy to my brothers— [A heavy footstep is heard coming down the stairs. YONKEL stops and they all look toward the door.]

MOISHA: Someone is coming! Who can it be?

MENDEL: [Goes to the door and opens it.] It is a policeman, Moisha! [The POLICEMAN enters and stands at the door, looking about suspiciously.]

POLICEMAN: [In a big, indulgent voice.] For Gawd's sake!

MOISHA: Abram, you know English! Speak to him!

POLICEMAN: What the hell's going on here? What are you Yits up to anyway?

ABRAM: [Meekly, in sing-song, broken Ghetto English.] It's nothing the matter.

POLICEMAN: Why, a feller just come up to me on my beat and told me there was a lot of Yits down here fighting like cats and dogs.

ABRAM: [With the same rising, sing-song accent.] Fighting? We should be fighting? No, sahr, we was only talking between ourselves, Mister.

POLICEMAN: You must've made a lot of noise with your mouths then! What'che talkin' about at this hour of the night, anyway?

ABRAM: Oh, I don't know—abaht money?

POLICEMAN: [Bursting into laughter.] Money? Money? That's good. Haw, haw, haw! that's a pippin. A lot of Yits talking at 3 A.M. in the mornin'—about money! That's rich! Haw, haw, haw! Money!

ABRAM: Yes, sahr?

POLICEMAN: [Wiping the tears of laughter from his eyes.] Well, fellow-citizens, blow out the candle, and don't argue no more about money. Leave it for tomorrow's peddlin', see? Go to bed now, an' happy dreams! [He goes out. ABRAM locks the door after him, stands there a moment, then blows out the candle.]

ABRAM: [In Yiddish, in which he has no accent.] He said we should go to sleep. He says we have talked enough. [They all lie down except YONKEL, who sits up and looks around him.]

MOISHA: Sleep, Yonkel, you too!

YONKEL: [Gives a little sigh and lies down.] Yes, Moisha.

[There is a silence as the men shift about on their mattresses, each occupied with his thoughts. Then the low, young, tender voice of MENDEL speaks in the darkness.]

MENDEL: I am younger than all of you, and I have not been a Talmud student like Yonkel, but have always worked. But once, I remember, I heard a man standing on the street corner here on the East Side, and he was saying that one day there would be no money, no rich and no poor, only everyone working together like brothers and sisters.

MOISHA: Yes? Who was the man said that, Mendel?

MENDEL: A Jew. A working man like ourselves.

ABRAM: [Lifting himself on his elbow.] But Mendel, did he say—

[They enter a new discussion on the endless problem of the world's misery and Money!]

NO CAUSE FOR COMPLAINT
BY GEORGE S. BROOKS

PERSONS IN THE PLAY

DETECTIVE CAPTAIN JOHN SHAY
DETECTIVE SERGEANT PAT GRADY
SAM BONOVITA
MARIA BONOVITA
HARRY SMITH
TONY LIBERTORE
FRANCESCA BONOVITO

NO CAUSE FOR COMPLAINT

DETECTIVE CAPTAIN SHAY'S office at Police Headquarters, East Side, New York City. It is a dingy
room, as such offices always are. There are two doors, one
leading to the Detective Bureau assembly room, and the other
to the detention room. CAPTAIN SHAY'S roll-top desk is
littered with papers and reports. Against the wall stands a
filing cabinet. There are cases of bound reports, identifica-
tion charts and all the scattered materials of a finger print
outfit in the room. There is also a dictaphone.

DETECTIVE CAPTAIN SHAY is seated at his desk. He is a
short, stocky, bald-headed, quick-tempered police officer. He
is shrewd in the same way that a ward politician is shrewd.
In other words, he is a quick judge of human nature and
has the self-assurance that comes from successfully weather-
ing the storms during thirty years of changing administra-
tions in the Police Department. This thirty years of experience enables him to scent lies and frauds with uncanny ability,
and his faults as an executive and director of detectives lie
in his lack of imagination and education. SHAY is dictating

153

a grand jury statement to a dictaphone. In the morning his stenographer will have considerable difficulty in transcribing the document, as the Captain includes his own comments in the phrases of the legal instrument.

SHAY: [Dictating.] I had my boys search his house. The search was made by Detectives Mally, Ginther, Ryan, and Schleyer and who the hell else was down there?—Oh, yes, Detectives Mally, Ginther, Ryan, Schleyer, and Nobles. They brought back to my office a quantity of stolen goods, valued by the property clerk at—I don't know what value he did put on them and it don't make any difference. It was over $50—valued by the property clerk in excess of $50. Then I showed the goods to the prisoner and asked him if he wished to make a statement. . . . [There is a rap at the door.] Come in!

[DETECTIVE SERGEANT GRADY comes in. He is a tall, well-built, athletic detective, about forty years old. He has the "flatfoot's" trick of never seeing anything except faces, as he meets people. His own features are a mask like a first-rate poker player's. He has an Irish sense of humor and a supreme contempt for "Wops" and "Padlocks" as he describes Italians and Poles.]

GRADY: Busy?

SHAY: What did you think I was doin'? Playin' pinochle? I gotto get out this grand jury statement.

GRADY: Them old people wants to see you. Them Wops. Parents of that kidnapped girl.

SHAY: Tell 'em we ain't found no traces of her, but we're workin' on it.

GRADY: I did. But they said we was to quit lookin' for her. They said she is all right now.

SHAY: Last night they was squallin' all over this office because we couldn't find her. Now they want us to stop lookin'. Ain't that just like Wops?

GRADY: Better talk to them. Somethin' wrong about it.

NO CAUSE FOR COMPLAINT

SHAY: [Pushing the dictaphone away.] Send 'em in.

GRADY: [Opening the door and motioning.] Come in, you.

[Enter SAM and MARIA BONOVITA. They are Sicilians. Both are dried up, wrinkled, timorous, superstitious. Thousands like them can be found upon the streets in any Eastern city.]

SAM: [Ducking his head to CAPTAIN SHAY.] Good evening, Captain. You know me, sure. My girl, Francesca, she runned away.

SHAY: [Jumping to his feet.] You lying thief! What do you mean, she ran away? Last night you told me she was kidnapped.

SAM: We thought she was kidnap. Oh, yes. Now we know she runned away. Me and my old woman, we come up to tell you, you don't look for Francesca no more. Sorry we mak-a th' troub'. [He grins engagingly.] Good-a-by, Captain. Some time you come by my store, me and my old woman give you good jug of wine. Good-a-by, Captain.

SHAY: [To GRADY.] Shut that door. [SAM and his wife are startled as they realize they are locked in.] Sit down, you. I'll learn you to come in here and lie to us. What makes you think your daughter ran away?

SAM: [Shrugging his shoulders.] Me no understand English.

GRADY: Sure you understand. I'll lock you up. Get that?

MARIA: [Weeping loudly.] Ai-ai-ai-ai, I told you it was bad luck when we hear the big eye chick in the park. . . . Hear him make so "Toowit-toowoo."

SHAY: What does she mean, "big eye chick"?

GRADY: Owl.

SHAY: [To MARIA.] Shut up, you old fool. [To SAM.] How do you know your daughter run away?

SAM: Feller tol' me.

SHAY: [With a cross-examination tone.] What feller? When? What did he say?

155

SAM: I don't know him. Honest, mister. I don' know him. He tell me my Francesca, she runned away and get herself marry. He tol' me to-night. I come up an' tell you, cause I don't want you to be trouble over nothing.

SHAY: That's a lie and you're a damned liar. Because she ain't been up to the city clerk's bureau to get a license. We had that covered. She can't get married without a license.

MARIA: Ai-ai-ai-ai, I tol' you it was no good to come here. I tol' you. Ai-ai-ai-ai, please, mister. Let us go 'way.

SHAY: [Shaking his fist.] You dirty garlic burners. Tell me the truth. Get down on your knees and tell me the truth. Where's your daughter? What become of her after they throwed her into the auto and carried her off? Who come to you and told you she was married?

MARIA: [Obviously telling the truth.] If we tell, we'll all be murdered.

SHAY: So that's it. Listen to me. Your daughter was kidnapped on Lafayette Street, yesterday morning. We have witnesses who seen four fellers grab her and throw her into an automobile. She dropped her purse when she fought 'em off and you identified it. Then you come up here, yesterday, squawkin' and squallin' like a pair of hyenas and wanted us to find her.

SAM: Yes, Capitano. That so. But she all right now.

SHAY: Don't lie to me. You come here because somebody told you they'd kill you if you didn't stop us lookin' for the girl.

MARIA: [To SAM, very angry with him.] You're a fool. You talk too much.

GRADY: Who threatened you? Who said he'd kill you?

SAM: Nobody. Honest, mister. Nobody.

SHAY: I'll lock you up. I'll send you to the workhouse for a year. Take 'em down and lock 'em up, Pat. You know what charge to put against 'em.

GRADY: Sure. Charge 'em with lyin' to a policeman. [He winks at SHAY.] You two will go to the workhouse for a year, as soon as the Judge hears about this.

SAM: What will become of my store while I'm in the jail?

GRADY: That's your hard luck. If you lie to us, we don't care what becomes of you or your store.

SAM: [Sinking upon his knees.] Please, mister. Don't do nothin' to me. I'm afraid. I tell you everything. My girl Francesca was kidnap, like I say yesterday. To-night, Tony-the-Wolf he come to my place and he say, Sam, if you don't stop the police makin' looks for Francesca, you'll never see her again. She die quick and I kill you and your woman, too.

SHAY: Where's Tony-the-Wolf now?

SAM: I don't know.

SHAY: You know where he is, because he told you where to meet him after you came away from here. Quick! Where is he? You'll be your daughter's murderer if you don't tell. [He makes a threatening motion.]

SAM: He's in that restaurant at the corner, by my store.

SHAY: That's the Bucket of Blood at Frank and State Streets. [He dives into a filing cabinet and brings out a card-index drawer.] Tony-the-Wolf, huh! His right name is Tony Liberatore. [He finds a card.] Here's his mug. We've had him in here for extortion and arson and murder, but we never hung nothin' on him. Take a couple of the boys with you. Bring him in. If he tries to pull his gun, don't kill him, because we want him to tell us where the girl is. Hurry back. [GRADY nods at these instructions.] Take her out in the other room. [Exit GRADY and MARIA.]

SHAY: Now, Sam, why do they call him Tony-the-Wolf?

SAM: It's a society. What you call blackhand.

SHAY: Another one of them college fraternities, I suppose.

SAM: Them fellers won't work. They make peoples give 'em money. They have womens workin' for 'em, too. If I don't give 'em $5 each week, my store is blowed up, maybe. Tony-the-Wolf, he is boss of the Wolves, so they say. I dunno. Very bad peoples, them Wolves.

SHAY: Why don't you come to the police when they attempt to extol money from you?

SAM: Oh, mister. We'd get blowed up if we told. We know all about them Wolves. We have 'em just like that in the Old Country.

SHAY: Why did Tony take your daughter?

SAM: Because he want her for his woman.

SHAY: Who was her fellow? Who did she go with? Here she is eighteen years old and she ain't married. What was wrong with her?

SAM: Now, mister. I tell you right. She didn't go with no Italian boys. She went to the High School, she did. She was goddam smart, she was. Then she went to college. Business college. She was a stenographer. She only go to shows with American fellow. She wouldn't have nothin' to do with Italians. That's why she ain't never marry and why she wouldn't look at Tony-the-Wolf.

SHAY: What American fellow did she go with?

SAM: Harry Smiths. His father works for the city. He's a big boss down to the Garbage Disposal Plant. Yes. His father is big mans in 23rd Ward. Yes.

SHAY: What does this Harry do?

SAM: He drive truck at Post Office, he does.

SHAY: [Opening the door.] Go out there and set down with your wife. [Exit SAM.]

SHAY: [At the telephone.] River six-one-hundred. Post Office? I want the Superintendent of Mails. This is Detective Captain Shay talkin'. Yes. Say, have you got a fellow named Harry Smith drivin' a truck? His father is a foreman down to the Garbage Plant. You have? When can I get hold of him? No. No. There's nothin' wrong with him. I want to ask him about a case I'm investigatin'. Send him up to my office. Room 14 at Police Headquarters. You'll send him right away? Thanks. You say he's a good boy? Well, don't worry. I'm not tryin' to hang anythin' on him at all. Thanks. [He hangs up the receiver, walks to the door and calls.] Send that woman in here. [MARIA comes in.] Sit down. Why didn't your daughter go with Italian fellows?

MARIA: Oh, mister. That's the troub'. I tol' her a thousand times it was no good for her to try to be American girl. I told her her fortune in the wine dregs and it showed she wouldn't come to no good. When she was borned, a lady come to me and warned me. . . . [She begins to weep again.] Ai-ai-ai-ai. . . .

SHAY: [Furious at her.] Shut off that sprinkler system and pay attention to me. [The telephone rings.] Shay speakin'. Hello, Grady. What? You've got the Wolf? And the girl, too? That's fine. Bring 'em in.

MARIA: She was bad luck to herself. Every time she go out of the house, the next door lady's black cat come to the door and "me-ouw" like that. I burned two candles for her, but it didn't do no good. . . .

SHAY: Oh, shut up. We found her. She'll be here in a minute.

MARIA: It's too late now. He's done it to her. Ai-ai-ai-ai. . . .

SHAY: [Shaking her.] Stop croaking. You're worse luck than a dozen black cats. What did Tony-the-Wolf say to you? What did he say he'd do to you if you didn't stop us lookin' for the girl? Did he say he'd kill you?

MARIA: All he can do now is marry Francesca. She is dishonor. She is his woman.

SHAY: Marry her? Hell no! Now we got a real case against him. We'll charge him with everything from abduction to malicious mischief and we'll put him away for life.

MARIA: No. No. No. It will be better for him to marry her.

SHAY: If she marries him, she can't testify against him. A woman can't testify against her husband. She's gotto rap to him in court.

MARIA: No! She must marry with him, quick.

SHAY: Get out of here, before I pound some sense into your thick Wop head. [He almost throws her out the office door.] Sit down out there and keep quiet. [MARIA goes out.] Is Harry Smith there? [Enter SMITH. He is a good-looking boy of twenty, wearing soiled riding breeches, puttees, flannel shirt and sheepskin coat.]

SMITH: Hello, Captain. The boss told me you wanted to see me.

SHAY: Have a seat. I hear you know this Francesca girl who was kidnapped.

SMITH: Yeah. I took her out, sometimes. She was a swell looker, even if she was a Wop.

SHAY: What sort of a girl was she? Was she a Wop in her habits, or was she white?

SMITH: Oh, she's like white folks. She don't like Wops no better than I do. She went through High School and Business College. She wouldn't have nothin' to do with the greaseballs.

SHAY: But did the greaseballs like her?

SMITH: You tell 'em they did. It used to burn 'em up, when I come down to her house and took her out to a dance or to the movies. They always tried to horn in. One time the greaseball they call Tony-the-Wolf put the death sign on me for goin' out with her. [SMITH bites his forefinger to illustrate Tony's action.] Her folks was scared half to death. They told me not to go there no more, for fear I'd be killed.

SHAY: What did you do? Did you stay away?

SMITH: Me? Stay away on account of a Wop? I ain't crazy. Next time I seen Tony-the-Wolf I clocked him one on the puss. Yessir. I give him a right hook to his jaw [Illustrates] and knocked out two of his teeth. He kept away from me after that. I don't let no Wop wisecrack to me. What the hell? If you don't show 'em their place, they'll walk all over you. Since I licked Tony, I can walk down through Guinea Town and every one of them rats on the corners takes off their hats to me.

SHAY: Was you engaged to this Francesca girl?

SMITH: Well, we hadn't fixed the day, or nothin', but I figured on it. So did she. The trouble was with my folks. They kept squawkin' because I was goin' with a Wop. My old man raised hell about it, every Sunday morning.

SHAY: He didn't have nothin' against the girl, did he? She was straight, wasn't she?

SMITH: Sure, she was straight. You couldn't even put a finger on her. She wouldn't even kiss you "good night." That was an idea she got off a teacher in High School. All Francesca wanted was to be an American girl and get away from the greaseballs. [There is a rap at the door.]

SHAY: [Calling.] Just a minute. [To SMITH.] I'll want you again. Go in there in the detention room and wait in the back. [He opens the second door. Exit SMITH.]

SHAY: [At the first door.] Grady, I want to see you. [Enter GRADY.] Did you find the girl?

GRADY: Sure. A Wop woman had her locked in a room over the Bucket of Blood. When the girl heard us, she screamed. I waltzed up the stairs and kicked the door in. We got Tony-the-Wolf downstairs. He had them in his clothes. [GRADY tosses a billy and a heavy automatic pistol on SHAY's desk.]

SHAY: Did he make a fight?

GRADY: [With a grin as he remembers it.] He reached for his gat, but I hit him first. When he came to, I had the cuffs on him.

SHAY: Bring him in. [GRADY goes out and returns a minute later with TONY-THE-WOLF. TONY is handcuffed. He is a typical second-generation Italian youth. His clothes are expensive and showy. His hair is slicked back with pomade. His eyes are shifty.]

GRADY: Here's your wolf. He looks more like a pole cat. [GRADY throws the young Italian into a chair, removes the handcuffs and expertly cuffs Tony's ears with the flat of his hand.]

SHAY: [Quickly.] Don't mark him. Don't mark him. We gotto take him into court in the morning and the Judge squawks if the prisoners is beat up. That's the trouble of not havin' practical men on the bench. [To TONY.] Now you damned cootie, we're goin' to learn you what happens when you kidnap a respectable girl. First, you're goin' to make a confession of your own free will, without duress, or under promise of immunity. [Slaps him.] Aren't you?

TONY: I won't say nothin' until I see my lawyer.

SHAY: So. You're a wise-cracker. You and your lawyer. Aren't you goin' to make a voluntary statement? [He kicks TONY's shins.] You won't see a lawyer. It will be an undertaker.

TONY: Kill me and be done with it!

SHAY: I'm goin' to kill you. What's your name?

TONY: [Weeping.] Tony Liberatore.

SHAY: Where do you live?

TONY: Over the restaurant at Frank and State Streets.

SHAY: How many women have you got out on the street, hustlin' for you?

TONY: Not any.

SHAY: How many women? [He kicks Tony's shins again.] How many women?

TONY: Only two.

SHAY: You intended to put Francesca out hustlin'. That's why you kidnapped her.

TONY: No. I'm goin' to marry with her.

SHAY: You won't marry with nobody. You're all caught

up. You get life imprisonment for the kidnappin'. Now tell us how you done this job.

TONY: I won't say nothin' until I see my lawyer.

GRADY: Let me take him back into the cell room. I'll tickle him until he'll be glad to talk.

SHAY: Don't mark his face, black his eye, or anything that the Judge can see. [GRADY and TONY go out, GRADY dragging him by the coat collar.]

SHAY: Send the girl in. [FRANCESCA comes in. She is an Italian beauty of eighteen. Even the harrowing experiences of the past thirty-six hours have not marred the beauty of her dainty features, her dark olive skin and her handsome dark eyes. Ordinarily, she would walk with a proud swagger. Now her shoulders droop as if she were ill.]

SHAY: I'm Captain Shay. I want you to tell me all about it.

FRANCESCA: It's no use, Captain. I might as well marry him and be done with it.

SHAY: Marry him? I should say not. We'll take care of him. Now tell me what happened.

FRANCESCA: I was walking down the street on my way to work, yesterday morning. An auto pulled up to the curb beside me. I didn't pay any attention to it, until I saw Tony-the-Wolf was driving and that he had his gang with him, They jumped out and then it was too late for me to run.

SHAY: Did you call for help?

FRANCESCA: Yes. But there was no one but Wops on the street and they were afraid of Tony.

SHAY: I see. Go on.

FRANCESCA: They grabbed me and tied a handkerchief over my mouth. They put me in the back of the car and drove to the saloon. The Bucket of Blood. They took me upstairs and locked me in a closet and left an old woman to watch me. Last night, they came back. They took me into a room—

SHAY: [Encouraging her.] Yes.

FRANCESCA: Then he— The old woman and the others held me. He said, "Now, you're my woman and you got to marry me." I spit on him and told him I'd kill him and myself, too. So they locked me up again.

SHAY: No. No. You don't want to marry him. You know he's got women out hustling for him. You know he's a no-good. You know he'll put you out hustling, as soon as he's tired of you. Come into court and tell the Judge what you've told me—

FRANCESCA: What's the use? I'm no good for any one else now.

SHAY: We'll see about that. [He opens the door into the detention room and calls.] Smith. Come here. [The girl starts.] You wanted to be an American and shake these Wops. Now is your chance. An American girl would go into court and convict this Tony. We'll send him away for life. [SMITH comes in.] Now, Harry. Here is Francesca. She had a hell of a time with this slicker. [The girl cannot face SMITH. She turns her back to him. Her shoulders shake.] Tell her, same as I have, that the thing for her to do is to go into court and testify against him. And Francesca. Don't bother your head about this. Do as I tell you and everything will be all right. [SHAY leaves the room.]

SMITH: [Wishing he were at the bottom of a deep well instead of in SHAY's office.] I'm awfully glad they found you, Francesca. I just wish I'd been there when that yegg grabbed you. I'd have put my trade mark on him, I would.

FRANCESCA: Do you remember the night we went to the dance at the lake?

SMITH: Sure I do.

FRANCESCA: Remember what you said, coming back?

SMITH: Uh-huh.

FRANCESCA: You told me you wanted to marry me. I said

NO CAUSE FOR COMPLAINT

you'd be ashamed of me. Because I'm a Wop. You said that didn't make any difference. Do you—I mean—well—would you say it again?

SMITH: [Generous for a moment.] Well, I don't care what you are. I told you I liked you.

FRANCESCA: Like Captain Shay said, last night don't make any difference to you . . . about liking me? [SMITH says nothing. FRANCESCA waits for him to kiss her, which he makes no attempt to do. Her shoulders droop again and she walks to the door and calls.] Captain Shay.

SHAY'S VOICE: Go on in there, you.

[MARIA and SAM come in.]

MARIA: [Weeping.] My baby! My poor baby! Ai-ai-ai-ai-ai. My poor baby. [She kisses FRANCESCA and then immediately begins to abuse her.] What did I tell you? You can't be American girl. Now you gone and done it. You must marry with Tony quick.

SAM: Sure. You marry with Tony.

FRANCESCA: I won't marry Tony. [SMITH sees that he is elected to be FRANCESCA's husband unless something turns up immediately. His one thought is to escape. He glances around and then quickly leaves the room.] I'll marry Harry Smith and send Tony to prison.

MARIA: So. You want all the peoples to point their fingers at Harry and say he took a girl Tony had first? They call him second-hand husband. You're Tony's woman. Marry him quick, or they point their fingers at you, too.

FRANCESCA: I tell you I don't care. I'm no Wop. I'm American. Isn't that so, Harry? [She looks around vainly for SMITH.] Where did he go?

SAM: He run away. Sure. He don't want to marry with Tony's woman. [SHAY comes in.]

SHAY: Bring him in here and we'll take his statement. . . . [GRADY comes in, leading TONY. TONY has been battered

165

until he is ready to admit anything. All his bravado has vanished.]

SAM: Sure. You marry with Tony.

SHAY: Where's Smith?

MARIA: He runned away, Captain. He runned away. He don't want to marry with Tony's woman.

TONY: I want to see my lawyer. She's my woman. I marry her now.

GRADY: [Cuffing TONY.] Take that for luck. You need a lynching party instead of a lawyer.

SHAY: Come, Francesca. We'll take your statement and fix Tony for a good long jolt over the road—

FRANCESCA: Yes. I'm an American girl—

SAM and MARIA: No. No. She must marry with Tony. She's his woman. Harry Smith run away.

FRANCISCA: [Beaten.] Yes. It's so, Captain. I—can't be an American. [Turning to TONY, her eyes blazing hate.] I'll be a Wop. I'll marry you and live in a pig-pen. I'll hate you and let you kiss me. Yes, I'll live with you and be your woman, you damned Guinea pimp!

SAM: It's all right now, Captain. She'll marry him.

SHAY: [Furious, not at the tragedy, but because his case against TONY has vanished into thin air.] Then get the hell out of my office, all of you. Why should I waste my time on cattle like you? [To GRADY.] Let him go, too. [GRADY releases TONY, with a parting kick.]

MARIA: I told you it was bad luck for you to be American girl— [SAM, MARIA, FRANCESCA and TONY leave.]

GRADY: I suppose I better make out a report on this. What shall I say?

SHAY: [Turning again to his dictaphone.] Mark it "No Cause for Complaint." What in hell else can you do?

WANDERLUST
By Paul Halvey

PERSONS IN THE PLAY

Isaac Pollant
Goldie Pollant
Bernice Pollant
Sidney Hein
Padriac Kerrigan

WANDERLUST

THE living-room of the POLLANT flat in the Bronx, New York. It is about seven o'clock of a late fall evening. The room is overfurnished and overcrowded with cheap furniture. The pictures are of the chromo variety: spirited horses rearing at flashes of lightning, chariot races, pastoral scenes. On a small table along one wall is a box-Victrola. It must be noted that at the opposite side of the room, near a well-worn rocker, is a small shelf-stand, filled with books. A door to the right leads into the dining-room and kitchen. On the opposite side of the room, a door leads to the outside hall. The room is illuminated by gas. There is a wall telephone.

MRS. POLLANT, a stout woman wearing a stiff black party dress, is sitting in a rocking-chair, knitting. She is talking to her daughter, who is in the next room dressing.

BERNICE: Ma, do something for me?

MRS. POLLANT: What do you want now, Bernice?

BERNICE: Turn on the phonograph, will you? I want to hear that new record—

MRS. POLLANT: [Rising heavily.] You should do it yourself. You're younger than me—

BERNICE: I'm dressing!

MRS. POLLANT: [Winding the machine.] By rights we oughtn't to play music in the house with Uncle Barney dead only three weeks and he our benefactor—

BERNICE: Oh, forget him!

[MRS. POLLANT starts the song on its way as BERNICE comes in. She is dressed in exaggerated imitation of the latest Fifth Avenue mode, and is a full-fledged product of the movie and dance palaces. She presents her back to her mother.]

BERNICE: Hook me up, Ma. Gee, this dress is a fright!

MRS. POLLANT: It makes you look so bold.

BERNICE: [Shaking her shoulders to the music.] I *am* bold. A bold bad gal from the Bronx!

MRS. POLLANT: Stand still!

BERNICE: Wait'll you see how I knock 'em dead up at the party to-night.

MRS. POLLANT: By rights we oughtn't go to the party so soon after your Uncle Barney—may he rest in peace—was taken from us.

BERNICE: Say, Ma, what's the use of kidding each other? You know we never thought a nickel's worth of that old tightwad when he was alive. It was the surprise of our lives he left us that money—

MRS. POLLANT: Of course in one way it don't do the dead no good to mourn for them. The best you can do is keep their memories in your heart—

BERNICE: Funny about Uncle Barney. We never knew the old boy was alive till he died. Say, that's a good one— never knew he was alive till he was dead—I'll have to tell Sid that one. [She is quite pleased with her *mot*.] The worst of going to this party upstairs is they'll think we're their friends for life.

MRS. POLLANT: The Vogels are nice people, Bernice.

BERNICE: First thing you know they'll be hanging around when we move up on the Drive. I tell you what, Ma, when we get into our new flat we got to cut out all these pikers around here—

MRS. POLLANT: You shouldn't treat your old friends that way.

BERNICE: [Turning off the Victrola.] There's something else I've been thinking—about Sid.

MRS. POLLANT: What about Sidney?

BERNICE: Well, Sid's a wonderful fella, but after all he's just a soda jerker.

MRS. POLLANT: It's a nice job—

BERNICE: I wonder does Sid expect me to marry him— now.

MRS. POLLANT: The way you two hug and kiss I'd hope so!

BERNICE: When we're up on the Drive, how can you tell who I'll meet—

MRS. POLLANT: I wouldn't let go of Sidney just yet— What's the rush?

BERNICE: [She looks thoughtfully at the ring on the third finger of her left hand.] I couldn't shake him very easy. I'll sure be tickled pink when we get out of here.

MRS. POLLANT: The movers promised for Monday. [Looking around her.] How I dread it!

BERNICE: But won't it be wonderful—! The trouble is, this old junk'll look fierce in the new place. It'll be a dead give-away.

MRS. POLLANT: Poppa won't let us buy new things just yet.

BERNICE: Oh, he makes me sick! If you left it to him we'd stay here the rest of our lives.

MRS. POLLANT: You can't blame Poppa so much. It's not as if Uncle Barney left us a fortune. It's just enough to live comfortable in a nice flat—

BERNICE: I don't care! Poppa don't consider us one bit. All he does is read those old books of his and spend his time gabbing with that Kerrigan fella. Makes me sick! That's what it does—

[At this point in BERNICE's diatribe ISAAC POLLANT comes in. He is a small, faded, baldish man. His clothes hang loosely on him, his eyes are faded, his skin faded. There is something quite gentle and likeable about him. He rather sidles in, gives a puzzled look around, as though he had not been living in this same flat for fifteen years and were not perfectly familiar with its details. He removes his overcoat, and almost at once edges to the rocker near the bookshelves. The conversation proceeds while he is engaged in these operations.]

MRS. POLLANT: Well, Isaac? You're late for supper, ain't you?

POLLANT: Not much, Goldie.

MRS. POLLANT: You want to go with us to the party upstairs at Mrs. Vogel's to-night?

POLLANT: I'm busy to-night—

MRS. POLLANT: What means busy?

POLLANT: I'm expecting Mr. Kerrigan.

BERNICE: Mr. Kerrigan! That kid!

POLLANT: [Polishing his spectacles.] What's the matter with Mr. Kerrigan, hey?

BERNICE: Why, he's one of those Socialists—Makes speeches on the corner. He'll be put in jail one of these days.

POLLANT: Don't worry yourself about Kerrigan, Becky!

BERNICE: How many times do I have to tell you not to call me Becky. My name is Bernice.

172

MRS. POLLANT: Your Poppa gets absent-minded from reading so much from books.

BERNICE: [Turning.] Let's go in and eat. Everything's ready, isn't it?

MRS. POLLANT: You go ahead. I'll wait for Milton. We ain't got much; Mrs. Vogel's got nice refreshments. You ought of seen what went up the dumb-waiter this afternoon—!

[BERNICE starts to go into the dining-room, when the hall door opens and MILTON, her brother, and SIDNEY HEIM, her beau, come in. MILTON is a tall, pimply youth. SIDNEY is a flabby individual with a drooping lower lip which makes his mouth seem perpetually open. He seems unable to stand still: his feet are always forming "steps," like a vaudeville dancer. Both youths wear the latest in natty clothes.]

MILTON: H'lo, folks.

MRS. POLLANT: [To her son.] I'd think you could get home to your meals on time. [To MR. HEIM.] How are you feeling to-night, Sidney?

SIDNEY: Not an ache or pain, Mrs. Pollant—not an ache or pain.

BERNICE: You didn't ring me on the phone to-day.

SIDNEY: I know it, Bernice. I got busy—

MILTON: I'll say he's busy. Vampin' all the broads that drink soda-water. Ladies and gentlemen: here he is! Behold the original drug-store sheik!

SIDNEY: [With a feint at hitting MILTON.] You big bum!

MRS. POLLANT: Boys, you shouldn't fight. [SIDNEY collars MILTON, puts his hand on his hip, and simpers effeminately in a high-pitched voice.]

SIDNEY: And this, ladies, take a look, is the Cigar Store's gentleman pet!

MILTON: Say! How do you get that way!

BERNICE: Sid, you're just killing when you act that way.

MILTON: It's a gift.

SIDNEY: Speakin' of gifts—that reminds me. A little package from Tiffany's. [SIDNEY presents a flat parcel he is carrying to BERNICE, with a ceremonial bow.]

MILTON: Don't get excited, Sis. It's a bum phonograph record he won in a raffle.

SIDNEY: It's a swell record—a red seal. Cost two seventy-five.

MRS. POLLANT: Now, isn't that nice?

BERNICE: "G Minor Ballade, by Chop-pin, played by Godowsky."

MILTON: Good night!

MRS. POLLANT: Put it on, and let's see what it sounds like. [SIDNEY takes record from BERNICE and puts it on the machine.]

BERNICE: I don't think I'm going to like it.

SIDNEY: You never can tell about this high-brow stuff— [The music begins. They all remain silent for a moment, appraising it.]

MILTON: You can have all of that you want—!

MRS. POLLANT: Sounds like somebody practicing—

BERNICE: I'll take it down and maybe they'll change it for one of Rudy Vallee's.

MRS. POLLANT: I think you better keep it, Bernice. It'll be nice for when we have visitors in our new apartment on the Drive.

POLLANT: Chopin—! Isn't that Chopin?

BERNICE: You can't prove it by me.

POLLANT: It's beautiful—!

BERNICE: Turn it off, Sid. Poppa can play it over when he's alone. [SIDNEY stops the machine.]

MILTON: Just so I'm not around—

SIDNEY: What's the snappy story you're so interested in, Mr. Pollant?

POLLANT: It's a copy of Baedeker.

SIDNEY: Baedeker. What's that—a disease?

MRS. POLLANT: Poppa reads books about travel. All the time—

BERNICE: And the only traveling he does is in the sub-way— [This remark causes laughter. POLLANT has returned to his reading.]

MILTON: On the way up to-night I took Sid around by the Drive and showed him the place.

MRS. POLLANT: That's why you were so late getting home.

SIDNEY: Some swell joint, I'll say! Oh boy!

BERNICE: Did you look inside?

SIDNEY: We tipped the nigger hall-boy a quarter, and he took us all through.

MILTON: It makes me feel rich just to walk through that marble lobby—

BERNICE: [To SIDNEY.] How'd you like the parlor with the windows looking out on 110th Street? You can see the River if you lean out enough. Did you show him my room, Milton?

MILTON: *Your* room! What are you calling your room?

BERNICE: The big one with the glass doors.

MILTON: And I'll be pushed into the little dark one, I suppose, where I get a fine view of ash cans!

MRS. POLLANT: Children, the rooms ain't decided yet! Now, hush!

MILTON: Well, Bernice gets everything in this family. What do you think I am—the goat?

MRS. POLLANT: We don't think no such thing.

MILTON: Well, I got some rights. And I'll tell you this —you might as well know it now—I'm leaving the store. Told the boss to-day.

MRS. POLLANT: Milton! You didn't!

BERNICE: You might know he'd do something foolish—

MILTON: Did you think I'd be stickin' to that job the rest of my life—!

MRS. POLLANT: [To her husband.] Poppa! Hear that, Poppa, Milton's quitting at the store.

POLLANT: [Looking up from his book.] What?

MRS. POLLANT: Milton—he's going to stop work.

MILTON: Well, what's the use of bein' left money if you have to work all the time?

POLLANT: But I specially told you not to give up your job!

MRS. POLLANT: [To her son.] Why didn't you mind Poppa?

POLLANT: How many times I told you not to give up your job? Didn't I tell you we got to go slow till we see how much expense we have if we do move?

BERNICE: If—!

MILTON: Oh, you're so scared of starving it's a wonder you don't die of fright—I'd look swell livin' on the Drive and sellin' cigars, wouldn't I?

SIDNEY: [Judiciously siding with the parent.] Something in what your Pop says, Milton.

MILTON: Say, you'd be satisfied jerkin' sodas till you was ninety. I've got ambition. I'm goin' on the road with a line of goods—that's where the money is—

POLLANT: I tell you you shouldn't give up your job till—

MILTON: Just because you been a stick-in-the-mud for twenty years is no reason I should be, is it?

BERNICE: Milton's right. If it wasn't that Uncle Barney died and left us this money we'd have to stay here the rest of our lives—

POLLANT: [Shrilly.] What's the matter with this place I'd like to know? What? It was good enough for Momma and me for twenty years, eh? What's your Riverside Drive? Eh? Who lives there? A lot of—a lot of low lifes!

MRS. POLLANT: Poppa, you shouldn't say such things!

MILTON: Let him rave—

POLLANT: There's better things to do with that money—than to move to the Drive—Finer things—! [The doorbell rings.]

MRS. POLLANT: See who wants us, Bernice.

POLLANT: [Rising.] That is Kerry, maybe.

MRS. POLLANT: You'd think he'd wait till after supper—

[BERNICE opens the door, admitting PADRAIC KERRIGAN. He is about twenty-five: a short, squat youth, with fine blue eyes and a lot of tangled black hair. His habitual expression is quite serious, but his eyes are full of humor.]

KERRIGAN: Good evening. [POLLANT gives an exclamation of pleasure, and crosses to shake hands with his friend. The rest of the family scarcely greet him.]

POLLANT: Come right here, Kerry—sit right here—

KERRIGAN: Fine night to be out. Stars, moon, and the air so sharp it makes your blood feel on fire.

MRS. POLLANT: Yes?

MILTON: Say, ain't it time to eat?

MRS. POLLANT: Yes, children. Go to the dining-room. No quarreling—

SIDNEY: I'm so hungry I can eat a house and lot—My arm? [He elaborately offers his arm to BERNICE, and the two go into the dining-room, followed by MILTON.]

MRS. POLLANT: Poppa, come eat something.

POLLANT: I don't want to eat now. Maybe—later.

MRS. POLLANT: What's the matter with you, Poppa? Maybe you'd like a little something, Mr. Kerrigan. We just got delicatessen—

KERRIGAN: No, thanks, Mrs. Pollant. I ate at the corner before I came up.

MRS. POLLANT: Well, you two—I don't know what to make of you—! [She goes out.]

POLLANT: How have you been, Kerry, my friend?

KERRIGAN: It isn't how have I been. It's how have you been? Have you told them yet?

POLLANT: No—that is, I haven't had a chance—

KERRIGAN: Not the chance! Make the chance. You're master in your own house, or ought to be. Why're you letting them do as they like with you—I tell you, Polly, your weakness disgusts me. If I weren't so damned fond of you —and if I weren't so damn grateful for the number of times you've helped me—I'd drop you—Yes, I would!

POLLANT: I know—I know—

KERRIGAN: For heaven's sake don't agree with me! Have some spunk about you—go in and tell 'em they can't move to their damn Riverside Drive—Do it now! Here you sit reading that Baedeker all the time—What's the use of reading that? Now I'll give you one more chance—and if you don't tell them—

POLLANT: Kerry, if I only had your tongue, your Irish tongue, your oratory—

KERRIGAN: It's true me family was a race of speakers.

POLLANT: O'Connell was a great orator—

KERRIGAN: Well, if it comes to that, how about Moses? He wasn't bad at kidding 'em along—Of course he didn't know anything about economics. Everything depends on that —I tell you, Polly, Economic Determinism. [Catching himself in time.] But that's neither here nor there—I'm going to give you one more chance, Polly, and if you don't tell 'em this time I'm through with trying to help you. You can go to your Riverside Drive and take the consequences—

POLLANT: But Kerry! They don't look at things the way you do. They don't know what I think of all the time—

KERRY: The money was left to you, wasn't it? You're the head of the family, aren't you? What a man you are, Polly! No backbone whatever—

POLLANT: I deserve what you say—

KERRIGAN: Don't agree with me—! Buck up! Tell 'em you won't move, and that you want to spend the money traveling— [Suddenly an idea strikes him, he takes up the Baedeker, opens it, and begins to read—he knows POLLANT's soft spot.]

KERRIGAN: "The Protestant Cemetery is open from 7 A.M. till dark. It is a retired spot rising gently towards the city wall, affording pleasing views and shaded by lofty cypresses. Of the old cemetery Shelley wrote that it might make one in love with death to think that one should be buried in so sweet a place. Close to the entrance is the tomb of John Keats, bearing the melancholy inscription: 'Here lies one whose name was writ in water'—The eye will fall with interest on the tomb of the poet Shelley, whose ashes are buried here—"

POLLANT: Don't read any more, Kerry—Don't—!

KERRIGAN: [Closing the book.] All your life you've wanted to go to places, see things, where the wonderful men of the world lived and died—Now a miracle happens, God himself drops the money into your lap, and you won't take advantage of it—Think of the golden places of the world! Italy, Spain, Germany, Cairo, Palestine—the immemorial home of your people—

POLLANT: I might make Momma see, but I don't think the children would come—

KERRIGAN: Then leave them behind—!

POLLANT: It sounds simple the way you say it, Kerry, but —you see—

KERRIGAN: Think, Polly! The graves of Byron and Keats, the waters where Shelley died, the Paris Villon knew—Why, with the present rate of exchange you can live in Italy for next to nothing, travel, do anything—

POLLANT: I must do it!

KERRIGAN: Call them in. Tell them now! I tell you it's a crime to squander your money on a vulgar apartment on Riverside Drive—develop in your family all the gilded parasitism of the Master Class—Why, they'll be worse there than here—a hundred times—It'll make them snobs as well as Philistines—

MRS. POLLANT: [Entering.] Poppa! You got to eat some supper; you'll be sick.

KERRIGAN: [Whispering.] Tell her now!

POLLANT: Goldie dear—I—I got to speak to you.

MRS. POLLANT: After you eat your supper, Isaac.

POLLANT: Now!

KERRIGAN: That's the stuff!

MRS. POLLANT: What's come over you two?

POLLANT: I don't know about this moving to Riverside Drive—

MRS. POLLANT: You don't know!

POLLANT: This Riverside Drive business don't appeal to me at all. Why should we spend all that money to show off with a lot of—lot of—

KERRIGAN: Parasites!

POLLANT: Parasites! That's right—parasites!

MRS. POLLANT: What's got through you, Isaac! Are you crazy? He picks to-night to tell us he don't wanta move—with the movers coming Monday—!

POLLANT: I never wanted to move—

MRS. POLLANT: Everybody knows Riverside Drive—what a fine neighborhood it is. And the air—right fresh from the River—

POLLANT: I know a place—better than Riverside Drive—it's not only better—it's cheaper—

MRS. POLLANT: Well—tell—

POLLANT: I'd like to move there with you and Beckie—

MRS. POLLANT: How long do I have to wait before you tell me—Where is it already?

POLLANT: Italy.

MRS. POLLANT: Italy!

POLLANT: Italy! I want to move to Italy.

Mrs. Pollant: Isaac! You don't mean where those dirty dagos come from!

Pollant: Italy! Where Shelley and Keats lived. It was good enough for them, I guess.

Mrs. Pollant: [Turning on Kerrigan.] It's you put him up to this!

Kerrigan: I put him up to nothing. He's always wanted to live in Italy.

Mrs. Pollant: Maybe you want he should make speeches over there against the government!

Pollant: Don't talk foolish, Goldie. With the rate of exchange like it is now between here and Europe we could live like lords—in Rome, in Venice, in Palestine—

Mrs. Pollant: Isaac! You're a Zionist!

Pollant: You see, Kerry. She don't understand—

Kerrigan: Mrs. Pollant, if I may be permitted to say so— you do not understand your husband. He is what you call romantic. He always has been—Poetry, music, literature— that's all he really cares for. An unkind fate and a ridiculous economic system has kept his nose to the grindstone when he should be free to study, to travel, to feed his starved imagination—Now that Providence has made him affluent—in a small way of course—he can satisfy the dream of a lifetime—He can visit all the places he's longed to see—

Mrs. Pollant: My God! [Milton strolls in from the dining-room, sucking a toothpick.]

Milton: What's all the shootin' for?

Kerrigan: He's worked pretty hard, Mrs. Pollant. He looks ten years older than he really is—This thing will mean everything in the world to him—

Mrs. Pollant: You really want this, Isaac!

Pollant: I'd like to see those lovely places—once—

Milton: Say, what is all this?

Kerrigan: The fact is, Milton, your father wants to travel. He wants to see the world.

MILTON: Why don't he join the Navy—? [BERNICE and SIDNEY come into the room.]

BERNICE: Momma, Sid and I are going on upstairs to the party.

SIDNEY: My motto is get there early and leave late. Hope they have good eats.

MRS. POLLANT: No—don't go yet. Wait—Milton— [MRS. POLLANT is convinced at last that something is the matter with her husband. She begins whispering to MILTON, and BERNICE and SIDNEY join them, listening to MRS. POL-LANT's words.]

KERRIGAN: [To POLLANT.] Now's your chance. It's now or never. If necessary you must defy them all. You've made a good start. I'm proud of you. Tell them you won't stand for this Riverside Drive business. Tell them after this you'll do the deciding—Will you tell them?

POLLANT: [Mopping his brow.] I'll try—

KERRIGAN: Your hand on it. [POLLANT presents a limp hand, which his friend shakes vigorously.] Courage! Remember—Byron, Shelley—Italy—Spain!

MILTON: [Leaving the others.] Now then, Pop, what is this new bug of yours?

POLLANT: Don't you talk to me like that—I won't have it! You're not the boss of this house yet— [MILTON is considerably taken aback by this firm tone; KERRIGAN's face is luminous with joy.]

MILTON: You needn't get so huffy—I'm only asking for information—

POLLANT: All right, I give you the information. All my life I work for nothing—to make a living. No time to read, no time to study—Now we get a little money, I don't want to waste it on nothing—I want to make a little something of myself—and Beckie, too—What I want with—with Riverside Drive—

BERNICE: Why, Poppa, all the finest people in New York live there—!

POLLANT: The richest, you mean—

KERRIGAN: Exploiters—

MILTON: [To KERRIGAN.] You keep your mug out of this!

POLLANT: Sure! Exploiters!

BERNICE: But we got the apartment all picked out and everything!

MRS. POLLANT: And the movers coming Monday—

POLLANT: Well, you can tell them not to come!

MILTON: Er—what's your idea, Pop?

POLLANT: My idea? You should keep on working. Books ain't for you. Your Momma and Beckie and me go for a trip—

MILTON: Good idea! But that needn't keep us from living on the Drive. You can take a nice trip to Niagara Falls —or Bermuda! Real ocean trip!

POLLANT: I don't mean a trip like that. I mean a trip for, maybe, a couple of years. All over Europe. Beckie can learn lots of languages and become really what you can call an educated lady—

BERNICE: Did you ever hear—! He wants me to be a school-teacher!

POLLANT: Why not? It's a fine thing, a school-teacher. Better than going to dances and spooning with that loafer, Sidney.

BERNICE: He's not a loafer—!

SIDNEY: Oh, well, if that's the way you feel about it, I guess I'll not trouble you any more—

MILTON: Stick around! The old man don't know what he's sayin'.

MRS. POLLANT: Poppa didn't mean nothing by it—

SIDNEY: [To door.] Nobody can call me a loafer and expect me to take it!

BERNICE: [Holding him.] Please don't go, Sidney!

SIDNEY: I'll come back to see you when your old man's out— [SIDNEY goes out the door, pulling BERNICE after him.]

MRS. POLLANT: Now look at what you done! Driven Bernice's sweetheart from the door.

POLLANT: May I never see him again—the *schlemiel*—!

KERRIGAN: Good for you, Polly—! [Suddenly MRS. POLLANT bursts into tears. MILTON tries to quiet her.]

MILTON: [To his mother.] It's all right—he'll be all right—

POLLANT: Goldie! What you crying for? Just because I want to take you and Beckie to Europe—? You'll have the finest time—you'll see all the finest pictures, and all the places where the greatest men in the world lived—all the men who wrote those books there—I'll read you the books, too—you'll see how fine they are—

MRS. POLLANT: Isaac, my crown, what's come over you?

MILTON: I guess you do need a little trip—change of air. Tell you what I'll do—I'll call up Dr. Schlossberg and we'll talk it over—

POLLANT: Dr. Schlossberg!

MRS. POLLANT: Dr. Schlossberg is fine, Isaac—Only the other day Mrs. Finkbaum was saying to me she don't believe in God but she believes in Dr. Schlossberg—You know what he did for my asthma—

MILTON: A few weeks in the country'll fix you up, Pop— No doubt about it—you're just run down—When you come back we'll be all fixed up in the new flat, and you won't want to go to Europe.

MRS. POLLANT: Sure, Poppa! A few weeks at Rockaway maybe—You'll be a new man again—

[As the truth suddenly dawns on POLLANT, he turns to look at KERRIGAN and finds KERRIGAN unable to meet his gaze. There is an embarrassed silence. MRS. POLLANT and MILTON stare at POLLANT curiously, as at a strange being from whom startling things may be expected.]

POLLANT: [Laughing hysterically.] They think I'm crazy, Kerry—

MILTON: Nothing of the kind, Pop—Just a bit run down, that's all—

MRS. POLLANT: God forbid—Isaac, my crown—

POLLANT: They think I'm crazy— [The telephone rings. BERNICE, who has just come in from bidding her beau goodbye, stops to answer it.]

BERNICE: Oh, that you, Mrs. Vogel?—Yes—Something's come up—Wait a second—[To the rest, her palm covering the transmitter.] It's Mrs. Vogel upstairs. She wants to know why we don't come up to the party.

MRS. POLLANT: Tell her Poppa ain't—feeling well—and we can't come.

POLLANT: Go to your party!

MRS. POLLANT: Isaac, my crown—!

POLLANT: Go to your party—I tell you you should go to your party—!

MILTON: Pop's right. Certain we go to the party. [To BERNICE.] Tell her we'll be right up.

BERNICE: [Into the telephone.] All right, Mrs. Vogel. We're just starting up. [She hangs up the receiver.]

MILTON: Why, Pop's perfectly well. Nothing the matter with him at all—Just a little run down—

BERNICE: [As the player-piano starts upstairs.] They've started dancing.

MILTON: Just take it easy, Pop. And if you want us, all you have to do is ring us—

MRS. POLLANT: Are you sure it's all right, Isaac?

POLLANT: Take them upstairs, Milton—

MRS. POLLANT: But, Isaac!

MILTON: Surest thing you know—[To his mother.]   Come on.   Pop don't want to be bothered with you.   He wants to be quiet and rest up a little—[He herds his mother and BERNICE out.]   See you later, Pop—Better not read too much to-night—Go to bed early—[The three of them go out of the hall door.]

POLLANT: It's funny, isn't it?   They think I'm crazy—

KERRIGAN: Are you going to let them get away with that! It was all I could do to keep from shouting at them.   Where's your spunk, man!   I'd be firmer now than ever—If they won't go abroad with you, go yourself—

POLLANT: Who knows?   Perhaps I am crazy—Perhaps they're the ones who aren't crazy—

KERRIGAN: Polly, you make me sick—you're hopeless—! You give in to them—

POLLANT: Well, maybe it's for the best—

KERRIGAN: Want to go down to 96th Street with me?   I'm addressing a meeting on Irish freedom.

POLLANT: No thanks, Kerry.   I'm too tired.

KERRIGAN: So this is the end of it—You're going to live on Riverside Drive after all.   It fairly breaks my heart that you won't have your wish—I tell you what it is, it's the System—It's not your family that's to blame, nor England, nor Capitalists—it's the System!   If we can just abolish the System—[But he becomes aware that POLLANT is not listening, and he is a bit ashamed of his tirade.]   Well, good-night, Polly, I've got to be running.

POLLANT: Good-night, Kerry, my boy—

[KERRIGAN goes out, closing the door softly.   The pianola upstairs is pouring out the latest song of the day.   POLLANT looks up resignedly at the ceiling.   His eye catches sight of the fat, red Baedeker.   He smiles, picks up the book and starts reading—slowly, his lips moving, pronouncing the words distinctly, one by one.]

POLLANT: "—cemetery Shelley wrote that it might make

186

one in love with death to think that one should be buried in so sweet a place. Close to the entrance is the tomb of John Keats, bearing the melancholy inscription: 'Here lies one whose name was writ in water—'" [The old man continues to read.]

THE GIRL IN THE COFFIN
BY THEODORE DREISER

PERSONS IN THE PLAY

WILLIAM MAGNET
JOHN FERGUSON
MRS. MAMIE SHAEFER
MRS. MARGARET RICKERT
MRS. HANNAH LITTIG
NICHOLAS BLUNDY
TIMOTHY MCGRATH

THE GIRL IN THE COFFIN

PATERSON, NEW JERSEY. The parlor of WILLIAM MAGNET's house, which is that of a well-to-do workingman. At the left is a door leading outside to the porch. On either side of the door are windows, with blinds drawn and heavy coarse white lace curtains. To the right is a wooden mantel with a plush lambrequin, an ornamental clock, a gilded plaster cast and a photograph in a celluloid frame. Over the mantel hangs a large "crayon portrait" of a woman in a heavy silvered frame. Toward the rear is a door leading to the dining room and the kitchen. In one corner stands a cheap mahogany upright piano with silk drapery hung over one corner. A large highly decorated vase and a chromo under glass representing St. Cecelia playing to the angels (this picture supported by a bracket) ornament the top of the piano. To the right of it is a standing lamp, unlighted. Near this are three tiers of section bookcases filled with "sets." Under the window at the left is a small upholstered plush sofa with a sofa cushion made of cigar ribbons. In middle of the back wall hangs a large

191

framed lithograph portrait of JOHN FERGUSON, strike leader, standing in an oratorical attitude. A real silk flag with gilt lettering and gilt fringe is draped over one corner of this portrait. On the floor directly below this picture—far enough out so that there is room to pass between it and the wall—stands a black coffin on trestles. The pallid profile and thick dark hair of a dead woman are barely visible.

To the right toward the front stands a small oak table with a lace cover and a large oil lamp with a painted china shade giving a dim light.

MRS. MAMIE SHAEFER is seated to the left of the table in a straight chair, crocheting lace edging. She is stout, neat, vigorous, red-cheeked, her hair brushed tightly back. She is dressed in tight-fitting black merino. To her left, MRS. MARGARET RICKERT occupies a cane-seated rocker. She also is stout and rosy, but of a more placid type. She wears a brown shawl and over her head a knitted scarf of pink wool. While MRS. RICKERT rocks and MRS. SHAEFER crochets, enter from the dining room door MRS. LITTIG, a little, thin, pale, vapid-looking old woman with scraggly gray hair, a gray calico dress and a small woolen shawl over her shoulders. She walks across the stage and lights the lamp by the piano.

MRS. SHAEFER: [Looking up from her crocheting.] Has Magnet come in yet, Mrs. Littig?

MRS. LITTIG: [Busy with the lamp-lighting.] No, he ain't come in. [She speaks in a mild, high, patient voice.]

MRS. SHAEFER: Where did he say he was goin'?

MRS. LITTIG: He didn't say. Most like he went to the cemetery.

MRS. SHAEFER: It's queer he wouldn't be back by now.

MRS. RICKERT: He might be at the depot to meet Ferguson's train. A quarter past seven he gets here. The crowds was thick already when I come up the street.

MRS. SHAEFER: To be sure, that's where he is. Are you

192

gettin' somethin' to eat, Mrs. Littig? Magnet'll need a good hot bite in case he goes to the hall.

MRS. LITTIG: There's coffee made and ham and eggs ready to fry ef he'll eat.

MRS. RICKERT: [To MRS. LITTIG.] Poor man, he ain't much appetite, I expect.

MRS. LITTIG: No, he don't eat very good. [When MRS. LITTIG has finished lighting the lamp, she walks to the coffin and stands stroking her cheek and wiping her eyes now and then with her hand. She is disregarded by the others, who go on talking. After a moment or two she goes out by the dining room door.]

MRS. RICKERT: I understand he takes it terrible hard, Mrs. Shaefer. My Jim met him on the street last night, and he says to him: "Magnet," he says, "I'm sorry trouble should 'a' come to you of all men in this town just at this time," he says, "when so many looks to you for help." And with that Magnet just give him a nod and walked on without a word to say. Jim was tellin' me he had a terrible look on his face like he was near to lose his senses. "It was a bad day for the workers o' this town, Maggie," Jim says to me, "when Magnet's girl took sick. You want to re- member," he says, "let the Tabitha run another week and this strike's lost; and run it will," he says, "as sure as I'm alive, without Magnet sticks on the job. Ferguson's a wonder," he says, "but he can't do everything alone. It's a shame for Magnet to draw out just now—there ain't nothin' ought to make him do it," he says.

MRS. SHAEFER: I heard say they got a message last night from Ferguson, one o' them secret telegrams. "The Tabitha walks out at noon Saturday," he says, "or the game's up. Drive them damn scabs"—that's what he says right in the telegram—"drive them damn scabs into Murray Hall at half past eight and look for me on the seven fifteen train. *Have Magnet there,*" he says. [A slight pause.] Ferguson

—ain't it surprising, now, what he's done in this town? Ain't he got a terrible strong will? "He's a great man" that's what Tim McGrath says to a crowd down there one night. "Talk about your kings and your emperors and your presidents and your millionaires," he says—"there ain't one of 'em all with the brains and the fists could stand up alone against Ferguson."

MRS. RICKERT: It's little Ferguson can do without others to help him. What do them nine-dollar-a-week scabs at the Tabitha know or care who Ferguson is? He can't talk no Eyetalian. He ain't never run a loom. It needs somebody can speak their own tongue and has lived in the same place and worked on the same job. Magnet's the man to talk to them men. Do you think he'll go to the meetin' tonight, Mrs. Shaefer?

MRS. SHAEFER: I don't know, I'm sure, Mrs. Rickert. I'm here to do what I can. "It's his duty," that's what my Joe says to me this mornin'—"it's his duty, and no man ain't got a right to go against his duty, no matter how black his trouble may be. Do you want we should 'a' starved and scraped ten weeks for nothin'?" he says. "Mill after mill will shut down," he says—"the Excelsior down a month since, the Maxwell down a fortnight this coming Wednesdays, the Junta down three weeks past—My God, think o' that!" Joe says to me, "the Junta—that miserable pesthouse o' poor, chatterin' Dago apes that you wouldn't 'a' thought would 'a' ever knew the difference between a strike and a bunch of spaghetti; and here they are holdin' together like human men, and who's done it?" Joe says to me. "Why, old Magnet's done it. Ferguson never could 'a' brought this strike where it is today without Magnet to back him. When the Tabitha shuts down," he says, "we've got the best o' them bloodsuckers that's tryin' to live off our carcasses, an' there's only one man can put a little reason an' backbone into them cowardly sponges o' furren scabs, an' that man's

Magnet. Magnet's in a bad place," he says, "with nobody but that one pore foolish old woman"—[She lowers her oice and motions toward the dining room door.]—"to look after him. She'd 'a' been in the almshouse long ago ef it hadn't 'a' been for Magnet's good heart. She's nobody to put nerve into a man. Now for God's sake," Joe says to me, "you go down there tonight, Mamie, and see he gets a good meal an' turns up at the hall an' gives his talk accordin' to the timetable. It's a great pity," he says, *for more reasons than one,* that Magnet's wife is no more alive. That house would 'a' been better this long time past for a good, strong woman in it," he says.

Mrs. Rickert: Seemed like he was terrible devoted to Mary.

Mrs. Shaefer: He made a great mistake to indulge her the way he did, Mrs. Rickert, a great mistake.

Mrs. Rickert: Seems queer she wouldn't 'a' got a man of her own before now—a bright, stylish girl like Mary. There was plenty courted her. They say as young Blundy, that's foreman of the warpers and twisters down at the Waverly, was after her to marry him this long time.

Mrs. Shaefer: [Severely.] She would never 'a' been content to be a mill worker's wife—Mary Magnet wouldn't. She'd too many notions for that. It takes a hard jolt to bring some off their high horse. [Significantly.]

Mrs. Rickert: [Leaning forward confidentially.] Ain't it surprising now that she should 'a' gone so quick? A strong, lively girl like that—she did look the very picture of health. What did *you* understand was the cause of her sickness, Mrs. Shaefer? I heard say the doctors wasn't able to give any satisfaction whatever.

[A sudden knock at the door intercepts the reply to this query. Mrs. Rickert rocks in silence, while Mrs. Shaefer opens the door and admits Nick Blundy, a tall, good-looking young workingman in a dark gray suit and flannel shirt.

He carries a large pasteboard box under his arm, and enters nervously, quickly removing his soft felt hat.]

MRS. SHAEFER: [In a subdued voice and with great solemnity.] Good evening, Mr. Blundy. You come to view the corpse? [She makes an impressive gesture toward the coffin and resumes her seat. The rocking and crocheting continue, while NICK stands for a moment or two by the coffin. The women glance furtively at him. When he moves MRS. SHAEFER speaks.]

MRS. SHAEFER: Won't you set down a minute, Mr. Blundy?

[She places a chair to the left of MRS. RICKERT. NICK seats himself gingerly on the edge of the chair, propping his package against it and turning his hat in his hand. The women assume attitudes and expressions of renewed gravity and importance. MRS. RICKERT almost ceases to rock.]

NICK: [In a subdued, nervous voice.] It's a terrible thing about Mary, ain't it? [Appropriately lugubrious sighs and murmurs come from the women.]

WOMEN: It is indeed, Mr. Blundy. Terrible. Yes, it's very sad.

NICK: [After a slight pause.] Where's the old man?

MRS. SHAEFER: We're expectin' him in any minute.

NICK: They say he grieves very bitter.

MRS. SHAEFER: Yes, he takes on a good bit.

NICK: Ain't he goin' down to the hall tonight?

MRS. SHAEFER: [With much gravity.] I can't say positive, Mr. Blundy. It's his *duty* to go. There's hopes he may be made to feel that.

NICK: [Spasmodically, after another slight pause.] I didn't know there was anything ailed Mary. I seed her only a week or two ago walkin' down Grant Street one night, and she says to me: "Nick," she says, "it's slow times these days, ain't it, with the girls and the fellows; but," she says, "what'll you bet when we win this strike we don't have more coin in our pockets than ever we did—and then for the good old Saturday nights!" Why, she was laughin' and carryin' on as lively as a kitten.

Mrs. Rickert: [Nodding.] She did enjoy a good time as much as any girl, Mary did.

Nick: [Shaking his head mournfully.] She must 'a' been took awful sudden. I heard she died Wednesday night down in the St. Francis. Is that right?

Mrs. Shaefer: Yes, Mr. Blundy, them's the facts.

Nick: Have you heard say what it was that ailed her? [Mrs. Rickert stops rocking entirely and looks expectantly at Mrs. Shaefer, who draws herself up with portentous dignity.]

Mrs. Shaefer: She was took very sudden, and they had need to operate to cure her. There's great danger in them operations. [A pause. Mrs. Rickert resumes rocking, folds her hands and looks wise. Nick gazes silently at the floor.]

Nick: [Sadly reflective.] She sure did have the ginger in her, that girl. There was few fellows could do with a loom what she could.

Mrs. Rickert: Mary was smart, all right. I guess there ain't nobody questions that.

Nick: [Lost in his own recollections.] Why, I seed her one day on a bet run six looms, at onct—seventy picks to the inch, mind you—and not a snarl on one o' them six machines. While we was standin' there watchin', the boss come by, and he says: "Mary Magnet," he says, "ef I could get the rest o' these chaps to work the way you kin work," he says, "I'd git a damn big raise to me wages," he says; and quick as a flash Mary says back: "Well, just because me and the boys *kin* make human shuttlecocks out o' our-selves, that ain't no reason why we're a goin' to *do* it," she says, "just to raise *your* pay. We know darn well we'd never raise our own," she says, all the time jumpin' around from one loom to another as springy as a cricket. [A pause.] Gee! [He shakes his head.] It sure is hard to believe she'd 'a' been took like this so soon.

[He fumbles after the box on the floor and lifts it to his knees, hesitates awkwardly and then removes the cover, displaying a white pillow of immortelles with the word "Asleep" formed upon it in large purple letters and tied across one corner with an elaborate bow of purple satin ribbon. There is a chorus of appreciative murmurs from the women. MRS. SHAEFER rises and takes the box, holding it up to full view.]

MRS. SHAEFER: Now, ain't that a beautiful thing?

MRS. RICKERT: Oh, that is *handsome*.

MRS. SHAEFER: Wait till I fix it on the coffin. [She walks across the room and props the pillow (which has a fixture for this purpose) on the lower half of the coffin which is closed, then backs away admiringly to get the effect. The others rise for the same purpose. At this moment the sound of shouts and band music, faintly audible outside in the distance for some few moments previous, becomes more distinct. MRS. SHAEFER lifts her hand.]

MRS. SHAEFER: It's Ferguson.

MRS. RICKERT: Yes, that's who it is. They're bringin' him up from the depot.

MRS. SHAEFER: Most like there'll be trouble with the police down here by the mill at the corner.

[A sudden loud knock comes. All walk toward the door, and MRS. SHAEFER opens it, admitting TIMOTHY McGRATH, a stocky, sandy-haired, smooth-shaven man in a black suit with a striker's button and ribbon conspicuous in his buttonhole. At the sound of the knock MRS. LITTIG creeps timidly in from the kitchen and stands in the background with one hand on the coffin.]

McGRATH: [Standing in the doorway.] Where's Magnet?

MRS. SHAEFER: He ain't come in yet.

MRS. RICKERT: Wasn't he at the depot?

McGRATH: [Rapidly and excitedly.] No, he was not, and Ferguson's been raisin' hell down there. "Where's Magnet?" he says the first thing he steps off the train. "Take away the band, take away the parade, take away that carriage," he says, "and get me Magnet. Why ain't Magnet here?" he says. "I told you to have Magnet here." Jack Flaven spoke up and says: "Mr. Ferguson, we done our best but we can't locate Magnet. You may not 'a' heard," he says, "but Magnet's had trouble. His girl's dead. He won't talk tonight," and Ferguson says: [He lowers his voice.] "I don't give a damn who's dead; I'll have no words with anybody till I've seen Magnet," he says. Can't none of you tell me where he is? When was he last home?

MRS. SHAEFER: I understand he ain't been home since noon, Mr. McGrath.

McGRATH: Well, for Christ's sake, any time he gets in send him down to the hall.

[NICK BLUNDY and McGRATH go out. MRS. SHAEFER and MRS. RICKERT remain standing just inside the open door. MRS. LITTIG moves aimlessly back and forth behind the coffin, her arms folded, gazing at the dead and now and then wiping her eyes. The band is now distinctly heard at the end of the street playing the "Marseillaise," and cheers, "Hurrah for Ferguson!" mingled with shouts.]

MRS. RICKERT: [Pointing excitedly.] There's Ferguson! See him there walkin' behind the band! Oh, he's a grand man! There ain't nothin' this town can do that's too good for Ferguson—that's what my Jim says. [They stand for a moment looking and listening, then close the outside door. MRS. LITTIG furtively leaves her stand by the coffin and starts toward the dining room door, but is intercepted by MRS. RICKERT, who crosses the stage and seats herself near MRS. SHAEFER, who has resumed her crocheting.]

MRS. RICKERT: Mis' Littig, you was at the hospital when

Mary died, wasn't you? I heard tell she suffered a good bit.

MRS. LITTIG: [Turning reluctantly on her way to the door.] She died very quiet, Mary did.

MRS. RICKERT: [Persistently.] Ain't you heard the doctors say what the matter with her?

MRS. LITTIG: No, I ain't heard.

MRS. RICKERT: Ain't they told her father?

MRS. LITTIG: I ain't heard him say.

MRS. RICKERT: I heard tell Mary was to be married in the summer, Mrs. Littig. Is that a fact?

MRS. LITTIG: I ain't never heard Mary was to be married.

MRS. SHAEFER: [Addressing MRS. RICKERT in a contemptuous whisper.] She don't know nothin'. [Exit MRS. LITTIG by the dining room door. MRS. RICKERT looks around to make sure that she has gone, then draws her chair close to MRS. SHAEFER and whispers a question. The latter responds by a very slow and preternaturally solemn nodding of the head, accompanied by a sideward glance full of the direst meaning.]

MRS. RICKERT: Oh, ain't that terrible now! [Parenthetically.] I had my suspicions! [She leans forward eagerly and whispers another question.]

MRS. SHAEFER: [Very impressively.] That I don't know, Mrs. Rickert. As far as I can make out there ain't *nobody* knows. "You can be sure o' one thing," Joe says to me this morning: "whoever it is, *Magnet has still to learn his name.* It's a short lease o' life for the man that wronged Mary Magnet, once her father finds out the truth. That's what ails Magnet," Joe says to me. *"He can't find out. Ef somethin' don't happen to take his mind off it he'll brood hisself crazy."*

MRS. RICKERT: [Shaking her head and clicking her tongue.] Tck! Tck! Tck! It certainly is awful. Now whoever do you suppose?

MRS. SHAEFER: In my belief it's some rich fellow she met up to the city. Many a Saturday night when work was over she's been seen take the train. I understand she spread round the report she was goin' to business college up there. I guess, if truth be told, it was the gay life she was after. Well, she's not the first girl foolishness has brought to her grave. [She nods wisely.] Them rich ones knows how to cover their tracks.

MRS. RICKERT: Ain't it a terrible shame now for a man like Magnet, a man as has worked hard and lived an honest life and everybody respects, that his girl should make a common woman of herself and his name be made a shame in the town?

MRS. SHAEFER: There's very few knows the real truth, Mrs. Rickert. "Whatever you do, Mamie," Joe says to me, *"don't talk*. It would be a bad thing just at this time," he says, "if many was to get the straight of how Magnet's girl come to her death. I wouldn't want Ferguson to know of it," he says: "why, Ferguson thinks the sun rises and sets in old Magnet," he says.

MRS. RICKERT: Mary always did seem like a right well behaved, sensible girl, too—for all her free ways and smart talk. It's queer about them things.

MRS. SHAEFER: She looked too high, Mrs. Rickert—she looked too high. That's the way with them smart, good-lookin' girls. They ain't never content with enough. That's what I says to Joe this mornin'. "Now there was a girl," I says, "that wanted to own the earth." Why, I used to see her go down to work in the mornin' her head way up in the air, swingin' her arms and steppin' along as proud as a peacock. You might 'a' thought she was some fine lady instead of a mill girl. An' now look what she's come to. A bitter dose she's had to take for her pride.

[There is a sound of voices and footsteps on the porch

outside. The women rise. The door opens and WILLIAM
MAGNET enters. He is a tall, spare man of over fifty, with
plentiful gray hair, dressed in a dark suit and flannel shirt.
He is pale and harassed-looking, and almost savagely grim
and abrupt in manner. He holds open the door, admitting
TIMOTHY McGRATH.]

MAGNET: [Abruptly, closing the door.] Take a seat,
Tim. I'll be with you in a minute. [To MRS. SHAEFER,
politely but sternly.] What is there I can do for *you*, Mrs.
Shaefer?

MRS. SHAEFER: [Ingratiatingly.] Put it the other way
round, Mr. Magnet. Ain't there nothin' we can do for *you?*
That's what we're here for. Won't you come out in the
kitchen and have a bite of somethin' before you talk to
Mr. McGrath? It'll do you a sight o' good, Mr. Magnet.
There's coffee right on the stove.

MAGNET: [Maintaining his direct and forbidding manner.] Thank you very kindly, but I ain't hungry just at
present. There's one thing you *can* do, if you'll excuse
my speaking very plain, Mrs. Shaefer.

MRS. SHAEFER: [Somewhat awed.] Well, now, what's
that, Mr. Magnet?

MAGNET: You can leave me to myself for this evening
if you'll be so kind. I'm willing those that wants to should
come in during the daytime, but at nights it suits me better
to be alone.

MRS. SHAEFER: [Swelling with offended dignity.] Why,
certainly, Mr. Magnet, just as you say. I've no wish to
thrust in my company anywhere I ain't wanted. [She goes
out promptly by the dining room door, followed by MRS.
RICKERT. MAGNET, quite unmoved, draws up a chair and
seats himself in front of McGRATH. He speaks restlessly,
and with a harsh, detached manner.]

MAGNET: Now, Tim, whatever you've got to say, make it
as short as you can. This is no time and place to waste

words. [He motions vaguely toward the coffin.] That ought to be plain.

MᴄGʀᴀᴛʜ: [Leaning forward and placing his hand on Mᴀɢɴᴇᴛ's knee.] You have us all wrong, Magnet, if you think you ain't got our sympathy. You've *got* it. But, man alive—[straightening slightly and shaking both hands in front of him]—we can't stop tonight to think of our feelings. We gotta think of the proposition we're up against. Inside of an hour that hall down there'll be chock full o' workers from the Tabitha. We've sweat blood to get 'em there. If they go back to work tomorrow morning this strike's on the blink. Who's goin' to hold that crowd, Magnet? Ferguson can't do it. He don't know the language.

Mᴀɢɴᴇᴛ: [Impatiently.] What's the matter with Bruno Bastido? He can make a speech all right.

MᴄGʀᴀᴛʜ: They're jealous of Bastido. They think he's got a graft. Magnet, do you remember what you says to us down at the hotel that night last January when Ferguson first come to town? You says: "Boys, it ain't no use tryin' to stir up the warpers an' the twisters an' the loom workers —they're organized so tight already they can hardly move. If you want to see a real strike in this town, there's just one way to do it, and that is *stop the looms*. Begin at the bottom of the ladder and get the dyers and the weavers out. Stop wastin' your breath on these gentlemen of labor that's enjoyin' good union wages, and talk to them poor devils that's starved so long they don't know they're hungry. Get out them at the bottom and the others 'll follow fast enough."—Wasn't that the advice you give, Magnet?

Mᴀɢɴᴇᴛ: [Indifferently.] I guess it was, Tim.

MᴄGʀᴀᴛʜ: Ain't we stuck pretty close to them tactics you proposed? Ain't that the way the Maxwell was shut down, an' the Junta? Wasn't you personally pretty much responsible for bringin' about them two walkouts?

MAGNET: [Wearily.] Well, suppose I was, Tim. What's that to do with it?

McGRATH: [With renewed earnestness.] Why, just this, Magnet. You *got* the men out, but there's some of the rest of us has had the devil's own time tryin' to *keep* 'em out. You know what the trouble is. Up to the middle o' last week we ain't never been able to get as much as a look-in on the Tabitha. That G—— d—— Vito Toccati they've got for a foreman up there has double-crossed us from the start. It's pretty hard on them poor devils from the Maxwell and the Junta that's livin' along from day to day on bread and potatoes from the relief station to see the Tabitha hands goin' to work an' know they're gettin' double pay and the promise of a big raise when the strike's over. They won't stick it out that way much longer. You can't put *too* big a strain on human nature. We've got to shut down the Tabitha. Why, Magnet, you was the first to say it. For two weeks we've kept a hundred pickets round that mill. It's been a grim game. Every day there's been as many as thirty out of the hundred arrested or sent to the hospital with a shot through the arm or a broken head, and every time the next morning we've had thirty new ones there to take their places. Well, we've made some progress. Out of the 425 that works in that mill there was only one hundred got through the picket lines this mornin'. But, my God, the fight's only just begun! We gotta get 'em *all* out an we gotta *keep* 'em out. We gotta clinch this thing, and tonight's the time. Ferguson's come down a' purpose. If this meeting falls flat the whole strike may go for nothing. You wouldn't want that to happen, would you, Magnet? Don't you feel like you ought to come down and help us put it through? [A pause. MAGNET rises abruptly and faces McGRATH squarely.]

MAGNET: Well, now, Tim, if you've said your say and feel satisfied, you can have my answer. It's the same I give you before we come in a few minutes ago. I can't do what you want me to. [Hastily, as McGrath starts to interrupt.] At least, I *won't* do it. There's no more chance of my goin' down to Murray Hall tonight than there would be if it was me instead of my girl lyin' in that coffin. Now that's all I have to say. I hope it's enough. I wish you'd go now and leave me to myself.

McGrath: Do you mean that, Magnet?

Magnet: [Savagely.] Do I *mean* it? O' course I mean it. Did you ever know me to say anything I didn't mean? [He turns his back.]

McGrath: [Rising.] Do you think you're doin' the square thing by Ferguson, Magnet? He's staked pretty heavy on you.

Magnet: [Desperately.] Square or crooked, Tim, have it as you please. I ain't goin' down to Murray Hall tonight. And what's more, I ain't goin' to argue about it any further. Now I wish you'd go.

McGrath: [Shaking his head.] I'm sorry about this, Magnet. I don't think you're doin' the thing that will give you the most satisfaction in the end.

[McGrath goes out. Magnet closes the door and stands for a moment stretching his arms back and forth with a weary movement of mental suffering and physical exhaustion. He walks to the coffin for a moment, shakes his head, moans a little and swears under his breath, then sinks into a rocking chair near the table, stretches out his feet, throws back his head, closes his eyes and lets his hands rest limply one above the other in an attitude of utter weariness and dejection. Mrs. Littig looks in from the dining room, retreats for a moment, and then reappears, carrying a pair of shoes, which she places on the floor beside him. He stirs a little, but otherwise pays no attention. Mrs. Littig returns to the kitchen and brings back a large bottle, cup and spoon. She pours from the bottle into the cup and touches MAGNET on the arm.]

MRS. LITTIG: Take a sup o' this.

MAGNET: [Rousing.] What is it?

MRS. LITTIG: It's hot spirits and Jamaicy ginger.

MAGNET: [Motioning her away impatiently.] No, no. I don't want it. [MRS. LITTIG places the cup on the table near him and starts toward the door.]

MAGNET: [Moving uneasily.] Mis' Littig! [MRS. LITTIG turns and walks slowly back.]

MAGNET: Mis' Littig. Come set here a minute. I want to ask you somethin'. [MRS. LITTIG seats herself in a nearby chair and rocks timidly with folded arms. MAGNET, with eyes still closed, twists about in great distress.] What did you say was the last thing Mary said to you?

MRS. LITTIG: She says: "Tell pap it's all right. Tell him he ain't to worry."

MAGNET: Didn't she never leave a message for anybody else?

MRS. LITTIG: Not as I heard.

MAGNET: That night you was settin' by her when her fever was so high—Ain't she never mentioned anybody's name?

MRS. LITTIG: [Shaking her head.] No, she ain't.

MAGNET: Didn't you ever hear the nurse or the doctor say there was somebody she was talkin' about?

MRS. LITTIG: No, I didn't hear.

MAGNET: [Reaching shakily over to the table for the cup and taking a long drink, then replacing the cup on the table and slowly beginning to unlace his boots and put on dry ones.] What ever become o' that ring Mary used to wear?

MRS. LITTIG: What ring?

MAGNET: Why, that gold ring with a little blue stone in it. You've seed her wear it. She told me she bought it out of her savings. It ain't on her finger now. What become of it?

MRS. LITTIG: I dunno, Mr. Magnet. I never noticed what she done with it.

MAGNET: I was upstairs this mornin' lookin' through all her things, and I couldn't find it. It ain't on her finger now. [A pause.] Them times last winter, Mrs. Littig, when Mary went up to the city so often, didn't she ever tell you nothing about where she went and what she done?

MRS. LITTIG: [Reflectively.] She wasn't ever much to tell.

MAGNET: Can't you recall she ever mentioned anybody she met up there, anybody that took her round and acted nice to her?

MRS. LITTIG: [Mildly.] Don't seem like I can remember she ever did. [A pause. MRS. LITTIG rises, takes the bottle and cup from the table and moves toward the kitchen. She turns as she reaches the dining room door.] Mebbe you would eat a little after a while. I got some supper in the stove. [She goes out.]

MAGNET: [Groaning despairingly and turning in his chair.] Her mother would 'a' knew! Her mother would 'a' knew! [There is a knock. MAGNET does not move.] Somebody else after me, damn it! Why can't they leave me alone? [The knock is repeated. MAGNET rises and goes savagely toward the door.] I'll teach 'em to stay out o' here for one night! [He opens and admits JOHN FERGUSON—a large man, tall, heavily built, smooth-shaven. He enters in silence. MAGNET succumbs a little under his steady eye.] Oh, why, good evening, Mr. Ferguson, good evening. [He holds out his hand, which FERGUSON takes silently.]

FERGUSON: I'm sorry to find you in trouble, Magnet.

MAGNET: [Walking toward the opposite side of the room. For the first time he speaks a little tremulously.] Yes, I'm in a bad way, Mr. Ferguson, a bad way. It's my girl, Mary. [He motions toward the coffin.] She's all I had. [While MAGNET's back is turned, FERGUSON glances swiftly about the room and in the direction of the open coffin with a look that is peculiarly painful, apprehensive and significant. Then he walks toward MAGNET and puts a hand on his shoulder.]

FERGUSON: I know you've had a hard blow, Magnet, but there's only one way to meet it. Pull yourself together. You have work to do. You're lucky there. Not every man has that comfort in his trouble.

MAGNET: [Half turning away.] It don't seem like I can take any comfort from that, Mr. Ferguson. I'd be glad to if I could. I wish I *could* talk to the boys tonight. I can't do it. I can't do nothing for a while but set here an' think. I can't believe Mary's gone. I can't get used to it. She was all I had. I'd better be dead myself. [Passionately.] My God, I wish I was!

FERGUSON: [Very quiet and repressed.] That's no thought for you to hold tonight, Magnet. If a man's no good to the world and he knows it, let him get out of it if he wants to. It don't stand that way with you. You've got a big responsibility. Why don't you be worthy of it? Why don't you stand up to it?

MAGNET: I can't think about that now, Mr. Ferguson. The way I see it I've got a right to be left alone with my own trouble. It's a privilege belongs to any man if he's a mind to claim it.

FERGUSON: [With sudden intensity.] Let me tell you, Magnet, it's a privilege no man ought to want to claim at the expense of fourteen thousand of his fellow workers. Things have got to a crisis, and you've had as much to do with that as anybody. If we can close out the Tabitha to-morrow and hold down it and the other mills till the end of next week, we're over the danger line. If we can't, we lose as sure as fate. If we lose, it'll take years, years—you know that, Magnet—to win back what we've gained. The outcome o' this strike don't rest on High, Magnet—[He makes a sardonic upward gesture.]—it rests right here in this room with you and me. [He pounds his fist softly on the table.] Now what are you going to do about it? [MAGNET shakes his head doubtfully. FERGUSON continues.] You want to remember how much depends on a big fight like this. What made the workers of this town listen to me when I landed here? It was because they knew I'd won a miners' strike out in Montana and a lumber jacks' strike in Oregon and a cotton workers' strike in North Carolina and a glass blowers' strike in New Jersey. They thought if I'd helped others to better wages and shorter hours I could help them. If we lose here, the next town where I go they won't be quite so ready to listen, now will they? To every big strike lost there's a hundred others lost in future. I've been holding off from this town a long time. I thought they weren't ripe for it. I looked over the ground a good while before I made up my mind. Do you want to know what was the chief thing made me decide to come here this winter and stick it out? It was because I found you here. When I heard you talk to that crowd outside the Excelsior one night last year, I said to myself: "When the time comes, there's a man I can depend on." Well, I have depended on you. You don't want to give me cause to regret that, do you, Magnet? If it hadn't been for you things here could never have come to a head the way they have. You know that. It's no time for you to desert me now. You can't do more to prove your sorrow than to meet it the way a man ought. Come on down to the hall, Magnet. The boys are waiting.

MAGNET: [Painfully, after a pause.] I'm sorry. I can't do it, Ferguson.

FERGUSON: *Why* can't you do it?

MAGNET: [Moving away a little distance and speaking with great feeling.] You're a big man, Ferguson. You've got a big mind. You've got a big power. You know how to fight, and you know how to put fight into other men. You put it into me. I shan't ever forget the day you come into this

God-forsaken town. It give me a feeling I ain't had for a good many years—a feeling I'd clean forgot I ever could have. Well—I followed it. I've fought for you, Ferguson, every day and every night for these past two months, and I'd 'a' fought for you to the end for better or for worse if it hadn't been for this. There's something, Ferguson, a man's mind don't seem to have no power to make him understand. He's got to 'a' been there himself. You ain't got no children of your own, Ferguson. You can't understand there's some troubles comes first with a man. The whole world might be waiting for him to save it, but it'd have to wait. Nobody wouldn't have any right to interfere. You don't know what it is to a man, Ferguson, when somebody —when somebody— [MAGNET's voice breaks. He pauses and looks about hopelessly as if driven into a corner. Then, with a sudden, desperate gesture, he breaks out fiercely.] Damn it, there's some rotten coward, some beast, some low-down scoundrel has ruined my girl. I don't know who he is. But I want to know! I want to find out! I want to find him! I want to kill him! It's the only thing I do want. Until I've done that, this strike can go to hell. You can go to hell. They all can go to hell. [He drops into a chair and covers his face with his hands. FERGUSON watches him steadily in silence, then as he quiets a little begins to pace up and down.]

FERGUSON: This man you say has done your girl so much harm—how do you know but what she loved him?

MAGNET: [In a savage tone, looking up swiftly.] Loved him! Loved him! The damn dog. Suppose she *did* love him! What's that to do with it?

FERGUSON: [Very quietly, still pacing up and down and looking at the floor.] A whole lot. No man ever lived that ruined the woman that loved him. It can't be done. [There is such a deep conviction in FERGUSON's tone that MAGNET gazes at him in silent astonishment. FERGUSON

seats himself slowly, remaining silent a minute.] There's
something I might as well tell you, Magnet, if you have
a mind to listen. [A long pause follows, FERGUSON gazing
at the floor. Then he speaks in a low voice.] You are not
the only man in this town tonight whose hopes are lying
in a coffin.

MAGNET: [Startled, looking closely at FERGUSON.] You?
[FERGUSON nods.] Somebody close?

FERGUSON: Yes, somebody close.

MAGNET: Dead?

FERGUSON: [Heavily.] Yes, dead.

MAGNET: [After a pause, drawing closer.] It ain't your
wife?

FERGUSON: No, not my wife. [He moves restlessly, and
speaks, after a pause, in a changed tone.] It's been some time
since your girl's mother died, Magnet—isn't that so?

MAGNET: Fifteen years.

FERGUSON: I suppose you and she lived happy together,
didn't you?

MAGNET: [Solemnly.] We did that.

FERGUSON: Well—I wasn't so lucky. My wife and I
haven't lived together at all this many a day. If we had I'd
never be here in a loom worker's cottage, fighting within an
inch of my life to win a strike. I'd be sitting in some hotel
parlor hobnobbing with a lot of bishops and politicians and
college professors, trying to patch up a peace between the
mill owners and the strikers. I'd wear a medal and have a
good fat bank account. I'd kowtow to ladies and gentlemen.
They wouldn't hate me the way they do now—they'd only
snub me. I wouldn't stick out my tongue at the minister.
When I drank champagne and ate at swell restaurants I'd
do it on the quiet. The newspapers wouldn't hound me—
they'd praise me. I wouldn't be a scoundrel, an anarchist,
a cut-throat revolutionist. I'd be a respectable labor leader
—that's what I'd be if I'd stayed with my wife. Maybe you

think I'd better have stayed with her. [He laughs sneeringly.] There's plenty would agree with you in that opinion. [MAGNET makes a protesting gesture, but FERGUSON pays no attention.] Well, I didn't stay with her, I left her. A good living is all she gets out of me. It's all she ever will get. Except my name. She hangs on to that. And my freedom. She's got that locked up safe enough, or she thinks she has. She claims I'm not good enough to marry any other woman. [He laughs cynically.] Maybe she's right about that. But I was good enough for another woman to love me just the same. [With a touch of boyish pride.] She did love me anyhow, this other woman, whether I was good enough or not. She didn't get a living out of me. She didn't get my name. She didn't get a right to blame me if I was unfaithful to her—and I wasn't always faithful to her. She didn't even get a right to tell anybody she loved me, and it seems like that's what a woman hankers after the most of all. I never told her I loved her. She just had a sort of an idea I was glad she loved me. I *was* glad—for a kind of a queer reason. She kept me from feeling lonely. I'll say that for her—she was the only human being I've ever known that could stand between me and mortal loneliness. Maybe that means I loved her. I don't know. I don't suppose I did. [A pause.] Well, tonight, just before I took the train to come down here, I heard that woman was dead. I didn't enjoy the trip down so very much. [There is so much suppressed suffering in his voice that MAGNET instinctively reaches forward and lays a hand on his shoulder. FERGUSON shakes it off, rises and faces MAGNET.] You said to me I don't know how it feels to be a father. You're right about that, Magnet, dead right. I don't know. Being the kind of man I am, nobody seems to think I'm entitled to any connection with a family. A courtroom or a jail cell is supposed to be the place where my disposition thrives to the best advantage. The only kind of a father I've ever had a chance

to be you wouldn't call a father at all. You'd call him a
beast, a low-down scoundrel, a man that ruins other men's
daughters. Since my mother died, when I was a ten-year-
old kid working on the bunkers in a coal mine out in Colorado,
I've never known but one home, and that's in a dead
woman's heart. I'm alone now and likely to stay so. I
haven't any more hope of happiness in this world than I
have of going to heaven when I die, and that's none at all.
[With sudden, passionate emphasis.] But there's one thing
I don't ever forget, Magnet—unhappiness is a lot easier
to bear when you've got clothes to cover your back and
food enough to hold your body and soul together. When
I come to a town in the dead of winter and find twenty-five
thousand people on the edge of freezing and starvation, I
remember the time when my own mother went cold and
hungry, and it don't seem to make very much difference to
me whether I'm happy or not. [He takes up his hat as if to
leave, and moves a little toward the door.] As long as I
can keep alive to fight for those poor devils, I'll fight for 'em.
There was a while I expected others to feel the same way,
but I've got over that. Nobody knows any better than I
do how few men you're likely to run across in a lifetime
that'll join the ranks to stay. I used to take it pretty hard
when an old comrade fell out, but it don't make so much
difference any more. I've swallowed that kind of a disap-
pointment with my daily bread for so many years now that
it's got to be a pretty old story. There's one thing that
always helps me to stand it. If there's nobody else in this
world I can count on, I know I can always count on myself.
As long as there's breath in my body I'll never lose heart
and I'll never give up the game. A good part of the world
seems to look on me as a kind of a devil. Well, if that's
the way they feel about it, let 'em think so. I don't mind
being the kind of an individual that can walk through hell
without being scorched any so's you'd notice it. Life can

kill and bury my happiness, but it can't kill and bury my courage. This strike that's on in this town is the biggest I've ever handled. Without you to help me, Magnet, maybe I'll lose it. Or maybe I won't lose it. Maybe I'll win it anyhow. This night may mean the beginning of the end for me or it may mean the beginning of the biggest success I've ever known. But whichever way it is, you can be sure of one thing—if ever I go down it'll be with every man's hand against me and my back shoved up against a hard high wall. [There is a knock. FERGUSON opens the door and McGRATH steps just inside.]

McGRATH: Are you ready, Mr. Ferguson? Time's getting short.

FERGUSON: All ready, McGrath.

MAGNET: [Rising suddenly.] Hold on there a minute, Tim. [He walks to the dining room door and calls to MRS. LITTIG.] You needn't set the table till I get back, Mrs. Littig. I'm going down to the hall. [He takes his hat and walks to the door.]

FERGUSON: You take the machine and go on over, boys. I want to walk. I'll be with you in a few minutes. [MAGNET and McGRATH go out. FERGUSON closes the door and leans against it, raising his head and laying one hand across his mouth. As he stands there MRS. LITTIG enters hesitatingly, looking about to make sure MAGNET has gone. She walks over to FERGUSON, and standing before him, pulls from the neck of her dress a long ribbon and from it unties a gold ring which she hands to FERGUSON. She looks at him sadly and timidly but simply and quite without reproach.]

MRS. LITTIG: She said I was to give you this. She said I was to say she died happy. [Without waiting for comment or reply, MRS. LITTIG leaves the room by the dining room door. FERGUSON slips the ring in his vest pocket and walks slowly to the coffin. He stands behind it and looks down.]

TOWN
By Marie Baumer

PERSONS IN THE PLAY

FLORRIE
CARL
EDDIE
SID HARKER
JIM HARKER
MRS. HARKER
DELLA HARKER

TOWN

A SOFT drink parlor, in a small Army Post town in southern Pennsylvania. There is a screen door opening onto the street, and on either side of it windows strung with colored electric lights. There are also a counter and two round-topped tables with wire chairs, the kind found in ice-cream parlors. There is a door behind the counter, opening into a store-room, and in the opposite corner a battered victrola. The walls are covered with garish posters, advertising soft drinks.

FLORRIE, a girl of twenty-four, heavily rouged and lipsticked, is standing behind the counter, arguing with two men in privates' uniforms, EDDIE and CARL. CARL is short and squatty; EDDIE tall and good-looking in a cheap way. Both men are slightly flushed, as though they had been drinking.

EDDIE: Aw, come on, baby. We'll pay you next time.

FLORRIE: Yeh, I've heard that before. What d'you shoot craps for if you lose every cent that you earn?

CARL: Well, my God, we gotta do something interesting

once a week, ain't we? [FLORRIE takes two bottles of ginger ale from under the counter and uncorks them.]

FLORRIE: Oh all right. Here—

EDDIE: Thanks, sweetheart. [He leans across the counter and kisses her, then they take the bottles and go to a table at back. As they do so, SID HARKER enters.]

FLORRIE: [Looking after EDDIE.] Fresh!

SID: D'you want me to beat 'em up for you, Florrie?

FLORRIE: Why, Sid Harker! [JIM HARKER, a big, hearty hill man, and MRS. HARKER, a faded, tired looking little woman, come in behind SID.] And, Mrs. Harker—and Mr. Harker! How are you all? My land, you're turnin' out in grand style tonight.

MRS. HARKER: Yeh, ain't we?

JIM: We even got Della with us this trip.

FLORRIE: Della? No!—

JIM: We sure have. Hey, where is she anyhow?

MRS. HARKER: I guess she's out watchin' the Salvation Army band. I notice it sorta took her eye.—[To FLORRIE.] She ain't used to crowds or anything.

JIM: Well, call her in or she'll be gettin' lost.

MRS. HARKER: Della! Della, come here—

SID: I'm goin' across the street, Pa. I'll meet you here when it's time to go home—huh?

JIM: Yeh, and don't keep us waitin'. We got a two hour drive back—

FLORRIE: You mean to say you spend four hours on the road for one hour in town?

JIM: Sure. Why not?

MRS. HARKER: Listen now, Sid, don't you go eatin' any more of them banana splits. Remember, last Saturday you was sick all the way home.

SID: It was worth it. [As he leaves.] And if I feel like eatin' banana splits I guess my stomach ain't goin' to stop me. [As he goes out he passes DELLA in the doorway.

DELLA is not quite eighteen, with work-worn hands and the face of a stolid child who has always accepted things without question.]

MRS. HARKER: Come here, Della. [Taking her by the arm.] This is Florrie Spoonhour—d'you remember?

FLORRIE: [Smiling at her.] How are you, Della? I ain't seen you in five years, I guess—not since I came to town.

DELLA: [Looking at her with wide, slightly vacant eyes.] Oh, yeh. How are you?

JIM: I'm goin' up street, Ma. And see you're right here when I'm ready to go home—even if you have to wait for me.

MRS. HARKER: All right. [As JIM starts out, CARL suddenly leans forward and hails him.]

CARL: Why, hello there, partner! I thought I recognized you. Don't you remember—we was both down at that house on—

JIM: [In consternation, glancing at MRS. HARKER.] Shhhh!

CARL: Oh, excuse me! [He and EDDIE go into a spasm of stifled laughter, and JIM hurriedly goes out. MRS. HARKER glances after him, then raises her shoulders in a barely perceptible, weary shrug.]

MRS. HARKER: Florrie, I wonder, would you mind if Della stayed here with you while I did some shoppin' in the five and ten?

FLORRIE: Not at all, Mrs. Harker—I'd be glad to have her.

MRS. HARKER: You'll stay here then, will you, Della?

DELLA: Yes, Ma—

MRS. HARKER: I'll be back in twenty minutes, at the most. [She smiles her tired little smile, and goes out.]

FLORRIE: [Leaning across the counter.] So this is your first trip to town—huh?

DELLA: Yeh, I always had to stay with the kids before, but Lucy's big enough to do that now.

FLORRIE: How d'you like it here?

DELLA: Gee, it's wonderful, ain't it! So many people— and lights—it's like somethin' in a book.

FLORRIE: Oh, well, you get used to it. Still, it's better'n seein' nothin' but a lot of hills all the time. You know, I heard about you.

DELLA: About me?

FLORRIE: Yeh, my brother was tellin' me about you the last time he was down here. He says you're the strongest girl he ever seen— He says you can chop wood and plow like a man. He says you'd be grand to have around a farm. It sounded to me like he was thinkin' of marryin' you.

DELLA: A lot of 'em want to.

FLORRIE: They would! The damn lazy good for nothin's! It's too bad a truck horse can't bear 'em children—they'd be matin' up with them as fast as they could. [DELLA hardly hears her. Her eyes are roaming around the room.]

DELLA: It must be nice, bein' in here— All them colors— [FLORRIE studies her with wise half-pitying eyes.]

FLORRIE: You work pretty hard at home, don't you, Della?

DELLA: I guess so—

FLORRIE: Don't you ever get tired, though?

DELLA: I don't have time.

FLORRIE: [Turning away.] My God! [EDDIE and CARL have been whispering together, and EDDIE suddenly smiles across at them.]

EDDIE: Say, Florrie, who's your girl friend? Has she got a friend? [DELLA turns and looks at them, and he grins.] Come on over, kid, and get acquainted.

FLORRIE: D'you want to?

DELLA: Yes.

FLORRIE: All right. [She takes DELLA by the arm and leads her to the table.] I want you to meet Carl Williams and Eddie Lane— This is Della Harker, an old friend of mine from up home.

CARL: Pleased to meet you.

DELLA: How are you?

EDDIE: Couldn't be better now that I've met you! Sit down and make yourself at home. [She sits down and he looks across at her.] So you're a little mountain flower just like Florrie, are you?

DELLA: Yes.

EDDIE: Well, I like the mountains and I like flowers, so that's O.K.

FLORRIE: To say nothin' of likin' yourself.

EDDIE: Never mind, young woman, no remarks from the cheap seats! [To DELLA.] I've never seen you around here before, have I?

DELLA: [Her eyes fastened on him.] No—

EDDIE: I thought there was something missing in this town. [Noticing her intent scrutiny of him, with his flashing grin.] What's the matter—are y'admiring my uniform?

DELLA: Yes.

EDDIE: Well, I'm only a private now, but in sixty years I'll be a Colonel. [DELLA smiles shyly, and he puts his hand over hers.] Gee, you're not so bad lookin' at that.

FLORRIE: Hey, go easy, will you?

EDDIE: Oh, shut up. Make her shut up, will you, Carl?

CARL: [Waggling his finger at her.] Shut up now, Florrie.

FLORRIE: [Backing away and beginning to giggle.] Stop it, you! Don't you dare tickle me—

[He begins to tickle her and she goes off into spasms of laughter.] Stop it—stop it, I say! You'll kill me. [They subside in the background, where CARL winds the victrola.]

EDDIE: [Turning his eyes back to DELLA.] She's a great baby, isn't she?

DELLA: Yes—

EDDIE: Say, is that the only word you know? [Putting his finger to his lip and winking.] Wait a minute, though, and I'll give you something that'll teach you the alphabet. [He takes a bottle out of his pocket. CARL has turned on the victrola, and he and FLORRIE dance forward. EDDIE pours the contents of the bottle into a glass.]

FLORRIE: Hey, don't give her any of that!

EDDIE: Why not? We gotta get rid of it, somehow. We can't take the bottle back to the barracks—

FLORRIE: But she's not used to it.

EDDIE: Aw sure she is, aren't you, sweetheart? There's plenty of likker in them thar hills. [Flourishing the bottle.] Just a moonshiner's gal, but I love her still!

FLORRIE: [Dancing away again.] Well, don't give her more'n a drop.

EDDIE: [Holding out the glass to DELLA.] Come on, try it— [She takes it and drinks it down.] Atta baby! More?

DELLA: [Choking a little.] I don't think so—

EDDIE: Then never mind about the thinking. [Pouring out more.] Women ain't meant to use their brains, anyway. They're just meant to be sweet and pretty like you are.

DELLA: Am I?

EDDIE: Didn't anyone ever tell you that before?

DELLA: No.

EDDIE: Go on, don't try to kid me. Do you mean to tell me fellows never paid you compliments?

DELLA: No, never. [EDDIE looks at her, then laughs.]

EDDIE: Do you like 'em?

DELLA: Yes—I guess I like 'em a lot.

EDDIE: You're a funny little cuss. I never met 'em like you before.

DELLA: I didn't, either—I mean, met 'em like you.

EDDIE: Gee, you're right there with the come-back, aren't you? You're improving, baby—d' you know it? [Lifting his glass.] **Come on, once again.** To us—[DELLA lifts her glass awkwardly and he clinks his against it. They drink.]

FLORRIE: [Stopping.] Say, didn't I tell you— [CARL starts to tickle her again and she turns from DELLA with a shriek.] Stop it! [CARL starts chasing her around the room, and DELLA begins to laugh; a joyous, untrammelled laugh. She is like one who has never laughed much before.]

DELLA: Look out, Florrie—he'll catch you!

EDDIE: That's right, Carl—show her who's master around here.

DELLA: [Turning her laughing eyes to EDDIE.] They're crazy.

EDDIE: It's nice to be crazy once in a while.

DELLA: Yes, it is—it is nice. [Twisting her glass around.] You—you get tired of actin' old—sometimes—

EDDIE: Old! How old are you?

DELLA: Seventeen.

EDDIE: Oh, my God! A regular antique—

DELLA: Well, it ain't so young, I guess. That's what they all say, anyhow—

EDDIE: Who says?

DELLA: My father—and other people. My sister Ella— she's nineteen, and she's been married four years.

EDDIE: Can y'imagine that! That's a hot one! You will have to hurry to catch up. But tonight you can be as young and skittish as you please—huh?

DELLA: Yeh—

EDDIE: That's right, always agree with me. [Holding out his arms.] How about a little dance?

DELLA: I don't know how—

EDDIE: Aw, come on, it's easy. [She gets up and he puts his arms around her.] Just keep in step with the music. [They dance a little.] That's right. Like it?

DELLA: Yeh— Gee, it's fun, ain't it? I wish we didn't ever have to stop—

223

EDDIE: Well, who says we do? [Putting both arms around her.] You know, I think we're goin' to get along better and better.

DELLA: Do you?

EDDIE: Why not? The minute I seen you I thought, now there's the loveliest little girl I'll ever have the good luck to meet.

DELLA: But I'm not lovely—

EDDIE: Oh, now don't begin that again. You know damn well you are. With hair like yours—and those beautiful eyes—and that pretty little mouth you got. [He winks broadly over her head at CARL and CARL grins.]

DELLA: I like you, too.

EDDIE: No! Honest? Gee, I can die happy then. [CARL and FLORRIE start whirling around.]

DELLA: Let's try the step they're doin'—shall we?

EDDIE: That's right—get ambitious. [He starts whirling her around, and they collide with CARL and FLORRIE.] Say, quit bumping into my girl.

FLORRIE: Who's doin' any bumpin'? Not us!

EDDIE: Oh, is that so! [He sticks out his foot and trips her up. Immediately there is a wild scramble and roughhouse; one couple bumping into the other, dancing faster and faster, chasing each other around, while FLORRIE keeps shrieking delightedly, "Stop it! Stop it, I tell you!" DELLA laughs, a feverish, excited laugh, and begins to do some pulling and pushing herself.]

DELLA: That's it—trip 'em up! Go on, trip 'em up!

EDDIE: [Rocking with laughter.] Atta baby, Della! You'll protect me, won't you? [She gives CARL a wild push that almost knocks him over.]

CARL: My gosh, she's comin' to life, all right.

EDDIE: I'll say she is!

DELLA: [Raising her face to EDDIE's.] He can't push us, can he? We'll show him—

224

CARL: Oh, will you! [He musses her hair and backs away, DELLA after him. But FLORRIE catches her by the arm suddenly sober.]

FLORRIE: Wait a minute! We've had enough of this. I told you not to give her that bum likker.

EDDIE: [Taking DELLA back into his arms.] Aw, boloney! She's all right.

FLORRIE: Well, behave yourselves then.

CARL: [Dancing with FLORRIE again.] Yes, you behave yourselves now, or we'll have to throw you outa this dance hall.

EDDIE: She hasn't had too much to drink, have you?

DELLA: No, I—I'm just beginnin' to enjoy myself, I guess—

EDDIE: That's the spirit. [They are dancing more slowly, EDDIE gazing down at her, their faces close together. He glances up furtively, sees that FLORRIE is dancing with her back towards them, then quickly bends his head and kisses DELLA, holding her tightly. After a moment she pulls away sharply and her eyes avoid his, but she does not release herself from his embrace. They dance in silence a moment. CARL and FLORRIE stand over by the victrola, winding it. Then EDDIE looks down at DELLA again.]

EDDIE: How about another one?

DELLA: No.

EDDIE: Just one more?

DELLA: [In a low voice.] I don't want to.

EDDIE: I might believe you if I didn't know women so well. [Tilting up her face.] And you got the wrong kind of face—you got the kind of face where everything shows. You don't know how to hide things, do you, sister? [They dance without speaking again for a second, and when she does speak it is in a scarcely audible voice.]

DELLA: All right.

EDDIE: All right what?

225

DELLA: You can if you want to. [EDDIE grins triumphantly and kisses her, then starts to whistle cockily. DELLA's face turned away from his, is alight with a dawning, half-bewildered radiance. After a moment, EDDIE stops and looks at his wrist-watch.]

EDDIE: Well, ladies, much as we hate to I guess we gotta be leaving you.

DELLA: Oh, no—not yet.

EDDIE: Why? Will you miss me?

DELLA: Yes, and—[glancing out the window] nobody else is goin' home yet, are they? It's still early—

FLORRIE: Not so early, at that. The stores'll be closin' in half an hour.

DELLA: But we only just came. It's only just started for us—all the fun and everything.

EDDIE: It's too bad, sweetheart, but I guess we can't turn back the clocks just for you. And the army is the army, ain't it, Carl?

CARL: And how!

EDDIE: But never mind—I'll never forget you till the day of my death, if I live to be a hundred!

DELLA: You mean it—honestly?

EDDIE: So help me God!

DELLA: Will I—will I be seein' you again?

EDDIE: Gosh, listen to her! Trying to date me up, no less—

DELLA: No, but I will see you, though—

EDDIE: Oh, probably. You might call at the barracks the next time you're in town.

FLORRIE: [Slipping her arm around DELLA.] Smarty! Think you're damn funny, don't you!

EDDIE: Sure—don't you? [With a half mocking little bow to DELLA.] And thanks for a very pleasant evening.

CARL: So long, kid. So long, Florrie. See you in the funny papers.

EDDIE: [Holding the door open and lighting a cigarette.] Come on, make it snappy. That Sergeant's got his eye on us as it is. [CARL and EDDIE go out, EDDIE not glancing back at DELLA. DELLA looks after them, then starts forward suddenly.]

DELLA: No, no, don't go. [She stops, and her arm falls to her side.]

FLORRIE: I'm sorry they got so fresh, Della. I was afraid of that when I introduced you.

DELLA: [Still looking after them.] They weren't fresh. Gee, he's good lookin', ain't he—and his uniform and all—

FLORRIE: A uniform helps, all right enough.

DELLA: I didn't know there was men like that—men who could say things like he did. Did you hear what he said about my eyes, Florrie? He said they was beautiful.

FLORRIE: Yeh, he's full of bull.

DELLA: [Looking around her, slowly.] I didn't know there was *anything* like this. Colors—and lights—

FLORRIE: [Anxiously, putting her arm around her.] Say, Della, that stuff didn't really make you drunk, did it?

DELLA: No.

FLORRIE: Because I'd hate to have your family think— [The door at back opens and MRS. HARKER comes in.] Oh, hello, Mrs. Harker—we were wonderin' where you were.

MRS. HARKER: I didn't mean to be so long, but I just couldn't tear myself away from the five and ten. My, they got wonderful things in there, ain't they? [To DELLA.] Your Pa ain't been back yet, has he?

DELLA: No.

MRS. HARKER: I thought my heart'd jump into my mouth when I looked up and seen the time. I run all the way over for fear he was waitin'. [DELLA stands silent as though her thoughts were far away. MRS. HARKER glances over her shoulder at FLORRIE who is clearing the bottles from the table, then moves closer to her daughter.]

MRS. HARKER: Look, Della, I wanta show you somethin' I bought— [She opens a bag and takes out a cheap little bracelet.]

DELLA: Ma!

MRS. HARKER: Ain't it beautiful? And only ten cents. They had pins, too, and diamond rings and strings of pearls —but I've always wanted a bracelet, somehow. [Slipping it on her wrist.] I don't know why—I won't be able to wear it. [Putting it back in the bag quickly.] Don't tell your Pa I bought it, will you?

DELLA: [Staring at her as though she were seeing her for the first time.] No! [FLORRIE joins them and they stand in a little knot, talking. SID and JIM come in.]

JIM: You mean to say you think she's good-lookin' with all that paint and powder stuck on?

SID: Yes, I do! At least, she don't look like the women up our way.

JIM: [Slowly.] Yeh, that's true. It *is* nice to see a woman with her hair fixed pretty once in a while. Oh, well, there ain't no use thinkin' of that. [Calling to the women.] Are you all set to go?

MRS. HARKER: Yes.

JIM: Then hurry up and stop dawdling. Florrie wants to close up, anyhow.

FLORRIE: I guess I'll go downstairs and switch off the lights, if you don't mind. And give the folks my love, won't you?

JIM: Sure will.

SID: You better come home for a visit soon, Florrie.

FLORRIE: [Starting to go out.] I will—some time. Good-bye, Mrs. Harker.

MRS. HARKER: Good-bye, Florrie.

FLORRIE: Good-bye, Della. [DELLA does not answer, but stands staring ahead as though she saw and heard nothing but her own thoughts. FLORRIE laughs a little and

228

turns back to the others.] Well, so long! [She goes out.]

JIM: Didn't you hear Florrie speak to you? Have you lost your tongue or what?

MRS. HARKER: [Taking his arm.] Oh, leave her alone, Jim, she's tired.

SID: Come on, Pa, or we'll just get caught in the jam. They're all startin' out right now.

JIM: Well, go and unhitch the buggy a while. [To his wife, as they start out.] You better sit in back goin' home so Sid can drive if I get sleepy.

MRS. HARKER: All right. I got a lotta bundles in back, too. [They go out, and DELLA is left standing by the counter. The lights in the windows along the walls go out, all except a little lamp on the counter which throws its light around her. JIM reappears.]

JIM: Della! What are you waitin' for? Don't you know we're in a hurry!

DELLA: I ain't goin'.

JIM: What! What are you talkin' about?

DELLA: I ain't goin'. [MRS. HARKER and SID appear.]

JIM: Come on, now, and stop this nonsense!

DELLA: [Jerking away from him, with sudden passion.] No! No! I won't go back there—I won't go back, I tell you!

SID: For God's sake, what's the matter with her! Is she crazy?

JIM: [Shaking her a little.] Della!

DELLA: [Backs away.] Leave go of me! You can't get me to go with you. All my life I done nothin' but work, work all the time and I never knew I was workin'! Just cookin' and plowin' and cookin' again. That's all I ever seen was a stove, and hills—hills shuttin' you up! And no people to look at but the ones you'd always seen—never anything new—or pretty. But now I'm goin' to stay here—here! [She buries her face in her hands and begins to sob.]

229

JIM: [Looking at SID, dumbfounded.] My God, she *must* be crazy.

MRS. HARKER: [Touching her arm timidly.] Della!

SID: Maybe she's drunk or somethin'—

JIM: [Lifting her chin.] Have you been drinkin'? By Judas, she has! [Shaking her.] Was it Florrie gave it to you? Answer me! [She stands motionless, like a statue, and he scratches his head helplessly. Then his anger floods back.] All right, young lady, don't answer me if you don't wanta. But this is the last time we'll ever bring you into town.

DELLA: No!

JIM: And as for stayin' here, you ain't got money to stay anywheres. And besides, you ain't of age yet—you know that.

DELLA: Pa—you didn't mean that—about not bringin' me in again—

JIM: Sure I mean it.

DELLA: No, no—please! I'll be good—I'll go home with you—

JIM: Well! That sounds more like it.

DELLA: Only you gotta bring me in with you again! You will, won't you?

JIM: That all depends on how you act—and how lively you step right now. [DELLA stares at him, then puts on her hat.]

DELLA: All right—I'm comin'.

JIM: [Wiping his brow as he goes.] I never heard of anything like that in all my born days!

SID: [Still looking at DELLA, dumbfounded]. Gee, what likker won't do to you—huh? [They go out and DELLA starts to follow after. MRS. HARKER timidly lays her hand on her arm.]

MRS. HARKER: Never mind, Della. Saturday night'll come round again.

DELLA: Yeh—

MRS. HARKER: [As they go.] It's only seven days off, and you'd be surprised how quick they go if you just sorta keep your eyes fixed on Saturday—that's all. Just keep on thinkin' ahead to Saturday. I know.

THE NO 'COUNT BOY
By Paul Green

PERSONS IN THE PLAY

Pheelie
Enos
The No 'Count Boy
An Old Negro Woman

THE NO 'COUNT BOY

THE small yard immediately before a Negro cabin. At the right front is a thick lilac bush with a bench beside it, and to the left from this a clumpy china tree with a rocking chair under it. At the left rear is a well, roughly boarded up, a chain and battered tin bucket hanging from a cross-piece above. In the back is the cabin. Rickety steps lead up to the door in the center. It is an afternoon late in summer.

PHEELIE, a neat Negro girl of seventeen, is sitting on the bench by the lilac tree looking through a book. She is dressed in cheap clothes—a white dress, white shoes and stockings. Presently there is the sound of an approaching buggy in the lane off at the left and a voice calls, "Whoa!" PHEELIE listens a moment, and then, without turning her head, gives it a toss and goes on fingering the leaves of her book. ENOS comes in and stands watching her. He is a short stocky Negro of twenty or more, dressed in a faded gray suit and black felt hat. His celluloid collar and scarlet tie shine out brilliantly against the black of his face.

235

Enos: [In a drawling voice that now and then drops into a stammer.] Well, Pheelie, heah I is.

Pheelie: I see you is, and you's 'bout a hour early.

Enos: But ain't you all dressed up to go?

Pheelie: I's dressed up, but I ain't ready to go.

Enos: Well, suh, now—I—I—

Pheelie: I des' put on dese heah clothes 'caze it was so hot in de house wid my work duds on. [He takes off his hat and discloses his naturally kinky hair combed back in a straight pompadour. He waits for her to notice it, but she keeps looking straight before her.] Set down and rest yo'se'f. [Somewhat ill at ease he sits down in the rocking-chair and watches her.]

Enos: I drapped by a little early hoping—a—mebbe you'd lak to take a small drive befo' church begun.

Pheelie: Thanky, I don't believe I wants to take no drive. [She becomes absorbed in her book.]

Enos: [Picking at the lining of his hat.] And I thought we mought stop by Buie's Creek and git some ice cream. [He watches her narrowly.]

Pheelie: Dat'd be nice, I reckon, but I don't want no ice cream nuther. [She is silent again. He pulls nervously at his fingers, making the joints pop.] And I'd be much obliged if you'd quit popping yo' finger j'ints.

Enos: [Jerking his hands apart and running his fingers over his greased hair.] 'Scuse me, Pheelie. [Somewhat timidly, but with a hidden touch of spirit.] You—you don't seem glad to see me much.

Pheelie: You didn't have no date to come over heah a hour befo' time.

Enos: I knows it. But whut's de matter wid you? You ain't mad at me, is you?

Pheelie: No, I ain't mad.

Enos: Seems lak you'd druther look at dat old book dan talk to me.

236

PHEELIE: Mebbe I had. [He feels his tie, twirls his hat, and spits softly through his teeth off to one side.]

ENOS: Whut sorter book is it, Pheelie?

PHEELIE: Whut difference do it make to you? You ain't int'rested in no book.

ENOS: 'Speck dat's right. But you sho' seems mo' tuk wid it dan anything I ever seed you have befo'.

PHEELIE: It's a fine pitchture book.

ENOS: Whah'd you git it?

PHEELIE: Dis mawning I was up to Mis' Ella's helping her hoe out de gyarden, and she told me a whole heap 'bout de places she and Mr. Jack went when dey was merried. And she give me dis book dat showed a passel of things.

ENOS: Hunh, dey had money to travel wid and enjoy deirselves.

PHEELIE: She said one place dey went to was some sorter Falls or something lak dat, whah de water poured over in a great river and made a racket same as de world was busting up.

ENOS: Dat ain't nothing—mostly talk, I bet a dollar.

PHEELIE: [Closing her book with a bang.] Dat's whut you allus says. You don't care a straw 'bout gwine off and seeing things.

ENOS: Ain't I done told you, honey bunch, we ain't gwine have no money to be traipsing round de world, not yit nohow.

PHEELIE: Don't you honey me no mo', I tells you.

ENOS: Whut'n de name of Old Scratch ails you? Ain't I gut a right to honey you? And you engaged to me.

PHEELIE: Engaged to you! It's you engaged to me.

ENOS: Aw right, I's engaged to you den, and you knows mighty drot'n well I's glad to be too. Dey ain't no put-on wid me.

PHEELIE: I reckon you is glad. But you mess wid me and you won't be engaged to nothing.

Enos: Now, Pheelie, you better th'ow dat book in de far and come on and le's go foh a drive, it's stirred you all up. Come on, I's gut a mess of news to tell you.

Pheelie: I ain't gwine on no drive. And I's 'bout decided not to go wid you to no meeting tonight nuther.

Enos: Lawd, don't talk lak dat. Heah I's been waiting all de week foh dis Sadd'y night, and you ain't gwine back on me, is you?

Pheelie: But, Enos, you's so samey, allus satisfied wid whut you has. You des' gits my goat.

Enos: If you means I ain't tuk wid no wild idees or sich 'bout trips way off yonder to see folks making fools of deirselves, den I is samey. But you listen heah, chile, dey ain't no meracles and sich off dere lak what you thinks. Onct I spent a good five dollars gwine on a s'cursion to Wilmington, and dey wa'n't a thing to see, not ha'f as much as dey is on dis heah farm.

Pheelie: You gut to have eyes to see things. Some folks is natchly bawn blind.

Enos: Well, mebbe when we's married we'll take a little trip to Raleigh or Durham and see de street cyars and big buildings.

Pheelie: But I wants to go furder, furder clean to de mountains, and right on den mebbe.

Enos: 'Y craps, must think I gut a can of money buried somewhah.

Pheelie: I don't nuther. Us could hobo, or walk part de way, des' fool along.

Enos: Hobo! Us'd hobo right into some white man's jail, dat's whut. And dey ain't nothing to dat walking business. We'd be a purty sight wid our feet blistered and somebody's bulldog tearing plugs out'n—well, you knows whut.

Pheelie: Setting dere looking through dat book I gut plumb sick and tar'd of you and all dis farming and sweating and gitting nowhah—sick of everything. And des looking at

238

old lazy Lawrence dancing over the fields made me want to puke.

ENOS: Honey chile, de last time I was heah you said you'd lak it working in de fields wid me and keeping de house and sich.

PHEELIE: I will, Enos, I reckons I will. But dat dere book set me to wanting to go off and git away.

ENOS: [Moving his chair over to her.] Listen to me. I knows I ain't fitten to breave on you, but I's gwine do my best by you. And whut you reckon? Mr. Pearson done told me today dat he's having de lumber sawed to build our house. September she'll be done, den you'n me kin have business—kin see de preacher.

PHEELIE: Mr. Pearson's good to you awright.

ENOS: Ain't he! Dat's a man whut is a man. And it ain't all foh me he's building dat house. He laks you and says he'll be glad to have you on his place.

PHEELIE: Whut kind of house is it—des' a shack wid a stick-and-dirt chimley?

ENOS: Now I was des' a-hoping you'd ax dat. No, suh, it ain't no cow-shed you could th'ow a dog through de cracks—nunh—unh. It's gwine be a nice frame house wid a wide po'ch, and it'll be ceiled. And listen heah, it's gwine have wallpaper. And, honey, Mr. Pearson said he wanted you to come up a-Monday and help choose de pattern. [He looks at her delightedly.]

PHEELIE: Oh, dat's so nice of you and him! [She bows her head.]

ENOS: Whut's de matter now?

PHEELIE: [Looking up with tears in her eyes.] You's too good to me, Enos, and I hadn't ort to allus be so onsatisfied.

ENOS: Sho', never mind now. [He puts his arm around her.]

PHEELIE: [Letting her hand rest on his hair.] Grannys alive! you done spent money to git yo' hair straightened.

239

ENOS: Yeh, yeh, I has. But it was to celebrate a little.

PHEELIE: Dat's th'owing away a dollar and a half. In a little bit it'll be kinky ag'in.

ENOS: Course it will, but I thought you'd lak it while it lasts.

PHEELIE: You sho' is a proud nigger. [She kisses him quickly and stands away from him.] Nunh—unh, I ain't gwine do it no mo'. [He drops reluctantly back into his seat, and she sits again on the bench.]

ENOS: You want to take dat little drive now?

PHEELIE: I mought, I guess.

ENOS: Hot dog, den le's go, honey!

PHEELIE: Lemme shet up de house and we'll be ready. Muh and Pap and all de kids is over to de ice cream supper at Uncle Haywood's befo' preaching. [She starts up.]

ENOS: [Standing up.] Aw right, honey babe. I sho' laks to see you jollied up. And I's gut anudder surprise foh you too.

PHEELIE: You has?

ENOS: Unh—hunh. But I'll tell you a little later.

PHEELIE: Naw, suh, tell me now—please.

ENOS: In course I cain't stand out ag'in you. Well, we ain't gwine drive behime no flop-yured mule dis time.

PHEELIE: We ain't!

ENOS: Naw, suh, I's driving Egyp' today.

PHEELIE: Mr. Pearson's fine hoss!

ENOS: Yeh, yeh, sho' is. I worked hard all de week, and dis mawning he come to me and axed me if I didn't want Egyp' to haul you wid tonight.

PHEELIE: Dere he is. Ain't dat fine, and is he safe?

ENOS: Safe! Safe as a cellar. But, Lawd, he kin burn de wind!

PHEELIE: Goody-good. Now come help me shet de house.

ENOS: [As they go off.] Mr. Pearson knows I ain't gwine beat his stock and bellows 'em lak some de niggers. I tells you, sugar lump, if we stays wid him and do right, some dese days we gwine have money to take dem dere trips you wants to.

[They have hardly disappeared when a slender Negro youth of sixteen or seventeen, barefooted and raggedly dressed in an old pair of overalls, shirt and torn straw hat, comes in and stands staring after them. He is whittling a green walking-stick. In a moment he pulls out a small mouth organ and begins playing a whirling jig.]

Enos: [Coming back around the corner.] Who's dat playing to beat de band? [He and Pheelie come back into the yard. Pheelie stares at the boy in delighted astonishment. Suddenly he winds up on a high note. As he beats the saliva out of the harp against his thigh, he bursts into a loud joyous laugh.]

Pheelie: Lawd, you kin play. Who is you?

Enos: Whut you want heah? I ain't never seed you befo'.

Boy: [In a clear childish voice, as he looks at Pheelie.] You ain't?

Enos: Naw, I ain't. Whut you mean walking up in people's yards and acting lak you was home?

Boy: I thought I mought git me a drink from de well dere.

Pheelie: Help yo'se'f. [He draws water and drinks. Enos and Pheelie watch him.]

Enos: I bet he's some boy run away from home. Mebbe a tramp, I dunno.

Pheelie: Dat boy a tramp! Hunh, he ain't no sich.

Enos: I bet you on it. Looks s'picious to me.

Boy: [Coming back from the well and wiping his mouth with his sleeve.] I thought I mought git a bite to eat heah mebbe. [He looks from one to the other, a lurking smile in his eyes.]

Pheelie: You mought.

Enos: Lak as not de lady wants to know whah you come from and whut yo' business is befo' she 'gins to feed you.

241

Boy: [Looking at Pheelie.] Would you?

Pheelie: Yeh. Whut's yo' name?

Boy: [Laughing and blowing out a whiff of music.] Mostly I ain't gut no name. [Beating the harp in his hand and scratching his leg with his toe.] 'Way 'way back down dere—[pointing indefinitely behind him]—whar I come from some of 'em calls me Pete, but mostly dey calls me de No 'Count Boy.

Enos: Why dey call you dat fo'?

Boy: 'Caze I don't lak to work in de fields.

Enos: Unh—hunh, unh—hunh, I s'picioned it.

Boy: S'picioned whut?

Enos: Aw, nothing. Anyhow dat's a good name foh you, I bet. Whose boy is you and whah'd you come from 'way back down dere as you calls it?

Boy: Cuts no wool whose boy I is. As foh whah I come from, I cain't tell you, bo, 'caze I dunno hardly. [Hesitating and pointing off in the distance.] You see whah de sky come down to de earf—'way, 'way yonder?

Enos: I sees it.

Boy: Well, I come from miles and miles beyont it. Lawd, Lawd, how fuh has I come?

Pheelie: You been all dat distance by yo'se'f?

Boy: Sho' has. And whut's mo' I walked it every jump. [Again he draws the harp across his lips in a breath of music, all the while watching them with bright eyes.]

Enos: Whah you gwine?

Boy: Des' gwine.

Pheelie: You mean you ain't gut no special place in mind —you des' hoboing along?

Boy: Dat's it, I reckon.

Enos: How does you git yo' rations—beg foh it?

Boy: I pays foh it when I kin git 'em. 'Times I goes hongry.

Enos: You ain't gut no money, has you?

242

Boy: Dat's awright. I pays foh it des' de same. [He stops and looks at Pheelie with big eyes.] You's as purty as a pink, ain't you?

Pheelie: [Turning away her head.] Why you ax dat?

Enos: You needn't be thinking you gwine git yo' supper on soft talk, hoss-cake.

Boy: Whut's yo' name?

Pheelie: My name's Ophelia, but dey calls me Pheelie.

Boy: [Staring at her admiringly and cracking his palm against his thigh.] Dawg-gone! des' lak me foh de world. I's named one thing and dey calls me anudder.

Enos: Heah, I 'specks you better be gwine on up de road. Me'n Miss Pheelie des' ready to go out foh our afternoon drive, and we don't want to be bothered wid nobody's no 'count boy.

Boy: I hates to hinder you, Miss Pheelie, and cain't I git nothing t'eat—a 'tater or anything?

Pheelie: I 'speck I could give you a snack in yo' hand right quick.

Boy: No sooner said'n done, I hopes. And I pays you foh it too.

Enos: Gut yo' pockets full of silver and gold, apt as not.

Boy: Naw, suh, I gut something better'n money. Heah she is. [Holding up his harp.] I plays you a piece or two pieces or three, and you gives me a bite and whut you pleases. [In mock seriousness he pulls off his hat and addresses them.] Ladies and ge'men, de fust piece I renders is called "De Dark-eyed 'Oman." It's music 'bout a 'oman whut had three little boys, and dey tuck sick and died one June night whilst de mockingbirds was singing. And allus adder dat dey said she had a dark shadow in her dark eyes. [He clears his throat, spits once or twice and lays the harp gently to his lips. Closing his eyes, he begins to play. Enos stirs about him as the notes flood from the boy's mouth, and now and then he looks questioningly at Pheelie's averted face. The boy's nostrils

243

quiver, and he makes a sobbing sound in his throat. Tears begin to pour down his cheeks. After a moment he winds up with a flourish.]

ENOS: Lawd Jesus, dat rascal kin blow!

BOY: [Looking at PHEELIE as he wipes his eyes.] I hopes you don't mind. Every time I blows dat piece I cries. [PHEELIE glances up with moist eyes.]

PHEELIE: I sho' don't mind. Whah you learn dat?

BOY: It's a made piece.

ENOS: Who made it?

BOY: Me.

ENOS: Hunh, you mought!

BOY: You believes I made it, don't you, Miss Pheelie?

PHEELIE: Dat I do.

BOY: Aw right den. And I'll play you anudder piece foh dat snack of grub.

PHEELIE: Dat one's enough to pay.

ENOS: You sho' you didn't git no rations down de road?

BOY: Not nary a chaw.

PHEELIE: Ain't you had nothing all day?

BOY: Nothing but some branch water and a little bitsy bird I killed wid a rock and fried. [His face takes on a sober look, and tears again glisten in his eyes.]

ENOS: You sho' is a quare fellow.

BOY: Dat little bird was singing so sweet and ruffling his breast in de wind, and I picked up a rock and des' th'owed devilish lak, never thought I'd hit him. But dat's de way it is —when you thinks you won't, you does, and I kilt him.

PHEELIE: And den you et him?

BOY: [Wiping his eyes on his sleeves.] I was so hongry den, and I built a speck of fire and baked him. Warn't it better foh me to eat him dan foh maggits to git at him?

PHEELIE: 'Twas dat.

BOY: But I sho' felt bad 'bout dat little bird. I cain't git his chune out'n my haid. He sot on dat limb and would give a long call and den a short one—des' lak dat.

ENOS: You's a mighty big fellow to be crying over a bird, seems lak to me.

PHEELIE: Enos, you quit dat making fun.

BOY: When I come through de creek back dere, a good-god was pecking in a high daid tree, and he turnt his haid sideways and whickered at me. I heahd him say he gwine ha'nt me foh killing dat bird.

ENOS: I swear! [PHEELIE gives him a cutting look, and he stops his laughing.]

BOY: I've hearn dat dem good-gods is old women turnt to birds 'caze dey was weeked. And you see dey's still gut on little old red caps.

PHEELIE: Dey won't hurt you.

ENOS: Pshaw, dey ain't nothing but great big sapsuckers.

BOY: How you know? Des' de same dis'n scolded me foh th'owing dat rock. I could tell it in his talk and de way he looked at me.

PHEELIE: You didn't mean to do it nohow, and you was hongry too. Now play us some mo'.

BOY: I 'speck mebbe den it's awright, I 'speck so. Now I plays you my udder piece to pay you plenty foh my eatings.

PHEELIE: 'Tain't dat, 'tain't dat. We laks to heah you. I'll feed you foh nothing.

BOY: Well, listen to dis, folkses. [He again pulls off his hat and makes his stage bow.] Ladies and ge'men, dis is a talking piece I's gwine render. It's 'titled "De Coffin Song," and tells 'bout a nice gal whut went away from home all dressed out in white and died, and dey sont her body back to her Muh and Pap. Dis heah's de Coast-Line coming down de track on a dark and rainy night wid her coffin on boa'd. [He closes his eyes and begins blowing the choo-kerr-choo of a starting train. He intersperses his blowing with short speeches.] De rain is beating on de window panes and

245

everybody is mo'nful. [The choo-kerr-chooing takes on a sobbing note, and the speed of the train increases.] De old man and de old 'oman is at de station waiting foh deir daughter's body, her dey loved so well, oh, her dey loved so well. "Don't cry, honey, she gone to heaven," de old man say, Lawd, Lawd, de old man say. Den he heah dat coffin-blow. [A long mournful wail of the engine's whistle follows, swallowed up in the growing speed of the locomotive. He opens his eyes and begins to chant forth his bits of dialogue.] Now she's balling de jack 'cross de river trustle. [He quivers and sings with the straining timbers of the bridge.] Heah she is passing by de gravel-pit. How she goes by, how she goes by! Lak a great black hoss, a great black hoss! And now she's blowing foh de crossing. [The whistle moans again.] Her Muh and Pap's on de platform at de station and dey feel deir hearts in deir moufs at de crying of dat train, Lawd, Lawd, de crying of dat train! [Again he gives the coffin-blow, long and heart-breaking.] De train she slow up. [The choo-kerr-chooing slowly stops.] Dey takes out de coffin and flowers and puts her in a huss, and dey all drives off slow, slow lak dis. [He plays a sort of dead march and stalks back and forth across the yard.] Den de next day dey takes her to de graveyard, de lonesome graveyard, and de preacher preach, and de people sing, shout—shout hallelujah—de preacher preach and de people sing, shouting glory to de lamb. And den dey 'gin th'ow dirt in on her. [He imitates the thump, thump of clods falling on the coffin.] Den de favver and muvver and sisters and bruvvers all cry out loud. Her Pap cries lak dis. [He gives forth a long deep groan.] And de sisters and bruvvers lak dis. [A medley of weeping sounds.] And de muvver cry lak dis. [A high piercing shriek.] And den dey roach up de grave and de preacher make prayer—"Lawd, Lawd Jesus, have mercy upon us!" Den dey all go off and dey ain't nothing left 'cepting a crow in a high scraggly pine a-saying: [He mingles his music with a raucous h-a-r-r-c-k,

THE NO 'COUNT BOY

h-a-r-r-c-k.] Den adder dat when night comes, dark and rainy night, de last thing is a small wind in de bushes lak dis: [A trembling flute-like note rises, bubbles and disappears. He beats the harp against his hand and looks uncertainly at ENOS and PHEELIE, the tears wetting his cheeks.]

ENOS: I cain't deny you gut de world beat handling dat baby, but whut'n de name o' God makes you cry so much?

BOY: [Watching PHEELIE's bowed head.] When I plays dat piece I feel so lonesome lak I cain't help crying, I allus cries.

ENOS: I's seed folks cry when deir people died, but, Lawd, I never seed no sich cry-baby as you.

BOY: You's hard-hearted. Look at Miss Pheelie, she's crying.

ENOS: Help my life! Whut ails you, Pheelie?

PHEELIE: [Hurriedly drying her eyes.] Don't make no fun of me, Enos. I des' had de blues ag'in.

ENOS: [Patting his hat anxiously.] Heah, don't you git to feeling dat a-way no mo' honey. Le's go on wid our drive.

BOY: You calls her honey!

ENOS: Dat I do. She's my gal, dat's whut. And listen to me—I don't want no no 'count fellow come piddling by wid a harp and wild talk to git her upsot.

BOY: I didn't know you was her man. I—I thought she was too purty and lak a angel foh dat. [PHEELIE looks at him tearfully and he gazes back warmly.]

ENOS: Look out, nigger, mind whut you's up to!

PHEELIE: Enos, you quit talking to dat boy lak dat.

ENOS: [Coming up to her and catching her by the arm.] Come on now and let dat fellow go on whah he's started.

PHEELIE: [Springing up.] Turn me a-loose. He's gwine stay right heah if he wants to and eat and sleep to boot.

ENOS: [Hesitating a moment and then flaring out, his timidity and slowness gone.] De hell you say! [He turns

247

suddenly towards the boy and points off to the left.] You see 'way, 'way yonder in de west whah de sun is setting in de tops of dem long-straw pines?

BOY: Yeh, yeh, I sees it.

ENOS: [Moving towards him.] Well, I wants you to git in dat road and in three minutes start dere.

PHEELIE: [Putting herself quickly before him.] He ain't gwine, I tells you.

BOY: You means you wants to run me off befo' I gits any rations?

ENOS: I don't keer whedder you gits any rations or not. I wants you to leave heah befo' you gits Pheelie all tore up wid you' foolish notions. You better git from heah!

BOY: [Swinging his stick before him and smiling with weak grimness.] Ah—hah—I ain't gwine. [ENOS makes another step towards him.] Don't you come towards me. I'll split yo' haid open wid dis heah stick. [ENOS stops and eyes him cautiously. The boy holds his stick in trembling readiness.]

PHEELIE: [Getting between them.] I tells you, Enos Atkins, you ain't gwine harm nary a hair of dis boy's head. You do and I'll scratch yo' eyes out apt as not.

ENOS: God A'mighty! done hyp'otized wid him a'ready, is you? Now, boy, cain't you see how 'tis wid me? We was des' ready to go off to church, and heah you pops up and sets yo'se'f in 'twixt us. [He feels in his pocket and pulls out a dollar.] Heah, take dis dollar and go on. You kin buy enough grub wid it to last you a week.

BOY: [Breaking into a loud derisive laugh.] Ain't he a sight trying to har me off from his gal!

ENOS: Dem dere laughs is lakely gwine be tacks in yo' coffin. [The boy closes his eyes in merriment. With a quick movement ENOS snatches his stick from him.] Now see'f you don't strak a trot up dat road. [He puts out his arm and

pushes PHEELIE back. Egypt is heard off the left pawing
the ground and shaking his bridle.] Whoa, Egypt!

BOY: Don't hit me wid dat stick.

ENOS: I ain't gwine hit you if you lights a rag out'n heah
dis minute. Scat, or I'll wring yo' neck. Make yo'se'f sca'ce,
nigger.

PHEELIE: Let him 'lone, let him 'lone, I tells you!

BOY: You better go tend to yo' hoss, bo. I heah him
trying to git loose.

ENOS: [Looking appealingly at PHEELIE.] Egyp's gitting
restless, Pheelie. You 'bout ready to be driving now? [He
steps aside and calls.] Whoa! whoa dere, Egyp'! Come on,
Pheelie, and le's go.

PHEELIE: [Shaking her head.] I ain't gwine on no drive
wid you, and dat's my last say.

ENOS: Oh, hell fiah! [He lowers his stick.] You des' wait
heah, you little pole-cat, and I'll fix you yit. [He hurries out.]

BOY: [Turning boldly back into the yard.] Hunh, dat
nigger ain't nothing but bluff.

PHEELIE: And he ain't gwine make you leave nuther. You
stay raght wid him.

BOY: He thinks you's gitting to laking me, dat's whut he
thinks. [He falls to staring at her intently.]

PHEELIE: Why you look at me lak dat?

BOY: How old is you?

PHEELIE: Seventeen.

BOY: Is? Den we's des' de same age. Cain't—cain't I
call you Pheelie?

PHEELIE: [Looking at the ground.] Yeh, yeh, you kin.

BOY: I feels des' lak I knowed you all my life, and I ain't
never seed nobody lak you in all my progueings, nobody—
and I's travelled a heap too.

PHEELIE: And you's seed a monstrous lot whah you travelled, ain't you? Yeh, you has, I bet.

BOY: I has dat—Lawd, Lawd!

PHEELIE: [Dropping into the rocking-chair.] Has you seed any big rivers and waters and sich?

BOY: Rivers! Lawd, yeh!

PHEELIE: Has you been by a place whah a great river pours over a steep hill roaring lak de judgment day?

BOY: [Dropping on his knees and marking in the dirt as he ponders.] I dunno—Yeh, yeh, dat river was two miles wide and you had to stop yo' yurs in a mile of it.

PHEELIE: Go on, go on, tell me some mo'. Has you been in any big towns?

BOY: Has I? I's been in towns dat had streets so long dey wan't no coming to de end of 'em.

PHEELIE: Was dey many people dere?

BOY: People! People! [He rolls over on the ground at the remembrance of it and then sits up.] All kinds and sizes. People running, people walking, some wearing diamont dresses and gold shoes. Rich, my, my, how rich! Ortymobiles as big as dat house wid hawns dat jar lak a earfquake and b'iler busting all to onct.

PHEELIE: Aw—

BOY: Hit's so. And street cyars running wid nothing pulling or pushing 'em. And buildings so high dat de moon breshes de top. High! Lawd, Lawd, how high! And people hauling money wid trains, big train loads whah dey keeps it in a big house wid a school breaking of folks to gyard it.

PHEELIE: I been looking at pitchtures in dis book, but nothing fine as dat. [She brings the book and shows it to him.]

BOY: Yeh, I's gut a book lak dat. [He begins picking his teeth meditatively with a straw.] It was give to me by a peddling man. But dat was befo' I went out travelling foh myself. Lawd, Lawd, 'pared to what I's seed in New Yawk dat book ain't nothing.

PHEELIE: New Yawk! You been dere?

BOY: Dat I has. She's a long ways yonder too, mebbe two

hundred miles, who knows? But, Pheelie, dat's de place to go, everything easy, people good to you, nothing to do but eat ice cream and mebbe now and den drink lemonade—and see people, people! worse'n de fair at Dunn. Never seed sich a mess of people. [ENOS is heard quieting his horse.]

PHEELIE: How'd you travel so fuh and pay yo' way? Must take a lot of money.

BOY: I walked, dat's how, bum my way. And when I gits hongry I plays my harp.

PHEELIE: Whah you sleep?

BOY: You don't know nothing 'bout travelling, does you? I sleeps on de warm ground. Come sunset, I stops in a hollow and breaks down bushes and rakes up pine-straw and sleeps lak a log. And in de mawning I wakes and sees de jew on everything and heahs de birds singing, and I lies dere a while and practice on my harp. Den I's off down de road breaving de fine air and feeling des' as happy as I kin.

PHEELIE: I done told Enos we could do lak dat. I sho' has told him time and ag'in.

BOY: Would you lak to live dat a-way?

PHEELIE: Unh—hunh, yeh, oh, yeh, I would.

BOY: Why cain't you, Pheelie?

PHEELIE: [Twisting her hands nervously.] I dunno—I wants to—I do wants to go and keep on gwine.

BOY: [Leaning quickly forward.] Pheelie, Pheelie, come on wid me and go tromping through de world. You kin leave dat bench-leg Enos behime.

PHEELIE: [Turning impulsively towards him and then dropping her head.] I cain't do it, I's 'fraid to. [ENOS slips in at the rear and watches them.]

BOY: I tell you we would have de best time gwine. Come on and go wid me.

PHEELIE: I—mought do it—I's half tempted to do it.

BOY: [Catching her hand.] I tells you whut—how 'bout

me waiting out in de woods dere till dark comes down and den you kin put on a old dress and j'ine me?

PHEELIE: [Pulling her hand unwillingly from him.] Dat'd be fine—fine, but wouldn't folks raise cain?

BOY: Let 'em. Whut you'n me keer? We'll be splashing in de rain and shouting in de sun. And we'll step along to-gedder, and I'll hold yo' purty little hand and you'll hold mine, and I'll teach you to sing songs. I knows a bushel of purty ones. And den I'll learn you how to blow my harp. And we'll slip down de roads at sunrise and sunset, singing and blowing de finest chunes dey is. Please'm say you'll go wid me.

PHEELIE: [With shining eyes.] You has de purtiest talk of any man or boy I ever seed, and, oh, I wish—wish— [With sudden abandon.] Yeh, yeh, I will—I will, I'll go. [Ecstatically he touches her arm and looks straight into her eyes.]

BOY: Birdie mine, birdie mine. [He stands up and bends over her chair.]

PHEELIE: [Her face alight as she leans her head against him.] Oh, it makes my haid swim to think of all we's gwine see and heah. [He timidly puts his arm over her shoulder. ENOS throws his stick behind him, springs forward and snatches the BOY away from PHEELIE.]

ENOS: Heah, you low-down rascal, trying to steal my gal, is you! Oh, yeh, I been heahing whut you said. [His nostrils dilating.] And I's gwine give you a kick in de seat of yo' britches dat'll send you whah you's gwine.

BOY: [Retreating behind PHEELIE.] I ain't trying to steal her nuther. She don't keer nothing foh you and wants to go on wid me.

ENOS: Dat's a lie, you little ficey fool, and you better look out befo' I gives you de lock-jaw.

BOY: She much as said she don't love you, now den.

ENOS: You didn't say dat, did you, Pheelie?

PHEELIE: I dunno whah I loves you or not.

ENOS: [Turning savagely upon the boy.] Damn yo' soul, I gut a notion to ham-string you. [He makes a movement towards the boy, who darts over to the left, sees his walking-stick, and seizes it.] You des' come heah rolling off yo' lies by de yard and tear up everything! Why don't you leave? Want me to bring out a fedder bed and wash yo' feet and sing to you and fan you and put you to sleep, does you? [Jumping forward.] I'll put you to sleep!

BOY: [Falling quickly behind PHEELIE and drawing his stick.] You make anudder move at me and I'll scrush yo' skull.

PHEELIE: Enos, stop dat, stop dat!

ENOS: Yeh, and who's you to order me—you lost every ray of sense you ever had! Wouldn't you be a purty fool running off wid dis heah woods-colt and sleeping in de jambs of fences and old hawg beds and scratching fleas lak a mangy hound! [His voice rising high in wrath.] Dat you would. And in winter weather you'd have yo' shirt-tail friz to you hard as arn. You'd be a sight for sore eyes!

PHEELIE: Shet up.—Boy, I wouldn't let him call me no woods-colt.

BOY: Don't you call me dat.

ENOS: [Taking off his coat.] Call you dat! I ain't started yit. I's gwine twist off bofe yo yurs and make you eat 'em widdout no salt. Hell, you ain't gut no mo' backbone dan a ground-puppy.

BOY: [Trembling and clinging to his stick.] Pheelie, Pheelie, don't let him git at me.

PHEELIE: Don't you hurt dat boy, I tells you ag'in.

ENOS: Hurt him! I's gwine crucify him. [He begins circling PHEELIE. The BOY keeps on the opposite side. ENOS reaches out and pulls PHEELIE behind him.] Now, my little son of a gun, whah is you?

BOY: [In desperation raising his stick.] Don't you come

253

neah me. [ENOS makes a dart at him. The BOY starts to flee, but as ENOS clutches him, he turns and brings his stick awkwardly down on his head. ENOS staggers and falls to his knees.]

PHEELIE: [Looking on in amazement a moment and then screaming.] Lawd, you's kilt Enos. [She stands uncertainly, and then runs and holds him to her.]

BOY: [In a scared voice as he drops his stick.] Muhcy, whut's I gwine do? Is—is you hurt, Enos? [ENOS groans.]

PHEELIE: Git out'n heah, you, you. You's murdered my husband. Enos, Enos, honey baby, is you hurt bad? [He groans again and she helps him to a chair.]

ENOS: [Twisting his head from side to side.] Hurt? Nothing but a little crack. Dat lizard ain't strong enough to kill a flea wid a sludge hammer. [He suddenly whirls around and runs his tongue out, snarling at the BOY.] Ya-a-a-h! [The BOY bounds backwards and, tripping over the bench, falls sprawling on the ground.] See dere, blowing my breaf on him th'ows him into fits. [The BOY lies stretched out still.]

PHEELIE: Oh, my Lawdy, you—l believes he's daid or something!

ENOS: Sho' nothing but de breaf knocked out'n him.

PHEELIE: [Shrilly, as she bends above the boy.] He's hurt, I tells you. Po' boy. [Turning towards ENOS.] Whut if you's kilt him?

ENOS: [Rubbing his head.] Shet up, he ain't hurt bad.

PHEELIE: You hateful mule-beating rascal, he is hurt. Oh, my sweet honey-boy.

BOY: [Sitting up.] Jesus, dat fall jarred de wind out'n my stomach. [Suddenly getting to his feet and eyeing ENOS fearfully.] Don't let dat man make at me.

PHEELIE: I don't reckon he will. You g'in him a dost to last foh a while.

ENOS: [Standing up.] A dost! Hunh, he cain't faze me

254

THE NO 'COUNT BOY

wid no little tap on de skull. [He begins rolling up his sleeves. There is a hail off at the right front.] And now I rolls up my sleeves foh de hawg-killing.

PHEELIE: You all stop dat rowing now. Yonder comes somebody. [The BOY reaches down and gets his harp out of the dirt.]

ENOS: Who is dat? Some old 'oman in a steer cyart.

BOY: Lawd Jesus, dat's—who's dat! Hide me, people, hide me quick so's she cain't git to me. [He looks around him in terror.] Whah must I go?

PHEELIE: Why you skeered of her?

BOY: Pheelie, put me somewhah, civer me quick!

PHEELIE: Drap down on yo' knees, she's coming up de paf. Better git behime de house mebbe.

BOY: [On his knees.] And if she axes foh me, don't you tell her.

PHEELIE: We'll tell her we ain't seed hair nor hide of you. But I cain't see why you so tore up. [He crawls rapidly off around the house.] Now, Enos, you keep yo' mouf closed. Dey's something up—dat boy 'fraid so.

ENOS: Dey is something up, and my s'picions is coming to de top.

OLD WOMAN: [Calling.] Heigho!

PHEELIE: Heigho! [A stout old Negress, dressed in rough working clothes, comes in. She carries a long heavy switch in her hand with which she cuts at the ground as she talks.]

OLD WOMAN: How you all come on?

PHEELIE: Well as common, and how does you?

OLD WOMAN: Well, I thanky. I's looking for my boy— seen anything of him?

PHEELIE: Whut sorter boy?

OLD WOMAN: Lawd, take me all day to gi'n you a pitchture of him. He's des' de no'countest fellow ever was bawn. He goes round playing a harp, and he's not des' right in his haid. He talks wild 'bout being off and travelling everywhah, and

255

he ain't never been out'n Hornett County. Gut all dat mess out'n pitchture books and sich. [A delighted grin begins to pass over Enos' face. Pheelie looks dejectedly at the ground.]

Pheelie: [In a choked voice.] I ain't seed him nowhah.

Old Woman: [Watching her closely.] I whupped him t'udder day 'caze he so sorry, and he run off. And when I ketches him dis time I's gwine cyore him foh good and all. You say you ain't seed him?

Pheelie: [Looking up.] Naw'm.

Old Woman: Dat's quair. I thought I seed somebody lak him standing heah in de yard. Last house down de road said he passed dere a hour ago, and dey ain't no road to turn off.

Pheelie: Naw'm, I ain't seed him. [Unseen by Pheelie, Enos makes a signal to the Woman that the Boy is behind the house. Cunningly she goes on talking to Pheelie.]

Pheelie: Mebbe he went by when we wan't looking. [The Woman darts around the house and is heard crying out.]

Old Woman: Ah—hah—heah you is, heah you is!

Pheelie: How'd she find out he's dere? [There is the sound of blows followed by loud crying.]

Enos: Listen at him cry, de baby!

Pheelie: [Who has started towards the rear.] Quit yo' laughing. [She chokes with sobs.] You set her on him, dat's whut you done. And I'll help him out, she shain't beat him so. [She meets the Old Woman coming in leading the Boy by the collar. He is crying like a child.]

Old Woman: Dry up! [He stops his sobbing and looks off ashamed.] Now ain't you a mess to be running off and leaving me all de cotton to chop! [Looking around her.] Well, we's gut to be moving, and I's gwine gi'n you a beating whut is a beating when you gits home.

Enos: Whah you live?

Old Woman: Down neah Dukes.

256

Enos: Oh-ho, I thought mebbe from yo' boy's talk you was from New Yawk or de moon or somewhah.

Old Woman: I be bound he's been lying to you. He cain't tell de trut. De devil must a gut him in de dark of de moon. [She brings the switch across his legs. He shouts with pain.] Step on now! [He struggles against her and holds back.]

Boy: Pheelie, Pheelie, help me, cain't you?

Pheelie: [Raising a face filled with wrath.] Help you! Dat I won't. [Coming up to him and glaring in his face.] You dirty stinking rascal, why you fool me so?

Old Woman: [Giving him another cut.] You put a move on you or I'll frail de stuffing out'n you. [They move off towards the right front, he looking back and holding out his hands to Pheelie.]

Boy: Pheelie, don't turn ag'in' me so. Pheelie! [They go out.]

Enos: Honey, don't—don't be mad now. See, if it hadn't been foh me, apt as not you'd a-let dat little fool gut you to gwine off wid him. [Pheelie bursts into wild sobs. He pulls her head against his breast, but she shakes herself from him. The loud voice of the Old Woman is heard outside.]

Old Woman: You git in dat cyart or I'll Pheelie you!

Pheelie: I don't want—I ain't never gwine to speak to you ag'in! Oh, he's done gone! [She calls down the road.] Heigh, Boy! Boy!

Boy: [His voice coming back high and faint.] Pheelie-ee-ee! [Pheelie falls on the bench, sobbing in uncontrollable grief. Enos stands looking at her with a wry smile while he gingerly rubs his bruised head. After a moment he goes over to her and puts his arms around her.]

'LIJAH
By Edgar Valentine Smith

PERSONS IN THE PLAY

JUDGE HOLMSTED
FIRST STRANGER
SECOND STRANGER
BAMA
'LIJAH

'LIJAH

THE living-room of Holmacres, a Southern Colonial home in what is known as the Black Belt of Alabama. The wall-paper is badly in need of repair. Upholstery of the furniture—which is of rosewood—is badly worn. There is everywhere the evidence of shabby gentility. A rosewood secretary stands in one corner of the room. There is an old sofa, two or three chairs, and a table on which is an oil lamp, and several ponderous law books. There are ancestral portraits in tarnished gilt frames on the walls. An arched doorway gives into the hallway where the bottom of a flight of stairs is seen. Opposite is a broad window looking out upon the fields. There is also a large stone fireplace with a mantel beneath which is an inscription. Between this and the broad window there is another door. On the mantel are two vases and between these an old-fashioned clock. There is also a glass jar on the mantel. The only modern thing in the room is a telephone on the wall.

Two STRANGERS come in from the outside.

JUDGE HOLMSTED: [Speaking from door.] Just make

261

yo'selves comfortable, gentlemen. I'll join you in a moment, if you'll pardon me. [The SECOND STRANGER is not so tall as his companion; more voluble; age about forty; typical "bustling" business man. Dressed in outing suit with knee-height laced boots.]

SECOND STRANGER: All right, Judge. [The FIRST STRAN-GER is tall; age fifty; hair graying at temples. Reserved in manner and speech. Dressed as is his companion.]

FIRST STRANGER: Fine old gentleman!

SECOND STRANGER: Yes. Regular story-book type. Thought they were all dead now. Makes our job a little harder.

FIRST STRANGER: How?

SECOND STRANGER: Well . . . it makes me feel kind of funny, accepting a man's hospitality when we're here for the express purpose of getting some of his property as cheaply as we can. How in the world are we going to talk business to a man who treats us like members of his family?

FIRST STRANGER: Simply talk . . . business. This is an acquisitive—a commercial age. If he isn't acquisitively in-clined. . . .

SECOND STRANGER: Sure! That's what we've come five hundred miles for. By the way, just as a feeler, I tried him out last night after you had gone upstairs. Asked him about his holdings, plantation lands, and so on. Incidentally, he mentioned that he owns what he calls the "hill forty," several miles from here. Took it in payment of a fee from a client. From the way he spoke of it, he doesn't even sus-pect its value.

FIRST STRANGER: Well . . . that simplifies matters—some.

SECOND STRANGER: Absolutely! If he has something of value and doesn't know it why—that's his misfortune.

FIRST STRANGER: Sh-h-h! [JUDGE HOLMSTEAD enters. Age about seventy. Tall, slender, the personification of

courtliness, with flowing white hair, moustache and goatee.
His shoes, though well-polished, are worn. Dressed carefully, after a "shabby genteel" fashion. Wears a long
"Prince Albert" coat, shiny from much usage, as are his
trousers. Wears low collar and black string bow tie and
double-breasted vest.]

JUDGE HOLMSTED: I'm sorry, gentlemen, to have kept
you waitin', but there was a little dispute among some of
the servants that I had to settle.

SECOND STRANGER: You find them quite a care—so many
of them—don't you, Judge?

JUDGE HOLMSTED: Yes, suh; they are.

FIRST STRANGER: Still, your kind of servants can be
depended on, can't they?

JUDGE HOLMSTED: Yes, suh. Particularly to do what
they're not supposed to do. [The SECOND STRANGER
chuckles audibly, while FIRST smiles appreciatively.]

SECOND STRANGER: [Glancing toward the telephone.] I
suppose the telephone connects with the town—Wynnesborough—doesn't it?

JUDGE HOLMSTED: Yes, suh. And we get pretty good
service, too. The lady in charge, Miss Effie—Miss Effie
Winsdale—belongs to one of our oldest families, suh. Splen-
did young woman. And very accommodatin'. She can
generally get the connection, too.

SECOND STRANGER: I suppose there's a garage in town
that we can call and get a conveyance?

JUDGE HOLMSTED: A conveyance? What for, if I may
ask, suh?

SECOND STRANGER: We'll be wanting to inspect the timber lands we spoke to you about. I believe you said they
lie on the river three or four miles from here? We'll need
to be going back and forth—

JUDGE HOLMSTED: Then use one of the hawsses on the
place, suh. I'll just have one of them hitched to a buggy.

Our country roads aren't suited to automobiles and for that reason I've never bought one. Will you be wantin' to leave right away?

FIRST STRANGER: We ought to be getting an early start, but as to accepting the use of a team from you, Judge, that would be unthinkable. We can't transgress on your hospitality—

SECOND STRANGER: No, no, Judge! We can't impose on you like that. Really, I feel that it's an imposition, accepting your invitation to stay here. Our inspection of the lands will require several days, perhaps a week—

JUDGE HOLMSTED: No imposition at all, suh! The idea of yo' rentin' a conveyance with all the hawsses we have on the place eatin' their lazy heads off! As to yo' stay here just think of me, gentlemen! I'm an old man—all alone, except for—except for the servants—and dreadfully lonely at times. I appreciate company. You'll be doin' me a real service by makin' Holmacres yo' home while you're in this vicinity. You *must* do it. I insist.

SECOND STRANGER: That's very kind of you, Judge. And if you insist—

JUDGE HOLMSTED: But I'm forgettin'. You said you wanted to be off. I'll have the rig hitched up for you. Just wait here till I call [hesitates, plainly embarrassed] till I call . . . er . . . 'Lijah. 'Lijah! [There is no answer. He calls again, more loudly.] 'Lijah!! . . . Oh, *'Lijah!!!*

['BAMA has entered the room through doorway, a typical plantation servant, born and reared on the place and assumes certain prerogatives. She is about sixty, fat and black. Holds something in her hand. Stops just inside room, gazing fixedly at JUDGE HOLMSTED. Evidently puzzled.]

'BAMA: *'Lijah?*

JUDGE HOLMSTED: [Turns from doorway, patently annoyed.] He's not in the house, evidently. [To FIRST

STRANGER.] You see how they are, suh: generally to be depended on to be somewhere else when you want them.

'BAMA: Judge, suh, you drapped yo' spec's on de dinin'-room flo'. [Hands him the spectacle case.] Speakin' 'bout 'Lijah, suh, don't you know whare he's at? Down behin' de bahn, diggin' yearthworms to *go fishin' wid!*

JUDGE HOLMSTED: I might have remembered, gentlemen. You'll learn somethin' about our Southern niggers if you stay down here a while. For one thing, it's almost impossible to keep a nigger and a river apart when the catfish are bitin'. Excuse me, please, while I step out to the barn. Maybe 'Lijah is still there. [He goes out.]

SECOND STRANGER: And who is 'Lijah?

'BAMA: Cap'n, suh, jus' think o' de mos' wu'thless nigger you is ever heard of . . . an' at's 'Lijah.

SECOND STRANGER: What does he do?

'BAMA: Fishes—day an' night!

SECOND STRANGER: *Day and night?* When does he sleep?

'BAMA: *Him sleep? 'Lijah* sleep. Don't you worry none 'bout 'Lijah not gittin' no sleep, Cap'n. All he needs is a sof' spot on de shady side of a tree when dey's somep'm needs to be done 'bout de house. He'll 'tend to de sleepin'. [The STRANGERS laugh heartily. 'BAMA leaves them.]

SECOND STRANGER: She's a character, too, it seems. These Southern planters must lead an ideal existence. [Takes a cigar from pocket, feels for match, fails to find one, and walks to mantelshelf. Leans over to strike a match which he finds there and has his attention drawn to inscription.] Hello! Have you seen this inscription—or motto?

FIRST STRANGER: [Has seated himself at table, casually scanning one of the law books.] What does it say?

SECOND STRANGER: [Leans closer.] "Be not forgetful . . . to entertain strangers . . . for thereby some . . . have entertained angels . . . unawares."

FIRST STRANGER: Angels!

SECOND STRANGER: Angels! I guess that's the main-spring of his hospitality. Kind of bred in the bone. Part of his inheritance, too. Probably placed there by his first ancestors who built this place. Well . . . I'll say that he's living up to the motto. But . . . we can't afford to be getting sentimental. Business is business. That's a bro-mide—but it's the truth, too. [JUDGE HOLMSTED comes in.]

JUDGE HOLMSTED: Caught him just as he was gettin' ready to leave, gentlemen. You'll find the hawss and buggy hitched at the front gate when you're ready. [JUDGE HOLMSTED turns toward secretary. 'BAMA comes in with a dusting cloth on her arm.]

'BAMA: Judge, suh, if you is lookin' foh seegars, you won't hahdly find none in 'at seceta'y. I seed 'Lijah sof'-footin' it 'roun' in here yistiddy evenin' when I was sweepin' de hall. An' if de seegars is gone, *he's got 'em!*

JUDGE HOLMSTED: 'Lijah? Oh . . . of course, 'Bama! The triflin' black rascal!

SECOND STRANGER: So he even pilfers your cigars, does he, Judge? [Takes out cigar-case and extends it to JUDGE HOLMSTED.] Try one of these.

JUDGE HOLMSTED: Thank you, suh. [Places cigar in his vest pocket.] I'll smoke it presently.

SECOND STRANGER: Guess we'd better be moving. [The STRANGERS, followed by JUDGE HOLMSTED, go to the door-way and disappear through it.]

JUDGE HOLMSTED: He's perfectly gentle, gentlemen. His name is Grover Cleveland. You see, I'm a Democrat. Hope you have a pleasant day. Come in any time you wish. Holmacres is always open. Good mawnin' . . .g-o-o-d mawnin'. [JUDGE HOLMSTED is thoughtful. Goes to mantel, takes top from glass jar, extracts long, thin, cheap black cheroot. Bites off end; starts to light it. Hesitates. Takes cigar from vest pocket. Compares the two. Re-places cheroot carefully in jar. Lights cigar. Seats himself. Blowing out a cloud of smoke.] Ah-h-h!! ['BAMA stops in her work of dusting the furniture to gaze fixedly at the JUDGE.]

'BAMA: Judge, suh, you mean to say you is gwine to let dem two mens drive *Grovuh Cleveland to a buggy?*

JUDGE HOLMSTED: Yes, 'Bama.

'BAMA: But how is you gwine to git back an' fo'th to yo' law office?

JUDGE HOLMSTED: I guess I'll have to take the mule from Eph.

'BAMA: My Lawd, Judge! Take de onlies' work muel dey is on de place, an' de Bermoody an' Johnson grass jus' chokin' de cotton to death? Can't dem gentlemens git deyse'ves a hawss an' buggy?

JUDGE HOLMSTED: You forget, 'Bama. Those gentlemen are guests at Holmacres.

'BAMA: Yes, suh. But . . . ain't dey *Yankees,* suh?

JUDGE HOLMSTED: They are gentlemen, 'Bama . . . and my guests! [JUDGE HOLMSTED sighs deeply.]

[A day now passes and the time is after dinner. A jumble of voices is heard. The STRANGERS enter, followed by JUDGE HOLMSTED. The boots of the STRANGERS are caked with mud.]

JUDGE HOLMSTED: It seems, gentlemen, that this was the nigger's favorite coon dog. As he told the story, the dog and the coon fought and fought until finally they got right in the middle of the railroad track. Then a train came along and put an end to fighting for both of them. And the nigger wound up the story with the most woebegone expression on his face by saying: "De on'y thing I hates 'bout it, Jedge, is 'at dawg always *will b'lieve* he wuz *kilt by a coon!*"

FIRST STRANGER: That's a good one. I'll have to remember it.

SECOND STRANGER: They're great characters, Judge—your

Southern Negroes. Wonderfully interesting, from what I've heard of them.

FIRST STRANGER: Very interesting. [Glances down at boots.] By the way, Judge, since we didn't have time before supper, I know you'll excuse us while we step up to the room and clean up a bit.

JUDGE HOLMSTED: Certainly, suh! [The STRANGERS leave and mount the stairs. 'BAMA comes in. JUDGE HOLMSTED calls after the STRANGERS.] Just leave your boots outside the door, gentlemen. I'll have 'Lijah clean them.

'BAMA: Judge, suh, did you git 'at lettuh what was on de seceta'y?

JUDGE HOLMSTED: A letter? No, 'Bama. [Goes to the secretary. Seats himself. Takes up letter. Looks at it.] Why . . . it's—from the bank. ['BAMA leaves the room.] I wonder . . . [Opens the letter nervously. Reads it. Is greatly perturbed. Looks at it again. Goes to the telephone. Takes down the receiver.] Hello! Miss Effie? Will you please, Ma'am, get Mr. Needham for me? No'm; he'd hardly be at the bank this late. Try his home. . . . Is that you, Mr. Needham? This is Judge Holmsted, suh. I . . . just got the bank's letter, Mr. Needham. I don't quite understand it. . . . Why—you don't mean that the bank won't renew the mortgage? . . . They've sold it? . . . It's in the hands of someone else, you say? . . . And this other person insists on settlement? But . . . but, Mr. Needham, I had counted on the bank's renewin' it as usual, suh. And it's due the fifteenth of next month? . . . I suppose so, suh . . . I suppose so . . . if the paper's passed into other hands. Yes, suh. I understand, Mr. Needham . . . I understand. Thank you for yo' trouble and I'm sorry I had to disturb you this time of night. Good-night, suh. [With a hand that trembles, he replaces the receiver on its hook, and turns away from the telephone. His shoulders droop; he is suddenly a broken old man. Slowly he walks to his chair and drops heavily into it. He stares moodily into the fireplace. 'BAMA enters.]

'BAMA: Judge, suh, dey's somep'm I oughta tell you. [She is plainly very much worried.] Hit's bad news, suh.

JUDGE HOLMSTED: All news seems to be bad news, 'Bama, since that ring of crooked politicians took the judgeship away from me. What is it now?

'BAMA: You remembuh, suh, I tol' you yistiddy 'bout de cow comin' home wid her laig all swole up like she was snake-bit? Well, suh . . . she died dis evenin'. An' bofe dem gentlemens likes cream in dey breakfas' cawfee, suh.

JUDGE HOLMSTED: I don't know that there's anything we can do about it, 'Bama.

'BAMA: Naw, suh. Jus' thought I oughta let you know, suh. ['BAMA leaves. The JUDGE resumes his attitude of hopeless musing. Voices are heard. The STRANGERS are seen descending the stairs. JUDGE HOLMSTED rises quickly. He straightens his tie; runs his hand through his tousled hair; tugs at the lapels of his coat; throws up his head and squares his shoulders. The STRANGERS come in through the doorway.]

JUDGE HOLMSTED: Come right in, gentlemen! Come right in! Seat yo'selves. [All three take seats.] I have to keep track of 'Lijah—or try to—and I forgot to ask you gentlemen if he brought hot water for your shaving this mornin'.

SECOND STRANGER: No, Judge; but that's all right.

FIRST STRANGER: Perfectly all right, Judge.

JUDGE HOLMSTED: I'm sorry, gentlemen. That trifling black rascal will be the death of me yet. If I don't wring his neck, first.

FIRST STRANGER: You Southerners treat your servants differently, Judge, from the way we do in the North. There they know that certain things are required of them. And they do those things—or get out.

JUDGE HOLMSTED: But they're not niggers, suh. There's the difference. Take 'Lijah, for instance. Been on the place all his life, goin' on sixty years. So was his father. I couldn't get rid of 'Lijah if I wanted to and I'll admit I don't *want* to. If I did, and were to discharge him, he'd simply refuse to stay discharged. He'd come sneakin' back —provided he were ever really to leave the place—and the first thing I knew 'Bama would be feedin' him again. So . . . there you are! ['BAMA, entering through the doorway, has a plainly worried expression on her face.]

'BAMA: Judge, you is jus' nachelly got *to do somep'm 'bout 'Lijah!*

JUDGE HOLMSTED: What's the rascal been up to now, 'Bama?

'BAMA: Nothin', suh! Excep' he's been 'mongst de chickens ag'in. [FIRST STRANGER smiles; the SECOND chuckles, shaking his head.] Took de las' ones I had, too, 'at I been fattenin'.

JUDGE HOLMSTED: Oh, well, 'Bama, I reckon we'll have to forgive him this time. He's probably givin' a party.

SECOND STRANGER: Doesn't he catch enough fish for his parties?

'BAMA: Yes, suh; he ketches plenty fish. But . . . but you see, suh, catfish is jus' a nigguh's regluh eatin' victuals. Dey uses de chicken kinduh foh—kinduh foh—dessert.

FIRST STRANGER: Does he give many of these parties?

'BAMA: 'Tain't no pahty he's givin', suh. It's a shindig —jus' a plain shindig! [The STRANGERS do not understand. They look at each other, then at the JUDGE, inquiringly.]

JUDGE HOLMSTED: A shindig, gentlemen, is a dance.

SECOND STRANGER: What? An old man like 'Lijah, dance?

'BAMA: Him *dance?* 'Lijah dance? Cap'n, suh, jus' you say "fiddle" to 'at nigguh, an' he stahts to shufflin' his

feets acrost de flo' right now! Age ain't purified him none.
[The STRANGERS laugh.] An' him wid gran'chillun! I'se
gwine to have him churched. I sho' Gawd is! [Goes
through the doorway.] Out dere diggin' yearthworms foh
fish bait an' lettin' all 'em cows an' ca'fs git together!
Co'se, he don't keer if us ain't got no cream foh de breakfas'
cawfee. De no 'count *bagavond!*

JUDGE HOLMSTED: You'll have to excuse 'Bama, gentlemen. 'Lijah aggravates her considerably. [The FIRST
STRANGER rises and walks to the window that looks out upon
the fields. The full moon is shining. He stands musing at
the window.]

SECOND STRANGER: This 'Lijah of yours, Judge, must be
a prize! I've read often about the Southern plantation
servants, but thought that 'Lijah's type existed only in fic-
tion. I simply *must* see him before I leave. I know,
though, just what he's like; a cigar-pilfering old Negro who
occasionally slips your bird dogs out and runs rabbits with
them. Guess he takes your foxhounds out, too, sometimes
at nights and hunts 'coons and 'possums with them. I can
see him grumbling a great deal and complaining of a "misery" in his back when he's told to do something he doesn't
want to do.

JUDGE HOLMSTED: You've described him very accurately,
suh. But . . . his type is disappearin'—disappearin' rapidly.
And the younger generation— Well . . . we won't mention them. We're attached—we Southerners are—and we
might as well admit it, to the old slavery-time nigger.
There's somethin' about him . . . Well—bein' from the
North, you could hardly understand—but there's somethin'
that draws us to him. The old things, though, are passin'.
Take the old families that used to live hereabouts. Nearly
all of them have gone to the cities, leavin' the plantations
in the hands of tenants and the places have gone to ruin.

FIRST STRANGER: And you, Judge? [He has turned

about from the window.] You've never felt any urge to leave the plantation yourself?

JUDGE HOLMSTED: Not the least, suh. We Holmsteds have always been lovers of the land and have always lived close to it. Maybe we were a little more firmly rooted in the soil than some of the others were. . . . Ye-e-s . . . things are different. Take the river, for one thing. Once we had an average of two steamboats a day on the 'Bigbee. Now . . . there's one a week. Then we always went to Mobile by boat. Those were great days, gentlemen! *Great* days! There was always a crowd of niggers on board with their fiddles and guitars. And dances! Many a time I've danced the polka and schottische until daybreak on a boat in midstream, gentlemen, with the *fairest partners* to be found in the *world!* [The SECOND STRANGER is leaning forward in his chair interestedly. FIRST STRANGER has faced about from the window again and is drinking in every word.] And the races between the different boats! Why, gentlemen, I've seen two of them pass our landin' here in the night, neck and neck, with their smokestacks flamin' red from top to bottom! You could see the niggers on the lower decks, stripped to the waist, the sweat pourin' from their brown bodies, as they fed the fat lightwood to the furnaces. I was a passenger on the *Nettie Belle* in seventy, when she beat the *Clay Jackson* in that famous race from Mobile to Demopolis by two hours, with a ten-foot rise in the 'Bigbee. And more than once, gentlemen—more than once!—I've seen a boat pull to the bank for two hot-headed young bloods to go ashore and settle their differences accordin' to the code!

FIRST STRANGER: With pistols, Judge?

JUDGE HOLMSTED: Yes, suh! In those days, gentlemen fought like gentlemen. And once . . . I saw a boat burned to the water's edge . . . not a half mile from our landin'. Ye-e-e-s . . . things were different, then. Goin' down in the fall, we'd stop at every landin' to load cotton, the boats racin' each other to see which could take in the biggest cargo. And I've seen fights—blood fights, gentlemen!—between cap'ns of different boats over the right to load cotton at landin's. [He checks himself, suddenly embarrassed.] But . . . pshaw! I'm becomin' garrulous. An old man, grievin' of the departed glories of his youth!

SECOND STRANGER: Not at all, Judge! Not at all! Go on!

JUDGE HOLMSTED: Some other time, gentlemen—if you please. Some other time. I'm monopolizin' the conversation.

FIRST STRANGER: It's positively enchanting here! What's that scent? Magnolia?

JUDGE HOLMSTED: No, suh; that's our cape jessamine. It's very fragrant this time of the year.

FIRST STRANGER: I don't think I ever saw such moonlight! The loveoaks look like they are bathed in a perfect mantle of silver dust. [He turns regretfully from the window.] I've just been thinking of the possibilities here for a stock farm, Judge. I understand that your native grasses—Bermuda and Johnson, I believe you call them?—make excellent pasturage and hay. They're volunteer crops, too, aren't they?

JUDGE HOLMSTED: So much so, suh, that we have to fight to keep them from takin' the cotton.

FIRST STRANGER: Probably, though, the idea of a stock farm doesn't appeal to you Southerners. You're so wedded to cotton.

JUDGE HOLMSTED: Wedded? [Smiles whimsically.] The word is well chosen, suh. And since the boll weevil hit us it looks like a weddin' with no chance of divo'ce. [The STRANGERS laugh.]

SECOND STRANGER: That's just what I would do if I owned this place, Judge. I understand that your land runs clear down to the river? Well, there's the water for your cattle. I'd stock this place with Angus or Hereford cattle and Berkshire hogs. Then divide it into pastures with a suitable number of fences. Your Bermuda and Johnson grasses would furnish spring and summer grazing. Then there are your river canebrakes for winter forage. Why, just think of it, man! Those rolling acres dotted with sleek, black cattle and fat hogs! And your bottom lands would raise what corn you needed. Romance? There it is for you! Why, a man under those conditions wouldn't have anything to do but sit and count his money as it came in!

JUDGE HOLMSTED: I've quite often thought of venturing some along that line, suh. I may even try it next year. ['BAMA enters with something in her hand.]

'BAMA: Judge, you dropped yo' fountain pen, too, suh.

JUDGE HOLMSTED: Thank you, 'Bama. ['BAMA leaves.] But I'm forgettin', gentlemen! You're probable tired from your day's tramp through the swamp. Any time you feel like retiring, don't stand on ceremony. Guests at Holmacres, you know, are home folks.

SECOND STRANGER: I'll confess I am a little tired, Judge. [Rises.] And if you'll excuse us—

FIRST STRANGER: Yes, Judge, that swamp mud was a bit thick. [The STRANGERS walk toward the doorway. JUDGE HOLMSTED follows them.]

JUDGE HOLMSTED: Good-night, gentlemen! Just leave your boots outside the door and I'll have 'Lijah polish them.

THE STRANGERS: Good-night, Judge. [As they mount the stairs.] Thank you. Good-night! [JUDGE HOLMSTED walks slowly to the window, folds his arms and gazes out, musing.]

JUDGE HOLMSTED: Blooded cattle . . . pastures . . . fat hogs. . . . [Turns abruptly from the window.] Pshaw! I'm dreaming! ['BAMA enters.]

'BAMA: Judge, de reason you is always drappin' things

outen yo' coat is dey mus' be a hole in de pocket. Better pull it off an' lemme fix it.

JUDGE HOLMSTED: All right, 'Bama. [Removes his coat and hands it to her. But let me have it early in the morning —early—remember.

'BAMA: Yes, suh. An' you better leave off 'at shirt an' git another one in de mawnin'. De cuffs is all frazzled an' I wants to turn 'em.

JUDGE HOLMSTED: All right, 'Bama. [Glances mechanically at his cuffs.] You may go now. I won't need you again to-night.

'BAMA: Yes, suh. Good-night, suh. [She leaves.]

JUDGE HOLMSTED: Good-night, 'Bama. [JUDGE HOLMSTED leaves and mounts the stairs. 'BAMA shuffles about, putting out lights, lowering shades, etc., singing softly to herself, "Swing Low, Sweet Chariot." Leaves through the doorway, JUDGE reënters, carrying two pairs of mud-stained boots and a lantern. Seats himself and begins cleaning the boots.]

[Five days now pass, and the scene is the same. The SECOND STRANGER is standing beside the window that looks out upon the field, gazing thoughtfully out. The FIRST STRANGER, seated beside the table, picks up a newspaper. There are a couple of suit-cases in the room. The two men are dressed for travelling. It is morning and they have finished breakfast. They are alone.]

FIRST STRANGER: [Reading.] "The *Wynnesborough Clarion.* Published weekly at Wynnesborough, Wynne County." [Stops and looks at his companion.] Well?

SECOND STRANGER: Don't ask me. I've been trying for three days to figure out a way to approach him. I don't know how to do it.

FIRST STRANGER: We'll have to be diplomatic.

SECOND STRANGER: Yes. And it'll take more money—a lot more—than we intended offering for the property.

First Stranger: I don't doubt it. And he's not the kind of man you can haggle with over price, either.

Second Stranger: Decidedly not! If we offend him— once—we might as well call the whole thing off. He'd very courteously, but very firmly, refuse to listen to any offer that we might make.

First Stranger: Ye-e-s. . . . And we know it's a valuable property—

Second Stranger: Valuable? Man, it's a mint—a Bonanza! It's the richest deposit I ever saw in a similar area. And I've got a hunch that we're going to have to pay for it, too . . . if we get it.

First Stranger: If we get it? Think there's any doubt of it? Do you imagine the Judge has any idea as to its value?

Second Stranger: Well . . . ye-e-s. I'm practically sure of it. [Takes a cigar from his pocket and lights it, but does not look directly at companion.] I—I saw . . .'Lijah —at last—yesterday afternoon. I gathered from him that the Judge has known of the deposit for a long time. 'Lijah even went so far as to say—

First Stranger: So-o . . . you've really *seen 'Lijah?* What does he look like?

Second Stranger: Just what I expected—only more so. You'll have to see him to appreciate him. [Laughs exaggeratedly.] He's quite a character. Just getting ready to go fishing when I ran into him. Got to talking with him and brought up the subject of the "hill forty," as the Judge calls it. 'Lijah said that he doubted if the Judge would sell at all unless he got a mighty good price for it. Ha! Ha! That's just the way he expressed it: a "mighty good price." Said the Judge is holding it as a sort of nest egg. Doesn't need to sell, you know. Why should he? Got this plantation, with a healthy income from it. Servants running all over the place. And he has no direct descendants. Last of his

race and that sort of thing. Then, there's his law practice.
I understand that he makes quite a bit out of that, too.
Keeps him busy and happy. Now . . . I'd suggest . . .

FIRST STRANGER: Just a moment! [Walks around in
front of the other and compels his attention.] Remember
. . . old man . . . we're partners. Let's be frank. Just
how long . . . have you known . . . the actual conditions
here?

SECOND STRANGER: Why . . . why . . . what do you
mean?

FIRST STRANGER: How long have you known that there's
no such person as 'Lijah? That he was created by the
Judge in his extremity solely in order to have something to
blame for the shortcomings in his hospitality? When did
you find out that the horse we've been driving every day is
the Judge's saddle horse and the only one on the place?
That he took the only mule on the place to ride to his office
and back? That he doesn't make enough out of his law
practice to feed himself? That this place is mortgaged to
the limit and that he couldn't borrow a hundred dollars if
his life depended on it?

SECOND STRANGER: I—I—

FIRST STRANGER: Listen! Two mornings ago I was
awakened by the singing of a mocking bird. I got up and
crept to the window without disturbing you to try to get a
glimpse of it. And what do you think I saw? The Judge,
under one of those China trees, *cleaning the mud from our
boots! He's your 'Lijah!*

SECOND STRANGER: And that isn't all! You remember
last night when I told you I couldn't sleep? Thought I'd
walk around a bit? I saw a light in the barn and walked
down that way, hoping to find 'Lijah. I saw him, too! By
the light of a lantern hung on the wall, the Judge, with his
coat off and his shirt sleeves rolled above his elbows, *was
washing the mud off of that damned old buggy* to have it

half-way decent for us to take out again and get more mud on it for him to wash off. My God! The hospitable, poverty-stricken old aristocrat—! [JUDGE HOLMSTED enters.]

JUDGE HOLMSTED: And you're really leavin' Holmacres, gentlemen? I had hoped for the pleasure of yo' company for several days longer.

SECOND STRANGER: Yes, Judge; as much as we hate to go. But . . . business . . . you know.

JUDGE HOLMSTED: Oh, I understand, gentlemen.

FIRST STRANGER: We can't begin to thank you for your hospitality, Judge, so we won't even try. We can only say that we appreciate it deeply.

JUDGE HOLMSTED: Don't mention it, gentlemen. I've been mo' than pleased to have you gentlemen with me.

SECOND STRANGER: It's certainly been a pleasure to us, Judge. [The STRANGERS appear nervous. They fidget about, glancing at each other suggestively. For once, the SECOND STRANGER seems willing for the other to take the lead.]

FIRST STRANGER: Er . . . before we go, though, Judge . . . there's a little matter of business that we'd like to talk over with you—if you've got time.

JUDGE HOLMSTED: Certainly, gentlemen. [He gestures toward the chairs.] Be seated.

FIRST STRANGER: When we came here, we told you that we were dealers in timber lands. We are. But . . . we also handle other properties, among them mineral lands. Do you know that there is a deposit of mica on that hill forty of yours?

JUDGE HOLMSTED: Oh, I'd heard, suh, that there was isinglass, as we call it, there.

FIRST STRANGER: Would you—er—that is—do you think you would care to dispose of the property?

JUDGE HOLMSTED: Why . . . if it would be any accommo-

278

dation to you gentlemen. It's several miles from the main body of the plantation.

FIRST STRANGER: My friend and I have talked the matter over. We realize that between gentlemen there should be no such thing as haggling over price, and we have decided to offer you the topmost figure that we can pay for the property. For the mineral rights, alone, we can give you fifty thousand dollars. [JUDGE HOLMSTED starts slightly, but regains his self-control. His hand, as he raises it to stroke his moustache, trembles slightly. But his voice is studiedly calm and indifferent, as he answers after a moment's wait.]

JUDGE HOLMSTED: I imagine, gentlemen, that the transfer can be arranged on that basis.

SECOND STRANGER: Good! Here's our check for five thousand dollars as earnest money. You can prepare the deeds and send them to our Chicago office and we'll remit the balance. [The STRANGERS prepare to leave. One of them pulls out his cigar case and offers it to the JUDGE.]

FIRST STRANGER: Have a cigar, Judge?

JUDGE HOLMSTED: Thank you, suh. [Places the cigar in his vest pocket.] I'll smoke it later. [The STRANGERS pick up their suit-cases.] Let me help you, gentlemen. I'll call 'Lijah. [Turns to the doorway.] 'Lijah! Oh, 'Lijah! [Faces the STRANGERS.] As usual, gentlemen, the black rascal isn't to be found. ['BAMA appears in doorway with the STRANGERS' hats.]

'BAMA: Judge, suh, 'Lijah ain't here. He went down to de river early dis mawnin' to see 'bout his trot lines.

JUDGE HOLMSTED: All right, 'Bama. Yo' visit here, gentlemen, has been an extreme pleasure to me. You must come again.

THE TWO STRANGERS: Thank you, Judge. [There are the customary adieus, with handshaking.]

JUDGE HOLMSTED: You'll find the buggy hitched, gentlemen. Just leave it at the livery stable in town. I'll send

'Lijah in for it. Good-bye! . . . G-o-o-d . . . b-y-e! . . .
[He follows them to the doorway. JUDGE HOLMSTED returns
to room. Comes to the center table. Picks up the paper.
Looks up, musing.] Blooded cattle . . . pastures . . . fine
hogs . . . servants. . . . [Glances at the paper. Seems
suddenly seized with an idea. Drops the paper and goes to
the telephone.] Miss Effie? Good-mawnin', ma'am! Fine,
thank you, ma'am! Fine! How's your mother's cold? . . .
Yes? Well, you just tell her to put a lard and turpentine
poultice on her chest. Yes'm. By the way, Miss Effie, could
you get me the *Clarion* office? Yes'm. . . . Good-mawnin',
Majuh. Is that you, suh? First rate, thank you, suh. No,
suh. The cotton ain't doin' at all well. Won't hardly pay
for raisin' and gatherin', suh. Oh, Majuh, I'd like to get
you to run a little advertisement in yo columns for me if you
please, suh. . . . WANTED: Nigra male servant, aged about
sixty, or thereabouts, for light work in plantation home.
Must be willing to answer to name of Elijah. Yes, suh; that's
right: Elijah. And, Majuh? Just mail the bill to me, suh.
Thank you, suh. Good-bye. [JUDGE HOLMSTED goes to the
fireplace. Takes one of his old cheroots from the glass jar
and starts to light it. Remembers the cigar given him by
the STRANGER. Takes it from pocket and compares the two.
Empties contents of the glass jar into hand and throws them
into the fireplace. Lights a cigar, and blows out a cloud of
smoke.] The trifling black rascal!

THE TIE THAT BINDS
By Orrelle Fidlar Cornelius

PERSONS IN THE PLAY

MELISSY MILLS
NAOMI
JEB
JUDITH
BEN WEBB
THE BABY

THE TIE THAT BINDS

THE living room of the MILLS' mountain cabin in the
Cumberland mountains of Tennessee. It is plain and
bare, but spotlessly clean. The bare board floor has experienced many scrubbings with the soft soap made by the
women folk. In fact, the entire room gives one the impression of being "home-made," from the rough table against
the left wall to the "split-bottom" chairs and the round
braided rugs on the floor. The walls are of hewn logs
chinked with mud which is falling out in spots, allowing the
afternoon sun to filter through in a golden haze. Strings
of red peppers, dried pumpkin and other evidences of the
fall harvest hang from the rafters. In the right wall is a
door leading onto the "go-between." At the center back,
a small, wood fire smoulders in a large, wide-throated, stone
fire-place, artistic in its design, although the builder had no
such idea in mind. To the left of the fire-place is a small,
square window with inside shutters of solid boards. This
looks out upon the mountain ranges which pile one upon

283

another until it is impossible to distinguish their haze from the soft blue of the sky.

JUDITH, a sweet, simple girl of about thirteen, stands near the fire-place working the dasher of an old-fashioned, wooden churn with a slow, easy rhythm as she gazes into space, lost in a day dream. She wears a plain calico slip and has a gingham apron tied under her chin. She is roused from her dreams by the entrance of her mother, and begins churning more energetically.

MRS. MILLS is a large, masculine woman of about fifty, with a natural dignity and firmness of manner and speech which hard work and trouble have intensified. Her features are hard and weather-beaten, and her hands betray the years of privation and drudgery she has known. When she speaks her voice is loud and harsh. She wears a faded calico wrapper with a gingham apron tied about her ample waist. She enters carrying a cedar pail of water which she places on the table. Then taking a gourd dipper from its nail on the wall, she drinks long from the cool spring water. Pouring the remaining water in the dipper into the tin washpan, she washes her hands and dries them on the roller towel which hangs near by. All this is done deliberately.

MRS. MILLS: [Removing her slat sun-bonnet and hanging it on a peg in the wall, then turning on JUDITH, harshly.] Ain't ye got that churnin' done yit? Lawsamassy, ye'r as slow as the seven y'ar eetch! What ails ye?—Hyar, give me a look at it. [Pushing JUDITH aside, she lifts the dash and examines the milk on the rod.] I 'low hit's a-beginnin' t' break.—Go fetch me some water. It's a mite too hot. [JUDITH brings a gourd of water which her mother pours into the churn through the hole in the lid. JUDITH then resumes churning. Meanwhile JEB comes in. He is a slender lad of about seventeen, clad in faded blue overalls. He has a listless air about him and is as slow of speech as of movement.]

JEB: [Throwing his worn straw hat carelessly onto the table and drawing a letter from his hip pocket.] I met Jim Riley over yander on 'Possum Ridge an' he give me this hyar. Said it war fer you, Maw.

MRS. MILLS: Huh! . . . Don't know who'd be a-writin' t' me, less'n it's the taxes. [JUDITH stops churning and listens attentively. This is a breath of air from the outside world.]

JEB: Jim said it'd been a-layin' thar in the Post Office nigh on t' a week. Warn't ary one frum these parts over thar lately.

MRS. MILLS: [Getting spectacles from the mantel, slowly adjusting them and tearing open the letter.] I reckon 'tis them thar taxes agin.— [Scornfully as she turns over the pages which she cannot read.] Huh!—Looks like Naomi's hand-writin'.

JUDITH: Naomi's?

JEB: [His face lighting up for the first time.] Is it frum sis? [MRS. MILLS draws herself up to her full height and crushes the letter angrily in her hand.]

JUDITH: [Running to her.] Maw, hain't ye a-goin' t' let Jeb read it to us?

MRS. MILLS: No! She hain't no gal o' mine no more!

JUDITH: Oh, Maw!

JEB: Better let me read it, Maw.

MRS. MILLS: Well—hyar—take it! [She throws the letter to his feet and takes up her basket of quilt scraps and begins sewing with an air of having washed her hands of the whole affair. JEB moves closer to the window to decipher the message while JUDITH peeps over his shoulder.]

JEB: Dear—Maw,—I—am—c-o-m-i-n—coming—h-o-m-e home—

JUDITH: Home! Oh, Maw, Naomi's comin' home!

MRS. MILLS: No, she ain't a-comin', nuther! Not ef my name's Melissy Mills!

285

JEB: For—a—l-i-t-t—little—v-i-s-i—t, v—i—s—i—

JUDITH: Skip it, Jeb, skip it! What else she say?

JEB: "I sh—shall—be—home—home—capital t—l—r—u—r—s—d—a—y—." Looks like hit's capital t—l—r—

MRS. MILLS: When she say she's a-comin'?

JUDITH: Don't ye know that thar word, Jeb?

JEB: Nope.

MRS. MILLS: Hyar I sont ye t' scule one hull term o' three months an' now what good does yer larnin' do ye!—Hum!—I allus said larnin' warn't no 'count, nohow!

JEB: [Turning slowly toward her.] The trouble hain't with the larnin', Maw, hit's 'cause I hain't 'nough of it.

MRS. MILLS: They hain't no kind o' sense but horse sense an' God A'mighty gives ye that.

JUDITH: What more she say, Jeb?

JEB: They's a heap more hyar, but I cain't make it out.

MRS. MILLS: Hit don't make no differ'nce, noway, 'cause Naomi Mills hain't a-goin' t' set foot in this house ef I know myself.

JUDITH: Oh, Maw!

MRS. MILLS: Shet yer mouth an' git t' yer churnin'! [JUDITH obeys meekly and churns spasmodically during the remainder of the discussion.] Ef we'uns warn't good 'nough fer 'er wunst, we hain't good 'nough fer 'er now!

JEB: [Slowly, as he leans against the window, looking out into the distance.] I've been a-thinkin' a heap lately, Maw, an' I calculate sis war right t' leave home an' go t' the city when them Scotts offered t' keep 'er an' school 'er like they did.

MRS. MILLS: Y-e-h! Them Scotts!—High-toned city folks, all on 'em!—An' now she's went an' married that pop-in-jay son o' their'n!—I tell ye, Jebie, they hain't no good in city folks!

JEB: They war mighty good t' sis, Maw. Give 'er a chanct t' be somebody.

MRS. MILLS: Now, don't ye argufy with yer Maw, Jeb Mills!

JUDITH: Naomi didn't think she war better'n us, nuther!

MRS. MILLS: Shet yer mouth til ye'r spoke to!—An' don't ye tell me I don't know what I'm a-talkin' about! Why wouldn't I know better'n you! Hain't I yer *Maw!*

JEB: I 'low Jude's right, Maw. You jes' didn't un'erstand sis. She didn't meant t' be uppish. But when she left hyar an' got t' larnin' things down thar in that school in the city, she jes' nacherly got differ'nt frum us. Warn't her fault.

MRS. MILLS: Y-e-h! An' when she cum home hyar o' summers, she tried t' upsot the hull kit an' bilin' of us by puttin' new-fangled, fool notions in yer head an' in Jude's. That's jes' what ails ye now. She's mought nigh ruinated both on ye!—An' she needn't think as how she cain cum back hyar agin with all 'er fine ways, 'cause I hain't a-goin' t' have 'er!

JEB: [Who has been so lost in his own thoughts that he is unaware of his mother's rising anger, speaks more to himself than to her.] Somehow—sis did make a feller feel as how he might amount t' somethin' ef he only had a chanct.— But, Thunder—! What cain a feller do hyar!

MRS. MILLS: What's the matter with this place, I'd like t' know! My folks an' yer pap's folks has lived right hyar in these hills fer y'ars an' y'ars. They war good 'nough fer them. Why hain't they good 'nough fer you'uns?—Ef ye'r half as good a man as yer pap war, Jeb Mills, ye'll be a-sailin'. Why, they warn't nary a man in these parts with a trigger finger like his'n. He cud bead a squirrel a quarter off.—An' jes' ye count the notches on his ol' gunstock yander! [She points to the gun which hangs over the fireplace.] You come frum good stock, Jeb Mills, an' don't ye never be 'shamed o' hit, nuther, like Naomi is.

287

JUDITH: Oh, I wonder what Ben Webb'll do when he hears Naomi's home!

MRS. MILLS: Ben Webb's forgot all about Naomi by this time.

JEB: No, 'e hain't, Maw, 'cause over t' the Settlemint t'other day some o' the fellers war a-pokin' fun at 'im 'cause Naomi wouldn't have 'im when he war so sweet on 'er. An' 'e got all-fired mad an' swore as how he'd kill 'er if 'e ever seed 'er back in these hills again.—Ben's a powerful good shot, Maw,—an' 'e's a reg'lar devil when thar's licker in 'im.

MRS. MILLS: Shucks! Ben Webb wouldn't be a dirtyin' up his gun t' shoot at her!—She oughter married 'im, nohow, an' staid right hyar with 'er own people.—Ben Webb's a'right. He's one o' the likeliest young fellers 'round hyar.— But 'e warn't high-toned 'nough fer her. She war bound t' have a city feller fer *her* man.

JEB: Maw, why air ye so sot agin Jack Scott?

MRS. MILLS: 'Cause his folks ain't our folks. City folks ain't no ways like mountain folks, an' ye cain't mix ile an' water. That's why! [Laying aside her piecing.] Give me that thar letter. I'm a-goin' over t' Clarindy Elrod's. Her Huldie's got more larnin' 'n you have an' maybe she cain make out what day Naomi said she war a-comin'. [She changes her apron for a clean one which hangs on the wall.] An' I'm a-goin' t' git her Huldie t' write a letter t' that Miss Fly-up-the-crick an' tell 'er that she cain save 'erself the trouble o' bringin' 'erself up hyar, fer I ain't a-goin' t' have 'er! She cast 'er lot with them city folks an' she cain stay thar.

JUDITH: Oh, Maw, I wisht ye wouldn't!

MRS. MILLS: You finish that thar churnin' an' be quick about it, too! Nex' thing I know you and Jeb'll be a-wantin' t' trapse off t' the city, I reckon. [MRS. MILLS takes her old cob pipe from the mantel, fills it, and picking up a shaving from the hearth, lights it from the fire in the fire-place. When her pipe is lighted to her complete satisfaction, she takes her sun-bonnet from the peg and starts toward the door. Turning at the door.] Jeb, you slop the hog an' pen up the calf, an' I'll be back in time t' milk the cow. An', Jude, you put some o' them sweet taters in the ashes t' roast fer supper. An' don't put 'em whar it's too hot, nuther.

JEB: Oh, Maw, I'm tired o' taters.

MRS. MILLS: Well—well, Jude, you make Jebie a corn dodger an' 'e cain have some o' that buttermilk ef ye ever git it churned. [She goes out. After she leaves, JEB stands gazing dreamily out the window. There is a moment's pause as JUDITH churns more and more languidly.]

JUDITH: [Ceasing to churn and resting her chin on her hands on the top of the dash rod.] Jeb—do ye reckon Ben Webb'd do like 'e swore 'e would?

JEB: I'm skeered 'e might. 'E's that kind. [He takes down the gun and sits near the hearth cleaning it. There is a brief pause as JUDITH watches him.]

JUDITH: Do ye reckon she'll come, Jeb?

JEB: I reckon so, less'n Maw skeers 'er out.

JUDITH: Oh, I hope she does. We hain't seed 'er fer so long.—She don't hardly seem rail, does she, Jeb?—Las' time we'uns heered from 'er war jes' arter she married—'member? An' she wanted ye to cum live with 'er an' go t' school, an' Maw wouldn't let ye.

JEB: No—Maw wouldn't let me. Maw's allus tried t' make us young'uns do jes' as she wanted. Hit makes 'er blood bile now 'cause Naomi war as headstrong as she war.— Naomi took the bit in 'er mouth an' lit out. Wisht I had!— Dadbustit!

JUDITH: Jes' think what ye might be now ef ye'd a-went down thar t' school that time, Jeb.

JEB: Yes—I might a-been pres—well, no tellin' what I might a-been.

JUDITH: No, they ain't.

[There is a short pause as both are lost in thought, then the door is pushed open and NAOMI enters carrying a small baby in her arms. She is well but not elaborately dressed, and is evidently a young woman of culture and refinement. JEB stands the gun in the chimney corner and leans against the mantel grinning.]

JUDITH: [NAOMI goes to her and kisses her.] Oh, Naomi, ye did come, didn't ye!

NAOMI: Judy, my little Judy! How are you, Jeb?

JEB: Howdy. [He picks up a stick from the hearth and begins whittling.]

JUDITH: [Noticing that the bundle in her sister's arms is not an ordinary one.] What ye got?—Why, it's a baby! —Whose is it?

NAOMI: Why, mine, of course. Whose do you suppose? You don't think I'd carry a strange baby all the way up this mountain, do you? [JUDITH takes the baby and dropping into a chair, begins cuddling it.] I certainly like the way you people come to meet your guests when they arrive.

JEB: We didn't know ye war a-comin'.

NAOMI: Didn't you get my letter?

JEB: Yes—we got it jes' this afternoon, but I couldn't make hit all out.

NAOMI: Oh, I see.

JEB: How'd ye git up hyar frum the Settlemint?

NAOMI: Why, I hired the store-keeper to bring me up on his mule. And such a ride! Gracious! I know that trail is steeper than it used to be— [Removing her hat and placing it on the table.] Where is Maw?

JEB: Over t' git Huldie Elrod t' read the rest o' yer letter.

NAOMI: I see everything is just as it always was.

JEB: Things don't change much hyar.

NAOMI: No, things don't change much here.—It's the same yesterday, today, and forever. And people like Maw are proud of it.—There is absolutely no progress up here. How in the world do you stand it, Jeb?

JEB: I got-a stand it.

NAOMI: Does Maw ever say anything about your coming down with me and going to school?

JEB: Lord, no! She'd a right smart druther I'd go straight t' the bad place 'n go down thar t' the city t' school.

NAOMI: [Shaking her head hopelessly.] The same old prejudice—and ignorance.

JUDITH: [Who has been completely engrossed with the baby.] What did ye name hit, Naomi?

NAOMI: I give you to understand, Judith Mills, that my baby is not an *it*. He's a *he*, and his name's Jack for his daddy.

JUDITH: Looky at 'im, Jeb. Ain't 'e cute!

JEB: Shore is.

JUDITH: [About to hand the baby to him.] Want t' hol' 'im, Jeb?

JEB: Huh-uh!

NAOMI: He won't bite you.

JEB: But—I—I—might drap 'im an' bust 'im.

NAOMI: Oh, you silly!

JUDITH: Ye'r an' ol' skeerdy-cat, Jeb Mills!

[The girls laugh gaily at JEB as he moves awkwardly back to the window and resumes whittling. NAOMI bends over JUDITH and the baby with her back to the door, which is pushed violently open. MRS. MILLS steps into the room with her head high, her eyes flashing and with a sneer upon her lips. At the sound, NAOMI turns, and seeing her mother, starts toward her with a word of greeting.]

NAOMI: Hello, Maw, I'm so— [Checked by the expression on her mother's face, she slowly steps backward, concealing JUDITH, who clutches the baby protectingly in her arms.]

MRS. MILLS: Don't ye "Maw" me! Ye don't belong t' us no more, Naomi *Scott*. [The latter name is hissed with all the venom of which she is capable. NAOMI stands rooted to the floor, regarding her mother blankly.] Ye thought ye'd slip in hyar while I war away, didn't ye? Didn't think I cud see ye a-comin' up the trail, did ye? [JEB, standing near the window, is attracted by something in the yard beyond. He peers out intently an instant, steps to pick up the gun, then returns to his watch at the window.] —Now, ye cain take yerself an' yer traps an' git out o' hyar.—Ef we'uns warn't good 'nough fer ye wunst, we hain't good 'nough fer ye now!—Thar's—the—door! [She indicates the open door with one arm extended rigidly. There is a pause as NAOMI stands with head bowed. JEB shifts position in order to keep his eyes on a moving object without. Speaking slowly and firmly.] I said—thar's—the—*door!*

JEB: I jes' seen Ben Webb cum in the wood lot, Maw.

MRS. MILLS: Ben Webb? Then she'll git t' see ef 'e's still so stuck on 'er. [MRS. MILLS remains standing in the same rigid posture, her extended arm indicating the door and her eyes fastened upon NAOMI. Slowly NAOMI turns to take her baby from JUDITH's arms.]

JUDITH: [Clutching the baby frantically to her and turning to her mother in tears.] Oh, Maw, don't make 'er go!

MRS. MILLS: [Sternly as she notices for the first time the bundle in JUDITH's arms.] What ye got thar in yer lap, Judith Mills?

NAOMI: He's my baby, Maw.

MRS. MILLS: Yer baby! [There is a flash of surprise in her voice and face which is instantly concealed by sternness as she draws herself back into her former rigidity and demands sharply.] Judith Mills, you give that baby t' hit's Maw! [JUDITH obeys reluctantly.] Now—thar's—

the—door! You an' yer— [She falters slightly at the word.] You an' yer—young'un—git out o' hyar!

[NAOMI slowly takes her hat, stoops to kiss JUDITH, looks sadly toward JEB, then starts falteringly toward the door. Before she reaches it, BEN WEBB lurches into the room past MRS. MILLS and meets her face to face. He is an uncouth fellow of about twenty-five, with a bit of bravado about him to conceal an innate cowardice. MRS. MILLS remains standing near the door, stiff and haughty, with her eyes riveted upon BEN.]

BEN: [Leering at NAOMI.] So ye've cum back, hain't ye! [NAOMI shrinks from him as JUDITH takes the baby from her.] Ye'd better a-stayed whar ye war!—Ye needn't think ye cain cum back hyar an' make me the laughin' stock o' these hills. [Moving closer to her.] I swore I'd kill ye ef ye ever sot foot hyar agin, an' I'm a-goin' t' do it! [As he reaches toward his hip, JEB steps between them with the gun in his hands. BEN straightens himself and looks at JEB with a contemptuous sneer.] Git out o' my way, ye chicken-livered runt!

MRS. MILLS [Stepping forward and taking the gun from BEN.] Give that hyar, son. This hyar's my job. [She motions JEB away, then turns on BEN fiercely.] Ben Webb, how-cum ye think ye got a right t' cum hyar an' threaten the life of a Mills?

BEN: [Quailing slightly under the piercing eyes of MRS. MILLS.] Naomi didn't treat me squar. She had no business a-turnin' me down an' makin' all the fellers laugh at me.

NAOMI: I never said I'd marry you, Ben Webb.

MRS. MILLS: Shet yer mouth, Naomi! This hyar's mine an' Ben's squabble.

BEN: [To MRS. MILLS.] An' *you* didn't treat me squar, nuther. You acted like ye stood up fer me, then ye went an' let 'er marry tha' thar city feller.

MRS. MILLS: I did stand up fer ye, Ben Webb, all along, 'cause I 'lowed ye war wuth it.—But I'm through with ye now! Mellissy Mills hain't no use fer nobody what cain't lose like a man, 'stid o' whinin' like a cry-baby!

BEN: Dad-gast-ye! Don't ye call me no names, er they'll be a Mills er two shy, I cain tell ye! An' no loss t' these hills, nuther. The Mills allus war pretty poor pickin's, nohow.

MRS. MILLS: Lawsamassy! I wouldn't speak o' the Mills in the same breath with the Webbs! The good Lord knows ye'r a low-downed lot, the hull kit an' bilin' of ye!

BEN: Low-down, air we! The Webbs hain't a pinch o' snuff t' the Mills fer all 'round cussedness, an' *yer* the bigges' ol' *she-man* o' 'em all! [JEB rushes forward to attack BEN.]

MRS. MILLS: Hol' on thar, son! Hol' on! Mellissy Mills cain take keer o' herself yit-a-while.

BEN: Y-e-h! Ye'r skeered yer little sweetie'll git hurt, ain't ye? Allus keepin' 'im under yer thumb like ye war skeered 'e couldn't take keer o' hisself! Afeered t' let 'im loose frum yer apern string, hain't ye? Ye won't let 'im out o' yer sight; skeered 'e'll do some divilmint, I reckon! Nothin' but a chicken-livered sissy, that's all 'e is!

MRS. MILLS: Ben Webb, shet yer dirty, lyin' mouth! I won't stand ye a-busin' my boy!—Why, they hain't nary a Webb what ever drawed the breath o' life what's fitten fer that boy t' wipe his feet on! [Speaking slowly and firmly as she draws closer and looks him straight in the eye.] An' the Mills hain't law breakers like the Webbs air, nuther. An' ef you darst t' try t' harm a hair on the head o' ary one o' my young'uns, I'll see that the law larns what you an' yer gang does fer a livin'! [She holds his eye for an instant before he begins to weaken.]

BEN: Huh!—Ye wouldn't do that. Ye'd be skeered t'.

MRS. MILLS: Melissy Mills hain't no reason t' be skeered

o' nobody, an' ef you think she wouldn't do hit, ye jes' don't know 'er! [There is a slight pause after which MRS. MILLS takes a few steps toward the door, indicating it with a stiffly outstretched arm.] Thar's—the—door!— Now, you git out o' hyar, ye skunk! Ye yaller dog! Ye snake-in-the-grass!

[BEN curls his lip in a sneer and draws himself up in a last attempt to bluff, but under her unswerving gaze, he weakens and slinks out through the open door. His departure is followed by a brief pause—a lull between storms —as MRS. MILLS watches him an instant before closing and fastening the door. Then she turns slowly toward NAOMI, regarding her sneeringly.]

MRS. MILLS: Hum!— Looks like Ben hain't as sweet on ye as 'e uster be!—How-cum ye brung yourself up hyar? —Is yer city feller tired o' ye, too?

NAOMI: Oh, for goodness' sake, Maw!—Jack wanted to come with me, but he couldn't be spared from the office. But after this disgusting scene we've just been through, I'm thankful he couldn't come.

MRS. MILLS: Then what brung ye up hyar?

NAOMI: I was homesick to see my family, but—I came mainly because—because of the baby.

MRS. MILLS: The baby? Judith, don't hold it so tight. Give it room t' breathe. [Harshly to NAOMI.] What's the baby got t' do with it?

NAOMI: Mother Scott insisted that I should come so that you, his other grandmother, could see him.

MRS. MILLS: Hum!—Wanted me t' see 'im, too? Hum! —How-cum?

NAOMI: Because she loves the little fellow so much, herself, she thought it wasn't fair to you not to let you see him and love him, too.

MRS. MILLS: Hum!—What's 'is name?

NAOMI: Jack.

MRS. MILLS: *Jack?*

NAOMI: Yes, he's named for his father. [Noticing that the name has further aroused her mother's prejudice and hatred, she continues hurriedly.] And Mother Scott feels that since the baby has come we all should be friends.—Then, too, the little fellow never has been very strong and she thought the mountain air might do him good.

MRS. MILLS: No wonder 'e's puny! God A'mighty never intended 'Is childrun t' live in the city in houses jammed together like grains o' corn on a cob! He meant 'em 't live whar they cud git the sunshine an' fresh, clean air er 'E wouldn't a-went t' the trouble o' making that fine gyarden, like 'E did, fer the fust folks t' live in.—[Slowly to herself after a moment of thought.] An' she wanted *me* t' see 'im, too. Well—let's have a look at 'im! [JUDITH jumps up eagerly and takes the baby to her mother, who examines him in an off-hand manner.]

JUDITH: [Hanging over the bundle in her mother's arms.] Oh, Maw, hain't 'e cute! Looky at 'is sweet, little nose!

MRS. MILLS: [Jerking herself up sharply as she realizes that unconsciously she has been patting the bundle which she holds.] I don't see nothin' oncommon about 'im. [To NAOMI.] How-cum ye didn't let us know ye had a baby?

NAOMI: Well, I wrote and wrote so many times before and had no answer that I just decided you didn't care anything about me. Then after the baby came, I was so busy, I—I—

MRS. MILLS: An' 'is Granny Scott made ye bring 'im up t' see *me?* Funny kind o' woman!— [Pushing JUDITH aside as she tries to take the baby from her mother's arms.] Git away frum hyar, Jude! You don't know nothin' about holdin' a young'un.—An' his t'other granny wanted *me* t' see 'im, too. There's some mountain blood in that woman, hain't they?

NAOMI: No, Maw. She was born and brought up in the

city there. Oh, I wish you knew her! There never was a kinder woman, or one with a bigger heart. She's been so good to me all these years!—And, Maw, she insisted that I bring you back with me to visit her.

MRS. MILLS: Me? Wants me to come see *her?*—Melissy Mills what hain't never knowed nothin' but these hills asked t' see rich city folks!—Hum!—Well—that do beat a hen-a-peckin'!—What makes 'er want me t' come down thar t' her house, I'd like t' know?

NAOMI: Just pure kind-heartedness, Maw. She wants you to be friends.

MRS. MILLS: Well—I didn't know the good Lord made *city* folks with hearts like that.—But what kind of a figger'd I cut down thar! Why, I hain't nary a thing fitten t' w'ar. My ol' black alpackie's jes' as brown as a ginger cake.

NAOMI: I thought of that, Maw, and I brought up clothes for all of you, but I had to leave my baggage at the Settlement.

MRS. MILLS: Go out thar in the smoke house, Judith, and fetch in the little old cradle what hangs thar on the wall. [As JUDITH goes out.] Mind ye bresh all the mud dobber nest out o' hit. [There is a pause as she sits and carefully examines the baby in her lap.] The little feller does look kinder puny-like.—I reckon maybe he does need both 'is grannies t' look arter 'im a spell. [Glancing up where NAOMI is still standing.] Draw ye up that cheer, Naomi. Ye look sorter pale.—Jeb, go down t' the spring an' git yer sister a fresh drink o' water.

NAOMI: [Sitting.] No, don't bother, Jeb. I'm all right.

MRS. MILLS: I wonder ef Judy put them taters—

JUDITH: [Breathlessly, rushing into the room with the cradle.] Maw! Maw! Ben Webb's still out thar a-settin' on the wood pile! [JEB picks up the gun and rushes toward the door.]

MRS. MILLS: [Thrusting the baby into NAOMI's arms, all

297

her softness gone like a flash.] Hyar, son, give me that gun! Give it hyar, I tell ye! Melissy Mills cain take keer o' that whelp! [Over her shoulder at the door to JUDITH, who has run with JEB to the window.] Judith, take the quilt thar on that cheer an' make a bed for the baby. [JUDITH grabs the quilt, then rushes back to the window where she and JEB watch the proceedings in the wood lot with great interest. NAOMI looks over their shoulders.]

JEB: Drat it, nohow! I wisht Maw'd let me a-went out thar. I'd a fixt 'im.

NAOMI: [Presently turning from the window in disgust.] Come on, Judy. Let's fix the baby's bed. [JUDITH leaves the window reluctantly and starts toward the cradle, then runs back for one last peep.]

NAOMI: Come on, Judy. [JUDITH obeys and the two girls are making the baby comfortable in the cradle when MRS. MILLS returns, contempt and disgust plainly written in her firmly set face.]

MRS. MILLS: [Standing near the door.] The Good Book says somethin' about the generations a-gittin' weaker an' wiser, but I think God A'mighty made a mistake.—He meant weaker an' ornerier. He'd a-thought so ef 'E'd a-lived in these parts now, nohow.—They's a change cum over these hills what I cain't make out.—They don't raise men like they uster.—Honest, God-fearin' men like yer pap war an' my pap.—The young folks now days is differ'nt an' the change ain't fer the better, nuther.—[She pauses a moment, lost in thought.]— Low-downed trash like them Webbs! [She stands the gun in the chimney corner.]

NAOMI: And, Maw, Ben Webb's only a sample of most of the boys around here. They can't help it. It isn't altogether their fault, for they've never had much chance to be anything better.—But I do hate to think of Jeb's growing up among them! [The light in the room gradually begins to fade as dusk slowly approaches.]

MRS. MILLS: An' he had the gall t' say I was skeered t' let Jeb out o' my sight! The mangy pup!—I reckon I have been wrong, fer I've larned this arternoon that they's good an' bad folks everwhars.—I reckon hit don't make much differ'nce whuther ye live in the city er in the hills.— Hit ain't the place ye live as much as that somethin' inside ye makes ye wuth yer salt er not.— [Coming out of her revery and looking sadly at JEB, who sits near the hearth whittling.] Cum hyar, son—I reckon I hain't never give ye much chanct t' try yer wings, have I? [Slowly putting her hand on his shoulder.] But you air the only boy I got—an' I allus dreaded fer ye t' leave me. But I hain't a-goin' t' have Ben Webb an' his gang a-t'antin' ye cause ye'r tied t' yer Maw's apern string!—Ef Naomi's willin' ye cain go down thar with 'er an' git that larnin' what I've seed fer quite a spell ye've been a-hankerin' fer.—An', Jeb, I want ye t' show them Webbs that a Mills cain stan' on 'is feet an' be a *man* no matter whar 'e is!

JEB: Oh, Maw, I—ef—Naomi—

MRS. MILLS: Dry up, now, an' go fetch me that bunch o' pener-ile a-hangin' thar in the go-between. I want t' make the baby some pener-ile tea. [As JEB goes out happily, MRS. MILLS goes to the window where she stands gazing into the rapidly gathering gloom without. There is just a suspicion that she whisks a tear from her eye with the corner of her apron. The light in the room has almost completely faded.]

MRS. MILLS: [Sadly, as she slowly closes the shutters and drops the bar into place.] The sun's gone down, now, 'hind Ol' Baldy, an' hit'll soon be a-gittin' night.—Punch up the fire a bit, Judith. [JUDITH obeys and the increased light from the fire casts a soft glow over the room. MRS. MILLS draws a straight "split-bottom" chair before it and sits looking into the fire.

MRS. MILLS: [Softly.] Rech me that baby, Naomi.

[NAOMI takes the baby from the cradle and places it in her mother's arms, then stands behind her chair in the firelight. JUDITH sits on the floor at her mother's feet. MRS. MILLS cuddles the baby in her arms a moment, then easing him to her knees, she looks at him fondly in the soft firelight.]

MRS. MILLS: He's got yer nose when you war a baby, Naomi.—An' 'e's got 'is Gran'pap Millses' chin. His Granny Mills is a-goin' t' make 'im some pener-ile tea—that's what she is.—Pener-ile tea is powerful good fer puny babies. [Softly, in a crooning voice.] An' we'll soon have the little feller as pink as a posy so 'is Granny Scott won't know 'im when we take 'im back down thar t' the city to 'er.—No—she won't know 'im. [She gathers him lovingly to her and rocks slowly backwards and forwards on the legs of her chair, crooning softly to him. With a contented smile she gradually drifts into—

Blest be the tie that binds
Our hearts in Christian love—

BUMBLEPUPPY
A COMEDY OF CLIMATE
BY JOHN WILLIAM ROGERS

PERSONS IN THE PLAY

ANDREW BUGG
HAMLET PRINNEL
GENTRY DAVENPORT

BUMBLEPUPPY

A SMALL clump of shade trees not far from the PRIN-
NEL farmhouse in Arkansas. Between two tree trunks
is hung an ancient and ragged hammock. Against a third
trunk an old cane-bottomed chair leans propped on its two
hind legs. At a carefully measured distance between the chair
and the hammock, stands a weather-stained table on which
have been placed—obviously with further regard as to equidis-
tance—two lumps of sugar. A second chair stands somewhere back of the table. Beyond the immediate shade of
the three trees, there is every evidence of the glare and heat
of a sweltering mid-afternoon in July.

ANDREW BUGG, an elongated, somewhat ancient-looking
individual of fifty, is discovered leaning back in the chair,
which is against the tree, a large palm leaf fan in his hand.
He is thoroughly rural-looking, and coatless and collarless.
His trousers are held up by a venerable pair of suspenders
and his shirt is the worse for at least two days' perspiration
and dusty roads. It being Wednesday, a three-day growth
of beard is on his face. On the ground beside him lie his

large straw hat and an empty mail pouch. Opposite ANDREW in the hammock sprawls HAMLET PRINNEL in faded overalls and a blue shirt. His legs dangle lazily down and he also holds a palm leaf fan. HAMLET, who at nineteen is a good-natured, somewhat appealing youth, will be a shambling, colorless, middle-aged farmer at thirty, unless something quite unexpected happens to him. Somewhere in the foliage a locust is droning his hot-weather zuree-zuree-zuree-z-z, and both men seem just on the point of being overcome by the languor of the afternoon, when HAMLET, using a minimum of effort, lifts his head enough to regard the lump of sugar nearest him. He yawns and speaks disgustedly:

HAMLET: Them flies ain't never comin'.

ANDREW: Give 'em time. Give 'em time.

HAMLET: [Sinking back into the hammock.] 'Tain't hardly worth fifty cents to keep awake so long.

ANDREW: I never did think you had no sportin' blood in you.

HAMLET: Oh, I'll keep awake all right. You watch your own lump er sugar.

ANDREW: I'm a-watchin' it. I'm a-watchin' it. [As if to prove it, he fans his sugar with a long sweep of his palm leaf.] I wus a bumblepuppy champeen 'fore you wus tallern a hog's back.

HAMLET: Bumblepuppy air a funny game.

ANDREW: What air funny about it?

HAMLET: Folks a-settin' waitin' for flies to come and light on two lumps of sugar.

ANDREW: Ain't no funnier than folks just a *settin'*, I reckon, and a heap er folks I knows does a lot er that.

HAMLET: Yeah. Settin' do seem to be popular.

ANDREW: Playin' Bumblepuppy, you can't never tell when you might win fifty cents. You can set all day and all you'll do is wear out the seat er your pants.

HAMLET: [Yawns.] Uh-huh. [HAMLET drowses, lying

on his back. Somewhere in the branches above, the locust begins his song again and is answered by another in the distance. ANDREW looks out into the burning glare and mops his face with a large grimy handkerchief.]

ANDREW: [Sighing deeply.] Whoopee. It's hotter 'n Miss Pharaoh's cook-stove. [He is just about to settle back in his chair when he notices something flying over the table. He becomes alert, looks quickly at HAMLET to make sure he is drowsing and uses his fan very gently to drive the quarry from his own sugar toward HAMLET's. On his face is written that beatific consciousness of being alive which comes to sportsmen in supreme moments of the chase. His movements are convulsive with excitement. He looks over at HAMLET, then stands up, pointing at the latter's lump of sugar, shouting triumphantly.] He's done lit on your sugar first. Gimme your fifty cents. [HAMLET, startled by ANDREW, almost falls out of the hammock. Then, after an examination of his sugar, he turns away with deliberate disgust and starts getting back into the hammock again.]

HAMLET: Shucks, 'tain't nothing but a gnat. Gnats don't count. Shoo. Shoo. [He drives the insect away with his fan]. What you want to get a feller out fer nothin' fer?

ANDREW: [Cheerfully, settling back in his chair.] I ain't seen you move so fast since a hen had teeth. . . . Say, Ham, if a snail in a well thirty feet deep crawls up three feet every day and falls back two feet every night, how long will it take that snail to——?

HAMLET: Aw, come on, Mr. Bugg, this ain't weather fer brain work. You always *was* a bird dog, though, fer that there higher mathymatics.

ANDREW: Well, mental arithmetic is just kinder my natural recreation, same as some folks likes to set and look through a Sears-Roebuck catalogue. [ANDREW's attention is suddenly attracted by something in the offing. HAMLET sees him looking.]

HAMLET: What's the matter?

ANDREW: Folks a-stoppin' at your front gate. You're a-goin' ter have company.

HAMLET: [Lying back in the hammock comfortably and stretching his arms.] I ain't. Comin' to see mom, I reckon. [Making a slight effort to see without taking the trouble really to raise himself up.] Who is it? I can't see.

ANDREW: Looks like Maria Abernathy's Ford. . . . They're a-gettin' out all right. She's got Gentry Davenport with her!

HAMLET: Gentry Davenport! [Interested, he sits up suddenly and looks.] Yeah, that's him. He come to see mama last week, the day after he got here. They both busted out cryin' as soon as they had a good look at each other.

ANDREW: Cryin'?

HAMLET: Yeah. Mom was a bride's maid or somethin' when he was married to his wife, and she's dead now.

ANDREW: Myrtle Horn she was. I used to kinder buzz around Myrt a little myself.

HAMLET: Mr. Davenport ain't been back here since they was married. Him and mom was a-talkin' it all over.

ANDREW: Your ma and Myrt used to be powerful close friends.

HAMLET: They was cousins.

ANDREW: When I used to go courtin' the gals, you never seen one er them without lookin' fer t'other. . . . Myrt's been dead quite a spell now.

HAMLET: But Mr. Davenport didn't never marry again. He said it was just like she'd went yesterday.

ANDREW: There's them as is one woman men, and others —well, as ain't so perticular. Personally, I always 'lowed I'd be a marryin' man.

HAMLET: I heard Newt Light say that Mr. Davenport owns four thousand acres of the best apple country in Oregon, and that he has at least fifty thousand dollars coolin' in the bank.

ANDREW: All that money and ain't no tellin' what's to become of it. It's a pity Myrt didn't have no children. . . . It's a dog-goned mixed up world, anyhow. Here I am—eleven children and no money.

HAMLET: Reckon what he'll do with his money?

ANDREW: Dunno. Wish he'd give me $39.15 I bin owin' on groceries at Kimbrough's store fer six months. A side er bacon at my house don't last no longer than a loaf er bread. . . . It do look like I have got the out-eatin'-est family in three counties.

HAMLET: [Fanning a bee away from his sugar.] Shoo. It's a bee.

ANDREW: [Fighting at the bee, which flies over to his sugar.] Git away. Git away, durn you. Sence Scena Mulberry tuk to keepin' bees, it's got so you can't have a comfortable game of bumblepuppy in ten miles, 'thout bein' pestered to death. Shoo. . . . Say, young feller, if you're a playin' bumblepuppy with me, you lie back in that hammock where you belong and stop inchin' up. How'm I gonner git that four bits out er your pocket and you a-crowdin' your sugar like a settin' hen?

HAMLET: [Lying back in the hammock.] All right. [He looks toward the house a little doubtfully.]

ANDREW: I don't suppose you want ter quit and go up to the house along of the company?

HAMLET: [Hesitating.] I reckon they ain't studyin' me.

ANDREW: Yep. We ought to finish this game. It would be a pity to stop without somebody winnin'—after we've worked this hard.

HAMLET: [Almost wistfully and a bit confessionally.] You know, Mr. Bugg, sometimes I think I'd like to go off to some fer place like—like Oregon—like Mr. Davenport done when he was young. Don't nothin' ever seem to happen around here.

ANDREW: Well, the boll-weevil gits worse.

HAMLET: To us, I mean. It would be a heap er fun to go off and do somethin' like Mr. Davenport. Looks like the folks that goes away from here has it all over us that stays.

ANDREW: Oh, I don't know. There was Bazzie Grimes. He went all the way to St. Louis and caught the pneumonia and died. He might have done as well as that if he'd stayed home.

HAMLET: [Almost dreamily.] I'd like to see Oregon. . . . Mr. Davenport says he's got an apple orchard more'n a mile square. That must be a pretty sight—all in bloom.

ANDREW: It must be a heap er work to pick all them apples.

HAMLET: He says in Oregon—

ANDREW: You know, Ham, Gentry Davenport was lucky. His pa died and left him with a mortgaged farm that couldn't nobody make a living on nohow.

HAMLET: You call that luck?

ANDREW: Yep. It was plain luck I tell you. 'Twarn't nothin' fer Gentry ter do after the bank sold off the farm to pay the mortgage, but to light out altogether. Now, if his pa had left him an everyday onery farm—the kind my Cousin Plutarch Pittard's been a-starvin' on fer thirty years, he'd be adown here settin' on it to-day, wonderin' where he was goin' ter find enough money to put a new roof on the spring house. Bein' tied to a little pore land have caused a heap er folks a lot er trouble.

HAMLET: Mr. Bugg, with your way of figurin' out things you'd orter be a rich man.

ANDREW: [Holding out his hand in protest.] Naw, sir. I figured it warn't worth while. Now, my chillun is goin' to have a chance equal to anybody. They ain't goin' to have nothin' to hold 'em down. [ANDREW abruptly gets up, and dropping his fan apparently tries to kill a fly between the palms of his hands. After one or two passes, he finally crushes it.]

HAMLET: Hey, what you a-doin'? How are we ever goin'
to finish this game and you a-killin' off all the ammunition?

ANDREW: [Seriously, holding out his hand, to which the
body of the fly has clung, for HAMLET to see.] 'Twarn't
nothin' but one er them yaller tassel flies, Ham. [He flecks
the fly away with his forefinger.] I know some folks counts
'em. But I never could take no comfort in a game er bumblepuppy with tassel flies. A tassel fly ain't got near as much
sense as one er these here little black cur flies. Look how
much easier they is to kill. I always says, if you're a-playin'
tassel flies, count me out. [Encouragingly, as he picks up
his fan and settles back into his chair again.] I seen a black
fly a-scoutin' around up there just now. He's already done
gone up to your house to tell some er his friends.

HAMLET: I'll bet they're all off somewhere havin' a nap.

ANDREW: Well, there's one thing to be said fer this climate,
Ham. Those on us that gits to Hell is more'n likely to feel
at home.

HAMLET: Mr. Davenport says it don't never get hot in
Oregon.

ANDREW: Yep, but I reckon the winters is powerful cold.
I'd ruther sweat a little than be froze to death. . . . [ANDREW
and HAMLET begin to be slightly more active with their fans
in guarding their sugar, as though the flies had begun to
gather around it.] You know, I used to go to school with
Gentry Davenport. He was a little spindle-legged feller—
always had his big toe tied up in a rag. He was everlastingly
stubbin' his toe. His voice had a way er slippin' up where it
didn't belong, and he always seemed to be tryin' to hide
behind somethin'. God-amighty, how he's changed. I was
at the station the other mornin' waitin' fer the mail when he
come in on Number Four. He walks over to the porch er
Kimbrough's store a-steppin' like a race horse and all curried
up in a blue suit and a collar and tie like a prize mule at a
fair.—"Hello, Andrew," he says right away, a-holdin' out his

hand to me. I thought he was one er them St. Louis drummers a-tryin' to be democratic fer business reasons.

HAMLET: Show nuff? [He fans away a persistent fly.]

ANDREW: Didn't none of us know him, he was that pepped up.

HAMLET: He do have a mighty active air about him.

ANDREW: What you might call too active, if you ask me— without meanin' no disrespect to Gentry, it always makes me kinder nervous to see a man bustin' with too much energy.

HAMLET: [Sympathetically.] It ain't comfortable.

ANDREW: It's a sign his nerves is inflamed. It's unhealthy.

HAMLET: I always had a feelin' it must be somethin' like that.

ANDREW: I reckon Gentry can't help it. . . . There warn't nobody to meet him at the station the day he come in—that there telegraph office in town had forgot to telephone out to Maria Abernathy and tell her he was a-comin'. I carried him down to her house as I come on with the mail.

HAMLET: [Fanning.] Shoo.

ANDREW: 'Course he wanted to hear about everything. You know, when you come to figure it up, there's been a heap er changes in this county in the last twenty years. . . . He didn't know about the lumber mill Tracy Minor and Abe Pittard had built back er Pigeon Roost, and he hadn't heard nothin' at all about the big fire when Uncle Charlie Taylor's store and the gin burned down. . . . I guess you was too young to remember that.

HAMLET: I kinder recollect.

ANDREW: Gentry was mighty interested in hearing about you. He said when Myrt got a letter from your ma tellin' that you was comin' into this world, she was that excited, it might have been a baby of her own. He wanted to know what kind of a feller you was. I told him that personally you seemed a pretty good sort, but it was the gals around here that was show-nuff enthusiastic about you.

HAMLET: Aw, come on, Mr. Bugg. . . . Quit yer hurrahin' me. [Both men become interested in defending their sugar from the flies.]

[GENTRY DAVENPORT comes in neatly dressed in a dark blue suit and panama. When he takes off his hat, which he does as soon as he gets into the shade of the trees, one sees that he is grizzle-haired, with the healthy, ruddy tan complexion of a man who has long been active out of doors. His movements are quick, and suggest vitality and impulsiveness. His collar is a bit too high and worries him a little now and then, so that while his appearance is decent enough—one feels he is very probably wearing his Sunday clothes and is slightly conscious of them.]

GENTRY: Hello, Andrew—afternoon, Hamlet.

ANDREW and HAMLET: [At once.] Howdy, Mr. Davenport. Evenin', Gen.

HAMLET: We wus just talkin' about you.

[ANDREW and HAMLET wield their fans against the flies.]

ANDREW: We seen you drive up with Maria.

GENTRY: Why, what's this—! Gosh ding it, if it ain't bumblepuppy! Haven't thought of bumblepuppy in twenty years. You still play that around here, do you?

ANDREW: Some on us do. . . . Shoo.

GENTRY: You still wet the lump and wait for the flies, eh? [He laughs heartily.]

HAMLET: Take a chair, Mr. Davenport.

GENTRY: [Sitting down and fanning with his hat.] Well, that'll be something to tell 'em about when I get back to Oregon—Bumblepuppy.

ANDREW: You want ter get in the game?

GENTRY: No, I guess I haven't got time. What's the stakes?

ANDREW: Four bits.

GENTRY: Well, you are getting reckless around here. Used to be a quarter in my day.

ANDREW: Waal, everything costs more these days. You used to could get a shave fer ten cents.

GENTRY: Did you ever play golf, Andrew?

ANDREW: Golf? Naw, what's that?

HAMLET: Cow pasture pool. You've heerd of cow pasture pool, ain't you?

ANDREW: One er them new-fangled games, I reckon. But I 'low it ain't no better than the rest. I've played 'em all in my time—parchesi, flinch, ping-pong, horseshoes, checkers, croquet— My gals is just mailed off a coupon fer one er them Chinese games—Ma's wrong er somethin'. But I tell 'em 'tain't no sense in sendin' off. There ain't no game that suits this climate like bumblepuppy.

HAMLET: Mr. Bugg is kinder partial.

ANDREW: Naw, sir. Sugar ain't hard to get and I ain't never seen flies no rarity. Shoo. A man can't afford to wear hisself out in this climate. He'll get all pulled down by the hot weather if he do.

GENTRY: [Turning to HAMLET, becoming serious.] I suppose you are going to be a farmer like your daddy, Hamlet?

HAMLET: [Sitting up in the hammock. He speaks with a slightly embarrassed little laugh.] 'Essir, I reckon so.

GENTRY: Well, I've always been partial to the land myself. A man can do well on a farm if he works hard and keeps his fence corners clean. I've done pretty well. I had to work hard, too—but I'm not sorry. A farm ain't any place for a boy that don't want to work. He just as well go to the city and have done with it.

HAMLET: 'Essir.

GENTRY: We've got some mighty bright boys out our way. Hard workers, too. Some of 'em are going to be rich men. [ANDREW yawns and makes a "ho-hum" sound. GENTRY turns to him.] What?

ANDREW: I didn't say nothin'.

GENTRY: But you know, Hamlet, I don't think those Oregon boys are any better than our boys here. I've been gone a long time, but I never have forgot that I grew up a boy in these hills round Pigeon Roost. I've always loved these old, rocky, red hills, poor as some of 'em are for making a living—and I don't believe there's a finer set of folks anywhere on God's Green Footstool. Now, the folks out in Oregon.—[ANDREW begins to fan vigorously. HAMLET'S attention is also distracted by the flies and he busies himself defending his sugar.]

ANDREW: [To HAMLET, as they fan vigorously.] Lay back—none er your inchin' on me. [HAMLET lies back in the hammock and for the next few moments they engage busily in the game. GENTRY is obviously annoyed with the interruption of his fine sentiments, but the players are too occupied to notice him. He looks from one to the other, purses his lips and apparently swallows down an irritation. Then, with an assumed patience, he waits for them to pay attention to him again. Eventually, the flies give the combatants a respite and HAMLET turns to GENTRY.]

HAMLET: You was sayin' something, Mr. Davenport.

GENTRY: Well, I—

ANDREW: Keep right on talkin'. It don't bother us, and the flies don't mind.

HAMLET: About Oregon?

GENTRY: Well, I was about to say—[ANDREW fans again] there's a great future for a young man in Oregon. Plenty of room and plenty of room to grow. [ANDREW fans again. GENTRY is annoyed, but continues, speaking meaningly, with a glance at ANDREW.] There's a different spirit, too. If I was a young man to-day, I'd go to Oregon. But, of course, every feller can't just pick up and leave. . . . For a long time, Hamlet, I've been thinking. A farmer can do a lot of thinking, if he's a mind to—

ANDREW: I does a heap er studyin' about things, myself. I reckon that's why I never did move into town. . . . I'm kinder philosophical. I come near movin' into Addle Junction, though, once. . . . Sorter wish I had.

GENTRY: [To HAMLET.] Before Myrtle went, I used to dream we might have a son. But that wasn't to be, and I've always had a feeling it was sinful for a man to let his thoughts go flying in the face of Providence.

ANDREW: Thoughts is pretty skittish things. Tryin' to drive 'em down this road and that is worse than herdin' a lot er young colts.

GENTRY: Those that do all they're put into this world to do, don't have time to let their thoughts go wandering off like a lot of young colts.

ANDREW: Shoo!

GENTRY: When I get thoughts that aren't practical, I try to find something in them for deeds that are. I began doing that a long time ago, Hamlet, and I found it paid. Our young men have got to dream dreams and see visions, but dreaming and seeing aren't enough.

HAMLET: No, sir.

GENTRY: There's doing.

HAMLET: 'Essir.

GENTRY: Providence put a lot of young folks in this world. If they aren't my sons, they are other people's, and I know what a helping hand means from the lack of one. I began to wonder—well, I'll explain a little more, first. I've been thinking a lot about Pigeon Roost, lately—

HAMLET: Shoo.

GENTRY: Somewhere in those hills, I says to myself, there's a young feller that might— [The two players begin to fan vigorously and grow excited in the game.]

ANDREW: Hep.

HAMLET: [Countering him.] Oh, no, you don't. [They

314

forget all about GENTRY, who rises angrily and paces the ground indignantly, glaring at the game.]

ANDREW: Waal, that was a real pert roun'. Flies round here just as lively as they ever was, Gentry. You know, folks devils a lot about flies and they is a nuisance, but summertime without flies would seem mighty queer. . . . You was a-sayin' somethin', Gentry?

GENTRY: Oh, well, I guess I'm the one that's changed. Trying to find things like you remembered 'em over twenty years—a man's got to be practical—I might as well try and see things— [HAMLET and ANDREW, who have been listening to GENTRY with one eye on their sugar, have started fanning again and once more forget GENTRY. This is too much for him and he loses all control. Bursting out.] Oh, hell!

ANDREW: What'd you say? [Having exploded, after a moment's hesitation, GENTRY seems to change his whole intention. He loses all his resentment and answers amiably.]

GENTRY: It's a hot day, ain't it? [He mops his brow with his handkerchief.] . . . Well, I reckon I better be getting back up to the house. Maria will be waiting for me. I just came down here to tell you folks good-bye. I'm going back to Oregon to-morrow. [HAMLET and ANDREW both stop the game in surprise.]

HAMLET: To-morrow!

ANDREW: Why, you ain't stayin' long to have come so fer.

GENTRY: That's home out there now, you know. Just wanted to look over the old stamping ground once more. [He starts over to shake hands with HAMLET, who begins to struggle out of the hammock.] No, don't get up. I'd hate to disturb your bumblepuppy. [Shaking his hand.] Good-bye, Hamlet, my boy. Come out to Oregon and see me some time. Bring your wife, it'll make a fine wedding trip. [He turns to ANDREW and goes over to him, shaking hands.] So long, Andrew. Take good care of yourself. I'm going to tell them out in Oregon what a bumblepuppy champion you are. Look out—there's a fly lighting on your sugar now. [ANDREW, startled, turns back to defend his sugar, and GENTRY makes a quick exit, calling "Good-bye." The bumblepuppy play becomes lively.]

HAMLET: Whoa! Keep down in your chair there. Hold steady! It's too late. Hey! Hey, stop. He's already on it.

ANDREW: [Jumping up and slinging his fan down, as an irate golf player.] Oh, mad-dog backward!

HAMLET: [Getting out of the hammock.] I won fair. Where's your money? [He holds out his hand. ANDREW hesitates a moment, looks uncertain, then reluctantly puts his hand into his pocket, carefully drawing out some change, which he examines, looking down sideways.]

ANDREW: [With resignation.] Well, Ham, here's fifteen cents. I had four nickels! There must be a hole in this pocket. [He turns the pocket inside out and examines it, then offers the fifteen cents to HAMLET.] Here, I'll just owe you thirty-five.

HAMLET: Any time, Mr. Bugg.

ANDREW: [Picking up his hat and mail sack.] I reckon I better be movin' on. I ain't gettin' no younger standin' here. Come, go home with me.

HAMLET: I can't. You come go home with me.

ANDREW: Much obleeged. [He starts to go, when he looks off in the distance and stops a moment.] Yonder goes Maria and Gentry. Did it strike you Gentry wanted to say something while he wus down here that he didn't never git out? . . . 'Peared to me he talked kinder jumpy-like—you know, I thought— No, I reckon I'm wrong. I guess that's just a way folks has er talkin' out in Oregon.

HAMLET: [Who has also turned to watch the departing visitors, speaking wistfully.] Gee, I wish I was going out to Oregon. [The two stand looking after GENTRY, making a picture for a moment; then HAMLET breaks the spell.] Oh, shucks! [He turns back.]

ANDREW: [Consulting a large Ingersoll watch on a leather thong.] Quarter to five.

HAMLET: Is that all? [Yawning.] I got time for a good sleep afore supper.

ANDREW: [As he goes.] So long.

HAMLET: So long. Play you another game of bumble-puppy some day. [He stretches himself and makes sleepy noises in a kind of yawn, then gets into the hammock and composes himself for a nap. Above, in the foliage, the locust takes up his song more droningly than ever—zureee—zureeeee-zureee-zzz-z. The hot afternoon sun has turned to ruddy gold, as a faint, reassuring, peaceful snore is heard from HAMLET.

THE MEDICINE SHOW
By Stuart Walker

PERSONS IN THE PLAY

Lut'er
Giz
Dr. Stev'n Vandexter

THE MEDICINE SHOW

THE scene is on the south bank of the Ohio River. An old soap box, a log and a large stone are visible. The river is supposed to flow between the stage and the audience. In the background, at the top of the "grade" is the village of Rock Springs.

PROLOGUE: This is only a quarter of a play. Its faults are many. Come, glory in them with us. You are a little boy once more lying on your rounded belly on the cool, damp sands beside the beautiful river. You are still young enough to see the wonder that everywhere touches the world; and men are in the world—all sorts of men. But you can still look upon them with the shining eyes of brotherhood. You can still feel the mystery that is true understanding. Everywhere about you men and things are reaching for the infinite, each in his own way, be it big or little, be it the moon or a medicine show; and you yourself are not yet decided whether to reach for the stars or go a-fishing. Brother!

[LUT'ER enters or rather oozes in. He is a tall, expressionless, uncoördinated person who might be called filthy were it not for the fact that the dirt on his skin and on his clothes seems an inherent part of him. He has a wan smile that—what there is of it—is not displeasing. Strangely enough, his face is always smooth-shaven. He carries a fishing pole made from a tree twig and equipped with a thread knotted frequently and a bent pin for hook. LUT'ER looks about and his eyes light on the stone. He attempts to move it with his bare foot to the water's edge, but it is too heavy for him. Next he looks at the log, raises his foot to move it, then abandons the attempt because his eyes rest on the lighter soap box. This he puts in position, never deigning to touch it with his hands. Then he sits calmly and drawing a fishing worm from the pocket of his shirt fastens it on the pin-hook and casts his line into the water. Thereafter he takes no apparent interest in fishing.

After a moment GIZ enters. GIZ is somewhat dirtier than LUT'ER but the dirt is less assimilated and consequently less to be condoned. Besides, he is fuzzy with a beard of long standing. He may have been shaved some Saturdays ago— but quite ago. GIZ doesn't speak to LUT'ER and LUT'ER doesn't speak to GIZ, but LUT'ER suggests life by continued chewing and he acknowledges the proximity of GIZ by spitting and wiping his lips with his hand. GIZ having tried the log and the rock finally chooses the rock and acknowledges LUT'ER's salivary greeting by spitting also; but he wipes his mouth on his sleeve. After a moment he reaches forward with his bare foot and touches the water.]

GIZ: 'T's warm as fresh milk. [LUT'ER, not to be wholly unresponsive, spits. A fresh silence falls upon them.]

GIZ: 'S *Hattie Brown* came in? [LUT'ER spits and almost shakes his head negatively.] She's a mighty good little steam-boat.

LUT'ER: She's water-logged.

GIZ: She ain't water-logged.

LUT'ER: She is.

Giz: She ain't.

Lut'er: She is.

Giz: She ain't. [The argument dies of malnutrition. After a moment of silence Giz speaks.] 'S river raisin'?

Lut'er: Nup! [Silence.]

Giz: Fallin'?

Lut'er: Nup!

Giz: Standin' still?

Lut'er: Uh! [The conversation might continue if Giz did not catch a mosquito on his leg.]

Giz: Gosh! A galler-nipper at noon day!

[Lut'er scratches back of his ear warily.]

Giz: An' look at the whelp! [Giz scratches actively, examines the wound and anoints it with tobacco juice. The play would be ended at this moment for lack of varied action if Dr. Stev'n Vandexter did not enter. He is an eager, healthy-looking man with a whitish beard that long washing in Ohio River water has turned yellowish. He wears spectacles and his clothes and general appearance are somewhat an improvement upon Lut'er and Giz. Furthermore he wears what were shoes and both supports of his suspenders are fairly intact. He is whittling a piece of white pine with a large jack-knife. Seeing Lut'er and Giz he draws the log between them and sits. After a moment in which three cuds are audibly chewed, Dr. Stev'n speaks.]

Doctor: What gits me is how they done it. [For the first time Lut'er turns his head as admission that some one is there. Giz looks up with a dawn of interest under his beard. Silence.]

Doctor: I traded a two-pound catfish for a box of that salve: an' I don't see how they done it. [Lut'er having turned his head keeps it turned. Evidently Dr. Stev'n always has something of interest to say.]

Giz: Kickapoo?

Doctor: Ye'. Kickapoo Indian Salve. I don't think no

Indian never seen it. [He looks at Giz for acquiescence.]

Giz: Y'ain't never sure about nothin' these days. [Dr. Stev'n looks at Lut'er for acquiescence also, and Lut'er approving turns his head forward and spits assent.]

Doctor: I smelled it an' it smelled like ker'sene. I biled it an' it biled over an' burnt up like ker'sene. . . . I don't think it was nothin' but ker'sene an' lard.

Giz: Reckon 't wuz common ker'sene?

Doctor: I don't know whether 't wuz common ker'sene but I know 't wuz ker'sene. . . . An' I bet ker'sene'll cure heaps o' troubles if yer use it right.

Giz: That air doctor said the salve ud cure most anything.

Lut'er: [As though a voice from the grave, long forgotten.] Which doctor?

Giz: The man doctor—him with the p'inted musstash.

Lut'er: I seen him take a egg outer Jimmie Weldon's ear —an' Jimmie swore he didn't have no hen in his head.

Doctor: But the lady doctor said it warn't so good—effie-cacious she called it—withouten you took two bottles o' the buildin' up medicine, a box o' the liver pills an' a bottle o' the hair fluid.

Giz: She knowed a lot. She told me just how I felt an' she said she hated to trouble me but I had a internal ailment. An' she said I needed all their medicine jus' like the Indians used it. But I told her I didn't have no money so she said maybe the box o' liver pills would do if I'd bring 'em some corn for their supper.

Doctor: Y' got the liver pills?

Giz: Uh-huh.

Lut'er: Took any?

Giz: Nup, I'm savin' 'em.

Lut'er: What fur?

Giz: Till I'm feelin' sicker'n I am now.

Doctor: Where are they?

Giz: In m' pocket. [They chew in silence for a minute.]

324

DOCTOR: Yes, sir! It smelled like ker'sene ter me—and ker'sene 't wuz. . . . Ker'sene'll cure heaps o' things if you use it right. [He punctuates his talk with covert glances at GIZ. His thoughts are on the pills.]

DOCTOR: Which pocket yer pills in, Giz?

GIZ: [Discouragingly.] M' hip pocket. [Again they chew.]

DOCTOR: The Family Medicine Book where I learned ter be a doctor said camphor an' ker'sene an' lard rubbed on flannel an' put on the chest 'ud cure tizic, maybe. [He looks at GIZ.]

DOCTOR: An' what ud cure tizic ought ter cure anything, I think. . . . I'd 'a' cured m' second wife if the winder hadn't blowed out an' she got kivered with snow. After that she jus' wheezed until she couldn't wheeze no longer. An' so when I went courtin' m' third wife, I took a stitch in time an' told her about the camphor an' ker'sene an' lard. [Ruefully.] She's a tur'ble healthy woman. [His feelings and his curiosity having overcome his tact, he blurts out.] Giz, why'n th' hell don't yer show us yer pills!

GIZ: Well—if yer wanner see 'em—here they air. [He takes the dirty, mashed box out of his hip pocket and hands it to the DOCTOR. The DOCTOR opens the box and smells the pills.]

DOCTOR: Ker'sene. . . . Smell 'em, Lut'er. [He holds the box close to LUT'ER's nose.]

LUT'ER: [With the least possible expenditure of energy.] Uh!

DOCTOR: Ker'sene! . . . Well, I guess it's good for the liver, too. . . . Gimme one, Giz?

GIZ: I ain't got so many I can be givin' 'em ter everybody.

DOCTOR: Jus' one, Giz.

GIZ: She said I ought ter take 'em all fer a cure.

LUT'ER: What yer got, Giz? [Calling a man by name is a great effort for LUT'ER.]

Giz: Mostly a tired feelin' an' sometimes a crick in th' back. [Lut'er displays a sympathy undreamed of.]

Lut'er: Gimme one, Giz.

Giz: Gosh! You want th' whole box, don't yer?

Lut'er: Keep yer pills. [He spits.]

Doctor: What's ailin' you, Lut'er?

Lut'er: Oh, a tired feelin' [there is a long moment of suspended animation, but the Doctor knows that the mills of the gods grind slowly—and he waits for Lut'er to continue] an' a crick in m' back.

Doctor: I'll cure yer, Lut'er. [Lut'er just looks.] If that Kickapoo doctor with the p'inted muss-tash kin cure yer, I guess I can.

Giz: [Who has been thinking pretty hard.] Got any terbaccer, Doc?

Doctor: Yep.

Giz: Well, here's a pill fer a chaw. [He and the Doctor rise. Giz takes a pill out of the box and the Doctor takes his tobacco from his pocket, reaches out his hand for the pill and holds out the tobacco, placing his thumb definitely on the plug so that Giz can bite off so much and no more. Giz bites and the Doctor takes over the pill. Lut'er not to be outdone takes a battered plug of tobacco from his pocket and bites off an unlimited "chaw." The Doctor takes his knife from his pocket and cuts the pill, smelling it.]

Doctor: Ker'sene! [He tastes it.] Ker'sene! Now I been thinkin' things over, Lut'er and Giz. . . . [He tastes the pill again.] Ker'sene, sure! [He sits down on the log once more, spits carefully and crosses his legs.] I got a business proposition to make. [Silence. Lut'er spits and crosses his legs, and Giz just spits.]

Doctor: There ain't enough home industry here in Rock Springs. We got a canning fact'ry and a stea'mill; but here comes a medicine show from Ioway—a Kickapoo Indian Medicine Show from Ioway! Now—what we need in Rock

Springs is a medicine show! [He waits for the effect upon his audience.]

LUT'ER: [After a pause.] How yer goin' ter git it?

DOCTOR: Well, here's my proposition. Ain't we got as much horse sense as them Ioway Indians?

LUT'ER: A damn sight more. [That is the evident answer to the DOCTOR, but LUT'ER develops a further idea.] We got the country from the Indians.

GIZ: [After a moment of accumulating admiration.] By golly, Lut'er, yer right.

DOCTOR: Now, I got some medicine science. I'd 'a' cured my second wife if it hadn't been for that busted winder.

GIZ: Yeh, but what come o' yer first wife?

DOCTOR: I could 'a' cured her, too, only I hadn't found the Family Medicine Book then.

LUT'ER: Well, what I wanter know is—what's yer proposition . . . I'm in a hurry. . . . Here comes the *Hattie Brown*. [The *Hattie Brown* and the whistle of the stea'mill indicate noon. LUT'ER takes in the line—removes the fishing worm and puts it in his pocket.]

DOCTOR: Well, I'll make the salve an' do the talkin'; Giz'll sort o' whoop things up a bit and Lut'er'll git cured.

LUT'ER: What'll I git cured of?

DOCTOR: Oh, lumbago an' tired feelin' . . . crick in the back and tizic.

LUT'ER: But who'll take a egg out o' somebody's ear?

DOCTOR: Giz'll learn that.

LUT'ER: [With a wan smile that memory illuminates.] An' who'll play the pianny?

DOCTOR: Besteena, my daughter.

LUT'ER: Where we goin'?

DOCTOR: We'll go ter Lavanny first.

LUT'ER: How'll we git there?

DOCTOR: Walk—unless somebody gives us a tote.

GIZ: We kin go in my John-boat.

Lut'er: Who'll row? [There is fear in his voice.]

Giz: We'll take turns. [Lut'er looks with terror upon Giz.]

Lut'er: How fur is it?

Doctor: Three an' a half mile. . . . Will yer go, Lut'er?

Lut'er. [Evidently thinking deeply.] How fur is it?

Giz: Three an' a half mile.

Doctor: Will yer go, Lut'er?

Lut'er: Uh-h.

Doctor: Huh?

Giz: He said, uh-huh. [Lut'er chews in silence.]

Doctor: I thought he said uh-uh.

Giz: He said uh-huh.

Doctor: He didn't say nothin' o' the sort—he said uh-uh. [They turn to Lut'er questioningly. He is chewing intensely.]

Lut'er: [After a moment.] How fur did yer say it wuz?

Doctor: Three an' a half mile. [Silence.]

Giz: We'll each take a oar. [Silence. A stentorian voice is heard calling Stee'vun. The Doctor rises, hastily.]

Doctor: What d'yer say, Lut'er?

Lut'er: It's three an' a half mile ter Lavanny—an' three an' a half mile back. . . . Pretty fur.

Doctor: We kin come back on the current.

Lut'er: Three an' a half mile air three an' a half mile—current or no current. [Again the masterful female voice calls Stee'vun. There is no mistaking its meaning. The Doctor is torn between home and business. Lut'er takes up his rod, rebaits the hook with the fishing-worm from his pocket and casts his line into the river.]

Lut'er: I'll think it over . . . but I ain't givin' yuh no hope. . . . Three an' a half mile one way air pretty fur . . . but two ways—it's turrible!

Doctor: Come on, Giz. We'll talk it over. [The Doctor

and GIZ leave LUT'ER to his problem. LUT'ER is undecided. He is at a crisis in his life. He spits thoughtfully and looks after the retreating DOCTOR and GIZ.]

LUT'ER: Three an' a half mile. . . . [He takes in his line and removes the fishing-worm. He rises and looks again after the DOCTOR and GIZ. He hesitates] . . . two ways . . . [He starts in the opposite direction, as he justifies himself to his inner self.] Rock Springs is fur enough fer me! [When he disappears the play is over.]

and Gra leaves Lu-ster to his problems. Lu-ster is undecided. He is at a crisis, isn't he?. He spits thoughtfully and looks after the retreating Doctor and Gra.]

Lu-ster: There on't half stuff . . . . [He takes in his line and removes the fishing-worm. He rises and looks again after the Doctor and Gra. He hesitated . . . two ways . . . . [He starts in the opposite direction, as he justifies himself to his finer self.] Black Springs is fur enough for me!

[When he disappears the play is over.]

THE COW WITH WINGS
A DOMESTIC COMEDY
By Elma Ehrlich Levinger

PERSONS IN THE PLAY

Ralph Gordon
Frances
Marion
Junior
Midge
Alice Graves
Mollie Glenn

THE COW WITH WINGS

MORTONVILLE is one of the many little college towns scattered through Ohio. Visitors are always shown its one beauty spot, the campus of the denominational college, dominated by the ivy-covered chapel. The other buildings are shabby and inadequate. To the Mortonville College faculty, with the possible exception of the "professor" of Greek and Hebrew, a retired minister with few sensual longings, the State Capital, about fifty miles away, represents all that the world holds of gaiety and culture. The president's wife, who gave up dancing upon coming to Mortonville as a bride twenty years ago, scans the society sheet of the *Columbus Dispatch* with painful interest. The young instructor of English goes up to State every summer for a few more credits toward his Ph.D., and dreams of a trip afterwards through the Wordsworth country he is so weary of describing to unmoved students. The "professor" of science (every schoolman, including the principal of the high school, is a professor in Mortonville) yearns for a real laboratory with upper classmen for assistants. His passion, by the way, is

333

entomology; at present he teaches zoölogy, which he loves, and botany, which he detests.

His name is Ralph Gordon and he may be seen every week-day morning at quarter to eight hastening down the tree-edged street on which he lives (exactly like every other residence street in Mortonville) past the Carnegie Library, the new American Legion Hall and the one movie palace, to his eight o'clock classes. But this is Saturday morning, so we will find him at home in the third house in "Professors' Row." All of the faculty live here except the "professor" of mathematics who married a rich wife and now occupies the ancestral mansion on the hill, where the town's six first families live. . . . But we may as well open the door—the children put the bell out of commission last week and Ralph hasn't got around to fixing it yet—and view the family in a typical Saturday morning atmosphere.

The dining-room of the Gordon home on a Saturday morning in early spring. The rather commonplace furniture shows intensive use by a young and lively family; but the room is brightened by all the touches advocated by the best women's journals: chintz curtains of a cheerful pattern, covers for the big chair and bumpy couch, a few flowering plants. The door to the left leads to the kitchen and stands open; a door to the right leads by way of the porch to the street.

All of the family but FRANCES are grouped about the breakfast table. RALPH is about thirty-five, slightly stooped, wearing a shabby alpaca coat and baggy trousers; with his quizzical, near-sighted eyes, he peers through a stack of magazines with formidable looking covers, searching for an elusive reference as he absently nibbles toast he has forgotten to butter. Not at all the caricature of the regulation professor, he is still the typical bookish soul, dreamy and ineffective.

MARION, a lovely child of eight, is peeling an apple; she is inclined, as the eldest of a brood that never knew any nurse

THE COW WITH WINGS

but an overworked mother, to be extremely competent for her age as well as a little domineering. JUNIOR, who is six, sits scowling above his bowl of cereal; as long as he can remember he has suffered alike from MARION's domination and the tyranny of a younger brother, than which there is no greater tyranny on earth. MIDGE, the tyrant in this case, is just past three. He has the face of a cherub and the manners of an Apache. It is his mother's most heart-felt prayer to survive his mischief until he is old enough for kindergarten. At present he amuses himself by shooting crumbs, casually but with science, across the table.

JUNIOR: [Whining.] Mother, Midge is shooting crumbs at me again.

FRANCES: [Calling in from the kitchen.] Tell your father.

JUNIOR: Dad, Midge is shooting crumbs in my milk, and I won't drink it neither.

RALPH: [Absently, not looking up.] Mmh—tell your mother. [Turns a leaf.]

JUNIOR: [Now shrieking with rage.] Mo-ther, he's doing it worse'n never and dad won't stop him.

MIDGE: [With a yell of triumph.] Hit him that time!

RALPH: [Not looking up.] Boys—boys! [As the noise increases, he puts aside his reading reluctantly.] Can't you let your poor dad enjoy a Saturday breakfast when there aren't any eight o'clock classes? [He is about to return to his magazine when MIDGE begins his crumb-shooting again.] If you shoot another crumb, Midge, I'll—I'll be very angry. Junior, go on with your breakfast.

JUNIOR: You let him fill my milk with his nasty old crumbs. [With a howl.] He's shooting at me again and you won't even hit him.

RALPH: [Cuffing MIDGE, not too hard.] Now I've hit him! Go on and drink your milk.

[JUNIOR obeys beamingly, but MIDGE bursts into heart-broken sobs.]

335

MARION: Mother, dad's hitting poor little Midge again. [Running over to pet him.] Don't cry, sweetheart.

[FRANCES enters from kitchen, carrying a large frosted cake, with eight pink candles and a larger white one in the middle. She is about thirty, heavy dark hair carelessly arranged, a figure that has grown too heavy and does not show to advantage in her graceless housedress; hers is the calm of an executive who knows that if she loses hold for a moment there will be all sorts of explosions; her voice although very quiet is strained.]

FRANCES: Junior, finish your cereal and stop picking fights or you won't go to the movie this afternoon. [She puts the cake before MIDGE, whose howls cease as suddenly as they began.] I know a big, big boy who never cries who's going to have a big piece of birthday cake for dinner. [Bending to kiss MARION.] Another kiss for my birthday girl. Like your cake, sister? [She takes magazine from RALPH.] Better drink your coffee while it's hot, dear. [All this has been accomplished with just a touch of scorn at her family's inanity, for this is the usual Saturday morning scene; now she takes the empty seat at the foot of the table, her body slumping with weariness.]

RALPH: [Over his coffee cup.] Better take something yourself, Fan. You look fagged. I told you it would be better to buy a cake instead of getting up at six to bake one.

MARION: [Coming to count the candles.] It's a shame to waste such a lovely cake on two pigs like Junior and Midge. [JUNIOR snorts at the insult; MIDGE grins like a cherub.]

FRANCES: Sorry, but we can't afford a birthday party this year, sister.

RALPH [In an undertone to FRANCES as the boys join MARION to examine the cake and peck at the frosting.] Hard work, isn't it, Fan, to raise three terrors on the same old salary year after year? They ought to have a successful plumber for a father instead of an assistant professor.

FRANCES: [Patting his arm.] They don't know a good teacher when they have one.

RALPH: You know I'm not a good teacher. I can't give flashy lectures; I'm just good for research. [Tapping his manuscript.] But if I ever finish my book on the mating habits of the beetle, I may get a little recognition . . . and a salary big enough for birthday parties. [Looks down on her hand still resting on his arm.] You burned your hand again on that old-fashioned oven! I hope it heals by the time you play at the president's reception.

FRANCES: [Shortly, pouring herself a cup of coffee.] I've decided not to play at the reception. I'm all out of practise.

RALPH: You ought to cut out everything for your music—

FRANCES: Cut out what? When the washing's over, there's the ironing; by the time I've got cookies baked, the pies are gone. [Nodding toward the overflowing basket on couch.] Look at that basket—not a bit of mending done this week.

RALPH: [Trying to smile; they have been over this so many times before.] I'm not much good at darning stockings, but if you'd only let me wash—or scrub—

FRANCES: I can't have you going to classes with your hands all red and rough from housework like mine. You just stick to your beetles and I'll tend to the scrub pail. And I didn't mean to be grouchy . . . my nerves. . . .

RALPH: If you could only quiet your nerves by picking up your violin once in a while!

FRANCES: I ought to break up my violin and use it for kindling wood.

MARION: [Running to her.] Oh, mamma, if you really don't want your violin any more, give it to me for my birthday.

FRANCES: [Shaking her head, before she wearily repeats her formula.] Junior, fold your napkin—put it in the ring— push back your chair. [As MIDGE jumps up.] Midge, have you eaten your toast?

MIDGE: [Surprised as he points it out under his chair.] Why, I dropped it!

JUNIOR: He threw it under, ma. I saw him.

FRANCES: [Separating them expertly as MIDGE begins battle.] Junior, go to the sink, wash the jam off your mouth, tie your left shoe, go out on your skooter. Midge, take this slice [butters a fresh piece of toast] and eat every crumb of it. Then put on your old sweater and go out and play. Marion, clear the table. Ralph, you'd better sit on the couch, so I won't have to sweep around you.

[All obey. FRANCES, pushing back her untasted breakfast, brings in broom from kitchen; RALPH tries to take it from her; she shakes her head unsmilingly; he retires to his magazines on couch; MARION piles dishes on tray; FRANCES sweeps as though her life depends upon it. MARION on way to kitchen with tray, stops to turn coaxingly to her mother.]

MARION: 'Cause it's my birthday, can't I go to the faculty concert to-night with you and dad?

RALPH: Let her have my ticket. I've got a lot of papers to mark.

FRANCES: [Ignoring him.] I'll let you have my ticket, Marion.

MARION: [Dancing into kitchen, singing happily.] I'm going to a c-o-n-c-e-r-t!

RALPH: You shouldn't give up one of your few pleasures to humor her.

FRANCES: [Banging the kitchen door savagely as she sweeps before it.] It's no pleasure to hear those amateurs murder Chopin. Anyhow, the less music I hear, the better.

RALPH: [Going to her as she bangs the last chair in place with unnecessary violence, taking her shoulders and forcing her to look at him.] Frances, what has got into you lately?

FRANCES: The devil! [With a grim laugh.] I looked to see if the door was closed before I said it. I don't swear in front of our angel children—yet. [Sits down on her heels,

338

throws her handbrush aside, and pushes her hair back wearily.] But I'm just at the end of my rope.

RALPH: [Patting her shoulder.] Why, dearest, you're not sick, are you?

FRANCES: Now don't ask to see my tongue, or tell me I've been drinking too much coffee. Or say I ought to take more exercise! [Hysterically.] Don't I walk to market every day with Midge chattering until I'm ready to scream? Then there's the excitement of wondering whether we can't afford grapefruit instead of dried apples and compromising on prunes. Then home to stew the prunes and bully Midge into taking his nap. . . . It's a gay life . . . and I'm beginning to weaken.

RALPH: What you need is a change. You'd better run up to Columbus for the next Symphony.

FRANCES: [Rising, speaking in a hard, cold voice.] I never want to hear a Symphony again. The last time I came home and cried all night. I told you it was a toothache; but music hurts more than a toothache now. Do you know why I'm not going to play at the president's reception or anywhere else? I can't play well enough even for an amateur audience any more. [Choking back a sob.] And once I played a solo—with the Symphony.

RALPH: If you could only manage to practise more?

FRANCES: My dear man, if you weren't the father of my children, I'd be tempted to strike you. Practise! Can I practise and be interrupted a dozen times with [she mimics JUNIOR's wail] "Mother—I can't find my rubbers." [MIDGE's howls] "Ma—Junior hit me." Or Marion needs help with her arithmetic. You know I've tried to practise at night, but after ten hours as cook, scrub woman, teacher, trained nurse, and society lady, if there's a faculty tea! Even when they're all asleep I keep wondering if Junior's kicked the covers off. [Quietly, without bitterness now.] I can't hold two jobs, so I'm giving up my music for good.

339

RALPH [Excited for once.] But you know when you graduated they said at the Conservatory—

FRANCES: [Crying out.] —that I had a future! [Quietly again.] Well, now my future's behind me. [She goes to windows to straighten the curtains; stares out; then finally turns to him, trying to control herself.] If I'd only had a chance to see what was really in me—a chance to practise all day—to hear plenty of real music—to lie at night and dream. . . . Just to work—and grow—and give my music a chance to come out. [The door bell rings; she speaks with her usual briskness.] I told you that coat was too shabby to wear any more. Go up and change quick.

RALPH: [Gathering up papers, books and magazines.] I'll just stay upstairs and read where I can't hear the children. [He goes out through the kitchen door, closing it behind him.]

FRANCES: [Opening the street door and stepping back astonished.] It can't be Alice Graves! [ALICE GRAVES enters; she is about FRANCES' age, but she seems at least ten years younger; trim figure, set off to advantage by expensively simple suit and light furs, modish bob, etc. Charming voice; rather dictatorial manner of lady patroness.] I didn't even know you were in town.

ALICE: [As they sit on the sofa together.] Just back yesterday to help settle father's estate. There's nothing left for me in Mortonville any more, so I'm going back to Paris next week. But I had to see you first.

FRANCES: When you didn't write for so long, I was afraid you'd forgotten what good friends we used to be at the Conservatory. Your father was always so wonderful about taking me along to concerts and the opera.

ALICE: He was always saying he wished he could do more for you. But I'm so stupid about business matters that I never knew poor father's plans for you until we went over the will yesterday. He was so disappointed that you got married as soon as you graduated from the Conservatory instead of going abroad to study at his expense.

FRANCES: [Slowly.] A year with Marretto would have helped—a good deal.

ALICE: Whenever we heard a great violinist abroad, father used to say, "Our Frances could have equalled him."

FRANCES: Don't!

ALICE: Father left a fund that you could go on with your music; study with Marretto for several years.

FRANCES: Study with Marretto! Several years of study— and rest—in Paris. [Trying to laugh.] Stop trying to tease me, Alice.

ALICE: If you'd rather talk over things with father's lawyer—

FRANCES: I didn't mean—but I'm so dazed—

ALICE: I thought you'd be after ten years of baby tending and housework. [Examining Frances' hand.] It's going to take some time limbering up these fingers again. Could you leave Monday?

FRANCES: [Still dazed.] Why in such a hurry?

ALICE: We'll cross together. If you were under my eye all summer, I could see that you practised and got yourself in trim again. Maybe we could persuade Marretto to take you in the fall.

FRANCES: [Resenting her tone of patronage.] How do you know I've slumped?

ALICE: A woman with half a dozen children—or is it three? —doesn't hurt herself practising.

FRANCES: [With a harsh laugh.] Thanks for reminding me. And how am I going to leave the children?

ALICE: Don't be a fool for the second time in your life, Frances. You wouldn't let father help you when you graduated—you wanted [in cruel mimicry] "a home and babies." Now give yourself a chance with your music.

FRANCES: I've got my job cut out for me here.

ALICE: You've sacrificed yourself for ten years. Let them sacrifice—just for a little while. Give yourself a sporting chance—and if you win—

FRANCES: [Breathing hard.] If I win—

ALICE: If you become a successful violinist, you'll earn more in a month than your husband can in a year. Think what that would mean to your children.

FRANCES: I wasn't thinking of the money. But the freedom—getting up in the morning to run to my violin as I used to at the Conservatory—no market list—no walk for Midge —no sweeping. I'm ashamed to say it, but I'm sick of everything here—ironing Marion's middies, or listening to Ralph talking about his everlasting beetles until I'm ready to scream. If I don't get out of this somehow, I'll go crazy.

ALICE: I wonder you've stood it this long.

FRANCES: A cow doesn't leave her pasture when the bars are up.

ALICE: But now the bars are down. You're coming to New York with me Monday; we'll pick up a few rags there and sail on Wednesday.

FRANCES: I can't. Even if Ralph would let me—and he's always wanted me to succeed with my music—I can't go. There's Midge; he's only a baby. He'd cry his eyes out.

ALICE: You had to neglect the others when he was born, didn't you? Your music is just another child; maybe the only child an artist ought to have, anyhow.

RALPH: [Thrusting his head through the kitchen door.] Somebody's been meddling with my papers again, Fan. [Annoyed but patient.] I can't find page 33 of my Mating Habits of the Beetle, and if it was thrown out during your Friday cleaning—

FRANCES: Come in, Ralph. [Sighing to see he hasn't changed his coat.] You remember Alice Graves?

RALPH: [Shaking hands absently.] Perfectly. [Begins

342

to rummage among the books on the side table.] I might have left it in the book I was reading before breakfast!

FRANCES: Sit down a minute, Ralph. This is just as important as your beetles. [He sits down, astonished at her tone.]

ALICE: You see, Mr. Gordon, my father always believed in Frances and thought she should devote her life to her music. He's left her enough in his will to work several years in Paris with Marretto. He'll make a real musician out of Frances.

RALPH: [Smiling up at FRANCES, on the arm of his big chair.] Why, she's the best violinist we have in Mortonville. Everybody says so.

FRANCES: Can't you understand? I don't want to be the best violinist in this silly little town; it doesn't mean anything to me. Or even in New York—or Paris. I want to feel I've reached just as far as I can possibly go. [Breaking down and sobbing on his shoulder.] I don't want to be a failure.

RALPH: [Soothing her.] Now that's no way to talk. How can you be a failure, Fan, when you've made such a lovely home for all of us?

FRANCES: [Wiping her eyes.] A lovely home? A prison, you mean! You're cramped in it, too, though you're too decent to say so. Sometimes I hate it all—the home—and the children—and even you—all standing between me and something I want more than all of you together—my music. Ralph, dear, please give me my chance. I know I'll be lonely over there; I'll just ache to give Midge his bath—when I don't have to every night!—or even to hear Junior's whining. It would be even harder for you, dearest, if you let me go. Though I could get Old Lady Browning to come and look out for things just for her board and she's a better cook than I ever tried to be. But I want my chance; if I don't get it soon I don't know what I'll do. I feel so burning up inside sometimes; hating the musicians when I see their pictures in my

Music Journal; just because they've succeeded and I haven't; hating my violin because I can't play any more as I used to; even hating you because you've robbed me of what I want more than anything else in the world. [Kneeling beside his chair, where he sits with face averted.] Don't let's go on this way, old dear. Give me my chance. Give me a chance to see what's in me.

RALPH: [Thinking it out slowly and carefully.] Maybe it's my fault. I promised you when we married you could keep on with your music. I was ambitious, too, then; I thought I'd soon get into one of the big colleges in a big city; a salary big enough for a maid; plenty of concerts for you and time to enjoy them; leisure to go on with your studies. You haven't had any of these things; but I did try to be a good husband to you, Frances.

FRANCES: It's not your fault; it's nobody's fault. We couldn't help falling in love, we couldn't help marrying. I know it's not easy for you either, teaching those stupid boys and girls when you want to be working in a lab., or helping me to put the children to bed, when you're wild to get to your writing. And doing at least half of the worrying over the bills! I ought to be contented, when you do everything you can for me, but something inside me won't let me be satisfied. I've given up ten years now, sacrificing my music for you and the children and the house. Not daring to think my own thoughts! Now I want to be free even for a little while. Just a little while, Ralph, to find out what I can do if I get a chance.

[ALICE goes to the table, picks up a book and tries to appear interested in entomology. RALPH rises and speaks heavily.]

RALPH: I'll try not to stand in your way, Fan. I thought when I brought you into this—too many babies and not enough to pay the rent sometimes—I thought I'd give you something just as good as your freedom. I'm not quick; I can't jump out and snatch ideas the way you do; but I'm

smart enough to see we oughtn't to go on like this . . . you
so restless and unhappy. I'll be rather—unhappy, too, without you; but I've been just as miserable watching you fretting
to get away. I guess Old Lady Browning can take care of
us all right. [Drawing her to him.] Anyhow, I'd be the last
to stand in your way.

[The door bell rings. FRANCES, wiping her eyes, opens
street door to admit MOLLIE GLENN, a wisp of a woman of
uncertain years, in shabby, genteel garments, hair slicked back,
spectacles before her peering, near-sighted eyes. Her voice
is high and sharp, her actions jerky and her manners in-
quisitive.]

MOLLIE: Just dropped in to tell you, Mis' Gordon, I could
come next week for the spring sewing like you wanted, 'cause
I ain't going to Mis' Randolph's like I planned. [With fine
contempt.] Mis' Randolph's going to Columbus to buy her
Sadie's wedding clothes, and they say they're buying the wedding dress and veil in Cincinnati. A fine way, when her husband's made all his money undertaking in this town, and she
up and takes the sewing right out of a honest woman's mouth.
So if you want me next week for the spring sewing—

FRANCES: [Prodded by ALICE, she manages to stop her.]
Miss Mollie, you remember Alice Graves?

MOLLIE: [With a screech of surprise.] Little Alice Graves!
Not Banker Graves' little Alice? Say, I made some of your
clothes before you thought of being born even. Turn 'round,
Miss Alice, please. So that's the length they're making 'em
in Paris—sort of up and down. Them Paris gentlemen-
seamstresses certainly do know how to make a maiden lady
look like one of them flappers in the movies. In them
clothes you don't look a day over thirty. [As ALICE is about
to make an indignant denial, she swings around to FRANCES.]
Now—about the spring sewing—

FRANCES: [After a long glance, first at ALICE, then at
RALPH.] I don't expect to be here, Miss Mollie.

345

MOLLIE: Going out of town? Who's going to be married or buried?

ALICE: Buy the lot in New York ready-made.

MOLLIE: Don't do it, Mis' Gordon, don't you do it, or you'll live to regret it. Them ready-made things don't hold together through the first wash; and they fades like the mischief. [Diving into her shabby satchel, pulls out several brightly covered fashion journals, pathetically eager to hold her customer.] Just you look here, Mis' Gordon, what I was aiming to make for your little Marion—no sleeves, 'cause she's got such nice little arms, and three ruffles—

FRANCES: Yes, Miss Mollie. Suppose you leave your books and patterns here; I think I'll be ready for you Monday morning.

ALICE: Frances!

[RALPH is about to speak, but thinks better of it.]

MOLLIE: [in the doorway.] But if you're going away, Mis' Gordon— [Her nose working impatiently as she scents news for her next customer.]

FRANCES: No, I'll be here Monday morning.

MOLLIE: And if you gives me scrambled eggs for my lunch like usual, don't forget to lay in a bit of bacon to go with 'em, Mis' Gordon. I know it's stylish to be thin, but my doctor says it ain't healthy to be undernourished like I am. Well, I certainly was pleased to see you, Miss Alice. Good-bye, Mr. Gordon. [She bows herself out.]

ALICE: [Angrily as the door closes.] If you expect to delay our sailing to fuss over a few rompers—

FRANCES: [Ashamed and uncertain.] Just a week— [Bursts into hysteric laughter.] A chance to study with Marretto—and I stand here worrying about Junior's summer blouses.

RALPH: [Looks toward the kitchen.] Be careful! . . . The children. . . .

FRANCES: [Steadying herself and speaking with just a

346

touch of bitterness.] No, I mustn't let myself go before the children! [Turning to ALICE.] You must think I'm crazy to act like this. But I was crazy even to think of going away with you.

ALICE: We've had enough foolishness. Dress yourself; we'll go downtown and buy the children enough to last till fall. Never mind—that's my treat—just to get that idiotic sewing off your mind. And Mollie Glenn can come anyhow and empty that terrible mending basket. [As FRANCES, looking rather dazed, goes out through kitchen.] We'll have to hurry her off before she changes her mind again.

RALPH [In the big chair again, heavily.] Frances won't change her mind if she can help it; she's too anxious to go.

ALICE: [Going to him, impulsive for once.] Don't hate me too much for tempting her to leave you, Mr. Gordon. I want her to live her own life.

RALPH: I thought she was—until you came.

ALICE: [On the sofa, dismissing the sex with a gesture before she begins to rummage in her make-up case.] Of course, a man wouldn't understand.

RALPH: I expected you to say something like that. A feminist would, and, of course, you're a feminist, aren't you, Miss Graves? [Lip-stick in hand, she nods, vaguely irritated by his air of quizzical patience.] I think I understand Frances and her troubles much better than you ever could, even if I am a man, only a stupid half-man as most of you practical people consider us professors. I know what it is for her to be starved for her music, listening to a few amateurs several times a year when the Elks give a benefit concert. Or running up to Columbus for a Symphony—after putting the house in order and retrimming a last year's hat, and coming home on the last bus so tired she's wondering how in God's name she's going to get up in time to get the children off to school and me to my eight o'clock. Or feeling that she's going to practise in spite of everything—and then Junior wakes up with a sore throat and has to be coddled all day, or I, God forgive me, bring home a basket of soft fruit I've picked up cheap at the market, and she has to drop everything to can it before it spoils. Oh, yes, I know what Frances has been going through ever since we've been married, for I'm in the same boat myself!

ALICE: [Snapping the case shut, says defiantly.] But you're a man—you can get out of the house for your work—you meet people—have fresh ideas—

RALPH: I'm afraid you don't realize, Miss Graves, that a man's work is often as puddling as a woman's. Take mine, for example. I wasn't cut out to be a teacher any more than Frances was meant to be a cook and a washwoman. I want a big, well-equipped laboratory, instead of the miserable hole and the cheap equipment which is all the college can afford; I want to spend hours and hours with my bugs—watch 'em eat and fight and make love and die and that sort of thing. And write 'em up afterwards. [With a half-smile.] Bugs aren't worth while to most people, although the money your father left for Frances's music probably was earned by some farmers a poor "bug-professor" like me taught to fight the corn pest. My work's just as important and as thrilling—yes, and as beautiful—as music or painting or even banking. [Shaken by his enthusiasm out of his usual air of indifferent dreaminess.] Yes, I want to do something worth while in my own line, too, instead of giving the same lecture year after year on the fertilization of the Easter lily, or watch Freshmen bungle the simplest experiments. But I've got to keep on with the grind.

ALICE: [Fencing for time.] I don't see why.

RALPH: I think you do. If I hadn't married, I could have kept on working for my doctor's; not worried about a job. I could have taken a year off, maybe, for research and writing. Now after teaching morons all day and marking papers half the night, do you think it's easy for me to settle down to my book [flipping the foolscap in his hand contemptuously], my book, I've tried to write between helping nurse Midge through the whooping cough, or doing the ironing when Fan has been flat on her back and couldn't prevent me. Why, even I know how rotten my book is, and when a man feels that way about his magnum opus— [With a helpless gesture.] But what's the use of talking?

ALICE: You ought to get a better paying job.

RALPH: [Again with his lazy good humor.] My profession is rarely overpaid, even for the good teachers. And I'm a poor one, though I might make out with fewer classes and not so many bills to worry about. The more we worry, the worse we teach; the worse we teach and the less we earn, the more we worry. It's a vicious circle, Miss Graves, and I admit it's tough on our women. But don't think we husbands have it much easier. [In his most academic manner.] If I may use a very old comparison you feminists like to ignore, but which I, as an entomologist, have seen worked out again and again, it's always the female spider that devours her mate. She has to be big and strong and healthy to look after the "kiddies"; the kind husband allows himself to be eaten—and the race goes on. [Smiling.] If the lady spider didn't eat up her husband and had to look elsewhere for food, I'm sure he'd sympathize with her as much as I do with Frances.

ALICE: Now you're disgusting!

RALPH: No—only scientific. I've found the two terms often mean about the same thing to feminists.

[Before ALICE can think of an answer sufficiently cutting, JUNIOR bursts in from the street.]

JUNIOR: Dad, Jack's going to the drug store for an ice cream cone; I want a nickel.

MARION: [Appearing at the kitchen door, which FRANCES has left open.] Mother never lets him have ice cream between meals.

JUNIOR: Mind your own business! Can't I have a nickel for a cone, dad?

RALPH: [Through force of habit.] Ask your mother.

FRANCES: [Entering.] What's the matter now? [She has changed into her best dress, a black velvet, which somehow fails to achieve the chic of ALICE's turnout; carries a small black hat.]

JUNIOR: Dad ain't going to give me a nickel for an ice cream cone.

FRANCES: [Mechanically, as she stands before the buffet mirror, arranging the lace at her throat.] "Isn't"—not "ain't." Now shake hands with mother's friend—the right hand, Junior.

JUNIOR: [Obeying.] Now do I get my ice cream cone?

FRANCES: No, Junior. [He goes out snivelling; she turns to RALPH who is going over his books on the side table.] Ralph, do you think you can ever make the children eat properly?

RALPH: [Waving the paper triumphantly.] I must have brought it down with my books— [Skimming to make sure.] Mmh, the "female beetle"—

FRANCES: Sometimes I think you're more interested in beetles than your own children. [Adjusting her hat at the mirror.] Alice, what is the matter with me? I know that this dress wasn't made in Paris, but why don't I look more like you when I'm fixed up? Why do I look so fat?

ALICE: Because you are fat. You'll have to train down a lot before you go on the concert platform.

[The street-door is flung open; MIDGE rushes in howling, his face very dirty, a grimy handkerchief pressed to one eye.]

MIDGE: I wanted to go to the drug store with the big boys and Junior threw a rock at me. My eye!

FRANCES: Let me see it!

MIDGE: My eye—Oh, my eye!

THE COW WITH WINGS

FRANCES: [Losing her self-control for the first time.] I've told you boys so often—if you've put your eye out as I've always said you would— [Appealing to RALPH.] I'm afraid to look at it.

[RALPH attempts to examine the eye; MIDGE jerks away and continues to howl.]

FRANCES: [Trying to catch hold of herself.] Maybe it's only a bruise—but a rock— [Kneeling beside him, trying to make him stand still.] Midge, please, please be good and let mother see the poor sick eye—she won't hurt it— Mother will put nice cold water on it— [To MARION, who has run in from the kitchen.] A wet rag, quick! [MARION hurries out.] And mother will get him some roller skates—just let mother see—! [Shudderingly to RALPH, who stands by, pale and helpless.] You remember the Dennison boy—both eyes! Do you think you ought to phone for the doctor? Please, please stop crying, Midge— [MARION returns with a wet cloth.] Now if you'll let mother see the poor eye—let mother see—and Marion'll cut you a piece of birthday cake right away— [She manages to get his hand down, disclosing an eye plastered with mud.] Let mother bathe it—so careful— [Does so.] Won't hurt a teeny bit— [Flops down on the floor, looks up at RALPH, lips trembling.] It's all right—and I was so certain Junior had put it out! [Turning on MIDGE.] Midge, are you sure brother threw a rock at you?

MIDGE: [With his cherubic smile, enjoying the lime-light.] It was hard like a rock. Can I have a big piece of birthday cake?

ALICE: If that was my child, I'd—

FRANCES: [Rising, suddenly aware of her guest.] Shake hands with mother's friend, Midge.

ALICE: [Drawing hastily back from his muddy sweater.] I'll excuse him this time.

MIDGE: Now do I get my cake?

FRANCES: You shouldn't spoil your dinner. [Wearily.]

351

Oh—give him a piece, Marion, but help him wash his face and hands first.

MARION: [Loftily, leading him into kitchen.] Come on, you pig!

FRANCES: [Sinking wearily into the big chair.] That's where all my energy goes— If his eye had really been put out!

ALICE: Snap out of it! Brush yourself off and we'll go downtown and buy those clothes before lunch.

FRANCES: [Absently, searching among the fashion journals on the couch.] The brush was here, but Mollie Glenn left such a mess— [Picks up open journal.] That little dress with three ruffles would look too sweet on our Marion. I'd never get anything so cunning ready-made. Really, Alice, I'd rather stay home a week and attend to the spring sewing.

ALICE: You're just looking for excuses!

FRANCES: Do you think I can go away and keep thinking all the time that terrible things are happening? Suppose Midge's eye is all right; maybe next week he'll really get hurt. Don't you remember, Ralph, how last spring Junior fell out of the cherry tree and almost broke his arm? And—

RALPH: [Who may understand women as well as beetles.] Frances, don't blame it on the children. You can't throw them overboard any more than I can. But if you really wanted to get away badly enough—if you were a real genius like Gauguin and those other fellows, you'd clear out no matter what happened to any of us.

ALICE: Aren't you willing to fight for your freedom?

FRANCES: You've brought my freedom too late. I've gone back in my music; I've ruined my hands; and I'm too fat. When Mollie Glenn flattered you before, Alice, I was jealous. But it isn't your Paris clothes and your stylish bob—you've taken care of yourself. And I'm afraid I couldn't ever diet and exercise to get my hips down again. My character's slumped along with my body. For ten years I've been telling myself, "If I only had a chance to practise all day!" [With a bitter laugh.] If I didn't have Midge to interrupt me, I'd probably lie on the sofa and read a story magazine. And then you talk about preparing myself to work with Marretto! I tell you I haven't the will to succeed any more.

ALICE: As soon as you're out of this mess—

FRANCES: No. I'd fail anywhere now—because I'm afraid of failing. You can't be a brave young girl again after ten years of slipping and letting go. I said I wanted to be free; but I'm afraid to break away. I'm mighty grateful to your father, and to you, Alice, but I wish you hadn't come. You've shown me how hopeless it all is. I'm just a cow—a nice, fat cow in a pasture. I was foolish to look over the bars. And it's not my fault that I'm a cow with wings.

RALPH: A what? Who ever heard of a cow with wings?

FRANCES: A new insect for your collection, Ralph. Everybody admires the poet's winged horse, a beautiful shining creature flying through the air. He isn't funny or wicked because he doesn't pull a plough; you expect him to rise to the clouds. But a cow, a stupid, discontented cow with wings on her fat, old shoulders—a cow who pretends to want to fly instead of giving her bucket of milk every day. . . . [With a hopeless shrug.] And then to find that the wings are useless even if some kind person does let down the bars and invites her to go flying over the moon. [Bitterly.] After this I'm not going to try to leave my pen.

ALICE: Yes, you are. You were discontented when I came; you'll be more so if you give up your only chance to make something of yourself. You can't really kill the music in you—

FRANCES: [Half sobbing.] I will—I will—

ALICE: It will be murder. And in revenge you'll go on hurting him and the children and yourself. You're giving up your freedom to stay and make a merry hell for them the rest of your life.

RALPH: [Soothing FRANCES, now in his arms.] You shouldn't have said that, Miss Graves. It wasn't kind.

ALICE: I was being what you call scientific, Mr. Gordon. [Going to the door.] I'm sorry I came and made things worse, Frances. Good-bye, both of you. It's not every professor who can keep a cow with wings in his collection.

RALPH: [Fencing with her, over FRANCES' bent head.] Am I supposed to answer something clever? You know I'm not clever.

ALICE: I wish I wasn't. It makes me feel so stupid in a mess like this. Good luck and good-bye for another ten years! [She goes out quickly.]

RALPH: My dear, my poor dear, I do wish things could have been different.

FRANCES: [Raising her head and speaking shakily.] We'll forget she was ever here—if we can. [Turns to the kitchen, trying to be once more the efficient Martha.] I suppose Marion's forgotten to put the butter in the ice box. [Opens the kitchen door; MARION stands there, a violin and bow in her hands.]

MARION: [Entering, a little abashed.] I didn't mean to, mum, but when I saw it up in your room—and you said you didn't want it— [Putting it under her chin.] I do hold it right, don't I?

FRANCES: No. This way! [Takes the violin; assumes the proper position; then suddenly holds it to her as passionately as she has clasped MIDGE.] Ralph—I can't give it up.

RALPH: [Very quietly.] I'll telephone to the hotel that you'll go with her.

MARION: Where, mother?

FRANCES: [With a laugh that must hurt her husband more than tears.] Over the moon! [Places the violin in MARION's arms.] I started to play when I was just as old as you are today, Marion. Now I'm going to teach you the little I

354

know. [Her voice breaks.] This is the biggest birthday present I am ever going to give you.

RALPH: She'll spoil it so, you'll never want to play on it again.

FRANCES: [A great renunciation in her voice.] I shan't try to play any more; it hurts too much. It will be better to be just a plain cow, not a cow with wings. Perhaps my wings will just moult and fall off. [With a cry of pain.] But, maybe, I never had wings at all, but just dreamed them. Maybe I was only a clever amateur, just an ordinary cow longing for the moon.

MARION: [Laughing.] Mamma, you do talk so funny sometimes.

FRANCES: I'm trying to break myself of the habit. [Catching the child to her and speaking with sudden passion.] But, baby, don't you be afraid of talking funny and having dreams. Don't let them cut your wings as you grow older; just keep on flying—and flying—and flying—and never stop.

RALPH: [Trying to smile.] Maybe she'll be as stupid as I am about music.

FRANCES: [Fiercely.] Let me keep my dreams about her as long as I can. Maybe they'll drive out the other dreams— a concert hall—people standing and crying "Encore"— But if Alice is right—if I can't stop dreaming about myself—if I go on torturing all of you—

RALPH: [With a glance toward MARION, before the buffet mirror, trying to assume the correct position with her violin.] I wouldn't—

FRANCES: [With resignation.] I'll be quiet. I'll learn to be a nice, stupid cow, pouring tea at college musicals and making snippy remarks about the soloist. I'll grow more and more bitter and disappointed. But I'll try to keep it to myself.

RALPH: [Going to her.] But you're going to let me help when it hurts too much, Fan. I'm blundering, but I understand. Because, dearest, my wings have started to moult and fall off, too. Only I'm sorry it had to come to you.

FRANCES: [Clinging to him.] But why was I given this longing for the moon if I haven't the courage to fly?

MARION: [Turning to her parents and making a sweeping bow.] And I'll bow like this, mums, and they'll all clap and bring me big bunches of flowers!

FRANCES: You see I'll have to believe in her from now on, Ralph. I can't believe in myself any more. I've thrown away my wings. I've made my choice. But it hurts a little . . . it hurts . . . [sobbing] O God, it hurts so much! [MARION comes to her questioningly; she tries to smile; goes to mending basket and picks up a pair of stockings and begins to hunt for holes as she sits in the big chair. MARION returns to her mirror and again practises her position. FRANCES, smiling crookedly, begins to darn. She looks up at RALPH; her voice is very tired.] And it's going to keep on hurting. . . .

[But MARION stands before the mirror; her eyes are big with dreams.]

THE TRYSTING PLACE
By Booth Tarkington

PERSONS IN THE PLAY

Mrs. Curtis
Lancelot Briggs
Mrs. Briggs
Jessie
Rupert Smith
Mr. Ingoldsby
The Mysterious Voice

THE TRYSTING PLACE

A ROOM just off the "lounge" of a country hotel in Indiana. However, this is not a "country hotel"; but, on the contrary, one of those vast and elaborate houses of entertainment that affect an expensive simplicity in what is called the colonial manner, and ask to be visited—by those financially able to do so—in the general interest of health and the outdoor life. The wall at the back of the stage is broken only by symmetrically spaced pilasters of an ivory color; each of the side walls is broken in the same manner; but here the pilasters help to frame two rather broad entrances, one at the right and one at the left, and beyond these entrances, on both sides, we have glimpses of the two corridors that lead to them. There are a few old prints —or new prints from old plates—upon the walls; and there are flowering plants on stands in the corners. The furniture consists of some chintz-covered easy-chairs, a light wicker settee with a chintz cushion and a valance that reaches the floor; and there are two wicker tables with a vase of jonquils upon each of them. In the rear right-hand corner of

the room, near the stand of plants, there is a tropical-look-
ing chair, wicker, with a back of monstrous size—a Philippine Island chair—and in the opposite corner is its mate.

Dance music is heard from a distant orchestra. Just after
the rise of the curtain two people come in together from
the left—a YOUNG WOMAN of twenty-five, or perhaps she
is even a little older, and a slim BOY obviously under twenty.
She is rather elaborate in her afternoon indoor dress, but
none the less effectively pretty; he is of a scrubbed and
sleeked youthfulness, in white trousers, a short black coat
and dancing shoes; and from the moment of his first appearance he is seen to be in an extremity of love. He leans
as near the young woman as he can; his eyes search her face
yearningly and without intermission; he caroms into her
slightly as they come in, and repeats the carom unwittingly.
They have evidently just come from the dancing floor and
are a little flushed; she fans herself with her handkerchief
and he fans her with his. They are heard talking before
they enter: "Oh, let's do find some place to sit down!" she
is saying; and he, simultaneously: "Oh, wasn't that divine!
You dance just simply divinely!" These speeches "bring
them on."

THE YOUNG WOMAN: Here's a place we can sit down!
[She immediately drops into a chair.]

THE BOY: Yes, this is a lovely place, where nobody is at
all. It's the only quiet place in the hotel: you never see
more than two people here at a time, because it's kind of
off, like this. That's why I wanted to walk this way. [Sit-
ting on a lounge and leaning toward her.] Isn't it divine
to be in a place where nobody is at *all?*

THE YOUNG WOMAN: [Still fanning herself.] Why, you
and I are here.

THE BOY: Yes; but I mean nobody else at all. We're
practically all alone, practically.

THE YOUNG WOMAN: [Laughing as she waves her hand to indicate the spacious corridors to the right and left.] Alone? Why, there are at least three hundred people in this hotel.

THE BOY: Yes, but they're all either outdoors, or dancin', or havin' tea, right now. It's practically the same as being alone. It is—practically, I mean.

THE YOUNG WOMAN: Yes, I've noticed that it was a rather secluded spot myself. [She glances about the room thoughtfully, then turns to him, smiling.] Don't you want to run and dance with some of those pretty young girls your own age?

THE BOY: [With pained earnestness.] Them? My goodness, no!

THE YOUNG WOMAN: Oh, but that isn't normal, is it?

THE BOY: I'm not normal. I don't want to be normal.

THE YOUNG WOMAN: Well, but it would only be natural for you to like those pretty young things, so— Well, *do* run and dance with one of 'em. Won't you, please?

THE BOY: [Interrupting.] No. They haven't got any experience of life. What I like is a woman that's had some experience of life, like you.

THE YOUNG WOMAN: But at your age—

THE BOY: Age hasn't got anything to do with it. The thing that brings a man and a woman together, it's when they have about the same amount of experience of life.

THE YOUNG WOMAN: [Absently.] You think that's it, Mr. Briggs? [She looks about the room thoughtfully as she speaks.]

MR. BRIGGS: [With intense seriousness.] I know it is. I had that feeling the minute I was introduced to you, night before last in the lobby—right by the third column beyond the office news stand, at a quarter after nine o'clock in the evening.

THE YOUNG WOMAN: You did?

MR. BRIGGS: It came over me, and I felt kind of--[he swallows] kind of drawn to you, Missuz—Missuz—Missuz—[He seems to hesitate somewhat emotionally.]

THE YOUNG WOMAN: My name is Mrs. Curtis. You seem to have forgotten it.

MR. BRIGGS: [Swallowing again.] I haven't. I know it's Curtis. The trouble is, it kind of upsets me to call you *Missuz* Curtis. I thought it was Miss Curtis when I was introduced to you. I didn't know your name was Missuz—Missuz—Missuz Curtis till the clerk told me, early the next morning.

MRS. CURTIS: [Frowning a little.] The clerk told you?

MR. BRIGGS: Yes. I asked him if he'd noticed whether you'd gone in to breakfast yet. He said, "You mean Missuz—Missuz Curtis?" Then I knew you must be married. [He shakes his head ruefully.]

MRS. CURTIS: [Smiling.] Well?

MR. BRIGGS: [Thoughtfully.] Well, it can't be helped.

MRS. CURTIS: I suppose not.

MR. BRIGGS: [Brightening a little.] Well, anyhow, I had that—that sort of *drawn* feeling toward you, the way I *would* get toward a woman that's had some experience of life; but a hotel like this is no place to explain feelings like that. You can't when you're dancing—not the way you want to—and all the rest of the time you had some o' those *old* men hangin' around, or else my mother and sister wanted me for something; because a hotel like this—why, it's terrible the way a young man's mother and sister want him to do somep'n for 'em *all* the time; so this is the first chance I've had.

MRS. CURTIS: [Rather urgently.] Don't you really think you'd better be dancing with some of those young things yonder?

MR. BRIGGS: [Puzzled.] Think I'd *better* be?

MRS. CURTIS: Yes; I do really wish you would. Wouldn't

it be a lot more fun than explaining something, as you said, to me?

MR. BRIGGS: No. No, it wouldn't. I want to explain how I feel about you.

MRS. CURTIS: Please go and dance, Mr. Briggs. I think it would be *much* better if you—

MR. BRIGGS: No, it wouldn't. I want to explain how I feel about you, so you'll understand. It's like this, Missuz [swallowing again] Missuz Curtis. I never used to think I'd ever get to feeling this way about—about somebody that was married, but it—it came over me before I knew you *were* married. I already *was* feeling this way before he said, "You mean—you mean Missuz Curtis?" It'd already —[he swallows] happened to me before I knew you were a—a married woman. [Shaking his head.] I certainly never *did* think I'd feel this way about a married woman.

MRS. CURTIS: But I'm not—not as you mean it. I'm a widow, Mr. Briggs.

MR. BRIGGS: [As in a dim perplexity.] A wid— You're a widow? [He jumps up suddenly, greatly amazed.] Oh, my!

MRS. CURTIS: What's the matter?

MR. BRIGGS: Oh, my!

MRS. CURTIS: What is it?

MR. BRIGGS: I guess I've got to get used to the idea of it. First I thought you weren't married, and then I was just gettin' used to the idea that you *were,* and now—well, I s'pose it's a good deal better, your bein' a widow, though, except—except for—

MRS. CURTIS: Except for?

MR. BRIGGS: Oh, I didn't mean except for your *husband!* I didn't mean your bein' a widow was better for— [He checks himself and swallows.]

MRS. CURTIS: Oh!

MR. BRIGGS: [Frowning with thought.] No. I meant

more on account of the way my family treats me. My mother and sister—well, to tell the truth, they always seem to think I'm about four years old. They can't seem to *realize;* and when I go and tell 'em you're a *widow*—

MRS. CURTIS: You think they'll be interested in hearing it? I haven't even met them.

MR. BRIGGS: No, but—but of course they've been *talkin'* about you quite a good deal.

MRS. CURTIS: They have?

MR. BRIGGS: You know how people are in a hotel like this: wondering who everybody else *is,* and whether some woman's some old man's wife or his daughter or just a trained nurse, and all so on. Of course my family noticed *you* right away and then after I *met* you of course then they said a *lot* more about you. Golly! [He shakes his head, indicating that the comment has been unfavorable.]

MRS. CURTIS: Oh, indeed!

MR. BRIGGS: [Ruefully.] They watch me like a hawk, and I know what they'll say now! When I tell 'em you're a widow, I mean.

MRS. CURTIS: Do you?

MR. BRIGGS: [Shaking his head.] I certainly never thought myself I would ever get to feeling this way about a widow *either!*

MRS. CURTIS: Don't you *really* think you'd better run and dance with one of those—

MR. BRIGGS: No. [Turning to her suddenly.] I was goin' to ask you—well, of course, in a—a technical way, so to speak, I mean in a strickly technical way, so to speak, I'm not exactly of age yet, and I suppose I'd have to get my mother's consent, because *she's* a widow, too, and got herself appointed my guardian besides; and the truth is, she's a pretty cold-hearted, bossy kind of a woman, and it's goin' to be a big difficulty gettin' her to see this thing right.

MRS. CURTIS: To see *what* right?

MR. BRIGGS: The way I feel about you. I know it's goin' to be difficult, because I started to talk a little about it last night to my mother and my sister—her name's Jessie—and they behaved—well, they behaved a good deal like two fiends.

MRS. CURTIS: They did?

MR. BRIGGS: I told 'em they didn't know you, and they *haven't* even *met* you, but they treated me like a—like a mere *jest;* and then they got so critical, the way they talked about you, it might be better if they didn't see me with you again for a few days. I can't stand the way they talk after they see me with you.

MRS. CURTIS: Indeed!

MR. BRIGGS: Well, what I was saying: I can't touch my principal till I'm twenty-one on account of the way my father went and tied up his will; but of course my mother and sister think a good many'll be after me on account of it; but, anyhow, I *have* got to feeling this way, and I know I'll *never* get over it, so what I wanted to ask you—well, it's—it's—[he swallows] it's just this: I know you *are* a widow and everything like that, but would you be willing to—[he swallows] well, of course I don't know how long since you lost your first husband—

MRS. CURTIS: [Incredulously.] What! [She rises.]

MR. BRIGGS: I mean I—I don't know how you *would* feel about gettin' married again yet, even if I didn't have my own difficulties about it, but—but—

MRS. CURTIS: [With increased incredulity.] Are you *proposing* to me, Mr. Briggs?

MR. BRIGGS: Well—uh—yes. [Then, looking beyond her down the corridor on the right.] Oh, goodness. They watch me like a hawk! Here comes my mother! [Dismayed, he turns to the left.]

MRS. CURTIS: [As he turns.] Perhaps it was time!

Mr. Briggs: There's my sister Jessie!

Mrs. Curtis: What of it?

Mr. Briggs: I told you they behave like two fiends when they see me with you. [Glancing right and left nervously.] Well, excuse me. [With perfect gravity he kneels at one end of the settee, which is in the rear, a little left of "center."] It'll be a good deal better if they don't see me, I expect. [He promptly crawls under the settee, and the valance conceals him entirely. From this invisibility he appeals with pathetic urgency in a hoarse whisper.] They'll prob'ly go right on. *Please* wait! Or—if you *haf* to go, come *back!*

[Mrs. Curtis stands dumbfounded for a moment; and then, controlling a tendency to laugh immoderately, she turns to examine a print on the left wall as Mr. Briggs's mother enters from the right. Mrs. Briggs is a handsome woman of forty-five or fifty, not now in a gracious mood. She comes in decisively, halts, and stares at Mrs. Curtis' back. Then she looks over the room in an annoyed and puzzled manner. Mr. Briggs's sister Jessie comes in from the left. She is a pretty girl of about twenty, but her expression is now rather cross. Her dress and equipment show that she has just come in from the golf course.]

Jessie: [Calling as she comes in.] Lancelot! [She halts, puzzled, and looks inquiringly at her mother.] Mamma, where's Lancelot? I was sure I saw him in here just a second ago.

Mrs. Briggs: [Grimly.] So was I. [After looking at each other, they turn their heads simultaneously and stare at Mrs. Curtis, who appears to be interested in the print.] It's very odd!

Jessie: Yes, very.

[The two again look at each other, and at a little distance appear to consult telepathically, without any change of expression; then they turn once more to look at Mrs. Curtis.]

MRS. BRIGGS: I beg your pardon, but I'm under the impression that you have met my son.

MRS. CURTIS: [Turning.] Yes?

JESSIE: Wasn't he here just now?

MRS. CURTIS: Yes, he was.

MRS. BRIGGS: Would you be good enough to tell me, did he leave here to go to his room?

MRS. CURTIS: [Casually.] I don't think so; he didn't say so. [She gives them a little nod, smiling politely, and goes out at the left. They stare after her.]

JESSIE: [Still staring after MRS. CURTIS.] She's a very bold type.

MRS. BRIGGS: [Seating herself on the settee.] Very.

JESSIE: [Turning to her.] I don't see how that little goose got away. You were coming from that direction and I from just yonder. I suppose he thought we'd say something that would embarrass him before her.

MRS. BRIGGS: I suppose she's thirty-five. I've heard of such people, but I never saw one before.

JESSIE: I regard her as distinctly the dangerous type of adventuress.

MRS. BRIGGS: Certainly. In the first place, her not having told the child frankly that she's a widow. One of the clerks told *me* she *was*.

JESSIE: Oh, she did that to flatter him into believing he's a real grown-up "man of the world" having an "affair"!

MRS. BRIGGS: So that when he's sufficiently entangled she can tell him she's a widow—and by that time we don't know *what* he'd do! A country justice of the peace probably!

JESSIE: Last night, when we were trying to teach him a little common sense about strange people in hotels, what was it he said she was? "An angel!"—oh, yes!—"One of heaven's highest angels."

MRS. BRIGGS: He said he wouldn't "listen to one of heaven's highest angels gettin' talked against by a lot o' women!"

I'm sure they heard him in the next suite. [She rises.] I suppose you'd better go and see where he slipped out to, Jessie. Of course, he'll try to find *her* again as soon as he can.

JESSIE: [Dropping into a chair.] I played three times round the course. Do you mind if I just sit here a while and rest?

MRS. BRIGGS: Then why don't you go to your room?

JESSIE: [Laughing feebly.] I'm just too tired. I will in a minute. [With a gesture toward the left entrance.] Hadn't you better—

MRS. BRIGGS: Keep her in sight? Yes. That's easier than trying to keep *him* in sight. You're going up to your room right away, aren't you?

JESSIE: Yes, in only a minute. I really think you'd better go, Mamma. He might—

MRS. BRIGGS: No, I'll see to that! [She goes out.]

[JESSIE stares after her for a moment, glances at a wrist watch, then rises and looks down the corridor beyond the entrance at the right. She appears to derive some satisfaction from what she sees there, returns to her chair and sits in a carefully graceful attitude, her expression demure. A moment later a YOUNG MAN—he is about twenty-five—comes in rather nervously from the right. He pauses near the entrance.]

THE YOUNG MAN: You!

JESSIE: [Softly.] You!

THE YOUNG MAN: Is your mother—

JESSIE: She's gone.

THE YOUNG MAN: [Nervously advancing.] I—I—

JESSIE: I was afraid maybe we couldn't have this nook to ourselves, after all. My absurd little brother was in here, hanging about that dreadful Mrs. Curtis, and I was afraid they wouldn't go away; but Mamma scared 'em both off providentially.

THE YOUNG MAN: [Moving a chair close to hers and sitting.] And so we're alone! [He speaks with a sentimental hushedness.] All alone!

JESSIE: All alone, Rupert! This is the only place in the hotel where you *can* be by yourself a while. That's why I said to meet here.

RUPERT: [Nervously.] You don't think your mother'll be back for a while?

JESSIE: No; she won't.

RUPERT: She hasn't found out I've come, has she?

JESSIE: She hasn't the remotest idea, thank heaven! Nobody dreams you're within hundreds of miles of here. That's one advantage of a big hotel.

RUPERT: Darling—

JESSIE: Yes, darling?

[The settee moves slightly at this, but it is behind them and they do not see it.]

RUPERT: I can't understand why your mother dislikes me so.

JESSIE: Well, I suppose her feeling about you is—well, she *says* it's because you're rather poor and I'm—not.

RUPERT: But what makes her think I care about you because you're not?

JESSIE: Well—

RUPERT: [Leaning toward her and lowering his voice.] Darling, there's something I want to ask you—

JESSIE: [Leaning toward him and almost whispering.] Yes, dearest, what is it?

[The settee slowly moves nearer them as their voices become more indistinct.]

RUPERT: I want to ask you—

JESSIE: Yes?

RUPERT: [With hushed tenderness.] Do you *really* love me, dearest?

JESSIE: [Gazing upward, tranced.] Oh, dearest, I do!

369

[The settee goes back to where it came from.]

RUPERT: But you don't think your mother'll ever change her mind about me?

JESSIE: She never does change her mind.

RUPERT: Then what can we do?

JESSIE: [In a low voice.] Darling, there's something I wouldn't say for anything in the world to anybody but you.

[The settee again approaches slightly.]

RUPERT: Yes?

JESSIE: I think Mamma really knows you're not mercenary, but the *real* reason for her opposition to you is pretty selfish. I think it's because she doesn't want me to marry and go away and leave her alone in the world.

RUPERT: But she wouldn't be. She'd still have the companionship of your young brother.

JESSIE: [Shaking her head.] That'd be the same as none. Lancelot seems to have scarcely *any* sense, you see.

[The settee once more retires.]

RUPERT: Then I don't see what possible hope—

JESSIE: [Warning him as she sees someone approaching in the corridor to the right.] Sh-h-h!

RUPERT: [Following her gaze.] Who *is* that old chap?

JESSIE: It's old Mr. Ingoldsby. He's some old friend of Mamma's that happened to turn up here.

RUPERT: [Moving as if to withdraw.] I'd better—

JESSIE: [Quickly.] No; he doesn't know you. Sit still. [She turns toward MR. INGOLDSBY with a smile as he enters.] Good afternoon, Mr. Ingoldsby. Did you do it in eighty-five again today?

[INGOLDSBY is a man of fifty-five or, possibly, sixty. He wears neat knickerbockers and is otherwise sprightly in his outdoor attire. He smiles rather absently as he replies.]

INGOLDSBY: Eighty-five? No, I—ah—no. I didn't go round today. Ah—has Mrs. Briggs been here?

JESSIE: Here?

INGOLDSBY: Yes, I mean—ah—here.

JESSIE: I think she's somewhere looking for Lancelot.

INGOLDSBY: Yes? Ah—I—

JESSIE: Is there something you'd like me to tell her when I see her?

INGOLDSBY: [Going toward the left entrance.] No; I— I— [He glances at his watch, and looks absently at JESSIE.] No, I believe I—ah— [He departs.]

RUPERT: Well, I *do* hope nobody else'll come poking about like that, because I—

JESSIE: No, darling; we're alone again now.

RUPERT: Darling—

JESSIE: Yes, darling?

RUPERT: We've had such difficulties in managing our little interviews; it does seem a precious thing to be near you again.

JESSIE: Oh, it does!

RUPERT: If we could only go away together, where it could *always* be like this—

JESSIE: Yes, with the world shut out.

RUPERT: Why can't we—

JESSIE: Hush, darling.

[She sees someone approaching in the corridor on the left. He looks dolefully in that direction.]

JESSIE: It's that dreadful woman.

RUPERT: I don't know her.

JESSIE: She's been trying to entangle Lancelot, and he's completely lost what slight intelligence he *had,* the little ninny! She's old enough to be his mother.

[The settee makes a slight convulsive movement.]

RUPERT: Sh! She'll hear you.

[MRS. CURTIS enters from the left. She looks about, with a faint embarrassment. JESSIE stares at her, then speaks coldly.]

JESSIE: I beg your pardon. Did you leave something when you were here with my little brother?

MRS. CURTIS: [Smiling constrainedly.] Did you happen to see a pair of white gloves?

[RUPERT rises and looks in his chair.]

JESSIE: No. There aren't any here.

MRS. CURTIS: I *may* have left them anywhere of course. [To RUPERT.] Don't bother, please. I thought just possibly— [She stoops slightly and looks behind the settee, and her expression shows a considerable illumination.] If I *had* left anything here I just wanted to see if it was still—

JESSIE: No; there aren't any gloves here. [She speaks in a sharp whisper to RUPERT.] Sit down! [He does so. Their backs are toward MRS. CURTIS.]

MRS. CURTIS: No. They don't seem to be. I'm sorry to have disturbed you.

[She moves toward the left entrance as she speaks. The settee follows her. She checks it with a sudden commanding push.]

JESSIE: I hardly think my little brother will come back *here*. My mother went to look for him.

MRS. CURTIS: [Politely.] No doubt she's found him by this time.

[She looks from the settee to JESSIE and RUPERT, and back again; and her eyes widen with an intense inward struggle.]

JESSIE: [Turning to look at her coolly.] Was there anything else?

MRS. CURTIS: [After a moment, during which her inward struggle prevents her from replying.] Oh—oh, no! I'm so sorry to have disturbed you! [Her voice threatens to break and she goes out hurriedly, at the left.]

JESSIE: [Staring after her.] Absolutely brazen! She came back after that idiot *boy!* Thought *he'd* probably come back!

RUPERT: Darling—

JESSIE: [Turning to him eagerly.] Yes, darling—

RUPERT: [Looking over her shoulder.] Oh, my goodness! [He speaks with intense anguish.]

JESSIE: [Seizing his hand feverishly.] What's the matter, darling?

RUPERT: [Rising.] It's your mother! [He strides hastily backward out of sight from the left entrance.]

JESSIE: Oh, murder!

RUPERT: She didn't see me, but she will if I try to go out there. [He points to the right entrance.]

JESSIE: She's coming!

RUPERT: This is awful! [His despairing eye falls upon the huge Philippine chair in the left rear corner of the room; he rushes to it, turns it round, with its back toward the front, and sits in it, concealed from view. He speaks in a hoarse whisper.] Darling—

JESSIE: Hush! [She has checked an impulse to rise and fly; and now, affecting carelessness, she brushes her left sleeve with her right hand, crosses her knees, swings her foot, whistles an operatic air and looks at the ceiling. MRS. BRIGGS enters at the left, frowning. JESSIE addresses her cheerfully.] Back again, Mamma? Where's Lancelot?

MRS. BRIGGS: [In an annoyed tone.] I don't know. I thought you were going straight to your room.

JESSIE: Oh, I am.

MRS. BRIGGS: Have you just been sitting here alone?

JESSIE: Mrs. Curtis came back a minute ago looking for the child.

MRS. BRIGGS: Yes; I saw *her*. Wasn't anyone else—

JESSIE: [Carelessly.] Oh, yes; that Mr. Ingoldsby was here, too.

MRS. BRIGGS: He was? [She looks at her watch and then toward the corridor on the left.] You told me you were very tired and were going straight to your room.

JESSIE: [Casually.] Oh, well, I feel rested now.

MRS. BRIGGS: You should lie down before dressing for dinner.

JESSIE: Why don't *you* do that, Mamma? You know how it brightens you up.

MRS. BRIGGS: [Frowning.] Brightens me up? Really!

JESSIE: Oh, I don't mean like a *terribly* aged person; but a nap every day's a good thing for everybody.

MRS. BRIGGS: I *took* a nap after lunch. Really, it's time you went.

JESSIE: Oh, I'll just sit around a while longer. I rather like to just sit around and do nothing, like this.

MRS. BRIGGS: You *said* you were going, and you ought to do things when you say you're going to do them.

JESSIE: But *why?* Why can't I just sit around here a little longer if I want to?

MRS. BRIGGS: Because you said you—

JESSIE: Oh, what if I did! Haven't I got a right to change my mind?

MRS. BRIGGS: I insist on your lying down for half an hour before you dress for dinner. What makes you so obstinate about it? Have you any *reason* for wishing not to do this simple thing? Is there anything you're trying to conceal from me, Jessie?

JESSIE: [Rising hastily.] Certainly not!

MRS. BRIGGS: [Severely.] You haven't any particular reason for staying here and not going to your room as you said you would?

JESSIE: No!

MRS. BRIGGS: Then—

JESSIE: Oh, I'll go; but I don't understand why you make such a point of it!

MRS. BRIGGS: [A little flustered.] A point of it? I? I'm not making a point of it! I don't at all, except—except for your health.

THE TRYSTING PLACE

JESSIE: [Going.] My *health!* [She halts.] What non-sense!

MRS. BRIGGS: Your health is the only thing to consider. You've started; why don't you *go?*

JESSIE: But what's the *hurry?*

MRS. BRIGGS: Hurry? Oh, none! I just meant, as you *are* going, why shouldn't you *go* and get it over?

JESSIE: What makes you so queer?

MRS. BRIGGS: [With quiet severity.] Queer? You call your mother queer? It seems to me you're the one that's be-having queerly. Jessie, is there anything you're trying to—

JESSIE: No! Don't get so upset. I'll go!

[She goes out at the left. MRS. BRIGGS stares after her for a moment; looks in the opposite direction; then seats herself upon the settee, and from the midst of a handkerchief which she has crumpled in her hand produces a small gold vanity box. She opens it, gazes in the tiny mirror, touches her hair, glances right and left, and uses a diminutive powder puff quickly; then she closes the box, conceals it in her hand-kerchief again, and hums a song to herself. MR. INGOLDSBY enters at the left. He has an air slightly embarrassed.]

MRS. BRIGGS: [As if surprised.] Oh!

INGOLDSBY: Ah—I was here a while ago. It was a little earlier than our—our appointment; if I may call it so. [He laughs nervously.]

MRS. BRIGGS: [Smiling.] Well, I suppose it *could* be called an appointment—in a way.

INGOLDSBY: I—I thought—that is, I've noticed this was about the only place in the hotel where there aren't usually a lot of people. I suggested it because—because I had some-thing to say—ah—I mean that I thought it would be as well to say it in private—as it were. That is, if we were alone together, I—ah—that is to say, it's something I couldn't very well say in—in public, so to speak. I mean it would be difficult with other people present.

375

MRS. BRIGGS: [Smiling nervously.] Is it something very mysterious, Mr. Ingoldsby?

INGOLDSBY: I wish you wouldn't call me that.

MRS. BRIGGS: [Seriously.] You want me to call you Henry?

INGOLDSBY: You did once.

MRS. BRIGGS: [Rising in some agitation.] Yes, but that was pretty long ago.

INGOLDSBY: [Sharply.] I called you Fannie then.

MRS. BRIGGS: [More agitated.] I don't think we should ever refer to it. When an episode is as long buried as—

INGOLDSBY: [His own agitation increasing.] Episode? See here, Fannie; you know why I stayed a bachelor. You do know.

MRS. BRIGGS: [Protesting quickly.] No, no! I have no responsibility for that!

INGOLDSBY: Haven't you? When you broke your engagement to me—

MRS. BRIGGS: [Crying out, though she suppresses the loudness of her voice.] It was a misunderstanding, Henry.

INGOLDSBY: It was not. I've held my peace in silence all these years because of my principles. I wouldn't refer to such things with you when you had become a married woman. But I can speak now. You deliberately broke off with me—

MRS. BRIGGS: [Choking.] I didn't!

INGOLDSBY: [With a suppressed passion.] You did! [He paces the floor as he goes on.] You decided Lance Briggs was the better man, and you sent me my ring and letters without a single word explaining why you did it.

MRS. BRIGGS: Oh!

INGOLDSBY: You did!

MRS. BRIGGS: Is it fair to attack me with that now?

INGOLDSBY: Fair? How *dare* you speak of *fairness* to *me?*

MRS. BRIGGS: But you knew why I did it.

INGOLDSBY: I did indeed! It was simply because you were

376

of a fickle nature. Of course you didn't have the courage to explain *that*.

MRS. BRIGGS: [With great emotion.] But you don't know the pressure, the awful pressure my mother brought to bear on me. She simply *made* me marry him, Henry. It was night and day, day and night, week in, week out—

INGOLDSBY: And you never for one moment had the simple bravery, the simple *loyalty* to the man you'd given your word to—

MRS. BRIGGS: I was worn out. I was—

INGOLDSBY: You didn't care enough for me to—

MRS. BRIGGS: I *did!*

INGOLDSBY: No! No! No!

MRS. BRIGGS: [Piteously.] Henry, you *must* listen to me! [She puts her hand on his arm.]

INGOLDSBY: [Moving away from her.] Why didn't you say that *then?* Why didn't—

MRS. BRIGGS: I loved you—I did, Henry! I simply let my mother break my will and wreck our two lives.

INGOLDSBY: What folly! You were perfectly happy with Briggs. I don't know *how* many people told me you were.

MRS. BRIGGS: I did my duty, and I tried to do it cheerfully; but the scar was always there, Henry.

INGOLDSBY: [Harshly.] I don't believe it!

MRS. BRIGGS: It was, Henry. [She sinks into the chair JESSIE has occupied.]

INGOLDSBY: [Swallowing.] What?

MRS. BRIGGS: [Feebly.] It was, Henry—the scar was always there. [Her head droops.]

[He walks across the room, then returns to her and looks down upon her.]

INGOLDSBY: [Swallowing.] Do you know what my life has been?

MRS. BRIGGS: [Tremulously, not looking up.] I—I heard you became very—very prosperous in—in real estate.

INGOLDSBY: Yes. What's that to fill a man's life? Look at the difference! You have children to be a comfort to you in your—your—as you approach middle age. I have nothing.

MRS. BRIGGS: [Pathetically, still looking down.] Oh, I'm sure you have something.

INGOLDSBY: I tell you I have nothing—nothing in the world to make life worth living, not a thing on earth! [He glances about, then sits beside her and speaks in a very low voice.] Fannie—Fannie— [The settee approaches a little nearer.]

MRS. BRIGGS: [Also in a very low voice.] Well?

INGOLDSBY: Fannie—I—I—Fannie—I— [His emotion is difficult to control and his voice fades out into a murmur of several slight incoherent sounds, whereupon the settee again moves slightly closer.]

MRS. BRIGGS: Yes, Henry?

INGOLDSBY: You said your life was wrecked, though you bore it dutifully and—and cheerfully. Mine—*my* life—it was withered!

MRS. BRIGGS: [Murmuring.] Oh—Henry!

INGOLDSBY: But, after all, our lives aren't over.

MRS. BRIGGS: [Shaking her down-bent head and protesting in a weak voice.] Oh, no, no! Don't begin to talk that way.

INGOLDSBY: Fannie, I never got over it. As time went on, I took up my work and tried to do my part in the world, but —but I never got over it, Fannie. I'm not over it now.

MRS. BRIGGS: [Turning to him mournfully.] Oh, yes, you are!

INGOLDSBY: [Shaking his head.] I'm not. I still—I still —I still—I still— [The settee again moves a little nearer.]

MRS. BRIGGS: No, no.

INGOLDSBY: I do. I still—I still—

378

MRS. BRIGGS: [In a faint and tearful protest.] No, you don't Henry. You only think you do.

INGOLDSBY: No, I really do. I—I—I care for you yet, Fannie.

MRS. BRIGGS: [Recovering herself enough to smile faintly as she shakes her head.] Oh, my, no!

INGOLDSBY: Fannie, let's—let's save these years that we still have before us. Let's try to make up for that old mistake.

MRS. BRIGGS: [Becoming a little brisker.] Why, how—how—why, we—why, I couldn't think of such a thing!

INGOLDSBY: [Solemnly.] Fannie, I ask you to marry me. [She stares at him; the settee moves an inch nearer.]

MRS. BRIGGS: What?

INGOLDSBY: I ask you to marry me.

MRS. BRIGGS: Why, good gracious! I wouldn't have my children know that anybody had said such a thing to me for all the kingdoms on earth!

INGOLDSBY: They needn't know it till afterwards.

MRS. BRIGGS: [Breathlessly.] Afterwards? After—after—

INGOLDSBY: You're not going to wreck us both *again,* are you, Fannie?

MRS. BRIGGS: [As in amazement.] Why, if I'd dreamed you were going to say anything like *this* to me when you asked me to meet you here this afternoon—

INGOLDSBY: [Solemnly.] Fannie, I want you to give me your answer, and to do it now. What do you say?

MRS. BRIGGS: [Feebly, with her hand to her breast.] Oh, my!

INGOLDSBY: Yes; you must.

MRS. BRIGGS: But I haven't had time to *think!* Why, I wouldn't have anybody know about this for—

INGOLDSBY: I want my answer, Fannie—Fannie *dear!*

MRS. BRIGGS: *Oh,* dear!

INGOLDSBY: Fannie, *dearest!* [He takes her hand.]

MRS. BRIGGS: Oh, I wouldn't have anybody know this—

INGOLDSBY: Dearest, dearest Fannie!

MRS. BRIGGS: Why, I wouldn't have anybody know that we—

[They are interrupted by a voice from a mysterious and invisible source. It is a male and adult voice, loudly and emphatically affecting to clear the throat of its origin in the manner of a person wishing to attract the attention of some other person.]

THE MYSTERIOUS VOICE: A-hem! A-a-a-*hem!*

MRS. BRIGGS: [Leaping in her chair.] Good heavens!

INGOLDSBY: [Jumping up.] What was that?

MRS. BRIGGS: [Rising.] Why, it was a man's voice.

INGOLDSBY: It was right here in the room with us.

MRS. BRIGGS: [Sinking into her chair.] Oh, murder!

INGOLDSBY: [Staring about the room, notices the Philippine chair with its back turned to the front.] There's somebody sitting in that chair! [He starts toward it angrily, but is checked by a suppressed scream from MRS. BRIGGS.]

MRS. BRIGGS: *Don't!* I'd *much* rather never know who it is. [Rising.] Let's get away! [She totters.]

INGOLDSBY: [Undecided, but very angry.] We ought to know who's spying on us like this.

MRS. BRIGGS: [Clutching at him.] Oh!

THE MYSTERIOUS VOICE: I'm not spying! This is a public room in a public hotel—

MRS. BRIGGS: [Moaning.] Oh!

THE MYSTERIOUS VOICE: [Continuing.] Any guest of this hotel has a right to sit here in peace, and if you *will* go on talking about your private affairs in a public room—

MRS. BRIGGS: [Leaning on INGOLDSBY's arm.] Oh, my!

THE MYSTERIOUS VOICE: [Continuing heatedly.] Why, it's your own fault, not mine. I was only warning you not to go any further. I've heard enough of other people's private affairs for one afternoon, anyhow.

MRS. BRIGGS: [Almost hysterically.] Oh, let's go! [She swings the reluctant and angry INGOLDSBY toward the left entrance.] Let's *go!*

INGOLDSBY: [Turning to call back angrily.] I don't know who you are, sir; but when I've seen this lady to a—a place of safety—I *intend* to know. I'll be *back* here, sir.

THE MYSTERIOUS VOICE: Fine!

MRS. BRIGGS: Oh, mercy! [She moves hastily away from INGOLDSBY as JESSIE suddenly comes in, from the left, confronting them.]

JESSIE: [Halting sharply.] What in the world's the matter?

MRS. BRIGGS: [In a shaking voice.] Nothing! Nothing at all, Jessie. Why should you think anything's the matter?

JESSIE: Why, you're all upset!

MRS. BRIGGS: [Trying hard to seem lightly amused, and failing.] Not at all—not at all! I was just sitting here a moment with Mr. Ingoldsby, chatting over old times and— and then we decided to leave. We decided to leave—that's all. I—I'm— [Suddenly she starts, and with an incoherent exclamation looks behind her. Then she faces JESSIE and, with a painful effort to smile, completes her sentence.] I'm all right.

JESSIE: Yes, you seem so. Mr. Ingoldsby, will you kindly tell me what you've been saying to my mother to upset her so?

MRS. BRIGGS: But I'm not—

INGOLDSBY: [Checking her sharply.] Miss Briggs, I should not be likely to say anything disrespectful to my old and dear friend, your mother. [Looking around angrily.] The truth is, there's an eavesdropping scoundrel concealed in this room, and I—

JESSIE: [Alarmed.] What! Oh, I'm *sure* there isn't.

INGOLDSBY: There is! An eavesdropping—

THE MYSTERIOUS VOICE: [Angrily.] This is a public room, I told you. How can *I* help it if you—

INGOLDSBY: I can't stand this. He's behind that chair. [He breaks away from MRS. BRIGGS and JESSIE, who both clutch at him.]

JESSIE: [Crying out.] Don't! *Please* don't!

MRS. BRIGGS: [Simultaneously.] Henry! *Don't!*

[But INGOLDSBY has already reached the Philippine chair that has its back turned toward the front of the stage; he seizes RUPERT by the collar and drags him forth. RUPERT is horrified.]

INGOLDSBY: Come out of there, you scoundrel. Come out to the light of day.

RUPERT: [Hastily.] I didn't do it. It wasn't *me*.

MRS. BRIGGS: Rupert Smith!

JESSIE: [Dolefully.] Oh, goodness!

INGOLDSBY: [Hotly.] What do you mean by terrorizing a lady?

RUPERT: I didn't! I didn't say a *word!* I *was* behind there, but I couldn't help it. It wasn't *my* voice talking to you.

INGOLDSBY: Then who was it?

THE MYSTERIOUS VOICE: If you're anxious for more witnesses, I suggest that you look under the settee.

MRS. BRIGGS: [Changing her mind as she is in the act of sinking down upon the settee.] What!

JESSIE: Look at it!

[MRS. BRIGGS screams faintly, as the settee moves rapidly to the left entrance, evidently meaning to leave the room.]

INGOLDSBY: [To RUPERT.] Stop that thing! Catch it!

[They seize the settee just as it is disappearing into the corridor. They drag it back into the room.]

RUPERT: [Trying to lift the settee.] Come out from under there!

INGOLDSBY: Come out, now!

THE SETTEE: I won't! You lea' me alone!

INGOLDSBY: Both together now—heave!

[They heave, and the settee yields, disclosing LANCELOT with his previously smooth hair disheveled and his clothes well rumpled.]

MRS. BRIGGS: Lancelot! Oh, gracious me!

INGOLDSBY: [To LANCELOT.] Shame on you!

RUPERT: Yes, shame on you!

LANCELOT: [Resentfully.] Well, you *would* get me; but I'll make you sorry you did it, both of you! [He rises, brushing himself and adjusting his attire.]

INGOLDSBY: [Irritably.] Don't you know better than to frighten ladies and eavesdrop and—

LANCELOT: I was abs'lootly honorable, because I couldn't help it, and you none of you ever gave me a single chance to get away. *My* conduct is the only one here that hasn't got a stain on it or anything. [He turns hotly upon MRS. BRIGGS and JESSIE.] I got nothing to reproach myself with, but I'd just like to know what either of you got to say for yourselves *now* about the way you been talkin' about Mrs. Curtis! If you either of you ever just *dare* to soil your lips with even her *name* again, why, I know more *things*—

MRS. BRIGGS: Be quiet, Lancelot.

LANCELOT: Quiet? *Me?* [He laughs shortly with an irony he could not express in words.] In the first place, don't call me Lancelot any more. You know how I hate that name, and I been tryin' to break you of it long enough—and now I will! I don't care what you call me, but don't call me *that!*

JESSIE: [Pointing to the settee.] How long were you under there?

LANCELOT: Long enough to get mighty tired of hearin' people callin' each other "Darling"! Good gracious! You don't think I *enjoyed* it, do you? Why, what I heard while I was under there—well, I got a pretty strong constitution, but—

MRS. BRIGGS: Hush! Oh, me!

INGOLDSBY: The voice that spoke didn't sound like Lancelot's voice—

LANCELOT: [Turning upon him ominously.] Did you hear me say not to call me Lancelot? I mean you, too.

INGOLDSBY: [With hasty meekness.] I'll call you anything you like; but I want to know who it was that *spoke*. You say it wasn't you—

LANCELOT: [Very emphatically.] No, it wasn't. I wouldn't 'a' told you to look under the settee, would I?

INGOLDSBY: [With a gesture toward RUPERT.] And this gentleman says it wasn't he.

RUPERT: Why, it spoke again after I came out.

INGOLDSBY: [Quite bewildered.] So it did. Then who—

LANCELOT: I don't care who it was; what I want to point out, right here and now, before we go any further, why, I'm in a position to say that I got some plans for my future life and I don't expect to have any intaference with 'em from my family, or from anybody that wants to *join* my family either. All up to now, I've spent my life in a dependent position, so to speak, but after what's happened here lately, and knowin' all the *things* I *do* know—

[His voice has risen during this oration, and JESSIE, after a glance to the left entrance, attempts to moderate him.]

JESSIE: Hush! There's somebody—

LANCELOT: I don't care *who's* comin', I'm goin' to say my say. I expect to settle my own future in my own way, and any lady that I may decide to make *another* member of this family—

JESSIE: *Hush!*

[The eyes of LANCELOT follow hers to the left entrance and his stern manner is instantly softened.]

LANCELOT: It's her.

[MRS. CURTIS comes in, but stops uncertainly near the entrance.]

MRS. CURTIS: Oh! I'm afraid I— [She turns to go.]

LANCELOT: Wait. I was just talkin' to 'em about you.

MRS. CURTIS: You were, Mr. Briggs?

LANCELOT: [To the others, reprovingly.] *She* never calls me Lancelot. Missuz—Missuz Curtis, I didn't have to tell 'em; they'd already found out you were a widow. We don't need to bother about that anyway.

MRS. CURTIS: *We* don't?

LANCELOT: I've found out a good *many* things since I saw you, and I'm goin' to tell you the whole biznuss.

MRS. BRIGGS: Shame!

JESSIE: [With a despairing laugh.] What would it matter? There's somebody *else* here that knows "the whole biznuss"!

MRS. CURTIS: [Struck by this.] What did you say, Miss Briggs?

INGOLDSBY: [Warmly.] She made a sensible remark, madam. There is a person concealed in this room—

MRS. CURTIS: [Impulsively.] Oh, dear! How did you know?

ALL THE OTHERS: What?

MRS. CURTIS: Nothing.

INGOLDSBY: All right! [To RUPERT.] I think I know now where he is, and I'm going to have him out.

MRS. CURTIS: [Gasping, then imploringly.] *Please* stop!

INGOLDSBY: [Halting.] Why?

MRS. CURTIS: It's a friend of mine.

LANCELOT: [Apprehensively.] A friend of yours?

MRS. CURTIS: I—I'll answer for him. He'll never mention—ah—anything. He really wouldn't be interested. He doesn't know any of you.

THE MYSTERIOUS VOICE: No; and doesn't care to!

INGOLDSBY: [Angrily.]   Now, I *will*—

MRS. CURTIS: *Please* don't!

INGOLDSBY: I mean to know who he is.

MRS. CURTIS: [Pleading.] Please! If you found him, you'd only see a total stranger to you. But he *wouldn't* be a stranger to quite a lot of people in this hotel that *I* know.

INGOLDSBY: [Now shaking his head.] I'm afraid I don't see it.

MRS. CURTIS: [In a faltering voice.] He's just here for one day and we—we didn't want anyone to know it. I had so many engagements I could only take a short walk in the country with him this morning and—and promise to meet him here at five this afternoon.

LANCELOT: [Who has been staring at her painfully.] But —but—see here!

MRS. CURTIS: Yes, I tried to get you to run away and dance with some nice young thing.

LANCELOT: So you could be here with—him?

MRS. CURTIS: I—I believe so.

LANCELOT: Oh, my!

INGOLDSBY: Madam, what you say doesn't excuse this person's eavesdropping.

THE MYSTERIOUS VOICE: [Belligerently.] Why doesn't it? A lady's got a right to keep her engagement a secret as long as she wants to, hasn't she? There are people in this hotel that would know all about it if they saw her with me. [With some bitterness.] That's why she said to meet her here, because it's so quiet!

INGOLDSBY: That doesn't excuse—

THE MYSTERIOUS VOICE: It's more your fault than anybody else's. I was awake all last night on a noisy train, and I was quietly *asleep* here—till you woke me up.

INGOLDSBY: Till *who* woke you up?

THE MYSTERIOUS VOICE: Till *you* did. I never knew a

man that made so much noise about proposing a second marriage.

JESSIE: [Amazed.] Oh, Mamma!

MRS. BRIGGS: [With severe dignity.] I'll speak to you and Mr. Rupert Smith after dinner. Henry, I don't see the propriety of continuing an argument with this interloper, whoever he may be. [She takes INGOLDSBY's arm.]

JESSIE: No. Let's *do* get away from here! [She moves toward the left entrance with RUPERT.]

INGOLDSBY: [Looking back, as he follows with MRS. BRIGGS; speaks reprovingly.] I hope you have some shame for your conduct, sir.

THE MYSTERIOUS VOICE: Bless you, my children!

INGOLDSBY: [Infuriated.] Now, I'll— [He turns to go back.]

MRS. BRIGGS: [Restraining him.] Henry!

[They go out the left entrance. JESSIE and RUPERT have passed out into the corridor.]

LANCELOT: Did he say "a lady's got a right to keep her— her *engagement*—a secret"?

MRS. CURTIS: Yes.

LANCELOT: To—to—to you?

MRS. CURTIS: Yes, dear.

LANCELOT: Oh—oh, pshaw!

MRS. BRIGGS: [Calling back.] Lancelot!

LANCELOT: Yes'm.

[He goes dismally across to the left entrance and pauses. INGOLDSBY and MRS. BRIGGS have withdrawn, preceding him.]

MRS. CURTIS: [As he pauses.] What is it, Mr. Briggs?

LANCELOT: [Swallowing.] Noth—nothin'. [He goes out.]

MRS. CURTIS: [Turning, after a moment's faintly smiling meditation.] You poor thing!

THE MYSTERIOUS VOICE: [In an aggrieved tone.] Well, I should say I am!

[She goes to the Philippine chair, near the right rear corner, and, moving a smaller chair close to it, seats herself and addresses the invisible person, who is evidently sitting in the shelter of the big chair.]

MRS. CURTIS: After all, there's nobody else here just *now*, darling.

THE MYSTERIOUS VOICE: No. We're alone, darling.

MRS. CURTIS: You poor darling!

[She glances about, then impulsively leans behind the huge back of the Philippine chair.]

THE ELDEST
By Edna Ferber

PERSONS IN THE PLAY

ROSE
FLOSS
AL
PA
MA
HENRY SELZ
A NEIGHBOR

THE ELDEST

THE dining room of a flat in a cheap neighborhood. It is evidently used as the common room. There are, besides the necessary dining-room furniture, one or two shabby armchairs and a small table. The room is in disorder. A small rug is rolled in one corner. The room, just cleaned, has not quite been set to rights. At the back, left, a door leading into outer hall. Another right, back, into bedrooms. At left a door into kitchen. At right, well down, door to MA's bedroom. This door stands open. The dining table is left center. On its bare top are two dining-room chairs back to back, as though they had been put out of the way during the scrubbing of the floor. A small stepladder against the wall. At the foot of the ladder a scrubbing pail, with a brush beside it and a moist gray rag hanging over the top. A telephone on a small table, back. An old-fashioned sideboard, left, near dining table.

ROSE enters from kitchen wiping her flushed face with a corner of her damp apron. She is a woman of about forty, grown heavy about the hips and arms as houseworking women do. On her face is the vague, mute look of one whose days are spent indoors at sordid tasks. Her features are good. She must have been pretty in her youth. She wears a calico work dress and apron. Her sleeves are rolled up, her hair wispy, but she does not look like a sloven. She is flushed and hurried. Rose comes quickly down to bare table, picks up the chairs that are on top of it and puts them in their places; unrolls the rug that lies in a corner and spreads it on the floor; goes to pail, stoops, wrings out the wet rag, meanwhile glancing anxiously about. All this is done hastily as one would hurry who is late with her work.

A doorbell rings. Rose gives an annoyed exclamation and drops her rag.

Rose: Who's there?

Neighbor: It's only me.

Rose: Oh, come right in. [Neighbor enters from kitchen. She is a stout, florid woman in a flowered kimono.]

Neighbor: What smells so good?

Rose: [Wiping her hands on apron.] I guess it must be my rhubarb pie. I just took it out of the oven.

Neighbor: My folks don't care for rhubarb in any form.

Rose: It does make the worst pie in the world.

Neighbor: Well, then, why in the world . . . !

Rose: [Almost sheepishly.] Oh, I don't know. I heard the vegetable man calling it down the street. And rhubarb, and spring, and housecleaning all seem to go together, somehow.

Neighbor: [Glancing swiftly around.] My land! You started housecleaning already!

Rose: [Triumphantly.] This morning.

Neighbor: Awful early, ain't it?

Rose: When I woke up there was a fly buzzing around the room. And I noticed the Burkes across the court had taken down their lace curtains. That started me.

Neighbor: It's catching. I guess I'll start in to-morrow.

It's certainly hot enough, for April. [Turns to go.] For goodness' sake, I'm forgetting what I came for! Can you let me have a cup of milk? Mine turned sour on me.

Rose: Just help yourself out of the bottle in the ice box. All I need's enough for their tea and ma's glassful. [Neighbor exits. Rose goes to sideboard, gets out tablecloth, begins to lay table for supper, with plates, knives, forks, etc. A sound, off, from kitchen, as though Neighbor has slammed the ice box door. Neighbor appears again at door, cup carefully held in hand.]

Neighbor: How's your ma to-day?

Rose: Just the same.

Neighbor: It's certainly awful. Keeps you tied right down, don't it?

Rose: Yes.

Neighbor: Well, I always say a person like that's better off out of their misery, really. It's been years, ain't it? How long?

Rose: Fifteen years this month.

Neighbor: You must have been just a young girl.

Rose: Floss and Al were hardly more than babies. We didn't think, at first, it would go on the way it has. The doctors said a few months—then a year—then five years. . . .

Neighbor: And everything on your shoulders. I s'pose you might of had a husband and a home of your own. I bet you wasn't bad looking.

Rose: I looked a lot like Floss looks now, they say.

Neighbor: No! [Shakes her head commiseratingly.] Well, I got to run along. [From kitchen, as she goes.] I'll return your milk to-morrow.

Rose: That's all right. [Rose listens to make sure that she has gone. Takes from the capacious pocket of her apron a little sheaf of time-yellowed letters, worn with handling, and a faded bit of blue ribbon. She comes over to sideboard and stacks the letters neatly, fingering them one by one. On her lips is a wistful, reminiscent half smile.]

MA: [From bedroom, in a high, thin voice.] Rose!

ROSE: [Startled, spills letters on floor.] Yes, ma! [Stoops, gathers letters in scrambling haste.]

MA: It's cold in here.

ROSE: I'll get you a hot bag in a minute. [Hurriedly ties letters together with the bit of ribbon, unlocks the top cabinet of the old-fashioned sideboard, thrusts the letters into it, locks the little door, pockets the key. Exits to kitchen, enters again almost immediately with rubber water bag. As she crosses to bedroom she is screwing the top on the bag and wiping its wet sides with her apron. Exits bedroom, off.] Where'd you want it this time, ma? Your head or your feet?

MA: Here. . . . Ain't the folks home yet?

ROSE: They'll be here any minute now. ⌐ ʒuess you've been dozing off a little.

MA: [Whining.] I haven't closed my eyes.

[The telephone rings. ROSE enters dining room, goes to telephone.]

ROSE: [At telephone.] Hello! . . . Al isn't home yet. . . . Well, I'll tell him as soon as he comes in. . . . I told you that before. . . . Yes, Hill 2163. [Hangs up receiver. Picks up pail and brush, carries them to kitchen. Reënters with dish of butter and milk pitcher. Busies herself at table. An outer door slams. PA enters. He is a fussy, gray-haired, sprightly old man of the hack bookkeeper type. He looks warm and irritable.]

PA: Whew! My God, but it was hot downtown! [Throws hat and coat on nearby chair.] What's all this muss?

ROSE: Housecleaning. [Back and forth between side-board, table, kitchen, with plates, bread, etc.]

PA: [To MA's bedroom door; peers in. With a false cheeriness.] Well, well! And how's the old girl to-night, h'm? Feel like you could punish a little supper?

394

MA: I couldn't eat a thing. My head's killing me again. My head. . . . [Her complaining voice goes on as PA stands a moment longer in the doorway. The outer door slams. AL enters. He is of the slim, furtive, weasel type. He walks lightly on the balls of his feet, like an Indian, but without the Indian's dignity. In figure a born fox-trotter. His coat is over his arm. He is wearing a flashy striped shirt.]

AL: Can you beat this for April! My shirt's stuck to my back.

ROSE: Al, put that stepladder away for me, will you?

AL: [To bedroom, back.] I will not. What d'you think I am! The janitor! [Exits bedroom. PA to armchair, newspaper in hand. Reads. ROSE folds ladder, places it against wall. AL enters from bedroom.]

ROSE: Oh, some girl's been calling you up. She said. . . .

AL: Well, why didn't you tell me! [Goes to phone.]

ROSE: I'm telling you now. Hill 2163. Pestering me all the time. I should think girls could wait till fellows call them. . . . [ROSE to kitchen; picks up pail.]

AL: [To operator.] Hill 2163. . . . No! Six three. . . . Yeh. [To ROSE.] Say, if they were all disappointed old maids like you, I guess they'd have to wait till. . . . Hello! [A complete change of tone.] That you, Kid? Say, listen. How about to-night, now? [Drops his voice very low during remainder of conversation. ROSE exits, kitchen. Outer door slams. FLOSS enters. She is about twenty, very slim, very pretty, rather cheap, in flimsy dress, cut too low, light-colored shoes, short skirt. As she enters she is breathless and excited. She carries a paper hatbag in her hand.]

FLOSS: Rose! Where's Rose? [ROSE enters from kitchen, carrying a dish.]

ROSE: What's the matter?

FLOSS: Did you press my pink georgette, like I asked you to?

ROSE: I didn't get time. I've been cleaning all day long.

FLOSS: But I've got to have it. I got to wear it to-night. Guess who was in the store to-day!

ROSE: Who? What's that? A hat?

FLOSS: Yes. But listen. . . .

ROSE: Let's see it.

FLOSS: [Whips it out of bag.] There! But let me tell you. . . .

ROSE: How much?

FLOSS: [Defiantly.] Nine-fifty—trimmed.

AL: [Who, having finished telephoning, has been regarding his sisters, leaning idly against the wall, cigarette in mouth.] Trimmed is right!

FLOSS: Shut up, Al! Well, but I had to have it, Rose. I'm going to the theater to-night. And guess who with!

ROSE: Who?

FLOSS: Henry Selz! [ROSE stares, then smiles uncertainly, puts the dish on the table with a hand that trembles a little.]

ROSE: What's the joke?

FLOSS: Joke, nothing! Honest to God! I was standing back of the counter at about ten. The rush hadn't really begun. Glove trade always starts late. I was standing there, kidding Herb, the stock boy, when down the aisle comes a man in a big hat, like you see in the western pictures, hair a little gray at the temples, and everything, just like a movie actor. I said to Herb, "Is it real?" I hadn't got the words out of my mouth when the fellow sees me, stands stock-still in the middle of the aisle with his mouth open and his eyes sticking out. "Register surprise," I said to Herb, and looked around for the camera. At that minute he takes two jumps over to where I'm standing, grabs my hands and says, "Rose! Rose!" kind of choky. "Not by about twenty years," I says. "I'm Floss, Rose's sister. Let go my hands!"

ROSE: [Vibrantly.] You said, "I'm Floss, Rose's sister, let go my hands." And then—?

ᴦʟᴏss: He looked kind of stunned, just for a minute. His face was a scream, honestly. Then he said, "But of course. Fifteen years. But I had always thought of her as just the same." And he kind of laughed, ashamed, like a kid. And the whitest teeth!

Rose: Yes, they were—white. Well?

Floss: Well, I said, "Won't I do instead?" Like that. "You bet you'll do!" he said. And then he told me his name, and how he's living out in Spokane and his wife was dead, and he had made a lot of money—fruit, or real estate or something. He talked a lot about it at lunch, but I didn't pay any attention. As long as he's really got it, a lot I care how. . . .

Rose: At lunch?

Floss: Everything from crab meat to coffee. I didn't believe it could be done in one hour. Believe me, he had those waiters jumping. It takes money. He asked all about you, and ma, and everything. And he kept looking at me and saying, "It's wonderful!" I said, "Isn't it!" but I meant the lunch. He wanted me to go driving this afternoon. Auto and everything. Kept calling me Rose and Rosebud. It made me kind of mad, and I told him how you look. He said, "I suppose so," and asked me to go to a show to-night. Listen, will you press my georgette? I got to have it.

Rose: I'll iron it while you're eating. I'm not hungry. [Turns. Goes to kitchen door.] Did you say he was gray?

Floss: [On her way to bedroom, beginning to unbutton her blouse.] Gray? Oh, you mean. . . . Why, just here and here. Interesting, but not a bit old. And he's got that money look that makes waiters and doormen jump. [At door.] I don't want any supper. Just a cup of tea. Haven't got time to dress decently, as it is.

Al: [Leaves wall and phone table, against which he has been lounging. Comes down.] Your story interests me strangely, little gell. But there's a couple other people would like to eat, even *if you wouldn't*. [FLOSS exits with a withering glance at AL.] Come on with that supper, Ro! Nobody staked me to a lunch to-day. [AL and PA to table, seat themselves. ROSE dishes out the supper to them, though she eats nothing herself.]

ROSE: I'll dish up for you, and then I'll get ma's tray, and press out that dress. I'm late with everything to-night, seems.

AL: [Eating.] Some doings ourself to-day, down at the store, believe me! The Old Man's son started in to learn the retail end of the business. Back of the cigar case with the rest of us, waiting on trade and looking like a Yale yell.

PA: [Looking over the top of his specs which he has put on while reading the paper.] Mannheim's son, you mean! The president of the company's son!

AL: Yep. And I guess he loves it, huh! The Old Man wants him to learn the cigar business from the ground up. I'll bet he never gets higher than the basement, that guy. Went out to lunch at one and never showed up till four. Wears English clothes and smokes a brand of cigarettes we don't even carry.

[ROSE has finished waiting on the men for the time. Goes to FLOSS's room. Out again at once with a pink georgette dress in her hand.]

PA: [Rises, picks up newspaper, which he scans while eating.] I see the Fair's got a spring housecleaning sale. Advertise a new kind of extension curtain rod. And Rose, Scouro, three cakes for a quarter.

ROSE: [Off.] I'm not wasting money on truck like that when half the time I can't make the housekeeping money last through the week, as it is.

PA: Your ma did it.

ROSE: Fifteen years ago liver wasn't seventy cents a pound. [Exits kitchen.]

FLOSS: [Calling from bedroom.] Rose, pour me out a cup of tea, will you? [ROSE, in kitchen, does not hear.]

AL: [Raises his voice.] Oh, Rose! Come on in here and pour out a cup of tea for the little lady.

ROSE: [From kitchen.] Well, then, carry in ma's tray for me.

FLOSS: [Enters from bedroom. She is in petticoat and flimsy kimono, evidently having stopped halfway in her toilette's progress. Her cheeks are very pink. Her hair is shiningly coiffed about her ears.] Tray! Well, I should say not. I haven't got time to eat. [Sits at table. Pours herself a cup of tea, which she gulps hurriedly.]

AL: [Sneering.] Every move a Pickford! And so girl-ish withal.

FLOSS: Shut up, Al. [ROSE enters from kitchen with tray. Crosses to MA'S room.] Guess who I waited on to-day, Rose!

ROSE: [Without interest. Into bedroom.] Who?

FLOSS: Gladys Moraine! I knew her the minute I saw her. She's prettier off than on, I think. She's playing here in "Our Wives." I waited on her, and the other girls in the department were wild. Bought a dozen pair of white kids and made me give 'em to her huge so she could shove her hand right into 'em, like a man does. Two sizes too big. All the swells wear 'em that way. And only one ring —an emerald the size of a dime.

PA: What kind of clothes'd she wear?

AL: [In a dreamy falsetto.] Ah, yes! What *did* she wear?

FLOSS: [Animatedly.] Just a suit, kind of plain, and yet you'd notice it. And sables! And a Gladys Moraine hat. Everything quiet and plain and dark; and yet she looked like a million dollars. [Sighs.] I felt like a roach while I was waiting on her, though she was awful sweet to me. . . . Hurry up with that dress, Rose.

Rose: In a minute. I've just got the collar to do.

Floss: [Rises.] He'll be here any minute now. And this place looks like the devil.

Rose: [Stops short.] Why—Floss! He isn't going to call for you, is he? Here?

Floss: Sure. With a taxi. Did you think I was going to meet him on the corner or something? [Goes toward bedroom.]

Rose: But listen! Floss!

Floss: Don't bother me. [Exits bedroom.]

Al: [Rises from table, yawning.] Guess I'll do a little beautifying myself. [Rubs an investigating hand over chin. Rose to kitchen, her whole figure drooping, shrunken somehow. Al to bedroom. Pa throws paper down, yawns elaborately, pushes back his chair. A sound as of some one pounding on a closed door, off.]

Al: [Off.] Hurry up and get through primping in there, will you! What d'you think this is—a Turkish bath!

Floss: [Shrilly, off.] Shave in your own room, can't you! [Rose enters from kitchen, the freshly pressed dress in her hand. She prinks out the pleatings and ruffles as she goes toward Floss's room.]

Pa: Well, I guess I'll just drop around to the movie.

Rose: Don't you want to sit with ma a minute, first?

Pa: When I get back. I don't want to come in the middle of the picture. They're showing the third installment of the "Adventures of Aline."

Rose: Ma'll be asleep by that time. You know it.

Pa: I been slaving all day. I guess I got the right to a little amusement! A man works his fingers to the bone for his family and then his own daughter nags him! [Snatches up his hat and coat from chair, stamps out. Rose looks after him, her shoulders sagging, her face drawn. The outer door slams noisily. From the bedroom comes the sound of Al's whistling and singing in an off-key tenor.]

FLOSS: [Enters hurriedly, making frantic passes at her finger nails with a dilapidated buffer. She is in petticoat and pink camisole.] Where's that dress?

ROSE: Here. [FLOSS clutches it impatiently. The door-bell rings, three long, loud rings.]

FLOSS: [Panic-stricken.] It's him! [Slips one arm into the dress.] Rose, you'll have to go.

ROSE: [Shrinking, cowering.] I can't! I can't! [Her eyes dart to and fro like those of a hunted thing seeking to escape. She runs to AL's door.] Al! Al, go to the door, will you?

AL: [In a smothered mumble.] Can't. Shaving. [The bell sounds again, three loud, impatient rings.]

FLOSS: [In a venomous whisper as though she could be heard downstairs.] Rose! I can't go with my waist open! For God's sake answer the door! [Runs back to bedroom, fastening gown as she goes.]

ROSE: [In a kind of moan.] I can't! I—can't! [And goes. As she goes she passes a futile, work-worn hand over her hair, plucks off her apron, casts it in a corner, first wiping her flushed face with it. She presses an electric button that opens lower door. Opens hall door. Stands there, waiting. A brief pause. HENRY SELZ is heard approaching with a springy step. HENRY SELZ stands in the door. He is about forty-two or three, well dressed, prosperous looking, almost youthful. He stares at ROSE uncertainly.]

ROSE: [Tremulously.] How-do, Henry.

HENRY: [The look of uncertainty changing to pitying incredulity.] Why, how-do, Rose! I didn't know you—for a minute. Well, well! It's been a long time. Let's see. Ten—twelve—about thirteen, fourteen years, isn't it?

ROSE: Fifteen. This month. Won't you come in and sit down? Floss'll be ready in a minute. [They sit, he a little ill at ease, ROSE nervously tucking back her wisps of hair, twisting her fingers.] Things look a little upset around here. I've been housecleaning.

HENRY: That's all right. [Dabs at his face with handkerchief.] Certainly is warm for this time of year. Well, and how've you been? Did little sister tell you how flabbergasted I was when I saw her this morning? Say, it was the funniest thing! I got kind of balled up for a minute and thought it was you. I'm darned if it didn't take fifteen years off my age—just like that! She tell you?

ROSE: Yes. She told me.

HENRY: She's the image of the way you used to look.

ROSE: I've changed—quite a lot.

HENRY: [Feebly.] Oh, I don't know, Rose. You're a pretty good looking girl yet.

ROSE: You've changed, too. But it's different with a man. You're better looking now than you were fifteen years ago.

HENRY: Things have kind of come my way. I was pretty late learning about golf, and caviar and tailors. But say, it doesn't take long. . . . I hear your ma's still sick. [ROSE nods her head.] That certainly is tough. And you never married, h'm?

ROSE: Never married.

HENRY: I guess you never held it up against me, did you, Rose? My marrying? When your ma took sick and we had to put it off, who'd have thought you'd be stuck here all these years?

ROSE: I never held it up against you, Henry. When you stopped writing I just knew. . . .

HENRY: [Glances around the room.] You've been going on like this, taking care of the family?

ROSE: Yes.

[FLOSS enters, a radiant, glowing, girlish vision. She is wearing the gown ROSE has pressed, and the pert new hat. HENRY SELZ rises. His eyes are fixed admiringly on FLOSS.]

HENRY: Ah! And how's the little girl to-night!

FLOSS: [Gives him her hand.] Did I keep you waiting a terribly long time?

HENRY: No, not a bit. Rose and I were chinning over old times, weren't we, Rose? [A kindly, clumsy thought strikes him.] Say, look here, Rose. We're going to a show. Why don't you just run and put on your hat and come along, h'm? Come on!

ROSE: No, thanks, Henry. Not to-night. You and Floss run along.

HENRY: Well, remember me to your ma.

ROSE: I will, Henry. I'm sorry you can't see her. But she don't see anybody—poor ma.

Henry: [Shakes her hand heartily.] Good-by, Rose. Glad I saw you.

ROSE: Good-by.

FLOSS: I hope we won't be late. [At door.] I hate to come in after the curtain's up, don't you? [FLOSS and HENRY go, FLOSS still chattering.] I went to a show one night and the woman behind us was simply furious because. . . . [ROSE peers after her, anxiously, as a mother would. The door closes. ROSE stands still, her arms hanging straight at her sides, staring after the door is shut. The outer door slams as before. ROSE turns, mechanically, and goes into her mother's room. She comes out immediately, carrying the littered supper tray.]

MA: [In her high-pitched, thin voice.] Who was that?

ROSE: [Over her shoulder.] That was—Henry Selz.

MA: [Wanderingly.] Henry? Henry Selz? Henry—oh, yes. Did he go out with Floss?

ROSE: Yes. [Goes slowly toward kitchen with tray.]

MA: [In a whine.] It's cold in here.

ROSE: I'll get you a bag in a minute, ma. [Exits kitchen. AL enters from bedroom, shrugging himself into his coat. He is shaved, brushed, powdered to a marvel. Glances

403

around, furtively, goes toward kitchen, encounters ROSE entering with hot water bag.]

AL: I'll take that to ma. [Takes bag to MA's bedroom. ROSE crosses to cluttered supper table, sits wearily. Pours a cup of cold tea. AL enters from MA's bedroom, over to ROSE, after regarding her speculatively for a moment. Lays a hand on her shoulder.] Ro, lend me a couple of dollars, will you?

ROSE: I should say not!

AL: [Douses his cigarette in the dregs of a convenient teacup, leans over, presses his pale, powdered cheek to ROSE's sallow one. His arm is about her, his hand patting her shoulder.] Oh, come on, kid. Don't I always pay you back? Come on. Be a sweet ol' sis. [Kisses her. ROSE shrugs away impatiently.] I wouldn't ask you, only I've got a date to go to Luna Park and I couldn't get out of it. I tried, honest.

ROSE: Don't you think I ever get sick of slaving for a thankless bunch like you! Well, I do. Sick and tired of it, that's what! Coming around asking for money as if I was a bank.

AL: Oh, come on, Ro. Just this once.

ROSE: [Grudgingly, wearily.] There's a dollar bill and some small change in the can on the second shelf in the china closet. [AL is off like a terrier. From the kitchen pantry comes the clink of metal against metal. He is back in a flash, snatches his hat, is out without a backward glance at ROSE. The outer door slams loudly. ROSE sits stirring her cold tea, slowly, as one does who will not drink it. She is gazing dully down into the cup. She turns her head and looks at the closed door of the sideboard cabinet, where the packet of letters lies. She crosses to sideboard, unlocks door, takes out letters, comes slowly back to table, stands a moment, tears letters across, crushes them in her fingers, and throws the pieces among the greasy supper dishes. Suddenly her face puckers up almost comically, like a child's. She sinks into a chair at the table, her head comes down on her outstretched arms among the supper things, so that the dishes jump and tinkle.]

MA: [Off.] What's that! Rose!

ROSE: [Raises her head, stifling her sobs.] Nothing, ma. [Wipes her eyes with the palm and back of her hand, sniffling. Sits staring down at the table. Her eye is caught by a head-line in the evening paper that PA has thrown down on the table. She picks it up almost unconsciously, scans it, her face, twisted with grief, gradually losing its look of pain. As the curtain descends she rises, gathers up a handful of dishes, and drags her accustomed way to the kitchen.]

THE FEAST OF THE HOLY INNOCENTS
By Samuel M. Ilsley

PERSONS IN THE PLAY

CORNELIA MILK
ELECTA MILK
MRS. OBERLY
JENNIE
MRS. OMAN

THE FEAST OF THE HOLY INNOCENTS

A WINTER afternoon of a recent year, in a house in Millet, Wisconsin. A little old-fashioned parlor, neat and comfortable, but showing age. There are a few pieces of old mahogany, but most of the furniture is plain and inexpensive. There is a small case of old books. One door leads to the street, another to the kitchen.

CORNELIA MILK, a maiden lady past forty, simply dressed, is sitting by the table putting fresh lace on a black silk waist. ELECTA, her sister, a year or two younger, is in a rocking chair darning stockings. MRS. OBERLY, the blacksmith's wife, is on the sofa. She is a heavy, middle-aged woman and wears a shawl and hat.

MRS. OBERLY: Well, I must be going home along.

CORNELIA: [Her needle flying.] Don't hurry, Mrs. Oberly, do sit awhile.

ELECTA: Sister and I don't get out much in winter.

MRS. OBERLY: I just stopped in to say good-bye.

CORNELIA: Oh . . . we forgot to tell you. . . .

ELECTA: We've about decided not to go.

MRS. OBERLY: Not going? Do tell!

CORNELIA: You see, it's so soon after Christmas.

MRS. OBERLY: For land's sake, I thought it was all settled!

ELECTA: Not settled, we are never sure beforehand.

CORNELIA: You never can tell what may happen.

MRS. OBERLY: After those grand invitations, and the weather so mild. . . .

CORNELIA: Yes, we never shall see another bishop consecrated.

ELECTA: We have seen four come and go in this diocese.

CORNELIA: But this man's young, and he'll outlast us.

MRS. OBERLY: Well, well, I am surprised, such great church ladies as you be! I says to John, I says, there wouldn't be no 'Piscopal church here if 'twarn't for them Milk sisters.

CORNELIA: Now, Mrs. Oberly . . .

MRS. OBERLY: True as I'm sittin' here, all Millet knows it. I warn't born 'Piscopal, but seein' as it's the only church here I'll do my share, and when it comes to finding delicate ladies like you be, down on your hands and knees scrubbin' the church floor, I says, you'd a better call on Joan Oberly first; scrubbin' is more in my line.

CORNELIA: Sister, do you hear her?

ELECTA: But you don't understand, Mrs. Oberly, we wanted to do it. It was only the altar steps.

CORNELIA: There is so little we can do.

MRS. OBERLY: Little! Fixin' that tree for the Sunday School all by yourselves, and climbin' on that rickety church ladder! I'm thankful neither of you broke your hip.

ELECTA: Don't suggest it: as if every time sister gets up on a chair. . . .

CORNELIA: It's you who will climb on chairs to reach down the jelly.

THE FEAST OF THE HOLY INNOCENTS

Mrs. Oberly: Excuse me, but I says to John, I says, if ever there was saints on earth the Milk sisters are them.

Electa: Now, now, now. . . .

Cornelia: Not saints!

Mrs. Oberly: I'd like to know, spending all your money on those young ones, and not havin' a trip to town to see the makin' of this new bishop?

Electa: You ask your husband about our being saints.

Cornelia: I guess John will tell you. . . .

Mrs. Oberly: Well, I must allow, husband did say. . . . There I won't repeat home talk.

Cornelia: Now, Mrs. Oberly!

Electa: Exciting our curiosity. . . .

Mrs. Oberly: Well, he did say as how he knew the Milk girls before I did. . . .

Cornelia: Yes?

Electa: Well, what else did he say?

Mrs. Oberly: It's time for me to be goin' home along. *stands*

Electa: Goodness, if I don't smell that sponge-cake! [She rises and hurries out.]

Mrs. Oberly: I was goin' to remark, if there warn't something in the oven.

Cornelia: Just like Lecta, she always forgets her oven. If she would only leave sponge-cake alone when eggs are high. I never say anything, for with her delicate digestion if there is any one thing she craves. . . .

Mrs. Oberly: Next to currant jelly there is nothing so uncertain as sponge-cake and a sponge-cake that don't rise. . . .

Cornelia: Oh well, the cat will eat it, with plenty of cream.

[Electa returns.]

Electa: Burnt to a crisp!

Cornelia: The full rule?

ELECTA: A dozen eggs. Oh, if there were only a man in the house to say something!

CORNELIA: My dear, before company!

ELECTA: I mean it! Of all the . . . mm-m . . . oh!

MRS. OBERLY: Just what John said, "Electa Milk had the old Nick in her when she was a girl." . . . Excuse me, I forgot!

ELECTA: Don't apologise, John knows. The other day when I went into his shop with our tongs to mend, and overheard some . . . well, pretty strong language. . . .

MRS. OBERLY: He was that mortified! But, he said, when it comes to shoeing a colt. . . .

ELECTA: Exactly! I told him there were times when even a lady would be glad of a man's tongue.

CORNELIA: Be careful, dear, if you say too much Mrs. Oberly will think. . . .

ELECTA: Oh—that burnt cake— Excuse me I must open the kitchen window. [She goes out.]

CORNELIA: Do be careful of draughts with your throat. Sister is so impulsive, she is like a child. I have to watch her.

MRS. OBERLY: John and I was saying how two such lovely ladies as you be . . . how you ever missed out with the boys?

CORNELIA: Oh, Mrs. Oberly! Somehow we had each other . . . and father.

MRS. OBERLY: Both so lively like. . . .

CORNELIA: My sister had chances enough, she was much sought after. There was one young man in particular . . . he wrote beautiful poetry. . . .

MRS. OBERLY: He up and died on her? That kind usually does.

CORNELIA: No . . . no . . . you'd be surprised if I told you who it was. He's president of a bank in Lakeport now.

Mrs. Oberly: You don't mean. . . ? I believe it was Charles Oman.

Cornelia: I mentioned no names.

Mrs. Oberly: His folks lived near here. And he off and married another girl. That's the city of it.

Cornelia: Please never mention it, Mrs. Oberly.

Mrs. Oberly: Well, I must say, I'm thankful I hain't got to raise my children in the city. All the temptations one reads about in the paper. . . .

Cornelia: Yes.

Mrs. Oberly: As bad for girls as boys. Ladies at their lunch parties drinking these 'ere cocktails. . . .

Cornelia: So they say.

Mrs. Oberly: And a smoking cigarettes. . . .

Cornelia: Dear, dear . . .

Mrs. Oberly: And playin' cards for money. I suppose you seen the Sunday paper?

Cornelia: I haven't had time to glance at a paper since before Christmas.

Mrs. Oberley: That French lady actor coming to Lakeport. . . .

Cornelia: You don't mean Bernhardt?

Mrs. Oberly: That's just who. In plays it made me blush to read about.

Cornelia: Aren't you mistaken, the paper said last week she was coming to Chicago? [She begins to turn over the papers on the table.]

Mrs. Oberly: Yes, but she was to come to Madison first, and the theatre burned, so she is goin' to Milwaukee tomorrow.

Cornelia: Dear, dear, and we have never seen her!

Mrs. Oberly: You don't mean you'd go!

Cornelia: No danger, we never shall have a chance.

Mrs. Oberly: I guess if you ever read the stories—"Camilly" and "Lay Toscay"—of all the . . . ! I tell you,

I got rid of that supplement before Mr. Oberly or the children got a hold of the paper.

CORNELIA: Really?

MRS. OBERLY: We have temptations enough in this country without bringin' in more from a foreign land.

CORNELIA: I can't imagine what Electa did with the Sunday paper, it usually lies here until we read it.

MRS. OBERLY: Well, I wouldn't 'a' mentioned the subject, but I thought you might like to burn that paper if your sister hadn't seen it.

[ELECTA comes in, and there is a meaningful silence.]

CORNELIA: Yes, I do think it is mild for this time of year.

MRS. OBERLY: Well I must be going home along.

CORNELIA: [Looking out of the window.] If there isn't the mail man already. . . . [She picks up a shawl.]

ELECTA: Now, Corny, with your neuralgia. . . .

CORNELIA: I'd like to know if you haven't a throat. . . .

ELECTA: Now don't stop and talk, no matter if it is mild. [CORNELIA goes out.] Sister is so impulsive, I have to watch her like a child. She looks to be stronger, but she has always been the delicate one. Like mother, so sensitive . . . the least thing. . . .

MRS. OBERLY: Well, if that's the mail man.

ELECTA: Oh, just a minute. What was it you were saying about the Sunday paper?

MRS. OBERLY: Did I mention the paper? Oh yes, I guess I did say how there didn't seem to be anything in it this week.

ELECTA: Exactly. I burned ours by mistake. In case Sister asks to borrow yours, you might say yours was gone too.

MRS. OBERLY: You read it, 'bout them plays?

ELECTA: I glanced it over; I didn't exactly read it . . .

MRS. OBERLY: I guess you felt as I did.

ELECTA: Sh . . . we won't say any more. [CORNELIA comes in.] Do come in again soon.

MRS. OBERLY: I feel terrible about your not goin' to the consecration, all on account of that Christmas tree for our young ones. It ain't right. [She shows embarrassment.] I suppose if John was to lend you a little something . . . just by way of a loan. . . .

CORNELIA: Oh, Mrs. Oberly, we couldn't think of it.

ELECTA: We have quite decided, we can't afford it.

MRS. OBERLY: Well, good afternoon.

CORNELIA: Good afternoon, Mrs. Oberly.

ELECTA: Good afternoon, Mrs. Oberly. [CORNELIA shows her out. ELECTA takes up the paper that has just come. There is a little pause after CORNELIA returns.]

CORNELIA: [Pretends to take up her sewing.] Do you realise, Electa, that to-morrow is the sixtieth anniversary of father and mother's wedding?

ELECTA: Goodness, don't remind me, the way time flies.

CORNELIA: That isn't the right spirit—our parents' diamond wedding—it is only proper we should celebrate it.

ELECTA: They never made anything of it when they were alive.

CORNELIA: All the more reason why we should do something, and besides, it is the Feast of the Holy Innocents.

ELECTA: I never heard of that before.

CORNELIA: The idea! It has always been in the Prayer Book in black and white.

ELECTA: You need not pretend you knew any more about it than I did until those invitations for the consecration came.

CORNELIA: Well now we do know about it we ought not let it pass, and to miss the consecration would be—well— almost a sin.

ELECTA: Cornelia Milk, it was you yourself decided . . .

CORNELIA: I never decide anything, I always leave it to

you. But I must say, if we miss this we never shall see another, and it will be a wonderful service in the cathedral, with candles, vestments, and everything.

ELECTA: But when it came to choosing between a tree for the children or going in town to the consecration. . . .

CORNELIA: We chose the tree, of course, but now that is over we can change our minds, rise to the occasion, and make a sacrifice.

ELECTA: Oh, sacrifice, I wish you would tell me one thing more we could sacrifice!

CORNELIA: I won't get a dress this year, that's all.

ELECTA: The idea, you haven't a dress fit to be seen. I might get on without one, perhaps, I don't wear my things so hard as you do.

CORNELIA: I'll wear calico.

ELECTA: Don't be flighty. We owe it to our position to appear like ladies even if we starve.

CORNELIA: Then we'll sell another lot along the road.

ELECTA: There will be precious little left for us if we sell another lot.

CORNELIA: I don't believe in hoarding at our age, any more than Carnegie.

ELECTA: We can't sell a lot this afternoon.

CORNELIA: We'll borrow money from Mr. Oberly, and give him a mortgage.

ELECTA: Cornelia, if you keep on tempting me! [She gets up.] I won't hear you. [The telephone rings three short and two long.]

CORNELIA: Was that our ring? You had better see anyway.

ELECTA: [At the telephone.] No it isn't for us. [She listens, and then hangs up.] It was Mrs. Oberly telling Mrs. Ashbridge we aren't going to the consecration of the bishop.

CORNELIA: Oh, passing the word around, is she? Explaining why, I suppose, as if that tree or their young ones. . . .

ELECTA: If they dared to offer us help! I . . . I won't stand it! Oh I'm willing to go, if you are so set on it.

CORNELIA: I'm not set. You are the one to decide. I only thought there is more than one reason why we should go now. I see the annual bargain sale is advertised at Baxter and Baxter's: if we got our new dresses there most likely we should save the cost of the trip to town.

ELECTA: Perhaps, but I wouldn't dare go to one of those bargain sales. Why, only the other day I read of a woman crushed to death at one in Cleveland, or somewhere.

CORNELIA: I wouldn't be so afraid of being killed as I would of getting the wrong thing in the excitement. I never can think when I am excited, and they won't let you exchange a thing.

ELECTA: Exactly . . . much better to deal with home merchants, we always did like to bring things home, and talk them over, before we decide, that's half the fun of shopping.

CORNELIA: I leave it to you.

ELECTA: Anyway, you'd get so tired most likely it would end in pneumonia.

CORNELIA: The idea! I'm not half so liable to things as you are. The least thing gives you a cold.

ELECTA: Now, Corny, dear, you know how imprudent you are. You're just like mother, so sensitive. . . .

CORNELIA: I'm not half so sensitive as you are, if I didn't look out for you at every turn. . . .

ELECTA: Very well then, we won't argue, let us settle it, we won't go.

CORNELIA: Just as you say, but when you think of the consecration, and that it is the Feast of the Holy Innocents, and father and mother's wedding anniversary, and everything else, it does seem. . . .

ELECTA: We can read about them all in the papers.

CORNELIA: Yes, I thought when we got our rural delivery, and could have a daily paper almost as soon as the people in town. I thought we should feel almost as if we lived there; but I declare, the more we read about what is going on the more tantalising it is. I sometimes wish we never saw a paper. [The telephone rings again, several long and short.]

ELECTA: Is that ours?

CORNELIA: I'd better see. [Takes down the receiver.] Same old story. . . . [Hangs up.] Mrs. Oberly telling Mrs. Linkum now . . . how we are giving up our trip . . . such saints. . . !

ELECTA: Saints! No, that is too much!

CORNELIA: Well then?

ELECTA: As if they could understand our position. When I think of what father was, and all the advantages he had.

CORNELIA: Precisely! If he had ever dreamed of his daughters being cooped up in a little country village all their lives. . . .

ELECTA: Don't blame poor father.

CORNELIA: I am not blaming him, I am proud of him. It wasn't every one went to Europe in those days, and learned French as he did in Paris.

ELECTA: If he hadn't put all his money into land just here.

CORNELIA: It wasn't his fault Millet didn't grow into a big city. No one could tell in those days which were going to be the large cities. I've been crazy to go to Paris all my life! [She finds an old encyclopedia in the bookcase. As she opens it various autumn leaves fall out.]

ELECTA: Paris, who wouldn't like to see Paris!

CORNELIA: "Paris. The history of Paris begins with the Commentaries of Julius Cæsar, wherein he speaks of Lutetia. Strabo calls it Lucotocia, Ptolemy Lucoticia, and the Emperor Julian Louchetia. . . ." [She sighs and stops reading.] That doesn't suggest Paris at all.

Electa: I think of a gay, brilliant place.

Cornelia: Of course . . . the opera.

Electa: And concerts . . . I adore music.

Cornelia: The beautiful palaces . . . with statues standing around. . . .

Electa: The galleries of paintings . . . don't you ache to see . . . to see a really famous painting?

Cornelia: I'd like to eat out of doors at a little table with lamps in the trees.

Electa: And to see the people . . . hundreds of people you don't know . . . one might have an adventure. . . .

Cornelia: And here we sit!

Electa: Shut in. . . .

Cornelia: And life passing away—

Electa: Passed away! [The telephone jingles again.]

Cornelia: You needn't listen, it will be the same old story. Every one in the village must know it by this time.

Electa: Let them talk. . . . I've decided to go.

Cornelia: Sister!

Electa: Yes, I've thought it out. We'll borrow the money as Mrs. Oberly offered and I'll telephone in to Lizzie Oman, and see if she will let us visit her for the night. We can't afford a hotel.

Cornelia: Electa Milk, are you willing to stay at Charles Oman's house?

Electa: I? You may not like to go, Cornelia.

Cornelia: It was you he was in love with.

Electa: No, I always said it was you.

Cornelia: Those poems were to you.

Electa: We never were sure.

Cornelia: Well, I am sure, he never proposed to me.

Electa: He never proposed to me.

CORNELIA: Now, Electa, if you think you can deceive me. . . .

ELECTA: Well, anyway, we can't deceive ourselves as to when it all happened. Let me think . . . it was. . . .

CORNELIA: Twenty-five. . . .

ELECTA: Thirty years ago.

CORNELIA: No matter, if you feel you can go to his house . . . I don't.

ELECTA: Lizzie has asked us more than once, and we have been there to lunch. [She takes up the telephone.] I want long distance. . . . Milwaukee. . . . Yes.

CORNELIA: Electa, long-distance is fifty cents!

ELECTA: I can't help it. . . . No, I'll hold the line. If she rings us up they'll all be on the line listening.

CORNELIA: Sister, I think you are hasty, deciding things in this off-hand way. We ought to talk it over first, and be sure.

ELECTA: Mrs. Charles Oman's residence. Yes. Is this Mrs. Oman's residence? She's out? Dear, dear! Oh, Louise, is that you? Is your mother out? This is Miss Milk of Millet. No, not Miller. Miss Milk, M I L K, you know, what cows give. Yes. What. . . . She is? Coming here? Now isn't that a coincidence! Yes . . . yes . . . yes . . . good-bye. [Hangs up.] Of all things, I should say it was the hand of Providence. Lizzie Oman came out to Beasely to-day to old Mrs. Park's funeral, you know the Parks are her cousins, and Louise says she is coming over here before she returns to town.

CORNELIA: Dear me, and your sponge-cake burned, we haven't a thing but bread in the house.

ELECTA: I'll run right over to the store. [She begins to get her cloak.]

CORNELIA: I oughtn't to let you go with your throat. . . .

ELECTA: I'd like to know if I'd let you run any risks with your neuralgia.

THE FEAST OF THE HOLY INNOCENTS

CORNELIA: Don't get ginger snaps.

ELECTA: I'll get some of those lovely wafers in a tin box. We can't spare expense at a time like this.

CORNELIA: Now don't be impulsive, and decide in a hurry. I really ought to go with you. Look over everything Mrs. Gunn has first, there may be some new cracker they are having in the city. I wish I knew just what they have at their teas.

ELECTA: Olives, or a little cream cheese?

CORNELIA: I'll make some marmalade sandwiches. I read about them in the paper. [The telephone jingles again. She addresses it without going to it this time.] Oh yes, tell them we are not going, tell them we are such saints, take up a subscription for us! [To her sister.] Do be careful of the steps, they are slippery, if you were to fall and break your hip.

ELECTA: If she has some of her own head cheese, or do you think sardines? [She goes out.]

CORNELIA: [Calling after her.] No, no, they are so old-fashioned. . . . Don't hurry. . . . I didn't say hurry, I said don't hurry. . . . No matter. Mercy, she will be sure to fall. I never should have let her go alone. [She picks up the paper eagerly, and scans it, then turns to the telephone.] Mame, I want long distance again . . . yes, I know it is fifty cents, it's horrid of the company to have such a charge . . . I want the Milwaukee Opera House . . . yes . . . line's busy. . . . Hello, is that the Opera House? Can I have two seats, no I mean three, for Thursday evening? Yes, Camille. . . . How much? . . . Oh, have you any for $1.50? Not any $2.00 either, only $2.50 in the sixth row . . . goodness . . . wait a minute . . . yes I'll take them. . . . Miss Milk . . . no not Miller, Milk . . . not Mick, Milk, M I L K, you know what cows give. . . . No, not Crosby, cows give, didn't you ever hear of cows? Yes, Milk. . . . Can't you keep them longer than that? . . . We can't get to

421

town before ten thirty. . . . Well, send them to Mr. Charles Oman's bank, he'll be responsible for them. . . . Be sure now. . . . [She hangs up and breathes in hard excitement. There is a knock at the door. She lets in a middle-aged lady, handsomely dressed. MRS. OMAN.] Lizzie Oman, of all things!

MRS. OMAN: I thought I'd surprise you. Isn't your sister here?

CORNELIA: She'll be back directly.

MRS. OMAN: I came out to old Mrs. Park's funeral.

CORNELIA: Yes, so we heard.

MRS. OMAN: You did? How in the world—

CORNELIA: We just telephoned to your house.

MRS. OMAN: To tell me that you were coming in to the consecration of the new bishop! I knew you would be sure to, such good church women as you are, it couldn't happen without you. Now I want you to come in with me this afternoon, and stay over Sunday at least.

CORNELIA: Impossible!

MRS. OMAN: Nonsense. Toss something into a suit-case, I'll lend you anything you forget. I've a carriage to take you to the station.

CORNELIA: There is so much to see to. . . .

MRS. OMAN: Not a word. I'll run over to see Mrs. Ashbridge, and leave you to get ready. I'll be back in twenty minutes.

[ELECTA comes in, her hands full of packages, which she tries to conceal. MRS. OMAN kisses her.]

ELECTA: Lizzie Oman—

MRS. OMAN: It's all arranged, you are coming with me to-day.

ELECTA: To-day? Impossible! You must have tea. . . .

MRS. OMAN: [Hurrying off.] No time for tea. I'll be back soon.

ELECTA: Did you ever!

CORNELIA: Just like Lizzie, she always was a whirlwind. That's the way she married Charles Oman. If you hadn't been so deliberate. . . .

ELECTA: Cornelia Milk, it was you never could or would decide anything.

CORNELIA: I will decide now. [She begins to tie up her head.]

ELECTA: You're crazy, you haven't packed yet.

CORNELIA: We have got to have some money first. I'm going right over to John Oberly's. . . .

ELECTA: Get ten dollars . . . no, twenty.

CORNELIA: Of course. I put my black silk in the valise this morning in case anything happened, so I haven't much packing to do.

ELECTA: And I packed the hand bag, but I didn't say anything, for I thought you would be so disappointed in case nothing happened. There now, do be careful, don't hurry, you will be sure to slip, you are so impulsive. [CORNELIA hurries off.]

ELECTA: [At the telephone.] Mamie, I wish you would hurry please and give me long-distance, Milwaukee. . . . I want the Opera House. . . . No, I will hold the line. . . . Is this the Opera House? . . . Well, I want three of your best seats for to-morrow afternoon for Bernhardt. . . . Yes, "La Tosca." . . . What, only box seats for three dollars? Well, yes, all right, three. . . . For Miss Milk, of Millet. What? Do I want them sent to Oman's bank? What made you think of that? . . . You can't keep them? Very well, but don't let him pay for them, charge them to me. Yes, plain Milk, you know—milk, cream, butter, eggs, . . . what cows give. Now don't fail to send the best you have left. [She leaves the telephone, and hurries to gather up her packages. CORNELIA comes in with JENNIE OBERLY, a fresh-faced girl of twelve.]

CORNELIA: Here's Jennie to see about everything while

we are gone. John will bring the money over before we go. [While they are talking, CORNELIA brings in an old-fashioned valise and is busy packing things she has brought in from the bedroom.]

ELECTA: Now, Jennie, you know how to run the base burner?

JENNIE: Yes'm, it's like ours.

CORNELIA: And you must feed Petkins.

JENNIE: Oh, yes'm.

ELECTA: But don't you give him meat. [She gets her hand bag and begins to pack also.]

CORNELIA: He'd be happier to stay right here at night.

ELECTA: You must give him all the cream—he will miss us so.

CORNELIA: And, Jennie dear . . . in case . . . in case anything happens to us. . . .

ELECTA: Sister!

CORNELIA: We must think of every contingency before going on a journey.

JENNIE: If you fell and broke your hip. . . .

CORNELIA: No, I mean, in case anything happened and we didn't come back, then, you are to have Petkins.

JENNIE: Oh, Miss Corny!

ELECTA: Yes, and I trust you, Jennie, to be very kind to him.

JENNIE: Oh, Miss Lecty!

CORNELIA: And Jennie, we shall be gone over Sunday. I hope you will learn your Bible lesson just the same.

ELECTA: We'll hear you when we get back.

CORNELIA: [Shutting the valise.] There, that is done.

ELECTA: Sister, there is still time to change our minds; are you sure we are doing the right thing to go?

JENNIE: Not go now?

ELECTA: There, Jennie, you run back to mother.

JENNIE: Mother, she says she don't blame you for changing your minds, any lady likes to change her mind; but father, he says, that last time you took back the dress to Beasely, he says. . . .

CORNELIA: Now, Jennie. . . .

JENNIE: He says, if you ladies had been married you couldn't 'a' changed your minds so easy, that's what he says.

CORNELIA: Now, Jennie, it isn't good manners to talk about your elders.

ELECTA: Nor to talk about marriage to unmarried ladies.

CORNELIA: Run along now, that's a good girl, and remember to keep the stove going, and to feed the cat.

ELECTA: And learn your Bible lesson. We'll put the key under the mat. [They show JENNIE out.]

ELECTA: Now we mustn't be hasty, Corny. . . . It's for you to decide.

CORNELIA: Because I am older you want to put all the responsibility on me.

ELECTA: Quietly, quietly, there is no need of getting excited. John hasn't brought the money yet. You must remember if we sell another lot it will put their back yard and all their Monday wash right where we can see it from our front door. Of course it is a church function, something we shall want to remember for the rest of our lives but still. . . .

CORNELIA: Very well, if you are afraid to go we'll give it up. [There is a knock at the door and MRS. OMAN comes in.]

MRS. OMAN: Well, are you all ready? Mr. Oberly met me at the gate and asked me to give you this. [She holds out an envelope to CORNELIA.]

ELECTA: Lizzie dear, we are not sure. . . .

CORNELIA: You see Electa has a very delicate throat. . . .

ELECTA: Oh, it isn't my throat half so much as sister's neuralgia.

MRS. OMAN: Not another word. Put on your hats. You may never see another consecration.

CORNELIA: Just like a man, taking vows for life.

ELECTA: As if one could ever be sure.

MRS. OMAN: There is a nice orchestral concert on Friday, you must hear that.

CORNELIA: We love music.

ELECTA: And out here there is not much music, except of course, sacred music.

CORNELIA: And graphophones, we have heard some beautiful records.

MRS. OMAN: And Saturday afternoon there is a card party at the club.

CORNELIA: So we saw by the paper.

MRS. OMAN: Fancy your noticing what we are doing in town.

ELECTA: Why not? We get our paper almost as soon as you do in the city.

CORNELIA: We always read all the society news, it's the only way we can take part.

ELECTA: It is so interesting. I don't suppose the ladies really do play for money as they say they do.

MRS. OMAN: You wouldn't have to see them. Perhaps two or three tables of the gay set in the back room might be playing for money.

CORNELIA: Dear me, I'd like to see ladies gambling, just once. . . .

ELECTA: Be careful dear, Lizzie might think. . . .

CORNELIA: I would, and I'd like to try it myself to see what it felt like.

ELECTA: Sister! you are too impulsive! You see our lives are so quiet.

MRS. OMAN: Of course. . . .

CORNELIA: Yes, and I'd like to see a lady smoking a cigarette.

THE FEAST OF THE HOLY INNOCENTS

Mrs. Oman: You wicked creature. I must think of some friend who indulges. I wish there was a play at the theatre you would enjoy. If it were only last week, "The Old Homestead" was playing. You would have loved it, all about the country. And the week before, "Mrs. Wiggs" was here, such a sweet wholesome piece.

Cornelia: Really?

Mrs. Oman: Of course Bernhardt is coming to-morrow, in some of her awful French plays, you wouldn't care for those, I suppose?

Electa: I don't know . . . perhaps not . . .

Cornelia: She is famous.

Electa: You didn't think of going yourself?

Mrs. Oman: Mr. Oman refused to take me. Not that we aren't old enough to stand anything, but he doesn't want daughter to go; and besides, he likes to be amused at the theatre and he hates those dreadful, sensational pieces and in a foreign tongue.

Cornelia: I suppose men do.

Electa: We wondered . . .

Mrs. Oman: You don't mean you would like to see her?

Cornelia: You see our father used to tell us a great deal about Paris.

Electa: He went there in 1847.

Cornelia: When Louis Philippe was king.

Electa: And we have longed to go there all our lives.

Cornelia: And we thought to see one of these plays would be something like going.

Electa: In a way it would be quite instructive.

Cornelia: But of course if Mr. Oman feels so strongly about it. . . .

Electa: As your guests we mustn't do anything. . . .

Mrs. Oman: Goodness, we're old enough and I'm dying to go. . . .

Cornelia: No one need know.

ELECTA: You can't understand, but we sometimes feel as if . . . well . . . something a little spicy might liven us up a bit.

MRS. OMAN: Not another word. We'll go if I can get seats so late. I must telephone before we start for the train. [The sisters exchange glances.]

CORNELIA: Oh, no, not now.

ELECTA: Let us decide tomorrow.

MRS. OMAN: It may be too late then.

CORNELIA: Let us go to the consecration first.

ELECTA: Yes, that is the important thing. That is what we are really going for.

CORNELIA: Then if we feel in the mood for a little . . . well . . . diversion . . .

ELECTA: We will take our chances. We never like to decide things ahead.

CORNELIA: One never can tell what may happen.

MRS. OMAN: Just as you say, but if we are going to get the 5:20 we must be off. [She starts to the door.]

CORNELIA: Sister, listen to me, we are not going on my decision. It was you that decided. I will take no responsibility.

ELECTA: Nor I, I left it entirely to you.

MRS. OMAN: Are you coming?

CORNELIA: Then we each go of our own free will?

MRS. OMAN: Come.

CORNELIA and ELECTA: [They speak together and go out slowly.] Yes—we are coming.

THE BARBARIANS
By Leo B. Pride

PERSONS IN THE PLAY

JAKE KNOWLES
FRANK BLAKE
BARTO
SNOWBALL
PETERS

THE BARBARIANS

A SIDE view of a chamber off the sub-entry in Stony Creek Coal Mine in the coal fields of southern Illinois. The chamber, or "room," as it is called, is only one of many tunnel-like openings driven into the coal. The section shows an irregular wall of coal streaked with veins of sulphur and gray patches of slate, and extends from right to left for some twelve or fifteen feet, where it is bounded by the "face" of the room, the farthest point of advance or digging. The method of mining employed is known as the "room and pillar" system of underground mining, the wall of coal in the background forming long parallel pillars of support for the roof, and the space shown being the room which serves as a haulage-way for the outgoing coal and as an intake for the fresh air that must be pumped into the room for the men at work. On the floor is the track on which stands, at the extreme right, a two-ton pit car loaded with coal.

Opaque blackness pervades the scene. No living thing with eyes can see. Out of the obscure atmosphere and re-

mote regions of the mine come the sounds of the underground industry—strange creakings, metallic noises harsh and
grating, faint and distant subterranean rumbles—all emanat-
ing from the black void, from which, during the momentary
intervals of silence, sounds the musical tinkle of dripping
water, somewhere close by.

Gradually the darkness becomes less intense; a pale and
leaden light shines from the right, then a single point of
light moving toward the left. A man is dimly seen. JAKE
KNOWLES, stripped to the waist, enormous, powerful, his
knotty muscles crawling under his grimy skin, is lifting
a huge lump of coal on the pit car. He grunts, standing for
a moment, panting hard. Another light is seen. FRANK
BLAKE, slender, poorly developed, his chalky-white skin
smeared with grime, struggles under a lump of coal which
he is trying to place on the car. KNOWLES helps him and
gives him a friendly slap on the back.

KNOWLES: That's the boy, Frank.

FRANK: I guess I haven't been much help, so far.

KNOWLES: You'll get used to it.

FRANK: Thanks. You're considerate. I know I'm a poor
buddy.

KNOWLES: That's all right. Well, suppose we eat now?
It's nigh on noon. We can't load no more coal till we get
more cars.

FRANK: I could eat a dog. [KNOWLES gets his bucket and
sits down with his back to the pillar of coal. FRANK takes a
paper of sandwiches from his jumper from behind the car.]

KNOWLES: Hungry?

FRANK: I'm not used to this kind of work.

KNOWLES: What brought you down here, anyhow?

FRANK: I needed a job.

KNOWLES: [Looking him over.] What was you doin'
before?

FRANK: I was a clerk on top. Got fired.

KNOWLES: Somebody put in your place, I reckon.

FRANK: How'd you know?

KNOWLES: That's the way them top jobs go. I thought you was the boy what worked in the office. Last night at the roadhouse, I says to myself, "That must be the lad who pays the boys off." Men like you don't often come down below.

FRANK: You were a good sport to take me on. I was trying to get on for a long time.

KNOWLES: My son used to work beside me, but he got caught under the slate. I needed a buddy, an' seein' as you needed a job, I didn't mind signin' up for you. You kinda look like my boy.

FRANK: I've got a real reason for coming down here. You see, I've studied mining, I'm educated, and I'm going to make these mines safe.

KNOWLES: [Chewing his food slowly.] I wish you luck, son.

FRANK: You believe me, don't you?

KNOWLES: Looks like you bit off a big bite. [He shakes his head and eats gloomily.]

FRANK: What's the matter?

KNOWLES: The old timers, I'm thinkin', might take you for a tenderfoot. Don't pay no attention to 'em, though.

FRANK: Everybody's got it in for me—I get so damn mad!

KNOWLES: How so? What seems to be the trouble?

FRANK: Oh, nothing much.

KNOWLES: You can tell me if you want to.

FRANK: I've got to stick it out, that's all.

KNOWLES: I've seen more'n one of them office guys come down, an' leave in a hurry. You're worried. Been here all mornin' an' ain't said a word.

FRANK: I've got to make more money. I've got a wife and kids.

KNOWLES: We all have. It takes a heap of brawn to keep the tots in school. You're troubled, all right.

FRANK: It's killing me.

KNOWLES: Tell me. I've got a wife an' tots.

FRANK: I couldn't make a living. She got disgusted with me. . . . It got worse and worse, we quarrelled.

KNOWLES: I see.

FRANK: I got madder than a boiled owl, told her what I thought of her, left her with the kids last night.

KNOWLES: Now you'll have to go back, Frank.

FRANK: She's impossible. I kept telling her I was coming below. She didn't want me to come to the pit. You see, it was like this. The company sent me down from the Chicago office. She hates this country . . . she's been used to things, and now I can't even make a living.

KNOWLES: What'd she say?

FRANK: She said if I came below, I'd be like the rest of the barbarians.

KNOWLES: [Swallowing a mouthful of food.] The what?

FRANK: Barbarians.

KNOWLES: Oh. That's somethin' like a gorilla, ain't it?

FRANK: No. They're a little higher than gorillas. I guess you'd have to know about evolution to understand. They are a race of men, I was reading, that's dumb. All backbone and no brains . . . can't think. That's how I lost my job, I was reading.

KNOWLES: So your wife, she don't like you to work below. We're just common, sweaty men.

FRANK: She's been used to things. She's afraid something might happen.

KNOWLES: Don't see how anythin' could happen. [Then with a blank stare on his face.] You've got a high-strung wife, boy. Barbarians . . . barbarians . . . so that's what people call us? [He looks at FRANK squarely.] Well. [The sound of footsteps is heard approaching. A moment

THE BARBARIANS

later, BARTO, a short, squat Italian with enormous shoulders, comes in. He is singing a folk song. He is followed by SNOWBALL, a big Negro. Both men are stripped to the waist, and wear heavy dungaree trousers and hob-nail shoes. BARTO has a radio under his arm, and his attitude toward this instrument is almost that of paternal affection. BARTO sits downs, the radio between his legs. He opens his dinner pail, takes a newspaper from his hip pocket and begins to read silently. SNOWBALL sits down against the car. KNOWLES watches them curiously. There is a pause.]

BARTO: [Reading his paper—chuckling.] Huh, huh.

SNOWBALL: What are you cackling about, Napoleon?

BARTO: Da Italian Princess, da paper say, marry herself to one coal miner. Golla, I wish I was da single man.

SNOWBALL: If you was, you'd be in jail.

KNOWLES: [Smiles and looks them over.] Barbarians.

SNOWBALL: [Leaning forward.] Eh? What's that?

KNOWLES: I say, you're a barbarian.

SNOWBALL: Ah didn't either.

KNOWLES: Now, there's Snowball . . . goes to church every Sunday. He can tell us about evolution. What's a barbarian?

SNOWBALL: Oh, Barbarian? Him's a man what did forget to evolute, says our new preacher.

KNOWLES: All backbone an' no brains. Barto, you're a barbarian, ain't you?

BARTO: [He receives the question with an air of indifference and takes a string of garlic from his pail. KNOWLES moves over and SNOWBALL holds his nose.] Barbarian? I do not geeve a damn. Worka vera harrd with da back and da hands. Maka da mon. Hava da wife and bigga da fam. Barbarian, maybe. Soma day, I own da American blind pig, am rich, then I leeva thees damn countree. [He shrugs his shoulders and attacks the garlic.]

KNOWLES: [Looking around and chuckling.] Barbarians

435

all. That's a good one on us, boys. I'll have to tell my wife she's married to a barbarian. She'd like to call me that—along with other things. [They remain silent, glancing at one another; finally their eyes become concentrated on FRANK, who has been sitting quietly. He moves uneasily in his seat as they appear to recognize him for the first time.]

BARTO: [Staring at FRANK.] Him barbarian, too? [He shrugs.] Huh, ees not bigga nough. [There is a pause.]

SNOWBALL: [Looking FRANK over—curiously.] You call us barbarians?

KNOWLES: [With a kind of detached air—himself curiously amused.] You punks make me tired. [He rises with an impatient gesture and walks behind the pit car and leans over facing the men.] What's the matter with you, say? [The men seem to listen, but after the fashion of men who work at back-breaking toil, continue to chew their food gloomily, paying little attention to KNOWLES.] That boy's all right, now. Didn't you know we was all barbarians, you, and you, and you, and you. [He points to himself.] An' Frank, there, he's one of them things too. His wife said so. Why, think we been livin' all these years without knowin' it. We're much obliged to you, Frank.

[BARTO and SNOWBALL continue to stare at FRANK, then at KNOWLES, silently resenting his interpretation as a joke. The men eat in silence, looking at one another. The dripping water, endlessly beating a musical tattoo, sounds close by. Finally PETERS, a vague shadow of a man, comes in via the break-through on the left and stands for a moment looking at FRANK. Finally he sits down. There is a suggestion of the pig and the fox in his face. His attitude is that of a man whose presence is not wanted. Feeling this curious desire to exclude his company, he rises and faces FRANK.]

PETERS: Well, baby, when did you get down below?

KNOWLES: This mornin'. He's goin' to be my buddy.

PETERS: Tenderfoot, eh? He's that smart kid from the office. [Stands before FRANK facing him with a sneer.] How long do you think you'll last, baby?

KNOWLES: Leave him alone, Peters.

PETERS: Take care you don't get your soft hands dirty, kid. [A silence falls upon the room.]

KNOWLES: [Casually pushes a pick over to FRANK.] Take up for yourself, boy. [SNOWBALL and BARTO stare at the old man.]

PETERS: Better go home to your maw, kid, or that doll-faced wife of your'n what hangs round the office with ye. [FRANK, taking the pick and facing PETERS, gets to his feet.]

SNOWBALL: [Also getting up.] Say, what fo' you come here to start a row, Peters? What fo', I asks you? [PETERS looks at SNOWBALL, grins, and then turns his back on him.]

BARTO: Who tella you to coma in bigga Jake's room? [He rises and faces PETERS with his hands on his hips.] Leeva da small barbarian alone. [The men gather close and finally they become engaged in a general argument. PETERS draws away and stands facing FRANK.]

PETERS: Now put that pick down, baby, before I smack ye down.

KNOWLES: Leave him alone, Peters!

SNOWBALL: Get out o' here!

PETERS: [Glowering at FRANK.] You damn chalky-faced clerk!

FRANK: [Swinging the pick over his shoulder and breaking out in a rage.] You can go to hell, you pig-faced idiot! If you had any brains, you wouldn't be here yourself. [PETERS rushes at him and KNOWLES blocks his attack.] Who are you to tell me what to do? Anybody can do your work. [He seems to forget for the moment that his anger has been aroused by PETERS and he turns on the men in

general.] Anybody, you wops, niggers, scum of the pit!
[As this insult is flung at them, PETERS springs at him, to be
knocked sprawling upon the floor by KNOWLES. BARTO
and KNOWLES, fired into action, now start for FRANK.
KNOWLES jerks the pick from FRANK and forces them back.
FRANK, raging with anger, stands defying the men.] You're
good for the dirty work of the world and that's all! Scum
of the earth! Barbarians! Barbarians!

KNOWLES: [Trying to keep the men back.] Cut it out!
What's the matter here?

FRANK: [Jerks the pick from KNOWLES.] Let 'em come.
Let 'em get me if they can. I'll put a hole in their heads.
[He stands defying them. KNOWLES, kicking and keeping
the men at their distance, protects the boy. The men be-
come suddenly arrested in attitudes of doubt and amaze-
ment, and stand transfixed for a moment, puzzled. Finally
KNOWLES confronts the men with a commanding stare.
There is a pause. He turns to FRANK.]

KNOWLES: Don't do that.

FRANK: Did I start it? Make 'em lay off.

PETERS: [Stumbling to his feet and holding his stomach.]
I'll smash his weasel head in! Who the hell kicked me?
[He groans with pain.]

KNOWLES: You touch that boy an' I'll sink this pick in
your skull. [The two glower at each other.] Now, you
sit down. [He forces PETERS to sit, standing over him a
moment.] Sit down, Snowball. You, too, Barto. [They
do so, not without a feeling of unwillful subordination.
There is a pause. KNOWLES moves back and forth in the
room, dragging the pick with him, glancing at the men. He
is master of the situation, ready to quell any outburst of
fresh trouble. Finally he pauses before PETERS, who faces
him with a cynical sneer.]

PETERS: This ain't the end of this.

KNOWLES: Dry up. You started this trouble. You're

438

always ridin' somebody about somethin'. That boy's got a right here. He's got to make a livin', ain't he? Now, you leave him alone or I'll have you thrown out of the mine. An' by God, if they won't throw you out, I'll do it myself! [He moves quietly up and down the room.] It's too bad grown-up men can't act like men. [The three men accept his decision with an air of silence. KNOWLES sits down, placing the pick at his feet.] Eat your dinner, Frank.

BARTO: I think it ees da fool I am. Wasta my time on da likes of you. Soma day I leeva thees damn countree.

KNOWLES: Pipe down.

BARTO: I should not talk to da likes of you.

KNOWLES: Shut up. [KNOWLES gives him an affected look of anger and BARTO looks down at the floor gloomily. The men try to eat their lunches, chewing their food slowly. Finally BARTO begins to tinker with the radio.] Will the blame thing work? What'd you do with it?

BARTO: See how I gotta da way to learna da Engleesh. I lika to spick da Engleesh. Soma day I am da American citizenship.

KNOWLES: I wish you luck, old man. [He taps BARTO on the shoulder, then he takes out a pack of cards and deals himself a hand of solitaire.] Guess I'll have a little game while my dinner settles. [The radio begins to squawk.]

SNOWBALL: How much that thing cost?

BARTO: Fifty dollar. American money.

KNOWLES: Sure you didn't forget your change? [The radio squawks again.]

PETERS: [Rising up on his elbow.] Turn that God-damn thing off!

BARTO: Da radio hava da bad cold. [He tinkers with the dial.]

FRANK: [He has risen and been standing for a time, deep in thought.] I guess I'm the cause of this trouble.

439

Peters, I'm sorry. [PETERS only stares at him, remembering the blow in the stomach. FRANK turns to SNOWBALL.] Snowball, old man, it's all right. [He turns to BARTO.] I'm sorry, Barto, old timer. [Finally he turns to KNOWLES.] Mr. Knowles, I'm sorry. I lost my temper. [He remains standing and looking at the men for a moment with an expression of regret on his face, leans against the wall and stares dully at the floor.]

KNOWLES: [Studying his cards.] It's all right, Frank. [He looks at the men.] Now, he's told you he's sorry. Let it go at that. [The men do not look up, apparently conscious of a kind of childish shame. They continue to eat gloomily. The musical tinkle of the dripping water beats endlessly. The wagging blazes of their carbide lamps cast a pale and sickly luminescence through the murky atmosphere of the room, accentuating the shadows in their faces and knotty bodies.]

SNOWBALL: It is very quiet. [The long drawn-out bray of a mule is heard in the distance.]

KNOWLES: Molly must be hungry.

BARTO: Nice mule, Molla. [Out of the obscure atmosphere of the mine comes a creaking sound, like the distant whine of a wagon axle.]

PETERS: [After a pause, listening and looking at the radio.] Listen, Wop, turn that thing off.

BARTO: What's the ma? Da radio ees not on. [The sound continues.]

FRANK: [Slowly lifting his head and staring at the ceiling.] Listen to that.

KNOWLES: [Glancing up.] Mother earth takin' on. [The sound continues.]

FRANK: [Motionless, still staring at the roof.] That's all, mother earth.

KNOWLES: [Trying to locate the sound.] It ain't up there. It ain't up there. It's farther down toward the neck.

[He jerks his thumb to the left.] The old earth moanin', that's all.

FRANK: [His eyes still fixed on the roof.] That's all . . . the old earth moaning. [He remains motionless. There is a long pause. The men, conscious of a strange tone in the boy's voice, look at one another and then turn to FRANK. The prolonged whine, like the squeak of a wounded mouse in flight, comes down the entry and ceases with an appalling quickness in the center of the room. It pulls the men up sharp. They look at the roof. Finally KNOWLES turns to FRANK.]

KNOWLES: [Looking curiously at FRANK.] Are you afraid? The way you talk, you'd almost scare a fellow.

FRANK: I'm not afraid. Let her groan. [He continues to stare at the roof, as if held by a spell. The men glance at one another.] Groan, groan, groan.

SNOWBALL: [Quietly to BARTO.] There's something the matter with the lad, maybe?

KNOWLES: [Finally getting to his feet and taking FRANK by the arm.] Listen here. What's the matter? There ain't nothin' to be afraid of. It's nothin' but a little noise, a little settlin' somewheres.

FRANK: [Gradually becoming conscious of what the men are thinking.] I say I wasn't afraid! What's needed here is teamwork, teamwork against this grand old mother earth you're dreaming about. Why don't you get together against the gases she vomits at you instead of fighting among yourselves? [The men look at him with a curious kind of admiration.] That's all. Teamwork! So that you can be sure you're going to walk out of the mine instead of being carried out on stretchers.

KNOWLES: [He turns to the men.] Did you know that Frank, here, has been away to them big schools studyin' minin' an' engineerin'? [The creaking sound begins again.] An' did you know that he's come back to make these mines safe? [For a moment there is silence, then PETERS bursts forth in laughter; then BARTO and SNOWBALL, seeming slowly to realize the incongruity of the idea, begin to chuckle.]

BARTO: [Putting the lid on his bucket and getting up. He waves KNOWLES aside.] Always you cracka da joke, bigga Jake. I am go home on that one. [He starts to go.]

KNOWLES: I don't see nothin' funny to laugh at. [SNOW-BALL and PETERS rise and start off.] Well, might as well call it a day, with no more cars to load.

SNOWBALL: The mine blowed over. There's no work this afternoon. Everybody's went home. [They all start off. The sound of sharp cracking breaks the silence. KNOWLES stops suddenly and FRANK cowers beside him. There is a subterranean rumble, a ponderous roar, stupendous crack-ing, the deafening tumult of falling rock, the tearing sound of timbers being smashed and riven, tremendous concussions and prolonged thunder. The men instinctively drop to the floor and put out their carbide lights. Save for the bright glare of the electric bug lights on the caps of KNOWLES and FRANK, the room is in ink-black darkness. From the left comes a rayless guff of coal dust. There is a long silence, broken only by the musical tinkle of dripping water.]

BARTO: Wat ees?

KNOWLES: Lay low.

SNOWBALL: A light.

KNOWLES: My flashlight. [He flashes on a light and plays it around the room.]

FRANK: Do you smell anything?

SNOWBALL: Afterdamp, big Jake.

PETERS: Gas! Afterdamp! Afterdamp!

KNOWLES: Quiet now! Stop that nonsense. Don't be a fool. How do you know we're caught yet? Pull yourselves together.

FRANK: I think the gas is coming in. I can smell it.

THE BARBARIANS

KNOWLES: Steady now. Hug the floor till we get our bearin'. [He coughs, and immediately the coughing is followed by the others, as if in imitation.]

FRANK: Hadn't we better get together?

KNOWLES: Listen men. It's teamwork that's needed now. [He plays the light round the room and into the faces of the men, then goes over to the left and passes into the break-through.] I'll see if I can find out anything. [The men can be heard and dimly seen getting to their feet.]

BARTO: [Speaking for the first time.] By golla, I leeva thees damn countree.

SNOWBALL: You been sayin' that ten year.

FRANK: You never know when a thing like this will happen.

PETERS: What're you cryin' about? Why don't somebody do somethin'? There's gas I tell you.

KNOWLES: [Appearing on the left and throwing the light in PETERS' face.] Now you keep quiet. [The dripping water beats endlessly.] Steady men. [The men stand waiting for him to speak.]

PETERS: For God's sake, what is it?

KNOWLES: The explosion's off this room, in the entry. We're blocked. Steady now. We've got to build a protectin' wall against the afterdamp. [There is a rush and a general skirmish.] Take your time. Take your time. All right, let's go to work. First, Barto, you take a pick an' go down an' kill the mule. We'll be needin' all the air we can get. Any old blinker can breathe four times as much air as a man. Get along, Barto. [BARTO takes the pick and hurries off to the left. KNOWLES plays the light on the pit car.] Push the car over here, boys. [He withdraws to the left, indicating a place for the car near the break-through.] Unload her, boys. We'll build the wall here. [He plays the light on the wall and floor. The men, obeying quietly, begin to unload the car.]

443

FRANK: Where do you want me, Mr. Knowles?

KNOWLES: Here, you hold the light. [He passes the flashlight to FRANK, then turns to PETERS.] Peters, put them buckets under the drip. Make slime. Fetch it quickly. [PETERS goes to work without a word. BARTO returns from the left and throws down the pick.]

BARTO: Molla, da mule, she die.

KNOWLES: Work with me, Barto. We lay the wall. [They get to their knees and begin placing the lumps of coal on the floor in a row at right-angles to the wall of coal in the rear. No one speaks. SNOWBALL, bending from car to the floor, mechanically unloads the coal. PETERS comes up with a bucket of mortar. They work quietly, timing their movements, no one speaking. FRANK stands alone playing the light on the rising wall.]

FRANK: That was a heavy blast, Mr. Knowles.

KNOWLES: 'Twas close by, too.

SNOWBALL: Wonder how many men got caught?

KNOWLES: It's noon, and the men on the way out, there's no tellin'.

PETERS: Hope the old hole don't catch fire. Got me clothes burnt off onc't. To hell with a job like this.

BARTO: Soma day I leeva thees damn countree.

KNOWLES: Get over, Barto, and less talkin'. More slime, Peters.

PETERS: [Comes with a bucket.] Righto.

FRANK: Wonder what caused the blast?

PETERS: The little butterflies out in the sunshine, they causes it.

KNOWLES: Another country heard from. [Someone coughs.]

FRANK: Who's coughing?

BARTO: Who maka da dust? Cut out.

PETERS: I didn't make no dust.

SNOWBALL: Shut up.

444

KNOWLES: Stop your fussin'.

SNOWBALL: Build a wall . . . build a wall . . . one, two, three, four. [The others add.] Build a wall . . . build a wall . . . one, two, three, four . . . one, two, three, four. [They work on quietly.]

BARTO: Golla! What time it ees?

PETERS: You ain't goin' nowheres, Wop.

FRANK: Smart guy, that Peters.

SNOWBALL: A punch in the nose'd help him a hell of a lot.

PETERS: Yeh? Who's goin' to do it?

SNOWBALL: I will. Right now. [Goes for him. BARTO starts to help.]

KNOWLES: Cut out that racket! Get back to your places, you punks. What's the matter with you? [They stand a moment glowering at each other, then go quietly back to work. The dripping water beats endlessly.]

BARTO: Who starta da fuss?

FRANK: He did, Peters.

KNOWLES: Stop that.

PETERS: Say, white-wash, your conduct is inexcusable. Get the hell out of the mine.

KNOWLES: Pipe down. Come on, more coal, more water. The gas is comin' in. Wake up, you punks. [They work lively for a time.]

SNOWBALL: Big Jake, you see any rats lately?

KNOWLES: Rats? Not for days. That ain't unusual, though. I don't leave 'em much scraps to eat these days, with only two days work a week.

BARTO: You maka bigga meestake, Bigga Jake. Da rat ees goot friend. Him tell da secrets. Him leeva da room quick when coma da explosh. Feeda da rat, you gotta da friend.

KNOWLES: You're right, old timer. I seen a bloody fight in the pit one time. Whew! Some new fellow killed a rat

445

for gettin' in his dinner bucket. The boys near mobbed the poor devil. Might as well kill a man as a rat down below. Get the hell off my foot, somebody!

SNOWBALL: Put your foot in your pocket.

PETERS: This here's sure luck. . . . I was goin' to knock off. I'm quittin' this shadow chasin' business.

KNOWLES: Less talk an' more water.

SNOWBALL: The mine blowed over for the day, and I was going home.

BARTO: Him blow over, but we worka just da same.

FRANK: Don't you think you'd better work a little faster? [He coughs.] I can smell something.

KNOWLES: Never you fear, my boy. The old wall's comin' right along. I was goin' home to work in my garden. What was you goin' to do, Barto?

BARTO: Oh, I maka da wine. Gotta da permit yesterday. American probish, huh! Goddam, I am hot. Snowball, what you do?

SNOWBALL: Ah wus going to work on my new home.

KNOWLES: Got it paid for yet?

SNOWBALL: Not yet, Mister Jake. But next winter, if the mines work steady. The realtor, he is very considerate. Ah only made him a payment last month, but he granted me a mortorium on the balance.

KNOWLES: I see. That's good. Will somebody scratch my back?

SNOWBALL: [Scratching his back.] And when Ah gets my new home paid fo', Ah'll be residin' on my own property, thank the Lord.

KNOWLES: Higher, that's better. Yes, a man ought to own his own home. I ain't selfish, but I always wanted more than to live from hand to mouth.

FRANK: Anybody does. About all I ever managed was a couple of pigeon holes somewhere in an apartment house.

PETERS: You guys give me a pain, talkin' about home. How d'you know you'll see home again?

SNOWBALL: Crape hanger.

FRANK: I guess everybody has troubles. Barto, you pay rent?

BARTO: [Tired out.] Shoo, boy, to da companee. Da companee taka da rent outa da pay check. I no getta behind. I senda da mon to Italy. Da sunshine there. But soma day, I getta rich, buy da blind pig, American style, smoka da big black cigar, den I. . . .

SNOWBALL: We know . . . you're going to leave this damn country.

BARTO: Shoo.

KNOWLES: [Himself almost exhausted.] Then you don't like America?

BARTO: [Breathing hard.] Yes, lika. Ees all right to maka da mon. Peeple in da bigga hurree in thees countree. American ees damn fool, buy da automobile, buy da home, buy da furniture, buy every damn thing. Then he dress up in da big red necktie and stall, sama time he work lika hell. That ees your America.

KNOWLES: There's all kinds of people in the world, my friend, all kinds.

PETERS: [Exhausted.] I'd give my wife for a cigarette.

SNOWBALL: You'll smoke hereafter.

PETERS: I don't care.

KNOWLES: It ain't nothin' to crow about, these mines. I often said to Annie, I'd as soon be in that hot place with my back broke, as in a mine in heaven. Just pick away, pick away.

BARTO: Work and eata. No worka, no eata.

SNOWBALL: Don't you worry. Build a wall . . . build a wall. . . . One, two, three, four. [The others repeat after him. Finally their voices become almost inaudible and they work for a time in silence.]

447

KNOWLES: Well, that ought to hold her. [He draws his bandana and mops his face laboriously.]

BARTO: [Quickly lying down flat on his back.] By Golla! Now I taka da vacash. No vacash in long time I gotta.

KNOWLES: Who ever heard tell of an underground savage takin' a vacation. [The men stand looking and examining the wall, paying no attention to BARTO and FRANK, who holds the light and stares at the protecting wall doubtfully.]

FRANK: How long will we have to stay down here?

KNOWLES: Depends on how bad the old hole blew up. Whew! I'm hotter'n a July baby. [He sits down and breathes deeply.]

FRANK: Hadn't somebody better try to get through, and take word? [This remark evokes a snicker or two.]

KNOWLES: No livin' thing with lungs can get through that afterdamp. [The men stare at KNOWLES.]

FRANK: But what if we don't get out?

KNOWLES: We'll get out. Better sit down an' take it easy for a spell. [FRANK remains standing.]

FRANK: How do you know? I got a wife and boy to think of.

KNOWLES: We all have.

FRANK: How long, at the most, will it be?

KNOWLES: I don't know. Sit down. [The men look at FRANK, who continues to stare at the barricade searchingly. KNOWLES takes up his cards and begins to deal quietly.] Suppose we have a little game, or somethin'? [The men nod.] Jacks or better, an' ten ton for the limit in this game. [The men pick up their cards.]

PETERS: Pass.

BARTO: [Without even looking at his cards.] Betta da ton of coal.

SNOWBALL: Stand and draw three. [He puts in.]

KNOWLES: [Dealing.] I'll stay. Hold the light. [He puts in.]

SNOWBALL: Two here. [They examine their cards.]

BARTO: Betta ten ton da coal. [He counts out lumps of coal.]

SNOWBALL: Stay. [He puts in.]

KNOWLES: [Scratches his head.] Looks like a fast game. Say, Barto, turn on that blame radio now. [BARTO does so and the radio makes a series of harsh noises.]

PETERS: Turn that damn thing off!

THE RADIO: Bur-r-r-r-r-r-r-r-rr—r-r-r-r-r.

PETERS: Turn it off!

KNOWLES: Let it go. There'll be plenty of time to rest. Maybe we'll hear somethin'. News. [The radio continues to squawk. KNOWLES looks at his cards, studies the faces of the men.] Let me see, Barto, he opened the pot. [There is an intense silence. The dripping water beats endlessly.]

THE RADIO: Bur-r-r-r-r-report . . . last minute news. . . .

KNOWLES: Listen!

THE RADIO: . . . Word has just been received that a great explosion wrecked Stony Creek Mine. . . . All men checked out at noon but six. . . . These men are lost. [A silence falls on the room. The men look at one another.]

KNOWLES: Whose play?

PETERS: I'll call that bet, Wop.

SNOWBALL: If you gamble, you lose, as the saying goes. Your play, Jake.

FRANK: How long will it be?

KNOWLES: [Studying his cards.] How long? God only knows. [KNOWLES lays down his cards.] Show your openers. [There is another series of explosions, violent thunder and roaring. The men spring to their feet. The barricade on the left crumbles to the floor. Silence. A red glare shines from the left.]

SNOWBALL: We are done for.

KNOWLES: The game is over.

PETERS: Gas! Fire!

KNOWLES: Quiet!

FRANK: Has anybody got a pencil and paper?

KNOWLES: We all have somethin' to write.

SNOWBALL: If anybody gets out, let him tell Mrs. Jackson that Ah was saved.

BARTO: Senda da word to my fam' in Italy, say I coma home, but first coma da explosh.

PETERS: I don't care. I just don't care.

KNOWLES: Come over by the car, boys. [They move wearily to the pit car.] Give Frank your big knife, Snowball. [He does so.] Give Snowball the light, Frank. [He hands the light to SNOWBALL and kneels before the car with the knife.] Write now, as I tell you. . . . "About noon, Saturday . . . gas bad. . . . Can't last much longer. . . . We are thinkin' of our wives . . . and children . . . and God. [The men stand in silence watching FRANK scratch the letters on the car. BARTO crosses himself. SNOWBALL kneels and prays in silence. PETERS stands motionless, his face frozen into an expressionless stare. They shake hands with one another kindly. Finally FRANK rises and takes KNOWLES by the hand. The red glare becomes brighter and the musical tinkle of dripping water continues its eternal beat.]

BREAD
By Fred Eastman

PERSONS IN THE PLAY

John Curtis
Martha Curtis
Grandma
Stella
Betty
Jim

BREAD

THE living and dining room of JOHN CURTIS and his family, a farm home in the valley of the River Kaw, in East-Central Kansas. At the rear is a door opening upon the front porch. Balancing it on the left is a rather wide window through which a window box of flowers is seen. In the middle of the right wall is a door leading to the kitchen; opposite, a door leading to a bedroom. The furnishings are simple, even meagre. A dining room table covered with a red tablecloth stands at right center, and at the right front, along the right wall, is a cupboard. In a rear corner of the room stands a what-not on which is a collection of basket-weaving materials and some large volumes. Upon the floor is a large rag rug, and upon the table an oil reading lamp with an old-fashioned shade. Directly in front of the window are two chairs, the one on the right an old-fashioned rocker; the one on the left a straight-backed dining room chair similar to half a dozen others about the room. In front of this particular chair is a small table, and upon it one of the large volumes. In the rocking chair sits GRANDMA CURTIS, JOHN's mother, darning hosiery. She is a woman of about seventy, with gray hair and a simple black dress. In the chair back of the little table is STELLA, a blind girl of fifteen, her face bright and filled with enthusiasm as her fingers touch lightly the pages of raised type before her.

STELLA: [Reading.] "Blessed are the poor in spirit, for theirs is the kingdom of heaven."

GRANDMA: That doesn't apply to this family.

STELLA: Why not, Grandma?

GRANDMA: There is nothing poor in spirit about us. Everybody around this house has too much spirit. That's the trouble. It makes 'em all so rambunctious.

STELLA: "Blessed are they that hunger and thirst after righteousness: for they shall be filled."

GRANDMA: That doesn't apply, either.

STELLA: Why Grandma!

GRANDMA: This family doesn't hunger and thirst after righteousness. Not so you could notice it. John hungers to make the farm pay; Martha hungers for a piano; Jim hungers for a job in the city, where he thinks he will have more fun and less work; Betty hungers for more eggs from her hens.

STELLA: And you—what do you hunger for Grandma?

GRANDMA: I hunger for a bathroom in this house. It's a shame the way we have to do without one year after year. Last winter when it was ten below zero—

STELLA: Yes, Grandma, I know. But how could father put in a bathroom when he couldn't even pay the interest on the mortgage?

GRANDMA: I'm not blamin' him. I'm just telling you what I hunger for.

STELLA: And me—what do I hunger for?

GRANDMA: You ought to know. Is it for righteousness?

STELLA: No, I'm afraid it isn't. I hunger to make enough

money from my basket weaving to buy some new books with this raised type.

GRANDMA: Well, that's no sin. You're the only one in this house has got any time to read, and if it wasn't for your readin' to me I don't know what I'd do. I would sure be lonesome. Darnin' socks all day! It's the holiest family that way I ever saw.

[BETTY comes in. She is a winsome lass of fourteen, dressed in a bright gingham, and carrying a basket of eggs. She fairly bursts into the room in her excitement, and leaves the door wide open behind her.]

BETTY: Hooray, Stella! Fourteen eggs today! That's all I need to make my twenty dollars!

STELLA: Fine, Betty! Has mother got her eighty yet?

BETTY: Almost. She had seventy-eight dollars and sixty cents last Tuesday. I don't know how much butter she got from her churning today. [Calling.] Hey, mother, how many pounds of butter did you make today?

[MRS. JOHN CURTIS comes in. She is a plump and hearty woman of about forty. She wears a cheap cotton dress, an apron, and cotton stockings. Her hair is in some disarray and her face is flushed, but pride shines from her eyes. She carries a bowl of butter.]

MARTHA: Six pounds! And as fine a lot as I ever made!

STELLA: Let me taste it, mother.

[MARTHA takes a spoon from the cupboard drawer, dips the tip of it in the butter, and gives STELLA a taste.]

MARTHA: Sure. I hope the customers like to eat it as well as I like to make it. There's something about butter-making that's real fun in spite of all the work. To see the yellow come, and then to pat it and roll it until the water is out of it, and then to shape it into a big ball—I don't know, but I feel like an artist makin' statues out of clay.

STELLA: [Tasting.] Mother, you *are* an artist. Tell me,

does it look as good as it tastes? Is it golden like the sunlight on the ripe wheat fields?

MARTHA: Yes, like the wheat before it begins to get brownish. You remember, don't you? I can't see how you do. You were only three years old when the fever came. I can't remember anything I saw when I was three.

BETTY: [Counting on her fingers.] Six times forty is two hundred and forty. That's two dollars and forty cents. Seventy-eight and two-forty is eighty-something, and my twenty makes one hundred, and—hot dogs! We've got it, mother! We've got the piano!

MARTHA: Have we? That's right! Your twenty and my eighty! Thank goodness! [She puts the bowl of butter on the table, and catching BETTY's hands, dances joyfully around the room.] A piano! We're going to have a piano!

GRANDMA: We need a bathroom before we need a piano.

MARTHA: No, we don't. We can get along without a bathroom a while longer, mother. But these children have got to have music lessons.

GRANDMA: Suppose they was to get sick—what good would a piano do 'em? But a bathroom—

MARTHA: [Shaking her head.] It's got to be a piano. We've saved for three years for this hundred and done without things we needed. If we was to wait any longer it would be too late. Betty is gettin' to be a big girl already and Stella has been so patient—

STELLA: Do you suppose I can learn to play as easily as I learned the reading?

MARTHA: I'll bet you will find it easier. Why, I never had but two lessons when I was a girl, but I took right to it; and you are smarter than I was.

STELLA: Why didn't you go on?

MARTHA: Our barn burned and there wasn't any more money for music lessons.

GRANDMA: Well, you better not count your chickens before they're hatched.

MARTHA: What do you mean, mother?

GRANDMA: What's happened once can happen again. If you are goin' to get a piano you had better get it before the barn burns or something else happens.

MARTHA: I guess you're right. Three years ago I almost had the hundred, and then Jim broke his leg falling off the roof. When we finished payin' the doctor I only had eleven dollars left.

BETTY: Mother! Let's get it today! Something might happen, and besides we could surprise everybody with it tonight. Just think! This very night!

MARTHA: I couldn't very well go to town today. Tomorrow the threshers come and I've got the ironin' to do yet.

BETTY: No, mother! Let's not wait another day. Jim is goin' to town in the Ford to get the binder twine. I heard him say so. He could take the butter and eggs to the grocery for us.

STELLA: Yes, mother, and then he could put the money in the bank as he always does, and you could give him a check to take to the piano store. You've got the piano all picked out, and they said they would deliver it whenever you gave them the check, didn't they?

MARTHA: Yes, they've held it three months for me. They said it was the best used instrument in the shop. But the money ain't on a checking account. I told Jim to put it in the savings department so it would draw interest.

STELLA: You could write a note to the bank, couldn't you, and ask them to let Jim have the money?

BETTY: [Dancing up and down.] And get it here tonight! Tonight!

MARTHA: I'll do it! And we'll have it here for tomorrow when the threshers come! Guess it will make them sit up some.

GRANDMA: Where you goin' to put it?

MARTHA: Right over where this old cupboard stands. The cupboard can go to the kitchen.

GRANDMA: That will make you walk farther with the dishes.

MARTHA: It doesn't matter. I can stand more walking if we can have a little music. Betty can play a march for me while I walk, can't you, Betty?

BETTY: I'll learn to play a march that will make you gallop. Won't that be fun? Let's shut our eyes and pretend. [She closes her eyes and pretends that the cupboard is a piano, and plays a rollicking tune while MARTHA dances about and STELLA beats time with her hands.]

[JIM comes in by the front door. He is a well-built lad of sixteen years, dark hair and eyes, and his skin shows the tan of the harvest fields. He wears overalls and seems tired and hot. He stands a moment watching the scene.]

JIM: Is it the heat or just natural?

STELLA: Oh, Jim, we've got something for you to do.

JIM: [Sinking wearily into a chair and wiping the perspiration from his face with a bandanna.] I'll bet you have. Everybody's got something for me to do. There's more work on this farm than—

BETTY: How soon you going to town, Jim?

JIM: Right away. And I wish to heaven I could stay there. Those town boys have it soft.

MARTHA: [Taking a bank book from a bowl in the cupboard.] Jim, we are going to surprise your father. I want you to take the butter to town with you and leave it at Collins's grocery. It's six pounds and ought to bring about two-forty. Take Betty's eggs, too; they will bring a quarter. Then take the money to the bank. I'll give you a note that will tell them to give you all I got there on the savings account—

JIM: Why? What's the matter? What you goin' to do with it?

BETTY: We're going to get the piano! We're going to get the piano!

JIM: You ain't got enough for that. You said it would take a hundred.

MARTHA: It will. The butter money will make it eighty and Betty will add her twenty. Then you take it to Porter's piano store and tell him to get the piano out here this afternoon sure.

JIM: [Swallowing.] I don't see how I could do it today, moth—

BETTY: [Who meantime has taken a purse out of the drawer in the cupboard.] Here's my nineteen dollars and seventy-five cents.

JIM: Wouldn't some other day do, mother? I'm awfully busy today. You see, I—I—

MARTHA: What else you got to do besides get the binder twine? That won't take five minutes.

JIM: Why, nothing especially in town, except I wanted to see some of the fellows about something, and—

MARTHA: You're not goin' around to that poolroom, Jim.

JIM: All right, all right. But a fellow is entitled to a little fun now and then, isn't he?

MARTHA: Not that sort.

JIM: And besides, father needs me back here in the field. The old mare was kind of sick this morning and we didn't get along very fast.

MARTHA: All we want you to do won't take long—not over twenty minutes at most. Go 'long now and get washed while I write the note to the bank.

[JIM hesitates awkwardly as if about to say something, looks at BETTY's purse in his hand, tightens his grip on it and starts toward the kitchen.]

JIM: A fellow don't get any rest around this place. Between father and that old horse and all these errands I'm drove pretty near crazy. [He goes out.]

MARTHA: [Looking after him.] What's got into that boy? He didn't use to be this way—so cantankerous and all. And he wanted that piano just as much as the rest of us a little while ago. [Taking ink bottle and paper from the cupboard.] Come on, Betty, tend to that buttermilk while I write this note. Stella, you can do the dishes, now the churnin's out of the way. [She goes into the kitchen, followed by BETTY, whose hands dance over the keys of an imaginary piano.]

GRANDMA: 'Pears to me like Jim was mighty leary of orderin' that piano.

STELLA: [Rising and feeling her way to the kitchen door.] Oh, Jim's all right, Grandma. He's just resentful at having one more chore to do.

GRANDMA: Mebbe so, mebbe so. Never can tell about boys. When they get the "I-don't-want-to's" or the "Gimmes" or the "Me-firsts" they just have to live through them like the whooping cough.

[STELLA goes into the kitchen. The front door opens and JOHN CURTIS enters. He is a middle-aged man of medium stature, his hair graying and his shoulders a bit stooped. He wears overalls and carries a wide-brimmed straw hat. He is hot and perspiring and limps painfully upon his left leg.]

JOHN: [Sinking into a chair beside the table.] That's about the last straw. [Rubs his leg.]

GRANDMA: What's the matter, John? Did you hurt yourself?

JOHN: No, I ain't hurt bad except in the pocket book. The old mare fell dead on me and kind o' wrenched my knee a bit.

GRANDMA: Tct! Tct! Ain't that too bad! I'll get the arnicky for you. [She rises.]

JOHN: All right, ma. Gosh! It's just one thing after another. First, the flood in the Spring, and I couldn't get the corn in soon enough. Then a cool Summer and it wouldn't ripen. Then that darned corn borer got busy in the stalks. The wheat ain't more'n two-thirds a crop, and the price is fallin'. And now the old mare ups and dies on me. Well, we'll manage somehow.

GRANDMA: One thing at a time, John. You got to rub that knee before it gets stiff or it won't be good for nothin' but a poker. [She goes into the bedroom.]

[BETTY comes in from the kitchen. She doesn't see her father at first and has evidently come just to picture the piano in the place of the cupboard, for she gazes wistfully at it as she wipes the churn-dash in her hands.]

JOHN: Hello, sis!

BETTY: Why, daddy, what are you home for? It isn't dinner time yet.

JOHN: Oh, I hurt my knee a little when the old mare fell dead on me this morning. Grandma is gettin' the arnicky for me.

BETTY: I'm so sorry, daddy. What did the mare die of?

JOHN: I don't know. I guess she just got discouraged waitin' for the government to do something for the farmer.

BETTY: Want I should rub your knee, daddy?

JOHN: No. I can rub it. I need cheerin' more than I need rubbin'.

BETTY: Daddy, I got a secret that will cheer you up when you hear it.

JOHN: Let's have it.

BETTY: I can't tell you now, but it's something *fine*. You'll hear it—I mean you'll see it tonight.

JOHN: I need cheerin' now.

BETTY: Do you think it would do you more good now than tonight?

JOHN: I couldn't feel any worse than I do now. But don't tell me if you oughtn't to.

BETTY: I'll tell. We're going to get a piano! Today!

JOHN: A piano? For us? Did someone die and leave it to us?

BETTY: No, sir! We're buying it! Mother's butter money and my egg money.

JOHN: How much you got?

BETTY: A hundred dollars altogether. Isn't it fine?

JOHN: A hundred dollars! [Half to himself.] I could get a new horse for a hundred dollars. Or better yet, I could make the first payment on a tractor.

BETTY: You don't seem so cheered up about it.

JOHN: Yes, I am, Betty. I'm certainly glad we got that hundred dollars. But I'm not so sure about the piano. We're havin' such hard times just now—

BETTY: Oh, but the piano's already ordered.

JOHN: Who ordered it?

BETTY: Mother. She gave Jim a note and the butter and eggs. He's going to get the money from the bank and pay it to the store and have the piano out here tonight!

JOHN: Where's Jim?

BETTY: He's gone to town. He ought to be there by this time. Aren't you glad about it, daddy?

JOHN: Yes, darlin', I *am* glad. And I want you to have your piano as much as any one. But I don't want you to go to the poor-house. They wouldn't take a piano to the poor-house, now, would they? Just you wait a minute. [He limps to the telephone and calls the operator.] Hello, Carrie, give me the bank. Yep, that's all I want today—just one bank.

BETTY: What are you going to do, daddy?

JOHN: Tell your mother to come here, Betty. [BETTY goes to the kitchen, weeping.] Hello, this the bank? This is John Curtis. Has my boy Jim been there yet? No?

BREAD

[MARTHA comes in from kitchen, and from the bedroom, GRANDMA, the latter carrying a bottle of arnica. They stand listening. MARTHA's back is stiffening and her face takes on a look of determination.] Well, Jim was coming to draw out some money. Just tell him not to bother about that today, will you, and to hurry home with that binder twine. Thanks. [He hangs up the receiver and turns to face MARTHA.]

GRANDMA: I smell a row. Well, a little excitement might be a relief after darnin' socks for a year.

MARTHA: Betty told me about the mare, John, and about your knee. I'm sorry. But why did you call up the bank? It wouldn't take Jim but a few minutes to do our errand.

JOHN: Sit down, Martha, and let me talk to you about that errand. [They all sit down. GRANDMA gives her bottle to JOHN and takes her rocking chair. JOHN rolls up his left trouser leg and rubs his knee with the arnica as he talks.]

MARTHA: There's nothing to be said about that errand, John. It's our money—Betty's and mine. We've saved it for three years. We are going to have that piano.

JOHN: I want you to have it, Martha. And I ain't the man to take the money away from you. I only want to borry it.

MARTHA: No, John. We won't lend it to you.

JOHN: Why not, Martha?

MARTHA: Because you couldn't pay it back, soon enough anyway.

JOHN: How soon?

MARTHA: Before these children get any older. We've waited long enough already.

JOHN: I know you've waited, Martha. And God knows I don't want you to wait a day longer than necessary. But it seems necessary.

MARTHA: Necessary for what?

JOHN: Necessary for a tractor.

463

MARTHA: No! You can't have our money for a tractor! Please, John. You don't know how hard we've worked for that money. It would break Betty's heart—and mine.

JOHN: Now, Martha, listen to reason. I can't farm without tools, can I? You couldn't make butter if you didn't have a churn, could you?

MARTHA: But, John, you can't take our butter and egg money for your tools. You wouldn't do that. Don't you remember when we were married and before that how you talked about the farmers that never gave their wives any money of their own? You said it would be different with us. You promised that I should always have my butter and egg money to spend on the home.

GRANDMA: That's what they all say before they marry. John, your pa promised—

JOHN: Never mind, ma. This is different.

GRANDMA: That's just what he said after we was married.

JOHN: Martha, I don't want to take your money. I only want to borry it.

MARTHA: It would be the same as taking it. You couldn't pay it back.

JOHN: Now don't take on so. Listen to reason, I say.

MARTHA: I don't want to hear any reasonin' that takes away our piano.

JOHN: You ain't got it yet, so you wouldn't miss it.

MARTHA: For six years we've saved, John. Don't you remember what happened last time, three years ago, when we almost had the hundred—about Jim's leg and the doctor's bills. You said you would pay that back, and I wouldn't let you. Jim was our boy, and I was willing to spend the piano money for that. But the mare, and a new tractor— that's different. Oh, John, I couldn't! I just couldn't!

JOHN: If you would only be calm a minute, Martha, I could make you see things straighter. You ain't quite well, I guess.

MARTHA: Say what you got to say; I'll listen. But I won't give in.

JOHN: If I could borry the money any place else I would. But I couldn't pay the interest on the mortgage, so the bank wouldn't lend me none. And there's no one else to go to. I ain't squandered any money, have I?

MARTHA: No. There ain't been any to squander.

JOHN: And it ain't my fault, is it, that the price of wheat and corn has been droppin' so low it hardly pays for the seed to plant 'em?

MARTHA: I didn't say it was your fault. What's that got to do with my piano money?

JOHN: It means that there is less money from crops, and *that* means that to buy a new tractor we got to borry the piano money.

MARTHA: Suppose there wasn't any piano money; then what would you do?

JOHN: If I couldn't get a tractor, or at least a new horse, I couldn't farm; and if I couldn't farm, I'd go bankrupt. Think of what it would mean, Martha, to hear the neighbors say, "There goes John Curtis; he's a failure." I couldn't stand that!

MARTHA: Is that all you got to say, John?

JOHN: I guess that's all.

MARTHA: Now you listen to me. You can't bear to have folks say you are a failure. I understand that. But I can't stand it to have the folks in town say of our children, "There's those Curtis kids; they're just ignorant country jakes."

JOHN: They ain't ignorant. They've been to school.

MARTHA: School ain't everything. They ought to have music and pictures and books. It's our job to see that they have them. But we've never had any music in this house, and no pictures, and mighty few books.

JOHN: Music and pictures and books are all right, Martha.

I want the children to have them. But they are luxuries—and we've got to have bread before we can have luxuries.

MARTHA: Luxuries! That's what you always said! But it ain't so, John. The children *need* them. And *I* do. We are starved for them. You can starve for such things as well as for bread. Ain't there something in the Bible what says you can't live by bread alone? For seventeen years I've done the washing and the cooking and the baking. I've patched the clothes of the family. I've had just four hats since we was married. I ain't never had a vacation. Something inside me has been dyin', John.

JOHN: I guess it's your love for me, Martha.

MARTHA: How can you say that, John?

JOHN: God knows I wouldn't blame you. I ain't been able to do much for you. I guess I am a failure.

MARTHA: [Going to him and kneeling by his side.] Oh, John, John! Don't say that! It ain't your fault. It's the way with most of the farmers. They don't get a square deal.

JOHN: But what am I goin' to do? What *am* I goin' to do?

GRANDMA: Keep rubbin' that knee, John. It'll freeze up on you if you don't.

MARTHA: There's nothing for you to do, John. You can have the piano money. There ain't nothin' else to do.

JOHN: When you act that way about it, I ain't got the heart to take it. Maybe we just better give up, sell the farm an' move to the city. I could get a job in a factory.

MARTHA: No, John. I've thought of that often. It would be easier. But we are goin' to stick by the old homestead as long as we got our strength.

GRANDMA: You better compromise. Instead of gettin' either a tractor or a piano, if you put a bathroom in this house—

JOHN: Now, ma, don't start on that. We've had enough trouble—

[JIM comes in by the kitchen door, followed by BETTY and STELLA. There is a look of grim determination about him and his fists are clenched. MARTHA rises quickly and faces him.]

MARTHA: What is it, Jim? Why you lookin' so queer?

JIM: There's no use beatin' about the bush, mother. There ain't any hundred dollars. I spent it, and I've come to take my medicine.

MARTHA: You *spent* it?

JOHN: What's that you're sayin?'

JIM: I spent it at cards, gamblin' in the pool room in the village.

MARTHA: Today? Just now?

JIM: No. All along. As you gave me the money, I took it to the pool room and gambled with it.

MARTHA: But you couldn't. You put it in the bank. The bank book says so.

JIM: I wrote those things in the bank book myself. It had the eleven dollars in there when you gave it to me. I wrote in all the rest. The eleven is still there. But the rest is gone.

MARTHA: And Betty's egg money—the twenty dollars?

JIM: [Shaking his head in misery.] That's gone, too. I lost it just now on a throw of the dice. I bet the whole thing trying to get back what I'd lost. [BETTY bursts into tears. STELLA takes her in her arms and strokes her hair.]

JOHN: You're a thief. That's what you are!

JIM: Yes, that's what I am. What are you going to do with me? Put me in jail?

MARTHA: Oh, God! I can't bear any more!

JIM: I wish I was dead. I didn't realize—mother. Honest, I didn't.

MARTHA: But why, *why* did you do it, Jim?

JIM: You remember three years ago when you gave me that first butter to sell? Well, I sold it and was on my way to the bank when I passed Griffin's window. There was a necktie there I wanted. It was seventy-five cents. I didn't have any money of my own. I almost never did. I had heard of some of the fellows at the pool room making money at cards. I thought I would risk it. So I got in a game. At first I won half a dollar. And then I began to lose, and the whole amount went. I didn't have the nerve to tell you. The next week I tried again, and so on week after week. Sometimes I made a little, but never enough to pay you back, so I kept at it. If I had had a gun this morning I would have killed myself. That's all there is to tell. You better call up the sheriff.

JOHN: I could forgive you, Jim, if it was my money. But it was your mother's and Betty's, and she's been so good—

JIM: I know! I know! I ain't got any excuse for myself.

MARTHA: Jim, I ain't holdin' it against you. You've been honest and come and told us like a man. You wouldn't do it again, now, would you?

JIM: I've learned my lesson. But that doesn't get you your piano.

MARTHA: Maybe that's worth as much as a piano.

JIM: But it wasn't my piano. It was yours and Betty's and Stella's—poor kids! [BETTY and STELLA go to him, and STELLA touches him on the shoulder.]

STELLA: It's all right, Jim. I still have my baskets and my books.

BETTY: And I've got my kittens to play with.

JIM: Don't! Don't be easy with me! Scold me! Hit me! Anything! I ought to be punished. You ought to lick me, dad! Go on and do it!

JOHN: I got in a scrape once like that myself when I was young. So I ain't for bein' hard on you.

GRANDMA: There wasn't goin' to be any piano anyway,

468

Jim. Nor a bathroom. Tell him what you was decidin', Martha.

MARTHA: The old mare died just after you left, Jim. We would have had to use the money for a new horse or a tractor.

JIM: Died? Nellie died? Gosh! Ain't we got trouble! What can you do now, dad?

JOHN: One thing at a time, Jim. The first thing to do is to bury Nellie. We'd better get out and do it. [He rises.]

JIM: Yes, and bury with her all our hopes for a piano or a tractor or anything else. You better just push me in the hole along with Nellie, and bury us both together. [He starts to follow his father to the door.]

MARTHA: Jim! [She opens her arms to him, and he comes into them, half sobbing. She kisses his hair while her own tears fall.] You are worth more than all the pianos and tractors in the world to me, boy.

JIM: I'll make it up to you, mother, and to Betty and Stella. Honest, I will! Gosh! I feel better already for getting it off my chest!

JOHN: Come on, son. We'll bury the past and start afresh. [They go out.]

[BETTY goes to GRANDMA and buries her head on the old lady's shoulder. STELLA returns to her table and begins weaving a basket. MARTHA starts setting the table for dinner.]

STELLA: Mother, if we had a tractor it would cheer up father and Jim a lot more than if we had a piano, wouldn't it?

MARTHA: Yes, it would. But we ain't.

STELLA: You know—I've been saving the money from my basket weaving. I've got almost sixty dollars. That would make a first payment, wouldn't it?

MARTHA: Now look here! There ain't no call for you to do that. Then there wouldn't be either music or books in this house.

STELLA: But we would all be happy again, wouldn't we? We'll arrange it this afternoon.

MARTHA: I can't seem to figure it out. I want you children to be cultured, like city folks.

GRANDMA: What is this here culture, Martha?

MARTHA: I don't know exactly, ma; it's knowin' what's what about the things you can't see.

GRANDMA: And you thought a piano would teach that?

MARTHA: Yes.

GRANDMA: Well, I guess you are something of a piano yourself, Martha.

STELLA: And you're a tractor too, mother.

MARTHA: [Her face lighting up.] What funny notions! You get me all flustered. Come on, Betty, let's get dinner. [BETTY lifts her head from GRANDMA's shoulder. She seems irresolute.]

GRANDMA: You ain't licked yet, are you, Betty?

BETTY: Not yet! Listen! [A hen is heard cackling in the barnyard.] Hear that cackle? It's a new egg! That's the first two cents on the new piano! I'm going to get it before it gets cold! [She runs out.]

MARTHA: [Following her, pride shining in her face.] Bless her heart! Ain't she got spunk? [She goes out.]

GRANDMA: Mebbe it's just as well not to get any more books, Stella. Too much readin' rots the mind. Anyway, you ain't read all that one yet. Go on with it.

STELLA: [Reading.] "Love suffereth long, and is kind; love envieth not; beareth all things, believeth all things, hopeth all things, endureth all things. Love never faileth...."

TRIFLES
By Susan Glaspell

PERSONS IN THE PLAY

GEORGE HENDERSON
HENRY PETERS
LEWIS HALE
MRS. PETERS
MRS. HALE

TRIFLES

THE kitchen in the now abandoned farmhouse of JOHN WRIGHT, a gloomy kitchen, and left without having been put in order—unwashed pans under the sink, a loaf of bread outside the bread-box, a dish-towel on the table—other signs of incompleted work. At the rear the outer door opens and the SHERIFF, HENRY PETERS, comes in followed by the COUNTY ATTORNEY, GEORGE HENDERSON, and LEWIS HALE, a neighboring farmer. The SHERIFF and HALE are men in middle life, the COUNTY ATTORNEY is a young man; all are much bundled up and go at once to the stove. They are followed by the two women—the SHERIFF's wife first; she is a slight wiry woman, a thin nervous face. MRS. HALE is larger and would ordinarily be called more comfortable looking, but she is disturbed now and looks fearfully about as she enters. The women have come in slowly, and stand close together near the door.

COUNTY ATTORNEY: [Rubbing his hands.] This feels good. Come up to the fire, ladies.

473

MRS. PETERS: [After taking a step forward.] I'm not—cold.

SHERIFF: [Unbuttoning his overcoat and stepping away from the stove as if to mark the beginning of official business.] Now, Mr. Hale, before we move things about, you explain to Mr. Henderson just what you saw when you came here yesterday morning.

COUNTY ATTORNEY: By the way, has anything been moved? Are things just as you left them yesterday?

SHERIFF: [Looking about.] It's just the same. When it dropped below zero last night I thought I'd better send Frank out this morning to make a fire for us—no use getting pneumonia with a big case on, but I told him not to touch anything except the stove—and you know Frank.

COUNTY ATTORNEY: Somebody should have been left here yesterday.

SHERIFF: Oh—yesterday. When I had to send Frank to Morris Center for that man who went crazy—I want you to know I had my hands full yesterday. I knew you could get back from Omaha by today and as long as I went over everything here myself—

COUNTY ATTORNEY: Well, Mr. Hale, tell just what happened when you came here yesterday morning.

HALE: Harry and I had started to town with a load of potatoes. We came along the road from my place and as I got here I said, "I'm going to see if I can't get John Wright to go in with me on a party telephone." I spoke to Wright about it once before and he put me off, saying folks talked too much anyway, and all he asked was peace and quiet—I guess you know about how much he talked himself; but I thought maybe if I went to the house and talked about it before his wife, though I said to Harry that I didn't know as what his wife wanted made much difference to John—

COUNTY ATTORNEY: Let's talk about that later, Mr. Hale.

I do want to talk about that, but tell now just what happened when you got to the house.

HALE: I didn't hear or see anything; I knocked at the door, and still it was all quiet inside. I knew they must be up, it was past eight o'clock. So I knocked again, and I thought I heard somebody say, "Come in." I wasn't sure, I'm not sure yet, but I opened the door—this door [indicating the door by which the two women are still standing] and there in that rocker—[pointing to it] sat Mrs. Wright.

[They all look at the rocker.]

COUNTY ATTORNEY: What—was she doing?

HALE: She was rockin' back and forth. She had her apron in her hand and was kind of—pleating it.

COUNTY ATTORNEY: And how did she—look?

HALE: Well, she looked queer.

COUNTY ATTORNEY: How do you mean—queer?

HALE: Well, as if she didn't know what she was going to do next. And kind of done up.

COUNTY ATTORNEY: How did she seem to feel about your coming?

HALE: Why, I don't think she minded—one way or other. She didn't pay much attention. I said, "How do, Mrs. Wright, it's cold, ain't it?" And she said, "Is it?"—and went on kind of pleating at her apron. Well, I was surprised; she didn't ask me to come up to the stove, or to set down, but just sat there, not even looking at me, so I said, "I want to see John." And then she—laughed. I guess you would call it a laugh. I thought of Harry and the team outside, so I said a little sharp: "Can't I see John?" "No," she says, kind o' dull like. "Ain't he home?" says I. "Yes," says she, "he's home." "Then why can't I see him?" I asked her, out of patience. "'Cause he's dead," says she. *"Dead?"* says I. She just nodded her head, not getting a bit excited, but rockin' back and forth. "Why—

475

where is he?" says I, not knowing what to say. She just
pointed upstairs—like that [himself pointing to the room
above]. I got up, with the idea of going up there. I
walked from there to here—then I says, "Why, what did he
die of?" "He died of a rope round his neck," says she,
and just went on pleatin' at her apron. Well, I went out
and called Harry. I thought I might—need help. We went
upstairs and there he was lyin'—

COUNTY ATTORNEY: I think I'd rather have you go into
that upstairs, where you can point it all out. Just go on now
with the rest of the story.

HALE: Well, my first thought was to get that rope off.
It looked . . . [Stops, his face twitches.] . . . but Harry,
he went up to him, and he said, "No, he's dead all right,
and we'd better not touch anything." So we went back
downstairs. She was still sitting that same way. "Has
anybody been notified?" I asked. "No," says she, uncon-
cerned. "Who did this, Mrs. Wright?" said Harry. He
said it business-like—and she stopped pleatin' of her apron.
"I don't know," she says. "You don't *know?*" says Harry.
"No," says she. "Weren't you sleepin' in the bed with
him?" says Harry. "Yes," says she, "but I was on the
inside." "Somebody slipped a rope round his neck and
strangled him and you didn't wake up?" says Harry. "I
didn't wake up," she said after him. We must 'a' looked
as if we didn't see how that could be, for after a minute
she said, "I sleep sound." Harry was going to ask her
more questions but I said maybe we ought to let her tell
her story first to the coroner, or the sheriff, so Harry went
fast as he could to Rivers' place, where there's a telephone.

COUNTY ATTORNEY: And what did Mrs. Wright do when
she knew that you had gone for the coroner?

HALE: She moved from that chair to this one over here
[pointing to a small chair in the corner] and just sat there
with her hands held together and looking down. I got

a feeling that I ought to make some conversation, so I said I had come in to see if John wanted to put in a telephone, and at that she started to laugh, and then she stopped and looked at me—scared. [The COUNTY ATTORNEY, who has had his notebook out, makes a note.] I dunno, maybe it wasn't scared. I wouldn't like to say it was. Soon Harry got back, and then Dr. Lloyd came, and you, Mr. Peters, and so I guess that's all I know that you don't.

COUNTY ATTORNEY: [Looking around.] I guess we'll go upstairs first—and then out to the barn and around there. [To the SHERIFF.] You're convinced that there was nothing important here—nothing that would point to any motive.

SHERIFF: Nothing here but kitchen things.

[The COUNTY ATTORNEY, after again looking around the kitchen, opens the door of a cupboard closet. He gets up on a chair and looks on a shelf. Pulls his hand away, sticky.]

COUNTY ATTORNEY: Here's a nice mess. [The women draw nearer.]

MRS. PETERS: [To the other woman.] Oh, her fruit; it did freeze. [To the LAWYER.] She worried about that when it turned so cold. She said the fire'd go out and her jars would break.

SHERIFF: Well, can you beat the women! Held for murder and worryin' about her preserves.

COUNTY ATTORNEY: I guess before we're through she may have something more serious than preserves to worry about.

HALE: Well, women are used to worrying over trifles.

[The two women move a little closer together.]

COUNTY ATTORNEY: [With the gallantry of a young politician.] And yet, for all their worries, what would we do without the ladies? [The women do not unbend. He goes to the sink, takes a dipperful of water from the pail and pouring it into a basin, washes his hands. Starts to wipe them on the roller towel, turns it for a cleaner place.]

Dirty towels! [Kicks his foot against the pans under the sink.] Not much of a housekeeper, would you say, ladies?

MRS. HALE: [Stiffly.] There's a great deal of work to be done on a farm.

COUNTY ATTORNEY: To be sure. And yet [with a little bow to her] I know there are some Dickson County farmhouses which do not have such roller towels. [He gives it a pull to expose its full length again.]

MRS. HALE: Those towels get dirty awful quick. Men's hands aren't always as clean as they might be.

COUNTY ATTORNEY: Ah, loyal to your sex, I see. But you and Mrs. Wright were neighbors. I suppose you were friends, too.

MRS. HALE: [Shaking her head.] I've not seen much of her of late years. I've not been in this house—it's more than a year.

COUNTY ATTORNEY: And why was that? You didn't like her?

MRS. HALE: I liked her all well enough. Farmers' wives have their hands full, Mr. Henderson. And then—

COUNTY ATTORNEY: Yes—?

MRS. HALE: [Looking about.] It never seemed a very cheerful place.

COUNTY ATTORNEY: No—it's not cheerful. I shouldn't say she had the homemaking instinct.

MRS. HALE: Well, I don't know as Wright had, either.

COUNTY ATTORNEY: You mean that they didn't get on very well?

MRS. HALE: No, I don't mean anything. But I don't think a place'd be any cheerfuller for John Wright's being in it.

COUNTY ATTORNEY: I'd like to talk more of that a little later. I want to get the lay of things upstairs now. [He goes to the left, where three steps lead to a stair door.]

SHERIFF: I suppose anything Mrs. Peters does'll be all

478

right. She was to take in some clothes for her, you know, and a few little things. We left in such a hurry yesterday.

COUNTY ATTORNEY: Yes, but I would like to see what you take, Mrs. Peters, and keep an eye out for anything that might be of use to us.

MRS. PETERS: Yes, Mr. Henderson. [The women listen to the men's steps on the stairs, then look about the kitchen.]

MRS. HALE: I'd hate to have men coming into my kitchen, snooping around and criticising. [She arranges the pans under sink which the LAWYER had shoved out of place.]

MRS. PETERS: Of course it's no more than their duty.

MRS. HALE: Duty's all right, but I guess that deputy sheriff that came out to make the fire might have got a little of this on. [Gives the roller towel a pull.] Wish I'd thought of that sooner. Seems mean to talk about her for not having things slicked up when she had to come away in such a hurry.

MRS. PETERS: [Who has gone to a small table in the left rear corner of the room, and lifted one end of a towel that covers a pan.] She had bread set. [Stands still.]

MRS. HALE: [Eyes fixed on a loaf of bread beside the bread-box, which is on a low shelf at the other side of the room. Moves slowly toward it.] She was going to put this in there. [Picks up loaf, then abruptly drops it. In a manner of returning to familiar things.] It's a shame about her fruit. I wonder if it's all gone. [Gets up on the chair and looks.] I think there's some here that's all right, Mrs. Peters. Yes—here; [holding it toward the window] this is cherries, too. [Looking again.] I declare I believe that's the only one. [Gets down, bottle in her hand. Goes to the sink and wipes it off on the outside.] She'll feel awful bad after all her hard work in the hot weather. I remember the afternoon I put up my cherries last summer. [She puts the bottle on the big kitchen table, center of the room. With a sigh, is about to sit down in the rocking-chair. Before she is seated realizes what chair it is; with a slow look at it, steps back. The chair which she has touched rocks back and forth.]

MRS. PETERS: Well, I must get those things from the front room closet. [She goes to the door at the right, but after looking into the other room, steps back.] You coming with me, Mrs. Hale? You could help me carry them. [They go in the other room; reappear, MRS. PETERS carrying a dress and skirt, MRS. HALE following with a pair of shoes.]

MRS. PETERS: My, it's cold in there. [She puts the clothes on the big table, and hurries to the stove.]

MRS. HALE: [Examining the skirt.] Wright was close. I think maybe that's why she kept so much to herself. She didn't even belong to the Ladies' Aid. I suppose she felt she couldn't do her part, and then you don't enjoy things when you feel shabby. She used to wear pretty clothes and be lively, when she was Minnie Foster, one of the town girls singing in the choir. But that—oh, that was thirty years ago. This all you was to take in?

MRS. PETERS: She said she wanted an apron. Funny thing to want, for there isn't much to get you dirty in jail, goodness knows. But I suppose just to make her feel more natural. She said they was in the top drawer in this cupboard. Yes, here. And then her little shawl that always hung behind the door. [Opens stair door and looks.] Yes, here it is. [Quickly shuts door leading upstairs.]

MRS. HALE: [Abruptly moving toward her.] Mrs. Peters?

MRS. PETERS: Yes, Mrs. Hale?

MRS. HALE: Do you think she did it?

MRS. PETERS: [In a frightened voice.] Oh, I don't know.

MRS. HALE: Well, I don't think she did. Asking for an apron and her little shawl. Worrying about her fruit.

MRS. PETERS: [Starts to speak, glances up, where footsteps are heard in the room above. In a low voice.] Mr. Peters says it looks bad for her. Mr. Henderson is awful sarcastic in a speech and he'll make fun of her sayin' she didn't wake up.

MRS. HALE: Well, I guess John Wright didn't wake when they was slipping that rope under his neck.

MRS. PETERS: No, it's strange. It must have been done awful crafty and still. They say it was such a—funny way to kill a man, rigging it all up like that.

MRS. HALE: That's just what Mr. Hale said. There was a gun in the house. He says that's what he can't understand.

MRS. PETERS: Mr. Henderson said coming out that what was needed for the case was a motive; something to show anger, or—sudden feeling.

MRS. HALE: [Who is standing by the table.] Well, I don't see any signs of anger around here. [She puts her hand on the dish-towel which lies on the table, stands looking down at table, one half of which is clean, the other half messy.] It's wiped to here. [Makes a move as if to finish work, then turns and looks at loaf of bread outside the bread-box. Drops towel. In that voice of coming back to familiar things.] Wonder how they are finding things upstairs. I hope she had it a little more red-up up there. You know, it seems kind of *sneaking*. Locking her up in town and then coming out here and trying to get her own house to turn against her!

MRS. PETERS: But Mrs. Hale, the law is the law.

MRS. HALE: I s'pose 'tis. [Unbuttoning her coat.] Better loosen up your things, Mrs. Peters. You won't feel them when you go out.

[MRS. PETERS takes off her fur tippet, goes to hang it on hook at back of room, stands looking at the under part of the small corner table.]

MRS. PETERS: She was piecing a quilt. [She brings the large sewing basket and they look at the bright pieces.]

MRS. HALE: It's a log cabin pattern. Pretty, isn't it? I wonder if she was goin' to quilt it or just knot it?

[Footsteps have been heard coming down the stairs. The SHERIFF enters followed by HALE and the COUNTY ATTORNEY.]

SHERIFF: They wonder if she was going to quilt it or just knot it! [The men laugh, the women look abashed.]

COUNTY ATTORNEY: [Rubbing his hands over the stove.] Frank's fire didn't do much up there, did it? Well, let's go out to the barn and get that cleared up. [The men go outside.]

MRS. HALE: [Resentfully.] I don't know as there's anything so strange, our takin' up our time with little things while we're waiting for them to get the evidence. [She sits down at the big table smoothing out a block with decision.] I don't see as it's anything to laugh about.

MRS. PETERS: [Apologetically.] Of course they've got awful important things on their minds. [Pulls up a chair and joins MRS. HALE at the table.]

MRS. HALE: [Examining another block.] Mrs. Peters, look at this one. Here, this is the one she was working on, and look at the sewing! All the rest of it has been so nice and even. And look at this! It's all over the place! Why, it looks as if she didn't know what she was about! [After she has said this they look at each other, then start to glance back at the door. After an instant MRS. HALE has pulled at a knot and ripped the sewing.]

MRS. PETERS: Oh, what are you doing, Mrs. Hale?

MRS. HALE: [Mildly.] Just pulling out a stitch or two that's not sewed very good. [Threading a needle.] Bad sewing always made me fidgety.

MRS. PETERS: [Nervously.] I don't think we ought to touch things.

MRS. HALE: I'll just finish up this end. [Suddenly stopping and leaning forward.] Mrs. Peters?

MRS. PETERS: Yes, Mrs. Hale?

MRS. HALE: What do you suppose she was so nervous about?

MRS. PETERS: Oh—I don't know. I don't know as she was nervous. I sometimes sew awful queer when I'm just tired. [MRS. HALE starts to say something, looks at MRS. PETERS, then goes on sewing.] Well, I must get these things wrapped up. They may be through sooner than we think. [Putting apron and other things together.] I wonder where I can find a piece of paper, and string.

MRS. HALE: In that cupboard, maybe.

MRS. PETERS: [Looking in cupboard.] Why, here's a bird-cage. [Holds it up.] Did she have a bird, Mrs. Hale?

MRS. HALE: Why, I don't know whether she did or not —I've not been here for so long. There was a man around last year selling canaries cheap, but I don't know as she took one; maybe she did. She used to sing real pretty herself.

MRS. PETERS: [Glancing around.] Seems funny to think of a bird here. But she must have had one, or why would she have a cage? I wonder what happened to it?

MRS. HALE: I s'pose maybe the cat got it.

MRS. PETERS: No, she didn't have a cat. She's got that feeling some people have about cats—being afraid of them. My cat got in her room and she was real upset and asked me to take it out.

MRS. HALE: My sister Bessie was like that. Queer, ain't it?

MRS. PETERS: [Examining the cage.] Why, look at this door. It's broke. One hinge is pulled apart.

MRS. HALE: [Looking too.] Looks as if someone must have been rough with it.

483

MRS. PETERS: Why, yes. [She brings the cage forward and puts it on the table.]

MRS. HALE: I wish if they're going to find any evidence they'd be about it. I don't like this place.

MRS. PETERS: But I'm awful glad you came with me, Mrs. Hale. It would be lonesome for me sitting here alone.

MRS. HALE: It would, wouldn't it? [Dropping her sewing.] But I tell you what I do wish, Mrs. Peters. I wish I had come over sometimes when *she* was here. I—[looking around the room]—wish I had.

MRS. PETERS: But of course you were awful busy, Mrs. Hale—your house and your children.

MRS. HALE: I could've come. I stayed away because it weren't cheerful—and that's why I ought to have come. I —I've never liked this place. Maybe because it's down in a hollow and you don't see the road. I dunno what it is, but it's a lonesome place and always was. I wish I had come over to see Minnie Foster sometimes. I can see now— [Shakes her head.]

MRS. PETERS: Well, you mustn't reproach yourself, Mrs. Hale. Somehow we just don't see how it is with other folks until—something turns up.

MRS. HALE: Not having children makes less work—but it makes a quiet house, and Wright out to work all day, and no company when he did come in. Did you know John Wright, Mrs. Peters?

MRS. PETERS: Not to know him; I've seen him in town. They say he was a good man.

MRS. HALE: Yes—good; he didn't drink, and kept his word as well as most, I guess, and paid his debts. But he was a hard man, Mrs. Peters. Just to pass the time of day with him— [Shivers.] Like a raw wind that gets to the bone. [Pauses, her eye falling on the cage.] I should think she would 'a' wanted a bird. But what do you suppose went with it?

Mrs. Peters: I don't know, unless it got sick and died. [She reaches over and swings the broken door, swings it again, both women watch it.]

Mrs. Hale: You weren't raised round here, were you? [Mrs. Peters shakes her head.] You didn't know—her?

Mrs. Peters: Not till they brought her yesterday.

Mrs. Hale: She—come to think of it, she was kind of like a bird herself—real sweet and pretty, but kind of timid and—fluttery. How—she—did—change. [Silence; then as if struck by a happy thought and relieved to get back to everyday things.] Tell you what, Mrs. Peters, why don't you take the quilt in with you? It might take up her mind.

Mrs. Peters: Why, I think that's a real nice idea, Mrs. Hale. There couldn't possibly be any objection to it, could there? Now, just what would I take? I wonder if her patches are in here—and her things. [They look in the sewing basket.]

Mrs. Hale: Here's some red. I expect this has got sewing things in it. [Brings out a fancy box.] What a pretty box. Looks like something somebody would give you. Maybe her scissors are in here. [Opens box. Suddenly puts her hand to her nose.] Why— [Mrs. Peters bends nearer, then turns her face away.] There's something wrapped up in this piece of silk.

Mrs. Peters: Why, this isn't her scissors.

Mrs. Hale: [Lifting the silk.] Oh, Mrs. Peters—it's— [Mrs. Peters bends closer.]

Mrs. Peters: It's the bird.

Mrs. Hale: [Jumping up.] But, Mrs. Peters—look at it! Its neck! Look at its neck! It's all—other side *to*.

Mrs. Peters: Somebody—wrung—its—neck.

[Their eyes meet. A look of growing comprehension, of horror. Steps are heard outside. Mrs. Hale slips box under quilt pieces, and sinks into her chair. Enter Sheriff and County Attorney. Mrs. Peters rises.]

485

County Attorney: [As one turning from serious things to little pleasantries.] Well, ladies, have you decided whether she was going to quilt it or knot it?

Mrs. Peters: We think she was going to—knot it.

County Attorney: Well, that's interesting, I'm sure. [Seeing the bird-cage.] Has the bird flown?

Mrs. Hale: [Putting more quilt pieces over the box.] We think the—cat got it.

County Attorney: [Preoccupied.] Is there a cat?

[Mrs. Hale glances in a quick covert way at Mrs. Peters.]

Mrs. Peters: Well, not *now*. They're superstitious, you know. They leave.

County Attorney: [To Sheriff Peters, continuing an interrupted conversation.] No sign at all of anyone having come from the outside. Their own rope. Now let's go up again and go over it piece by piece. [They start upstairs.] It would have to have been someone who knew just the—

[Mrs. Peters sits down. The two women sit there not looking at one another, but as if peering into something and at the same time holding back. When they talk now it is in the manner of feeling their way over strange ground, as if afraid of what they are saying, but as if they cannot help saying it.]

Mrs. Hale: She liked the bird. She was going to bury it in that pretty box.

Mrs. Peters: [In a whisper.] When I was a girl—my kitten—there was a boy took a hatchet, and before my eyes—and before I could get there— [Covers her face an instant.] If they hadn't held me back I would have— [catches herself, looks upstairs where steps are heard, falters weakly]—hurt him.

Mrs. Hale: [With a slow look around her.] I wonder how it would seem never to have had any children around.

[Pause.] No, Wright wouldn't like the bird—a thing that sang. She used to sing. He killed that, too.

MRS. PETERS: [Moving uneasily.] We don't know who killed the bird.

MRS. HALE: I knew John Wright.

MRS. PETERS: It was an awful thing was done in this house that night, Mrs. Hale. Killing a man while he slept, slipping a rope around his neck that choked the life out of him.

MRS. HALE: His neck. Choked the life out of him. [Her hand goes out and rests on the bird-cage.]

MRS. PETERS: [With rising voice.] We don't know who killed him. We don't *know*.

MRS. HALE: [Her own feeling not interrupted.] If there'd been years and years of nothing, then a bird to sing to you, it would be awful—still, after the bird was still.

MRS. PETERS: [Something within her speaking.] I know what stillness is. When we homesteaded in Dakota and my first baby died—after he was two years old, and me with no other then—

MRS. HALE: [Moving.] How soon do you suppose they'll be through looking for the evidence?

MRS. PETERS: I know what stillness is. [Pulling herself back.] The law has got to punish crime, Mrs. Hale.

MRS. HALE: [Not as if answering that.] I wish you'd seen Minnie Foster when she wore a white dress with blue ribbons and stood up there in the choir and sang. [A look around the room.] Oh, I *wish* I'd come over here once in a while! That was a crime! That was a crime! Who's going to punish that?

MRS. PETERS: [Looking upstairs.] We mustn't—take on.

MRS. HALE: I might have known she needed help! I know how things can be—for women. I tell you, it's queer, Mrs. Peters. We live close together and we live far apart. We all go through the same things—it's all just a different kind of the same thing. [Brushes her eyes, noticing the bottle of fruit, reaches out for it.] If I was you I wouldn't tell her her fruit was gone. Tell her it *ain't*. Tell her it's all right. Take this in to prove it to her. She—she may never know whether it was broke or not.

MRS. PETERS: [Takes the bottle, looks about for something to wrap it in; takes petticoat from the clothes brought from the other room, very nervously begins winding this around the bottle. In a false voice.] My, it's a good thing the men couldn't hear us. Wouldn't they just laugh! Getting all stirred up over a little thing like a—dead canary. As if that could have anything to do with—with—wouldn't they *laugh!*

[The men are heard coming downstairs.]

MRS. HALE: [Under her breath.] Maybe they would—maybe they wouldn't.

COUNTY ATTORNEY: No, Peters, it's all perfectly clear except a reason for doing it. But you know juries when it comes to women. If there was some definite thing. Something to show—something to make a story about—a thing that would connect up with this strange way of doing it—

[The women's eyes meet for an instant. Enter HALE from outer door.]

HALE: Well, I've got the team around. Pretty cold out there.

COUNTY ATTORNEY: I'm going to stay here a while by myself. [To the SHERIFF.] You can send Frank out for me, can't you? I want to go over everything. I'm not satisfied that we can't do better.

SHERIFF: Do you want to see what Mrs. Peters is going to take in?

[The LAWYER goes to the table, picks up the apron, laughs.]

COUNTY ATTORNEY: Oh, I guess they're not very dangerous things the ladies have picked out. [Moves a few things about, disturbing the quilt pieces which cover the box. Steps back.] No, Mrs. Peters doesn't need supervising. For that matter, a sheriff's wife is married to the law. Ever think of it that way, Mrs. Peters?

MRS. PETERS: Not—just that way.

SHERIFF: [Chuckling.] Married to the law. [Moves toward the other room.] I just want you to come in here a minute, George. We ought to take a look at these windows.

COUNTY ATTORNEY: [Scoffingly.] Oh, windows!

SHERIFF: We'll be right out, Mr. Hale.

[HALE goes outside. The SHERIFF follows the COUNTY ATTORNEY into the other room. Then MRS. HALE rises, hands tight together, looking intensely at MRS. PETERS, whose eyes make a slow turn, finally meeting MRS. HALE's. A moment MRS. HALE holds her, then her own eyes point the way to where the box is concealed. Suddenly MRS. PETERS throws back quilt pieces and tries to put the box in the bag she is wearing. It is too big. She opens box, starts to take bird out, cannot touch it, goes to pieces, stands there helpless. Sound of a knob turning in the other room. MRS. HALE snatches the box and puts it in the pocket of her big coat. Enter COUNTY ATTORNEY and SHERIFF.]

COUNTY ATTORNEY: [Facetiously.] Well, Henry, at least we found out that she was not going to quilt it. She was going to—what is it you call it, ladies?

MRS. HALE: [Her hand against her pocket.] We call it—knot it, Mr. Henderson.

things about, disturbing the quilt pieces which cover the box. Stops back.] No, Mrs. Peters doesn't need supervising. For that matter, a sheriff's wife is married to the law. Ever think of it that way, Mrs. Peters?

MRS. PETERS: Not—just that way.

SHERIFF: [Chuckling.] Married to the law. [Moves toward the other room.] I just want you to come in here a minute, George. We ought to take a look at these windows.

COUNTY ATTORNEY: [Scoffingly.] Oh, windows!

SHERIFF: We'll be right out, Mr. Hale.

[Hale goes outside. The Sheriff follows the County Attorney into the other room. Then Mrs. Hale rises, hands tight together, looking intensely at Mrs. Peters, whose eyes make a slow turn, finally meeting Mrs. Hale's. A moment Mrs. Hale holds her, then her own eyes point the way to where the box is concealed. Suddenly Mrs. Peters throws back quilt pieces and tries to put the box in the bag she is wearing. It is too big. She opens the opera box, starts to take bird out, cannot touch it, goes to pieces, stands there helpless. Sound of a knob turning in the other room. Mrs. Hale snatches the box and puts it in the pocket of her big coat. Enter County Attorney and Sheriff.]

COUNTY ATTORNEY: [Facetiously.] Well, Henry, at least we found out that she was not going to quilt it. She was going to—what is it you call it, ladies?

MRS. HALE: [Her hand against her pocket.] We call it knot it, Mr. Henderson.

MINNIE FIELD
By E. P. Conkle

PERSONS IN THE PLAY

Alt Page
Jim Day
Mel Clark
Corine Young
Tip Field

MINNIE FIELD

FIVE men sitting up with Tip Field's wife's corpse. The men sit in the kitchen of a small farm-house in Nebraska; the corpse and coffin are in the spare front-room just beyond. It is three o'clock in the morning. Jim Day has his feet cocked up on the stove-hearth. He leans back and smokes his pipe. Alt Page leans against the wall on the other side of the stove. Cornie Young sits at the table nibbling at this and that. Mel Clark stands at the door looking out into the night through the glass pane. Tip Field sits in a small rocker with his nose in a newspaper. He reads and rocks and reads and rocks. Things go slowly, quietly.

Alt: Settin' up with a corpse is like goin' a-courtin'.

Jim: How so, Alt?

Alt: A feller'll think-a some-a th' dad-blamdest things sometimes.

Cornie: Don't they, though.

Mel: I reckon Tip's a-thinkin' 'bout Minnie in thur . . . dead. Et's too bad.

493

CORNIE: You shore got my sympathy, Tip. I don't know what I'd do ef I was t' lose Emmy.

ALT: A man's losin' his wife's 'bout like him a' losin' his best mare.

JIM: Feller cain't break in a new one t' no account.

CORNIE: Leastwise, not one like Minnie was.

MEL: Don't take et too hard, Tip.

TIP: I wonder ef . . . ef that sow's gone an' laid on her pigs.

[The men glance at one another.]

JIM: Oh. Well. . . . I ain't heard no squealin'.

TIP: Guess we'd-a heard et if she had-a.

ALT: Them little devils shore does squeal.

CORNIE: Feller cain hear 'em in th' next county on a clear night like this'n.

MEL: I wudn't worry none, Tip. You got s'many other things t' worry over.

TIP: I ain't worryin' none. I was just . . . wonderin'. [Silence.]

CORNIE: Say, fellers . . . here's this card's got t' be wrote on. [He motions to a card on the table.]

JIM: What'll we write on et?

ALT: What you think, Tip? Et's your folkses funeral.

TIP: You fellers is payin' for th' flowers. Say what you're a-mind to. You can't hurt me none what you say.

MEL: Say as how th' flowers was given by all th' neighbors to th' diseased.

JIM: Might put in a little verse or so.

CORNIE: Anybody know any verse t' put on?

MEL:

> Roses is red;
> Vi'lets is blue;
> Sugar is sweet;
> So're you.

ALT: That's all th' po'try I know of.

TIP: Et's good enough.

JIM: Might say:

> Roses is red;
> Vi'lets is blue;
> Sugar is sweet;
> So *was* you.

. . . since Minnie *ain't* no more.

CORNIE: You ain't got no objections to us callin' Minnie "sweet" have you, Tip?

TIP: I reckon not. They always say nice things 'bout th' dead even when they mayn't be true. Cain't hurt me none.

MEL: Us folks allus thought Minnie was about *it.*

JIM: We all liked Minnie, too. She allus was a doin' somethin' for Amy and th' kids.

ALT: Funny how Minnie come t' die, ain't et?

TIP: Nothin' funny. She just kicked up her heels, passed in her checks, an' died. That's all.

MEL: Minnie was allus a workin' perty hard whenever I seen her.

TIP: That was one thing about Minnie. She went an' killed herse'f-a hard work. I give her credit for that.

CORNIE: Everybody's got to die sooner as later. Some-a 'em got to die a-workin'. A feller gets ketched that-a-way sometimes.

JIM: I reckon it won't never ketch you that-a-way, will et, Tip?

TIP: I ain't aimin' fer et to, Jim.

[The men laugh, except TIP, who reads. Then the men become conscious of their place and the corpse. Silence.]

MEL: Et's a funny thing. . . . Death is.

CORNIE: Et strikes when a person ain't lookin' for et.

ALT: And et strikes where a feller ain't lookin' fer et, too.

JIM: Et struck Jenny's pa right below th' collar-bone

when et struck him. They was a black-an'-blue spot there big as a goose-egg whur et struck him. We all seen et when they was layin' him out.

MEL: Et's like lightnin' strikin' a forked tree.

TIP: Minnie was carryin' up a bucket of warter from th' well at th' foot of th' hill. Ag'in she got ha'f way up, she keeled over an' spilt all th' warter out. That's about all they was to et. I called up th' doc an' he come an' worked on her. I had t' fetch up another bucket-a warter m'se'f.

MEL: Eet's too bad, Tip.

TIP: Shore . . . is.

[Silence. CORNIE eats.]

CORNIE: These yeller t'mater p'serves is fine, Tip.

TIP: Minnie put 'em up for th' winter. She was allus a doin' some durned-fool thing like that. Got a whole cellarful-a that kinda truck.

CORNIE: Cudn't a been better if I'd a put 'em up m'se'f, Tip. Yummmm.

JIM: I hear none-a your folks is comin' to th' funeral, Tip.

TIP: I . . . reckon not.

ALT: So I heard. How come, Tip?

TIP: They didn't like Minnie none. They said she was allus too smart. She was allus trying t' git me t' pull my freight an' git away from 'em. Minnie was plannin' big on that. Th' day she died she got a letter from Montana or somewheres 'bout new land. She even drawed a plan for a new house out there. My folks didn't like that none.

JIM: Well . . . us folks all liked Minnie real well. Mighty well.

ALT: Us folks, too.

MEL: Minnie was allus smilin'. I never seen her when she wasn't smilin'.

TIP: She cudn't tolerate none-a my folks none.. I reckon my folks was as good as hern.

JIM: [Pointing with his pipe-stem at TIP.] Wasn't nobody good as Minnie, Tip.

TIP: I . . . reckon not.

[Silence.]

MEL: Who put that rose on her coffin in thur, Tip?

TIP: She done et herse'f.

JIM: *She* done et?

ALT: How'd *she* do et, Tip?

TIP: Couple-a years ago she set them posies out in th' back yard. An' she says to me: "Ef I ever die when those-there roses are in bloom, Tippy dear, put one of them on my coffin." So . . . her ma went an' done et.

JIM: Et looks mighty perty and simple. Naturally I don't go much on beauty. But that-there was a beautiful idea, I say.

MEL: My Haley's that-a-way, too. Women-folks is durned funny critters.

CORNIE: They shore put th' trimmin's on a feller.

ALT: I didn't 'mount to a durn b'fore I was married.

JIM: Y' don't 'mount t' much more now, do you, Alt?

ALT: I reckon me and you is on a par, ain't we, Jim?

JIM: That suits me, Alt.

[The men laugh loudly.]

CORNIE: Oh, hummmm. Kind-a sleepy. You reckon th' corpse is all right, in there?

ALT: Take a look, Mel.

MEL: Et makes me creepy t' snoop 'round a corpse. Cornie, you look.

CORNIE: Nothin' to that, Mel. [He goes to the left door and opens it.] They ain't nothin' could hurt a person 'bout a corpse.

MEL: Mebby not. But they're like cold mashed p'taters; they ain't got no life to 'em.

CORNIE: Ever'thing's all O.K. 's fur's I can see. Minnie's women-folks is snorin' like all-git-out in th' spare bedroom. Sounds like a hog-pen.

TIP: Et is . . . with *them* in it.

CORNIE: [Looking in.] You got a nice front-room in there, Tip. Fixed up a sight better'n ourn is at home.

TIP: Et was . . . her.

CORNIE: [Closing the door.] Whur'd you git th' pianner at?

TIP: She got et. She usta thump on et in th' evenings. "In th' Gloamin'" and "Darlin' Nellie Gray" and such.

JIM: Must-a cost a sight. Emmy got a parler-organ and et kept me poverty-struck for five years hand-runnin'.

TIP: Didn't cost *me* nothin'. She got et with her butter 'n egg money. Took seven years. There et is in there now. Doin' nobody no good. She was just thet-a-way.

ALT: You cain cut et up for kindlin' wood, Tip.

CORNIE: Et'd make a good hen-coop for yer little chickens. All you got t' do is t' take out th' works and put a strip-a tar paper on top.

TIP: May do that.

MEL: Well . . . who's goin' t' write out that card? There et is on th' table.

JIM: I cain't write so's a person can read et.

TIP: Don't worry . . . nobody's goin' to read et.

CORNIE: I can't draw my X's so's a person can make 'em out. And my Z's has got curley-cues on 'em. You write et out, Alt.

ALT: I wud . . . but I sprained my ankle an' I'm stiff all over so's I can't even scratch my own back.

JIM: A-course, we couldn't ask Tip t' do et.

TIP: Stick th' durned flowers on without a card. Who cares for style? I been a-gettin' my belly-full-a style fer th' past ten years.

CORNIE: Just's you say, Tip. We just thunk et'd be kind-a nice, that's all.

[MEL looks out the window.]

MEL: Et's gettin' daylight out, boys. I got t' be goin' on home.

JIM: Me, too. Them calves got t' be tended to.

[The men start to put on their coats and hats.]

TIP: You fellers is comin' back t' carry th' woman to th' grave, ain't you?

CORNIE: I reckon so. We was 'pointed pall-bearers. Won't be hard to carry Minnie. She didn't weigh no more'n a bag-a feathers.

ALT: I guess I orta be hikin' on home, too. I got some chores t' do.

JIM: You goin' my way, Cornie?

CORNIE: Guess I'll cut across the hog pasture—it's shorter.

MEL: Whut'll you do without Minnie to do your milkin' now, Tip?

TIP: Reckon I'll have t' . . . git me another woman.

[The men stop still.]

CORNIE: You . . . got anybody . . . in mind, Tip?

TIP: I got Annie Smith in mind.

JIM: Ab Smith's dorter?

TIP: Yeh. I've had her in mind for some time. When I seen Minnie was . . . ailin'.

[The men look at one another. They say nothing.]

ALT: Well . . . I . . . I guess I'll be . . . goin' on, boys.

JIM: Me too, Alt.

TIP: I may need you fellers later t' help me bust up that pianner in there . . . when we git Minnie out of the way.

CORNIE: Any time. *Ef I ain't doin' somethin'.*

ALT: Me, too. Most likely I *won't* be.

MEL: I guess . . . I'll just take another look . . . at Minnie in there . . . b'fore I go.

JIM: Me . . . too.

[MEL opens the door. The men look in.]

MEL: Th' sun . . . looks perty . . . shinin' on that . . . rose, Tip.

JIM: Shore . . . does.

ALT: Et's tough luck t' lose a woman like Minnie.

MEL: She was allus smilin' and bright.

TIP: I'll git over et all right. Don't worry none 'bout me.

CORNIE: I reckon . . . we won't . . . much.

[ALT opens the outside door. The men start out.]

MEL: [Turning toward Tip.] I s'pose th' baby is inside th' coffin with Minnie, ain't it?

TIP: It's layin' on her breast. [Pause.] They wa'n't no use wastin' *two* coffins.

[The men leave. TIP resumes his reading and rocking. The sunlight washes out the pale of the lamplight.]

THE CAJUN
By Ada Jack Carver

PERSONS IN THE PLAY

ARMIDE
JULIE
PAPITE
ANATOLE
PIERRE
FATHER MARTEL

THE CAJUN

AMONG the so-called Lost Peoples of the South, around whom romance and legend cling, are the Cajuns of Louisiana. The name "Cajun"—a corruption of "Acadian"—was originally restricted in the La Fourche and Bayou Teche parishes to descendants of the unfortunate but worthy French farmers, who in 1755 fled from the English invasion to Louisiana. The "Acadians," descendants of these refugees, have grown and prospered and still dwell on the banks of the Teche. But the term "Cajun," dissociated now from its etymological origin, has gradually gained a broader, a popular significance; and—distinctive from "Creole," which to the Louisianian denotes an aristocrat— is now loosely applied to the illiterate lower-class French of South Louisiana.

The action of the play takes place in the year 1900, when in certain rural districts of the state there were no telephones nor telegraphs, and the roads were almost impassable; when, brought about by intermarriage, conditions such as are portrayed in this story existed in not a few isolated communities, necessitating the passage of what is known as the First Cousin Law.

The Cajun mood is wistful, naïve, shifting from comedy to tragedy and back again. The Cajun talks with his eyes, with his hands, and his shoulders. He is ecstatic, impulsive, lovable; easily excited over trivial matters, but possessing strength and dignity under stress of real emotion. In writing this play, no attempt has been made to portray in spelling the Cajun patois, the author for the sake of clearness relying for the effect in dialect upon the characteristic arrangement of words and sentences.

The scene is laid in what is known, pridefully, as the "front-room" of a Cajun home. It is a charming room, although it reveals poverty; for the presence of at least one piece of nice old furniture and the loveliness of a portrait on the left rear wall (the life-size painting of a woman in the dress of 1850) impress one with the fact that this family in past generations has known better days.

In the rear corner right is a four-poster bed, spread with a gay pieced quilt. On the wall above the bed are pictures of the saints and the Virgin Mary; and between the bed and the door, which is in center rear, a crude little altar hung with snowy lace supports a crucifix; before the crucifix are candles, a rosary, and a vase of fresh flowers. The old blue batten door in rear center is opened within, disclosing a scrubby cane-patch and trees draped in Spanish moss. On the left center wall is a wide old-fashioned fireplace, from which are hung iron pots and pans, and a turkey-feather fan; and which is festooned with strings of red pepper and garlic. A large black stew kettle hangs over the fire, suspended by a crane; and on a trivet in front of the fire is a coffee pot. In the corner by the fireplace is an old home-made broom, and an antique clock graces the mantel.

The chairs are home-made, with cow-hide bottoms. The

table, although a crude kitchen one, is spread with a snowy cloth; and for a reason: on this cloth reposes, conspicuously and pretentiously, a stacked wedding cake, duly embossed, on the topmost layer of which is a tight little nosegay, tied with a white satin bow. On the table near the cake is an old-fashioned cake knife; and disposed about the room are jars of Southern spring flowers, giving the room an air of gayety, of festivity. Clearly an event of some importance is soon to take place in this family.

On the right, front, is a window, with the panes out. Opposite is another door.

ARMIDE, JULIE, her daughter, and PAPITE, her witless son, are present. PAPITE is seated before the fireplace at left. His face is drawn, expressionless. He is pitiful rather than repulsive, and during the entire play he remains seated in his place on the floor, only vaguely aware of what is happening about him. At intervals, and with exaggerated absorption, he plays with a piece of string, humming a mournful minor strain that dies away on an unfinished note. PAPITE serves as a norm, as part of the atmosphere of the play, dominating the brave festivity of the wedding cake, and even the presence of JULIE clad in her wedding gown.

ARMIDE, her mouth full of pins, is down on her knees intensely doing something with needle and thread to the dress of JULIE. Around her neck she wears a small gold cross; and although weary with trouble and toil ARMIDE shows traces of what once must have been beauty, animation.

JULIE's frock is a quaint, ruffled muslin, and she wears a white japonica in her hair. She is young, lovely, wistful; but no blithe bride is she, for JULIE appears anxious, harassed; and her nervous, pretty hands are forever in motion.

PAPITE is humming.

JULIE: Mama, for today . . . my wedding day . . . for why you not make Papite stop sing that song? . . . It cause me ache in my heart. I try in my mind to sing wedding march . . . but Papite, he drown it all out. [She breaks away from ARMIDE, trembling and hiding her eyes from the pitifulness of her brother.] It make me upset, full of nerve . . .

ARMIDE: [She removes the pins from her mouth, then looks with concern from PAPITE to JULIE.] For shame, chère '. . . I don't know what come into you—your own poor brother, and him not to blame for up there— [Taps her forehead.] Stand still, mon enfant, so I make this to hang—so! I have see many bride in love, but not like to you—so full of jump and tremble. Stop fidget, chère, with your hand and foot.

JULIE: [Sighing and glancing toward the window.] But it make me feel faint . . . to stand up so long. And just for suppose I not ready, time Pierre he get back. Hurry—make haste, Mama!

ARMIDE: Mais non—make haste pourquoi? . . . Look! your grandmama clock she say quarter to five, and you know that mean it just four.

JULIE: [Breaking away and going to the window.] But it seem so long since my Pierre gone to town . . . since daybreak, yes. All day, me, I have wait and watch. Look like by now he be back.

ARMIDE: [Throwing out her arms.] Bah! Such a child! Is it something to worry, because a boy take his time in town? Your cousin Pierre he been gone to get marriage license— how you make marry, I like to know, without any license? . . . and a license mean much of red tape. It is not as if Pierre he depart to take pleasure—no! Your cousin he gone to get license, and license take time . . . Viens-ici! [JULIE reluctantly quits her watch at the window, and ARMIDE bends again to her task, which, it is plain to see by her airs, is quite to her liking. She sews, then she leans back on her heels and gazes at JULIE with pride.] Voilà! How sweet, what a

506

love she look! And how full of smell, like a flower! . . .
Beside, you must remember, my child, it been a flood, *hein?*
. . . and the road is ter-ri-fic! Let me see—this been nineteen hundred—well—

JULIE: Oh, I know, me . . . this been the worst flood
since come the year fifty-nine!

ARMIDE: Well, it's so, *hein?* No one in Louisian' she see
such a flood, with two river pouring together, and rushing
like mad. And you know yourself, since the bayou overflow,
today is first time for as more as five month since a man get
to town—way out here where *we* stay. . . . And Father
Martel, he been gone to town too. For suppose Pierre return
quick? What good that do? You can't go to church 'till
the Father get back. How you make marry without the
priest, *hein?*

JULIE: If it had not to been for them river, rushing and
pouring together . . . me and Pierre we was marry by now.
I feel me like something . . . was going to happen, again
like before. It make me feel faint. . . .

ARMIDE: [Pulling at JULIE's skirts, with her head on one
side.] Be still, *ma fille*—you too much of impatient. Such a
girl, and so much of in love! Well, me, I'm glad you make
marry today . . . it not well to put off the wedding of
young folk engage' . . . Ooooo! But you must not faint on
your wedding day—that bad luck, *cherie.* I hear your grandmama tell how one time a girl faint on her wedding day and
pouf! . . . the groom he run off with another! [She gasps
in dismay at what she has said, while JULIE throws out her
hands.]

JULIE: Mama, my Pierre he is not like to that. It is not
my Pierre make me fear . . . I . . . look like I not sleep.
I think of my marry all the long of the night.

ARMIDE: Bah! No eat, no sleep, no pray—for love!

JULIE: Mama, five month ago, when flood come . . . and
there was much of sorrow . . . we put off the wedding. To-

day I feel just like to that. Look like we wait so long to make marry—it come to arrive that my heart . . . is afraid—[Makes the sign of the cross.] And just suppose something happen to Pierre, with all the road wash away! For just suppose Pierre . . . he fall in the bayou!

ARMIDE: I never see so worry a child, always to think something happen to that Pierre of hers! . . . Maybe some friend give Pierre little drink.

JULIE: Mama!

ARMIDE: Ah, not to hurt—just make him feel good on wedding day. *Viens-ici!* [JULIE approaches sullenly, holding up her skirts.] Bah! Do not make foot to expose like that! Is you forgot your convent training? Is you forgot your grandmama was aristocrat? Stop pull at your skirt. Pierre can take care of himself, a big strapping boy.

JULIE: [Clasping her hands tragically.] Ah, but, Mama —you do not know. My Pierre—he so easy to kill!

ARMIDE: [She sits back on her heels, rolls her eyes, and lifts her hands to high heaven.] Such a daughter I got! Always you see of thing what don't be! Bah! You are fierce —like French Opera. . . . [JULIE stands and gazes out of door at back.] Come, *chère*—no tear on your wedding day. That bad luck— [ARMIDE sits down by the table.] A girl with a trousseau all laid away, and *verteverre* in it—so sweet! To say nothing of your grandmama' dress all made over. And linen, too—ain't I just off the iron with your linen? Linen what I sell my own heifer to buy, 'stead of wait to sell him next fall. Ah, *chère,* I plan to go to New Orleans next year, to Mardi Gras, on my heifer. But I sell him to get you fine linen, the best I can buy, though time she is hard, and it—what you say?—a strain to make end stretch to end, both end to meet. [Gazes at the wedding cake.] A girl with a fine wedding cake, she ought to sing and dance, and not cry! A cake what I save the egg for two week! . . . What more you ask? . . . And your grandmama' cake knife to cut it. [She picks up the knife and kisses it lovingly.] Ah, *chère,* this knife is cut many a wedding cake. *Pour* your grandmama and your grandpapa, and your *morrain* and all her child, what were Pierre' cousin, too. And Mathilde and Placide and your *Tante* Mimi, what was own twin sister to Louise—[JULIE, pouting, shrugs her shoulders]—and Henri and his child, and your cousin Pierre' grandmama on his papa' side, what is Phillipe' grandmama, *too;* and Phillipe' *porrain,* and he was name Paul . . . and him, and his child—

ANATOLE'S VOICE: [Outside the window.] Julie! Sweet-heart! [JULIE turns joyfully, while ANATOLE, a rustic, appears in the window and points a derisive finger.] Ah, I fool you! You think all time I was Pierre!

ARMIDE: Anatole! You must not to do that! Don't you see Julie is upset—on her weddnig day?

ANATOLE: Oh, I sorry! I no mean to hurt—just make little tickle . . . Julie, *viens-ici, viens-ici!* . . . [Lifts a market basket in through the window.] *Les cadeaux,* from your *Nonc* Paul, your *Tante* Marcelline, your Cousin Justin. . . . [Dangles a paper bag before JULIE's eyes.] And this little one is from Poleon-Fiset, for *lagniappe!*

ARMIDE: What is it, Julie?

JULIE: Just some more wedding gift, Mama—

ARMIDE: Oh, la, la!

ANATOLE: Julie! Don't worry! If Pierre no come back, I make marry with you! Ha! Ha! [Laughs elfishly as he disappears from the window.]

ARMIDE: [With indignation.] *Vas-t'en, fou!* [She sits down and examines contents of the basket, while JULIE, at the rear door, again takes up her vigil.] More coffee, *chère* . . . and three more coffee pot! [Places the coffee pots on the table.] And a bolt of fine nainsook from your *Nonc* Paul' store cross the bayou. . . . Ah, two bit a yard! . . . Well—*I* put him away! [She lays the material away in a drawer of the chest, in rear of room.] Maybe some day you need him, *hein?* [Shakes her head.] Oh, I never yet see girl so cold to her fine wedding gift! Ah, well. . . . [Shrugging.] Come now, *chère,* let's put on the veil. See how you look, all *fini . . . tout ensemble.* [Takes wedding veil from back of chair and adjusts it fondly, gazing at JULIE from all angles.] *Très bien . . . très jolie . . .* my pretty daughter, my sweet one. . . . Wait! [ARMIDE's demeanor suddenly changes. She stoops, and, lifting JULIE's dress, counts her petticoats.] For shame, *cherie!* Just three petticoat! When I make marry I wear six. . . . But, of course, time is change. . . . [JULIE, with weariness, starts to sit down.] Oh, la, la! Wait! Don't sit, Julie, please! You mash me the dress in the back. You spoil all what I do this whole day. . . . Wait. . . . [Adjusts JULIE's ruffles.] Now . . . *assis-toi—eh bien!* . . . [She gazes at JULIE speculatively.] Is you got something old, and something new? . . . something borrow and something blue?

JULIE: My grandmama' dress, that is old, Mama. My petticoat, she is new. And my bustle, I think it is . . . blue— ARMIDE: Where is your something borrow?

JULIE: I—I don't know, Mama. . . . Oh, lend me . . . lend me your cross—to wear—

ARMIDE: [She drops her attempt at gayety, and clasps the cross to her breast.] *Non!* No—no—

JULIE: For why, Mama?

ARMIDE: I have never tell you, *chère*—concern this cross, what it mean. I have plan to myself to tell you . . . come when you marry. But now, since you ask, this is good time—

JULIE: What do it mean, Mama?

ARMIDE: [She sits in chair by the fireplace, while PAPITE crawls to her side and puts his head in her lap. ARMIDE gazes upon him with terrible, pitying love.] *Chère,* I—I have never tell you—that I am to blame for your poor brother, being like this in his mind—

JULIE: Poor, poor Mama—

ARMIDE: It happen the year of the cholera, not long after I marry . . . when I help nurse the cripple, and them what ain't right in their mind. For I do not know then, *chère,* that I . . . was with child. There was your *Tante* Angelique' son, and your papa' own brother. And there was Pierre' Cousin Phillipe. And as I look at them—so! . . . and stare, poor thing . . . my baby . . . he was mark. [She makes the sign of the cross.] For two, three year I pray . . . I make novena for Papite. But no, it God' will he be like he is. Something break—snap! . . . in his head—and he not get no better. Papite, poor little son—

JULIE: [Hiding her eyes from PAPITE.] Hush, Mama, don't cry. Poor mama. But, Mama—the cross—

ARMIDE: Listen, *chère.* This cross— [She kisses it tenderly.] This must I say, before you make marry; for the time is come when in the sight of God it is well to speak of such thing, of such sacred thing. When, after long time, I find another little one is come to me . . . my mama, your grandmama up there—[points to the portrait on the wall]— what was Pierre' grandmama, too . . . she give this to me. She say this was bless' by the Pope. And she say to me— "take it and wear it" . . . and peace will be yours.

JULIE: Bless'—by the Pope!

ARMIDE: *Oui,* Julie . . . bless' by the Pope. Ah, *cherie,* so I wear it, this cross . . . long month for you. And then, when you come, you such a beauty of baby! Of such straightness and dearness! Such a joy, and so much of mischief, too —*mon Dieu!*—just like a rose. And so this cross is a charm; and I say to myself . . . when Julie she make marry, and time come to have little child . . . I . . . I give it to her—

JULIE: The . . . cross—

ARMIDE: [With her arms round JULIE.] And so when the time come, *cherie,* after you make marry with Pierre . . . and you know that God is to give you little child . . . just come to mama. Since your grandmama die, and your papa he

die, no one know this but just you and me, and Father Martel.
. . . So come and say to mama: Give me the cross. Mama
will know . . . she will understand, *chère*.

JULIE: Yes, yes, Mama. I will . . . say . . . Give—me—
the—cross—I—I— [There is the sound of wagon wheels
outside, and JULIE breaks away and runs to the window.]
I—I know that is Pierre! [She gazes out of the window,
then turns dejectedly.] *Non!*

ARMIDE: [Shaking her head sorrowfully.] Ah, *chère* . . .
he will come soon. [Suddenly ARMIDE sniffs in alarm, and
starts toward the fireplace.] *Voilà!* You make me so distract . . . I let the gumbo boil over! [She lifts the pot lid,
and stirs the gumbo; then raises her hands ecstatically.] Ah,
such garlic! Such onion! [ARMIDE pronounces "onion" as
if it were God.] . . . There, there, *cherie* . . . no more tear,
and sad thought. Come, let me fix you a plate—so divine!

JULIE: *Non!* Gumbo would stick in my throat. [She
kneels before the altar, while ARMIDE feeds PAPITE.]

ARMIDE: Gumbo would make you brace up, feel good again.
No breakfast, no dinner—and all for love! I bet me, Pierre
he been stuff in town! There, there, we must not let him
come . . . and find you with tear—

JULIE: Mama, you say Pierre he be back, time gumbo is
finish. [She walks up and down disconsolately.] Long time
we been love and engage—

ARMIDE: There! Such a child! Come, look at your fine
wedding present. A bride with five coffee pot, she ought to
be gay! [A button rolls to the floor; PAPITE retrieves it, and
JULIE takes it from him.] Another button off—you see?
Bah! I must sew you up again . . . I don't know what you
will do to your dress, time Pierre get here. [Sews vehe-
mently.] You just like your grandmama up there on the wall.
I hear them say when she marry, she so much in love, she
keep them wait—the Father and all—while they sew her up
in the sacristy— [There is again the sound of a wagon, and

ARMIDE and JULIE listen, motionless, ARMIDE's needle poised in the air. JULIE breaks away and flies to the window.]

JULIE: [Looking out.] It is Pierre! It is my own true love, come back safe and sound. Ah, Mama . . . it is Pierre—

ARMIDE: [Still on her knees.] Thank God he has come at last.

JULIE: Pierre! [She waves, then appears bewildered. She stares and waves again, uncertainly, while PAPITE begins to hum. JULIE turns from window.] Something . . . something done happen to Pierre. He don't . . . wave . . . back! Mama, he is worry, unhappy . . . while he cross the long bridge. He don't . . . wave back. It—it make me afraid. . . . I . . . do you think he stop love, all of a quick?

ARMIDE: Silly child. Pierre, he is come. He will explain. [ARMIDE makes the sign of the cross, and they watch the door for PIERRE's entrance.]

[PIERRE appears in the doorway, and pauses on the threshold. He is a slender, quiet-looking boy, about twenty. He stares at JULIE, starts toward her. He seems to be dazed and troubled.]

PIERRE: Julie . . . Julie, my love— [He takes her in his arms.]

JULIE: Pierre, what has happen? Pierre—

ARMIDE: Where is license, my son? Let me see.

PIERRE: [Passionately.] We . . . Tante Armide, we must go out of state, Julie and me, for get marry.

ARMIDE: [Throwing out her arms.] Out of state! . . . What you mean?

PIERRE: Tante Armide . . . I . . . when I get to town I find the law make object for us to get marry, Julie and me. I go to the court, and the court say no! . . . Two month ago —a law, she was pass . . . in the state. The judge he say he try to get word to the Father, through all the parish . . . but the road was so bad he can't reach us.

ARMIDE: But the law, the law! What kind of law?

PIERRE: The law—wait, I try make you explain. The law it say first cousin can't marry. Can't get license. They call it the First Cousin Law—

JULIE: [She holds out her arms, then drops them.] But we must to get marry! Our . . . bann, she been read. I—I feel marry already.

ARMIDE: What law is this, my son? What a way to treat good Catholic citizen—make law to say who they must marry! And how come they wait to pass law like that 'till you and Julie fall in love! . . . Bah! What they think, them man what make law! A minute it take to fall *in* love, but a long, long time to fall *out*—

PIERRE: Come, come, we talk all that later. This is no time for discuss. We must go . . . to the state line, to Mississipp'. They say we can't marry here, in Louisian'? . . . Huh! Then come, sweetheart, go get your cloak— [JULIE goes out.]

ARMIDE: Her cloak! Eloping like child with no raising! . . . And me not to see her get marry, with a veil and a priest and all proper! And beside, Pierre, her dress . . . it will not last to the river. She will come all to piece. . . . Wait, not so fast, not so fast. Let me think. . . . This is no way to treat a mama, and gumbo made and a fine wedding cake. Pierre, ain't they no way to get license? Have you talk to Father Martel?

[JULIE reappears in her cloak.]

PIERRE: I tell you there ain't no way! No way . . . I do all I can. I told the Father, ain't you got dispensation? . . . and he ask me no—he won't give it.

JULIE: It is not our fault we are cousin. The law! . . . I will choke, I will kill him!

PIERRE: Julie! . . . Listen, *Tante* Armide. We must hurry. Father Martel, he went to town too, you know. I see and I talk to him there, but I left for home first. He will come here when he return; and if he come, if he catch us, he will not permit that we go. He will say we must stand by the law!

JULIE: [Frantically.] Pierre, come—

ARMIDE: Wait . . . be still, *chère*. Pierre, you say the Father don't think this is right? Then *why!* Pierre, *I* want to talk to the Father—

JULIE: Pierre! Come!

ARMIDE: Julie, you go on of such way as I find myself crazy! Ah! . . . [FATHER MARTEL appears in the doorway, and JULIE and PIERRE turn away, clinging together. ARMIDE makes the sign of the cross. FATHER MARTEL is an old French priest; his hair is white; he appears troubled, distressed. He blesses the household.] Father—

FATHER MARTEL: Madame Armide. . . . My poor, poor children. My heart goes out to you. This is hard, a sore trial for us all. [He observes JULIE in her cloak.] Ah, my child . . . surely you would not defy the law of your state!

PIERRE: But, Father, I love her. . . . We love each other—

JULIE: Father, it is not our fault we are cousin— I don't want to marry . . . no one . . . ain't *kin* to me. It would be like marry a stranger.

ARMIDE: Father, they . . . they want to go to Mississip' for get marry there, she and Pierre, of which she is engage so long a time. And Father, you know a long engage—it make for no good. Either you fall *out* of love, or too much of *in!* Such a law!—and me to know nothing about it, so I keep Pierre and Julie apart. . . . Why, look—[brightening] —I—I marry my first cousin. Julie' papa and me, *we* was first cousin!

JULIE: [Hopefully.] Yes—

FATHER MARTEL: Ah, I know, madame . . . but. . . . Has Pierre then not told you everything? . . . the meaning, the wherefore of this law. . . . [He turns to PAPITE; the others, with dawning realization, gaze at PAPITE with shrinking and pity.] I talk with the judge, with the doctors . . .

and they say to me . . . that first cousin must not make
marry—here where we have live so long isolate. . . . It is
like those two surging river, those river that flowed and
joined . . . and wrought such havoc, such sorrow, and woe.
. . . This girl, Julie . . . do you want her to have a child—
like Papite?

JULIE: No! No! But we must go—do not stop us—

ARMIDE: Wait, my child. Julie, wait. We must have patience. The Father would not tell us what is not so. Let me
think. . . . Father, I don't . . . understand—

JULIE: I—I don't . . . understand. [She leans against the
table.] Tell me, tell me again. Would my child—and Pierre's
—[PIERRE takes her hand]—would it be like Papite? Would
it be like—*that?*

FATHER MARTEL: Julie, look at your *Tante* Angelique'
son, your papa' own brother . . . and Pierre' cousin Phill-
lipe. And now Papite . . . poor little Papite.

ARMIDE: No . . . no . . . Papite, he was *mark*—

FATHER MARTEL: Madame Armide, it is in the blood.

[ARMIDE gropes for the chair, and sits down. JULIE, swaying, reaches for the nosegay on the cake, and crunches the
flowers, flinging them to the floor. She turns, hysterically,
and her groping hands encounter the cake-knife.]

PIERRE: Julie! [He takes the knife from her.] Father,
you must marry us!

FATHER MARTEL: The law forbids, my son.

PIERRE: *Tante* Armide—

ARMIDE: Father Martel, he is priest, Pierre—

JULIE: What is law to say? Who is priest to say? Oh,
Mama . . . can't you see? Don't you understand? . . . I
. . . I. . . . Give—me—the—cross—Mama! *Give—me—the
—cross—*

[JULIE kneels and buries her head in ARMIDE's lap. FATHER
MARTEL makes the sign of the cross; and PAPITE hums his
little song.]

ADDIO
By Stark Young

PERSONS IN THE PLAY

Monkey Tom
Harry Boyd
John
Susa

ADDIO

THE room in JOHN'S place, New Orleans, looks out through a sort of triple door, or French windows, all open, into an arcade with columns of old brick and plaster. In the street outside the last of the afterglow shines. A few street cries are heard, but they, too, are going like the daylight. The high walls, with traces of decoration still on them, show that the old room has seen better days, when New Orleans was a part of France and the Cathedral was the heart of the town. Showcases with bread and cakes stretch across the back of the shop. JOHN has put some paper flowers among the loaves, and on one of the cases a vase of these flowers and some palmetto fans. Opposite the door are the entrances to the kitchen and two or three tables.

JOHN stands behind a showcase sorting loaves of bread and humming to himself. He is a big, ruddy, middle-aged fellow and speaks with a lazy, good-hearted drawl.

HARRY enters, fanning himself with his hat.

JOHN: Hello, Harry! How's your character? You're looking dapper enough. Yais, ain't it hot!

519

HARRY: Zat you, John? How goes it, John? I say, how long is Canal Street, anyway? And then if you stop at Raynor's—what time is it? [He sits down by a table to the right.]

JOHN: 'Bout six, I reckon.

HARRY: Just six? Lucky dog!

JOHN: Supper time in the world, all right.

HARRY: What time do you have supper?

JOHN: Oh, generally 'bout six, I reckon; 'long there.

HARRY: What time d'you say it was?

JOHN: 'Bout six. Got some fine crabs to-day. From the island; reckon these Cajuns are poaching for 'em; but they're fine crabs now—yes, siree, they are—fine ones.

HARRY: What time is it, now, John?

JOHN: Good Lord, I'll put in a clock! It's five after six. Catching a train?

HARRY: Promised to meet Susa here at six.

JOHN: Susa? Oh, ho! And how is Susa? I haven't seen her for weeks.

HARRY: Straight and quick as ever. That girl's got spirit. I got a little roan from Kentucky, same spirit—damn me!— you oughter seen her, John, when the oyster chap—you know Fernandez—dirty sliver—well, he asked her for a kiss yesterday. She smacked him so hard everybody in the market jumped. "Say, Dollie, give me a kiss," he says. "Give you a smack," she says. And old Potted Plants, when she heard it, yells out, "Holy Virgin! Who knocked it off?" She was noddin', you see. [HARRY sits down by one of the tables. JOHN chuckles as he drifts about the place.]

JOHN: Susa's all right!

HARRY: Yes, Susa'll come out all right, but——

JOHN: I used to see Susa passin' here, walkin' down the banquette with her head in the air—and those there young chaps along behind, but she'd go by herself, she would.

HARRY: I used to be one of 'em. I'd hang round, but she

wouldn't see me. Sometimes I'd try to speak to her, but she'd give me such a look my knees were water. She wouldn't see any of us chaps at first. Not for a long time.

JOHN: Aw well, who knows? Women's eyes are different, maybe. But I ain't seen Susa pass by here in a long time.

HARRY: No; you see they've moved. Gone over to Esplanade, near Pacco's.

JOHN: Good-night! Some style! She and her ma still at the market?

HARRY: Yes, at her mother's stand—the blue stand next to the oysters. But I reckon business is pretty slow for 'em.

JOHN: A pretty girl like that oughtn't to have no business but a husband. And how is your business?

HARRY: Booming, John. By George, if I'm not making fifty dollars a week with my teams now, clear!

JOHN: Fifty dollars! Say! Why—then you can marry! Easy as fallin' off a log.

HARRY: If Susa will only say the word, I'm ready for it! She seems to love me sometimes, John, and sometimes she doesn't.

JOHN: 'At's a' right. They're all that way. Sometimes they do and they don't, and sometimes they don't and they do.

HARRY: She had a sweetheart in Sicily once, and I think she remembers him sometimes; but then—

JOHN: Aw naw; she's forgotten him.

HARRY: I don't know; you can't tell about these things. I ask her sometimes if she loves me, John, and she just stands there looking at the oranges. I asked her, I says, "Susa, do you love me?" and she picks up an orange and says, "You oughter see the oranges in Palermo." "But don't you love me now," I says, and she says—

JOHN: Listen, Harry, they kin forget. I'm a married man, and I know. My wife's done forgot all those other fellows—every mother's son of 'em.

HARRY: Has she?

JOHN: She's about forgot me, too, I reckon. [A long pause. JOHN goes on with some business about the showcases. HARRY lights a cigarette and begins to smoke impatiently. TOMMASO's hand-organ is heard outside playing the "Merry Widow Waltz."]

JOHN: Pst! Listen, there's Monkey Tom—

HARRY: Who?

JOHN: Monkey Tom; here he is. [JOHN goes and stands in the door, speaking to someone outside.] 'S 'at you, Tom?

TOMMASO: Buon giorno, Signore—howdy!

JOHN: Well—hello, Tom! Don't he speak English now? [TOMMASO enters from the street, carrying by a strap his organ, which is supported from beneath by a pole. He is a young man of twenty-four, but his lameness makes him look far older.]

JOHN: Mr. Boyd, Signor Tommaso.

HARRY: Howdy; how are you, Signore? [TOMMASO bows. Then he sets down the organ, half leaning on it.]

JOHN: How's this for weather, Tom? Nearly as hot as Sicily, eh?

TOMMASO: Sicilia, that is not hot!

JOHN: Not hot? Now, Harry, I ask you what about a country where the whole island is a cook-oven?

TOMMASO: Oh, dio santo, Signore! [HARRY laughs.]

TOMMASO: In Sicilia—ah, Signore, I see you make 'a me fun.

JOHN: All right, Tom. You want your bread and the cake for Gigia, eh?

HARRY: Does he buy cake for the monkey?

TOMMASO: How Gigia love de cake!

JOHN: Harry, you saw Gigia dance, yes?

HARRY: [Shaking his head.] No, never did. Seen Bessie Bliss.

TOMMASO: You got a monkey, too, Signore? [JOHN gives a chuckle.]

TOMMASO: [Solemnly.] Oh, a lady—scusi, Signore.

HARRY: [Smiling over the lady idea.] If you like.

JOHN: [Bringing out a tray.] Aye, aye, what do you think of this?

TOMMASO: No, no cake to-day, Signore. Gigia, Gigia's dead—dieda last night—poor Gigia—all I had!

JOHN: Dead? Aw now, come along! Cheer up; some people ain't never had a monkey. And you'll pick up less money, but you'll need less to buy. What's the bread, long or short? To-day's or yesterday's? To-day's 5 cents; yesterday's 2 cents.

TOMMASO: Short; and dat's too mucha wivout Gigia.

JOHN: Yesterday's?

TOMMASO: Si, si, I no lika to-day's bread. It is too—too—

JOHN: Hot? Yais, yais, I see—[laughing.] I see, Tommie. To-day's bread's too hot, yes. Yesterday's, well, yon 'tis.

HARRY: How do you like America, Tom?

TOMMASO: Me? Oh, I no like America, Signore. Fast, so fasta! I say, "Permesso, Signore,"—he say, "Git out a de way!" [He comes down to the front.] I work all week, and den Sunday comes, domenico—ai, ai, ai, no festa, no wine—no—oh no!

HARRY: How long have you been over?

TOMMASO: Two year and half. Longa time, Signore!

HARRY: Played the organ all the time, eh? Made any money?

TOMMASO: Si, si, but only little, poco, poco, Signore—pocino, Signore. You see, Signore, I lame and weaka—

JOHN: Aw, come on now, Tom's gettin' rich! [He finds his wire brush and stands guard over the case of bread.]

TOMMASO: No, no!

HARRY: Why do you stay then, if you make no money?

TOMMASO: Ah, Signore, I no come for money.

JOHN: Aw, shucks, what then? [Striking at a fly.] For love? For love, oh la, la!

TOMMASO: [Excitedly.] Listen, Signore—me—I lookinga for someone.

HARRY: Well, get that, will you! A vendetta, eh? to kill?

TOMMASO: No, Signore, not kill.

HARRY: No?

TOMMASO: To love—to love, Signore, si.

HARRY: A woman?

TOMMASO: Si, [with a shrug] altro. Si, Signore.

JOHN: Aye!—[He hits hard and gets his fly.]—these women!

HARRY: And have you found her?

TOMMASO: Found her? No, Signore, mai. Mai, Signore. Never found.

HARRY: Yes, America's a big place, ain't it, Tom? Oh, well, there're other fish in the sea.

TOMMASO: Scusi, Signore?

HARRY: I say this is not the only woman in the world. There're other—

TOMMASO: No, Signore, I no think.

HARRY: Eh?

SUSA: [Outside.] Er, Pietro, ecco! Domani due kili! E cirassi— [At the sound of her voice TOMMASO starts violently, and, as she enters, retreats to the rear of the shop.]

A MAN'S VOICE: [From the street.] Si, si, ho capito, domani mattina a buon ora.

SUSA: [In the door.] Allora, senza mancanza, va bene. [She enters hastily and angrily.]

HARRY: [Going towards her.] Susa! Why I thought you had forgotten!

SUSA: [Motioning him back from her.] Forgotten—io —I?

HARRY: Why!

SUSA: You have forgotten! You say you come for me

524

by the market—and I—[half sobbing] I wait, waita till everyone go away—waita, wait, wait, and I was afraid—and so—so I come—epoi, senta, listen—

HARRY: No, no, Susa, I'm sorry. You got it wrong. I said I'd meet you here at John's. [She turns her back on him.] Why, you're not mad, are you? Are you, Susa? [TOMMASO meantime at the back has left his organ propped against the showcase, and stares at SUSA with wild, eager, large eyes.]

HARRY: Are you angry, Susa?

TOMMASO: [Under his breath.] Susa—oh!

HARRY: Susa, it wasn't my fault.

SUSA: Oh, basta, basta, it's a lie!

JOHN: Oh, Lord, these lovers and loveresses! And this love! Give me the oven for mine! Come, come, don't you all be scrappin'—I've got a nice supper for you—all hot.

TOMMASO: [At the back, stretching out his hands to her and speaking to himself.] Susa, Susa, Susa!

HARRY: [By the table on the right.] Come, Susa, you're wrong! [She stamps her foot.] Come, let's eat a bite. All right, John, let's have your feast. [Susa stands with her back to him, without moving. HARRY takes off his hat, hangs it on the chair back, and straightens his tie. TOMMASO at the back looks steadily at HARRY, studying him from head to foot, then at himself; back to HARRY, then at himself again, and down at his crippled leg, and shakes his head.]

HARRY: [Reminding him.] John—

JOHN: [Going out.] All rightsky, zwei minute! JOHN goes out. TOMMASO puts on his hat, pulls it down over his eyes, and walks over toward the organ.]

SUSA: I won't eat any supper!

HARRY: Why, Susa, you ain't really mad, are you? Oh, come now, honest, I said I'd wait here.

SUSA: It's a lie—you dodged me—you lie to me—oh—

Posse mori a ches! I hate you. [JOHN comes in with a tray of plates.]

JOHN: All rightsky—better'n the fat o' rams!—waffles, crab gumbo à la— [SUSA moves toward the door.] Hello, where you goin'? Ain't you goin' to eat anything?

SUSA: I'm a goin' home.

JOHN: Home!

HARRY: Susa, you don't mean it! Then I'll go, too.

SUSA: No, sacramento, mai—never—e senta, senta, Harry, listen! Don't you come near me again—don't touch me—or —or I'll kill you, briconaccio—leave me be! And I'll go to Napoli again, my country; I hate you Americani, cold fish! I'm disgoosted and disgraced! [She thrusts him aside and starts toward the door.]

JOHN: Susa! Oh, now! Now, Susa!

SUSA: [Stopping for a moment.] Oh, you! basta! [She clasps her palms together.]

HARRY: Susa—

SUSA: Accidente!

TOMMASO: No, no! [He moves quickly in front of her and stands across the door, his hat still down over his eyes.] No, no, you musta no go. You too quicka—

SUSA: Che, che? Who's goin' stop me? Let me pass!

TOMMASO: You are too quicka, Signora—non c'è de l'amor —no mucha love—no any place—don'ta throw it away—don't throw it away. Pardone—be gentile—

SUSA: I'll show you how to move!

TOMMASO: [His manner gathering force as he stops her with his hand outstretched.] Aspetti, wait, waita, wait till you hear—

SUSA: Hear what? John, he's crazy!

TOMMASO: There was a man in my country—Italia— [He pauses. They all grow quiet to listen. SUSA moves a step backward.]

SUSA: Well? Epoi?

TOMMASO: [Speaking very slowly at first] who love a woman—anda she loveda him. And one other personne made lies to them. And she taka and crede the lies—and leave him and go to America—epoi—and so—dey lose each oder.

JOHN: Why man— [SUSA comes down nearer the table on the right and stands looking into space, clasping and unclasping her hands. HARRY watches her anxiously.]

JOHN: [Speaking low to TOMMASO.] Why, man, I see—I see—take her—speak! You take what's yours!

TOMMASO: [Almost in a whisper.] La mia—mia fanciulla —Susa—allora perche—Signor? why? Oh no—

JOHN: Sure, sure, Tom— [TOMMASO looks at HARRY, then at himself; then points to his crippled leg, and shakes his head.]

HARRY: Sure—fight for your rights—speak up!

TOMMASO: Shh! Hush, Signore, hush!

SUSA: [Raising her head and looking at no one.] Well? —che ha fatto? What did he do? What dida that man do?

TOMMASO: What do? [He makes a little gesture of putting his hand to his eyes for a second.] Piange. She go to America, and he cry and cry for her, but never, never found—

SUSA: And then? And then?

TOMMASO: And then the fever take him and molto miseria—

SUSA: And did—and did he follow her?

TOMMASO: Si, when he was well—longa tim' after—to America.

SUSA: And found?

TOMMASO: Mai. And never found. [JOHN makes an impatient step forward.]

SUSA: [Whispering as to herself.] Ah, never? Madonna! Never?

TOMMASO: But if she hadna been so quicka, so fast, so angry—dey had not lost each oder.

Susa: No, maybe not. [She is silent for some time, working her hands together. Her voice changes entirely when she speaks.] Oh, no, no! Eh, altro! Someone tells you this, in the markette maybe.

Tommaso: The Mercato—no, Signora—no.

Susa: [She faces him as she speaks; he stands with his hat still down over his eyes.] Ma che, tell me—what was his name? What was this man's name?

Tommaso: Tommaso. [John and Harry look at each other, but remain as they were standing.]

Susa: [Taking a step toward him.] Tommaso? Tommaso?

Tommaso: Si, Tommaso.

Susa: How did you know? Tommaso! That was his name? You say? What do you say?

Tommaso: I speaka to make you not to leave your man, there— [He fumbles at his hat, pushing it at last further down to shadow his face.]

Susa: But you—but you—what your name?

Tommaso: [Slowly, with a great effort.] My name? Luigi—is my name. [Harry and John look suddenly at one another, but seem unable to act.]

Harry: Why—why—you will not—? [Susa snaps her fingers at Harry to silence him].

Tommaso: [In a firm voice.] Luigi.

Susa: [She unclasps her hands and waits a little before speaking again.] But—how did you know the storia?

Tommaso: How did I know? I see it in the play at— Pisa. You see, Signora, it was a very grand teatro—you see, Signora—I say a play—there was—you see, Signora— when they loved each oder, eh, you see, Signora, that night— [He limps a step nearer her. Susa looks at him a moment, gives a sudden start, and shivers, then turns away, slapping her hand on the table and leaning against it. She has decided not to recognize Tommaso.]

528

Susa: Oh dio, I was a fool to think that— My Tommaso—

John: Oh, Susa!

Tommaso: No broka like me, eh? Your Tommaso, no—no like— [touching his breast]—me. [He pauses.] In the play at Roma—at Pisa, Signora—Allora—I go. Ricorda, Signora—

John: Stay, stay. Tommaso—Luigi—old chap—and take some supper with me; it won't cost you nothin'—I invite you!

Tommaso: No, I no eat. I am a little seeka to-day. I think I joosta taka de bread. [Susa stands near the table, looking at the floor, struggling to master herself. She has forgotten the three men. After a while she shakes her head and throws out her hands in a little hopeless gesture, then stands quite still.]

Harry: Susa!

Susa: Oh, wait! Please, wait! [The three men stand watching her. Harry still seated on the far side of the table. Tommaso at length raises his hat from his face and takes one long look at her. Then he goes back and puts the strap over his shoulder, and then leans suddenly against the organ and buries his face in his arms.]

John: Hey, kiddo;

Tommaso: [Rousing gaily and striking up the waltz.] Si, si, addio! Where's Gigia! Addio. Goodabye—[Outside.] —goodabye!

John: Good-bye.

Susa: Good-bye—Luigi. [She stands motionless, resting one hand on the table. Harry has risen from his chair and stands, waiting, doing nothing. The organ plays farther and farther away.]

John: Oh! his bread! [He takes up the bread that Tommaso has left and starts after him, stops, puts the bread back on the showcase, and without turning wipes his eyes on his sleeve.]

SUSA: Harry—

HARRY: Yes?

SUSA: Scusi—I'm sorry. [Without turning, she holds out her hand to him. The strains of the waltz die away in a far-off street.]

THE RESIGNATION OF
BILL SNYDER
By John D. Shaver

PERSONS IN THE PLAY

BILL SNYDER
EDWARD MCDONALD
GRANT WILLIAMS
RALPH RILEY
SHERMAN FISCHER
GEORGE GUYER
HANK PHILLIPS
JESS MILLS
GUSTAVE ANDERSON
BEN PERRY
DOCTOR GOODSON

THE RESIGNATION OF
BILL SNYDER

THE lobby of a small-town post-office in northwest Missouri. It is probably the little town of McFall where the author once lived, and where the original of BILL SNYDER once carried the mail on route three for nearly a score of years. This section of the state is a pleasant land in summer, and ordinarily the winters are mild enough, but lying just to the east of the great plains with no protection from their wintry blasts, it is occasionally swept by fierce blizzards from the northwest that bring down the intense cold and the great snows of the northern mountains and plains.

Such a blizzard is now beating against the door of the little post-office about seven o'clock in the morning on the second day of January. The lobby of the post-office is simply furnished. In the center of the room is a big box stove set in a shallow box of cinders. By the stove is a goods-box and a stool. Against the rear wall is a bench, and in the upper right-hand corner is a large waste-basket. Out to the left is the mail room. In the partition between the lobby and the mail room are the general delivery windows, and slots for mailing letters and packages. The door leading into the mail room is in the upper left-hand corner. Center right is the door to the street. Around this door and around the stove snow has been tracked in from outside. Everyone who comes in is well wrapped up in overcoat and muffler.

SHERM FISCHER, the postmaster, is poking the fire and sweeping up the snow around the stove. He is about fifty years old, thin and slightly stooped. He is wearing a very ordinary business suit, rather old and unpressed.

GUSTAVE ANDERSON, the new storekeeper, enters. He is a round, bustling person, in his forties, a progressive business man and a good citizen. He is carrying some small packages.

FISCHER: Well, how-do-you-do, Mr. Anderson? What are you going to think of our town, having such weather as this?

ANDERSON: By Jims, I thought I was coming to a warm country. Why, we never had it any worse than this in Minnesota. [He notices the snow he has trailed in.] I didn't get much off my feet outside, did I? If everybody that comes in tracks in that much it'll keep you sweepin' all day.

FISCHER: Oh, I won't mind. I won't have anything else to do. There won't be many in.

ANDERSON: [Stamping his feet, and going to the stove.] Ain't it terrible?

FISCHER: It sure is. Worst I've seen in years. I had ten below this morning, but it feels worse'n that when the wind hits you.

ANDERSON: I had twelve. That sleet cuts like glass. I nearly froze coming across the street. Are the carriers going this morning?

FISCHER: Sure! They'll start. Some of them may not get around, but they'll try it, and go as far as they can. We've got a fine lot of boys, Mr. Anderson. I'm going on my second term as postmaster and I don't recollect any of 'em not starting. We're mighty proud of our record here in the office.

ANDERSON: That's fine.

FISCHER: The boys sure can do some braggin' at the association meetings. We got one of the best records of any office in the state.

ANDERSON: Who have you got to take route three?

FISCHER: Well, we haven't got anybody yet.

ANDERSON: Well, here's a little more for each of the boys. [Shows the packages.] Got to let people know we're ready for business.

FISCHER: What are they?

ANDERSON: They're some ads. I got 'em up as New Year's greetings for everybody on all the routes. I've got some of my prices on 'em, and a suggestion to compare with mail order house prices. Here, take one. [He takes a small, neat folder from his pocket and gives it to FISCHER.] I'm going to try to clear out that stock and make a real store out of it. These would have gone out before this, but I didn't want to send them till I was in charge and done invoicing. We'll finish this morning.

FISCHER: [Looking over the circular.] Pretty nice, all right. Did the *Ledger* do 'em?

ANDERSON: Oh, you bet. I believe in patronizing our own folks, wherever I am. Besides, they do good work. I'm going to have them do a lot for me.

FISCHER: This is a bad day for the boys to take 'em.

ANDERSON: That's just the point. Soon as we saw last night what the weather was liable to be this morning we wrote on all of the ads, "We serve in spite of the weather; can the mail order house do more?" That's the reason they've just got to go out this morning. I want to get 'em on route three especially on account of having Bill in the store. That's something that counts.

[Enter RALPH RILEY, the youngest of the carriers, a husky boyish young fellow in his late twenties.]

RALPH: [Going to the stove, unwrapping and blowing on

535

his fingers.] By Jacks, let me to a stove. What'll we do today, Sherm? Freeze?

FISCHER: You'll sure have to keep moving and stop in an' warm about every box.

RALPH: Ain't the other boys going?

FISCHER: Sure. Mack's in putting up his mail now.

RALPH: Well, what's the matter with Bill Snyder? When I came by his place he was standing at the window and he waved and came to the door and hollered and asked if I was going. I said yes, and rode on. If he don't go, it'll be the first time route three's missed a day in his fifteen years, won't it?

FISCHER: Why, Bill's resigned. Didn't you know it?

RALPH: Resigned! Go 'long. Has something really happened that he can't go?

FISCHER: No. I'm not joking; he's quit, actually. Handed in his resignation when he came in off the route day before yesterday, last day of December. I supposed you'd heard it.

RALPH: No. You know I was first one in that day. We was over visiting at my wife's folks yesterday and I didn't come in. Grant put up my mail. What's the matter? What'd Bill resign for?

FISCHER: Well, you know he's over the age limit and finished his fifteen years of service last October, so he could retire any time and get his pension.

RALPH: Well, what put it into his head to quit now?

FISCHER: Oh, we've had all this bad weather and mud and he's had a lot of breakdowns and other bad luck and when he came in off the route Tuesday he said he'd been thinking, and he just believed he'd quit right then at the last of the year. Said his wife and their daughter had been begging him to; and we'd have New Year's Day off to get somebody, so that route three wouldn't miss a day and the new man could start right in with the new year. So he just set down and wrote out his resignation to take effect immediately.

THE RESIGNATION OF BILL SNYDER

RALPH: Have you sent it in yet?

FISCHER: No, not yet. I've got it in my pocket.

RALPH: Read it. I'll never believe it till I hear it.

FISCHER: Here it is: "Fourth Ass't. Postmaster General, Wash., D. C. Dear Sir: Having served over fifteen consecutive years in the United States Civil Service as a rural mail carrier, and having passed the retirement age of sixty-five years, I beg leave to present, through my postmaster, my resignation from the service to take effect immediately. Yours respectfully, William Snyder, carrier route three."

RALPH: Well, that's just like Bill. When anything's to do, do it! Who's going to take his place? This is the kind of day we need Bill.

FISCHER: I don't know yet. I told Bill I'd appoint anybody he recommended as temporary carrier. You know he's never had to have a substitute. [The telephone rings in mail room.] I wonder who that is now. [To ANDERSON.] I'll take these ads in. [He goes into the mail room.]

RALPH: Well, that beats me! I can't imagine this post-office without Bill Snyder on route three. Why, he's the only carrier ever been on the route, and he's never missed a day. That route is the pride of the state. Them people out there's got more confidence in Bill's getting there than they have in the sun coming up. And he always got there too. I've seen him go it worse days than this. It's the way Bill does that keeps the rest of us going so.

ANDERSON: Yes, I've heard about Bill. That's why I grabbed him for the store.

RALPH: For the store?

ANDERSON: Yes, Bill was over there Tuesday right after he resigned. As soon as I heard it, I knew he was the man I wanted, and I made him a proposition and he took me up. He's to start in as soon as we finish invoicing. We'll get done this morning, I believe.

RALPH: Might know Bill wouldn't set down on a pension and do nothing.

[FISCHER comes in from the mail room.]

FISCHER: That was Bill, then, wanting to know who was taking route three. Might know he'd be stewing about it. Said a lot of the boys were down to see him yesterday, and he just told 'em all that the first one down here this morning he'd recommend. But he didn't know this was coming. There ain't everybody like Bill, ready to start out on a day like this.

RALPH: Well, they'd better be showing up, and I'd better be getting to work. [As he comes into the mail room.] Hello, Mack! Did much come up on nineteen?

MACK: [In mail room.] Not much.

ANDERSON: Who all is wanting Bill's place?

FISCHER: Oh, three or four; Hank Phillips, Tom Beeks, Jess Mills, Larry Mathers, George Guyer. I think they every one went down to see Bill yesterday.

ANDERSON: I thought they got these carriers' jobs by examination.

FISCHER: They do, but you never can tell when they'll be held; maybe three weeks; maybe three months.

ANDERSON: That temporary carrier job might be a pretty good thing then.

FISCHER: Yes, and the fellow that is on as temporary carrier learns a lot that helps him in the examination. He generally gets the regular job anyway. That's why these fellows want it.

[GRANT WILLIAMS comes in wrapped up, but cold; he goes to stove as he takes off gloves and muffler; a stocky, heavy-set man of about forty.]

GRANT: Br-r-r-r-r! Ain't this a day?

FISCHER: It's sure bad. That snow'll drift twenty feet deep by night if it keeps up.

GRANT: Lord help the fellow that's taking Bill's place on

route three. He has to start right out facing it. Who's taking it?

FISCHER: I don't know; one of the boys that's applying, I guess. Bill just now phoned and said give it to the first one that come down. Said that would be a test for 'em.

GRANT: Well, I know one that's out. Larry Mathers was down to the barn and said he was glad he hadn't signed up for it. Said he wouldn't go this morning for a million dollars.

FISCHER: Well, some of 'em better be showing up. Their mail's all up and waiting. Your mail up?

GRANT: All but what came up on nineteen; that won't be much.

FISCHER: You needn't take any fourth class stuff this morning.

GRANT: I'll take that package for little Alice Thompson. It's a Christmas present from her brother in the Marines. Clear from the Philippines; that's why it's late.

ANDERSON: It'll be a job taking it horseback.

GRANT: I'll manage some way to get it there, and stop in and warm and she'll show me what it is. I hope it's nothing that will freeze.

ANDERSON: I want that route three mail to go if possible. I've got to get back to the store now. If any of the boys that want the route are there, I'll send 'em over. If Bill comes in, tell him to come over. I expect we could use him this morning, but I hate to call him out in this blizzard.

FISCHER: All right, I'll tell him;—and send some of them boys over. [ANDERSON goes out.] That Anderson is a live wire; I'm glad he's come here; he'll make a real store out of Davison's old place.

GRANT: Yes, and specially now that he's got Bill. But I can't imagine Bill selling dress goods and wrapping up sugar.

539

FISCHER: Bill will make a good clerk, though; knows everybody in the county.

GRANT: Bet he'll be a pardner in a year.

FISCHER: Well, them two would make a good pair. [BEN PERRY comes in; he is the railroad station agent, about thirty years old, a likeable fellow, but of few words.] Good-morning, Ben. When'd you ship in this weather? That snow and sleet'd cut a man's face off.

PERRY: And it nearly has mine! [Like the others, he goes to the stove to warm.] Are the carriers going?

GRANT: Yes, don't you envy us?

PERRY: No, but I'm glad you're going. Load of cattle came in last night for Charley Ward, and they'll die if he don't get 'em to shelter, and his wire's down and I'll have to write him. [He gives FISCHER an envelope.]

GRANT: He's on route three, ain't he?

PERRY: Yes.

FISCHER: Well, Ben, I don't know whether route three will go or not. Nobody was signed up for it, and I don't know whether we can get anybody to go on a day like this, or not.

PERRY: Didn't anybody apply for Bill's job? Two or three told me yesterday they was going down to see Bill to try to get his recommendation.

FISCHER: Yes, but this won't look good to them. One's backed out already.

PERRY: Well, I've got to get that notice out there some way.

[GEORGE GUYER comes in, a young fellow in his twenties.]

FISCHER: Come in, George. Did Anderson send you over?

GEORGE: Yes, what's this about having to take route three this morning if you want the temporary job? Anderson said he had a lot of stuff that had to go out and he was going to get somebody to take it.

PERRY: Yes, and I've got something that's got to go out. The company may be held for a lawsuit if a lot of them cattle die and it might all come down on my head. Besides, I've got some feeling for the cattle.

GEORGE: Well, what's that got to do with carrying the mail twenty-five miles through this blizzard?

FISCHER: Uncle Sam's mail has to go, George, blizzard or no blizzard. And this is route three, that ain't missed a day since Bill Snyder carried the first round, over fifteen years ago. You've been wanting to get in the service; now's your chance. You know what it means to get the temporary carrier job.

GEORGE: Why, what's the use of starting out in this? You wouldn't get half-way around. None of you will.

GRANT: We'll try it anyway. I've been on five years and never was afraid to start.

GEORGE: Well, I'm not afraid either, and I want the job, but I don't see the sense in starting something you can't finish.

GRANT: We don't know we can't till we try. The mail has to go, George. You can't tell what you're carrying or how much it might mean to somebody.

GEORGE: Well, I'll go down and see how my horse is, and if things don't look too bad, maybe I'll go.

GRANT: [Going to the mail room.] That's the stuff, George. Only cut that "maybe" out of it.

GEORGE: [As he goes out.] Well, I'll see how it feels.

FISCHER: I don't believe he'll go.

PERRY: I don't either.

[RALPH comes to the door of the mail room.]

RALPH: What's George going to do?

FISCHER: Said he'd go look at his horse and come back and tell us.

RALPH: He'd make a good carrier if he ever got the spirit. I don't think I'd 'a' gone my first day in such a storm as this, either.

FISCHER: Oh, yes, you would, Ralph. You used to sub for Haley on just as bad days as this.

RALPH: I was afraid not to; the other boys would have laid me out.

FISCHER: Ha! Ha! Well, they'd 'a' felt like it. Remember the day you upset in Black Creek and like to 'a' drown'd getting the mail out?

RALPH: Do I? Say, if I ever was sick of a job I was that day. I don't see how Doc ever kept me from getting pneumonia.

PERRY: Was that the time that all you had with you was one letter?

RALPH: No, that was Mack. He went all the way round one raw November day with one letter; great big fat one from New York City for Amanda Jacobs. She met him at the box and opened the letter and it was a washing machine ad. Lord! Mack was mad.

[Enter HANK PHILLIPS, a lean, rat-faced fellow about forty years old, inclined to shiftlessness, not so well-dressed as the others, chewing tobacco and expectorating with much energy.]

HANK: By gosh, it's gittin' colder every minute.

FISCHER: Good-morning, Mr. Phillips, you coming in to see about carrying the mail on route three?

HANK: See what?

RALPH: You coming in to take Bill's route?

HANK: Yes, like thunder! A man would freeze to death before he got out of the first drift.

FISCHER: Well, I was going to say you was probably too late. George Guyer's been here and spoke about it. He's down to the barn now looking over his outfit to see if he wants to tackle it.

HANK: Why, anybody's a fool to start out such a day as this. I'll bet George won't take it. I'll wait for the examination. That decides the thing, anyhow.

542

PERRY: Look here, Hank! Bill Snyder's went worse days than this. Anybody that's after Bill Snyder's job will have to do Bill Snyder's work.

HANK: To hell with Bill Snyder's work. I don't look like a fool, do I? What do you care about it?

FISCHER: Ben's got a carload of cattle in for Charley Ward, and he's got to get him word, and the wire's down.

HANK: They can go to the devil for all of me.

[Enter DOCTOR GOODSON, a tall, grave, elderly man.]

FISCHER: Good-morning, Doc! Is it cold enough for you?

DOC GOODSON: Yes, and there's wind enough and sleet enough. Have the carriers gone?

FISCHER: No, but they'll be going in a few minutes.

DOC GOODSON: Good! I've got some medicine to go out. This is for John Taylor on route one; and put this in for Herbert Pierson out on route three. [He hands FISCHER a small package.] It's medicine for his wife. She's awfully bad, but she has a fighting chance. I was out yesterday and left her all of those drops I had made up, but it wasn't enough. I called out this morning and Herbert said they thought she was a little better, but they were about out of medicine. I could hardly hear him and just as I started to tell him I couldn't come, but would send some by the carrier, something snapped and I couldn't hear him at all. Central said she thought the wire went down.

PERRY: Yes, I tried to call to Ward's a bit ago and I couldn't get anything.

DOC GOODSON: What's the matter at Ward's?

PERRY: He's got a carload of cattle in. They'll some of them die if he doesn't get 'em to shelter.

DOC GOODSON: Who'd you get to take route three now, Sherm?

FISCHER: We ain't got nobody, Doc. That's just the trouble. They won't take it in this storm. The other boys are going, but it looks like route three won't, unless George Guyer takes it.

[GEORGE GUYER enters in time to hear the last sentence.]

DOC GOODSON: Here's George now. He's just the boy for a carrier's job. Give it to him.

GEORGE: Not on your life you don't. It's getting worse every minute. My horses ain't fit to face this anyway; they couldn't make the drifts. I'd go if it wasn't for that.

DOC GOODSON: You can have my horse, George.

GEORGE: I—I—I don't want to take anybody else's horse out into this and kill him.

FISCHER: One of 'em'll just have to go now. You all know Martha Pierson. She's mighty sick. [The telephone rings inside.] Answer that, Mack. Me and the carrier boys wants the mail to go because that's our job, and because route three ain't never missed a day since it was started. You may not care anything about that, but you can't turn down Doc Goodson when he's trying to get medicine to Martha Pierson.

GEORGE: Is she worse?

DOC GOODSON: No, she's some better and may have a chance to pull through if I can get some more medicine out to her.

GEORGE: Why can't you go, Doc?

DOC GOODSON: I've got to take care of the Bradley twins. Diphtheria. I'm going down there right now.

[FISCHER and the DOCTOR talk aside.]

GEORGE: [Speaking rather low to HANK.] Was you figuring on taking it, Hank?

HANK: Not in this blizzard, I won't. Go on and take it if you want to.

GEORGE: Man, a fellow'd freeze to death! Let Doc take his own medicine; that's his business.

HANK: He'll have another patient if he can get somebody to go out in this storm.

[Enter EDWARD MCDONALD with mail pouches. He is a small, wiry man about forty-five years old.]

MACK: That was Bill again wanting to know if you'd got somebody for his route yet. Said he'd called down to Tom Beeks and he wouldn't take it. I told him some of the boys were here now and I thought would go.

GEORGE: Well, you've got another think coming if you were thinking of me.

MACK: Well, Bill says his mail has to go whether anybody else's went or not. Said his record shouldn't be broke.

DOC GOODSON: It's got to go for Herbert Pierson's wife, and you fellows ought to be ashamed not to take it.

MACK: That's what I say.

HANK: George's the first one applied.

GEORGE: What's Bill interested for? He's quit.

DOC GOODSON: A man like Bill Snyder never quits.

FISCHER: Well, here's somebody's chance for a hundred-and-fifty-dollars-a-month job and the mail's got to go this morning.

GEORGE: Some fellows may want the job bad enough to face this blizzard for it, but I don't.

HANK: Days like this don't come once in ten years. A fellow might carry that route half a lifetime and never hit a storm like this again. Bill said I stood as good a chance as the next fellow in the examination. I'll take it when it comes, and try to get on that way, but I'm going right back to my fire on a day like this. Give me my mail, Sherm; that's what I came for. [FISCHER goes behind the general delivery window and hands out mail.]

GEORGE: Same here. [As he gets his mail.] Let everybody look out for their own business.

HANK: If you want to send that medicine, Doc, go hire somebody to take it. It'll be lots quicker than mailing it.

DOC GOODSON: That's what I'll do, but with a storm like this on I'd rather trust Uncle Sam's carrier to get there than anybody I can hire. That was Bill Snyder's way. If he knew Martha Pierson was depending on him for medicine that might be all that could save her life, he'd get there and laugh at a blizzard.

MACK: Have you tried Jess Mills yet? He said yesterday he was going to take the examination.

FISCHER: [Who has returned from handing out the mail.] No, I ain't tried him.

GEORGE: He'll be over at the garage.

DOC GOODSON: Well, I don't know what to do. I can't wait much longer. Those drops have got to start out there pretty soon. I wish Bill Snyder knew how bad that mail ought to go.

PERRY: He wouldn't give a damn. He'd go the round just as quick with nothing but a last week's newspaper.

[Enter GRANT from the mail room with pouches and a parcel post package.]

RALPH: Ready, Grant?

GRANT: Yes. Your mail up?

RALPH: All but about three miles. I'd better get to it; I'll be the last one out. [He goes out.]

GRANT: Ready, Mack?

MACK: Yes, we'll stop at the garage and have them send Jess over.

FISCHER: Do. As quick as you can.

HANK: [To GEORGE, at one side where they are looking at newspapers.] What's he got to do with it?

GEORGE: Oh, he's got some ads he wants somebody to freeze to death to carry around.

HANK: Some people ain't got no sense at all.

[The telephone rings inside.]

FISCHER: I'll bet that's Bill again.

RALPH: [In mail room.] Sherm, here's Bill wants to talk to you again.

FISCHER: Coming. [FISCHER goes out.]

546

ANDERSON: I wish Bill would come down. We could use him in putting on some tags.

[PERRY goes to the general delivery window.]

PERRY: [Speaking through the window.] Is all the mail up?

RALPH: Yes, all for the boxes.

[PERRY goes to a box and takes out some mail which he starts to look at. ANDERSON does the same.]

[Enter JESS MILLS. Under his overcoat he has on a pair of greasy mechanic's union-alls. He has the grimy appearance of a garage hand just called from his work.]

JESS: By Whilikers, what d'you know about such a day? It's gettin' worse all the time. Where's Sherm? The boss said he wanted to see me.

PERRY: He does, Jess. Didn't you want Bill Snyder's job as carrier on route three?

JESS: I sure do. I went down yesterday and seen him about it, and he said I stood as good a chance as anybody.

ANDERSON: Well, you stand a better. The other applicants have all laid down on the job this morning, and you're the last one. You're the man we're looking for. I knew we'd find somebody to go.

JESS: Go! The carriers ain't going this morning, are they?

Doc GOODSON: Sure they are, Jess. Uncle Sam's mail has to go.

JESS: Well, they don't get this chicken out on a day like this! Not much!

GEORGE: Another guy with brains.

Doc GOODSON: Jess, I've got to get some medicine out this morning to Martha Pierson.

JESS: Well, take it yourself, or have somebody.

HANK: That's what I told him, Jess.

FISCHER: [Entering from the mail room.] Jess, Bill just phoned again. It's the third time. Said his mail never had missed a day and it had to go this morning.

Doc Goodson: Did you tell him about Martha Pierson?

Perry: Did you tell him about the cattle?

Anderson: Did you tell him about the ads?

Fischer: No, he hung up before I could tell him anything except they had all laid down on the job but Jess. If you take the mail to-day, Jess, Bill will see that you get the regular job all right. You know there's some politics in choosing the appointee from among the highest in the examination and you're in the right party and so's Bill, and he's got a pull with the Congressman. I can swear you in as temporary carrier right now.

Jess: You'll swear the devil! I'm not risking freezing to death to carry a bunch of letters to some darn farmers. I've got too good a job in the garage. Bill's too particular about this route three. Let it go to-day. He's quit anyway. One miss in fifteen years won't hurt 'em. The other boys didn't go, did they?

Fischer: Sure they went.

Jess: Well, they're damn fools.

[Ralph comes in with mail pouches.]

Ralph: Yes, that's what I'd 'a' thought once, but after you're with it you see it different.

Doc Goodson: Ralph, can't you skip the regulations once and take route three? He can, can't he, Sherm? You haven't anything important to go.

Ralph: How do I know, Doc? I can't tell what's in these mail sacks. They've got to go.

George: Hop to it if you want to. It's not for me.

Hank: You don't get any thanks for it.

Ralph: Don't you believe it. [Begins wrapping up and putting on mail pouches.] Those people out there swear by us. They're waiting for us now, phoning down the line as far as they can to ask if we're coming. They're getting ready to meet us at the big drifts and have something hot to drink at the box, and if night catches us or we can't go on or come back, every house out there's got a hot supper and a good bed for us.

JESS: Well, not for mine.

DOC GOODSON: Boys, I don't know just what the pay is on this route, but I'll give ten dollars extra to the one that will take the mail this morning. Herbert Pierson's wife has got to have that medicine.

PERRY: Yes, and I'll give ten more.

JESS: Well, one of you guys go. You ain't got nothing else to do.

HANK: Why, God Almighty, man, I wouldn't ride that twenty-five miles in this blizzard for twenty-five dollars a mile. Why, a man would freeze to death stuck up on a horse with a half bushel of mail around his waist.

JESS: Well, Sherm, it wouldn't pay me. I'll make ten dollars today in the garage. George, you take it.

HANK: Sure! You were the first one down here.

GEORGE: Oh, I might not get the route if I did go. I'm not in Bill's party.

HANK: I'm not either. That's the trouble nowadays; you got to have pull for everything.

PERRY: Well, here's your chance to get it. I know Bill Snyder. He'll pull for the man that's got nerve enough to take this mail this morning.

JESS: Oh, I don't know, I stand pretty well with the county chairman.

DOC GOODSON: Well, if the mail isn't going I'll have to get somebody to take that medicine out. Can I get it back, Sherm?

FISCHER: Sure.

PERRY: I'll pay half of it, Doc, and have him stop at Ward's and tell Charley about the cattle. Who do you suppose we can get?

FISCHER: It's somebody's duty to take this mail.

GEORGE: Duty, hell!

549

[BILL SNYDER now comes in. He is a small man, white-haired, bronze-faced and wrinkled; as straight as an arrow and his keen blue eyes show a man of iron nerve. Though over sixty-five, he has a face of fifty and a walk of thirty. He speaks clearly and sharply. Of all those who have come in he is the only one who doesn't go to the fire shivering with the cold. He speaks as he comes in.]

BILL SNYDER: Who's taking the mail on route three?

ANDERSON: Why, here's Bill. Bill, there's a—

PERRY: Bill, I've got a—

DOC GOODSON: Bill, Martha Pierson needs—

BILL: Which one's taking it?

FISCHER: Can't get anybody, Bill. The fellows that wanted it yesterday and day before don't want it this morning.

DOC GOODSON: Bill, I wish—

PERRY: It's just the day—

BILL: George? Hank?

GEORGE and HANK: No.

BILL: Jess, don't you want the route?

JESS: Not this morning.

BILL: You're going, ain't you, Ralph?

RALPH: Bet your life.

BILL: Mack and Grant gone?

RALPH: Just left, and I've got to start. My horse will freeze standing out there. Fight it out, you boys.

[He adjusts his pouches and goes out into the storm.]

BILL: [To FISCHER.] My mail up?

FISCHER: Yes, the boys put it up yesterday, and I put up number nineteen.

[BILL whirls on his heel and goes into the mail room.]

ANDERSON: I'll give Bill five dollars if he'll take that mail this morning.

DOC GOODSON: I'll give ten.

PERRY: So will I.

THE RESIGNATION OF BILL SNYDER

[BILL comes out of the mail room, strapping on mail pouches.]

BILL: You sent in my resignation yet, Sherm?

FISCHER: No, here it is.

BILL: Give it here. [He takes the resignation, tears it in two and tosses it into the waste-basket.]

HANK: Now what the devil does that mean?

PERRY: That means you won't be a rural route carrier.

ANDERSON: But see here, Bill, what about the job in the store? I thought you was going to work for me.

BILL: Work? This is my work! You boys needn't mind about that examination. Route three mail goes. [He goes out, and the others look after him for a minute.]

THE RESIGNATION OF BILL SNYDER

[Bill comes out of the mail room, strapping on mail pouches.]

Bill: You sent in my resignation yet, Sherm?

Feretier: No, here it is.

Bill: Give it here. [He takes the resignation, tears it in two and tosses it into the waste-basket.]

Hank: Now what the devil does that mean?

Perry: That means you won't be a rural route carrier.

Anderson: But see here, Bill, what about the job in the store? I thought you was going to work for me.

Bill: Work? This is my work! You boys needn't mind about that examination. Route three mail goes. [He goes out, and the others look after him for a minute.]

RECKLESS
By Lynn Riggs

PERSONS IN THE PLAY

HANNIE RADER
PAP RADER
BUZZEY HALE
RED IKE BRAZIER
BLACK IKE BRAZIER

RECKLESS

BY the side of a road through the woods, in Indian Territory, many years ago. The back end of a covered wagon, with a box for stepping down out of it, can be seen at the left. The road, coming in at the back from deep in the woods, has been widened here by hundreds of campers. Trash and tin cans litter the roadside. A large black pot with a fire under it stands at the right. Some old camp chairs, a battered stool or two, dishes, tin pans, etc. It is near sundown of a day in June, and the air is summery and sweet.

BUZZEY HALE, a little, bluish, dried-up man, is sitting disconsolately by the fire. PAP RADER, a tall, wiry, good-natured old man, with dirty, falling-apart clothes, comes from around the wagon.

PAP RADER: Set there a-pinin'. Damned if you doan look like a ole turkey buzzard! No wonder Hannie called you Buzzey.

BUZZEY: That ain't it. Buzzey is short—fer beautiful.

PAP: Beautiful! Huh! If you're beautiful, I'm a bob-

555

tailed witch. Looky here, I doan see whut you make outa follerin' us around anyway, Mister Turkey Buzzard. They ain't nothin' dead around here fer you to chaw on. Clappin' yer wings! An' damned if that sorry face o' yourn ain't blue, too, same as a buzzard! After you've et, things must be a sight. I doan wanna be around.

BUZZEY: I ain't wantin' you around.

PAP: I'm gonna *be* around, though. Smoke that.

BUZZEY: Yeow, you'll be. If it hadn't a-been fer you, Hannie wouldn't a-left me in the first place. You done it with yer damned ole covered wagon. Tellin' her about the roads again. Remindin' her of when she uz a girl ridin' hell-bent from Arkansaw to Panhandle alongside you an' yer old womern. You brung her up. I'll say you brung her up, with her ways! Wonder I ever married her a-tall an' her with a ole man like you couldn't read a sign on a hitch-post. Whut'd you think about? Ridin' on the road, that's all you think about. From here t' Texas, and back to Wyoming and all over the cattle roads, and little shike-poke towns from here to Missouri. Stealin' chickens an' roast'n'-ears an' sich, t' keep you alive. The road! That's all you think about!

PAP: Whut you think about is plowin'.

BUZZEY: Yeow, an' makin' hay an' plantin' corn an' oats an' feedin' cattle an' shoats—livin' outa the ground, is whut I think about. I'd like to know whut's better?

PAP: This *here's* better. An' I'm tellin' you Hannie'd *orter* divorced you like she did. You ain't no kind of a man, an' yore life ain't no kind of a life fer Hannie t' be havin'. She's a strappin' girl that wants to roam, like me, an' see life 'stid of a milk churn.

BUZZEY: I'll git her back, you'll see. If I have to foller you up Salt Crick.

PAP: If you foller us too long, yer crops'll all be ruint. Here it is June an' I'll bet yer hay ain't even first cut.

BUZZEY: It's cut, Pap Rader. I got money t' h'ar me h'ard hands.

PAP: An' while you ain't there how hard you reckon they work? I used t' be a h'ard hand myself. When ole man Hardgraves uz away we'd se' down an' not git up till his buggy wheels rattled the pike comin' home from Joplin.

BUZZEY: When *I* h'ar men, I h'ar *men*. Red Ike and Black Ike Brazier—that's the kinda men *I* h'ar. I've knowed em from boys up. Ever since Hannie married me, Red Ike an' Black Ike has worked on my farm same as if it uz theirn, an' ud git the last drap of growin' out of it.

PAP: Well, I hope yer right. 'Cause if you ain't, you'll git sick an' turn bluer'n you be a'ready.

BUZZEY: I'm right, Pap Rader.

PAP: Ain't nobody right fer too long at a time, I noticed.

HANNIE'S VOICE: [From inside the wagon.] Pap!

PAP: Whut is it?

HANNIE: Pap, come 'ere!

PAP: Come 'ere, yerself. I'm busy. [To BUZZEY.] If you doan git sense enough to stop follerin' us from county to county the way you been doin' fer a week, you'll sleep here on the cold ground till you die of the shakin' aygers.

HANNIE: [From the wagon.] Pap! You heard me, you tarnation ole fool! Come a-runnin'! Cain't you hear nuthin'?

PAP: Well, whut is it? Come out here an' tell it.

HANNIE: [Sticking her head out.] I ain't got s' many clothes on. An' I doan 'spect t' come out an' give that old buzzard no free show. He's crazy enough fer a womern 'thout seein' one naked. Case you'd like t' know it, that hound of yourn is eatin' up yer hog shoulder.

PAP: [Flying around the wagon and out of sight.] Well, why in blazes diden you say so!

HANNIE: I said so. [She withdraws her head. A hound lets out a dismal wail and a series of short yelps.]

557

BUZZEY: [Going up to the wagon.] Whur'd yer Pap git a hog shoulder, Hannie? Guess he bought it—

HANNIE: [Putting her head out again.] Bought it, huh? Stole it offen the slaughter house at Claremore.

BUZZEY: I knowed it.

HANNIE: You're s' smart. [She withdraws.]

PAP: [Coming around the wagon.] I saved that dog from drownin' an' this is the way he does me. A good hog shoulder plum ruint. [He holds up a mutilated hog shoulder.] Here, might as well have it all now you've ruint it, you yeller cur. [He throws the shoulder back to the dog.] I'm goin' down along the crick bank an' see whut I c'n see.

BUZZEY: Watermelons ain't ripe yit, Pap.

PAP: Who said watermelons?

BUZZEY: Roast'n' ears 'll be ripe in July, though.

PAP: I'm gonna git a mite of hay fer the horses. Stir that stew if you're gonna stick round here. You'll be wantin' some in yer measly gullet afore long. [He starts out.] I'm gonna jist look t' see if they's any fish while I'm about it. [Turning back.] Looky here, you let Hannie alone. She ain't gonna marry you *again*. An' she ain't gonna have no *truck* with you 's long 's I'm around, you hear me?

BUZZEY: I hear you.

PAP: You better heed me. [He goes out. BUZZEY stirs the stew, tastes it, and is about to pour some in a bowl when he hears singing down the road. He puts the bowl down hastily, wrinkles his forehead, trying to make out something. HANNIE comes out of the wagon and down the steps. She is a buxom, well-made girl about twenty, with black snapping eyes and a rich, vulgar, earthy humor. She crosses over past the fire.]

BUZZEY: Hannie. [She stops.] Hannie, you ain't runnin' away from me, air you?

HANNIE: I doan know you from Adam.

BUZZEY: Don't you do me this a-way, Hannie.

558

HANNIE: What a-way?

BUZZEY: Not havin' no words with me, even.

HANNIE: Why're you follerin' us all the way from Vinita, me and Pap?

BUZZEY: I cain't he'p it. Cain't you come back to me?

HANNIE: Not to you ner no one like you. I want me a man, not a broomstick. Besides, I had enough of bein' a farmer's wife.

BUZZEY: It uz cause you'd been s' sharp to me, I done whut I done. You wouldn't a-got no divorce from me if someone hadden fixed it up fer you t' find me the way you did.

HANNIE: Oh, woulden I? Sich a womern I found you with too! You must been in a bad way. Who fixed it then?

BUZZEY: I ain't sayin'.

HANNIE: Well, whoever fixed it, you fixed yerself with me.

BUZZEY: Hannie, come on back! The—the ca'ves even doan know me. Old Roan kicks at me ever time I go in the barn. They won't have nuthin' t' do with *me*. They're missin' you, I reckon.

HANNIE: Well, I been missed by ca'ves and horses afore. I'm that kind of a womern. But I never heared of no dumb animals dyin' of a broke heart. Quit a-botherin' me now.

BUZZEY: Aw, Hannie, lemme go with you. Air you goin' to pick up sticks?

HANNIE: No, I ain't.

BUZZEY: Er find wild ingerns? I'll help you do whutever you're a-goin' fer. Guess I'll foller you.

HANNIE: Guess you won't, Mister Buzzey Hale. I ain't gonna do nuthin' you c'n he'p me do. [She goes out.]

[The song down the road comes nearer. BUZZEY listens, uncertain and worried. Then he straightens up decisively

and is a rod of cold anger, when RED IKE and BLACK IKE
BRAZIER burst into sight through the trees along the road.
They have on straw hats, overalls, dirty blue shirts, heavy
brogans, and are leaning on each other's shoulders, singing
loudly. BLACK IKE's hair is coal black, RED's a flaming red.
They are stupid and elfin at the same time. Seeing BUZZEY,
they stop short, and make a sudden instinctive move to run
away, which they quickly suppress.]

BUZZEY: Well, by God! It's you, is it?

RED IKE: [Swallowing hard.] Yeow, it's us.

BLACK IKE: Red Ike and Black Ike—*both* of us.

BUZZEY: Red Ike and Black Ike, hell! Of all the sorry,
mangy—dirty— Whut in hell're you doin' here anyhow?
Whut 'd you mean flyin' off leavin' my farm t' run itself?
How long you been gone? You're two days away now!
I'll bet the hogs've died fer slop! I'll bet the hay's
burnt up in the field! I'll bet the corn's jist bakin' in the
row—

RED IKE: Is this yore campin' outfit?

BUZZEY: [Outraged.] Campin'!

BLACK IKE: You a campin' man now, Mister Hale? We
didden know whur you'd went at.

RED IKE: You got some soup?

BUZZEY: Soup!

BLACK IKE: We're powerful hongry. Ain't et in a day.

RED IKE: Been a-singin' t' keep up our sperrits.

BUZZEY: Singin'!

BLACK IKE: Et some strawberries, though.

BUZZEY: I don't keer if you starve! Whut'd you leave
my farm fur! Thought I could trust it to you.

BLACK IKE: Mister Hale, we never thunk to a-run onto
you, I swear t' my time. We didden know whur you wuz,
not showin' up. Thought mebbe you drowned in the bottom
some'ers.

RED IKE: We uz a-lookin' fer someone else.

560

BLACK IKE: Is this the—? [He is looking over past the wagon.] By gum it is!

RED IKE: It's the horses.

BUZZEY: You git back quick 's you c'n hotfoot it, both of you. I'd orter thrash you 'thin a inch of yer lives! *Git*, I tell you!

RED IKE: We're gonna stay. [He sits down, cross-legged.]

BLACK IKE: [Following suit.] We're gonna set here and stay, ain't we, Red?

BUZZEY: You're f'ard, both of you!

RED IKE: Suits me. Cain't make *me* mad.

BUZZEY: I'd orter f'ar you.

BLACK IKE: We're a 'ready done f'ard.

BUZZEY: No, you ain't! You 'greed t' he'p me git the hay in an' stay th'ough the thrashin'.

RED IKE: We'll he'p you.

BUZZEY: Well, don't set here. Git back like I told you.

RED IKE: We jist come.

BUZZEY: Look here. I'd orten't t' do this—you're both so onnery—but I'll give you five dollars.

RED IKE: Le's see it. [BUZZEY hands him a bill.]

BLACK IKE: Le's see another'n. [BUZZEY hands over another. RED IKE and BLACK IKE look at each other, then hand the bills back.]

RED IKE: Don't hurry us.

BUZZEY: You better take it. Why, you're damn fools! It'll buy you near ten plugs of Horseshoe.

BLACK IKE: [Spitting.] 'Druther chew Star Navy.

BUZZEY: Well, Star Navy.

BLACK IKE: Chew Star Navy an' spit ham gravy.

BUZZEY: Look here, if I give you ten dollars apiece—no, I won't give you ten dollars.

RED IKE: Woulden take it.

BUZZEY: How much you tryin' t' bleed outa me?

RED IKE: Not any.

BUZZEY: Whut'd you come fur anyway?

RED IKE: Oh—jist seen the purty road an' started off a-follerin' it.

BLACK IKE: You cain't keep no colt in the pasture when it's summer. We uz puttin' up the mules an' I says t' Red, "Red," I says, "How about it?" An' Red says, "How about it yerself?" So up we got an' away we went till we come t' Verdigree Switch. There they uz a great to-do of a man shootin' his way into jail, so we hurry up and here we be.

BUZZEY: You got sump'n up yer sleeve.

RED IKE: Why, Mister Hale, no. No, we ain't. Mebbe you're right though. Mebbe we have got sump'n up our sleeves. [Breaking off, excitedly.] Oh! [He scrambles to his feet.]

BLACK IKE: [Doing likewise.] It's her.

RED IKE: She's a-comin'!

BLACK IKE: She's here!

HANNIE: [Coming in, ecstatically.] Hello! Howdy! Red Ike and Black Ike! *Thought* I heared yer voices!

RED IKE: Thought we'd find you!—

BLACK IKE: *Knowed* we'd find you!—

RED IKE: 'f we looked long enough—

BLACK IKE: 'n in the right place—

RED IKE: 'n on the right road.

HANNIE: If I ain't missed you!—

RED IKE: We missed *you.*

BLACK IKE: Come on back, what you say?

RED IKE: 'Spect us to work 'thout you around?

BLACK IKE: Marry the old buzzard again.

RED IKE: Put up with him.

HANNIE: Quit it! I'm s' glad to see you, I'll be promisin' to, in a minute!

BUZZEY: Hannie! Go on, promise! I'll be good to you if you come back. Git you a carpet sweeper.

BLACK IKE: Go on, promise! Think of me an' Red. Not hardly able to do no work 'thout you around.

RED IKE: Think of me an' Black. In the field honin' fer you.

BUZZEY: Think of me, why don't you, Hannie?

HANNIE: Now, now! Quit it! I'm gonna think of my-*self* a while. Here, set down and eat some soup.

BUZZEY: You ain't said you *wouldn't* come back.

HANNIE: An' I ain't said I *would*. [She gives them all soup. They sit down and eat.]

BLACK IKE: We're hungry.

RED IKE: Ain't et in a day.

HANNIE: 'S jist like ole times. Me an' Buzzey an' you Ikes settin' around. If I ain't missed you! Ever once in a while I git so homesick I'd purt' near kick paw in the pants, an' hotfoot it back. I wanta set quiet once in a while, an' drink milk out of a cold well.

BUZZEY: We got milk, Hannie. Ever since ole Reddy come in with her calf—

HANNIE: But paw's sich a goer. Has to cross that next crick, or make the next aidge of town 'fore sundown. Lissen to me, I'm gonna tell you sump'n. Men is s' crazy. Some wants to set on a farm till they dry up an' blow away—like Buzzey here. Or some wants to go streakin' across the country, hell-bent, like a dose of salts th'ough a widder womern—like paw. If they uz jist a half-way crazy man who liked to streak, an' liked to set—*both*. A nonsensical strappin' man who had a good time settin' *or* streakin'— but who had a *good time*— [She breaks off.] Now tell me things.

BLACK IKE: Whut about?

HANNIE: Oh, anything. The way you used to.

BLACK IKE: [To RED.] 'Bout the ghostes?

RED IKE: On Mabel Gardner's bed post?

HANNIE: I heared that.

BLACK IKE: I know! The man in the sack.

RED IKE: Chinaman!

BLACK IKE: Sewed in a gunny sack.

RED IKE: Mad as a steer!

BLACK IKE: Hung up to the ceiling!

HANNIE: I heared that, too.

BLACK IKE: Oh! She's heared that. Oh, I know! We'll tell her about Reckless! Wanta hear about Reckless?

HANNIE: Who's Reckless?

BLACK IKE: Well, we seen sich a sight. Didn't we, Red?

RED IKE: Down at the Switch as we come th'ough.

BLACK IKE: A man th'owed in the jail fer gettin' drunk.

RED IKE: He got drunk an' crazy an' wild. An' he yelled. My, how he yelled!

BLACK IKE: Whut wuz it he yelled? "Borned in Texas—" How'd it go?

RED IKE: [Loudly.]

> Wild an' reckless,
> Borned in Texas,
> Suckled by a bear,
> Steel backbone,
> Tail screwed on,
> Twelve feet long,
> Dare any son of a gun to step on it!

HANNIE: Purty!

BUZZEY [Disgusted.] Purty!

RED IKE: 'Nen the law got a-holt of him, an' the jedge said "Twelve days in jail, one fer ever foot of yer long tail." So they went to th'ow him in jail an' he kicked the jedge offen the bench an' made jist plum hash outa the court room first 'fore they got him in the calaboose.

HANNIE: Good!

BUZZEY: [Disgusted.] Good!

RED IKE: My, a big hulky, curly-headed, han'some ring-tail-tooter, wuzn't he, Black?

HANNIE: An' whur is he?

RED IKE: Sh! Down the road a piece.

HANNIE: Outa jail?

BLACK IKE: Shore. Lissen. Me'n Red seen him, s' we come along. Like to scairt us to death, too. Come up on us, and said, "I broke outa jail, an' if you tell on me, I'll break yer head." My, we woulden tell on him, would we, Red?

HANNIE: Down the road there.

BLACK IKE: [Pointing back.] That road right there.

BUZZEY: You ain't interested in a man like that, air you, Hannie? A man 'at breaks laws, an' don't have no home, an' goes shootin' around—

HANNIE: Shet up about it. I hate a man like that.

BUZZEY: That's whut I thought. Here comes yer pap. [PAP RADER comes in with an armful of hay for the horses. He drops it in astonishment.]

PAP RADER: Red Ike and Black Ike! [Gleefully.] I knowed it, I knowed it! [To BUZZEY.] Whut'd I tell you about h'ard hands!—Hee! Hee! Knowed they wouldn't work 'thout you around! [There is a pistol shot at back, quite near.]

HANNIE: [Rushing over to PAP.] Hey, Pap, they's a man comin' along the road! [In an excited rush, thumping PAP on the chest at every sentence.] Wild an' reckless, borned in Texas! A tail twelve feet long! He shot his way into jail and outa jail, an' he's comin' along that road there, an' heavens an' earth, whut're you gonna do!

RECKLESS' VOICE:

> Wild an' reckless,
> Borned in Texas!

HANNIE: Hear that! It's him. I'm gonna run in the wagon, quick!

PAP RADER: Why, Hannie! Nuthin' won't hurt you. We got guns.

BUZZEY: Don't you be afeard, little womern. I'll pertect you. An' in the mornin', we'll go back home.

HANNIE: Why, you little dried-up, stinkin', blue-nosed ole buzzard smellin' of a dead cow in the summer time! Go home with you? [She laughs uproariously.] Go home with a dead stick! I got better idys 'n that. I'm gonna go in the wagon.

BUZZEY: Whut fer, Hannie?

HANNIE: I'm gonna put flour on my face, an' purty myself up—that's whut fer! [She goes up into the wagon.]

BUZZEY: Now whut on earth's come over her?

PAP RADER: Damned if I know. Whut's this about a man?

BUZZEY: Why, Red an' Black says this is a wild crazy han'some man, who don't respect no law, ner live nowhur, an' says he uz borned in Texas, an' he's comin' along the road an'—

PAP RADER: Hmm. Oh! Texas.

BUZZEY: Whut'd you mean—*Texas?*

PAP RADER: [With an amused chuckle.] Hannie. That's whur *she* uz borned at.

RECKLESS' VOICE: [Coming nearer.]

Steel backbone,
Tail screwed on,
Twelve feet long,
Dare any son of a gun to step on it!

ACROSS THE BORDER
By Colin Clements

PERSONS IN THE PLAY

MRS. HOPPER
ED HOPPER
FRANK HENDERSON

ACROSS THE BORDER

THE main room of an adobe ranch house somewhere
north of El Paso, Texas. The only bit of color in
this somber low-ceilinged room is the homespun curtains
which are drawn over the small window at the back—a
feminine touch in a masculine world. A heavy door opens
into the patio; in the opposite wall is a square hole, from
which a short ladder is hung, opening into the sleeping loft.
Near the center of the room stands a heavy table. A lighted
lantern, hung on a wire from a rafter above, throws a circle
of yellow light on the table and catches part of a kitchen
chair which is pushed up close to it. The rest of the room
is in shadow. Against the wall at the left is a rough Spanish
cupboard, the lower part of which has swinging doors, kept
in place by a heavy lock.

Throughout, there is the suggestion of howling wind and
the sound of fine sand blown against the window.

MRS. HOPPER is seated in the chair near the table. She is
a woman of thirty-six or -seven. Although her body is slight,
there is in her quick nervous movements a suggestion of un-

derlying reserve power. Her large eyes have a haunted look; her face is drawn.

The wind outside becomes louder, then gradually dies away. The howl of a distant coyote is heard, a clock in the loft strikes twelve.

MRS. HOPPER starts suddenly, moves to the window, pushes back the curtain, and stands for a moment looking out into the night; slowly she shakes her head, goes to the door, makes sure the bolt is in place, then turns and walks back to the chair near the table. She looks toward the sleeping loft, half smiles, then sinks down wearily into the chair.

There is a soft rap at the door. MRS. HOPPER lifts her head and waits. The rap is repeated. She rises and moves to the door.

MRS. HOPPER: [Softly.] Who's there?

ED: It's me! Ed.

MRS. HOPPER: Say it louder.

ED: Oh, hell, open the door! It's Ed, I tell you! Can't you recognize your own husband's voice when you hear it? Open the door!

MRS. HOPPER: I am! I am! [She pushes back the heavy bolt.]

ED: [Stands in the doorway for a moment bewildered, as if the light blinded him.] For God's sake, woman! [He turns and bolts the door, then turns toward his wife and stands brushing the thick yellow dust from his clothes as he speaks.] Did y' want me to stand out there all night! [He walks toward the table, into the light. ED HOPPER is a tall, thin man with shifting eyes and a narrow, weak face. He is unshaven and dirty.]

MRS. HOPPER: Ed! You're back! You can't know how glad I am to see you. And Jackie hasn't slept for nights— just waitin' for his daddy to get back. [She holds up her arms, but he brushes her aside and moves closer to the

570

table.] What is it, Ed? What is the matter? I'll make you a hot cup of coffee. Are you sick?

ED: [Unbuckles his belt and holster, throws them down on the table.] There ain't anything the matter . . . and I ain't sick, either.

MRS. HOPPER: [Coming closer to her husband.] Ed, you've brought back the cattle they stole from us? You've brought 'em back, ain't you?

ED: Aw, don't stand there askin' damn fool questions. Can't y' see I don't feel like talkin'?

MRS. HOPPER: Oh, then I'll make you some coffee, Ed. Won't take a minute.

ED: Don't want any coffee.

MRS. HOPPER: Warm you up. Always cold ridin' at night this time of year.

ED: I said I don't want no coffee.

MRS. HOPPER: [Stands looking at him several moments.] Ed, what is it? What's the matter with y'? You been down in Mexico for five days and naturally I want to know about things. Five days is a long time without a man in the house.

ED: Only five days? That's all I been gone? Five damn long years it seems to me.

MRS. HOPPER: You caught the thieves? You caught them?

ED: What?

MRS. HOPPER: Y' wouldn't come back till you'd caught 'em, I know.

ED: That's where you're damn wrong.

MRS. HOPPER: [Sinks down into a chair.] Y' haven't brought 'em back . . . you haven't brought back our cattle, Ed?

ED: No; we ain't brung back your cattle. At least, I didn't.

MRS. HOPPER: What'll we do now, I wonder?

ED: Just like you! Like you. What about me, eh? Why don't y' ask about me? Hell of a lot you care, don't y'?

Think more of a few damned head of steers than y' do your own husband.

MRS. HOPPER: You know better than that, Ed. It's just . . . I . . . what'll we do?

ED: I don't know what you're plannin' o' doin' 'n' what's more I don't give a damn. But I can tell you right now I know damn well what I'm going to do. [He takes out his watch.] What time is it? M' watch is stopped—every damned thing's stopped! Sand! Sand! Sand! I can feel it between my teeth. Sand! What time is it? D' y' hear what I'm askin' y'? What time is it? D' y' hear what I'm askin' y'? What time is it?

MRS. HOPPER: [Whose thoughts have been wandering.] It's a little after midnight, Ed.

ED: [Looking at his watch disgustedly.] There. Guess that's done for, too. Plugged with sand. I'll leave that turnip behind for you. [He flings the watch across the room.]

MRS. HOPPER: Did Henderson . . . and the other ranchers . . . come back with you?

ED: What? Come back with me? I don't know what they've done 'n' let me tell you I don't care. I don't give a damn if that's any consolation to y'.

MRS. HOPPER: [Rises slowly.] But you wouldn't come back and let them go on without you!

ED: Oh, wouldn't I? What do y' think this is standing here talkin' to y'? A ghost?

MRS. HOPPER: You couldn't let them go on alone, Ed.

ED: [Leers at his wife.] Well, that's just what I did do. I gave 'em the slip.

MRS. HOPPER: Ed!

ED: Sure, gave 'em the slip. And what's you or anybody else goin' to do about it? A man don't have to go on lookin' for cattle thieves all his life 'less he's a mind to.

MRS. HOPPER: [Stands looking across the table; the lines

of her tired face harden; she pauses a moment before she speaks.] I'm ashamed of you. I'm ashamed of you, Ed.

ED: I don't give a whoop in hell if you are . . . or if you ain't. One way or 'nother is the same to me. It's not my game, this ridin' across the desert for days, ridin' across hell after a gang of dirty greasers. Shootin' 'em down like dogs because they happen to rustle a few head of cattle. It's not my game, I tell y'! And, by God, I can't stand it . . . I can't stand it. This life down here in this God-forsaken hole is drivin' me crazy. I can't go through with it. I can't go through with it! [MRS. HOPPER takes several steps toward the sleeping loft, then turns back.]

MRS. HOPPER: We've got to get back what those Mexicans have stolen from us, Ed.

ED: That ain't so easy.

MRS. HOPPER: If we can get back the cattle they've taken from us, another two years will see us clear, Ed. Clear, with our heads above water. Clear, with a little money in the bank and a sure future. Clear, with a chance of making good in a big way—all the chance in the world. But if we don't get back those cattle, Ed, we'll have to start all over again. We'll be right back where we were eight years ago.

ED: Not me! I ain't droppin' no more sweat into this here desert. Not me! I'm through!

MRS. HOPPER: There's no other way out . . . just hard work.

ED: That may be your way of lookin' at things.

MRS. HOPPER: I tell you, Ed, there's no other way of lookin' at them.

ED: Oh, ain't there? I'm not so sure about that as you seem to be. [His mouth curls into a sneer.] You're always so damned sure about everything. Look here, Martha, I might as well tell y' straight. I'm clearin' out.

MRS. HOPPER: What do y' mean, Ed?

ED: Just what I said. I'm leavin'. You know how I hate

573

ranchin'. Hated it to begin with—every year I've hated it worse 'n' worse, until—well, the last couple of years have been hell on earth. I hate this life. Hate it! Now, do you understand?

MRS. HOPPER: Hate it? Who hasn't hated it at times? But when y' start a thing you've got to go on to the finish. You and I have got to see this thing through. When we ride out of El Paso it's got to be with our heads up. I tell you—

ED: Maybe that's your way . . . I guess it is. I wish y' luck. You always was so damned superior. Comes from readin' books 'n' things, I s'pose. Well, you can do as you like. I'm goin' . . . I'm clearin' out the quickest 'n' shortest way. I'm through.

MRS. HOPPER: Then you mean this place of ours is for sale? You're selling out, is that it?

ED: Don't ask so damned many questions.

MRS. HOPPER: I've got a right to know. Why shouldn't I ask questions?

ED: 'Cause I don't want y' to. I'll tend to my affairs in my own way.

MRS. HOPPER: I'm your wife, Ed.

ED: Wife, hell! You've been the man of this ranch ever since I can remember. Always nagging at me to do this . . . nagging at me to do that till I'm damn near out of my head.

MRS. HOPPER: That's a lie! I've never nagged you!

ED: Well, maybe not nagged me. Leastwise y' ain't done it like other women do . . . but your damned coldness . . . that's what gets me. Hell! To you this old adobe shanty 'n' a few head of cattle is everything there is in life.

MRS. HOPPER: [Turns and looks at the ladder, and shakes her head.] No; not everything. He's everything. This is just a beginning . . . a beginning. Look here, Ed, you know why we came out here and—

ED: You've been throwing that up in my face ever since

574

I can remember. You're damned right I know why we came out here. But I guess by this time my lungs is as good as anyone else's, if that's what y' mean. Anyhow, what's lungs compared to a lot of other things in life, eh? What's th' use livin' if y' got t' just keep on grubbin' . . . slavin' out your heart 'n' soul in a rotten place like this? I won't stand it, I tell you!

MRS. HOPPER: [Moves over and lays her hand on his shoulders.] You'd best turn in and get some rest, Ed. You're tired out . . . that's the trouble. You're talkin' wild tonight, but after a good rest you'll feel better about things.

ED: Bah! That's always your attitude. Always know better than anybody else about things. So damned high 'n' mighty.

MRS. HOPPER: Ed, I'll do anything within reason. [There is a tense pause.] What is it, Ed? Tell me what's the matter.

ED: I s'pose if I was a steer you'd call me locoed. Well, I ain't. I know what I'm sayin' 'n' why I'm sayin' it.

MRS. HOPPER: Ed, we've had other nights like this. We've gone through all this a hundred times before. I tell you, Ed, we've got to stick here. There's no other way out right now. Sometime . . . somehow, we'll be on top. [She holds out her hand.] I'm still your partner, Ed.

ED: [Ignoring her hand.] Partner, hell! Yes; maybe we have been through all this before . . . and I've heard all this talk of yours before, too. I've heard it so often that it's gettin' funny.

MRS. HOPPER: Then what are we going to do? What do you want us to do?

ED: I told you before what I'm goin' to do. [He pounds on the table.] Martha—

MRS. HOPPER: Sh-h-h. You'll wake up Jackie!

ED: I know damned well what I'm goin' to do. Eight years ago, or something like that, we come out here to Texas

. . . a couple of greenhorns. Just like kids. Everything was fine . . . everything was an adventure. But, my God, we've paid for that adventure ten times over. We've paid for it! Why, I'm an old man and you—you—

MRS. HOPPER: What . . . what am I, Ed?

ED: Y' was purty once, Martha.

MRS. HOPPER: Ain't I any more?

ED: Just a slave to a piece of grazin' land. Just a chunk of gumbo . . . mud . . . like everybody else down here. That's what soil does to you . . . drags y' down till you're just like it. I tell y' there's more in life than this 'n' I'm goin' to find it.

[He moves to the window, takes down a heavy key from a nail, walks to the cupboard and throws open the lower doors. He takes out a battered tin box, moves to the table and, under the light of the hanging lantern, fills a small bag with gold pieces.]

MRS. HOPPER: [With astonishment.] Money?

ED: [Shaking the bag in her face.] See that? See that? I'm goin' out where it can buy things . . . I'm goin' out 'n' see if there ain't something left in life but drudgery 'n' backaches 'n'—well, I'm taking a fling.

MRS. HOPPER: Ed, where'd you get that money? Where did you get it?

ED: Who wants to know?

MRS. HOPPER: I do, Ed . . . I do.

ED: Well, it's like this . . . where I got this money ain't none of your business, Martha. See?

MRS. HOPPER: It is.

ED: I reckon y' thought you was the only clever one around this ranch, eh? Well, you've got another think comin'. I can pull a deal off once in awhile myself.

MRS. HOPPER: Tell me, Ed. Where did you get that money?

ED: The ranch is sold, in a manner o' speakin'. Sold, see?

Jim Marston, they call him Texas Jim around here, is movin'
in tomorrow. Now you know.

MRS. HOPPER: [Speaking with tremendous difficulty.]
You mean we don't own this place any more? You mean,
you've sold us out?

ED: That's it. Yes; out from under. [He puts the money
into an inside pocket.] Plumb clean. I'm ridin' the pinto
pony over to the depot 'n' takin' the early train for 'Frisco.

MRS. HOPPER: You're ridin' over tonight?

ED: Heard me, didn't y'?

MRS. HOPPER: You mean—you're going alone?

ED: Yes; damn it—alone.

MRS. HOPPER: Y' can't do it, Ed. You can't just go out
like this without—

ED: Eh?

MRS. HOPPER: Y' can't do it! Y' can't leave us like this—
me and Jackie. What is it? What's happened, Ed? What
are you holding back on me? What makes you like this?
Tell me. There's something you're keeping from me.

ED: I tell y', Martha, this country has got me . . . it's
got under my skin. I'm gettin' out of it . . . I'm gettin'
out of it fast.

MRS. HOPPER: You've done something, Ed. You ain't
tellin' me the whole truth. [She rushes to the door and
stands before it.] You ain't leavin' us. You ain't goin'
out alone, either.

ED: Alone? Aw, hell, what kind of a woman have you
been to me? Tell y', Martha, if y' want to know, there's
a dame up in 'Frisco who—

MRS. HOPPER: So that's it?

ED: What of it?

MRS. HOPPER: Just leavin' us flat.

ED: You'll get along. I ain't worryin' my head none
about you. You've got the guts to make anythin' go. I'll

say that for you. I ain't worryin' about how you'll make out . . . and I ain't holdin' anythin' against you, Martha. It's just that you 'n' me don't pull together in the same harness.

MRS. HOPPER: I ain't thinkin' about me, Ed. I'm thinkin' about our boy. What about Jackie—what about him?

ED: Aw, you're his mother, ain't y'? What's the brat t' me?

MRS. HOPPER: [Shuddering involuntarily.] Ed!

ED: He's nothin' t' me—nothin'.

MRS. HOPPER: He's yours and mine together. He's the one thing we've got that's worth goin' on for.

ED: He's your kid, not mine. Dead spittin' image of y'. He speaks your language, not mine—gets more like y' every day. What's he t' me? Nothin'. We ain't got a damn thing in common—not a thing. [He shrugs his shoulders.] Aw, hell, what's the use standin' here arguin' all night? I'm off.

MRS. HOPPER: No, y' ain't neither, Ed.

ED: You ain't stoppin' me.

MRS. HOPPER: Y' can't, Ed, y' can't go!

ED: Get out of my way.

MRS. HOPPER: You can't just go away and leave me alone with the kid like this—you can't do it, I tell y'.

ED: Get out of my way or by God—get out of my way, woman.

[He grabs his wife's arm, twists it until she winces with pain, then throws her back into the room. He reaches for the heavy bar and is about to lift it, when there is a sharp rap. In surprise and fear ED backs away. The rap is repeated. He turns toward the window at the back and makes sure the curtains are drawn. There is a frightened, haunted look in his eyes as he glances hopelessly around the room for some means of escape.]

MRS. HOPPER: It's somebody.

578

ED: There's somebody out there in the patio.

MRS. HOPPER: I'll see who it is.

ED: Wait!

MRS. HOPPER: No; I'm opening the door, Ed.

ED: Wait, damn y'! [He points to the cupboard.] If it's anyone t' see me, y' don't know nothin' about me. See? Y' don't know where I am—y' ain't seen me since I started out with the others to look for the cattle thieves. See? Martha, what you said a little while ago about us bein' partners with me. We're stickin' together in everything. You've got to see me through—I'm your husband, ain't I? You're stickin' by me, ain't you? [He grabs his wife by the arm.] An' by God, if y' don't stick by me I'm putting both you 'n' the kid in hell—in hell, understand? I'm speakin' plain, Martha. [He points to the cupboard again.] I'm goin' in there. [His face close to MARTHA's.] You hold the key.

[The rap at the door is repeated and voices are heard. ED moves quickly across the room and crawls into the lower part of the cupboard. MRS. HOPPER, nursing her bruised arm, follows him, hesitates a moment, turns the key in the lock, and moves slowly toward the door. Again the knock is repeated, louder this time.]

MRS. HOPPER: Who's there?

HENDERSON: It's me, Martha—Frank Henderson.

MRS. HOPPER: [Brushes back her hair, glances quickly around the room, then opens the door slowly.] Come in, Frank. [HENDERSON steps in. He is a tall, gaunt, angular man, slightly bow-legged and pigeon-toed. His hair is iron gray; his face is thin and hard lined, but his blue eyes are kind.]

HENDERSON: 'Evening, Martha. [He laughs.] More'n likely it's mornin', though.

MRS. HOPPER: [Trying to smile.] Yes; it's way past midnight.

HENDERSON: [His hand reaches for his gun.] Hate t' bother y' thisaway. S'pose y' was in bed, sleepin'?

MRS. HOPPER: No; I was sitting up.

HENDERSON: That's like womin folks. [He looks about the room.] Always a stayin' up while their men is away.

MRS. HOPPER: [Nodding toward the chair.] Won't y' sit down, Frank?

HENDERSON: No; I ain't stoppin' but a jiffy, Martha. Got t' git over 'n' see how my woman is makin' out. Ain't seen her for a spell now.

MRS. HOPPER: [Glances at the cupboard, then quickly turns her head.] How'd y' happen t' get back before the others?

HENDERSON: Did I? I thought mebbe—

MRS. HOPPER: How about the cattle?

HENDERSON: Got 'em back—most of 'em.

MRS. HOPPER: Thank God! I mean Ed's back then too, ain't he?

HENDERSON: That's what I come here to find out.

MRS. HOPPER: He's back then?

HENDERSON: Ain't he?

MRS. HOPPER: Is—he—why do you ask me like that, Frank?

HENDERSON: Well, Martha, it's like this—I'm sorry t' put y' out but I thought mebbe—I had a 'spicion mebbe—

MRS. HOPPER: What is it, Frank? I've been waiting here alone, except with Jackie, for the men to get back.

HENDERSON: Yes; I know. [An awkward pause.]

MRS. HOPPER: You said the cattle were back safe?

HENDERSON: [Watching her closely.] Yes; most of 'em.

MRS. HOPPER: Why did you come here first—I mean before you went to your own ranch? You said you hadn't seen your wife yet. Frank, is there something you want to tell me?

HENDERSON: See here, Martha, I always play square.

MRS. HOPPER: [Backing toward the window.] I know you do, Frank. Yes; you do play square, Frank.

HENDERSON: I always had an idea you was on the square, too, Martha.

MRS. HOPPER: Ain't I?

HENDERSON: Are you?

MRS. HOPPER: [Becoming hysterical.] Ain't I—ain't I? Oh, God—what are you men trying to do to me—trying to do to me? You all go away and leave me alone for days and nights—nights—nights, and when you come back—back, y' stand askin' me questions and— [She suddenly realizes what she is saying.] I tell you I am on the square. I am, Frank. Maybe my way of seeing things ain't your way, but it's just as square as your way is. I tell you I am square, Frank.

HENDERSON: [Now near the table.] I don't want t' press y', Martha, but if y'are as square as y' say y'are, then— then what's this gun doin' here?

MRS. HOPPER: [Throws back her head and takes a step forward.] I told you I've been alone here for five days— just me and Jackie. [She nods toward the sleeping loft.] We've been here alone and—

HENDERSON: I see. Y' might have had need for a gun, eh?

MRS. HOPPER: You never can tell what might happen down here when none of your own men are on the ranch.

HENDERSON: [Suddenly.] You're a good woman, Martha.

MRS. HOPPER: What did you say, Frank?

HENDERSON: [Moving toward the door.] I said you're too good for the man y' got—too good. I ain't one t' step between a man 'n' his woman, but just the same I'm tellin' y' what I think.

MRS. HOPPER: He's my man—yet.

HENDERSON: [Turns at the door.] Yeah; I s'pose he is,

581

MARTHA. I s'pose when a woman loves a man she's just dumb blind about him until something opens her eyes.

MRS. HOPPER: He's the father of my boy, ain't he?

HENDERSON: Yeah; y' know all of us down here have always liked y' ever since the day y' moved in—like th' way you've stuck it out—plucky like. But I don't have t' tell y' none of us ever trusted Ed Hopper any too much. Y' know that as well as I do.

MRS. HOPPER: I s'pose I do. I know how all you old timers have felt about him. I'm sorry—I'm sorry. I guess it's just his way of not fitting in with most people.

HENDERSON: [Hesitates a moment, awkwardly.] I s'pose I've got t' tell y' the truth, straight out, Martha. 'Tain't any too easy but you'll find it out purty soon.

MRS. HOPPER: What have you got to tell me, Frank?

HENDERSON: I told y' the cattle was back.

MRS. HOPPER: Yes.

HENDERSON: We didn't kill no greasers t' get 'em back nuther. Them cattle warn't stole out 'n' out. No. They were sold. Yeah, sold. We was double-crossed by a certain party that lives on our side of the river. Yeah, a bunch of Mexicans paid for them cattle before they drove 'em down into Old Mexico.

MRS. HOPPER: Y' don't mean my husband—?

HENDERSON: I'm sorry, Martha, but that's what I do mean.

MRS. HOPPER: [Moves away to the table, throws back her head.] And that's the man who called my boy a—a—a—

HENDERSON: What's that y' are sayin', Martha?

MRS. HOPPER: Nothing—nothing.

HENDERSON: [Scratching his head.] We'd 'a' got back sooner with them cattle, but we was damn fools enough to let Ed act as guide for the outfit 'n', of course, he kept puttin' us off the track. 'Course he knowed where them cattle was all the time. Soon's we'd hit the right trail he turned his ho'se and cleared out—gave us the slip. I'm mighty sorry, Martha, for you 'n' the kid. I ain't aimin' t' stir up no trouble, but I calc'late the boys'll want t' see Ed Hopper. He'll have t' answer t' them for a thing or two.

MRS. HOPPER: [Who has been listening to HENDERSON intently.] You'll come over first thing in the morning? Maybe he'll be here then.

HENDERSON: Yeah, I'll be over early. I s'pose some of the boys'll want t' hang around outside to give Ed a rousin' welcome if he shows up. Two of 'em are ridin' over t' put up a sign in the Post Office at El Paso.

MRS. HOPPER: You mean—

HENDERSON: [Nodding.] Dead or alive. Y' know as well as I do, Martha, what stealin' ho'ses 'n' cattle means down in this part of the country.

MRS. HOPPER: Don't let them do it, Frank—don't let them put up that sign! Talk t' them, they'll listen t' you—they'll do whatever you say, Frank. Oh, for God's sake, don't let them put it up. Think of my boy—think of Jackie! It ain't right, Frank—no; it ain't right.

HENDERSON: But y' know what the laws out in this country are, Martha, I mean the laws that all of us hold to.

MRS. HOPPER: There's also a law out here that every man gets a square start. My kid can't start life straight with a blot like that against his name, Frank. He can't, I tell you! Nobody could.

HENDERSON: Laws is laws. I reckon it's up t' you t' give the boy a new start. Leastwise it looks thataway. I ain't aimin' to' be stubborn, but cattle thieves is cattle thieves 'n' there's only one way of dealing with 'em. But I just want t' say this, Martha, if you 'n' the kid have any need for it, why me 'n' the missus'll help y' out any way we can. Y' can ask us anything y' got a mind to.

MRS. HOPPER: Then I'm askin' y' now, Frank. Don't let that sign go up in the Post Office over in El Paso. [She looks up into his face searchingly, grimly.] I'll turn your thief over t' y' in the morning.

HENDERSON: You'll turn him over? Y' know what it means? Hangin' ain't a purty word t' say t' any man's wife, but that's what it means, Martha.

MRS. HOPPER: [Takes a step toward HENDERSON.] I said I'd turn your cattle thief over t' you in the morning, Frank.

HENDERSON: You will?

MRS. HOPPER: [Throws back her head and looks HENDERSON straight in the eye.] I promise you.

HENDERSON: I believe y', Martha. I'll send one of the boys over t' see that that sign don't go up. Y' are a brave little woman, Martha. We've knowed y' for some years now. Y' are like one of our own kind. I've seen you havin' some purty hard ridin' 'n' I'll say y' sure don't pull leather.

MRS. HOPPER: [Who has not heard what he is saying.] Thanks, Frank, about the sign.

HENDERSON: Well, I'd best be movin'. [He offers her his hand.] 'Night, Martha.

MRS. HOPPER: Want a lantern t' light y'ur way?

HENDERSON: No, the sun'll be streakin' over the desert soon. Near time for it, I guess.

MRS. HOPPER: Good-night.

[She closes the door after him, pushes the bolt into place, stands there for a moment, then turns and starts toward the table. Her mouth is set with grim determination. There is a sound from the cupboard. MRS. HOPPER turns like a startled deer. She remembers her bruised arm and begins to nurse it. A soft rap from the cupboard is repeated.]

MRS. HOPPER: [Laughing softly, hysterically.] Now you're locked up—for eight years you kept me that way— locked up—locked up—workin' for you night and day— drudging for you—starvin' and eatin' my heart out for you —locked up inside myself. [ED's voice is heard from the cupboard.] Then you steal and try to run away—steal all we've worked for and try to run away with it all for some woman in 'Frisco, leavin' us behind to starve—leavin' us behind to bear the shame of it—the shame of it. [Slowly she takes the key out of her pocket and looks at it.] Now it's you that's locked up! Bringin' shame on your own kid and then runnin' away from him! [She beats on the cupboard with her fists.] But you can't do it, Ed, you can't do it! You can't! You can't! [ED's voice is heard inside. MRS. HOPPER nursing her arm moves back around the table.] Stealin'—callin' your kid a brat—hurtin' me—killin' me. Killin'—killin'— [She has reached the table as she says these words and her eyes look down upon ED's gun.] Killin' —they hang cattle thieves—hang 'em by the neck. They'll say my kid's father was hung for stealin' cattle. They'll say —no—no. I won't let 'em say that—I won't let 'em. D' hear me, Ed, nobody's ever goin' t' say you was hung for stealin' cattle. [Calmly she removes the revolver from its holster. Her hand is steady now. She raises the gun slowly, points it toward the cupboard, and fires. There is a long pause. A child's voice is heard from the loft.]

JACKIE: Mother, are you there? Mother, do you want me?

MRS. HOPPER: [Lets the gun slip from her hand to the table. She straightens. Her tired face is changed, the hard lines have disappeared, there is the light of freedom in her eyes; her face is almost radiant as she brushes the hair back from her eyes.] I'm coming, son, I'm coming up to rest now.

[She takes down the lantern and starts toward the ladder of the loft. The room is left in shadow with only the sound of the wind outside and the fine sand blown against the window.]

THE ORGAN
By G. Edward Pendray

PERSONS IN THE PLAY

HENRY PETERSON
MYRA
MARVIN
CALVIN JASPER
MRS. CALVIN JASPER
TUDE MEEKER
MRS. TUDE MEEKER
JOE WESTON
ELMER FLAMMER
JIM LANGDON
COL. OKAYNE
THE CLERK
A GROUP OF HOMESTEADERS

THE ORGAN

THE front yard of the PETERSON homestead in eastern
Wyoming. At the left stands the house—weatherbeaten
and dilapidated. To the right, though not in sight, are the
barn, sheds, and corral. In the distance may be seen the
open prairie, gently rolling and bluish-purple with sage-brush.
A barbed-wire fence which seems to enclose all the buildings
is visible. The ground about the house is beaten bare by
the tramp of feet, and on it is piled furniture in great con-
fusion, just as it has been carried from the house. It is
awaiting public sale by auction. Chairs, beds, bedding, a
sewing-machine, a tin wash-tub, an old dresser, a kitchen
stove with utensils, and the like, are in the collection. Somewhat by itself, near the wall of the house, stands a shiny
golden-oak upright organ of the kind advertised in the mail
order catalogues. It is open, and a copy of the Methodist
hymnal is upon the music rack. A three-legged upholstered
organ stool stands some distance away with the other furniture.

It is early afternoon of a hot summer's day. From the

direction of the barn come the sounds of an auction sale: the auctioneer with his singsong, the staccato bark of an occasional bidder, the undertone of conversation. These noises continue intermittently until the auctioneer and the crowd come in.

MYRA PETERSON is seen seated beside the organ in a straight-backed chair. Her hands are folded helplessly in her lap and she is staring blankly in front of her. She is gaunt, gray-haired, not over forty, but hard work and privation have taken their toll. After a few moments MARVIN PETERSON, an undersized, anemic boy of about fifteen, comes out of the house carrying a dining-room chair which he places with the others. He is dressed in overalls and is barefooted.

MARVIN: There, Maw, that's all the chairs.

MYRA: All right, Marvie.

MARVIN: You a-settin' out here like a gypsy!

MYRA: We are gypsies now, ain't we? We ain't got no home.

MARVIN: We'll have one soon as Paw gits back to Des Moines. He'll get took back into the shops. No use worryin' about it—

MYRA: Bein' sold out ain't jist a picnic.

MARVIN: I know, Maw, but they can't nothin' be done about it now.

MYRA: I never thought I'd see the day. I figgered somethin'd turn up. I been fearin' this fer a year—an' now it's come! [She pauses for a moment, listening to the auctioneer.] I hope it don't take 'em long. I feel kind of faint.

MARVIN: They's a good crowd. Paw says stuff ought to go perty high.

MYRA: Lot of good that'll do us! The money all goes to pay debts an' back taxes. Here we been workin' hard fer years to make this place a home. I been cleanin' it up an' dustin' it up every day, an' now they're takin' it away from us, Marvie.

MARVIN: Let's not talk about it. You'll jist git started cryin' again.

MYRA: It's all I got to talk about. Look at the dining-room set there. We bought it before we left Ioway. An' that dresser. Yer grampa gave it to me when yer Paw an' I first started housekeepin'. That rocker yonder's been in the Loomis family fer three generations. I recollect seein' my maw rockin' in it, an' her maw before her.

MARVIN: We'll git together some more things better'n them when we git back to Ioway. I kin git me a job, too, an'—

MYRA: We'll never git such stuff together again. How'd we ever git enough money to buy another organ? I jist can't bear to see that organ go, Marvie. Right when you're doin' so well with yer music, too!

MARVIN: I'll sure miss it to play on.

MYRA: Every time you come back from yer lesson over at Mule Creek I could notice you improvin'. There ain't hardly a hymn you don't play now. It wouldn't be long 'till mebbe you could play good enough to git a job as a musician.

MARVIN: Maybe in one of them pitcher shows Miz Jasper's always sayin' she seen over in Cheyenne—

MYRA: But *now* what chance you got? They're takin' the organ!

MARVIN: Don't you think mebbe when we git settled in Des Moines—

MYRA: We might git another organ? We'll be lucky if we got enough to eat. We'll never git another organ like that again. [She sighs. Both are quiet a moment.] Marvie, git the organ stool an' play me a piece. It'll comfort me.

MARVIN: Aw, Maw, I don't feel like it now—with all them folks down at the barn.

MYRA: Play soft—they won't hear you.

MARVIN: I can't play very soft.

MYRA: It'll prob'bly be the last time I'll ever hear you play the organ, Marvie. Do it fer me. [MARVIN reluctantly carries the stool to the organ and sits down.]

MARVIN: What you want to hear, Maw—a hymn?

MYRA: Play that last piece Miss Simpson give you.

MARVIN: "The Jolly Hunter's Polka"?

MYRA: That's the one. You know most of it by heart. Jist don't pump too hard, Marvie.

[MARVIN begins laboriously to pick out the first notes. MYRA listens as one entranced. He is halfway through the "piece" when HENRY PETERSON enters hurriedly from the direction of the barn. He is about fifty years old, with unshaved face, faded patched overalls, and an old blue shirt rolled up at the sleeves and open at the neck—a broken man with defeat written in his face and voice.]

HENRY: Marvin! Stop that! Ain't you got no sense? [MARVIN stops playing at once, turning on his stool.]

MYRA: What's the harm in him playin'? I ast him to.

HENRY: With all them folks down at the barn! I'm s'prised at you, Myry.

MYRA: What do I care about them!

HENRY: Now don't be so high-strung, Myry. You oughta went to town like I wanted, an' waited 'till it was all over.

MYRA: It's my things they're sellin', same as yours. You're stayin' to see yer cattle an' implements done right by; I'm stayin' to see my house an' furniture done right by.

HENRY: It makes it harder to stand—with you here, Myry.

MYRA: I reckon we'll both have to stand it, Henry.

HENRY: I don't see why you think so much of this place, anyhow. It ain't what you was brought up to. [Shaking his head.] I been an awful poor provider, Myry.

MYRA: Don't blame yerself. If I hadn't of been in the hospitle so long we might of got a little ahead.

MARVIN: Now, Maw, quit talkin' so! It wasn't yer fault no more'n anybody else's. It jist happened.

HENRY: That's right. We jist had bad luck. Crops failed, an' there was the fire, an' the cow market dropped—

MYRA: An' me in the hospitle.

HENRY: Well, everything'll come out all right.

MYRA: All these years I've been prayin' it would—but it never has.

HENRY: We're goin' back to Des Moines, an' then everything'll be better.

MYRA: Yes, we're goin' back to Des Moines an' start in again right where we did fifteen year ago.

HENRY: Don't worry about it. We'll git a new start—

MYRA: A new start! That's what you're allus sayin'! We can't do it, I tell you. We're too old, an' I ain't got no heart fer it. A new start! What we got to start with? Furniture gone, cattle an' farm tools gone, an' our spirits gone. They're even takin' Marvie's organ. It ain't fair! It ain't fair, an' if you was half a man, Henry Peterson, you wouldn't let 'em!

HENRY: Hush up, Myry! Here comes someone.

[There come from the direction of the barn MRS. TUDE MEEKER and MRS. JOE WESTON. MRS. MEEKER is a stout woman, clad in pink gingham—evidently her Sunday best. Her hair is coiled back in a knot on her head and a black straw hat trimmed with ancient red cherries perches on it. MRS. WESTON is tall and angular. Her clothing has no frills or decoration. Her head is protected by a sunbonnet. Both women are ill at ease, endeavoring to be kind to an old neighbor who has met with misfortune.]

MRS. MEEKER: Well, Myry, they're about through down there. An' the farm things are a-goin' right high, too.

MRS. WESTON: My Joe jist bought yer plow team, Henry.

HENRY: I'm glad, Ella. He'll not work 'em too hard like

some folks. That's allus been a good team to me. I remember once when I—

MRS. MEEKER: The sun's right warm here, Myry, an' you without no hat! I allus miss the shade-trees in this homestead country. I say to Tude, "Wyoming'd be all right if we could only grow some trees like we had back in Illinois."

MRS. WESTON: Here, Myry, take my bonnet. [Removing her sunbonnet.] You'll git sunstroke if you ain't careful.

HENRY: She can go in the house.

MYRA: I wouldn't feel right, a-settin' inside without my furniture. I'm goin' to stay right here.

MRS. MEEKER: I know jist how you feel. It's hard. We was sold out in Illinois. You don't never want to see the inside of your house again.

MRS. WESTON: I kin jist imagine, Miz Meeker. [MARVIN has left the organ stool, and is slipping off quietly in the direction of the barn.]

MYRA: Where you goin', Marvie?

MARVIN: Down to the barn.

MYRA: You be careful, with all them horses millin' around in that old corral! [MARVIN goes out.]

HENRY: Reckon I'd better be gittin' back. [To the others.] Look after Myry, will you?

MYRA: I don't need no lookin' after.

HENRY: Colonel Okayne ain't goin' to be much longer. . . . [He shambles off toward the barn, almost apologetically.]

MYRA: Set down, won't ye? Plenty of chairs.

MRS. MEEKER: Myry, we thought we'd come ahead to tell you. That Miz Jasper's come out to git yer organ.

MYRA: Miz Jasper . . . !

MRS. WESTON: She's tellin' everybody that's what her an' her husband come to this sale fer.

MYRA: What does she want with an organ? She don't play.

MRS. MEEKER: She's goin' to git Miss Simpson over at Mule Creek to give that Leroy boy of her'n lessons.

MRS. WESTON: The little sissy ought to learn how to do something. If he was mine I'd have him in dresses.

MYRA: He'd never learn as quick as Marvie does. Miss Simpson says Marvie's got a natural gift fer it.

MRS. MEEKER: It's a shame an' a disgrace he can't go on learnin' to play.

MRS. WESTON: That's what I say!

MYRA: I wisht you'd heard him a while ago. He was playin' that new piece Miss Simpson gave him, "The Jolly Hunters." It sounded sweet as church music. An' just to think mebbe he won't ever git to play again.

MRS. MEEKER: There, Myry—I wouldn't take it so hard.

MRS. WESTON: Here comes Miz Jasper now! Don't let her see you cryin', Myry.

MRS. MEEKER: Look at the fancy clothes on her! I'd like to know what they got, to put on such airs! [MYRA hastily dries her eyes.]

MRS. WESTON: That's what comes of seein' too many toorists go by. I say to Joe, "I'm glad we ain't direckly on the highway," I say— [MRS. CALVIN JASPER comes in. She is a pudgy woman with reddish skin and thick ankles who seemingly has the delusion that she is pretty. She is dressed in a blue skirt, too small for her broad hips, high button shoes, and a white shirtwaist. She carries a palm-leaf fan.]

MRS. JASPER: Hullo, Miz Peterson! I sorta thought you'd be in town.

MYRA: I ain't the sort to run away.

MRS. JASPER: No, I s'pose not. Why'n't you have yer sale in the mornin', when it's cooler?

MRS. WESTON: Afternoon's as good as any.

MRS. JASPER: 'Course when you have it in the afternoon you don't have to serve 'em lunch.

MRS. MEEKER: If anybody's small enough to want free lunch, let 'em stay away, I say.

MRS. JASPER: Oh, *there's* the organ! Cal's goin' to buy it fer our Leroy.

MRS. WESTON: You can never be *too* certain you'll git a thing when it's up at auction.

MRS. JASPER: Well, we're ready to bid with the next one. [She goes over to inspect the organ, while MYRA stifles an involuntary motion to prevent her.]

MRS. WESTON: I wish we could afford an organ. Joe spends all his extry money on our radio.

MRS. JASPER: One of your ivory keys is loose, Miz Peterson.

MYRA: It don't affect the music none.

MRS. MEEKER: If I'm any judge, it's a good insterment. Good as new. . . .

MRS. JASPER: This here stool ain't none too solid. My husband'll have to glue it together again. [Pumping the bellows and trying a note or two.] It ain't very loud, is it? I like organs lots louder.

MYRA: It was good enough for us. We had it goin' on five years.

MRS. JASPER: Well, you can't expect to git much fer it— the shape it's in.

MYRA: Nobody's askin' you to buy it!

MRS. JASPER: You needn't git so short with me, Miz Peterson.

MYRA: Besides, I—I don't know as we want to sell it.

MRS. JASPER: I don't see how you can help yourself. It's a sheriff's sale, an' everything has got to go.

MRS. WESTON: 'Tain't none of your business, Miz Jasper!

MRS. JASPER: Well, you needn't git so smart, Miz Weston. I guess it's my business if I want to bid on this organ.

MRS. MEEKER: There'll be other bidders. You ain't the only one got a chance to git it.

MRS. JASPER: I reckon my Cal is prepared to bid as high as the next one. You can't bluff him, once he makes up his mind about anything. We'll see who gits it!

MRS. MEEKER: [Her arm about MYRA.] If it's all the same to you, Miz Jasper, would you mind goin' back to the corral? Yer gettin' Miz Peterson all upset.

MYRA: Never mind about me.

MRS. JASPER: Oh, very well. I thought this was a *public* auction. I didn't know you couldn't speak your mind! I thought it would be doin' Miz Peterson a favor to take that old organ off her hands! [She flounces off toward the barn.]

MYRA: I can't stand to see her git it! It's *my* organ. Her Leroy don't need it. We bought it for Marvie, an' it's his by right!

MRS. WESTON: Chances are *she* won't git it. She jist likes to talk.

MRS. MEEKER: That husband of her'n is awful bull-headed once he gits an idee. . . .

MRS. WESTON: She ain't allowin' fer other folk's outbiddin' him.

MYRA: Bid or no bid, she don't git it. *I made up my mind!*

MRS. WESTON: If I was you, Myry, I wouldn't make no trouble. It don't do no good in the long run.

MYRA: They's some rights a body has, auction or no auction. [HENRY comes in from the direction of the barn.]

HENRY: Myry, they're about through down there, an' Colonel Okayne wants to know if you're ready fer him to start sellin' the stuff up here?

MYRA: I reckon I'm as ready as I'll ever be.

MRS. MEEKER: We'll stay by her, Henry.

HENRY: That's neighborly of you, Marthy. She's so high-strung.

MRS. WESTON: I'd like to know who wouldn't be high-strung at a time like this!

MYRA: Never mind about me. I'm all right. But they ain't goin' to git Marvie's organ!

HENRY: What you talkin' about, Myry?

MRS. MEEKER: Miz Jasper allows she's goin' to git the organ fer her Leroy.

HENRY: Well, if she pays the price. . . .

MYRA: She ain't goin' to have it, d'ye hear me?

HENRY: Talk sense! You sound like you was out of your head. The organ's got to go, along with the rest of the truck. You don't seem to realize this is a sheriff's sale, Myry.

MYRA: What do I care about the sheriff? It's Marvie I'm thinkin' of! We got the organ fer him. It's his organ! We ain't got no right to sell Marvie's organ, jist when he's learnin' to play on it! [HENRY is about to remonstrate with her when the crowd is heard approaching from the barn.]

HENRY: Now you behave, Myry. They're a-comin'!

[COL. OKAYNE, the auctioneer, comes in, followed by some twenty or thirty homesteaders, including TUDE MEEKER, JOE WESTON, ELMER FLAMMER, JIM LANGDON, MR. and MRS. CALVIN JASPER, and the CLERK. The COLONEL is a very large man in a shiny black suit and broad felt hat. He carries a hickory stick. THE CLERK follows at his heels, with a square pad upon which the sales are recorded. The homesteaders are all talking at once. The women stand more or less together, except for MYRA, who keeps her place by the organ. MARVIN crosses to his mother and takes her hand. The auctioneer greets MYRA perfunctorily and raps his stick on the table-top for silence. The crowd subsides as he begins to talk.]

COL. OKAYNE: Here we are, folks! All you need to set up housekeepin'! Young fellers, here's where you git that start in life. You supply the girl, an' we supply the rest.

Nothin' could be fairer. All this here furniture is in A-one shape, folks, an' absolutely g'aranteed to be as represented. Look it over all you please!

[At this invitation several advance and paw over the furniture in a half-hearted fashion, rather ill-at-ease in the presence of MYRA. COL. OKAYNE takes advantage of the lull and deposits a huge chunk of chewing-tobacco in his mouth.]

THE CLERK: Colonel, are the terms same as they were at the barn?

COL. OKAYNE: Yep, same thing. Same thing. Now, folks, if you've had your look around, let's get down to cases. As I said down yonder, we're all sorry to see the Petersons sold out, but what has to be has to be. What's one man's loss is another's gain. It's the way of life! [He pauses a moment, clearing his throat importantly and assuming his professional voice.] Now, folks, the terms of this sale is the same as they was at the barn, with this leetle exception: everything in the lot sells for cash. Them's the usual arrangements with house furniture in small sales, an' them's the arrangements here. Everything goes to the highest bidder, an' folks, I'm goin' to sell this stuff fast! It's gittin' late, an' all of you has got cows home waitin' to be milked. Any questions about this sale? All right, then! [He mounts a chair and begins calling for bids in his wooden, singsong voice, hoarse and strident from long ill-usage. Occasionally he uses his hickory stick for emphasis.] This stuff's goin' cheap an' fast. Somebody's goin' to git some rare bargains here. Think fast an' act accordin'. What'll we put up first? As the feller says, "If you don't see what you want, ask fer it." Call out what you want to bid on first. I'm at your service!

A NEIGHBOR WOMAN: The sewing-machine!

TUDE MEEKER: The dinin' table!

CAL JASPER: The organ!

ELMER FLAMMER: The bed!

COL. OKAYNE: Wait a minnit! Wait a minnit! Not so fast. One at a time. All right, Elmer, we'll take the bed first—just to please you.

JOE WESTON: I seen Elmer out ridin' with a girl in his new flivver!

JIM LANGDON: Oh, you Elmer!

COL. OKAYNE: Never you mind, Elmer. We was all young once. Y'know, folks, Elmer's plannin' about gittin' hooked up. When these young bucks begin lookin' around fer a bed— [He is interrupted by a burst of laughter from the men.] Now, then, folks, the bed. Bounce them springs. Look at them legs. Genu*ine* golden oak, folks. Bid on it, covers an' all. The quilt goes, too. It's a good bed, ain't it, Miz Peterson?

MYRA: We've had it since we was married. Got it fer a weddin' present from Henry's Paw. That quilt belonged to—

COL. OKAYNE: Well, somebody start it. What am I offered? How about you, Elmer? What do I hear for this lot?

ELMER: Two dollars.

COL. OKAYNE: What! Two dollars? For a bed like that? Wouldn't pay for the varnish on it! Two I'm bid. Who'll make it five? Five. Five. Five. [A homesteader shouts "Five!"] I've got five. Who'll make it ten, make it ten, make it ten?—Don't you people sleep at night? Step up an' examine it. You act like you was scared it'd bite! [A few do as COLONEL OKAYNE suggests. Another homesteader holds up seven fingers.] That's more like it! Seven is bid. I've got seven. Seven. Now, Elmer! Say ten. Make it ten.

ELMER: Eight!

COL. OKAYNE: I've got eight. Eight. Eight. Eight. Honest, folks, I don't believe you know a fine bargain when you see one! This han'some bed an' covers fer eight dollars! Eight, I'm bid. Eight. No higher? Last call! All done? I'm bid eight—once. Eight—twict. Eight— [Striking his stick against the side of the chair.] Sold! To Elmer Flammer fer eight dollars. An' with it, Elmer, goes my wishes fer a long an' happy life in double harness. [The crowd relaxes and stirs about. ELMER advances to THE CLERK to pay for his purchase. The auctioneer shifts his chew from one cheek to the other and takes a reef in his snakeskin belt in preparation for the next sale]

COL. OKAYNE: Look at this here wonderful chiffonier with the beveled glass in it. Almost bran' new. Jest like what you see in the Sears Roebuck catalogue. Take this home to yer wives, men, an' it won't take 'em so long to git dressed mornin's. What you say we auction it off next, folks?

MRS. JASPER: Colonel, put up the organ next.

COL. OKAYNE: The organ?

CAL JASPER: My wife an' me got to start back perty soon, an' we want to bid on the organ.

COL. OKAYNE: Anything to oblige. I'm here to accommodate the public. You all heard? Cal Jasper's asked a chance to bid on the organ. The organ goes next.

MYRA: No, no! [There is a stir of interest.]

HENRY: Hush, Myry!

MYRA: Well, she ain't goin' to git it! [MARVIN puts his arms about her.]

MRS. JASPER: Go ahead, Colonel—put up the organ.

MYRA: It belongs to Marvie, an' it's his'n by rights.

COL. OKAYNE: All right! Miz Peterson says it's her son's own personal insterment, an' her guarantee of tone purity an' mechanical perfection goes with it. [COLONEL OKAYNE gets off the chair and helps THE CLERK push the organ into better position for inspection. A woman in the crowd whispers something to him.]

COL. OKAYNE: What's that, lady? Yep, the stool sells with the organ. You bet! An organ without a stool would be like a tom cat without a tail. [He laughs loudly at his joke, and pumps the bellows, striking a few keys.]

TUDE MEEKER: Play us a tune, Colonel!

JIM LANGDON: He couldn't carry a tune in a bucket!

COL. OKAYNE: That's one on me, boys. Truth is, I couldn't. But you ought to hear me on a fiddle. . . . [Mounting the chair again.] As the feller says, "Music has charms to soothe the savage beast."—Take this melodeon home fer your women-folks, fellers. It's the chanct of a lifetime to git such an insterment, mellered with age—an' here's a religious hymn book goes with it. You git yer music an' religion together, all fer the price of one. All right, now, bid fast! Who'll start it? Who'll say ten? [MYRA steps in front of the organ defiantly, her face bloodless with excitement, her voice harsh and determined.]

MYRA: I tell you, you ain't goin' to sell it! [HENRY hurries to her side, and tries to pull her away.]

COL. OKAYNE: What's that, Miz Peterson?

MYRA: I ain't goin' to let you sell it!

HENRY: She don't mean nothin', Colonel.

COL. OKAYNE: Miz Peterson, the tail goes with the hide! Everything here sells, if anybody'll bid on it. Them's my orders. Sorry, but it can't be helped!

HENRY: [Trying to lead her away.] Myry, we can't do nothin'! You better go in the house.

MYRA: You leave me be! I ain't goin' to let him sell my organ.

MRS. JASPER: How you aim to keep him from it?

COL. OKAYNE: Sorry, but I take my orders from the sheriff. Everything goes, fair an' square, to the highest bidder, come one, come all! Now, folks, if Miz Peterson will kindly step out of the way, we'll—

MYRA: I won't, I tell ye! I won't git out of the way. You can't sell the organ, an' that's all they is to it!

MRS. MEEKER: [Stepping to her side.] You won't do nothin' 'cept make a scene, Myry. Come on back an' set down. [But MYRA refuses.]

COL. OKAYNE: All right, folks. Let's not mind the interruption. Women folks is bound to git hysterical at times. It can't be helped—it's their nature. Now what am I offered to start off this melodeon? You heered it play. It's a daisy. What am I bid to start her off?

MRS. JASPER: Go on, Cal, speak up! You ain't goin' to let her scare you out?

COL. OKAYNE: There's a lady knows a good thing when she sees it! Speak up, Cal. How much?

CAL JASPER: Five dollars.

COL. OKAYNE: Five is bid. Who'll make it ten? I got five. Five. Five—

MYRA: Don't none of you bid. It ain't fer sale!

COL. OKAYNE: Now looky here, Miz Peterson. . . .

[MYRA mounts a chair beside COLONEL OKAYNE. The crowd is hushed. HENRY hurries toward her.]

MYRA: There's somethin' I got to say to all of ye—

HENRY: Myry, git down off'n there!

MYRA: Not 'till I've had my say! I'm goin' to tell this crowd somethin' 'fore I have to leave the country. I been a good neighbor to every one of you. There's Jim Langdon over there. I stayed up nearly every night fer a month with his wife when she had the pneumony an' liked to died. I done her washin' besides. And Tude Meeker. Where'd you of been if we hadn't sent you butter an' milk an' truck the year hail got yer crops an' you couldn't keep no cows? Not that I b'lieve in throwin' it up to any of you—we been proud an' glad to help. That's the only way when you're homesteadin'—

603

COL. OKAYNE: Now, Miz Peterson, you been a good woman, but this ain't hardly the place or time—

MYRA: I ain't through yet, an' I'm goin' to finish! As I was sayin', when you're homesteadin' you got to help one another. All stick together. An' now *I* want somethin'. I want to keep that organ. It's all I got to give Marvic. If he gits a chanct he'll be a big musician some day. Most of you've heered him play, an' know how well he does.

MARVIN: Aw, maw!

COL. OKAYNE: Well, Miz Peterson, all you say is very interestin', an' I'd like to oblige you, but we already got one bid.

MYRA: One bid! Five dollars! An' from Cal Jasper, too. I done more for Cal than I done for anybody. You ain't fergot, Cal, the time when you used to live at our house, before yer shack was built, an' how I mended yer clothes an' did yer washin's—'fore you had this here woman to do 'em for you? We fed you an' kept you like one of our own, an' never so much as charged you a cent. An' this is how you pay me back!

COL. OKAYNE: Well, Cal, do you wanta withdraw yer bid?

MRS. JASPER: I'll answer that fer him. He don't!

COL. OKAYNE: That settles it. Five dollars I'm bid fer this beautiful upright organ. Five dollars! [MYRA becomes hysterical and breaks down completely. MARVIN and MRS. MEEKER help her down from the chair. The crowd stirs uneasily. Pretending not to notice her, COLONEL OKAYNE goes on with his patter.]

COL. OKAYNE: Five dollars I got, now. Five dollars. Who'll say ten? Folks, you don't know what you're missin'! Course we all feel sorry fer Miz Peterson, but business is business. The organ's worth twenty-five if it's worth a penny. I got five. Make it ten. Ten . . . What's the mat-

604

ter, folks? You gone on a strike? [The crowd remains stolid and silent.]

Tude Meeker: Colonel, you can't git no decent man to bid on that organ. [He looks meaningly at Cal Jasper.]

Col. Okayne: Come on now, Tude! Don't git chicken-hearted!

Tude Meeker: Everybody here knows what he owes Myry Peterson. We know what's right an' what's wrong, an' if Cal Jasper wasn't married to that woman of his he'd withdraw his bid in a minnit! [There is a rustle of approval in the crowd.]

Col. Okayne: But Cal ain't withdrawin' his bid, an' I'll have to sell the organ at five dollars. Folks, it's a shame to sell a fine organ like that fer five—

Tude Meeker: Cal, here's yer last chance to withdraw that bid an' let Miz Peterson have her organ! [There is a tense silence. Cal Jasper thrusts out his chin.]

Cal Jasper: I ain't to be bluffed out by nobody. If I want to withdraw my bid, I don't need to be reminded by no homesteader!

Col. Okayne: All right, then! Five I'm bid. Five dollars once—

Joe Weston: That organ'll cost you a lot more'n five dollars, Cal. There's my seeder you borrow every spring an' my binder every fall. You'll never git the loan of 'em again!

Cal Jasper: I guess they's others!

Elmer Flammer: You allus count on me to help you with the thrashin'. I'll never help you again if you buy that organ!

Tude Meeker: Ner me! I won't help! I'll see you in hell first.

Mrs. Weston: He won't be able to hire no help no-where. [The crowd echoes similar sentiments.]

Jim Langdon: [To Cal Jasper.] Next time that heifer

of your'n gits in my corn, I'm goin' to shoot her. I warned ye enough about her.

MRS. JASPER: You don't care about that, Cal. Let 'em talk!

TUDE MEEKER: You can't git very far without yer neighbors if you expect to stay on a homestead, Cal. You know that. Better think it over!

MRS. JASPER: Colonel, hurry up an' sell us that organ. I'm tired of hearin' all this gab!

CAL JASPER: Go ahead, Colonel.

COL. OKAYNE: Five I got. Five once. Five twice—

MYRA: Oh, Marvie, they're gonna sell it—

COL. OKAYNE: Three times, an' *sold* to Cal Jasper over there fer five dollars. Cal, you got a bargain! Now, folks, let's git right busy on the—

MRS. MEEKER: Ain't you ashamed of yourself, Cal?

CAL JASPER: Jist hold yer horses, Miz Meeker! [Loudly to the crowd.] Now, then, *I* got somethin' to say. I bought the organ an' it's mine. I can do what I like with it. I ought to be mad, after all you said, but I ain't. I'm goin' to give this here organ to Miz Peterson, with my compliments an' thanks fer what she's done fer me. [He pauses a moment. The crowd shows signs of being suspicious at his sudden burst of generosity.] That agreeable with everybody?

TUDE MEEKER: Well, I'll be damned!

MYRA: [Going to him, uncertainly.] Cal, d'you mean it?

JIM LANGDON: He knows better'n not to mean it.

JOE WESTON: You ain't foolin' nobody, Cal. You're just doin' that to save your face!

MRS. JASPER: Cal Jasper, you come home. I want to talk to you.

MYRA: Marvie, you thank 'em fer both of us. They're the finest neighbors a body ever had!

LAST DAY FOR GROUSE
By Orin Mack

PERSONS IN THE PLAY

MARGARET
ELMER
MARTIN

LAST DAY FOR GROUSE

THE interior of a log cabin in Colorado, twenty miles from one of the famous mining towns of the West, at an elevation of 11,000 feet, on the eastern slope of the mountains. It is a section which has promised big strikes in zinc and silver, and intrigued prospectors for half a century. A door and window at the rear, both open, show the steep, barren sides of a long mountain ridge which shoulders up into the sky like some gaunt monster. Beyond, a patch of sky. The base of the ridge seems to be creeping ominously down upon the cabin.

The window is wider than it is high and is equipped with a door that swings upward and is propped open with a heavy stick. Between the doorway and the window is a shelf with lamp, pistol, shell-box, etc. In one corner a small cook-stove; a pan of biscuits in the open oven; a frying-pan on the hearth; a wood-box. Nearby a home-made bed with a hilly mattress; a curtain strung on a wire and serving as a screen is pulled back. A table with legs of young pine logs. In another corner two bunks; the lower with bedding; the

609

upper piled with boxes, old clothes, ropes, cable, tools, etc. On a wall hangs a double-barreled shotgun. Two or three nondescript chairs; empty powderboxes used as stools. Some drills laid out in orderly array on one of the boxes. On the floor several ore sample bags of canvas; on top of the bags a large magnifying glass.

MARGARET is seated at the table, which is set for breakfast. She is reading a cheap magazine and smoking a cigarette. She looks up now and then as if listening. She rises and goes to the window; hurries back and furtively conceals the magazine under a board in the floor. The clump and grind of hob-nailed shoes on gravel is heard outside.

ELMER comes in. He is not tall, but is physically powerful; walks slowly and heavily; uses his hands with quick, deft movements; is about twenty-five years old.

MARGARET: I got your breakfast all ready for you, Elmer. You must be hungry carrying those logs up all by yourself.

ELMER: I only got 'em half up.

MARGARET: Looks like someone ought to help you once in a while. I heard you tell him to last night.

ELMER: Yeh, dad knew I wanted to get that timber packed up this morning early.

MARGARET: All I can say is, Martin ain't crazy about work.

ELMER: Where'd he hike off to this morning?

MARGARET: He said something about grouse when he went out.

ELMER: After grouse again! He ain't done a shift at the mine for a week. He laid off all day yesterday chasin' round and bangin' at grouse.

MARGARET: I wouldn't be surprised if he was figurin' on layin' off today, would you, Elmer?

ELMER: [Glancing at the shotgun on the wall.] He didn't take the shotgun.

MARGARET: Oh, he'll be back for it, likely. We don't want any grouse, do we, Elmer?

ELMER: Naw. [He sits at the table.]

MARGARET: Ham and bacon's all right for us, ain't it, Elmer?

ELMER: Sure—it's all right.

MARGARET: Martin's just trying to get out of work.

ELMER: Yeh, don't you s'pose I know it!

MARGARET: And the way he used to fight the booze so he couldn't do his bit at the mine.

ELMER: Yeh.

MARGARET: But we got his booze hid all right, all right, now, ain't we?

ELMER: Uh-huh.

MARGARET: You and me's enough for the old man—what say, Elmer?

ELMER: I say, what's eatin' you! Cheese it. I'm 'bout fed up hearin' you talk about him—and I'm sick hearin' you and him jaw at yourselves when you get in sight of one 'nother. Come on with the eats.

[MARGARET looks a little crestfallen. She carries biscuits, coffee, etc., to table. They eat in silence. ELMER is preoccupied. MARGARET is constrained and restive. She wishes he would speak, but he reaches the magnifying glass, takes some ore samples from his pocket and examines them with absorption. He is oblivious of MARGARET's presence; he treats his food as a matter of secondary interest.]

MARGARET: Gosh, Elmer, wouldn't you ever open your mouth if I didn't start!

ELMER: What's to talk about? [He continues to examine the samples.]

MARGARET: Anything—I don't care—anything! Seems like I'd bust sometimes if I don't talk to someone.

ELMER: Humph.

MARGARET: I been livin' in a big burg all my life, I have,

and I'm used to seein' crowds, and meetin' people and talkin' and hearin' noise. It's what I like, I do. I ain't made for a dump like this place. God, but it's still up here. And that mountain—seems like it's goin' to crawl right in the door sometimes and smash me. But I could stand it a little better if you'd spark now and then with some talk.

ELMER: [Putting down the glass and samples as if he has finished with them in his own good time.] I got a lot to think about.

MARGARET: Well, tell me what you're thinkin', then. I can't stand this bein' still all the time.

ELMER: I wonder how far I'll have to sink that cord to cut the vein. Just where I was figurin' on cuttin' into a nice body of ore with the tunnel they was a fault in the rock and you never can tell for sure how deep them faults is.

MARGARET: But I don't get that line of talk, Elmer.

ELMER: Well, you wanted me to say somethin'. Maybe you get this: sinkin' that cord's goin' to keep us up here till God knows when.

MARGARET: You can finish by next month, can't you?

ELMER: Next month! It might take a year.

MARGARET: A year! Why, you said when we come up here you'd have things in shape so as to get some rich guys to take up with it by next month and we'd get out o' this hole and be in town for a while.

ELMER: Well, she can't be done now I hit that fault. Say, you don't seem to savvy I'm figurin' on opening some little body of high-grade carbonate. Get me? That hill's got the stuff tucked away in it somewheres, it has.

MARGARET: What's high-grade?

ELMER: It's what puts a guy on easy street. I stand to make some little pile when I cut that vein. Say, she must be a peach!

MARGARET: Is it a sure thing, like you talk, Elmer?

ELMER: I got the right hunch this time, all right.

MARGARET: They say about one prospector in a hundred makes good.

ELMER: Who says?

MARGARET: Well, that's what Johnson told me.

ELMER: A hell of a lot that kid knows about minin'! When you been talkin' to him?

MARGARET: I ain't been lately. What you got it in for Johnson so strong for?

ELMER: What's he come round here buttin' in on my job for, makin' me cut my timber a mile farther down the trail and drag it a mile back!

MARGARET: He don't make the rules about where you can cut your trees, does he? The gover'ment does that. He can't help it; he's just the ranger.

ELMER: Seein' as how you know him and his damn regulations has slowed up my work, I wouldn't be standin' up so strong for him if I was you, 'specially as you say you're so keen on gettin' out of here in a hurry.

MARGARET: I ain't standin' up for him, Elmer. But you ain't got no right to get sore at him for what the gover'ment makes him do, and tell him to keep away from the house.

ELMER: He can see me at the mine. He's too fresh around a woman, and you didn't seem to object any to it.

MARGARET: All he ever done was bring me up a bunch of stuff to read once a week and stop to talk a while.

ELMER: Well, I told him to cut that out.

MARGARET: Made it look like there was something between him and me—like you don't think I'm straight with you.

ELMER: Well, you wasn't so straight when I picked you up.

MARGARET: Aw, cut that, Elmer. Don't throw that up at me. Didn't I come up here because I was sick of that life in the city? Ain't I begged you a dozen times to go down to the town and get married regular by a judge or a preacher —ain't I?

ELMER: Yeh, you have been at me, all right, to do that.

MARGARET: I don't see why you can't lay off and do it. It'd only take two or three days to go down and back.

ELMER: How long d'you s'pose my grubstakers would stand for me using their money to support a woman up here, married or not. I ain't tyin' up anyway, not until I make a stake.

MARGARET: We don't need a stake, Elmer. Couldn't you get a job in the mines around the town?

ELMER: Could I! You just know it. I'm the best timber man in this neck of the woods—bar none. Goss, foreman at the Corona, says to me, he says, "Elmer, any old time you want a job you just signal me and I'll hoist one up for you." That's how I stand round this distric'.

MARGARET: It'd be swell to settle down in a town and you gettin' regular pay.

ELMER: Not for mine. I'll turn a big one out o' these hills someday. I'll make this old mountain hum. I ain't settlin' yet a while.

MARGARET: Well, we could get hooked up regular, anyway, couldn't we?

ELMER: Ain't I said I ain't hookin' up?

MARGARET: What'd you bring me up here for, then?

ELMER: What d'you s'pose? I like a woman about. What'd you come up for?

MARGARET: I like you a lot, Elmer. I thought we'd hit it off together—make it regular. I don't want to go back to the way I was—not knowin' what's comin' next—never sure of anything. [She tries to take his hand.] Can't you see, Elmer, I'm crazy about you?

ELMER: You ain't got it so bad up here. You got your grub and a snug shack to flop in and you don't have to go out lookin' around for a livin' every night.

MARGARET: Aw, I know it. And I could stand bein' lonely

if I could just look ahead to a sure thing. 'Tain't that I'm a little older than you that you stall on marryin', is it, Elmer?

ELMER: Well, you ain't no spring chicken.

MARGARET: What's a few years got to do with us lovin' each other?

ELMER: Aw, cut the slush.

MARGARET: Seein' you're set on not stoppin' your work, I don't suppose you'd mind if I went down for a few days and bought some things and maybe saw a movie or two. I'd come back, Elmer. I wouldn't go for good.

ELMER: Naw, I wouldn't mind. Only I thought you didn't know the trails.

MARGARET: I don't; I get all mixed up in the mountains. But Johnson's goin' down Friday. I could go along with him.

ELMER: How'd you find that out?

MARGARET: Martin told me—Martin saw him the other day.

ELMER: Well, you don't go with that guy.

MARGARET: Who with, then?

ELMER: Martin could take you down.

MARGARET: Martin! You make me laugh, Elmer, actin' like you was jealous of Johnson and then tellin' me Martin can take me. Why, it's Martin, your old man, that's always tryin' to get fresh with me.

ELMER: How d'you mean?

MARGARET: Ever since he come up here, when he ain't been jawin' me, he's tried to get soft with me.

ELMER: Well, the old man's a he-man, ain't he? And he knows you ain't been a innocent little lamb all your life. What d'you expect?

MARGARET: Anyway, he hates me good and plenty 'cause I won't stand for him comin' round me that way, and he's always razzin' me 'cause I ain't married to you. That's another reason why I want us to go down and get spliced, if I'm goin' to stay up here along with Martin. It'd maybe shut him up a little. I tell you, I'm just about to my limit; I can't stand Martin's tongue any longer.

ELMER: There you go on the old man again. He ain't much to brag about when it comes to work, damn his lazy hide! But outside that I can't see where you work up all this grouch against him.

MARGARET: Oh, you can't! Well, I could stand it up here in this God-forsaken joint if it wasn't for him. Ugh, I hate him—I could kill him, sometimes, when—

ELMER: Say, ain't you talkin' a little strong! Any old time you don't like it up here you can beat it.

MARGARET: Sure, I know I can.

ELMER: Beat it for keeps, too, is what I mean.

MARGARET: Aw, come now, Elmer. I ain't wantin' to leave you. I'll stay. I won't go down with Johnson. [She caresses him.] You'd want me to come back, wouldn't you, Elmer? It's nicer with me here, ain't it, Elmer?

ELMER: I guess it is, old girl.

MARGARET: You like me pretty well, don't you, Elmer?

ELMER: You're a good old scout.

MARGARET: Say, Elmer, I got a dandy idea to help you with the work.

ELMER: Let's have it.

MARGARET: Martin'll be back here for the gun to go grouse shootin' pretty soon.

ELMER: Well, he don't get it, see?

MARGARET: But he'll take it away from me when you're at the mine. My idea is to hide it.

ELMER: Good idea. Where?

[MARGARET takes the shotgun off the pegs and looks about the room for a hiding-place. ELMER nods toward the board under which MARGARET has hidden her magazine.]

ELMER: There's a board looks like it was loose. Put it under there.

MARGARET: That board ain't loose. I tried it the other day.

[From some distance on the outside a lusty, untrained voice is heard singing "I've Been Working on the Railroad." The singer is approaching.]

MARGARET: There he comes. Listen to him—always bawlin' some song—thinks he can sing. [Surveys the room hurriedly, and moves toward the bed.] We'll hide it here. [Puts gun under the mattress. Goes to shelf at rear and takes a square box. Glances about.] And the shells here. [Empties the box and puts a handful of shells in ELMER'S sample bags.] I'm glad that gun's hid. He's always flashing it around at me. Remember how he did when I wouldn't tell him where we hid his booze? Shoved it right in my face, didn't he?

ELMER: Yeh, he's too handy with a gun.

MARGARET: Gosh! He looked wicked enough to shoot.

ELMER: I didn't like the way he was fingerin' the trigger. The old man's always been hot-headed and quarrelsome-like when he don't get his booze regular.

[The singing is heard quite near the door.]

MARGARET: Sh! [Smiles with mischievous and malicious satisfaction.]

[MARTIN enters. He is tall, straight, rather graceful. His bearing is jaunty, insolent and defiant. He is about forty-eight years old. Humming, he continues the air of "I've Been Working, etc.," and moves about nonchalantly under the patently hostile and accusing looks of MARGARET and ELMER. He throws his hat and coat on his bunk and proceeds to get biscuits, coffee, etc., from stove. He turns and glances with defiant mockery from MARGARET to ELMER, who are watching him tensely. He throws a cigarette butt on the floor. MARGARET glances sharply at it but restrains herself. MARTIN grins at her discomfiture. He sits at the table and begins to eat. ELMER begins to sort out some drills. MARGARET remains standing, tense and hostile, watching MARTIN.]

MARTIN: [Turning to MARGARET with a mock gallant air.]

617

For a lady that's been moving in swell high society in the city like you, I can say you make damn fine biscuits, Mag.

[MARGARET shrugs and gives him a poisonous look. He continues to eat.]

MARTIN: Saw a fine bunch of grouse down the trail.

[ELMER lifts his head slightly from his business of sorting the drills. Resumes the work. After a slight pause the whistle of a woodchuck is heard outside.]

ELMER: Them damned woodchucks hollerin' again. I shot a couple of 'em yesterday—one at a hundred yards and on the move, too.

MARTIN: You're a good hand with a pistol, Elmer, even if I do say it as learned you how to shoot. They ain't no one quicker'n you to get the drop on what you're shootin' at, and you ain't likely to miss, either. I'm figurin' on doin' a little shootin' myself today.

ELMER: How d'you mean?

MARTIN: I mean I'm layin' off; I'm goin' after them grouse.

ELMER: You laid off yesterday to shoot grouse.

MARTIN: Well, what of it?

ELMER: This much—someone's got to pack up the rest of that timber, and you're the guy what's goin' to do it.

MARTIN: Who says so?

ELMER: I do. Time you get through with the timber I'll have these drills sharpened up and then you and me's goin' to wheel out that dirt I shot away yesterday. Get me? You're goin' to do some work round this here claim today.

MARTIN: Like hell!

[ELMER pauses at the door and turns as if to speak further. The cry of a woodchuck is heard again. He picks up the pistol from the shelf.]

ELMER: There they go again. Gets my goat them devils pokin' their noses over the rocks and yellin' at me all the time. I'll show 'em. [He examines the cylinder of the pistol.]

MARGARET: They ain't hurtin' anything, Elmer. I like to hear them whistle. It's kind o' company.

[ELMER turns and walks through the doorway. He pauses at the window.]

ELMER: No monkey-work now, dad. You'll be healthy to get at that timber and dirt soon's you finish eatin'.

[MARTIN clamps his coffee cup angrily into the saucer. He glares at Margaret.]

MARTIN: Your doin's—been settin' Elmer against me ever since I come up here. [MARGARET begins to pick up the dishes. ELMER is sharpening the drills. The ringing tattoo of his hammer on the anvil is heard for some moments. MARTIN scrapes his chair back impatiently from the table. He rolls and lights a cigarette, tossing the match carelessly on the floor, as if to taunt MARGARET.] By the eternal mountain! I'm goin' grouse huntin' today.

MARGARET: You—you, Martin—you ain't done much but drink and loaf since you been here.

MARTIN: Oh, ain't I, now! Well, I'm his dad and that's more than you can say. If Elmer's grubstakers found out he was keepin' a woman up here I guess they'd shut down on puttin' up any more money. Anyway, I'm goin' after them grouse.

MARGARET: Didn't you hear Elmer say he wanted you to work today?

MARTIN: Yeh, course I heard him. You give me a pain talkin' like I was hinderin' Elmer when you stand to spoil all his chances of workin' the claim at all.

MARGARET: I guess Elmer knows what he's doin' lettin' me stay.

MARTIN: Yeh, he knows he'll chuck you good and plenty when he gets tired of you. My notion is he's gettin' tired of you already, Mag, my dear.

MARGARET: Elmer and me's going to get married soon's he can get to town. He said so this morning.

MARTIN: Fat chance you got with Elmer. I've seen him ditch one or two skirts 'fore you come along.

MARGARET: Elmer thinks a lot of me, he does.

MARTIN: Say, you don't think he's goin' to hook up with the likes of you when they's plenty of young ones squawkin' round. Not Elmer! Take a tumble to yourself—why, you're old enough to be his old maid aunt. [Tries to take her hand.] Now if it was me you was tryin' to grab they'd be some sense to it, wouldn't they, Mag?

MARGARET: Leggo!

MARTIN: Well, why not? What's the matter with me I'd like to know. I ain't so damn old for the likes of you, am I? I ain't exactly a dead one, either, am I? And I got some life in me, I have, but Elmer, there—good Lord! All he thinks about is work.

MARGARET: Aw, cut this stuff. You'd better be thinkin' about work, too.

MARTIN: Didn't you hear me tell Elmer what I was goin' to do today?

MARGARET: Well, you better not.

MARTIN: S'pose you'll put him wise 'fore I start.

MARGARET: S'pose I do?

MARTIN: You just try it and I'll—

MARGARET: What'll you do?

MARTIN: Why, I'll just see to it that Elmer hears about you goin' down to the Big Rock to meet that young ranger feller Johnson last week.

MARGARET: A lot you know! I ain't been down that way for a month; I ain't seen Johnson since him and Elmer had a row.

MARTIN: Oh, ain't you, now?

MARGARET: [Holding out a plate for his inspection.] What makes you always waste twice too much syrup?

MARTIN: [Looks closely at a calendar on the wall.]   October tenth, ain't it?

MARGARET: There's enough syrup left on your plate to do two men.

MARTIN: Last day for grouse—season closes today.   And say, I hear that syrup talk every morning.   Get something new.

MARGARET: Watch your ashes—knock 'em in the saucer. There they go on the table cloth.   You been strewing up the floor, too, ever since you come in.

MARTIN: [Rises, shoves back his chair and advances threateningly toward MARGARET.]   I'm hittin' the down gulch trail pronto and you're not tellin' Elmer when I hit.   Where's that gun?

MARGARET: I guess Elmer put it away.   How do I know?

MARTIN: You know, all right.   S'pose you thought someone'd shoot you.

MARGARET: Well you acted crazy enough with the gun when you said I hid your booze.

MARTIN: Well, you did, didn't you?   But I don't need a gun to bring you round.   All I have to do is mention that ranger feller to Elmer.

MARGARET: Oh, dry up about Johnson.

MARTIN: You sure do like 'em young.   Even Elmer's looking kind o' old to you, eh?

MARGARET: Ugh—you—you—

MARTIN: Well, I guess this place ain't so big but what I can find a gun in it.   [He starts toward the board where the magazines have been concealed.]

MARGARET: Wait—wait—it ain't there.   I'll get it.   [She gets the gun from the bed.]

MARTIN: Thought I'd bring you round.   You ain't keen about Elmer seein' what's under that there board.

MARGARET: There ain't nothin' under it.

MARTIN: Ain't they, now? Don't I know where you stow them papers and magazines Johnson give you last week?

MARGARET: Well, ain't I got a right to keep some of them old magazines he give me before Elmer told him to keep away from the house?

MARTIN: Them old ones was burnt long time ago to build fires with. I s'pose that bunch he left for you yesterday was old ones, too. I seen 'em this morning at the Big Rock. You missed seein' him yesterday 'cause you was a-scared if you waited any longer you'd be late gettin' Elmer's supper, and Elmer might ask some questions. Johnson come up the trail 'bout ten minutes after you left.

MARGARET: Been spyin' around, have you?

MARTIN: Sure—it pays.

MARGARET: What of it, if I do get some stuff to read from Johnson?

MARTIN: Oh, nothin'—only you wouldn't like Elmer to know you see Johnson now and then, would you?

MARGARET: They's nothin' between Johnson and me and you know it.

MARTIN: Yeh, but you'd have a fat chance makin' Elmer believe that. He don't love that young ranger any too much, now, does he, Mag?

[The high eerie note of a woodchuck, rather near, is heard. The tattoo on the anvil ceases. A pistol shot is heard. MARGARET and MARTIN stand motionless, listening for a moment.]

MARTIN: Elmer's got a woodchuck. [Goes to shelf and picks up the shell box. Discovers it is empty.] Hid the shells, too, did you? Where the hell are they? Hurry up—get 'em—quick! Elmer'll be in here in a sec to show us the chuck he killed.

[While MARTIN is searching at the rear, MARGARET steps forward and furtively breaks the shotgun. She extracts the two shells and puts them into her apron pocket—a shallow pocket. She hands MARTIN the gun as he comes toward her.

MARTIN trying to appear half in jest, but really in earnest, brandishes the gun at her.]

MARTIN: Where's them shells? Jump—you!

[MARGARET coolly stares at the muzzle of the gun and pushes it away.]

MARTIN: What kind of a game you playin'! I'll show you. [He aims at her with no pretense of a half-joke.]

[ELMER appears at the window holding a woodchuck proudly by the tail. He stops dead at the scene before him and lets the woodchuck fall abruptly. An instant later he enters, carrying the pistol at his side in his right hand.]

ELMER: What you doin' with that gun?

MARTIN: What d'you s'pose? [He lowers the gun.]

ELMER: I told you once not to be flashin' that iron round at people, didn't I? Where you goin'?

MARTIN: Grouse huntin'—ain't I told you? She's hid the shells on me.

ELMER: Well, I told her to. You're goin' to wheel out that dirt today.

MARTIN: You got another guess.

ELMER: I'm tellin' you, now. By God! I'm about sick o' you layin' off.

MARTIN: Well, you can stay sick.

[MARTIN swaggers defiantly out the door, ELMER watching him intently and following him one or two steps. ELMER is near the window. Through it MARTIN's arms with the gun suddenly appear. The gun is drawn on ELMER.]

MARTIN: [From the outside.] You ain't got the old man's goat yet. Now hustle, you over there, and get them shells or I'll blow Elmer's head off.

[MARGARET is standing pressed back against the wall. ELMER bends forward, his gaze riveted on MARTIN's trigger finger.]

ELMER: Hey, you fool, your finger's gettin' a little too nervous on that trigger!

MARTIN: I'll have them shells.

[ELMER leans forward farther. His pistol hand is tense and poised. The pistol points rigidly behind him.]

ELMER: By God! I believe the way you're fingerin' that trigger— Cut it—d'you think even if you are my old man—

[MARGARET is struggling to speak. She screams. Almost simultaneously ELMER swings his right arm forward, up, down for a drop-shot. He fires. The shotgun tumbles inside and MARTIN's arms disappear. ELMER leaps to the window and looks out for an instant with terror. He then rushes out the door.]

ELMER: Good God! Yes—I have—I done it—my own dad!

[A short pause. MARGARET is still standing, frozen with terror. ELMER enters, looking stupidly dazed. He pulls a blanket from MARTIN's bunk and carries it outside. In a moment he re-enters and sits heavily in a chair. He is still dazed. After a long pause it is evident that he is beginning to consider with some alarm the consequences of his act.]

ELMER: He made me do it. You saw him, didn't you, Mag? You saw the way he was fingerin' that trigger. I thought he was goin' to blow my head off. What's the matter with you? Can't you talk? You'll testify it was self-defense, won't you? Say you will—say it—talk up!

MARGARET: Yes, I'll testify. [She crumples to the floor. The two shells rattle out on the boards from her pocket. ELMER sees them and starts. He looks sharply at her. Then he picks up the shotgun, breaks it and discovers that it is not loaded.]

ELMER: Good God! It wasn't loaded. You knew that all the time? [MARGARET nods.] Well, why didn't you say something?

MARGARET: I tried.

ELMER: Tried—what d'you mean?

MARGARET: I couldn't speak; somehow I was too scared;

my tongue wouldn't work; my throat was—but I did yell just when you done it. It wasn't soon enough.

ELMER: What I want to know is, why you didn't yell before.

MARGARET: I couldn't, Elmer, I tell you, I couldn't.

ELMER: Naw, you couldn't talk, you couldn't.

MARGARET: I couldn't, Elmer, honest I—

ELMER: Course not—not without spoilin' your frame-up on the old man and me.

MARGARET: You don't say—you don't think, Elmer—

ELMER: I think you hated the old man enough to want anything to happen to him.

MARGARET: I hated him, all right. He was threatenin' me. But I didn't figure on this, Elmer. I'd a-told you if I could. I was tryin' to keep him here to work. You know that—say you do, Elmer. [She rises, crawls toward him and tries to fondle him. He pushes her away.]

ELMER: Get away, you damn she-devil! Wasn't you sayin' this morning you could kill him sometimes?

MARGARET: Oh, I know I was—I was only talkin'. He made me sore; he was always pesterin' me. He was just before you come in.

ELMER: Sure—and so you roped me in on your dirty work.

MARGARET: No—no—you ain't got me right, Elmer, to say it. I didn't. [She stops and thinks. A look of doubt and alarm comes over her face.]

[Slowly and as if terrified at the thought.] I don't think I did. I—I—

ELMER: Don't think! Well, don't you know?

MARGARET: I can't understand just how it all happened. I was plumb scared—and he'd been bullyin' and insultin' and makin' love to me—but if I could of thought I wouldn't of really wanted him to get killed—I wouldn't of wanted you to do it. Sure I wouldn't, Elmer. You see, don't you, Elmer, how everything can be all mixed up in your head at once—

how you'd want to do something and not want to all at the same time—and then before you could make up your mind, to have something happen too quick for you, like when you shot. I seen your hand gettin' tight and I thought you was goin' to shoot and I thought I'd better tell you the gun wasn't loaded. It seemed like a hour I was tryin' to speak out and then—that's the way it was inside me. See, Elmer?

ELMER: Naw, I don't get you. Look here, though [picks up the two shells and slips them into the shotgun] you're goin' to say on the stand that gun was loaded even if it wasn't.

MARGARET: All right. Can't you believe I'll do anything I can to clear you without keepin' askin' me about it?

ELMER: You better, 'cause if you don't I'll bring you in on this business and we'll both do our time—a good stiff one, too. One of us might even get it here. [He makes a gesture toward his neck.]

MARGARET: They won't send us up, will they, Elmer? They ain't no danger, is they? I was in the cooler six weeks once 'cause a guy I was with said I glummed his cuff-buttons. It's hell, Elmer, being locked up—I couldn't stand it.

ELMER: They ain't no danger if you come through with the right story, see?

MARGARET: How many times I got to tell you? [ELMER puts on his coat.] And when the trial's over we can get out of this place, you and me, can't we, Elmer?

ELMER: Get out! Not on your life. I'm comin' back to open that body of high-grade.

MARGARET: Elmer, we can't live here after all that's happened. Can't you see we can't? Let's quit this for a while and live in a burg.

ELMER: Well, they's nothin' stoppin' you.

MARGARET: No—nothing—'cept I ain't no quitter, Elmer.

ELMER: What I mean is, I'm comin' back here by my lonesome.

MARGARET: But I'd come, Elmer—I wouldn't kick.

ELMER: You and me's done, see? Think I'm living with someone what fixes it so I kill my own dad? [He picks up his hat and moves toward the door.]

[MARGARET watches him. She looks very tired.]

MARGARET: Don't go, Elmer.

ELMER: The quicker I get down and give myself up to the sheriff the better it'll look for me.

[He goes through the doorway. MARGARET gives a terrified glance outside the door where MARTIN has fallen. She shudders and rouses herself to cry out.]

MARGARET: Elmer! [He stops at the window.] I can't stay here alone—I'm afraid.

ELMER: You can go down to Johnson's shack and stay there till he goes to town the end o' the week.

[ELMER goes. MARGARET puts her hands on the floor and leans forward on her arms. She remains thus inert.]

THE END OF THE TRAIL
By E. H. Culbertson

PERSONS IN THE PLAY

BILL WATSON
MARTHA HINLEY
JOHN HINLEY

THE END OF THE TRAIL

THE small, bare, cramped living-room of a shack in the Cascade Mountains, Oregon. There is a door at the back, and when it is open one gets a view of a narrow valley with beetling mountains towering skywards on the opposite side. There is a small four-square paned window at the left, and a similar one opposite. There is a door leading into the other room of the house. In one wall is a shelf on which stand a number of old pasteboard boxes, half a dozen or so partially filled medicine bottles, and an oil lamp. Underneath the shelf on nails and hooks, hang a variegated assortment of old coats, aprons, hats, etc. Immediately below on the floor stand several pairs of old boots and shoes. Nearby stands a small bed. There is no spread on it—just a pair of blankets over the mattress and two pillows at the farther end. The pillow slips are soiled and mussy. In the center of the room stands a small, rough-hewn table covered with a red and white checked tablecloth. Near the door, there is another table—still smaller—and on it stands an unlit red lantern. Four or five rough kitchen chairs stand here and there about the room. There is an antiquated wall telephone on the wall near the window, right—of the style in use in the middle and late nineties. On the wall at the back there is a crayon portrait of an eight-year-old boy, and also on the wall near it, another of a girl about eighteen. On the wall, right, hangs an old shotgun and several mounted horns.

MARTHA HINLEY is seated near the table patching a pair of old trousers. She is a woman of about fifty-two. The events of a hard, bitter life have taken their toll and she looks old and broken—much older than she really is. Her hair is gray and thin and drawn back tightly from a wrinkled forehead. Her cheeks are shrunken and drawn. The expression in her eyes alternates between one of angry, bitter protest and brooding, tragic despair. She works, now with the listlessness of one for whom the burdens of life have come to weigh too heavily, and now with a feverish, impetuous vigor, as though to drive out the thoughts which crowd into her mind. Once she drops her work with a little cry of anguish, jumps up and goes to the window, right, where she stands with clenched hands, staring fiercely out, and breathing convulsively. She returns to her work at length. Presently, as though from some distance down the mountain side, there comes a far-away "Hallo!" MARTHA rises and hurries to the door, back, opens it and steps out. She peers down, and into the distance, and in the course of a moment or two, spies some one and waves her hand.

MARTHA: Hello thar!

BILL: [From below.] Hello! Hello, Marthy!

MARTHA: Hello, Bill!

BILL: This trail gits steeper every time I travel it.

MARTHA: Takes all the steam a body's got.

BILL: An' when yuh're old an' ain't got no steam—

MARTHA: Yuh're steppin' like a two-year-old!

BILL: [With a laugh. He is quite near now.] Don't give

me no belly-wash like that—w'en yuh kin hear my j'ints creak from har to Chilton. [Pause. Then he speaks as though only a few steps away.] Whewee! The more yuh ile 'em the wuss they git!

MARTHA: Spokane "red-eye" ain't the right kind-a ile.

BILL: Not even Injun "red-eye" 'ud make 'em swing easy. [He appears at the door.] Been nigh onto three weeks since I was up har. Thought I'd drap over an' see how John was treatin' yuh—an' what yuhre ideas is on politics an' religion —and the natur'-a things in gineral.

MARTHA: Him an' me was jist talkin' 'bout yuh last night. [MARTHA comes in, followed by BILL.]

BILL: Now I know why my ears was itchin' like blue hell.

[MARTHA smiles—faintly. BILL WATSON is a big, gruff miner. His hair is dark and scraggly, and the lower part of his face is covered with a stubble beard. He wears overalls, a leather coat, boots, and carries an old battered felt hat in his hand. He closes the door after him.]

BILL: Whar's John?

MARTHA: Out on the tracks. He—he's down toward O'Fallon's sidin'. [Steps to the window and stares out apprehensively.] Couple of slides down that-a-way last week. He don't hardly sleep nights from worryin' for fear thar'll be more.

BILL: When a lot-a loose dirt an' rocks git restless an' hit the trail down'ards all hell an' a year of lyin' awake nights ain't goin' to stop 'em.

MARTHA: [Turns away.] That's what I keep tellin' him. But it don't make no difference what yuh say to him.

BILL: No, I s'pose not.

MARTHA: Sit down!

BILL: Don't mind if I do. [He reaches in his pocket and pulls out a short clay pipe and a bag of tobacco and proceeds to fill the pipe painstakingly. MARTHA drops down in a chair on the opposite side of the table.]

MARTHA: Slides—slides! If it ain't them—it's somethin' else.

BILL: This is the time of year fer' em. Gotta take things as they come, Marthy, in this har world.

MARTHA: Easy enough ter say that.

BILL: Yuh take life too serious.

MARTHA: Most anybody would—who'd been through what me an' John have.

BILL: Life ain't no easy, greased slide fer nobody.

MARTHA: It's give us nothin' but kicks an' slams.

BILL: Yuh stick too close to home, Marthy—if yuh don't mind me tellin' yuh.

MARTHA: Somehow I don't take ter none of the people out this har way.

BILL: John could easy git yuh transportation back to St. Paul—whenever yuh want it.

MARTHA: Don't never want to see St. Paul again. The— the only time in my life when I been a little bit happy was back thar. It—it's whar I first knowed John—me an' him was married thar—an' my first baby was born in a little house down on Lisner Street—an'—an' well—yuh jist see—

BILL: [Nods, lights his pipe and blows a mouthful of smoke at the ceiling.] I understand, Marthy.

MARTHA: Never seen nobody so conscientious as John.

BILL: Alla's on the job, ain't he?

MARTHA: As long as he kin crawl he'll be out thar doin' his part.

BILL: I knowed he was a hustler the first day I sot eyes on him.

MARTHA: The limited's due in half an hour—an' yuh couldn't drag him off them tracks till it gits through.

BILL: Kind-a stuck on that ole rattler, ain't he?

MARTHA: Like as if it was a pet or some teeny child. He's half sick from worryin' whenever it gits held up—just a little bit. As if he could stop a washout or a slide or keep it from snowin'!

BILL: [With a contemplative, understanding smile.] He's jist built that way—that's all.

MARTHA: If he'd only let up—just a little. He's gittin' old an' he ain't strong. The company don't half 'preciate him. Never did an' never will!

BILL: Men like John don't git their due in this world. The best they kin hope fer is to store up glory fer "kingdom come."

MARTHA: He ain't got no right to be out thar now. He— he was walkin' them tracks till half-past twelve last night— till after Number Two went through. Then up ag'in at five—an' out most-a the day.

BILL: Don't wanter take no chances. Couldn't if he wanted ter.

MARTHA: [Rises, goes to the box and lights the red lantern.] Liable to rush in har any minute fer this. May as well git it ready fer him. [Returns slowly to the chair and sits.] What credit does he git fer takin' his job serious? Fer not sleepin' nights—fer bein' out in all kinds of weather —gettin' his feet an' hands near froze off—fer killin' himself by inches? Let a little wreck happen along somewheres —an' they make him out responsible—an' all them thirty years' work for the road ain't goin' to count fer nothin'.

BILL: I wouldn't swim no river till I come to 'em, Marthy.

MARTHA: Allus—ever since he started out workin' fer it—it's been the road. The road! He's so sweet an' gentle- like—an' tries to reason it all out. Now an' then he gits took down with a spell of sciatica an' he lies thar on the bed an' talks to me by the hour 'bout it. Keeps goin' on 'bout this har road—an' the others bein' to the country what a vein or artery is to your body—an' that we are doin' some- thin' patriotic an' noble by helpin' keep 'em in shape. He calls our road "a gateway to the Orient." Says somebody's got to do the work to keep it in order an' clare, an' it might as well be us.

BILL: [Blows a mouthful of smoke at the ceiling.] That's one way a-lookin' at it!

MARTHA: I don't see it that-a way—an' never will! I don't see nothin' noble in slavin' an' slavin'—year in an' year out—an' most-a the time so onhappy an' half-sick yuh wish yuh was dead! Thar ain't nothin' in it!

BILL: Yuh an' him have had it hard.

MARTHA: An' it keeps gittin' harder—the older we git—

BILL: Yuh an' John been pretty close-mouthed. Yuh ain't never tol' me how yuh happened to come up this har way.

MARTHA: He—he started out as a wiper on the engines in the roundhouse in St. Paul. It was his first job—Joe Ferris give it to him—an' I met him 'bout a year or two after. It wasn't long 'fore they made him a hostler an' then him an' me got married. After he'd been thar 'bout ten year they made him a foreman. He hadn't had this job no more 'an a year or two 'fore his health got so bad he couldn't hardly drag one foot after 'nother. The smoke an' grease an' dirt was too much fer him. [She taps her chest. BILL nods.] The company give him a job as assistant section boss out at Minot. He done so well that the boss got scar't he was goin' to git his job, an' made complaints to the superintendent. After that they made him engineer at a water tank out in the bad lands. Not a tree, or a house, or a fence within ten mile of it. Most God-forsaken place yuh was ever in. [She hesitates a moment and gives a dry, racking sob.] The climate thar didn't agree with our daughter Minnie an'—an' she died. An' no more had she been dead an' John hurt his hands—an' was laid up ever so long. It crippled him fer life. Ever since he ain't been able to do no liftin' or handlin'.

BILL: I notice he allus favors his left hand.

MARTHA: Then Sam Bartlett—he was assistant to the master mechanic—got him a job as agent at a little station called Ulm on the Butte branch. [Glances up at the picture.] It was while we was thar that little Harry died. The—water done it—we allus thought. We couldn't stand stayin' thar after that. Then they give John this track walkin' job. [She jumps up and strides to and fro with clenched hands and a wild, malevolent glitter in her eyes. BILL smokes in contemplative silence. The wind outside now rises to a mournful howl.]

MARTHA: Listen to that wind! Listen! A storm's comin'—

BILL: We may git a little snow.

MARTHA: Blizzard more likely.

BILL: Oh, I dunno. They tell me the Chinook's goin'-a blow steady this winter.

MARTHA: What does anybody know how the Chinook is goin'-a blow? [Raising her voice to a plaintive, raucous wail.] Oh, fate has been ag'in us—beatin' us down, grindin' us in the dirt, pushin' us under! When I look at these har mountains—so high an' turrible—they seem to be mockin' us! Mockin' us, I say!

BILL: I git to feelin' that way sometimes myself, Marthy. But it don't do no good. It's usually when I ain't had my sleep an' this har cantankerous liver-a mine is cuttin' up didoes.

MARTHA: [Goes to the window and stares out, then turns away at length—with a shudder.] Back in the shops in St. Paul—in the winter—when they're gittin' the sleepers ready fer the run to the coast, the men keep sayin' to each other, "Well, I hope she gits through the Cascades." An' they keep askin' each other an' the crews that come through from Seattle an' Portland, "How are the Cascades? Did yuh make the Cascades all right?" At Minot when Number One west bound passes Number Two east bound yuh can't hear nothin' but the nigger porters on Number One shoutin' at them on Number Two. "How are the Cascades? Are they chock full of snow? Are we goin' to git caught?" Or in the summer, "How are the Cascades? Any fires? Are the Cascades clare?" At St. Paul, Minot, Havre, Kalispell or Seattle—it's allus, "How are the Cascades?" The whole road stands in fear of 'em—like some great divil that kin cast a spell. An' when the snow begins to fly yuh kin feel the fear settlin' down on everybody—like a pall—east an' west.

BILL: I know, I know. They allus been hell in winter.

MARTHA: An' now, har we are—right up in 'em—agin 'em —facin' another turrible winter! I git chucked right up agin the very things I hated an' feared. If—if it wasn't fer John —Gawd bless him—I don't know what I'd do. He's all I got now! Why should we be doin' this so rich people from back east kin ride through in fine upholstered coaches—sleepin' safe— Oh, I hate 'em—I hate 'em—an' these har turrible mountains!

[Suddenly the door bursts open, and JOHN HINLEY staggers in, deathly pale; blood streams from a deep gash on his forehead. He is a middle-aged man, with weather-beaten face, mild blue eyes, and thin gray hair. His shoulders are stooped. Normally, his manner is kindly, philosophic, mild. He wears a pair of worn and patched overalls, a jumper, and over this a short leather jacket. In one hand he carries an old cloth cap, with ear flaps turned down. MARTHA leaps to his side with an agonized cry. BILL rises and hurries to him.]

MARTHA: [Grabs his arm.] John! John, honey! What's the matter?

BILL: [Supporting him on the opposite side.] What hit yuh, ole man?

JOHN: A slide! It got me!

MARTHA: Oh, my Gawd!

BILL: Whar did it hit yuh?

JOHN: Mostly on—on the side—seems like—I dunno— A rock hit me on the head. Knocked me out—fer a few minutes.

MARTHA: I knowed somethin' like this was goin' to happen! I knowed it!

JOHN: It—it's a good thing I was out—an' seen it— Right thar—two hundred feet west-a the tool house— [Points off.]

MARTHA: You're pale—an' yuh ain't breathin' right—my pore honey! Whar—whar does it hurt yuh? Tell Marthy!

JOHN: [Weakly, as he makes a pathetic attempt to smile.] I—I ain't bad off. Don't take on. All I got was a bad bumpin'. To—to please yuh we'll have the company doctor come out on Number Four in the mornin'—an'— [His knees suddenly give way and he starts to sink to the floor. They exert their full strength and manage to keep him on his feet.]

MARTHA: John—honey! [Searches his face with an anguished gaze.] Yuh're weak as a rag—! Whar does it hurt? [In an hysterical undertone to BILL.] He ain't goin' to—?

BILL: No, no! Git him over on the bed.

JOHN: I'm—I'm goin' to—to be all right. Just a bad bumpin', that's all. [They half carry him to the bed and lay him on it. MARTHA, with BILL's help, slowly takes off his leather coat.]

MARTHA: No, no—don't try to set up—! Thar—thar—! We'll git it off— Be careful— Oh! [They contrive to get one sleeve off without much difficulty. He winces and groans as they turn him gently over on his side preparatory to getting off the other one.] Does it hurt yuh thar?

BILL: His shoulder, I reckon. Easy, ole boy!

JOHN: My—my side—jist a little—

MARTHA: [While BILL holds him on his side, she pulls off the other sleeve with the greatest care.] Thar—! Thar—! Up easy like—jist a little. That's it! Now—now—

639

[She tosses the coat on a chair, then with BILL's assistance places him gently back in position.] Git me a pan-a water an' a rag, Bill—quick—!

BILL: Yes, ma'am. [He jumps up and goes out, hurriedly. She goes to the table, opens the drawer, takes out a small roll of bandages and a towel, then returns to the bed and sits down again.]

MARTHA: [Bends over.] Honey, are yuh hurt bad—d'yuh think? Tell me! Tain't goin' ter do no good if yuh make out yuh ain't—if yuh are. It's only goin' ter make things worse.

JOHN: Just side-swiped me—that's all. Set me down kind-a hard. Now, don't you worry, Marthy. I'll be up an' around an' spry an' chipper as ever—in a day or two— [His face contorts and he breaks off as though suffering a sudden twinge of pain. BILL comes in again, carrying a small tin pan of water and a ragged wash cloth. He pulls up a chair to the side of the bed near MARTHA, sets the pan on it and hands the cloth to her.]

MARTHA: I'll git that blood an' dirt off yuh're face.

JOHN: Looks as though—I got handed—a kind—a rotten deal.

BILL: One-a them things yuh can't figur', ole boy. [MARTHA proceeds to wash JOHN's face.]

MARTHA: [Examines the cut.] That's—that's a bad 'un, honey.

JOHN: Did git me kind-a square.

MARTHA: Might-a been one-a them big 'uns that 'ud mashed the life clean out-a yuh.

JOHN: But it wasn't, Marthy—an' a miss is good as a mile. [She wipes his face, then carefully adjusts one edge of the bandage over the cut, winds it about his head and pins it. All at once a wild look comes into his eyes and he raises himself up on one arm with a tremendous effort.]

JOHN: Marthy!

640

MARTHA: What is it?

JOHN: The limited!

MARTHA: [Glances at the clock.] 'Tain't due in Chilton yet. We got plenty of time. An' it may be late.

JOHN: The slide—it took down the lines—! See if yuh kin git Chilton—! [The woman rises quickly, goes to the telephone, turns the crank rapidly several times, then takes down the receiver and puts it to her ear.]

MARTHA: Hello, hello! Hello, hello! [She presses down the receiver bar and gives the crank several rapid turns.] Hello, hello!

JOHN: See—! I told yuh! They're down—! [MARTHA hangs up the receiver, and comes back to the bed.]

BILL: Couldn't git 'em?

MARTHA: No.

JOHN: Somebody'll have ter flag her now! Somebody'll have ter git out thar with the lantern—!

BILL: I'll hike down ter O'Fallon's an' swing it thar at the head of the canyon.

JOHN: Yeah, yeah, Bill—that's what yuh do—! Give 'em the "high ball" thar—! Marthy, d'yuh hear—?

MARTHA: Don't yuh worry, honey! We'll take keer of that all right. 'Tain't the first time it's happened this way. Thar, thar, now! You remember— [JOHN's face suddenly contorts in pain, and he gasps and sinks back on the bed.] What is it? What is it? Tell me, honey! Does it hurt yuh so bad?

JOHN: It's gittin' me—right thar—

MARTHA: Yes, yes. Let Marthy rub it fer yuh. [She starts to open his shirt. He groans.]

JOHN: Some—somethin' hot, Marthy—reckon it'll do more good 'an rubbin'.

MARTHA: [Jumps to her feet.] The bag-a hops! [JOHN smiles faintly and nods. BILL starts toward back, as though to get the lantern.]

MARTHA: [With a convulsive sob as she hurries to his side and lays a restraining hand on his arm.] Bill—!

BILL: Yeah?

MARTHA: Stay har with him till I git the hops het up. Only take me a minute or so. Then yuh kin go.

BILL: Sure, Marthy—jist as yuh say—

MARTHA: Thar's plenty-a time— [She turns and moves quickly toward the door. Just before she reaches it, she pauses and glances at JOHN, gives vent to several prolonged sobs, then goes out. BILL returns slowly to the side of the bed and sits. JOHN gives another little gasp, rolls his eyes for a moment or two, then groans softly.]

BILL: Givin' yuh hell, eh? [JOHN nods.] Yuh will step in front of the side of a mountain jist to save the company a little time an' money. [Laughs.] I'm kind-a hefty meself —but I never figured I could buck a ton-a flyin' dirt an' rocks an' git away with a whole hide.

JOHN: Didn't git no chanct ter look her over.

BILL: Wouldn't put it past yuh—even if yuh had. No, siree!

JOHN: [With another mighty effort raises himself on one elbow.] Listen—! [He glances apprehensively toward the door then reaches over and grips BILL's hand tightly.] I'm pretty bad off. It—it was a big 'un an'—an' it caught me square. I—I heard her comin' but I warn't spry enough. She caught me an' carried me down thirty feet this side of the track. Right out har—three hundred foot from the house. Knocked me plumb out. When I come to they warn't nothin' but my head stickin' out. Mouth was full of dirt— an' my eyes, too—so I could hardly see. I—I had to dig an' claw my way out. Didn't have no strength—an' I don't know how long it took me ter git out. Seemed like hours. [He pauses, breathing with considerable difficulty. MARTHA can be heard sobbing hysterically.]

MARTHA: Oh, Gawd! Why d'yuh bring things like this

642

on us? Why d'yuh? I knowed somethin' like this was goin' to happen! I knowed it!

JOHN: Listen to her! Jist listen!

BILL: Takes it hard, don't she? [Her lamentations stop momentarily.]

JOHN: [Speaks with greater effort now.] I had-a crawl on my hands an' knees—most all the way har.

BILL: [Bends over and peers into his face.] Yuh don't look none too good!

JOHN: Somethin's busted inside.

BILL: Yuh think so?

JOHN: It feels that way. An' I seem ter be gettin' weaker.

BILL: We oughter git a doctor har quick.

JOHN: I dunno—I might be able ter hold out—until mornin'—

BILL: But McCafferty won't send no doc out on Number Four—'cause thar ain't no way of lettin' him know what fix yuh're in.

JOHN: Then—then thar ain't nuthin' ter do—but sit tight.

BILL: I could hitch up them broncs-a mine an' git over to Hooper Springs in a couple of hours. If ole Doc Fletcher ain't out somewhars I kin pick him up an' maybe with luck git back by midnight—or a little after. That's quicker 'an goin' ter Busby or Chilton.

JOHN: Don't bother ter do nothin' like that.

BILL: Hells-fire, thar ain't no use takin' chances.

JOHN: Kin yuh drive that road at night?

BILL: I drove it when yuh couldn't see yer hand before yer nose. [JOHN closes his eyes for a moment or two, as though yielding to weakness and pain. Suddenly he opens them, with a look of fear, and clutches BILL's arm tightly.]

JOHN: Bill—!

BILL: Yeah—?

JOHN: Git down to O'Fallon's with the lantern—as fast as yuh kin—!

BILL: Jist a minute. I want to tell Marthy whar I'm goin' after.

MARTHA: [From the other room.] Oh, Gawd! Ain't we never goin' to have it easy? Ain't it ever goin' to be nothin' but trouble, an' accidents an' death? Oh, Gawd!

JOHN: [Sinks back on the bed.] Listen to her, Bill! Jist listen! [He is now perceptibly weaker.] That's the way she goes on when anything happens to me. Yuh see, she ain't got no one else now. She—she's a good—woman—! Faithful—an' hard workin' an' kind—! They—Gawd listen! They don't make 'em no better. But—but life seems to be —gittin' too much fer her. She—she don't stop—don't stop to figur' things out. I—I was careless—same as this time maybe—when I hurt my hand. An' if we'd been more careful—as we had a right to be—'bout the water at Ulm little Harry 'ud still be alive. The—the company ain't no charity organization. It's allus done the best it could fer me. Them people back east, an' the passengers on the limited, an' these har mountains an' the snow—they ain't got nothin' to do with our bad luck. [MARTHA gives vent to a mournful wail.] But she— [Shakes his head despairingly.] Yuh can't make 'em reason it out—logical-like to a finish. Now an' then, they seem ter git the whole lay-out twisted—an' grab at things. It's—it's the tiger in 'em, Bill! The tiger in 'em.

BILL: Yuh can't figur' 'em. But I wouldn't bother 'bout that now.

[MARTHA comes in, carrying the bag of hops. BILL rises. MARTHA goes to the bed, bends over and carefully places the bag at JOHN's side. He moans softly, makes an effort to smile, then closes his eyes. She notes that he has grown considerably weaker, and picks up his hand and feels his pulse.]

BILL: [In an undertone.] Guess I'll be travelin'. [She gives a quick nod, and he moves to back, and picks up the lantern. MARTHA gives a little gasp of suppressed anguish, and drops JOHN's hand.]

MARTHA: [Turns and calls.] Bill—! [She hurries to his side.] His—pulse is awful weak—an' unsteady—! An' —an' Gawd—the way he's breathin'—!

BILL: He's in kinda bad shape, Marthy.

MARTHA: This is turrible. We oughter have a doctor— quick.

BILL: I'm goin' to Hooper Springs an' fetch Doc Fletcher —as soon as I stop this har train— [MARTHA turns and gazes at JOHN.]

MARTHA: How—how long'll it take yuh ter git him— d'yuh think?

BILL: With luck I'll git back by midnight. [MARTHA stands in tense thought for a moment or two. BILL consults his watch.]

MARTHA: [Impulsively, at length.] The—the limited may be an hour or two late. Yuh kin never tell. Sometimes she's right on the dot an' then ag'in she ain't—!

BILL: Well—of course—figurin' that way—

MARTHA: Go on an' git the doc—an' I'll give her the "high ball."

BILL: Yuh'll git out an' swing it—?

MARTHA: Done it twic't before—when John was laid up with sciatica.

BILL: Go hikin' down them tracks with the wind blowin' forty mile an hour?

MARTHA: I done it already, I tell yuh—onc't after a blizzard when the snowplow was stuck in the cut by Shimmer's. Went down to O'Fallon's an' give 'em the "high ball." An' onc't I stood on a rock out thar by the tracks an' give it to 'em. On a clare night—like this—the engineer kin see two miles down the canyon—an' they allus whistle an' slow up east of O'Fallon's.

BILL: Well—if yuh figur' yuh kin do it all right— [Sets the lantern back on the box.]

MARTHA: I could almost set it in the window an' they'd see it. [With a little cry of despair.] He's so bad off, Bill— don't yuh see—! I never seen him worse. Oh, Gawd! A half hour might make all the difference in the world.

BILL: Jist as yuh say, Marthy.

MARTHA: Mighty good-a yuh ter go, Bill—!

BILL: 'Tain't nothin' at all. Good-by. I'll git back as soon as ever I kin.

MARTHA: I know yuh will. Good-by. [BILL goes out. MARTHA goes over to the bed and sits on the side. Bending over him, she speaks in low, gentle tones.] Honey—! [JOHN opens his eyes and gazes at her with a dazed look.]

JOHN: That—that yuh—Marthy—?

MARTHA: Yes, yes. How d'yuh feel now?

JOHN: A-all right—all right—but— [Breaks off and smiles faintly.] Slides—yuh kin never tell—when they're comin'—yuh kin never tell—

MARTHA: Don't yuh try to talk!

JOHN: Never—never got caught before. Allus think-a— poor Hogan—who got carried down with his engine!— If the roadbed thar—at Flathead hadn't been soft—it 'ud never happened. Roadbed—roadbed—that's—that's what Nichol- son used ter say— 'Member, Marthy, it's the best road— in the country, now—a—a—great link 'tween east an' west— an' to the Gateway of the Orient—! The—the great steel trail—ter—ter Asia! Heavier rails, though—if they're goin' ter put them giant "hogs" on the mountain division.

MARTHA: Thar, thar, honey!

JOHN: Rails—rails—rails—an' steel goin' up—! They— they say the Japan trade is goin' ter pick up in the spring— But—but me an' you'll keep the road clare—won't we, Mar- thy? Let 'em send a dozen extras through. We'll do it!

We gotta do it. Greatest road in the world. A—a great arter—

MARTHA: Honey—please stop—!

JOHN: [Rises, struggling to get his breath.] Marthy—I —yuh an' me—

MARTHA: [Puts her arm about him.] Lie down, honey —yuh ain't—! [She attempts to force him gently back on the bed, but he struggles desperately to sit erect.]

JOHN: [Breathing with great effort.] Gotta git over ter— ter the shops, Marthy—Joe—Joe Ferriss'll be wonderin' why I ain't back—

MARTHA: Hush! Hush! Yuh ain't seen Joe in thirty years—

JOHN: He—he's thar at the shop—now— [At length he gives up the effort to sit up, and sinks limply back in her arms. He tries to speak but is unable to do so; his eyes roll and he struggles for breath. From time to time his body twitches and his face becomes distorted with pain. After a brief interval he grows very calm, and his breathing seems to become easier. He looks up at her with an expression of great placidity and a faint smile plays over his face.]

JOHN: [In a whisper.] Marthy—yuh allus been—my— [He breaks off, his eyes close and his head sinks down on his chest. MARTHA stares at him in horror for a moment or two, then gives a cry of wild, passionate anguish, lets his body sink prone on the bed, and leaps to her feet.]

MARTHA: Oh, Gawd—! Oh—oh! [She presses her hands tightly against her forehead and closes her eyes.] Oh! Oh! What shall I do? What am I goin' ter do? [She drops to her knees at the side of the bed, stretches out her arms and babbles hysterically.] John! John! Yuh ain't goin' ter leave yuhre Marthy— Oh, John—don't leave me—don't! Thar ain't nobody else! John! Oh, Gawd, don't take him from me! He's all I got—all that's left! Oh! Oh! Oh, Gawd, don't take him from me! Oh, Gawd, don't take him from me! [Abruptly, from far off, comes the sound of a train whistle. MARTHA does not hear it.] John! open yuhre eyes an' look at me! Look at yuhre Marthy an' smile! [She jumps to her feet with clenched hands and an expression of tigerish challenge.] Thar ain't no Gawd! Thar ain't no Gawd! If—if thar is one he's a black-hearted divil! That's what he is! Curse Him—an' His world—an' all the people in it! [The whistle sounds again in the distance—a little louder this time.] Curse Him! Curse Him! Curse Him! [Again the whistle sounds. She pauses and listens—as though in a daze. A prolonged blast—and still louder. She realizes suddenly that the limited is coming up the canyon. She gives a gasp, jumps to the table, turns down the oil lamp, then staggers to the window and peers out. She stands there for a moment, then goes swiftly to the back of the room, picks up the red lantern and moves to the door. She puts her hand on the knob, as though to open it, then something impels her to face about. Her eyes rove about the room and she presents a picture of tragic woe. The whistle again—still nearer—marked by a discernible canyon reverberation. She stands tense, listening and deliberating for a brief interval. Then hoarsely.] At—at the edge of the canyon—blowin' fer O'Fallon's— [Her eyes wander to the bed, and she stares fixedly at the still form on it. Suddenly she gives way to a series of prolonged, dry racking sobs. Presently she brings herself up short, and with a wild cry raises the lantern in the air, and dashes it down across the back of a chair. The light vanishes, the glass flies in all directions and the lantern falls to the floor with a dull thud. She moves unsteadily to the window, stands for a moment gazing out, then comes back and clings to the table for support. The whistle sounds again—shrill and penetrating. A shaft of light shoots in the window—faint and eerie—and dances about. The limited's whistle—quite near. The shaft of light grows larger and brighter. Suddenly it strikes her full in the face, revealing an expression which is a combination of insane hate and fear. It plays on her face for several moments, then disappears. The roar of the oncoming train can now be heard. MARTHA gives way to an outburst of hysterical laughter. The train thunders past the house. A brief interval ensues, dominated by the roar of the flying train, then comes the sound of a tremendous crash, as it dives into the slide and is wrecked. MARTHA gives a piercing shriek, puts her hands over her ears, and sinks to the floor.]

DAY'S END
By Alice Pieratt

PERSONS IN THE PLAY

SARAH KROAN
MOLLY
SALLY
SKIFFENSON

DAY'S END

A FARMHOUSE kitchen in a remote part of the mountains of Nevada. An old oak tree covers the one window with its heavy foliage, allowing what little light the day affords to fall in fantastic shadows upon a large, much worn armchair. To the left, some distance away, a door opens onto the back porch. There is a living room door to the right. A cupboard, a table, a stove and a few chairs complete the furnishings. The kitchen, as we see it, is quite dim, then as though the sun has broken through the clouds, a few rays of light play into the room and upon the old chair.

SARAH KROAN comes in, followed by MOLLY and a second later by the reluctant SALLY. SARAH, in the late forties, is dressed simply in black. She seems the typical hard-working farm woman of a period some thirty years back, but this impression is belied by the deep tones of her voice and a peculiar lightness in the movements of her hands. MOLLY is about the same age, though her round eyes and slightly petulant mouth might indicate that she was considerably younger. She is also dressed in black, but not so simply as SARAH. Jet ornaments dangle from her hat and there is a bit of fur on her coat. Her daughter SALLY is about eighteen, her black outfit is a makeshift affair, as though the various garments had been gathered from as many people to serve for this emergency.

SARAH: [Going to the range.] I put plenty of wood in the stove this morning so's there'd be some coals left. [She adds fresh fuel.] It'll catch in a minute.

MOLLY: [Dabbing at her eyes with a black-bordered handkerchief.] That range always did hold fire. I remember when Gran bought it. She bought it from Skiffenson, when I was still a girl home here on the old place. Poor Gran! She always was a good customer to Skiffenson. And you know, Sarah, I think she missed him not coming up here the last few years. Just last week she was trying to mumble something about him to me, when I brought her over that cheese-cake—remember? It was the last thing she ate from me. She always liked cheese-cake. [She weeps and sniffs.]

SALLY: [Holding the door open slightly.] Aw, now Moms!

SARAH: [Has been standing very still near the range, her eyes away, a light on her face. At SALLY's voice she turns.] Better come in, Sally, and shut the door.

MOLLY: You're letting all the heat out, Sally. It's cold enough in here.

SALLY: Moms, you said you wouldn't stay.

MOLLY: Now don't go telling me what I said or didn't say at a time like this. I can't remember nothing from one minute to the next.

SARAH: Shall I make some tea?

MOLLY: [With an apprehensive glance toward the large chair.] I—yes, make some, Sarah. [Sits on the chair near the range.] A body feels the need of something hot after a funeral.

SALLY: Oh, now we'll be here for an hour. I want to go home.

MOLLY: Listen to her, Sarah. The way that young one talks!

SARAH: She's tired . . . the water's getting ready to boil.

MOLLY: [Weeping and settling herself comfortably.] I've seen Gran sitting in that old chair for so many years, seems I see her sitting there still. It don't seem real . . . she's gone.

SARAH: [Moving toward the sitting room door.] Yes . . . she's gone. [Her voice rises on a note of pain.] She's . . . dead . . . at last. [Her eyes fall for an instant on the old chair and a haunting doubt creeps into her voice.] You —are gone? [She turns from the chair and faces MOLLY.] Like you, Molly, I thought for an instant I saw her—sitting there.

MOLLY: Sarah, you take it so queer. I know you're just her daughter-in-law and blood's thicker'n water, but you've lived with her for nearly thirty years. And God knows you been good to her. Better'n Otto, her own son, ever was. He's terrible anyhow. He wouldn't speak at the funeral this morning. Anybody'd think he was dumb, the little he talks. Making motions for this and making motions for that. . . . [A sudden, sharp whistle is heard outside. SARAH takes a step forward, then stands with a quick intake of breath.]

MOLLY: [Drops her wet handkerchief.] What's that?

SARAH: It's Otto. It's the whistle he uses when he wants Chad to help him in the field. One long whistle . . . like that.

SALLY: No wonder he can't keep a hired man on the ranch. Chad said he wouldn't stay here any longer than it took to get a job somewhere else, he likes some sociability. [Turns to SARAH.] Then I guess Uncle Otto will have *you* working out in the fields.

SARAH: No, no, Sally, no. I'll not be working in the

fields any more. I'll not plow the near end orchard this spring to come, nor ever again, not ever any more.

MOLLY: [Picking up her handkerchief.] You're too old to work in the fields, Sarah. [Looks belligerently toward the door.] If that ain't just like Otto! Blowing a whistle when he wants the hired man. And what right's he got working in the fields today? With Gran not cold in her grave . . . her own son not showing more respect . . . he's my own brother but I . . . I'd like to tell him what I think of him. [She weeps again.]

SARAH: The water's boiling. You make the tea, Molly. I'll be right back . . . there's something I want to . . . do. . . . And, Molly, put out the old blue cups, I'm going to use them today. . . . Gran's precious old blue cups. [She goes, quickly.]

MOLLY: [Getting up.] Blue cups! Sarah, did you say the old blue cups? Did she say the blue cups, Sally?

SALLY: [Listlessly turning over the pages of a catalogue.] I don't know. I wasn't listening.

MOLLY: I don't know what's got into Sarah. She don't act natural. I don't like the look on her face. What does she want to use Gran's old cups for . . . at a time like this. Gran never used them blue cups except for weddings and christenings and . . . farewells . . . like when your Uncle Joey went away to sea. . . .

SALLY: Maybe Aunt Sarah's going away. She hasn't been off this ranch in thirty years.

MOLLY: Tisht! Sarah going away. Where'd she go, who's she got to go with? How many times didn't we invite her to take a trip down the valley with us, but you couldn't budge her from this place.

SALLY: Well, why don't you use the blue cups if she wants 'em. What good are they up on the shelf?

MOLLY: [Straightening the table.] Them cups are valuable, Sally. More'n a hundred years old they are. I know

Gran wouldn't like 'em used at a time like this and I ain't
going to set 'em.

SALLY: I wish we were home. How Aunt Sarah ever
lives in this place is more'n I can see.

MOLLY: [Waving her handkerchief.] Where else would
she live? This is her home, the only home she's known in
thirty years. She ain't never left these mountains since she
came up here to teach in the old school what was burned
down before you was born. She was teacher here a few
months . . . and then she married Otto—and I tell you we
never thought she'd have him—but Gran said Otto was like
herself and always got what he wanted. [She weeps again.]

SALLY: Oh, well, I wish you'd stop crying. Poor old
Gran is better off dead and you know it. Last few years
she couldn't do anything but sit and mumble. And I didn't
see the family coming over and doing anything for her either.
They left all that to Aunt Sarah. Gran's better dead.

MOLLY: [Puts her handkerchief on the oven door to dry
and takes a fresh one from her pocket.] I never thought to
hear you speak so heartless. Now I know it'll be the same
when I'm gone. Never a tear nor a word of praise for all
the years I've raised you young ones . . . just nothing but
"she's better dead."

SALLY: [Comes over and fusses with her mother's hat.]
Now, Moms, don't feel bad. I didn't mean it the way you
took it up.

MOLLY: [Brightening, she continues to clear the table.]
Well . . . I know Gran lived a full life and it was her time
to go. But she did hold on, Sally. I never knew anyone
so strong for wanting her own way. And she was hard
to the end. She wouldn't send a word of forgiveness to your
Uncle Joey—and him off in a heathen land across the sea.

SALLY: [With conviction.] I think Uncle Joey is one
member of this family I'd have liked . . . besides you, Mom,
of course.

657

MOLLY: Your Uncle Joey did a terrible thing. Gran never forgave him, and she prayed extra for him every day of her life. He married a divorced woman.

SALLY: What's so terrible in that?

MOLLY: Sally! That's a mortal sin. When people are married they have to stay married no matter what.

SALLY: There's some people I wouldn't stay married to— no matter what!

MOLLY: [Weeping.] Sally! Wherever do you get such ideas. Anybody'd think I didn't raise you right. Seems you're always crossing me here lately.

SALLY: Oh, don't cry, Moms. I didn't mean it. [Pats her shoulder.] Make the tea for Aunt Sarah.

MOLLY: [Fussing with the table.] Yes, poor Sarah. She's been a good wife to your uncle, Sally. She's never crossed him by a word.

SALLY: Hmm! Might have been better all around if she had.

MOLLY: Sally! I can't stand the way you are talking. Where do you get such thoughts? You can't say things without thinking 'em first. I declare!

SALLY: I'm sorry again, Moms. Anyhow I'm going outside and wait for you. I don't want any tea.

MOLLY: But it's cold out there, Sally.

SALLY: Maybe it is, Moms. But this coat that you borrowed from Mrs. Anders would keep me warm on top of Shasta. [She spreads her arms and turns about displaying the size of the garment.]

MOLLY: I don't know what we'd do without Mrs. Anders. She's that good-hearted about lending her coat for funerals. For all of twenty years its been goin' the rounds in these mountains. She's getting on herself, Sally. I don't think she'll last many more winters. Then I guess her sister down in Wooden Valley'll get the coat. Though I've done a lot for Mrs. Anders myself.

DAY'S END

SALLY: Well, I hope I never have to wear it again. Make the tea, now, Moms, and I'll be outside. [She moves to the door.]

MOLLY: I guess it's all right, Sally, but I think you ought to stay in if only to show respect.

SALLY: [Has opened the door.] Moms, here comes old Skiffenson with a pack on his back.

MOLLY: Skiffenson? Why he never peddles these mountains in the winter. And as I was sayin' to your Aunt Sarah he hasn't been up this way for a couple of years. I know what, Sally, somebody in the valley must have told him that Gran . . . was gone. Lots of the old timers heard about it. Someone must have told old Skiffenson. Bad news travels fast.

SALLY: Maybe that's it, Moms. But he didn't forget to bring his pack. Leave it to that old peddlar to mix business with pleasure.

MOLLY: [Sinking into a chair.] Sally, you keep saying such things!

SALLY: I won't say another word, Moms. But listen now, don't buy anything for *me* from *him*. He's carried the same stock around since the year one. He might have been all right in the old days, when you couldn't get to town and they didn't have stores in the valley, but no one wants his stuff now.

MOLLY: You just be still, Sally. Gran traded with old Skiffenson all her life and so did I up until . . . a few years ago. Let me tell you his stuff *wore*. Anyhow, who's thinking of buying anything at a time like this?

SALLY: I just wanted to tell you. It might be a good idea if you let me keep your purse. You got the butter money in it.

MOLLY: I can take care of my own purse. You . . . You're too sassy, Miss. [Rises.] Come in or go out but shut the door!

659

SALLY: Don't be so mad at me, Moms. I'll wait out in the rig. [She smiles as she is about to go out.] You like me, don't you, Moms?

MOLLY: Go on with you, Sally, you're letting all the cold in. [As SALLY is half through the door.] If you sit in the rig wrap the buggy robe around you.

SALLY: All right, Moms. [She goes.]

[MOLLY pours water into the teapot and puts fresh wood in the stove. There is a knock on the door and at MOLLY's "come in," SKIFFENSON enters. He is bald-headed and old, long and thin. His glasses rest almost on the tip of his pointed nose. He has a habit when talking of blowing upward and so placing the glasses higher. But they never stay there long, and most of the time he peers over them, his head swaying on his long neck when he wishes to emphasize his words.]

SKIFFENSON: [Surprised at seeing MOLLY.] Hah! Well, for all! You here, Mully? [He takes the pack from his shoulders and slips it onto the floor.] Wh-r-r! The cold right through this stuff what they sell for wool, now, goes. [Flips off his scarf with contempt and holds it, up.] Wool what never saw a lamb's back, Mully. . . . My! My! How is't with you, Mully?

MOLLY: [She wipes her eyes.] Well—

SKIFFENSON: My! My! The years like the birds they go, hah? In this kitchen I ain't seen you since you was married with Salvin. I brung your weddin' linen. Thirty years, I bet, Mully.

MOLLY: Thirty-two, but it seems longer.

SKIFFENSON: Yah! Yah! In them times I did the good business, Mully, and had no rheumatiz and all. Skiffenson was the man to buy off in them days. Now alls got rigs, or wasting money in damned autymobiles, and down they go buying, to the valley. And them storekeepers what are reapin' benefits from trade what I built . . . they ain't givin' no tick . . . they ain't trustin' nobody . . . and they don't sell honest but set traps in winders, to catch fool people what don't know wool from shoddy. [He kicks the scarf which has fallen to his feet away from him.]

MOLLY: Times change. The young ones want things different. . . .

SKIFFENSON: [Has not listened to her and now his eyes are on the old chair. A fantastic pattern plays on the worn back cover. He speaks slowly.] My! . . . My!

MOLLY: Course you knew about . . . Gran?

SKIFFENSON: Yah! Yah! Poor womans! [Blows his glasses.]

MOLLY: She went, but it was her time. We all got to go. Too bad you missed the funeral. Lots came even if it did look like another storm. And we had one wreath made special at the valley florists, too. Mrs. Anders led the singin' —but she always sings too high. Still it was nice. It's too bad you didn't get here earlier.

SKIFFENSON: My! My! . . . For funerals I wouldn't take this long trip the mountains over. Not anyways till it comes summer and good roads. [Touches his heart.] In here I keep what I feel for old customers like what Gran was.

MOLLY: You didn't come for the funeral? Then what brought you?

SKIFFENSON: [Peering over his glasses.] Long in the past I promised Mis' Kroan to come right here . . . when the old lady . . . went. . . . [He raises his finger upward with a simple gesture.]

MOLLY: You got your wagon—you come up in it?

SKIFFENSON: Yah, down in the road bend I left it. [Looks at her doubtfully.] Bein's you're here, Mully, you know all right that Mis' Kroan goes with me down the valley?

MOLLY: [Pours a cup of tea and gulps it down.] She said

661

something . . . but I think now . . . she changed her mind. When was it she asked you to come now? I forgot.

SKIFFENSON: She asked me—come thirty years back next Easter. [Blows his glasses.]

MOLLY: Thirty . . . Yes, that's how long she's been married to Otto . . . I can see . . . but since then she ain't thought of going to the valley. We ask her'n', ask her, but she won't budge a step. You made your long trip for nothing, Skiffenson.

SKIFFENSON: Yah! Right you might be, Mully. But I made promise to Mis' Kroan and old Skiffenson don't forget. My! My! Mully, I brung her up here to teach in the school and she rode in the same old wagon that's waitin' now down in the bend. My! What a smiley she was. Mind, I mean before she was married with Otto—when she was sweetheartin' with that artist man what was boarding with Mis' Anders.

MOLLY: You mean Peter Farrel?

SKIFFENSON: His name is no matter. But Mis' Kroan made no laugh on me when old like I was, even then, I asked her the way to make numbers and writing.

MOLLY: I know, we had t' laugh t' see you writing on a slate. You never held the pencil right.

SKIFFENSON: [Blows his glasses.] To laugh was all right, Mully. But from then on I got no cheatin' done to me. But more'n that, for myself I could read words what one who once loved me, wrote me, back in the old country— far years past—and a long time she's been up. And now come every Christmas I write the words over . . . it wears the paper out here [touches his heart] against me. And . . . it seems new again—the letter—like it was fresh from [the upward gesture] her what once loved me.

MOLLY: Oh . . . poor thing. But it was long ago . . . and them things we forget . . . except sometimes . . . and then . . . we remember . . . I know . . . how 'tis.

SKIFFENSON: So for Mis' Kroan I have thanks for the learnin'.

MOLLY: Sarah *was* a good teacher.

SKIFFENSON: Yah! I had no thought then, that long spring past, that come next summer I'd find her married with Otto Kroan. My! My!

MOLLY: And you wasn't the only one that had no thought of such to happen. I think she had a fallin' out with Peter Farrel and married Otto for spite. Though she never said so.

SKIFFENSON: By the road bend she was standin' when I came that summer. "I scarce to know you, Miss Sally," I sez. "You lookin' so lost in your face . . . like somethin' what's been sucked dry" . . . "I don't be Miss Sally anymore," she tells me, "but Mis' Kroan—I want a promise from you—when you hear—when once you hear old Gran's dead—come in your rig what brought me here—and take me back home to the valley!"

MOLLY: I bet Sarah forgot all about it years ago. Course if she wanted to go below *then* she might've asked you to call for her. The roads was a fright and the men didn't go down month in, month out. But the last ten years—she could've gone any time. If you start off now, Skiffenson, you'd make the Anders place by night.

SKIFFENSON: Yah? Mully, here I stay till I see Mis' Kroan. My! My! What a booty she was.

MOLLY: Yes, she was, but no more, Skiffenson. You get the idea out of your head that she's going down with you.

SKIFFENSON: [With a stubborn look.] Here I wait till I see Mis' Kroan. I take her if she wants.

MOLLY: She can't take that trip to the valley with you in that old rig. Everybody'd be talking. A woman can't get up and leave her husband like that. Gran would never stand for anything like that—she'd turn in her grave.

SKIFFENSON: [Watching the light on the old chair.] Sit down, Mully, start no goings on. Something fine, so fine I'll show to you. [He lifts his pack and removes a few yards of crimson cloth.] Now, just look and see.

MOLLY: [She sits down and watches him from the corner of her eye.] How should I care to look . . . at a time like this?

SKIFFENSON: Never will come a better time, Mully. Forty years I been through these mountains peddlin'—and at weddin's and funerals is best to look for the eyes something better to do than weepin' it gives. [With a quick movement he spreads the cloth before her.] See now, hah, how is that for a bootiful?

MOLLY: [Rises and feels material expertly.] Oh, lands. [Her face falls.] Such a color! Gran wouldn't like it. Anyway at a time like this I couldn't think to buy anythin'.

SKIFFENSON: It bootiful makes you, Mully.

MOLLY: Red always was the color I liked best . . . but Gran . . . No, I wouldn't buy it.

SKIFFENSON: [Folds material.] No? Mis' Dodgers then maybe will like it.

MOLLY: Let me feel of it again. [Does so and sighs.] I couldn't wear it. The color . . . the neighbors'd talk. I got to wear mournin' now for always.

SKIFFENSON: [Blows his glasses and speaks mysteriously.] Mully, you could wear it *under*.

MOLLY: Such a talk! Waste it under?

SKIFFENSON: Wait now, something I'll show you. [Draws a booklet from his pocket.] Here it tells from the people what makes the stuff that ladies can use it for things *under*. [She peers over his shoulder eagerly.] Wait, I find it. Here . . . here is where it says it. [He adjusts his glasses and reads.] "This goods is un-ex*celled* for the fashioning of. . . ." [At this moment the same whistle that

was heard earlier sounds piercingly, but this time there are
two short blasts. They both start.]

MOLLY: [Moving away.] That's Otto again. He must
want something. Sarah's such a long time in there. Sarah,
what are you doing in there?

SARAH: [Comes into the room carrying an old valise, a
black hat and a coat.] It—took longer than I thought—
to get—things together. [She sees SKIFFENSON and her
face lights up, as she goes to him.] I knew you wouldn't
forget to come— I knew all the time that you remembered.
Although—it's been a little bit long—to wait—but you got
the rig—the same old rig?

SKIFFENSON: Yah! Down at the bend I got it.

SARAH: How is it down home in the valley, Skiffenson?

SKIFFENSON: [Shaking his head.] My! My! Mis'
Kroan for me there is no business there no more. [The
two whistles are heard again. SARAH stiffens.]

MOLLY: What does Otto want, Sarah? You seem to
understand his whistlin'. You must've heard him a minute
ago.

SARAH: Yes . . . I heard. . . . But I thought this once
I wouldn't. . . . I thought this once I won't. . . . [Her eyes
seem drawn to the old chair.] But maybe. Two whistles
short like that, means Otto wants a change of horses. I
. . . I don't want to see . . . him. Will you take them
down for me, Skiffenson?

SKIFFENSON: To see Otto I'm not longin'. But for you
I'll do it, Mis' Kroan.

SARAH: Don't tell him that I'm going.

SKIFFENSON: Have no fear for me makin' loose of my
tongue. [He is at the doorway.]

SARAH: Bring him the two grays, Skiffenson. [Re-
luctant to go.] He . . . doesn't like to wait . . . for things.

SKIFFENSON: I hurry. [He goes.]

MOLLY: My Heavens, Sarah! What's all this about you

going down to the valley with Skiffenson? If you hadn't been actin' so queer yourself, and having such a funny look on your face, I'd have thought the old man was crazy. He said you asked him thirty years ago to come and get you . . . when he heard that Gran was . . . gone.

SARAH: Yes, I did. I asked him then. I've been waiting all the while . . . to go.

MOLLY: Oh, Sarah, you could've gone down the valley for a trip any time with us. It's out of the question you going in that old rickety wagon.

SARAH: You don't understand, Molly. It was Skiffenson who brought me here—I remember— how the wheels crunched and crunched in the brown road—and how everything was still except for that sound—it sang "Peter . . . Peter . . . Peter . . . Peter." [The two whistles are repeated, the animation dies from Sarah's face.]

MOLLY: Can't he wait a minute. I don't see how you put up with that whistling for things. I don't see how Gran ever put up with it.

SARAH: She liked it—and she liked it more and more toward the last. She used to say . . . she guessed I wouldn't forget I was a Kroan . . . when Otto whistled.

MOLLY: [Wiping her eyes.] Gran was . . . she had a powerful mind. She was a good woman . . . she always made people do just what she wanted. I remember . . . when I didn't want to marry Salvin . . . when I liked . . . someone else. . . . It might sound funny, Sarah . . . but I wonder how it'll seem to Gran being . . . where what she wants . . . don't count. . . .

SARAH: [With a start, looking at the table.] You didn't put on the blue cups.

MOLLY: Gran wouldn't like it, Sarah. Anyhow, I wouldn't set them, now I know what you want to use 'em for. You think you're going to stay in the valley.

SARAH: I'll get one for myself. [She takes a blue cup

from the shelf and smiles strangely.] I'll drink from it
. . . and as it has meant God Speed to others, let it mean
the same to me. [She holds it out.] God Speed me!
[Her eyes dart to the old chair and an involuntary shiver
runs through her body, and the cup crashes to the floor.]
Oh!

MOLLY: Sarah! You broke it. [She stoops and picks
up the pieces.] I wanted them cups to pass on to Sally.
[SARAH stands white and motionless; a sudden pity stirs
MOLLY and she goes to her.] Here, sit down, Sarah. Now
drink from this. [She hands SARAH an ordinary cup and
SARAH drinks.]

SARAH: Thanks. Where is Sally?

MOLLY: She's waiting out in the rig. She didn't want
any tea.

SARAH: I'm sorry about the cup—because of Sally.

MOLLY: [Fitting the pieces.] We might be able to glue
it together. Sally'll like this set . . . she feels worse about
Gran than she lets on.

SARAH: She's a good girl.

MOLLY: Well, I don't know, Sarah. It's hard work understanding your own young ones. I used to feel sorry for
you not having any when mine were small—but now—I
don't know—it may be just as well.

SARAH: Just as well.

MOLLY: [A pause while SARAH stares straight ahead and
MOLLY sugars her tea noisily against the cup.] You always
been a good Christian woman, Sarah.

SARAH: If you call me good because I stayed with him
you'll have to begin calling me bad, I guess. I'm leaving
these mountains—right away, with Skiffenson.

MOLLY: [Spilling her tea.] Sarah! If you want to go
down let someone in the family take you, don't go with
that old peddlar.

SARAH: You don't understand, Molly. I have to go with

667

him—if I went down into the valley with anyone else—
I'd never find myself again—myself—you know—my real
self that got lost when I married Otto. [She draws her
hand over her brow.] You see, Molly, I . . . I have not
been here at all—ever. I have been lost somewhere on the
road to the valley and I need Skiffenson's rig to carry me
over the road. . . . I need to hear the wheels crunch and
crunch. . . .

MOLLY: Sarah, what do you mean? You better take a
rest when I go. You're upset about Gran. I know you
haven't had any sleep for a week.

SARAH: There'll be lots of time to sleep. I don't have
to stay here any more now that Gran's gone. And she is
gone, isn't she, Molly?

MOLLY: You know she is. But if you wanted to leave
Otto for so long I don't see how a helpless old woman like
Gran could've held you here.

SARAH: She was strong, Molly, strong enough—to do
with me anything she wanted—while she lived. [She puts
her arms on the table and leans toward MOLLY.] She knew
something—and she promised never to tell—so long as I
stayed here—and now she's dead—and what she knew—is
buried with her.

MOLLY: What'd she know?

SARAH: I'll never tell. I gave myself to the long slow
years—years eating into me, in and out and in and out like
worms in a dead tree, so you nor anybody else would hear
what she knew.

MOLLY: [Weeping.] It's awful to hear you talk this
way, Sarah. But if what she 'knew kept you here, when
you've felt this way—it must have had something to do with
Peter Farrel!

SARAH: [Rising.] She never said so! She never spoke
of him to you?

MOLLY: No. But you know everybody expected you to

marry Peter Farrel. We was all dumfounded when he went off so sudden—and nobody never heard from him again.

SARAH: Never again.

MOLLY: I remember so well because Peter went the night somebody killed Aspin, the old hermit. And robbed him of the money he had sewed in his mattress. I remember Gran was the first on the scene. She always was everywhere first.

SARAH: [Her hands gripping the table hard.] Pour me a little more tea, Molly.

MOLLY: [Pouring.] But that's all past and done with. God knows where Peter Farrel is. And you're too old to begin a new life. I don't think Gran would've died until she was sure nothing—could make you break your marriage vow. "Till death do us part" was what she always preached for married people. [She sighs.] Gran was religious. [Shakes her head.] You're set now, Sarah.

SARAH: That's not true! I tell you that's not true. I've been keeping watch on myself all the while—I've been waiting and waiting for her to die. In my soul—in that part of me that really lives—I've never been here at all. I've lived ever and always in a world you know nothing of—and I'm not old . . . not so very old.

MOLLY: Anybody but me'd think you were out of your head, Sarah. I know you're just worn out. Sit down.

SARAH: [Glancing at the clock, her spirit droops.] Why —it's time to mix the bread. [She begins mechanically to make preparations.] It's so cold the yeast doesn't raise, my bread's been kind of heavy.

MOLLY: Sarah, you haven't any folks in the valley no more, it's been five years since your last cousin died. And you haven't any more blood folks.

SARAH: That doesn't matter. I have myself down there. It's myself I want to be with again.

MOLLY: Suppose—even if you do go with Skiffenson—you can't find—what you're looking for down there?

SARAH: Molly, I never thought of that, I always felt so sure [she puts her hand to her heart] here. And while I was longing and praying to be free to go—it seemed so simple. The first few years I used to go down to the bend and I'd pretend to myself—"this is the day I am going away, this is the day, this is the hour." . . .

MOLLY: But you don't do that no more, Sarah?

SARAH: I've always done it in my mind.

MOLLY: Well, keep on doing it in your mind. That won't hurt nobody. But you know Sally and Ned are going to school in the valley next term and they'd feel terrible if you went off and left Otto. Everybody'd be talking—these mountains'd just buzz with the talk. The Kroans've always held up their good name.

SARAH: I know . . . but I'm going.

MOLLY: Who's going to bake the bread, Sarah, if you won't be here to-morrow?

SARAH: What? Why, that's true. I forgot for a minute. It's just . . . just habit . . . Gran always liked the bread set at this time. [She pushes the mixture away and goes back to her seat.]

SALLY: [Opening the door.] Moms, are you never coming? I'm nearly froze. It'll take two hours to get home. You know Dolly's got a sore foot.

MOLLY: I'll be right out. Go on, I've got something to say to Aunt Sarah.

SALLY: Bye, Aunt Sarah. I'll come over next week and help you some.

SARAH: I wish you would, Sally.

SALLY: I will sure. Now hurry up, Moms. [She goes.]

MOLLY: How can you tell Sally to come next week when you're leaving? [Rises.]

SARAH: [With a bewildered fluttering of her hands.]

Why . . . that's right. I forgot again. I've dreamed of going for so long . . . you know . . . that now . . . I can't realize . . . I . . . I'm going. [She starts again to mix the dough.]

MOLLY: Sarah, you keep spilling flour on the floor.

SALLY: [Opens the door.] There's a big black cloud in the sky, Moms. Looks like a real storm's coming. You better hurry, you know Dolly shys at thunder.

MOLLY: That horse is an old fool. I've got to go, Sarah. [She feels the handkerchief, now dry on the oven door, and begins to weep into it afresh.] I can't say nothing more to you, Sarah. I'm just wore out. You try to think about the rest of us a little bit. [She moves to the door.] Your best years are gone. You don't know enough to teach the young ones nowdays. I'm going, Sarah. [She stands undecidedly for an instant.] Good-bye. [Goes.]

SARAH: Good-bye, Molly. [She crosses slowly and stares out the window. She adds more wood to the stove, then returns to the window.]

SKIFFENSON: [SARAH does not hear him enter the door, which MOLLY had not closed.] I brung Otto the grays. And now it's better to start, Mis' Kroan. Already the storm I smell.

SARAH: Skiffenson, Skiffenson, if you knew how I've hated that tree. The branches always seemed like big live hands choking the life out of the sun.

SKIFFENSON: [Tightening his pack, folding the crimson material into it regretfully.] These mountains is thick with 'em like that. Better to chop it down from there.

SARAH: Oh, no! I'm used to it now. I'd feel . . . queer with it gone.

SKIFFENSON: Better to put your hat on now, Mis' Kroan.

SARAH: [Moving to the table eagerly.] Skiffenson, call me, "Miss Sally."

SKIFFENSON: [Averting his face.] Miss Sally!

671

SARAH: [A hurt expression on her face.] Why . . . it doesn't sound the same . . . it doesn't reach deep down in me . . . and make me sing . . . I. . . .

SKIFFENSON: Better to put your hat on now, Mis' Kroan.

SARAH: [Doing so.] It seems strange to put my hat on this time of day. [Looks at the clock.] It's almost time to feed the turkeys. [She looks at him helplessly, appealingly.]

SKIFFENSON: [At the door, looks at her sadly.] I'll pass by here again—come summer time.

SARAH: In the summer? Everything is different in the summer, isn't it, Skiffenson?

SKIFFENSON: My! My! Yes. The roads are more better.

SARAH: That's true. I didn't think of that. The wheels couldn't crunch happily in the mud. No . . . they'd slither along, like the years sneaking by on you.

SKIFFENSON: We better to start, Mis' Kroan . . . if you're going. . . .

SARAH: Yes. [She stoops and picks up the valise, and at the same instant three long whistles ring out. She drops the valise.] Three? Was it three whistles? Did you count three whistles?

SKIFFENSON: Three. [He opens the door.]

SARAH: [Her eyes are drawn irresistibly to the old chair, a single line of light plays among its shadows.] Three. [Removes her hat slowly.] That means Otto wants . . . me. . . .

SKIFFENSON: I got to go now, Mis' Kroan. No longer can I wait. The storm I feel it heavy in the air.

SARAH: [She takes a few swift steps toward him.] I'm going with you. I'm going with you. Wait for me! [As she is about to put on her hat again, the whistles are repeated. She stands still and the light dies again from her face, her body wilts, and she looks, as SKIFFENSON would

say, "sucked dry."] Next time . . . you come . . . maybe
. . . in the summer? Everything is different in the
summer.

SKIFFENSON: Yah! All's different then . . . in the summer. [He opens the door.] Good-bye to you—good-bye to
you—Miss Sally. [He goes.]

SARAH: Miss Sally . . . oh. . . . Skiffenson, say my old
name in that tone again. [She takes an eager step.]
Skiffenson! Wait! [The whistles sound again more urgently. She moves back to the table. Her eyes are no
longer eager, but deeply shadowed.] I hear you . . . I
hear you. . . . [She takes an apron from the door and puts
it on, her eyes on the chair all the while. She seems drawn
to it irresistibly, and for an instant she stands with a look
of fear upon her face. Suddenly she straightens, her hand
on the back of the chair.] I hear you. . . . [She sinks
into the chair.] But I'm not coming. [The light plays
upon her face.] I'm not—coming.

GOOD VINTAGE
A PLAY OF CALIFORNIA
By Dan Totheroh

PERSONS IN THE PLAY

JULIA GARCIA
MAMMA GARCIA
JOE GARCIA
AUNT ANNIE
AUNT ROSE
LEONORA
MARIE
HARRY BARTO

GOOD VINTAGE

JULIA GARCIA'S bedroom in her father's ranch house, Sonoma County, California, not very far from the Valley of the Moon. It is the typical room of a young Italian girl whose father is now wealthy and can afford to give her a room to herself. Before Prohibition, when JOE GARCIA was a struggling vine-grower, JULIA slept in the same room with four brothers and sisters. The room is box-like and unimaginative, with white-washed walls. The white-wash is fresh and clean, however, and gives the room a singularly virginal appearance. JULIA's highly-polished brass bed is at the center, with a sky-blue counterpane, now flung back, for it is early morning and the bed is not made up. The rest of the furniture is a shiny mission set, bought in Napa at the Star furniture store, the leading one in the county. It is golden oak, highly polished, outdoing the glittering brass of the bed. On the dresser are many little girlish trinkets such as souvenir pin trays, a pin cushion shaped like a silver slipper, a burnt-wood box for handkerchiefs, some fancy bottles of cologne, a white ivory toilette set

painted with small pink roses and a red porcelain vase for
flowers. There is also a little chalk statue of the Virgin
in a bright blue robe edged in gold. Over the bed is a wooden
crucifix from which dangles a string of rosary beads, and
there are numerous holy pictures on the walls. The Virgin
holding up her red and gleaming heart, Christ holding out
his pierced hands, The Visit of the Wise Men, etc.—all
highly colored lithographs. JULIA's communion veil and
wilted wreath are also hung up on a peg near the dresser.
The carpet on the floor is gay and garish with bright pink
and red roses on a field of dove-gray. The early fall day is
already warm, the sun streaming through the flowered curtains of JULIA's room, bringing a promise of baking heat
at noon. Indeed, the morning could not be more propitious
for a Grape Festival. This is real grape-weather—the sun
kissing the grape into sweetness on the vine—and even
though the day will be a scorcher, the nights in the valley
are always cool and there will be a moon for dancing on the
open-air platform in the square.

JULIA GARCIA is discovered standing in the center of a
fluttering group of relatives, being dressed in the robes of
the Queen of the Vineyards. She is lithe and Latin—
dusky as a purple grape herself—her hair thick and blue-
black, and her eyes liquid brown, swimming with dreams.
She has been up since dawn and so has the GARCIA household. JOE GARCIA has outdone himself, sparing no expense
in costuming his daughter. The voluminous gown is of
varied-colored silks, and there is a heavy satin cloak ter-
minating in a long train. The colors of the gown are the
colors of the grape, the leaves of the vine and the wine of
the vintage. There are touches of young green also—the
whole dress symbolic of the grape from the time it is green
on the branch to the time it ripens. MAMMA GARCIA, fat
and swarthy of skin, with gray streaks in her once satin-
black hair, is just putting the dress over JULIA's head.

JULIA'S AUNT ANNIE, thin and wiry with a beak-like nose and brown, leathery skin, is helping her. Then there is AUNT ROSE who is small and all shriveled up like a dried apricot. She is in a lachrymose state for she has recently lost her husband and cannot forget it. Her hair is white with a tinge of yellow like an old bone, and she is dressed in shoddy black. Around her neck is a black chain, dangling a crucifix of yellowed ivory.

JULIA'S cousin, LEONORA, a girl of fourteen, overgrown and thin, her skirts too short for her spindly legs, sits on the edge of the unmade bed, watching JULIA with an envy which she attempts to conceal under a childish cloak of nonchalance.

AUNT ANNIE: [Clasping her hands in ecstasy as the folds of the dress drop to the floor.] Beautiful! Beautiful! *Dio Mio,* how beautiful!

AUNT ROSE: [Tearfully.] Ah, pretty Julia *mia*— She is like a saint. [She blows her sharp nose which is always red from blowing.] The little Saint of the Flowers.

MAMMA GARCIA: [Who is always practical.] No, no, not of the *flowers,* Rosie—of the grapevines!

AUNT ANNIE: [Who always agrees with her wealthy sister.] Yes, that is right—little Saint of the Grapevines. [To her daughter, sitting on the bed.] Ain't she beautiful, Leonora?

LEONORA: Swell.

AUNT ANNIE: [Laughing and winking at AUNT ROSE.] Swell, she says! That's all she learns in high school.

MAMMA GARCIA: [Straightening out the folds of the dress.] How does that feel, Julie?

JULIA: Fine—but warm, Mamma.

MAMMA GARCIA: Warm, of course! What do you think? An' you will be warmer than this when you ride on the float. It's what you must expect.

JULIA: Yes, Mamma.

MAMMA GARCIA: Didn't you almost faint last year, when you was maid-of-honor? [JULIA nods.] But then you had to ride down hot Main Street all that time with no cover over your head. It's dif'rent bein' queen, Julie. You get to ride on the throne with grapevines to keep the sun off.

JULIA: Yes, Mamma.

AUNT ROSE: It was hotter last year.

AUNT ANNIE: What are you talkin' about, Rosie? You can't tell so early in the mornin'.

AUNT ROSE: But I remember last year— Tony, he says to me, right after breakfast— [Crossing herself.] You know, Tony was alive this time last year— [She blows her nose.]

MAMMA GARCIA: Now, Rosie, you promised not to talk about Tony till next Sunday mass, didn't you?

AUNT ROSE: Yes, but I remember he said, "Rosie *mia,* this is the hottest mornin' in August since I come to Sonoma an' that was fifteen years ago."

MAMMA GARCIA: All right, but that is over now. Now, walk up and down, Julie. Let Mamma see how the train goes. [JULIA, with the dignity and pride of a little queen, walks up and down the room.]

AUNT ANNIE: Beautiful! Wonderful! *Dio Mio! Dio Mio!*

AUNT ROSE: The little Saint! Like in a church window she is!

MAMMA GARCIA: That is fine, Julie. Never was there such a beautiful queen in Sonoma county!

AUNT ANNIE: Or in all California!

AUNT ROSE: Cara Arbini was so ugly last year. So fat! When the float bumped she jiggled like jelly.

LEONORA: [Giggling.] An' she has a mustache! [They all laugh, in spite of the fact that MAMMA GARCIA has a mustache of her own.]

MAMMA GARCIA: Cara Arbini is a fool.

AUNT ANNIE: *All* the Arbinis are fools.

AUNT ROSE: They are dangerous people.

AUNT ANNIE: Poof! Don't talk crazy, Rosie.

MAMMA GARCIA: [To JULIA who is still walking up and down, pausing to preen in front of the dresser mirror.] Now turn around slow, Julie, an' make your bow like when they crown you queen. [JULIA stops, turns, and makes a low bow, bending her head.]

THE TWO AUNTS: Beautiful! Wonderful! Don't she do it beautiful! Just like a dancer!

AUNT ANNIE: See. She stays like that till they put the crown on her and read the speech.

MAMMA GARCIA: [As JULIA rises again, flushed and with sparkling eyes.] That was good, Julie.

AUNT ANNIE: Just like a movie queen.

MAMMA GARCIA: Shall I call Papa?

AUNT ROSE: [Blowing her nose again.] If Tony could only see her. Tony always loved Julie.

AUNT ANNIE: Yes, call Joe, Amelia. He will be so proud of her.

MAMMA GARCIA: [Going to the door and calling down the stairs.] Papa! Oh, Papa! Come up an' see Julie all dressed.

JOE GARCIA: Just a minute, Amelia.

AUNT ROSE: All the girls will be so jealous of her.

JULIA: I don't *want* them to be jealous, Auntie.

MAMMA GARCIA: Of course not! Julie is a sweet girl.

A YOUNG GIRL'S VOICE: [From downstairs.] Oh, Julie, can I come up?

JULIA: [Eyes dancing.] It's Marie! Tell her to come up, Mamma!

MAMMA GARCIA: Come up, Marie! We are in Julie's room. [JULIA walks up and down again, her little chin tilted. In a moment, MARIE rushes in, a girl of JULIA's age, dressed as a maid-of-honor. She is a plain-looking girl with chestnut brown hair and many freckles scattered across her snubby nose. She pauses a moment in the doorway, eyes round with admiration; then she squeals and rushes to JULIA with outstretched arms.]

MARIE: Oh, Julie—Julie—you look simply wonderful! [The girls kiss each other, squealing, giggling, half crying.]

MAMMA GARCIA: [Studying MARIE with keen, analytical eyes.] *You* look nice, too, Marie.

MARIE: [Stepping away from JULIA to get a better view.] Yes—but I'm only a maid-of-honor. *Julie's* the *queen!* I *never* saw anybody look so *wonderful!*

JULIA: I'm glad you like it, Marie.

MARIE: I just been down to see the float. It looks *simply* beautiful—just like a big wedding cake!

AUNT ANNIE: Wedding cake! That's funny.

MARIE: Yes, it does. A beautiful, big wedding cake.

AUNT ROSE: A wedding cake with grapes on it. That's a good one.

MARIE: The throne's awful high. Everybody'll see Julie easy—above everybody else. Some of the maids-of-honor were there already, picking out the best seats. Helen Raymond was acting like a pig.

LEONORA: She only got twenty-five votes. I saw the list in the drug store.

MARIE: [Giggling.] Who would buy votes for Helen Raymond!

AUNT ANNIE: Her papa is stingy. He makes a lot of money with plumbing.

MARIE: The Native Sons' float looked pretty.

LEONORA: They decorated the new fire wagon.

MARIE: My brother Johnny's going to drive the horn of plenty.

JULIA: What time is it, anyway?

MARIE: Almost ten.

JULIA: I didn't know it was *that* late. The parade's supposed to start at eleven.

AUNT ANNIE: They *never* start on time.

LEONORA: I haven't heard the firemen's band yet.

MAMMA GARCIA: They can't start without the queen.

AUNT ROSE: That would be bad luck, an' the grapes would be bad next year.

AUNT ANNIE: Such crazy talk, Rosie. You talk like the old country.

MAMMA GARCIA: This is California, Rosie.

AUNT ROSE: [Shaking her head.] Grapes are the same here as in Italy.

AUNT ANNIE: You talk old-fashion, Rosie.

AUNT ROSE: What do we have the festival for? It is to make thanks for a good vintage, is it not? What is Julie a queen for?

MAMMA GARCIA: It is all for fun! [As JOE GARCIA comes in.] Oh, here's Papa. Look at her, Papa! Look at your Julie! [JOE GARCIA is a thick-set, middle-aged Italian with a round stomach and a red-brown face. His eyes are small and good-natured, and his coarse black hair, a little greasy, is streaked with gray. He is dressed for the occasion in a flashy, chocolate-brown suit and wears a red vest which fits over his stomach as snugly as red feathers fit a robin's breast. His cream-colored satin tie has a ruby stick-pin in it and there is a ruby ring on his little finger. He is inordinately proud of his daughter and now becomes almost hysterical over her appearance.]

JOE GARCIA: Oh, Julia *mia,* you are wonderful! Wonderful! You are like—like all the leaves in my vineyard! [His eyes fill with tears.]

MAMMA GARCIA: Walk up an' down for Papa, Julie—up an' down. [JULIA walks up and down.]

JOE GARCIA: [Wringing his hands in ecstasy.] Beautiful! Wonderful! Everybody will be so jealous of her!

My beautiful Julie! She is the most beautiful queen in the world! If only Mussolini could see her. *He* would say she was beautiful! Oh, Julie—Julie—you make your old Papa cry. [He sniffs and clasps and unclasps his pudgy, red hands. AUNT ROSE weeps a little in her handkerchief.]

MAMMA GARCIA: Now bow for him, Julie—just like you did for us. Look, Papa—this is how she'll bow when they put the crown on her. [JULIA turns and bows, sinking gracefully to one knee.]

JOE GARCIA: [Clapping his hands like an excited small boy.] *Dio Mio,* you are an angel. Everybody will cry when you do that—*everybody*—even people who are jealous of me—even my enemies. They will all cry!

MAMMA GARCIA: See? She stays like that till the mayor puts the crown on her.

MARIE: And we'll all bow behind her, like this. [MARIE bows awkwardly.]

AUNT ANNIE: Good!

MAMMA GARCIA: Get up now, Julie.

JULIA: [Rising.] It's about time for us to go, Mamma.

JOE GARCIA: I am going to take you down in the new car, Julie. [He rubs his hands together.] You'll look beautiful in the new car.

MAMMA GARCIA: Ain't that fine, Julie? You'll be the first to ride in Papa's new Pierce Arrow.

MARIE: [Squealing, quite beside herself.] Oh, Julie— Julie— [She crushes JULIA in her arms.]

MAMMA GARCIA: Look out, don't mess her, Marie. [A bell rings downstairs.]

JOE GARCIA: Ain't that somebody at the door?

MAMMA GARCIA: Mary'll answer it.

AUNT ANNIE: We're forgettin' all about dressin'. Come on, Leonora, get yourself washed.

AUNT ROSE: I must get my corset on.

684

MARY: [The servant, calling at the foot of the stairs.] It's Mister Barto, Mr. Garcia.

JOE GARCIA: [Still excited.] Harry! Harry must see my Julie!

MAMMA GARCIA: He can see in the parade, Papa.

JOE GARCIA: No, I want him to see her here. Have him come up, Mary.

MARY: All right, Mr. Garcia.

MAMMA GARCIA: Well, don't be long, Papa. We got to go.

AUNT ANNIE: [To LEONORA who is looking out of the window.] Come along, Leonora. You got to get your new pink dress on.

LEONORA: There was a man lookin' up at this window from the grape arbor.

JOE GARCIA: Huh?— Somebody lookin' up here? [He trots to the window and peeks out, rather cautiously.] Who was lookin' up at my Julie's bedroom?

LEONORA: He ain't there now. [Pointing out the window.] But he was right over near that wine barrel.

JOE GARCIA: What did he look like?

LEONORA: I couldn't see very well. The leaves was in front of his face.

JOE GARCIA: A tall man?

LEONORA: I don't know. Maybe. I just saw him and then he went away.

AUNT ANNIE: Funny the dogs didn't bark.

MAMMA GARCIA: Just one of the new pickers, Papa.

JOE GARCIA: [Rubbing his chin, thoughtfully.] Maybe, an' maybe not. Maybe one of my enemies. I got lots of enemies since I got rich.

AUNT ROSE: That is always the way. When you was poor, everybody liked you.

JOE GARCIA: [Rubbing his hands.] They are all jealous of me. They laughed at me when Prohibition came in.

They made believe to be sorry for me. "Poor old Joe Garcia," they said— "All them grapes planted an' now no place to sell his wine." They made believe to be sorry, but they was all glad. [Chuckling.] But—but I fooled 'em— They laughed too quick. Yes, I got lots of enemies.

MAMMA GARCIA: Don't talk like a fool, Joe—an' don't go talkin' so loud. The windows are open. [Enter HARRY BARTO, a short, very dark Italian, younger than JOE. He wears a heavy, black mustache and his eyes are beady-black and snapping. Usually a placid little man, he is now excited. He too is dressed for the festival, but his attire is less conspicuous than GARCIA's, although he wears a very bright red necktie and his suit is a light gray with a thin stripe.]

HARRY: Hello.

MAMMA GARCIA: Hello, Harry.

JOE GARCIA: Harry—Harry—you are just in time— [Trotting over to him, shaking his hand and dragging him into the room toward JULIA, who stands before the mirror.] Look at my little Julie—my little queen— Is she not beautiful, huh? [Turning JULIA around as though she were a wax model.] All real silk, Harry—*real* silk. How much did it cost in Napa, Mamma?

MAMMA GARCIA: Thirty dollars, Joe.

JOE GARCIA: Do you hear that? Thirty dollars just for a costume, Harry—but it's worth it, eh?

HARRY: Sure.

AUNT ANNIE: An' the cloak, Joe—real *satin.*

JOE GARCIA: Yes, real satin. How much was that, Mamma?

MAMMA GARCIA: Twenty-five dollars, Joe.

JOE GARCIA: Twenty-five dollars, just for the cloak. [Chuckling.] An' that's only part of it. One hundred dollars for votes. One hundred dollars to make Julie queen. But what do *I* care? I showed all my enemies. Last year

Arbini bought all the votes. He thought he was so smart. Julie could only be maid-of-honor. They laughed at me, but I showed 'em. Julie will look so beautiful on the float— [Pinching JULIA's cheek.] Won't you, Julie—huh? You will hold your head up way, way high, huh, Julie? He-he-he, look at her blushing. She is so happy— Now, make one of them pretty bows for Harry, Julie, like you did for me. A bow for Papa's best friend. [Pulling HARRY back a little.] Now, now look, Harry— Watch. She will bow like this when Spegenni puts the crown on her. Go ahead, Julie. [JULIA bows as before.]

JOE GARCIA: Ha, ha, ha—beautiful, eh?—beautiful! My God, Julie, you are beautiful! [Slapping HARRY on the back.] What say, Harry?

HARRY: Fine, Joe—just fine. [He shuffles his feet impatiently.]

MAMMA GARCIA: Get up, Julie—don't you get tired now. [Putting her arm around her as JULIA rises.] Come in my room a minute. I want to give you something. A present Mamma has for you.

JULIA: A *present,* Mamma?

MAMMA GARCIA: Yes, a little surprise, Julie. [They go toward the door.]

AUNT ANNIE: Let us see too, Amelia.

MAMMA GARCIA: Yes, you can all come.

JULIA: Come on, Marie.

AUNT ANNIE: Come on, Leonora. Then you must get dressed an' look pretty.

JOE GARCIA: Don't be long, Amelia. I got the new car waitin'.

AUNT ROSE: [Pointing to a wreath of grape leaves and artificial grapes lying on the bed.] You forgot the wreath, Amelia.

MAMMA GARCIA: We'll get that in a minute. Come on. [All the women crowd out, following MAMMA GARCIA.]

Aunt Rose: [Shaking her head and blowing her nose.] This is a sad day for me. No Tony— Tony he used to like the festivals. In Italy we would dance all day an' night when it was a good vintage. Everybody would get drunk but nobody would hurt each other— [She goes out, mumbling.]

Joe Garcia: What's the matter, Harry? You don't act right.

Harry: [Looking around him and speaking in a low, cautious voice.] They're all in town, Joe.

Joe Garcia: The Arbinis?

Harry: Yep. They came over from Santa Rosa in a truck, early this mornin'. It don't look good.

Joe Garcia: [Purple in the face.] Let him try anything!

Harry: There's a lot of 'em. Ten, I think. They all got guns.

Joe Garcia: Guns!

Harry: Yep. Eddie thinks they mean business.

Joe Garcia: Goddam—just let 'em try things. I ain't scared of them.

Harry: They think you'll be off guard, tendin' to the festival. Eddie says two or three of 'em was talkin' in the barber shop an' not carin' who heard 'em. They came right out about hi-jackin'.

Joe Garcia: They better keep out of my territory!

Harry: We went into theirs, didn't we?

Joe Garcia: That was dif'rent. Jesus, I don't carry no guns to go around killin' people.

Harry: No, but I do. An' you better carry one today, Joe. In them crowds there's no tellin' what they'll do.

Joe Garcia: Is that Goddam Arbini here, too?

Harry: Not yet—just his gang. But he'll come over later, I'll bet, when things get goin'.

Joe Garcia: That Goddam wop! Let him start tryin' things. I wouldn't mind killin' him. Ever since he come

688

up from 'Frisco he's been dirty with me. [He trots up and down.]

HARRY: We don't want no scraps at the festival, if we can help it.

JOE GARCIA: Of course we don't. We all ought to be happy. *Everybody* in Sonoma ought to be happy. We ought to give thanks to God, Harry. He gave us a good vintage this year—*never* such a good vintage. We ought to thank God an' make merry.

HARRY: Arbini's crop wasn't so good. That early frost got him, you remember?

JOE GARCIA: It got *him* an' left *me* alone.

HARRY: Yes. Well, maybe that's what makes him so sore.

JOE GARCIA: Serves that wop right! Goin' around with guns—hatin' people. Serves him right!

HARRY: Well—we got to be careful today, anyhow. You better not go ridin' around in that new big car. You'll be a regular target in that.

JOE GARCIA: Like Hell! I'll go around in that car, all right. [Mopping his perspiring forehead with a flashy handkerchief.] Hot, ain't it? We better tell the sheriff to keep on the job, Harry.

HARRY: Sheriff knows we hi-jacked over in Santa Rosa, last week.

JOE GARCIA: Sure, but he won't say nothin'. I got him fixed, all right. I'll phone George downstairs. He's a good feller.

HARRY: I don't trust him a inch. If Arbini gave him more money, he'd—

JOE GARCIA: Arbini *won't!* That Goddam wop, he pinches every nickel. He won't even give to the church! But look at *me*. I give a fat sum every month, an' two weeks ago I gave Father Roni one hundred dollars to put a new wall on the mission.

HARRY: Sure, *I* know. You're a good man, Joe. But all them things make Arbini more mad, all the time. He don't like to see you act so rich—so, so we better watch out today. See?

JOE GARCIA: Sure, I see. [Patting HARRY on the back, affectionately.] You're a good friend to me, Harry—a damn good friend. You help me lots. I don't forget, see? Come on, I'll phone George an' then you an' me'll have a big drink of vino. Then we go downtown, huh?

HARRY: Sure.

JOE GARCIA: Don't let the women know about Arbini, Harry. We can't get them scared. I want them to have a good time today.

HARRY: Sure. [They start for the door, when the women return.]

JULIA: [Bursting in, flushed excitedly. MARIE follows; then LEONORA and the three sisters, MAMMA GARCIA beaming broadly.] Look, Papa— Look at the present Mamma gave me! [She runs over to her father and shows him a chain of bright blue beads around her neck which terminates in a little blue-lacquered crucifix.] Isn't it pretty, Papa?

JOE GARCIA: Ah—it is very pretty, Julie. It goes pretty with your costume. You'll wear it today, huh? [JOE, somewhat sobered, kisses the little crucifix.] It will protect you from harm.

JULIA: Yes. Mamma had Father Roni bless it for me.

JOE GARCIA: That was good, Amelia. That was very good. [Letting the cross drop back against JULIA's little breast.] You did right. It will protect my little Julie from all harm.

MAMMA GARCIA: You talk like there is some sort of danger, Joe.

JOE GARCIA: [Shrugging and glancing at HARRY.] You never can tell.

AUNT ROSE: [Blowing her nose.] No, you can't. Look

what happened to Tony. This time, last year, he was stronger than anybody—drivin' a big truck, good as anybody—then, all of a sudden—

AUNT ANNIE: Rosie! Today we are all goin' to be merry!

MAMMA GARCIA: What a lot of crazy jabber. This is a festival, not a funeral! [Picking up the wreath of vine leaves from the bed.] Here, put on the wreath, Julie. Then we must go. [The wreath is placed around JULIA's blue-black hair. It is very lovely with her dark skin and eyes.]

AUNT ANNIE: How beautiful!

MAMMA GARCIA: She'll wear that until they put the crown on her.

MARIE: The crown is *simply* beautiful. It looks like real gold an' has rubies an' emeralds in it.

LEONORA: They ain't real! [She turns to the window and looks out.]

JOE GARCIA: They wanted to give her the old one they used last year, but I bought a new one for her, out of my own pocket. It was the best I could get in 'Frisco.

AUNT ANNIE: Imagine usin' the one Cara Arbini wore!

JOE GARCIA: This one will be mine after the festival is over. Julie can hang it up in her room. Would you like that, Julie?

JULIA: Oh, yes, Papa.

HARRY: Come on, Joe—we got to phone.

JOE GARCIA: All right—[Turning to look once more at JULIA.] *Dio Mio,* I can't get enough of her. She is so beautiful. Walk up and down just once more for your Papa, Julie—just once more, a little bit.

MAMMA GARCIA: Listen to him! You are so crazy, Papa.

JOE GARCIA: [Winking at MAMMA GARCIA.] Like I was about *you,* Amelia. [He puts his hand on his heart and sighs loudly.] Ha, ha, ha, just like that!

AUNT ANNIE: Don't *I* remember them days, Joe. She thought you'd *never* ask her. Ha, ha, ha.

MAMMA GARCIA: What a lot of foolishness!

JOE GARCIA: Go on, Julie. Walk up an' down for Papa, once more!

AUNT ANNIE: You'll get her all tired out, Joe.

JOE GARCIA: Shut up, Annie. Go on, Julie. [JULIA walks up and down, tilting her chin.]

LEONORA: [At the window, drawing back a little as JULIA is walking.] Look! There's that man again, Uncle Joe!

JOE GARCIA: Where? [He cautiously tiptoes toward the window. JULIA, in her glory and pride, is still walking, looking back to see herself in the dresser mirror.]

LEONORA: [Suddenly crouching.] Look out, Uncle Joe! He has a gun. He's pointin' it right at you!

HARRY: [Nearer to the window.] For Christ's sake, duck, Joe— Duck! [JOE GARCIA drops down to his knees. There is a shot outside. JULIA screams. She stands still as though transfixed; then crumples up and falls in her glory of robes to the floor.]

MAMMA GARCIA: Julie! Baby—Julie. [She drops to her knees beside JULIA.[

HARRY: It's one of Arbini's gang! [He pulls out his gun and runs swiftly down the stairs.]

LEONORA: [Peeking out.] There he goes! He jumped the fence. He's runnin' down the road!

JOE GARCIA: [Dazed and stumbling to JULIA.] Julie— my little Julie— That was meant for your papa—not for you—not for you—not for my baby—for her bad papa— [He, too, is on his knees, lifting JULIA in his arms.] Julie— my little girl—

MAMMA GARCIA: Run, Annie—quick—quick—telephone the doctor.

AUNT ANNIE: Yes, yes—the doctor— [She is running out.]

AUNT ROSE: Get Father Roni, quick!

AUNT ANNIE: Yes, Father Roni— [She stumbles down the stairs and out of sight.]

JOE GARCIA: [Stroking back JULIA's hair.] Julie—speak to Papa—speak to Papa— Julie, open your eyes— Look at Papa.

JULIA: [In a whisper.] Papa—

MARIE: [Sobbing wildly.] Julie—Julie—don't die—

MAMMA GARCIA: Put her on her bed, Papa. [JOE GARCIA lifts up JULIA and carries her to the shiny brass bed and puts her down gently, her head on the pillow.]

JOE GARCIA: There, Julie—that's all right—you'll be all right— There, Julie—

JULIA: [Whispering.] Papa—Mamma—

MAMMA GARCIA: Yes, Baby—here I am, Baby.

JULIA: [Her hands flutter a moment; then she dies without another sound.]

JOE GARCIA: [Patting her hands.] You're all right— you're all right, Julie— You're a queen, Julie—the queen— You got to ride on the float, Baby—don't forget that— Papa is so proud of you—

MAMMA GARCIA: Oh, blessed Virgin— Oh, blessed Jesus— [Stroking her brow.] She's gone, Papa— She's gone—

JOE GARCIA: [Fiercely.] What are you talkin' about, Amelia! What are you talkin' about! Julie's here—Julie's here— [Suddenly, far off, the town band is heard, playing rather discordantly, one of Sousa's marches.]

MARIE: [Between sobs.] There—there comes the band— They're—they're getting ready for the parade—

MAMMA GARCIA: Make 'em stop— Make 'em stop— They don't know what they're doin'—

AUNT ROSE: [Sinking to her knees beside the bed and slowly crossing herself.] Thy will be done — [She pats

Julia's hand.]   Tony will take care of you now.   [The town band draws nearer, up the dusty road, the brasses blaring.   It drowns out the sound of weeping around the bed.]

PRODUCTION NOTE

The acting rights for all the plays in this volume are fully protected by copyright. The text of each play bears the necessary copyright notice on the reverse of the half title. Regarding the production rights, both amateur and professional, and all other rights including public reading, radio broadcasting, etc., it is necessary to apply to the agent or owner.

In the case of the following plays included in this volume, the agent is Samuel French, 25 West 45th Street, New York, N. Y.: LAST DAY FOR GROUSE, GREASY LUCK, THE RESIGNATION OF BILL SNYDER, RECKLESS, TOWN, BLOOD O' KINGS, THE TIE THAT BINDS, THE NO 'COUNT BOY, BUMBLEPUPPY, THE GIRL IN THE COFFIN, MINNIE FIELD, CHUCK, MONEY, THE CAJUN, BOUND EAST FOR CARDIFF, QUARRY, THE FEAST OF THE HOLY INNOCEN'S, BREAD, GOOD VINTAGE, THE ORGAN, and BARBARIANS.

Regarding the following plays application must be made to D. Appleton & Company, 35 West 32nd Street, New York, N. Y.: THE LAST STRAW, THE COW WITH WINGS, THE MEDICINE SHOW, THE ELDEST, ACROSS THE BORDER, ADDIO, and THE END OF THE TRAIL.

For amateurs to produce THE TRYSTING PLACE application must be made to the Editor of *The Ladies' Home Journal,* Philadelphia, Pa.

Regarding the following plays application must be made to Walter H. Baker Company, 41 Winter Street, Boston, Mass.: TRIFLES, 'LIJAH and WANDERLUST.

Application for production rights of DAY'S END must be made to Professor Frederick H. Koch, University of North Carolina, Chapel Hill, N. C.

Application for production rights of NO CAUSE FOR COMPLAINT must be made to Miss Margaret Christie, 200 Madison Avenue, New York, N. Y.